The Lur

BERKELEY SERIES IN INTERDISCIPLINARY STUDIES OF CHINA

Published in collaboration with
the Center for Chinese Studies
Wen-hsin Yeh, Editor

1. *The Lure of the Modern:*
Writing Modernism in Semicolonial China, 1917–1937
by Shu-mei Shih

The Lure
of the Modern

Writing Modernism in Semicolonial China,
1917–1937

Shu-mei Shih

UNIVERSITY OF CALIFORNIA PRESS
Berkeley   Los Angeles   London

Cover: Chang Yu, *Pink Nude,* 1929; oil on canvas (45 × 81 cm.).

Chapter 10 was previously published in the *Journal of Asian Studies* 55:4 (November 1996): 936–956. Reprinted with the permission of the Association for Asian Studies.

University of California Press
Berkeley and Los Angeles, California
University of California Press, Ltd.
London, England
© 2001 by
The Regents of the University of California

Library of Congress Cataloging-in-Publication Data
Shih, Shu-mei, 1961–
    The lure of the modern : writing modernism in semi-
  colonial China, 1917–1937 / Shu-mei Shih.
        p.   cm.
Includes bibliographical references and index.
ISBN 978-0-520-22064-5 (pbk. : alk. paper)
1. Chinese literature—20th century—History and criticism.
    2. Modernism (Literature)—China.   I. Title.
PL2303 .S57   2001
895.1'09112—dc21   00-062855
                                        CIP

Manufactured in the United States of America
14   13   12   11   10   09   08   07   06
11   10   9   8   7   6   5   4   3   2

CONTENTS

PREFACE

In the fall of 1990 I visited Shi Zhecun, the only surviving modernist from the 1930s, then eighty-five years old. His flat was in an old building from the Republican era standing in crowded proximity to many other similar buildings on a narrow tree-lined street in the heart of Shanghai. In the main room of the three-room flat, moldings along the edges of the ceiling, a fireplace, and a small veranda with iron railings were all remnants of bygone Shanghai, particularly conspicuous in a nation filled with functionalistic architecture born from a Marxist-nationalist, ascetic ideology in the preceding decades. Had the fireplace been operational or the veranda filled with potted plants, one might have thought the room had been frozen in the time of the late 1920s and early 1930s, when a European lifestyle was the trend among the Shanghai cosmopolitan cultural elites. The fireplace was empty though, and there were no tools. Since they were made of iron, the tools had been taken for smelting during the Great Leap Forward and had never been replaced. From the veranda, there was also no view to speak of. In the middle of this crowded but otherwise clean and pleasant room that served simultaneously as the writer's study, bedroom, dining room, and living room was Shi Zhecun, seated grandly at his desk, wearing a green terry cloth bathrobe over a white dress shirt and black-grey dress pants tightened around the waist with an old-fashioned leather belt, smoking a pipe. Wearing a hearing device in one ear, Shi had an oval face with gentle and delicate features befitting a Southern gentleman. For three full days, he graciously entertained my questions about his work and the time of his youth as a writer in old Shanghai. He talked passionately not only about French symbolists, Emily Dickinson, and Virginia Woolf, who had been some of his favorite writers back then, but also about various contemporary Western writers, including the latest developments in literary theory such as deconstruction.

I was all ears for his nostalgic reconstruction of his youthful days as a young, aspiring writer and editor, and was especially struck by how deeply he remained so "contemporary" and well-informed. It was as though we were connecting in a place where all the gaps between us—of history, geography, gender, age—evaporated and his participation in the great upheavals of modern Chinese history were but detours that could be readily sidestepped or forgotten. Many cultural critics have noted the similarity between the Republican era and the 1980s, noting that the 1980s was an age of "new" enlightenment that pursued similar goals of cultural cosmopolitanism. An important writer and editor in his youth, Shi was predictably "rehabilitated" in this period of new enlightenment as a major modern writer, his main works all reprinted, and even entire sets of the journal he edited, *Les Contemporaines,* made available in bookstores. One could say that in the 1980s there was a wave of nostalgia for the literature of the Republican era, as young writers of various persuasions found in the earlier generation justification as well as inspiration for a more transnationally articulated form of culture writing. This kind of culture writing was crucial to the "culture craze" or "culture fever" (*wenhua re*) zeitgeist of the 1980s, whose motto was "walk out into the world" (*zouxiang shijie*),[1] a neologism that in the 1990s would be transformed to "going global." From a historical perspective, this nostalgia was by no means an accident. From 1949 to the death of Mao Zedong in 1976, the so-called cosmopolitan and modernist writers were categorically dismissed as Westernized, i.e., ideologically backward and morally decadent, and marginalized in all literary histories. But the tables were turned during the culture craze, as the same modernists became models to recuperate and to emulate. When I visited Shi in the fall of 1990, it was at the tail end of the culture craze, as the Tiananmen massacre of the previous year had brought it to a dramatic close.

The 1980s nostalgia for the Republican era is an understandable, yet extremely curious phenomenon. The objects of this nostalgia were, to some degree, the cultural products of semicolonialism, a political, social and cultural formation rejected by the Chinese Communist Party's agenda of anti-imperialism. Ironically, then, one may say that this nostalgia for the past was a *colonial nostalgia, not by the colonizers but by the ex-colonized,* a peculiar cultural phenomenon perhaps only possible in China due to the Party's cultural isolationism and ideological inflexibility. Passionate in their criticism of the government, though expressing it obliquely, the culture-craze proponents utilized this colonial nostalgia as a counterdiscourse to domination by the

1. For the 1980s "culture craze," see Jing Wang, *High Culture Fever: Politics, Aesthetics, and Ideology in Deng's China* (Berkeley: University of California Press, 1997), and Xudong Zhang, *Chinese Modernism in the Era of Reforms* (Durham: Duke University Press, 1997).

Party-cum-government. No text better captures this nostalgia for semicolonial Shanghai than Wang Anyi's widely acclaimed novel *Song of Sorrow* (*Changhen ge,* 1995), replete with a celebration of capitalist bourgeois sensibilities and lifestyle and a categorical negation of the intervening years. The culture craze of the 1980s was sublated into a popular passion for the reinstitution of capitalist economy and lifestyle of the Republican era in the 1990s. The availability of calendars, posters, and numerous other artifacts from the Republican era in the 1990s marked a retro trend which commodified precisely the nostalgia for semicolonial cultural products. In this sense, we see a continuation of the 1980s culture craze in the 1990s commodification of culture, with the latter displacing the high seriousness of the former after a violent chastening by the Party.

Nostalgia for the past also had important implications for the temporality and spatiality of a Chinese modernity. If Republican-era culture was being recuperated as "modern," the literature of the intervening years appeared to belong to a different category, while the 1980s connected to the Republican era by somehow miraculously jumping over the intervening years. It is as if Chinese modernity, as a construct that is always defined along the lines of Westernization, can only exist in spurts, without historical continuity, and as if it is always ineluctably a by-product of some form of capitalism, whether protocapitalism, semicolonial capitalism, or a market economy with socialist characteristics. Hence the discourse of enlightenment from the Republican period, in a leap of space and time, endured in the period of the new enlightenment, repeating issues of Chinese modernity and literary modernism, albeit of course with significant variations. One can only imagine, if the earlier enlightenment continued in the decolonized terrain without the leap over the intervening years to the 1980s, how questions of Chinese modernity would have been posed and interrogated differently. If Chinese modernity was in any way emblematic of Third World modernities in general as a by-product of colonialism and capitalism, the continued and sustained investigation into its problems, limits, and possibilities might have given us a different scenario of how modernity in the Third World is to be construed. What this scenario might have been, or whether such a scenario would even have developed, we of course do not know. This does not mean that semicolonialism should or would have persisted, but rather that, without violent ruptures of history, the Chinese might have been able to conceive of modernity in ways not imaginable today in their rush to integrate with capitalist modernity, and could have been spared the anxious and some may say hopeless resistance to capitalist modernity among the so-called New Left intellectuals in China in the 1990s.

Is this book, one that theorizes and studies semicolonial modernism of the Republican era, then party to the nostalgia of the 1980s and 1990s? Although as an ethnic Chinese who is not a Chinese national, I could deny any participatory role in the collective nostalgia in China, semicolonial Shanghai has also been the object of considerable nostalgia for scholars in the United States in the past decade, with many conferences held and books published on the subject, and Shanghai modernism has itself become a fashionable topic in Chinese literary studies. During one conference on Shanghai, I once asked the self-reflexive question of why we loved to study old Shanghai so much. Instead of a reasoned response, I received an emotionally charged dismissal of the question. If there was any complicity between scholars of China and the collective nostalgia in China, these nostalgias were nevertheless, of course, qualitatively different, and colored by individual subject positions. Multiply diasporic and having been exposed to the Taiwan modernism of the 1960s, my own perspective had to be more self-reflexive of the ways in which our discourses are partly structured by various experiences of colonialism: how Taiwan modernism was aided by the Guomindang's anticommunist hysteria in the 1960s, which promoted Western cultural prestige and sanctioned Western modernism; how growing up in modernization-crazy postwar South Korea may have induced me to cultural expressions of capitalist modernity without serious reflection; how earning degrees in English and American literature has paradoxically prepared me for the study of Chinese modernism. It is no secret that various humanities departments, when reviewing applicants from East Asia, look for some background in English and American literature: for linguistic proficiency, but also for conceptual frameworks that are compatible with those in the United States. We live every day with these subtle subjections to and exercises of neocolonial cultural domination, glossed over in the name of cosmopolitanism or academic rigor.

But it would be too easy to reduce the complex processes of subject formation to neocolonial influences today, just as it would be unfair to examine Chinese modernism of the Republican era from a strictly colonial framework. Just as I would not reduce my own subject formation to being a passive process of subjection to Western cultural imperialism, neither could I do so when thinking and writing about Chinese modernists such as Shi Zhecun. Thus the desire to think through the historical, political, and cultural exigencies of Shi's and others' modernism in Republican China across the local/global divide has motivated and energized the writing of this book over the years.

When I embarked on the project, I had not anticipated that the historical, textual, and theoretical matrix of Chinese modernism would be as expansive as it turned out to be. This matrix involved, first of all, local contingencies and exigencies in modernist articulation, hence I theorize semicolonialism as a social formation distinct from formal colonialisms. Secondly, it involved the linkages of Chinese modernism to other modernisms (particularly Western and Japanese), its transnationalism expressed within multiple fields of discursive and political power. These are what I term the local and global contexts of Chinese modernism, whose interactions account for diachronically changing constitutions of meaning and agency. From my own discursive predilections, the matrix further involved comparative consider-- ations of theories of Third World modernism, colonialism and postcoloniality, and local/global cultural studies.

The result is a book that I hope offers something to a range of readers. To scholars and students of modern Chinese literature and history, I offer an account of Chinese literary modernism from the beginning of the May Fourth era in 1917 to the outbreak of the Sino-Japanese War in 1937, combining textual and historical coverage with theoretical inquiries. To theorists of modernism in the West, I chart modernist crossings among China, Japan, and the West, and delineate the cultural politics of this transnational circuit as tracing multiple colonial trajectories and cultural encounters, thereby unsettling the center-periphery and East-West binaries often assumed in comparative studies of culture. To theorists of colonialism and postcoloniality, I theorize how Chinese semicolonialism registered a set of cultural politics and practices different from formal colonialism. Situated at the intersection of the local and the global, Chinese modernism, in my view, was always defined by both axes simultaneously, albeit differently. It seems to me that the synchronic and diachronic implications of the local and the global outline a much more complex circulation and articulation of Chinese agency than previously assumed.

These different directions of analysis also required me to develop a methodology that integrates the historical, the textual, and the theoretical. These three perspectives crisscross in application, and it is often impossible to delineate where one ends and another begins. I use this methodological amalgam deliberately against the compartmentalization of research methods: the traditional "empirical" and "theoretical" divide in historical studies, the "textual" and "extratextual" divide in literary studies, and the "Western theory" and "non-Western text" divide in cross-cultural studies. As to the organization of the chapters, this book is divided into three parts—covering the May Fourth era, the Beijing School, and Shanghai's new sensationism—after an introductory chapter, where I lay the theoretical and historical groundwork for my discussion of Chinese modernism. Each part starts with an opening chapter where I attempt to theorize the cultural zeitgeist of the moment under examination, within which specific definitions of sociocultural modernity give rise to different formulations of aesthetic modernism. Then follow chapters on particular modernist writers and their works, in which I analyze the specific ways they negotiated issues of cultural modernity in expressive forms.

Finally, a word about the title of the book, *The Lure of the Modern*. By "lure,"

I suggest both the processes of subjection and sublation. Chinese modernists saw modernity as alluring, enticing, and desirable, an external category to which they were subjected both involuntarily and voluntarily. This subjection can be said to have produced Chinese cosmopolitan subjectivities. In a different sense, Chinese modernists proactively desired and lured modernity, turning modernity into an internal category as in a process of Hegelian sublation, thus revising, redefining, and reinventing modernity on the local terrain. Subjectivities were also thus engendered. The entanglement of the two processes of subjection and sublation, I argue, are endemic to semi-colonial subject formation in modern China. Thus the writing of modernism both subjected and subjectivized Chinese writers within the local and global contexts, disrupting any Manichean assumptions of cultural colonization and agency.

Like all academic endeavors, this book is helplessly indebted to numerous friends, colleagues, mentors, students, and family members. For their guidance and continuous support, I'd like to thank Leo Ou-fan Lee of Harvard University and Yan Jiayan of Beijing University. For reading the entire manuscript, Steven Day, Prasenjit Duara, David Der-wei Wang, and Wen-hsin Yeh. For reading chapters, Stanley Abe, Michael Bourdaghs, Arif Dirlik, Gail Hershatter, Yibing Huang, Ted Huters, Gregory Lee, Seiji Lippit, Lydia H. Liu, Yue Meng, Leslie Pincus, Lisa Rofel, Haun Saussy, Miriam Silverberg, and Chaohua Wang. For early inspiration, my godfather Chen Tzu-wen and Hong Kong poet Ping-kwan Leung. For being supportive, critical interlocutors, the members of the "Colonialism and Modernity in East Asia" resident group at the Humanities Research Institute of the University of California (Yoko Arisaka, Chungmoo Choi, Tak Fujitani, James Fujii, Amie Parry, and Lisa Yoneyama, as well as Ted, Gail and Lisa Rofel, already acknowledged). Also, for critical dialogue in many conferences together, the members of the Transcultural Studies Network (Stephen Chan, Yvonne Chang, Benjamin Lee, Leo Lee, Steven Lewis, Ping-hui Liao, Lydia Liu, Richard Smith, Hui Wang, Jing Wang, and Jianying Zha). On the L.A. home front, I thank Jean Hamilton, Katherine King, Jinqi Ling, Françoise Lionnet, Robert Buswell, Don Nakanishi, Herman Ooms, and many others for intellectual and emotional support. For research assistance, Eileen Cheng, Yibing Huang, Kelly Jeong, James Lee, and Mary Wang. Finally, my gratitude to the Fulbright-Hays Foundation and Committee on Scholarly Communication with China for funding my dissertation research in China, to the Center for Chinese Studies at the University of California, Berkeley, for a Postdoctoral Fellowship, and to UCLA for a career development award and for yearly academic senate grants. A grant from the Center for Chinese Studies at UCLA helped defray the cost of indexing the book. My colleagues in three departments in which I teach,

East Asian Languages and Cultures, Comparative Literature, and Asian American Studies, are gratefully recognized here for their support and camaraderie as well.

My family more than deserves a separate paragraph of acknowledgment: my husband Adam, my sons Timothy (little Tian) and Raymond (little Ray), my parents Shou-pu Shih (1935–1994) and Kuei-lan Chang, and my wonderful sisters (Shu-tsui, Shu-yen, Shu-hsiang, Shu-hui, and Shu-ping). My deepest gratitude for tolerating the endless and obsessive toiling that took time away from my being with them. To them collectively, I dedicate this book.

The Global and Local Terms
of Chinese Modernism

Formal analysis . . . [has to be] firmly grounded in formational analysis.
RAYMOND WILLIAMS (1989)

It is at the end of capitalism—during the era of imperialism . . . that Kipling eulogized British imperialism in his poetry, and Italian futurists became the hired poets of Fascism.
HU QIUYUAN (1931)

Suppose a being which is neither an object itself, nor has an object. Such a being, in the first place, would be the unique being: there would exist no being outside it—it would exist solitary and alone. For as soon as there are objects outside me, as soon as I am not alone, I am another—another reality than the object outside me. For this third object I am thus an other reality than it; that is, I am its object. Thus to suppose a being which is not the object of another being is to presuppose that no objective being exists. As soon as I have an object, this object has me for an object.
KARL MARX (1844)

What does need to be recognized, if the area studies tradition is to be revitalized, is that locality itself is a historical product and that the histories through which localities emerge are eventually subject to the dynamics of the global.
ARJUN APPADURAI (1996)

The deployment of Western critical terminology in the analysis of non-Western writing can readily unsettle Eurocentric paradigms of cultural discourse. This is particularly the case when we use the term *modernism*, which has been invested with decades of scholarly attention and has acquired a kind of hegemonic cultural value in the West.[1] Although Western discourse con-

---

1. Besides referring to the nations of Europe and North America, I also evoke the West as a symbolic construct, following its definition by the Indian Subaltern Studies group as "an imaginary though powerful entity created by a historical process that authorized it as the home of Reason, Progress, and Modernity," a construct distributed and universalized by imperialism and

ceived modernism as an "international" movement, it systematically denied a membership in its pantheon to the nonwhite non-West. A quick look at the geography of modernism as mapped by the classic textbook of modernist criticism and history, *Modernism,* edited by Malcolm Bradbury and James Mc-Farlane, is sufficient to illustrate that no city with a nonwhite majority inhabits the landscape.[2] Geopolitical, cultural, and racial centrisms discredited the participation of nonwhite peoples in modernism even while the West heralded the supposedly international tenor of the movement. These centrisms sanctioned the way Euro-American modernism displaced the significance of the periphery and constituted and justified itself as center, hence various evidence carrying the critical potential for challenging the center-periphery notions of modernism went unnoticed. It has been pointed out, for instance, that use of the term *modernism* to designate an aesthetic movement is an appropriation from the Latin American *el modernismo* founded by the Nicaraguan poet Rubén Darío in the early 1890s.[3] In this historical example of the metropolitan center appropriating the discourse of the periphery,[4] a relationship of discursive domination is made explicit, exposing the blindspot in literary histories that construct the center as origin. Discursive domination was explicit not only in the way modernism was characterized as exclusively Western, but also in the way modernisms in the non-West, if recognized as such, were later examined as but variations of Western modernism. Tautologically, Western modernism defined itself as the ultimate criterion and frame of reference for all "belated" non-Western modernisms, contextual differences constituting merely "variations." Modernism was always described as moving to non-Western sites, its place of origin without question the metropolitan West. That modernism was the agent of cultural power over non-Western sites necessitates a geopolitically situated critique of cultural imperialism. That modernism's travel was viewed as one-way traffic further exposes the discursive imbalance between the West and non-Western sites.

In recent years, attempts to challenge the colonizing conceptions of metropolitan modernism have resulted in various revisions, although no fundamental questioning of the one-directional travel narrative of modernism has been articulated. Recent theorizations of non-Western modernism have marked modernism as a heterogeneous event, exposing the parochial, Eu-

---

nationalism. See Gyan Prakash, "Subaltern Studies as Postcolonial Criticism," *American Historical Review* 99 (1994): 1475–1490.

2. Malcolm Bradbury and James McFarlane, eds., *Modernism* (New York: Penguin Books, 1976).

3. Matei Calinescu, *Five Faces of Modernity* (Durham: Duke University Press, 1987), 69.

4. I use the word "metropolitan" chiefly to designate the West as an industrially developed, geopolitical location. I also use it to make a distinction: "the metropolitan West" for the geopolitical West outside China, and "the colonial West" for the West's imperialist presence in China.

rocentric, racial, and patriarchal biases in the very ways metropolitan modernism was theorized. Third World critics working inside and outside the United States have demonstrated that modernism in the non-West not only co-opted but also challenged metropolitan modernism. Recuperative efforts have also been made within the metropolitan centers by modernism's perennial Others: feminists have rewritten the history of modernism from the perspectives of feminist critique and women's literary history;[5] minority views have exposed the racial and cultural biases in the conception of modernism.[6] The new emphasis in international modernist studies is on the specific "situatedness" of non-Western modernisms in Asia, Africa, and Latin America, which were dialogically connected to Western modernism but fundamentally different from it. Non-Western modernisms arose from different notions of modernity, nationhood, and nationalism, and in many cases were closely linked to the history of colonialism and imperialism. Each had its own mode of negotiation with the West, ranging from willing, unpoliticized participation in the Western modernist movement (though unacknowledged by the West as such), to modulating modernism for local needs and negotiating anxieties about the colonial legacy of modernism, to a thorough subversion of Eurocentric modernism. Periodization of modernism also differs in each situation, disrupting Western chronologies of modernism and registering different histories, each "belatedness" becoming a distinct marker of the local.[7]

Difference and similarity therefore inform non-Western modernisms precisely because they were closely related to Western modernism. Where their difference from Western modernism is emphasized, we perceive them as offering different experiences and narratives of modernity, and we understand that they hybridize and heterogenize metropolitan concepts of modernity and modernism. Where similarity is emphasized, we perceive a transnational and deterritorialized modernism that promises the possibility of a cosmopolitan cultural politics, even as it necessarily hides a fundamentally hierarchical notion of center and periphery. When concerns over cul-

---

5. Feminist critics have attempted to "write" gender into modernism. In particular, American feminist critics have been working to resuscitate undervalued work by women modernists and establish a countertradition of female modernism. See, for instance, Bonnie Kime Scott, ed., *The Gender of Modernism* (Bloomington: Indiana University Press, 1990), and Suzanne Clark, *Sentimental Modernism: Women Writers and the Revolution of the Word* (Bloomington: Indiana University Press, 1991).

6. African American modernism receives excellent treatment in Houston Baker, *Modernism and the Harlem Renaissance* (Chicago: University of Chicago Press, 1987), and James William Coleman, *Blackness and Modernism* (Jackson: University Press of Mississippi, 1989), to name only two.

7. For situated Third World modernisms, see, for instance, Iris M. Zavala, *Colonialism and Culture: Hispanic Modernisms and the Social Imaginary* (Bloomington: Indiana University Press, 1992); Coleman, *Blackness and Modernism*; and Simon Gikandi, *Writing in Limbo: Modernism and Caribbean Literature* (Ithaca: Cornell University Press, 1992).

tural domination are projected onto similarity, however, non-Western modernisms become sites of anxiety and paranoia. All of these modes of seeing non-Western modernisms acknowledge a *necessary* confrontation with the West.

It is from the perspective of this necessity that Chinese modernism must also be understood. But this necessity is different for China, not only because of historical and contextual differences but also because China was not simply the destination of Western modernism. Historical interactions between the West and China in the cultural arena in general, and in the writing of Western modernism in particular, have shown China to be an important part of the non-Western alterity that constituted Western modernism. According to recent "multiculturalist" arguments, China was one of the major "influences" on Western modernism[8]—it was the "misuse" of Chinese culture that contributed to the making of such modernist giants as Ezra Pound.[9] I will be explicating this interrelationship between Western modernism and China in fuller detail later, but it suffices here to suggest that Chinese modernism both challenges the constructed history of modernism as primarily a Euro-American event, and destabilizes Western modernism's claim to ontological primacy and aesthetic uniqueness.

Chinese modernism departs further from the usual binary models of the non-West's confrontation with the West—"China versus the West" or "East versus West." Most significant in this regard was the prominent role played by Japan as the mediating transmitter of Western culture and a potent force in the formation of Chinese modernism. This triangular relationship is indicative of the political and cultural condition of China under multiple domination from Euro-American and Japanese imperialisms, which in turn problematizes the China/West binary model privileged in comparative culture studies. "Modern Japan," which was dramatically transformed by the modernization campaigns in the wake of the Meiji Restoration (1868), played a number of important roles for Chinese intellectuals. Japan was the sole Asian example of successful Westernization and hence the primary model for similar efforts in China; it was the pan-Asianist ally in the struggle against Western imperialism for nationalists like Sun Yat-sen; it loomed as the imperialist tiger hungering for Chinese territory; and it also mediated Western literature through Japanese translations and other productive cultural forms. The complex relationship between Japan and China not only refracts the China-West binary model of confrontation, but sometimes displaces the role of Western modernism entirely. The binary model therefore limits under-

---

8. Zhaoming Qian, *Orientalism and Modernism: The Legacy of China in Pound and Williams* (Durham: Duke University Press, 1995), 1–6.

9. Xiaomei Chen, "Rediscovering Ezra Pound: A Post-Postcolonial 'Misreading' of a Western Legacy," *Paideuma* 23:2 and 3 (Fall/Winter 1994): 81–105.

standing of non-Western modernism by solipsistically honoring the hegemonic, narcissistic West as the ultimate frame of reference, and reinforces
the construction of the West as the Hegelian third term triumphant in its
successful absorption of the non-West.

Debunking the myths of Eurocentric modernism and the binary model
of cultural confrontation is thereby a central task in any discussion of Chinese modernism. In the sections below, this introductory chapter first exposes the mythmaking strategies of Western modernism by analyzing the ways
in which "China" operates within those strategies, which foregrounds the intimate discursive and historical relationship between China and the West.
This intimate relationship underlies my contention that Chinese modernism
must be considered within the intersecting contexts of the local and the
global, wherein the question of Chinese agency has to be dialectically posed
in its historical specificity and difference across contexts, not via tropes of
equivalence. This chapter then presents a historically specific argument regarding the relationship between Japanese and Chinese modernisms, troubling the binary model of cross-cultural studies, before moving on to a theorization of semicolonial cultural formation as the manifestation of global/
local intersections.

WESTERN MODERNISM AND CHINA

*While the imperial metropolis tends to understand itself as determining the periph-
ery, . . . it habitually blinds itself to the ways in which the periphery determines the
metropolis.*
                              MARY LOUISE PRATT (1992)

The connection between European realist travel literature of the nineteenth
century and the geographical expansion of British imperialism and colonialism has been persuasively established by Edward Said. His by now famous
argument is that Western realist literature helped legitimate and consolidate
the empire through a discourse that posited the Orient as the colonizable,
self-consolidating Other. Until recently, however, the similar connection between Western *modernism* and expansionist politics has seldom been the subject of critical attention, chiefly because Western modernism has been canonized (through the endeavors of New Critics and those I call New Critical
deconstructionists such as Paul de Man) as a conglomeration of autonomous
textual entities, disconnected from politics and history. Contemporary
Marxian literary critics, however, have challenged such a perceived discon-
nection as the mark of something else. Fredric Jameson argues that it is precisely modernism's willful aloofness from the history of Western imperialism from the late nineteenth to early twentieth centuries—the era of Western
literary modernism—that reveals how the "structure of imperialism" marks

the "inner forms and structures" of modernism. Modernism's alienation from the history of its time mirrors the imperialist practice of occluding the colonized on the discursive level, and separating metropolitan life, though vitally reliant on imperialist expansion, from the colonized. Jameson calls such a practice "a strategy of representational containment."[10]

In a later work, Said outlines the link between Western modernist formal practices and Western empires. He suggests that the absence of the colonized in modernist literature is manifested as a set of formal techniques that exemplify the invisible threat modernists felt from the presence of the contending natives and other rising nation-states, a threat which challenged the hegemony of Western empires. Modernist sentiments such as dislocation, displacement, discontinuity, and self-consciousness were responses to external pressures on Western culture. Modernists such as Joseph Conrad, T. E. Lawrence, and Ezra Pound, whether writing travel literature or not, shared this sense of crisis, from which the prime agenda of modernism arose: the desire for cultural regeneration. This sense of crisis is manifested in modernism's "self-contemplative passivity" and its "paralyzed gestures of aestheticized powerlessness" produced by the writers' anxiety in the face of an alterity that was becoming increasingly powerful.[11]

A more explicit, cruder management of that alterity was conducted through recourse to the familiar technologies of Orientalism. By traveling to the frontier, the non-West, modernism hoped to regenerate a decadent society and culture. These journeys consolidated Western theories of race, class, and eugenics, which were the discursive foundations and justifications of empire.[12] According to Said, specific cases of Orientalist practice can be seen in Joseph Conrad's imperialist, "paternalistic arrogance"[13] toward the Orient and Paul Valéry's presentation of the Orient as a passive object for the Occident to manage, consume, and dispense with.[14] From the overt fascist propensities in Ezra Pound, T. E. Hulme, Wyndham Lewis, and the Italian Futurists, to the more latent fascism of Luigi Pirandello, and T. S. Eliot's royalist politics, a "virulently antidemocratic politics" (Terry Eagleton's words) persisted in modernism. According to William H. Gass, "the camps of the early modernists in most of the arts were full of fascists, fascist sym-

10. Fredric Jameson, "Modernism and Imperialism," in Fredric Jameson, Edward Said, and Terry Eagleton, *Nationalism, Colonialism, and Literature* (Minneapolis: University of Minnesota Press, 1990), 43–66.

11. Edward Said, *Culture and Imperialism* (New York: Alfred A. Knopf, 1993), 188–190.

12. David Trotter notes that T. S. Eliot and Ezra Pound at different times resort to such discourses in their work, and are guilty of encoding a specific vocabulary that promoted an imperialist mythology. See his "Modernism and Empire: Reading *The Waste Land*," *Critical Quarterly* 28:1–2 (1986): 143–153.

13. Said, *Culture and Imperialism*, xviii.

14. Edward Said, *Orientalism* (New York: Vintage Books, 1979), 186, 190, and 250–251.

pathizers, and other lovers of on-time trains; there were many anti-Semites, sexists, denigrators of colored races, upper-class apes and royalist snobs."[15] Antidemocratic politics was also reflected in modernism's assimilating power, appropriating non-Western cultures for its own social and discursive ends. Modernism's formal strategies—such as textual fragmentation and the use of contradictory genres—and its antinormative aestheticizing impulse are both made possible by this assimilative power.[16] Western modernism, then, is ineluctably associated not only with imperialism, but also with "cultural expansionism,"[17] and is constituted in a dialectical relation with non-Western alterity.

Besides formal and thematic links between Western modernism and imperialist politics, Western modernism as a historical formation would not have been possible without imperialism as an economic agenda. Raymond Williams remarks that the specific historical form of modernism was made possible by "the magnetic concentration of wealth and power in imperial capitals and the simultaneous cosmopolitan access to a wide variety of subordinate cultures."[18] As mentioned, not the least of these "subordinate cultures" was China. As is well known, Britain, the United States, Japan, France, Germany, and several other European nations had competing economic interests in China throughout the late-Qing and Republican periods. They "carved up" Chinese territory along the coast into pockets of extraterritoriality, where they could amass wealth through militarily protected capitalist ventures and repatriate it to the Euro-American metropolitan centers. The direct access to China and Chinese culture that was afforded by these economic activities was significant for the formation of Western modernism. Just as China was a vast resource for economic exploitation, China offered rejuvenating cultural inspiration for the West, which in turn served imperialist expansion. This Western use of China as both exploitable political and economic entity and assimilable exotic cultural material can be partially explained in terms of a psychological mechanism. Jonathan Arac and Harriet Ritvo argue that exoticism served as the "aestheticizing means by which the pain of [imperialist] expansion is converted to spectacle, to culture in the service of empire."[19] In providing the means for avoidance, exoticism became an enabling

15. Quoted in Stanley Sultan, "Was Modernism Reactionary?" *Journal of Modern Literature* 17:4 (Spring 1991): 447.

16. Stephen Slemon, "Modernism's Last Post," *Ariel* 20:4 (1989): 5–6.

17. The term "cultural expansionism" comes from Rey Chow. See her *Writing Diaspora: Tactics of Intervention in Contemporary Cultural Studies* (Bloomington: Indiana University Press, 1993), 55.

18. Raymond Williams, *The Politics of Modernism* (London: Verso, 1989), 44.

19. Jonathan Arac and Harriet Ritvo, "Introduction," in *Macropolitics of Nineteenth-Century Literature: Nationalism, Exoticism, Imperialism,* ed. Arac and Ritvo (Philadelphia: University of Pennsylvania Press, 1991), 3.

factor of imperialist expansion and was thereby complicit with it. In the case of China, economic domination and cultural access by the West led to Western manipulation of Chinese literary traditions, ranging from outright Orientalism to subtler approaches. While China as a historical and political reality was systematically absented from Western modernist writing, Western modernists traveled to China as diplomats, luminaries, and pleasure-seekers, some explicitly for the purpose of gathering Chinese cultural materials.

One of those travelers to China was the 1960 Nobel Prize winner, French poet St. John Perse (1887–1975), who wrote his most acclaimed poem "Anabase" (published 1924) while serving as a diplomat in China (1916–1921). Perse thirsted for "risk, excitement, and amusement," as one biographer described without irony, and he enjoyed his stay in China, particularly when experiencing the *"bonne petite rupture d'équilibre,"* which included the devastating plague of 1918 in northern China. Other details his biographer notes admiringly: Perse had only a small number of servants—"a chief 'boy,' a cook and his assistant, a coolie for heavy housework and another for errands in town, but no gardener or laundress, nor a groom for his stables"— and an entourage of animals including Mongolian horses, a lizard, a frog, crickets, a dog, and a mosquito (!), all of which joined him at his table.[20] While China was in the throes of upheaval, including the May Fourth movement of 1919, Perse enjoyed his secluded life surrounded by exotica in the name of "solitude."

As one would expect, the main theme of "Anabase" is the enjoyment of heroic solitude against the backdrop of the military conquest of Asia, described as an expansive, visionary adventure. In his preface to Perse's *Collected Poems,* T. S. Eliot writes that images in the poem form "one intense impression of barbaric civilization."[21] Exoticized, barbarized, China was Perse's metaphor for the infinite expanse of Asia waiting to be conquered by the "civilized" West, a space that provided room for heroic action and solitude. It is interesting that Perse's poem was translated into English by modernist Eliot (an admirer long before the Nobel Prize committee recognized Perse's talent). It attests to the fact that high modernism considered conquest a natural part of the heroic magnitudes of modernist experience. The complicity between the Nobel Prize committee, Perse, and the modernist translator of Perse's poetry can be located in their shared barbarization of Asia, and more specifically China. The alterity of China sharpened the image of the solitary Western traveler, who was the emblematic protagonist in the narratives of alienation that Western modernism valorized. Less obvious exam-

20. Erika Ostrovky, *Under the Sign of Ambiguity: Saint-John Perse/Alexis Léger* (New York: New York University Press, 1984), 79–104.

21. T. S. Eliot, "Preface," to St. John Perse, *Collected Poems,* trans. W. H. Auden, T. S. Eliot, et al. (Princeton: Princeton University Press, 1971), 676.

ples of Western modernism's use of China can be found in other French poets and diplomats, including Paul Claudel (1868–1995), who went to China in 1895 and wrote a collection of prose poems called *Connaissance de L'Est* (*The East I Know,* 1900). Victor Segalen (1878–1919), who lived in China for seven years, started writing poetry there as he witnessed the "decay" of Chinese civilization, and produced stories, plays, and poems grafted from Chinese culture. These works set in China portray China as the repository of difference and femininity against which the masculine subjectivity of the modernist is formulated.[22]

Ezra Pound's work is perhaps the most prominent example of how Chinese materials were used in Western modernism. Typically, they were used for the peculiar, individual purpose of "conquer[ing] new poetic territory"[23] without paying homage to the materials themselves. Pound's numerous "creative renderings" of classical Chinese poetry and Confucian writings showed little respect for the texts adopted and adapted, which he exuberantly tailored for his specific poetic purposes. As one scholar argues, Pound translated Chinese poetry in order to "propagate his poetic views, [and] to attack what he considered to be the current poetic demise by using a foreign force."[24] China was the treasure house from which poetic materials could be freely grafted and redisplayed, so that Pound's uniqueness as a poet could be foregrounded. Of course, that Pound imitated Chinese authors in order to appear unique is only one of the ways Western modernism simultaneously included and excluded China, heralding the appropriation as evidence of modernism's international nature and suppressing the evidence of modernism's colonialist roots.

Interestingly, Western modernism's two modes of using "China"— orientalizing it and appropriating its cultural material— roughly follow the genre division of narrative and poetry. Orientalism most commonly manifests itself in narrative containment of the Other, while formal appropriation manifests itself in poetic grafting. Narrative requires China as a setting and therefore involves Chinese characters and scenes, but poetry can simply lift fragments out of the Chinese context; in either case, "China" as a historical and cultural entity disappears. That is, narrative renderings of "China" displace the "real" China and instead project a land of the writer's imagina-

22. William Burgwinkle, "Veiling the Phallus: French Modernism and the Feminization of the Asian Male," in *Gender and Culture in Literature and Film East and West: Issues of Perception and Interpretation,* ed. Nitaya Masavisut et al. (Honolulu: University of Hawaii and the East-West Center, 1994), 29–39.

23. John Gould Fletcher, "The Orient and Contemporary Poetry," in *The Asian Legacy and American Life,* ed. Arthur E. Christy (New York: Asia Press, 1945), 146.

24. William Tay (Zheng Shusen), *Literary Relations* (*Wenxue Yinyuan*) (Taipei: Dongda tushu, 1987), 176. Also see Wai-lim Yip, *Ezra Pound's "Cathay"* (Princeton: Princeton University Press, 1969).

tion, while poetry's use of "China," as conditioned by its short, fragmentary form, allows for partial appropriations without giving "China" a tangible presence at all. Both uses of "China" absent China as a historical entity in their texts and turn it into an embodiment of cultural exotica.

Western modernism, thus implicated in the repression and appropriation of China through imperialism and Orientalism, was imported into China. What happened in the course of this movement? In Edward Said's much cited configuration, the traveling of any theory or idea occurs through four common, consecutive stages: (1) a point of origin, (2) a distance transversed through the pressure of various contexts, (3) conditions of acceptance and resistance, and (4) the now accommodated or incorporated idea transformed by its new uses and its new position in a new time and place.[25] As many critics have pointed out, this model for the movement of ideas has problematic implications. In the specific case of China, it is nettlesome for at least one important reason: Said's notion, with its premises about origin and context conceived in unilinear terms, posits a sequence in one direction and cannot account for the complexities of cross-fertilization between China and the West. As I have argued earlier, China and Chinese culture formed an important part of that non-Western alterity constituting Western modernism (though through an uneven play of power). When Western modernism traveled to China, its point of origin was already ambiguous.

A few examples suffice here to problematize Said's first stage and to show how China shaped this Western "origin." Hu Shi's (1891–1962) famous "Eight Don'ts" (*babu zhuyi*), which heralded a new literature in the beginning of the May Fourth era, were partially taken from the Imagist manifesto,[26] which in turn had earlier been influenced by the tenets of classical Japanese and Chinese poetry. In the 1930s, Shi Zhecun (b. 1905) translated the English word "image" as *yixiang*, and advocated what he called "image poetry" (*yixiang shi*). Again, this poetry crystallized because of the two-way traffic between classical Chinese poetry and imagism. As Shi noted in his correspondence, he considered the origin of imagism to be China, then it was fully accomplished in the United States, and later brought back to China by himself.[27] Is *yixiang shi* Chinese or Western in origin then? Ernest Francisco Fenollosa's classic essay that inspired Ezra Pound and other modernist poets, "The Chinese Written Character as a Medium for Poetry," was also im-

25. Edward Said, *The World, the Text, and the Critic* (Cambridge: Harvard University Press, 1983), 226–227.
26. Tay, *Literary Relations*, 166. The "Eight Don'ts" include prescriptions such as "Don't imitate the ancients," "Don't use allusions," "Don't avoid colloquial words and expressions," and "Don't use clichéd expressions." For the contribution of Hu Shi's "Eight Don'ts" to the May Fourth literary revolution, see Qian Liqun et al., *Thirty Years of Modern Chinese Literature* (*Zhongguo xiandai wenxue sanshinian*) (Shanghai: Shanghai wenyi chubanshe, 1987), 21–28.
27. Shi Zhecun, personal correspondence, March 16, 1989.

ported into China in 1926.[28] Shi mentioned to me in an interview that Amy Lowell had a friend in Shanghai who helped Lowell with her understanding of Chinese poetry. This was Florence Ayscough, with whom Lowell translated a book of Chinese poems and carried on an extensive correspondence.[29] In narrative writing, the explicit traces of such cross-travel are less apparent, but the fictional technique of montage, based on a filmic technique developed by Sergei Eisenstein, was also reputedly inspired by Beijing opera and the juxtapositional quality of Chinese written characters.[30] Note also Fei Ming's (1901–1967) detour from modern Western poetry to Six dynasties and Tang dynasty poetry, in a search for sources of syntactic and semantic structures akin to the stream-of-consciousness narrative. His work is an interesting case of correspondence of styles between two divergent traditions. What remains most striking, however, is how similarities were recognized only *after* Western traditions were incorporated; that is to say, the initial catalyst for the Chinese recognition and adaptation of traditional Chinese aesthetics was often their endorsement by the powerful West, not an innocent reinvention of native aesthetics. After all, Fei Ming did not study classical Chinese poetry in earnest before he had been exposed to Western literature as an undergraduate in the English department at Beijing University.

Clearly, modernism never traveled one way from a point of origin to a place of destination. But it was consistently conceptualized as such due to the imbalance of discursive power between China and the West. Most often, it was only when Western modernists "validated" Chinese aesthetics by appropriating it that Chinese culture was seen as having the capacity to be modern. And it was only when the Chinese modernists self-consciously modeled themselves after Western modernism that "modernism" was supposed to exist in China. For inasmuch as modernism did travel from the metropolitan West to modern China, it did so endowed with the power of cultural supremacy bestowed by imperialism. That both Western metropolitan and Chinese critics saw China as cultural recipient reflects the lack of discursive alternatives for Chinese writing caught within unequal power relations. The vast aesthetic heritage of classical China was not seen as a viable resource to those Chinese

28. Zhang Yinlin, "Fenollosa on the Strengths of Chinese Written Characters" (*Fennuoluosa lun Zhongguo wenzi zhi youdian*), *Critical Review* (*Xueheng*) 56 (August 1926): 1–28.

29. See *Fir-Flower Tablets*, trans. Florence Ayscough and Amy Lowell (New York: Houghton Mifflin, 1921), and *Florence Ayscough & Amy Lowell*, a book of correspondences between the two edited by Ayscough (Chicago: University of Chicago Press, 1945). Interview with Shi Zhecun, October 22–24, 1990.

30. Zheng Peikai (Cheng Pei-kai), "The Cultural Impact of Mei Lanfang on World Theater" (*Mei Lanfang dui shijie jutan de wenhua chongji*), *Con-Temporary* (*Dangdai*) 103 (November 1994): 43 n. Wai-lim Yip also argues that montage was a "concept inherited from the Chinese character." See Yip, "Modernism in a Cross-Cultural Context," in his *Lyrics from Shelters: Modern Chinese Poetry, 1930–1950* (New York: Garland Publishing, Inc., 1992), 4.

writers who wanted to enter the modern, for the modern could only be out-lined by Western time and history. To enter the modern moment, they had to look to the West for models, tacitly acquiescing to the notion that mod-ernism came from the outside, and actively asserting the same to legitimate their status as the harbingers of the modern within their local contexts. This shared construction of the unilinear travel narrative of modernism by West-ern and Chinese discourses points to a peculiar collusion between metro-politan hegemony and local Chinese elites' cultural hegemony, though each for very different purposes.

The fourth travel stage that Said proposes—that each theory becomes modified for local use in a different context—is also problematic, as Said did not contextualize this stage in Western imperialism. The "traveling" of Western culture is never innocent; it is foremost an exhibition of the desire for conquest and a display of power. The conditions that allowed Western modernism and modernists to travel to China were those of military and eco-nomic power acquired from a century of incursion on Chinese territory. In Bertrand Russell's unambiguous words, "Apart from war, the impact of Eu-ropean civilization upon the traditional life of China takes two forms, one commercial, the other intellectual. Both depend upon the prestige of ar-maments."[31] The cannons of Western imperialism beginning in the mid-nineteenth century are what shocked the Chinese intelligentsia into what Lin Yü-sheng called the "crisis of Chinese consciousness."[32] Desperate for na-tional survival, intellectuals in Republican China launched various literary and cultural renovation campaigns. Literary modernism was espoused as a solution to national degeneration mostly due to its affinity to modernization, despite the fact that many strands of Western modernism were generally crit-ical of modernization, and that modernism was part of the ideological legit-imation and neutralization accompanying imperialist expansion, instituted through propagating the imperialists' literature among the colonized in the name of a civilizing mission.

One of colonialism's most efficient technologies of social containment and control in formally colonized countries was the dissemination of canon-ical European literary texts through the colonial education apparatus, as a means of soliciting consent from the indigenous people for their domina-tion.[33] In a partially colonized country such as Republican China, Western imperialism's mechanism of social containment and control was also edu-cation, which reached the more "progressive" (read: Westernized) native elites. Most of the writers who negotiated with Western modernism were ed-

31 Bertrand Russell, *The Problem of China* (New York: The Century Co., 1922), 72.

32. Lin Yü-sheng, *The Crisis of Chinese Consciousness* (Madison: University of Wisconsin Press, 1979).

33. Slemon, "Modernism's Last Post," 7.

ucated either in the West or in Japan, the "honorary West." Those who did not go abroad were educated in missionary-run institutions, such as Aurora University and St. John's University in Shanghai, or in the foreign language departments of native institutions manned by returned elites educated in the West or Japan.[34] Literary historians categorize such foreign-educated writers into two groups: the "Euro-American School" (*Oumei pai*) for those who were educated in Europe and the United States, and the "Japan School" (*liu Ri pai*) for those educated in Japan.[35] During the Republican era, writers who advocated new techniques and consciousness were almost always mediators of literary trends from abroad; they often translated Western and Japanese literature into Chinese and boldly borrowed their techniques and ideas. The "foreign" connection, albeit to different degrees, explains much of the critical and creative impetus of Republican modernists.

The question remains to what extent such borrowing was cultural or intellectual capitulation to Western hegemony. Lydia Liu, in discussing what she calls "translingual practice," argues that patterns of domination and resistance in cross-cultural exchanges are never unilinear. She emphasizes the notion of "co-authorship" in the translation and adoption of Western discourses in China. She places Chinese translators as equals to the Westerners from whom they borrowed because they engaged in "productive distortions" or "parodic imitations" of Western discourses based on local needs and purposes.[36] Similarly, Xiaomei Chen analyzes the use of the West in what she calls Occidentalist discourse. She posits that Occidentalism in China is much akin to Orientalism in the West in its willful manipulation and "misunderstanding" of the Occidental Other for distinctly local purposes.[37] (I will analyze this notion of Occidentalism in greater detail in chapter 5.) It is important to me, however, to reconsider the tropes of equivalence posited by Liu and Chen in specific reference to modernism of the Republican period. I think the key point here is to distinguish, for the sake of clarity, be-

34. The institutions of higher learning in modern China are thus characterized by Wen-hsin Yeh as the "alienated academy," that is, alienated from traditional cultural authority, from the past, from the customs and values of the older generation. In all, the academy's alienation from tradition and "sensitivity to stimuli existing outside the established order" reflected a hierarchy of tradition (as China) placed below modernity (as the West). Wen-hsin Yeh, *The Alienated Academy: Culture and Politics in Republican China, 1919–1937* (Cambridge: Council on East Asian Studies, Harvard University, 1990).

35. In general, writers who studied in the United States and England tended to advocate realism and lean toward capitalism, while writers who studied in Japan and France had modernist tendencies, such as those around the Creation Society (*Chuangzao she*) and the Zhou brothers (Lu Xun and Zhou Zuoren), many of whom turned to the left in the 1930s.

36. See Lydia Liu, "Introduction: The Problem of Language in Cross-Cultural Studies," in *Translingual Practice* (Stanford: Stanford University Press, 1995), 1–42.

37. Xiaomei Chen, *Occidentalism: A Theory of Counter-Discourse in Post-Mao China* (New York: Oxford University Press, 1995).

tween two discursive contexts —the *global* and the *local*—and to examine the different and often mutually contradictory constitutions of power within these two overlapping contexts.

As suggested earlier, Chinese modernism never competed for global discursive power, even though China was an important alterity of Western modernism; there was instead a willing acceptance of the unilinear travel narrative of Western modernism. In a perfect illustration of how "imperialism as ideological domination succeeds best without physical coercion"[38] through the colonization of consciousness, many Chinese writers valorized Western modernism as the signifier for the modern and the tool to delegitimize traditional Chinese culture, binding modernism to a kind of masochistic denial. Not surprisingly, therefore, what is often missing in Chinese modernist writing is a self-conscious investigation of the ideological content of Western modernism. Instead, in a kind of principled naivete, writers saw modernism as a liberating discourse and literary style, one that, like other Western "isms," would help the Chinese "reach" modernity and modernization. Cosmopolitans such as Guo Moruo (1892–1978), working in the early to mid-1920s, and Shi Zhecun, up until the mid-1930s, saw Chinese literature as a member of the global literary community or a tributary of Western literature, opting to disconnect the imperialist presence of the West in China (the "colonial West") from the Western cultural discourse they were importing (the "metropolitan West"). The connection between Western modernism and imperialism was masked with a utopian cosmopolitanism, or what Guo Moruo called "supranationalism" (*chaoguojia zhuyi*). In the case of self-proclaimed cosmopolitan writers, then, Chinese modernism was the willing site of colonial inscriptions when seen in the global context, and its Occidentalism thus cannot be posited as the reversal of Orientalism. Occidentalism did not have the economic and political agendas of subjugation that Orientalism did. Rather than any "representational containment" of the Western Other, Occidentalism promoted the Other as having universal value over the now particularized Chinese culture.

The question of capitulation needs to be broached differently when our attention turns to the local discursive context, and it is this context that Lydia Liu and Xiaomei Chen mainly examine. I agree with their views that Chinese writers manipulated their borrowings for discursive ends within China, but the Chinese context was never entirely independent of inherent global hierarchies. The local discursive context was arguably the most immediate arena of cultural negotiation and displays of power, and modernism needs to be situated and understood within that context. Nevertheless, the Chinese modernists' adoption of modernism would have lacked legitimation without the lure of global modernity. May Fourth writers justified their appropriation

38. Chow, *Writing Diaspora*, 8, 26.

of modernism as a counterdiscourse to Chinese tradition (however problematic that may be), as a means to accelerate the arrival of modernity, and as a mark of their cultural power as iconoclasts. The constructed "universality" of Western modernity gave them ammunition to assault other so-called "conservative" positions. The global context of imperialist expansion, which successfully instituted modernity as the telos of all histories, was the condition of possibility for modernist cultural positions in the local context. Thus when we prioritize the local over the global in reading modernism, we restore agency to the Chinese modernists as actors in the local area of cultural production, where they could contest cultural power with other local agents. But we must also contextualize this agency in the global arena of unequal cultural and political relations, the local manifestation of which was semicolonialism.

One might argue that there is yet another reason to prioritize the local over the global in our understanding of Chinese modernism. The Chinese modernists' blindness to the imperialist constructs of modernism might have paradoxically neutralized its imperialist intent: imported and taken out of context, Western modernism's ideological meanings were perhaps voided. Western modernism could then be seen as a pure literary practice in China: formal experimentation, psychological investigation, and hybridized linguistic expression, to name a few of its formal practices. One could appropriate the very argument that many modernists themselves made and conclude that literature was a pristine arena where utopian, aesthetic ideals could be realized and relations of power neutralized. Lu Xun's (1881–1936) famous "grabbism" (*nalai zhuyi*) is an example of a theory that advocates eclectic, confident borrowing from the foreign without fearing the possibility of enslavement by what one borrows.[39] While I will grant that one can borrow a foreign discourse in an unpoliticized manner, an examination of Chinese usage of Western discourse reveals the unfailing presence of embedded biases within Western discourse. The conundrum here echoes the dilemma of nationalism in Third World countries: Can a discourse borrowed from the West be truly liberating without implicating its users in its epistemological and power hierarchy?[40] One must ask to what extent modernism as a social, ideological, and cultural choice was self-empowering, given its ineluctable imbrication in the unequal relationship between China and the West. As I will show in chapter 1, the discursive biases that some Western modernist discourses inherently contained—such as explicit assumptions of superiority in Western modernism and implicit racism and sexism in Freudian

---

39. Lu Xun, "Upon Gazing in a Mirror" (*Kanjing yougan*), in *Complete Works of Lu Xun* (*Lu Xun quanji*) (Beijing: Renmin wenxue chubanshe, 1980), 1:197–200.

40. For a thorough delineation of this dilemma in the context of India, see Partha Chatterjee, *Nationalist Thought and the Colonial World: A Derivative Discourse* (Minneapolis: University of Minnesota Press, 1993).

psychoanalysis—undermined the liberating potential of the Western discourse thus borrowed and appropriated in the local context.

This is not to deny the local agency of Chinese writers, who deployed what they conceived to be features of Western modernism in their contest for local cultural prestige, but rather to point out that their agency needs to be conceived in specific reference to time and space. Agency is not a stable condition: contexts shift. In the case of the Beijing School (*jingpai*), for instance, we see an important attempt by a group of philosophers and writers to theorize a notion of modernity transcending the East/West binary. Particularizing Western modernity as arising from a specific Western historical context and criticizing its militaristic and materialistic tendencies, these intellectuals expanded the notion of global modernity to include aspects of Chinese culture. As I elaborate in Part Two of this book, they saw global modernity as having the potential to merge the best of Eastern and Western cultures, when both are conceived as particular entities with equal claims to universality. Their task of consolidating local agency was aided by the work of Western philosophers such as Henri Bergson and Rudolph Eucken in Europe and the American New Humanists, led by Irving Babbitt, who confirmed for them the value of Chinese culture, and with whom the Beijing philosophers communicated or studied. The Beijing School is a complex example of how the local becomes recognized as having agency in the global setting after having been spotlighted by Westerners.

In sum, situating Chinese modernism across the local and global divide destabilizes facile determinations of agency and alerts us to tensions and contradictions in its constitution. Local empowerment in modernist appropriation can be undermined in the global discursive context and vice versa. The relationship between local and global agencies cannot be clearly conjugated and coordinated as each modernist articulation enters into this relationship differently, depending on the moment and space of articulation.

JAPANESE MODERNISM AND CHINA

The relationship between Western modernism and imperialism in China is further complicated by the mediating role of Japanese modernism, itself not innocent of Japanese imperialist cultural and political agendas in China. Beginning during the May Fourth movement, Chinese writers, many of whom (particularly those associated with the Creation Society) were educated in Japan, translated Japanese modernist writing and Japanese discussions of Western modernism.[41] Additionally, these writers' knowledge of Western lit-

---

41. A general statistic may be illuminating here. Shi Zhecun estimates that between the late Qing and the May Fourth period, eighty percent of all translations of Western literature were retranslations from the Japanese. Interview with Shi Zhecun, October 22–24, 1990.

erature was mediated through Japanese translations, available to them during their educational sojourns in Japan and in Japanese bookstores in China such as the famed Uchiyama Bookstore (*Uchiyama shoten* in Japanese; *neishan shudian* in Chinese) in Shanghai. While Japan's expansionist ambitions in China grew, Chinese writers went to Japan,[42] brought back Japanese and Western books, and engaged in literary debates across the Sea of Japan, including the May Fourth debate on "art for art's sake" (*wei yishu er yishu*) and the modernist debate on new sensationism (*shinkankakuha* in Japanese; *xin'-ganjuepai* in Chinese). If the Chinese reception of Western modernism should be viewed with ambivalence because of Western imperialism, the role of Japanese modernism doubles this ambivalence.

To better explicate the literary and political relations in modernist crossings across the transnational terrain, it helps to provide a short overview of the changing role "Japan" played in Chinese cultural imaginary and "China" in Japanese cultural imaginary. Imperial China traditionally regarded Japan as a vassal state, a fiction not entirely undermined until China's defeat in the first Sino-Japanese war of 1894–95. Japan followed this victory with a series of imperialist actions. From the Russo-Japanese War of 1904–1905, Japan acquired Russian privileges in Manchuria. During World War I, Russia, France, and Great Britain sold their rights in China to Japan to secure Japan's neutrality. In 1915 Japan imposed the infamous "Twenty-One Demands" on the outraged Chinese. In the 1919 Treaty of Versailles all German rights and titles in Shandong province were "turned over" to Japan by the Western powers. Post-1919 events turned increasingly bloody, and by the early 1930s Japan began its brutal campaign to conquer all of China.

Throughout all of this, Chinese intellectuals nevertheless saw Japan as a model of successful modernization/Westernization. The logic of this contradictory perception of Japan as both aggressor and exemplar operated thus: Japan was able to defeat Russia and conquer parts of China due to its program of Westernization. By emulating the ways Japan learned from the West, China could also become Westernized and strong. During the Republican era, until the outbreak of the Sino-Japanese War in 1937, an intellectual could become influential in literary circles through knowledge of modern Japanese literature, as did the critic Xie Liuyi (1898–1945), or by importing Western modernism via Japan and appropriating Japanese modernism, as did the writers Yu Dafu (1896–1945), Liu Na'ou (1900–1939), and many others. Traditional Chinese ethnocentric prejudice against the Japanese and decades of Japanese incursions on Chinese territory did inspire strong nationalist resistance to Japan, but Japanese cultural products and mediated presentations

42. See Jerome B. Grieder, *Intellectuals and the State in Modern China* (New York: Free Press, 1981). He notes that by 1914 there were an estimated 5,000 Chinese students studying in Japan.

of Western culture were valued and deemed necessary for China to understand the West and "Asianize" it for Chinese use. More than a model, Japan
was the medium and the shortcut to Westernization.

Just as the West was bifurcated into the metropolitan and the colonial,
there was a similar differentiation made between the culture from metropolitan Japan on the one hand, and Japan's imperialist culture in China on
the other. Zhou Zuoren, the famous Beijing School essayist and literary theorist, for instance, wrote numerous articles about the necessity of bifurcating Japanese culture. Throughout his essays of the 1910s and 1920s, he noted
the important contributions Japanese culture had made and argued against
interpreting Japanese culture as solely militaristic. He distinguished between
metropolitan Japan and colonial Japan by saying that the former produced
an admirable culture while the latter produced imperialists and barbaric big-
ots. He accused Japanese colonialists of being the outcast elements in metropolitan Japan, trafficking in morphine and heroin, running drug dens,
and degrading the Japanese samurai spirit with random acts of violence, thus
rightly inciting the anger of the Chinese. This colonial Japanese culture
should be criticized and overthrown. To repudiate metropolitan Japanese
culture would, however, amount to a great loss for the Chinese, according
to Zhou. While colonial Japanese culture necessitated an emotional recourse
to nationalism and resistance, metropolitan Japanese culture called for rational consideration of its objective value.[43] Hence, Japanese cultural imperialism in the form of colonial control was forcefully repudiated in Zhou's
essays from the 1930s, in which he deplored Japanese involvement in the
Chinese educational system as "imperialist inculcation" and Japanese newspapers as producing nothing but "international pornographic news" deepening China's crisis.[44] Differentiating the metropolitan and colonial Japanese cultures allowed Chinese intellectuals such as Zhou to evaluate Japan
as a cultural exemplar for China, while denouncing its militaristic colonial
culture.

Another dimension of the contradictory perception of Japan as mediator, aggressor, and exemplar was the view of Japan as an ally in the struggle
against Western imperialism. This view was less commonly held but nevertheless influential. The pan-Asianist idea that "Japan derived its special position by protecting other Asian nations from the corrupting influence of
Western capitalism," while undoubtedly self-serving in legitimizing Japanese
imperialism in the region, also helped stimulate the nationalist zeal of Sun

---

43. Zhou Zuoren, "Discussion on Anti-Japanese Sentiments" (*Pai Ri pingyi*, 1927), in *About Tigers* (*Tan hu ji*) (Shanghai: Beixin shuju, 1936), 519–523. Also see the many essays on the subject in *Zhou Zuoren's Essays* (*Zhou Zuoren sanwen*), ed. Zhang Minggao et al. (Beijing: Zhong-guo guangbo dianshi chubanshe, 1992), for example 3:169–172, 182–196, 235–236, 264–272.

44. See the essays collected in *About Tigers*, 495–524, especially 508.

Yat-sen and others who fought Western imperialism.[45] One also cannot disregard the racial affinity between the Chinese and the Japanese in the Chinese perception of Japan. In the prestigious 1930s modernist journal *Les Contemporaines* (*Xiandai*), for instance, there were several articles celebrating the sympathy between Japanese and Chinese leftist writers as both struggling against Japanese imperialism.[46] The writer Liu Na'ou was rumored to be half-Japanese (although evidence suggests that he was full-blooded Taiwanese), but he was readily assimilated into the Shanghai literary scene, and became the leading proponent of Chinese new sensationism. However, to overemphasize the solidarity between the Japanese and the Chinese or the "positive" role Japan played for China runs the risk of parroting the very justifications used by Japanese imperialism.

Japan's view of China was equally contradictory. On the one hand there was modern Japan's "anxiety of influence" due to China's past cultural hegemony, and on the other Japan's rising expansionist ambitions in China. Both were conjoined in Japan's China policy during the period between the Meiji Restoration and the Pacific War. Itself recently the object of Western imperialism, Japan was striving to become the first modern Asian imperialist power on par with the West, an agenda which demanded and produced cultural justifications. The prominent Meiji intellectual leader Fukuzawa Yukichi (1835–1901) preached the concept of "parting with Asia," because he was convinced of the superiority and universality of Western culture. He urged his fellow countrymen "to discard their cultural ties with China and treat Asian neighbors such as Korea and China the same way the Westerners treated them."[47] Japan's narrativization of its distinctiveness from and superiority over China, and its assertion of equality with the West, were expressed through the creation of modern Japanese neologisms such as "Shina" (the Japanese transliteration of the Western word "China") and "tōyōshi" (Oriental historiography) to replace the older terms "Chūgoku" (Middle Kingdom) and "kangaku" (sinology).[48] Japan's appropriation of "Shina" from the West displaced China's centrality, implied in the name Mid-

45. Prasenjit Duara (paraphrasing Marius Jansen), *Rescuing History from the Nation: Questioning Narratives of Modern China* (Chicago: University of Chicago Press, 1995), 14–15.

46. See Zhu Yunying, "Japan Correspondence" (*Riben tongxin*), *Les Contemporaines* 3:1 (May 1933): 169–171. See also Yu Dafu, "Proclamation Addressed to the Japanese Police on the Assassination of Kobayashi" (*Wei Xiaolin de beihai xi Riben jingshiting*), *Les Contemporaines* 3:1 (May 1933): 4, in which Yu Dafu protests against the secret murder of proletarian writer Kobayashi Takiji (1903–1933) by the Japanese police. This solidarity with the Japanese writer-activist was expressed in conjunction with Yu's outcry against the Japanese invasion of Manchuria (1931) and bombing of Shanghai (1932).

47. K. H. Kim, *Japanese Perspectives on China's Early Modernization* (Ann Arbor: University of Michigan Press, 1974), 32.

48. Stepan Tanaka, *Japan's Orient: Rendering Pasts into History* (Berkeley: University of California Press, 1993), 1–28.

dle Kingdom, and degraded China as backward and "temporal[ly] inferior" to Japan.[49] The *genbun itchi* (unifying writing and speech) movement of the Meiji era was another instance of constructing Japanese modernity on anti-Chinese sentiments, in this case by abolishing the use of Chinese characters or *kanji*.[50]

As one scholar has noted, Japan's academic and cultural perceptions of China manifested a close partnership with its political and military goals.[51] One example of such complicity was the connection between the Oriental Historiography Group (*tōyōshigaku*) and the Research Bureau of the South Manchurian Railway Company.[52] Unlike other imperialist powers in China, Japan actually administered formal colonialism in Taiwan and Manchuria, replete with colonial policies that couched "military preparedness in civil garb" (*bunsō teki bubi*), as the first president of the South Manchurian Railway Company revealingly put it. The company established a program entitled "Cultural Invasion" to study and analyze Chinese culture so as to solidify Japan's colonial control. The Research Bureau of the South Manchurian Railway Company lasted thirty-eight years, its long lifespan testifying to the ongoing need for and success of scholarship in the facilitation of colonial control.[53]

Another important example was the East Asia Common Culture Academy (*Tōa Dōbun Shoin*, 1900–1945) in Shanghai, which educated Japanese China hands who served as trained manpower for the Japanese penetration of China. The military directly benefited from the political intelligence funneled by Academy graduates, and their voluminous research from extensive field trips became confidential material for the perusal of the Japanese government, and was later published as encyclopedic studies of China. Most of the Academy graduates who found employment in China worked for Japanese imperialism directly in occupied Manchuria, for example in the Research Bureau of the South Manchurian Railway Company itself.[54]

Part of the legitimation that colonial institutions such as the East Asia Common Culture Academy depended on was the rhetoric of common culture

49. Ibid., 20. See also Joshua Fogel's chapter on "The Sino-Japanese Controversy over *Shina* as a Toponym for China," in *The Cultural Dimension of Sino-Japanese Relations: Essays on the Nineteenth and Twentieth Centuries* (New York: M. E. Sharpe, 1995), especially 75–76, where he discusses how in 1946 the Japanese government bowed to Chinese pressure and abolished the use of the term *Shina*, which the Chinese consistently saw as derogatory.

50. See Karatani Kōjin, *Origins of Modern Japanese Literature*, trans. and ed. Brett de Bary (Durham: Duke University Press, 1993), 45–75.

51. Ibid., 106.

52. Tanaka, *Japan's Orient*, 26.

53. Fogel, *The Cultural Dimension of Sino-Japanese Relations*, 118–121.

54. Douglas R. Reynolds, "Training Young China Hands: Tōa Dōbun Shoin and Its Precursors, 1886–1945," in *The Japanese Informal Empire in China, 1895–1937*, ed. Peter Duus, Ramon Myers, and Mark R. Peattie (Princeton: Princeton University Press, 1989), 210–271.

within East Asia, more specifically between Japan and China, as summed up in the phrase "*dōbun-dōshu*" ("common culture, common race"). Intellectuals as diverse as Okakura Tenshin and Yamagata Aritomo upheld this notion to show that "the Japanese had a special sympathy for China or a depth of understanding that the Westerners did not."[55] This idea, which was inevitably co-opted by imperialist propaganda, obliged Japan, as the successfully modernized, superior nation, to help its Asian brother to modernize. In the 1890s, this obligation was expressed in the idea of "the yellow man's burden"; in the wake of World War I, it was changed to a nobler sounding "civilizing mission" (*kyōka*).[56] For the Oriental Historiography Group mentioned earlier, Japan also had a clear mission in China: "as a Westernized nation, Japan should bring the gospel of Western civilization to China for her regeneration."[57] Japan's cultural diplomacy failed miserably, however, due to the prevalent Chinese suspicion that its aim was to ultimately reduce China to becoming Japan's colony.

The Japanese belief in their cultural superiority took the literary forms of cultural treatises, travel narratives, and novels, reminiscent not only of nineteenth-century Western Orientalist writing, but also of Western modernism's appropriation of China. The so-called *Zhinatong* personalities (the "China hands") wrote books on the Chinese national character, describing it as antimodern, antirational, and antimoral. Chinese intellectuals avidly read many of them.[58] According to Naoki Sakai, the *Nihonjinron* ("discourse on Japanese uniqueness") travelogues, for instance, deployed a "subjective technology" which posited the Japanese self as the Other of the Chinese through a kind of "imperialist superiority complex," and established the Chinese national character as anarchistic, apathetic, and disorganized.[59]

The celebrated China travelogue by Akutagawa Ryūnosuke (1892–1927) deserves some analysis, because it captures both the Japanese propensity to celebrate their superiority, and the Chinese intellectuals' surprisingly uncritical reception of such views. Akutagawa, author of the acclaimed *Roshōmon*

55. Peter Duus, "Introduction," *The Japanese Informal Empire in China*, xxvi.

56. Ibid., xiii, and Sophia Lee, "The Foreign Ministry's Cultural Agenda for China: The Boxer Indemnity," in *The Japanese Informal Empire in China*, 272–306.

57. K. H. Kim, *Japanese Perspectives on China's Early Modernization*, 34.

58. Two of the most notable examples are Zhou Zuoren and Liang Shuming, who thought these narratives were more or less correct renderings of Chinese failings and thus should be studied with care. See Zhou Zuoren, "*Zhina* National Character" (*Zhina minzuxing*, 1926), in *About Tigers*, 547–549, and Liang Shuming, *Eastern and Western Culture and Their Philosophies* (*Dongxi wenhua ji qi zhexue*, 1921) (Taipei: Liren shuju, 1983). Also see Ching-mao Cheng, "The Impact of Japanese Literary Trends on Modern Chinese Writers," in *Modern Chinese Literature in the May Fourth Era*, ed. Merle Goldman (Cambridge: Harvard University Press, 1977), 63–88.

59. Naoki Sakai, "Subject and/or *Shutai* and the Inscription of National Culture," paper presented at the "Imaging Japan: Narrative of Nationhood" conference, Stanford University, May 13, 1993.

and an early modernist known for the dense textuality and linguistic opacity of his work as well as his famous suicide, went to China in 1921 under the sponsorship of *Ōsaka mainichi shinbun*, the *Osaka Daily*. Intended as a major "publicity coup" by the newspaper owners, Akutagawa wrote *Travels in China* (*Zhina youji* in Chinese; *Shina yūki* in Japanese), which became a bestseller in Japan.[60]

A translation of portions of the travelogue appeared in Chinese in 1926, the work of a leading intellectual/educator, Xia Mianzun (1886–1946). Xia relates the story of his encounter with the Japanese book in the preface to his translation, a story that offers more than a glimpse into how the Chinese intellectual valued Akutagawa's diagnosis of China and elided its imperialist implications. When Xia was in Shanghai, he went to the Uchiyama Bookstore and bought Akutagawa's *Travels in China* upon this recommendation of the proprietor, Uchiyama Kanzō: "Sir, you may not find this book very interesting, but it is a recent best-seller in Japan and is full of derision about your country!" Upon reading the travelogue, Xia felt compelled to translate "important" parts of it so that the Chinese people would have the benefit of Akutagawa's "correct" vision of Chinese society:

> The book is indeed full of sneers and derision. But if we observe the actual situation [in China], in all fairness, his perceptions are correct. He does not make any presumptuous exaggerations. Even if the author appears before me, I cannot defend and argue for my own country. I cannot wait for all Chinese to read this book. [We should] use his observations as a bright mirror to look at our own ugly faces! Upon thinking this, I translated those parts of the book that need to be introduced [to the Chinese]. I also wanted to borrow the tone of the Japanese proprietor and warn my countrymen thusly: "You may not find this book very interesting, but it is a recent best-seller in Japan and is full of derision about your country!"[61]

The patronizing manner in which Akutagawa comments on China and its customs—as his choice of the word "Shina" instead of "Chūgoku" amply indicates—is painfully obvious in Xia's translation. Akutagawa's China is full of dirt, urine, prostitutes, and fossilized, snobbish intellectuals, all of which function to confirm Akutagawa's sense of his own cultural purity and vibrant youth. Akutagawa makes judgments regarding the Chinese national character based on randomly observed details. He ruminates at length, for instance, on the shape and texture of Chinese prostitutes' ears as compared to those of Japanese women.

60. Joshua A. Fogel, "Akutagawa Ryūnosuke in China," *Chinese Studies in History* 30:4 (Summer 1997): 6–9.

61 Mianzun (Xia Mianzun), "Mr. Akutagawa Ryūnosuke's Views on China" (*Jiechuan Longzhijie shi de Zhongguo guan*), *Short Story Monthly* (*Xiaoshuo yuebao*) 17:4 (1926): 1–26. Joshua Fogel's English translation of the travelogue is available as "Travels in China" in *Chinese Studies in History* 30:4 (Summer 1997): 10–55.

For my purpose here, the book raises two interlocking issues that need consideration. One pertains to Akutagawa's "Japanized Orientalism" which constructs China as the alterity to confirm Japanese cultural superiority, particularly in the context of Akutagawa's own cultural identity crisis. The other is the Chinese reception of this Orientalism as having inherent value for the regeneration of Chinese society. I will deal with the second point first. Xia's unquestioning acceptance of Akutagawa's perception of China is immediately revealed by his transliteration of the derogatory "Shina" in the title of Akutagawa's book as "Zhina," as well as Xia's respectful address for Akutagawa with the honorific "*shi*" (Mr.). Since the Chinese routinely felt humiliated when called "*Zhinaren*" (the Zhina people), this willingness to engage in self-deprecation is striking. Furthermore, transferring Uchiyama Kanzō's demeaning words to his own lips exemplifies Xia's self-imposed colonized perspective, which mimics and reinforces a negative perception of oneself. What Xia did in his translation of *Travels in China,* other writers such as Lu Xun, Guo Moruo, and Yu Dafu did in their unforgiving sketches of the Chinese character and social ills.

A similar anecdote revealing the Chinese willingness to accept negative criticism of themselves is also recorded by Bertrand Russell: "Shortly before I left China, an eminent Chinese writer pressed me to say what I considered the chief defects of the Chinese. With some reluctance, I mentioned three: avarice, cowardice, and callousness. Strange to say, my interlocutor, instead of getting angry, admitted the justice of my criticism, and proceeded to discuss possible remedies."[62] A partial explanation for the willing self-criticism of modern Chinese intellectuals lies in the intensity of the crisis of consciousness they experienced as their country confronted Japan and the West, and their passionate belief that societal ills needed to be properly diagnosed before cures could be devised. Russell explained this commitment to rationality as an open-mindedness that exemplified the "intellectual integrity" of Chinese intellectuals, which he called "one of China's greatest virtues."[63]

Perhaps they had intellectual integrity, but an inferiority complex also informed this self-critical sensibility[64]—a common phenomenon among ed-

---

62. Russell, *The Problem of China,* 220–221. Russell's book, like Akutagawa's travelogue, was promptly translated into Chinese and published in China. See Lydia Liu, *Translingual Practice,* 46.

63. Russell, *The Problem of China,* 221.

64. Even in positive accounts of May Fourth iconoclasm, such as the work of C. T. Hsia, we see the critical spirit toward things Chinese described as "masochistic." Talking about Chen Duxiu, Lu Xun, and others, Hsia remarks: "Perhaps in their younger days they had been proud of China, but this pride had turned into a frankly masochistic admission of what they saw as inferiority in every department of endeavor. Disgusted with pigtails, bound feet, and opium— palpable symbols of China's backwardness—they were no less ashamed of her art, literature, philosophy, and folkways." See his *A History of Modern Chinese Fiction, 1917–1957* (New Haven: Yale University Press, 1961), 11.

ucated native elites in colonized countries, according to postcolonial theorists.[65] This inferiority complex resulted from the negation of what is Chinese, and a desire to be accepted as equals with the powerful West and Japan. The negative self-perception mimicking that of the imperialists also carried with it a class dimension, however. The target of harsh criticism in most cases was the uncultured and irrational masses, contrasted to the intellectual who presented himself as a rational critic of Chinese society. The object of criticism—the category of the "people"—most often did not include the intellectuals themselves, as their position as critics of Chinese society placed them above and beyond it.[66] If the intellectuals felt inferior to the West and Japan then, this inferiority translated into superiority over the masses. This may be a form of mimicry prevalent in both the colonial and the semicolonial cultural conditions.[67] For those intellectuals who subscribed to the perception that Japanese and Western cultures were superior, the masses became the site of objectification or anxiety, to be observed and dissected, then to be reformed or, in unfortunate cases, rejected. When obsessed with their accountability to the masses, intellectuals and writers expressed their moral anxiety in writing;[68] more often than not, however,

65. Frantz Fanon discusses the situation of educated elites in the Antilles, particularly those who were educated in Europe, returned to Antilles, and became extremely critical of their compatriots. They suffered most intensely from an inferiority complex and required "white approval" for their thoughts and actions. I am tentative about directly applying this to Chinese intellectuals, because China was never thoroughly colonized (see my discussion of semicolonial cultural politics below). The comparison is useful, however, in so far as many Chinese intellectuals did, without hesitation, agree with Western and Japanese Orientalist views of China and its culture, siding themselves with the West or Japan in order to prove themselves more enlightened than the masses who supposedly held onto the traditional China that they were rejecting. For Fanon's discussion, see Black Skin, White Masks, trans. Charles Lam Markmann (New York: Grove Weidenfeld, 1967), 12–51. In this regard, it is useful to look at the genealogy of Lu Xun's famous character Ah Q via Japanese translations of European missionary Arthur Smith's Orientalist characterization of Chinese national character; see Lydia Liu's Translingual Practice, chapter 2.

66. There were rare exceptions, such as Lu Xun's stories "Blessing" (Zhufu) and "Hometown" (Guxiang), in which the intellectual returning from the city to the countryside is portrayed as an ineffectual and powerless agent of modernity, morally more suspect than the countryfolk themselves.

67. Homi Bhabha considers mimicry a potentially disturbing feature of the colonized who, by imitating the colonizers, unsettle the clear distinction between the colonizer and the colonized, a distinction that colonizers are intent on preserving. My specific delineation of mimicry is historically rooted, and does not follow Bhabha's utopian notion of mimicry as resistance par excellence. See Homi Bhabha, The Location of Culture (New York: Routledge, 1994), 85–92.

68. See Marston Anderson's discussion of the moral implications of the realist form in Chinese literature in "The Morality of Form: Lu Xun and the Modern Chinese Short Stories," in Lu Xun and His Legacy, ed. Leo Ou-fan Lee (Berkeley: University of California Press, 1985), 32–53.

they supplanted this anxiety with a desire to remake the "people" to fit the cultural modernization paradigms that supported their leadership positions.[69]

Turning now to the first issue raised by Akutagawa's book, Japanized Orientalism, it should be noted that Akutagawa was at the time plagued with a sense of fragmentation and contradiction in terms of his cultural identity. He found no ready confirmation for a stable identity in Japanese culture, from which he felt distant and alienated. His suicide has been attributed to this tormented struggle with fragmented subjectivity, and a "collapse of a coherent cultural identity."[70] Seen in this light, his traveling to China was an encounter with difference which brought into relief what *did not* constitute the Japanese cultural identity so as to delineate what *did*. For a time, the difference he witnessed could arrest his identity crisis and allow him to articulate a coherent cultural identity.

Japanese cultural identity in *Travels in China* is resolutely, and almost absolutely, differentiated from that of the Chinese. The Japanese people he encounters, planting cherry blossoms in their gardens and doting on Akutagawa as a cultural messenger from their home country, all long to return to Japan. Even Mr. Jones, a British journalist who travels with him on the same ocean liner to China, notes how "awfully sentimental" he would get when thinking of Japan. Akutagawa also visited the East Asia Common Culture Academy, and his seemingly innocent account of the visit shows an unmistakable tinge of imperialist pride, and, only a few weeks after having left home, nostalgia for Japan:

> When I went to the East Asia Common Culture Academy, walking on the second floor of the dormitory, we saw a sea of blue young barley through a window at the end of the hallway. Here and there in that barley field, we saw a cluster of ordinary rape blossoms. Far beyond them we saw a huge carp streamer over a number of connected roofs. The paper carp was blowing in the wind and animatedly fluttering up into the sky. This one carp streamer changed the whole scenery for me. I wasn't in China. I felt as though I was in Japan. But when I approached the window, I saw Chinese farmers working in the barley field before my eyes. I felt angered as though they weren't supposed to be there. Coming all this way to see a Japanese carp streamer in the Shanghai sky gave me a bit of joy.[71]

Japanese-ness, captured in one singular image of the carp streamer, is brought into sharp relief against the Chinese farmers. At this moment, there is no doubt as to what constitutes Japanese-ness. Throughout the book,

69. Duara, *Rescuing History from the Nation,* 90–95.

70. Seiji Lippit, *Japanese Modernism and the Destruction of the Literary Form: The Writings of Akutagawa, Yokomitsu, and Kawabata,* Ph.D. dissertation, Columbia University, 1997, 140–142.

71. Fogel, trans., Akutagawa's "Travels in China," 37.

derogatory commentaries on China's problems foreground the absence of such problems in Japan. The terms of contrast and opposition, used to emphasize the difference between China and Japan, mark a moment of certainty for a Japanese cultural identity. The years between his return to Japan and his suicide marked a gradual loss and eventual disintegration of this certainty.

Japanized Orientalism, in the larger context of the triangular relationship between China, Japan, and the West, underscores the ambiguous position held by Japan, caught in and perpetuating a circle of discursive oppression by simultaneously being the object of Western Orientalism and the subject of its own version of Orientalism against China. Leslie Pincus rightly calls for a reconsideration of Japan's role in global imperialism from the perspective of postcolonial studies, because Japan's initial choice "to become a 'civilized' nation in the image of the West was exercised under threat, imagined or real, of colonization." To survive in an "era of rapacious imperialism," Meiji Japan had to model itself on its Western predators.[72] Bertrand Russell also points out that "the responsibility for Japan's doings in China rests ultimately with her white teachers."[73] Not only did Japan empower itself vis-à-vis other Asian nations through learning from the West, becoming, in E. J. Hobsbawm's words, an "honorary Western imperial power,"[74] it also directly relied on the West's cooperation in its imperialist endeavors in China.[75]

Posing as a modernizing agent, Japan legitimated its invasion of China with the support of cultural work, as did its Western partners/competitors, but with a greater facility since it shared a written aspect of language—*kanji*—with the Chinese. Japan's difference also lay in the singularity of motivation and the direct and conspicuous way the Japanese conducted the propagation of Japanese modernity through books (travelogues, novels, sociological studies) and films about China.[76] Furthermore, Japan's military policy

72. Leslie Pincus, "Epilogue," in *Authenticating Culture in Imperial Japan* (Berkeley: University of California Press, 1996), 239.

73. Russell, *The Problem of China*, 8.

74. See E. J. Hobsbawm, *Nations and Nationalism Since 1780*, 2d ed. (Cambridge: Cambridge University Press, 1992), 151.

75. As mentioned earlier, Western powers in China conceded much of their rights to Japan in exchange for Japan's neutrality during World War I. See Russell, *The Problem of China*, 142.

76. See, for instance, Amar Lahiri's book *Japanese Modernism*, written in English and published by the Hokuseido Press in Tokyo in 1939 for dissemination in Western countries, as part of the legitimation for Japan's imperialist endeavors in China. The book argues that Japan's prime modernizing goal is "Asia for Asiatics," hence it annexed Korea to save it, fought the Russo-Japanese war to protect China from the incursion of the Russians, joined the Western forces in suppressing the Boxer Rebellion to ensure China's long-term interests and stability, and so on. See also the popular film *Nights in China* (*Shina no yoru*), directed by Fushimizu Osamu and released in 1940, in which Japanese colonization of the Chinese subject is rendered as the sanitization and modernization of a Chinese woman (played by a Japanese actress who

in China was endorsed by leading intellectuals in Japan, especially during the late 1930s and early 1940s. By then, even previously self-proclaimed apolitical aestheticians unabashedly allowed their writing to serve Japanese imperialist interests. Cultural discourse in Japan moved squarely into the domain of the state, which suppressed the autonomy of culture in the mobilization for Japan's militarist mission.[77] One can trace a cultural imperialist trajectory from Fukuzawa in the Meiji era to the intellectuals in the interwar years, justified by Japan's self-appointed mission to "enlighten" China and guard it against Western imperialism. Japanized Orientalism was the legitimating mechanism throughout; Japan was both the transmitter, intermediary, and Asian embodiment of Western Orientalism, diverting the original one-way traffic between the West and Asia into an equally hierarchized, top-down, but now *layered* traffic among the West, Japan, and China.[78]

A more direct relationship between Japanese imperialism, Japanized Orientalism, and literary modernism, can be seen in the work of Yokomitsu Riichi (1898–1947), who was very influential among Chinese new sensationist writers and had direct contacts with at least Mu Shiying (1912–1940). Known as the most important proponent of the modernist new sensationism, Yokomitsu's work was translated into Chinese, and he himself wrote a novel about China entitled *Shanghai* (*Shanhai*, serialized 1928–32), as well as several articles, diary entries, and letters about Shanghai. His novel illustrates how imperialist ideology operates on the textual level. If Akutagawa's *China Travels*, written in straightforward prose, marked a moment of certainty or stability for the tormented Japanese subject, Yokomitsu's novel, which prominently displayed the idioms of new sensationism and depicted Shang-

---

spoke fluent Chinese, Yamaguchi Yoshiko). Zhou Zuoren deplored the Japanese "cultural invasion" as much worse than that of the British, as I mentioned earlier (see his *About Tigers*, 509–513). For a good summary of Japanese colonial cultural institutions in China, particularly Manchuria, and institutions promoting the study of China in Japan, see also Akira Iriye, *China and Japan in the Global Setting* (Cambridge: Harvard University Press, 1992), 41–88.

77. See Pincus, "Epilogue," *Authenticating Culture in Imperial Japan*, 209–247.

78. Ultimately, therefore, the postcolonial reading of Japanese imperialism—which sees this imperialism as derivative of its Western models and created under the threat of Western imperial powers as a means of self-preservation—cannot annul the atrocities committed by Japanese imperialism in China. In other words, theoretical conceptualizations make themselves obsolete as soon as the concrete, material history of violence and bloodshed is evoked. It was precisely the naked and bloody form of Japanese domination that shocked the Chinese intellectuals into political action, even as they earlier espoused a culturally cosmopolitan outlook that incorporated Japanese perspectives. During the Sino-Japanese War of 1937 to 1945, the confluence of ideologies earlier considered to be in conflict—political nationalism and cultural nationalism—became inevitable for many. The participants and proponents of this cultural nationalism were the same self-avowed cultural cosmopolitans who, though politically nationalistic all along, had earlier bifurcated culture into metropolitan and colonial categories. This bifurcation increasingly lost purchase as colonial violence vitiated the draw of metropolitan culture, and blood was shed on street corners.

hai as a city of decay and decomposition, propagated his modernist agenda that dismantled literary form and fractured subjectivity.[79] Using the term "Shina" for China, as in Akutagawa's *Travels in China*, Yokomitsu depicts Shanghai as a center of moral, spiritual, and physical degradation, a vast "waste dump of Asia" filled with all the forms of filth by then familiar to readers of Japanese accounts of China. Shanghai embodied "the grotesque and the bizarre"[80] for Yokomitsu. Given the marked racial difference between the Japanese and Euro-American residents of Shanghai, the racial similarity between the Chinese and the Japanese produced anxiety. Japanese characters in the novel fear being mistaken for being Chinese, a confusion that threatens to obliterate the hierarchy painstakingly manufactured by the Japanese.[81] The repudiation of the Chinese Other, that is to say, is built upon a recognition of commonality: the mirror reflection that is Chinese haunts the Japanese who have modeled themselves on the West. When the male protagonist Sanki renounces his attachment to Japan and wears Chinese clothes, for instance, he is treated as a Chinese and thrown into a boat filled with excrement, the boat being the symbol of Shanghai.[82] Hence, when a Japanese person falls into disgrace, he or she symbolically "becomes Chinese," as do Sanki and the prostitute Osugi. This symbolic relegation of deviating Japanese subjects to the excrement-filled "Chinese" realm suggests the inflexibility of the Japanese national subject, and the fiercely felt need to protect this national subject by punishing those who do not conform. Indeed, it is the Japanese colonizers' anxiety about not maintaining the absolute superiority which Western colonizers enjoyed over the Chinese (due to their race) that produced Japan's fervent need to fix the boundaries of Chinese-ness and Japanese-ness. The desire for conquest intersecting with anxiety about the self-same Other contributed to the intensity with which Japan exploited Chinese raw materials and labor, took aggressive military action on Chinese territory, and persistently dehumanized the Chinese. These colonial consequences can be partly explained as the extreme expression of the Japanese desire to maintain difference and contain similarity.

Yokomitsu's novel also evokes the rhetoric of Sino-Japanese unity, despite this fear of becoming Chinese. The threat of global capitalism is used to jus-

---

79. Pincus, *Authenticating Culture in Imperial Japan*, 59.

80. Ibid., 196.

81. I am indebted to Leslie Pincus and her students in her class on *Shanghai* for sharing with me their insights. My reading of *Shanghai* is based on the version in *Japanese Literature* (*Nihon no bungaku*) (Tokyo: chūō kōronsha, 1966), 37:156–307. I am also indebted to Seiji Lippit's reading of *Shanghai* in his dissertation cited above.

82. Lippit, *Japanese Modernism and the Destruction of the Literary Form*, 59, 194. Lippit notes that the novel was treated as a nationalist text (178), but he also reads the novel as depicting the destruction of national identity. Either way, the novel highlights what is Japanese and what is not, and sets matters of national and cultural identity against China and Chinese-ness.

tify Japanese economic exploitation as a form of protection ("If we don't use Chinese materials and labor then the Euro-Americans will"). This capitalist exploitation has literary implications, since Yokomitsu went to Shanghai for the deliberate purpose of collecting "raw material" for literary production. Japanese imperialist subjectivity was produced from a discursive exploitation of the Chinese as object: the modernist traveler's relationship with the cultural material mimics capitalist exploitation of native resources. Thus capitalism not only justified Japanese imperialism in the political and economic spheres, but its process also informed the Japanese modernist mode of writing.

The most intriguing episode in the relationship between Japanese new sensationism and Chinese new sensationism was probably the interaction between Yokomitsu and Mu Shiying (discussed further in chapter 11). Yokomitsu was in China more than once, and Mu Shiying visited Japan sometime between 1933 and 1934, and once again in 1939. Though poorly documented, their relationship has important implications, since Yokomitsu increasingly became a staunch nationalist, writing and speaking on behalf of Japanese imperialism while eschewing his earlier formalist conception of art. From the only extant essay written by Yokomitsu about Mu (upon the latter's assassination in 1940), we can glimpse how the two new sensationisms diverged, the Japanese one shifting to serve the imperialist state. Asked by Mu why his new sensationism took such a decidedly traditionalist and nationalist turn, Yokomitsu answered: "New sensationism valorizes rationalism and scientism, which is a shared tendency of all modern East Asian youth due to [shared] history. Although each is rooted in its own national tradition, this tendency forms a congealing, not separating, force within East Asia."[83] The sentiments expressed here come uncomfortably close to the rhetoric of the Greater East Asia Co-Prosperity Sphere, heralding a shared history to emphasize unity, and claiming cultural uniqueness (each according to one's tradition) to emphasize the right to build a multiculturalist empire.[84]

Akutagawa's and Yokomitsu's work demonstrate the ways in which Japanese modernism is linked to Japanese imperialism. We are still left, however, with the question of Chinese cultural subordination and agency, asked earlier vis-à-vis Western modernism. Even if Chinese writers thought their heavy borrowing from Japan—the forms, techniques, and often the very vocabu-

83. Yokomitsu Riichi, "The Death of Mr. Mu Shiying" (*Mu Shiying shi no shi*), in *Literary World (Bungakukai)* 7 (September 1940): 174–175. *Bungakukai* was one of the leading journals in Japan at the time and in 1942 it sponsored the "Overcoming Modernity" (*kindai no chōkoku*) conference which marked an explicit nationalist turn in Japanese literature. My gratitude to Seiji Lippit for information on *Bungakukai*.

84. For a more detailed analysis of the literary relations between Chinese and Japanese new sensationism, see chapter 9. In chapter 11, devoted to Mu Shiying, I also explicate in some detail what I mean by "multicultural imperialism."

lary used to depict modernist experience —was purely a utilitarian means to approach the West, the ideological imprints of that borrowing on Chinese writing was unavoidable. This was most notable in the way Chinese new sensationist writers curiously replicated an ideological shift from the left to the right found in the members of the Japanese new sensationism, and kept intact the racial and sexual prejudices in Freudian psychoanalysis as mediated by Japanese texts. Similarly, that Japanese new sensationists such as Yokomitsu and Kataoka Teppei turned to support the imperialist cause further stirs up the political implications of Japanese new sensationism as a model.

Nationalist sentiment against Japan threatened the place of Japanized Chinese modernist writing in modern Chinese literary history, as age-old ethnocentricism against Japan and abhorrence of recent Japanese militarism and racism against the Chinese prompted even self-styled cosmopolitans to lament, if not openly criticize, Japanese assertions of supremacy. Xia Mianzun's willing acceptance of the Japanese criticism of China was thus understandably set against a prevailing sense of melancholia, loss, and anxiety in modernist stories set in Japan by writers such as Yu Dafu and Guo Moruo. This is because, unlike the resistance against Western culture, which was largely confined to ultranationalist groups, anti-Japanese sentiments found a much wider audience. This meant that Japanized modernist writing was forced to confront its own affinity with Japanese culture: torn between modernism and nationalism, between longing and hatred, and hence suffused with a predominant tone of melancholy. Since much Chinese modernist writing was written by Japan-educated writers, its beleaguered reception further illustrates the conflict between nationalism and modernism in China.

THE CULTURAL POLITICS OF SEMICOLONIALISM

As I have argued above, Western and Japanese modernisms were intimately connected to their respective political contexts of colonialism and imperialism. Produced within these contexts, they also served crucial purposes of legitimating and disseminating imperialist ideologies. It is within the same conjunctural moment that Chinese modernism also needs to be situated. For China, this is the political condition of multiple imperialisms. It has been argued that the discourse of the nation-state and nationalism emerged in modern China due to the invasion of Western powers, but less prevalent is the notion that imperialism, or its forms of practice in the colony, fundamentally affected modern Chinese cultural production.[85] Rather, the communist Chinese state's agenda of anti-imperialism, which formed the basis

---

85. A recent exception is Prasenjit Duara's *Rescuing History from the Nation,* where he critiques the consequences of imposing Hegelian historical consciousness as the teleology of the nation in modern China. Also see my discussion of May Fourth teleology in chapter 1, and Tani

of its early legitimacy, confined the discussion of imperialism to the political domain. Since the political uses of imperialism reduced the examination of its cultural effects to facile dismissals, my invocation of the term imperialism needs to be clearly distinguished from that of the Chinese state. I do not mean to imply that all literary production was a reaction to imperialism, but that modern Chinese literary production was enmeshed in a historical condition where Western and Japanese imperialisms had instituted what I call semicolonialism. The necessity to contextualize literature in its historical and political milieu is born out of my conviction, shared with Raymond Williams, that literary analysis has to be firmly grounded in historical formational analysis.[86]

Starting from Edward Said's useful distinction between imperialism as the "practice, the theory, and the attitudes of a dominating metropolitan center ruling a distant territory," and colonialism as "the implanting of settlements on distant territory" as a consequence of imperialism,[87] I use "semicolonialism" to describe the specific effects of multiple imperialist presences in China and their fragmentary colonial geography (largely confined to coastal cities) and control, as well as the resulting social and cultural formations. Like imperialism, the term "semicolonialism" has been previously inscribed with communist rhetoric as the partner of "semifeudalism" in forming a dual structure of oppression in China, but the cultural politics of semicolonialism is yet to be charted. Before a cultural definition is possible, however, semicolonialism as a political formation must first be delineated.

Republican China has been variously called a "semicolony" (*ban zhimindi*) and a "subcolony" (*ci zhimindi*) because of the obvious limitations of the term "colony" as applied to China. "Semicolony" is a term used since the 1920s and 1930s by Marxist critics, including Mao Zedong, as a way to describe the coexistence of colonial and native feudal structures. Jürgen Osterhammel explains that the term originated with Lenin and was developed by Chinese Marxists as integral to a "comprehensive theory of China's semi-feudal semi-colonial society": "The theory tried to make sense of a historical process in which 'feudalism' obviously disintegrated, but no significant transition to capitalism took place. A feudal system was penetrated, but not superseded, by colonialism, thus giving rise to a hybrid social formation that had not been anticipated by classical historical materialism."[88] Mao's use of the term repeatedly underscored semicolonialism as a unique social formation, not only

---

Barlow, editor's introduction and "Colonialism's Career in Postwar Chinese Studies," *positions* 1:1 (Spring 1993): v–vii and 224–267.

86. In *The Politics of Modernism*, Raymond Williams emphasizes that formal analysis has to be "firmly grounded in formational analysis," and that there is a "profound connection between forms and formations" (79).

87. Said, *Culture and Imperialism*, 9.

88. Jürgen Osterhammel, "Semi-colonialism and Informal Empire in Twentieth-Century

because of its coexistence with residual feudalism, but also because of the multiplicity of colonial powers involved[89] "Subcolony," in contrast, was coined by Sun Yat-sen, the founder of Republican China, to emphasize the worse-than-colonial situation of China, because the Chinese were not just the "slaves of one country, but of all."[90]

Whether "semicolony" or "subcolony," Marxists and Nationalists alike used the terms to explain the singularity of China's social formation, and to help legitimize their respective political agendas. Despite their different ideological positions and emphases, both felt the need to modify the term "colonialism," which points to its essential limitation in the Chinese context. Most significant is the term's inability to describe the rivalry among foreign powers, and the multiple layers of domination among the foreign powers and China. Also significant is its inadequacy in reflecting the relations of cooperation among the foreign powers in China, which had the effect of snowballing exploitations. In my use of "semicolonialism," I partially invoke the Marxian discussion of early-twentieth-century imperialism as the moment of "inter-imperialist" rivalry, when the imperialist powers had to a large degree completed dividing the world into "spheres of influence" and competed over these already divided spheres.[91] Fredric Jameson identifies the Berlin Conference of 1884, which parceled out Africa among the imperialist powers, as the moment that codified this new imperialist world system.[92] For China, the Versailles Conference of 1919 epitomized the collusive cooperation of foreign powers in deciding its fate. China, though only one geopolitical nation-state, was an Africa of multiple imperialisms struggling over spheres of influence.

Arguing for the uniqueness of twentieth-century imperialism, Jameson overemphasizes inter-imperialist rivalry and underemphasizes the exploitative relationship between the imperialist and the colonized. In contrast, my purpose in raising the inter-imperialist rivalry narrative is to illuminate the relationship of domination and subordination, rather than to occlude it. That is, the multiple and multilayered domination of China by competing foreign powers vying for more power and profit resulted in specific forms of colonial relationships. As eighteen foreign powers competed with each other, they

---

China: Towards a Framework of Analysis," in *Imperialism and After: Continuities and Discontinuities,* ed. Jürgen Osterhammel and Wolfgang J. Mommsen (London: Allen and Unwin, 1986), 276.

89. See *Selected Writings of Mao Zedong* (*Mao Zedong xuanji*) (Beijing: Renmin chubanshe, 1968), 47–312.

90. Quoted in Elizabeth Lasek, "Imperialism in China: A Methodological Critique," *Bulletin of Concerned Asian Scholars* 15:1 (Jan.–Feb. 1983): 50. The original can be found in *Three Principles of the People* (*Sanmin zhuyi*) (Taipei: Zhongyang gaizao weiyuanhui, 1950), 39.

91. Anthony Brewer, *Marxist Theories of Imperialism* (London: Routledge, 1989), 7; see also chapter 6 on Bukharin and Lenin, 109–135.

92. Jameson, "Modernism and Imperialism," 44.

forcefully colonized various parts of China and enforced extraterritorial rights in some fifty treaty ports beginning in the mid-nineteenth century. If we posit that a degree of "care" had to be exercised by a single imperial nation in its formal colony, if only to assure the quantity and quality of production to serve the imperial center, the inter-imperialist rivalry and cooperation among the foreign powers in China had the effect of exempting them of any responsibility or pretense to colonial benevolence. Sun Yat-sen argued, in this regard, that if a formal colony encounters such natural disasters as famine and flood, the imperial nation feels obligated to provide relief, befitting the role of the master. But when northern China suffered from a natural disaster in the early 1920s, no imperial nation took it upon itself to provide relief.[93] In effect, informal imperialism saved the "costs of administering the local state or controlling the local population," hence it made better economic sense.[94]

Another case in point is the opium trade. The United States began selling opium to China in the early nineteenth century, as soon as the British started. In order to compete with the British, whose Indian opium was superior in quality to U.S. Turkish opium, the United States increased volume in order to cut into British profit. Britain then responded by increasing its production.[95] Bypassing Chinese laws prohibiting the opium trade, these foreign powers challenged the sovereignty of the Chinese state. Furthermore, their mutual competition magnified the volume and destructive effects of the trade. Subsequently, two Opium Wars were fought in China, the resulting spoils enjoyed by the British and other foreign powers. Since the "most favored nation" clause in the Treaty of Nanjing mandated that each foreign power should receive all benefits China accorded to any other power, each unequal treaty signed with a foreign power forced China to extend the same benefits to all other powers.[96]

Whether the foreign powers (Britain, Russia, Japan, Germany, France, and the United States, to name the major ones) were competing or cooperating with each other, their intention was to maximize profit and to devise new ways to exploit China. Japan's rising ambition in China was also part of the effects of imperialist competition. As Peter Duus explains, Japan after its successful modernization felt entitled to an equality of status with the West, which meant seeking unequal treaties with China, following the Western precedents. Signing the Treaty of Shimonoseki in 1895 gave Japan the most favored nation clause and other new rights, which were then extended to all

93. See Sun Yat-sen, *Three Principles of the People*, 39–40.
94. Peter Duus, "Introduction," *The Japanese Informal Empire in China*, xvii.
95. James C. Thomson, Jr., Peter Stanley, and John Cutis Perry, *Sentimental Imperialists* (New York: Harper & Row, 1981), 31–43.
96. Ibid., 122.

powers; thus they presented themselves as promoting the interests of the Westerners as well as their own.[97] This is a classic case of a "competitive imperialism," with imperial powers working both in competition and cooperation with each other.[98]

The cooperative and competitive domination of China was of great consequence for its domestic politics. Arthur Ransome, a British philosopher visiting Shanghai in the 1920s, noticed how extraterritoriality deepened domestic political corruption because officials, politicians, and warlords could use the situation to their benefit. Ransome gave the example of foreign banks in which corrupt personalities deposited their loot. These foreign banks, Ransome argued, like the concessions which provided safe havens for criminals, contributed largely to the "amenity of Chinese civil war and political strife."[99] Along similar lines, the Marxist thinker Qu Qiubai (1899–1935) called China an "international colony" (*guoji de zhimindi*), accentuating that such a condition contributed to the fragmentation of domestic political spheres and the aggravation of their conflicts.[100] The impossibility of forging a unified political front among the various domestic power groups due to multiple colonialism naturally had cultural consequences as well. Most predictably, it spelled a lack of cohesion and an abundance of strife within the cultural sphere.

I choose to use "semicolonialism" to describe the cultural and political condition in modern China to foreground the multiple, layered, intensified, as well as incomplete and fragmentary nature of China's colonial structure. The "semi-" here is not to denote "half" of something, but rather the fractured, informal, and indirect character of colonialism, as well as its multilayeredness. Unlike many other Third World nations that were formally colonized, China was never systematically colonized and did not have a central colonial government implementing extensive colonial institutions and structures. The fact of China's linguistic integrity[101]—China was never forced to supplant its native language with a colonial one and its official language remains Chinese—is cultural proof for the incompleteness of colonialism in

---

97. Peter Duus, "Introduction," *The Japanese Informal Empire in China*, xx-xxi.

98. The term "competitive imperialism" is from Bernd Martin, "The Politics of Expansion of the Japanese Empire: Imperialism or Pan-Asiatic Mission?" in Osterhammel and Mommsen, *Imperialism and After*, 63.

99. Arthur Ransome, *The Chinese Puzzle* (New York: Houghton Mifflin Company, 1927), 121–127.

100. Qu Qiubai, "Eastern Culture and World Revolution" (*Dongfang wenhua yu shijie geming*, 1923), collected in *Collected Essays from the Debate on the Question of Eastern and Western Culture During the May Fourth Period* (*Wusi qianhou dongxi wenhua wenti lunzhan wenxuan*), ed. Chen Song (Beijing: Zhongguo shehui kexue chubanshe, 1989), 591–602.

101. The term "linguistic integrity" is Rey Chow's; see her *Primitive Passions: Visuality, Sexuality, Ethnography, and Contemporary Chinese Cinema* (New York: Columbia University Press, 1995), 61–62.

China. Paul Cohen therefore also described the Chinese colonial experience as partial, multiple, and layered.[102]

This definition of semicolonialism has multiple implications. First, as a condition of asymmetrical relationship between the foreign powers and China, semicolonialism implies that the powers did not assume "outright domination and formal sovereignty" over China,[103] and that domination was exercised through less formal, although no less destructive or transformative, channels. Second, the absence of outright control means that semicolonialism, in regards to economic penetration, racial discrimination, and limited territorial jurisdiction, was closer to neocolonialism than to formal, institutional colonialism.[104] Third, the fragmentation and multiplicity of foreign powers implies that each power potentially occupied a different place within the Chinese cultural imaginary, as indeed was the case in the distinction most Chinese made between Japanese and Euro-American imperialisms. Fourth, and most important for our purpose, while multiple colonial presences multiplied controls and augmented exploitation, they made impossible a tight-fitting, unified colonial management and containment of native spheres of activity. This afforded Chinese intellectuals more varied ideological, political, and cultural positions than in formal colonies where the ordinary Manichean division of nationalists and collaborators held sway.

Fragmentation in the political and cultural spheres, then, actually allowed for multidirectional pursuits among Chinese intellectuals. I hasten to add, however, that this "freedom" of pursuit should by no means be mistaken as the "gift" of benevolent imperial powers, but rather should be seen as the paradoxical emergence of culture in the fissures among different agents of control. The multiplicity of intellectual positions largely reflected the state of emergency of the Chinese cultural imaginary, infused with a heterogeneity of often ambivalent and shifting positions, searching in different directions for answers to China's problems. Nationalism, in many cases, took a backseat in these searches. Throughout the decades, cosmopolitan thinkers and writers, though by no means procolonial, saw Western culture as the prize to be attained. The May Fourth enlightenment project, for instance, had an ambivalent, almost contradictory, relationship with nationalism, as evidenced by its prioritizing of "enlightenment" (*qimeng*) over "national salvation" (*jiuwang*). Enlightenment was heavily coded as antifeudal and pro-Western, so the enlightenment thinker was a putative nationalist who in

---

102. Paul Cohen, *Discovering History in China* (New York: Columbia University Press, 1984), 144–145.

103. For this aspect of semicolonialism, see Osterhammel, "Semi-colonialism and Informal Empire," 308.

104. See Gregory Lee on the Chinese condition as similar to neocolonialism, in his *Troubadours, Trumpeters, Troubled Makers: Lyricism, Nationalism, and Hybridity in China and Its Others* (Durham: Duke University Press, 1996), 74.

actuality was a self-appointed cultural critic and vanguard. For the enlightenment thinker, the urgency of criticizing feudalism and forwarding Westernization often displaced the immediate need to confront and criticize colonial domination.

Such displacement was often accompanied by a split in the concept of "the West," between the metropolitan West (Western culture in the West) and the colonial West (the culture of Western colonizers in China). In this dichotomy, the former was prioritized as an object of emulation, which often resulted in diminishing the latter as an object of critique. By bifurcating the two, the intellectual could proselytize for Westernization without being perceived as a collaborationist—he could be the "third" term in the nationalist/collaborationist dyad. In a similar way, Japan was a medium for Western knowledge, hence Japan's political domination could be set apart from the exigency of cultural enlightenment (albeit with greater difficulty given Japan's role as a new aggressor). This capacity to displace colonial reality through the discourse of cultural enlightenment was endemic to semicolonial cultural politics.[105] Hence, in the context of this book, "semicolonialism" is a term meant to encapsulate multiple and multilayered colonial domination as well as the fragmentary and incomplete nature of such domination, which contributed to a discursive formation that bifurcated the metropolitan and the colonial.

Such displacement or non-engagement with colonial reality points to a fundamental ambivalence toward colonialism, but should not be taken as an acceptance of it. The structure of this particular ambivalence can be broadly explained in terms of the absence of a uniform colonial infrastructure. In other Third World nations, the presence of a tight-fitting formal colonial structure often meant that there could be an epistemologically clear distinction between the inside and the outside: the enemy was easily identified and native culture could be unproblematically assumed to be the site of resistance.[106] In Republican China, this usual colonial scenario did not apply. The multiplicity of colonial powers, and their both cooperative and competitive forms of domination, meant that it was difficult to target the enemy clearly. Furthermore, since native culture had been systematically dethroned

105. This point is argued throughout this book, but, for a quick example, I note the disappearance of Caucasian characters in May Fourth writing, in contrast to their prominent appearance in late-Qing fiction. The disappearance indicates the desire to displace and avoid the colonial presence. I thank Theodore Huters for providing this important observation.

106. Regarding the epistemological clarity distinguishing inside and outside in a colonial situation, I am appropriating Rey Chow's argument about Hong Kong, in her "Between Colonizers: Hong Kong's Postcolonial Self-writing in the 1990s," *Diaspora* 2:2 (1992): 151–170. For other examples of a clear distinction between the inside and outside, and native culture as the site of resistance, see Partha Chatterjee's discussion of nineteenth-century nationalist discourse in India in his *The Nation and Its Fragments* (Princeton: Princeton University Press, 1993).

by Chinese enlightenment thinkers themselves, it was neither readily established nor available as an untainted and untroubled sanctuary of resistance against colonialism. The condition of semicolonialism hence made articulating resistance much more difficult, as native culture had already been "deconstructed" and could not serve as the unquestioned locus of resistance, not even for those who argued for the recuperation of native culture. Diverging from the binary colonial model, therefore, the semicolonial condition undermined the clarity of colonial relationships, infusing the Chinese cultural imaginary with uncertainties and ambiguities in its relationship with colonial reality.

Prasenjit Duara also attributes the absence of strong critiques of (Western) modernity in modern China to the indirect nature of colonial control. In India, the full encounter with colonial ideology enabled someone like Mahatma Gandhi to produce a coherent antimodern and nonmodern discourse. But the encounter was of a different kind in China:

> In China, the imperialist presence was, of course, widely resented and anti-imperialism was at the core of political movements for the first half of the twentieth century. But the absence of institutionalized colonialism in most parts of China also meant that the colonial ideology was not entrenched among both colonizer and colonized in the same way as it was in India and other directly colonized countries. The opposition to imperialism was chiefly political and economic and did not present the urgent need to root out imperialist ideology in the very self-perception of a people.[107]

Caught up in the May Fourth enlightenment discourse—which, by dismissing alternative narratives of Chinese culture and nation as conservative, largely cut off the possibility of a critique of modernity—modern Chinese intellectuals saw even less urgency or legitimacy in a critique of the cultural ideologies of imperialism. Charlotte Furth notes that even among the nativist camps of the National Essence school (*guocuipai*), there was no principled opposition to modernity as a Western construct.[108] As the May Fourth discourse of cosmopolitan modernity increasingly gained hegemony, aided by the absence of a critique of modernity and the importation of Hegelian notions of unilinear history, the emergence of a truly anticolonial cultural discourse became less and less viable.[109] Semicolonialism thereby sanctioned a degree of cultural colonization that was self-imposed and left unexamined, and operated like neocolonialism, through diffused ideological and cultural interpellation rather than institutionalized, formal domination.

107. Duara, *Rescuing History from the Nation*, 224.

108. Summarized in ibid., 207–208.

109. See Duara's book on the suppression of alternative narratives of the nation by the hegemonic May Fourth discourse of modernity and enlightenment.

Reflecting the incomplete nature of colonial domination, then, reactions to colonial reality were equally fragmented, allowing neither the development of a coherent, consistent, and comprehensive discourse of anticolonialism nor the formation of a coalition among the disparate camps of intellectuals. Not until the emergence of a consonant political and cultural nationalism during the anti-Japanese war did Marxist ideology herd disparate ambivalent positions into ideological unity. Until then, the ambiguous and heterogeneous attitudes toward imperialism reflected the worldwide trend of pacifism after the experience of World War I, as Akira Iriye has usefully delineated, when international economic and cultural relations became more dominant than military ones (until China was swept away again in a protracted war with Japan in 1937 and the world became embroiled in World War II).[110] Reflecting the popular pacifist tendencies of Western intellectuals in the interwar years, Chinese intellectuals also supported the higher ideal of global peace and did not directly support the military dimensions of anti-imperialist endeavors. The failures of the late-Qing reforms, which were mainly military in character, also revealed to them the futility of such endeavors. Furthermore, by the early twentieth century, the Euro-American presence in the treaty ports of China had settled into a seminormalized state: no further military aggression was launched against China except for a few small-scale clashes. Semicolonialism, in this sense, is akin to neocolonialism, the main purpose being economic rather than political. Hence an enlightenment thinker such as Hu Shi could say that Euro-American imperialism was not really the problem for China, since China had been poor even before the imperialist invasion. And since China had no capitalist class to speak of, criticizing Western capitalism was also off the mark.[111] In this post–World War I climate, then, intellectuals were not considered out of line when adoring metropolitan Western culture without confronting the colonial culture in China. The bifurcation strategy itself enjoyed the legitimation of a worldwide pacifist trend, even though this pacifist trend, couched in the rhetoric of cultural internationalism and economic interdependence, did not serve China, and made its struggle against imperialism more arduous.

Akira Iriye also claims that the relationship between China and Japan in the 1920s was mainly economic and cultural, not militaristic, as it was "characterized by the absence of large-scale direct military confrontation between the two countries or Japan's blatantly aggressive designs to control China." But even as he idealizes their relations, we cannot fail to notice that the same economic and cultural relations consistently served Japan, using Akira Iriye's

110. Iriye, *China and Japan in the Global Setting*, 41–45.

111. Hu Shi, "Which Path Shall We Take?" (*Women zou natiaolu*, 1930) and "Reply to Mr. Liang Shuming" (*Da Liang Shuming xiansheng*), in *Which Path Shall We Take?* (Taipei: Yuanliu chubanshe, 1986), 6, 30.

own evidence. Japan replaced Britain as the leading trading nation in China, which would prove to be "the key to a successful economic transformation of Japan" from a market for U.S. goods into an industrial producer and exporter to China. While Westerners were quick to respond to the Chinese call for tariff autonomy in 1928, Japan refused to grant it to China until two years later. With the money it received from the Boxer Indemnity Fund, Japan instituted student exchange programs (as the U.S. had done a few years earlier), and the travels of such writers as Tanizaki Jun'ichirō and Akutagawa were lauded as examples of genuine cultural communication.[112] Zhou Zuoren's critique of Japanese cultural imperialism mentioned earlier (so tragically convincing because he was later branded a Japanese collaborator and traitor for his life-long study of Japanese culture) and Akutagawa's colonialist attitudes lead us to further question Akira Iriye's argument. The use of the Boxer Indemnity Fund by Japan was by all means controversial: the Japanese Foreign Ministry strictly controlled the use of the fund and dictated that those Chinese who used it to study in Japan had to "swear reciprocity" to the Japanese emperor,[113] while the Europeans and the Americans basically allowed the Chinese to decide on the use of the fund by themselves. The Chinese were offended by the high-handed manner in which the fund issue was dealt with by the Japanese government.[114]

Here, my point is that the Chinese *differentiation* between Euro-American imperialism and Japanese imperialism complicated the multilayeredness of colonial domination. While Euro-American imperialism was taken for granted by some Chinese intellectuals, Japanese imperialism was persistently repudiated. Japan was a new imperialist power in China (since the first Sino-Japanese War in 1895), unlike the Euro-Americans who had carved out their extraterritorial rights in the mid-nineteenth century. Japan's behavior was also perceived as comparatively more violent, naked, destructive, and threatening to the Chinese. Throughout the 1920s, Japan backed the puppet regime of Yuan Shikai and the warlord Zhang Zuolin; in the 1930s, their occupation of Manchuria, bombing of Shanghai, rape of Nanjing, incursion into Inner Mongolia and other parts of Northern China, and the Sino-Japanese War (1937–1945) all contributed to the image of Japan as an eager imperialist coveting the territorial occupation of China as a formal colony, as it did with Taiwan, the Penghu islands, and Korea. Bernd Martin therefore notes that Japan exercised both formal, colonialist imperialism and informal economic penetration in China.[115] This is also why Mark R. Peattie

---

112. Iriye, *China and Japan in the Global Setting*, 41–67.
113. See Sophia Lee, "The Foreign Ministry's Cultural Agenda."
114. See the editorial, "Sino-Japanese Cultural Enterprises," that appeared in *The Chinese Nation* 1:44 (April 15, 1931): 1165–1166.
115. Martin, "The Politics of Expansion," 78.

concluded that Japan was the most "rapacious military presence" in China, its government the "most outrageously provocative of all the foreign gendarmeries," seeking predominantly violent military solutions to perceived problems.[116]

My purpose in delineating the Chinese differentiation of the Japanese and Euro-American presence is not to absolve the latter of their imperialism, but to foreground the uneven colonial relations between the Chinese and the multiple imperialisms in China, again spelling out the complexity of semi-colonialism as a cultural, political, and economic formation. Even among the Euro-American powers, the Chinese related to each differently. As Gregory Lee points out, while the British acquired economic dominance, the French were more involved in cultural dominance, having failed in their bid for economic exploitation. Hence there was more aversion to the British and their culture, and a preference for the French and their culture.[117] The Chinese perception of the different powers also varied over time and in different places. My argument recognizes historical mutations in those relations over time, while vigilantly delineating spatial specificities of a given Chinese cultural articulation vis-à-vis the West and Japan; hence this book's focus on Chinese modernist writers' heterogeneous cultural positions by charting the shifting locality (Beijing and Shanghai) and temporality (from 1917 to 1937) of their modernism.

CHINESE MODERNISM IN LITERARY HISTORY

Through the 1980s and early 1990s, Chinese literary criticism began to debunk the state-sponsored literary ideology of socialist realism, and a small but influential literary movement self-consciously announced its antecedents in Western modernism.[118] Prior to these decades, modernism was a dismissed, if not forbidden, topic. The imposition of ideologically overdetermined criteria in literary histories systematically displaced the works of writers with overt modernist tendencies. These literary histories linked the development of modern Chinese literature to the political advance of the communist revolution, judging literature according to its degree of participation in and documentation of the changing revolutionary reality, thus making (socialist) realism the *sine qua non* of authentic literary production. Since realism was generally understood as a writing style that "reflected reality" (*fanying xianshi*), it was readily canonized as a mode befitting the pressing revolu-

116. Mark R. Peattie, "Japanese Treaty Port Settlements in China, 1895–1937," in Duus, Myers, and Peattie, *The Japanese Informal Empire in China*, 201–207.

117. Gregory Lee, *Troubadours, Trumpeters, Troubled Makers*, 74.

118. For discussions of 1980s modernism, see Jing Wang, *High Cultural Fever: Politics, Aesthetics, and Ideology in Deng's China* (Berkeley: University of California Press, 1997), and Xudong Zhang, *Chinese Modernism in the Era of Reforms* (Durham: Duke University Press, 1997).

tionary agendas during and after the Republican period, and therefore as sufficiently transplantable and sinicized to avoid being implicated in the cultural power politics with the West. Within this paradigm, modernism's role in literary history was predictably troubled. It was perceived as a threat to the autonomy of Chinese culture because its mode of expression and philosophy, some claimed, exhibited a willing capitulation to Western cultural hegemony and its capitalist decadence. However, since realism and modernism were both imported in the early twentieth century, the canonization of the former and the denigration of the latter reveals less about the two modes' essential characteristics than about the politics of culture and ideology behind such a selective endorsement.

The standard, still unsupplanted literary history written by Tang Tao and Yan Jiayan, *A History of Modern Chinese Literature* (*Zhongguo xiandai wenxue shi,* 1979–80, three volumes), remains mute on the issue of Chinese modernism. The earlier classic that had defined modern Chinese literature as an academic discipline, *Manuscript on China's New Literary History* (*Zhongguo xinwenxue shigao,* 1951) by Wang Yao, clearly exemplifies the extent to which ideology dictated the writing of literary history. Analyzing Dai Wangshu's modernist poetry, for instance, Wang Yao recognizes Dai's technical efforts but summarily concludes that his poetry was a form of escape from social practice and was therefore "unhealthy."[119] Shi Zhecun, the prominent Shanghai modernist discussed in my preface and mentioned above, unambiguously claimed in 1990 that there was no literary history in China, only the "literary constitution" (*wenxue xianfa*) promulgated by the government.[120] After the relative thaw in political control of culture in the 1980s, a few "revisionist" literary histories recognized the existence of modernist writings, but their authors still qualified this recognition with an ideological critique, portraying modernism as a slavish imitation of Western literary styles and as a capitulation to Western capitalist bourgeois decadence. Except for the compulsory ideological critiques, Yan Jiayan's later work *Schools of Modern Chinese Fiction* (*Zhongguo xiandai xiaoshuo liupai shi,* 1989) and Yang Yi's voluminous *History of Modern Chinese Fiction* (*Zhongguo xiandai xiaoshuo shi,* 1986–91, three volumes) are exemplary in partially recuperating Chinese modernism from the Republican era.[121] Indeed, it is due largely to Yan Jiayan's meticulous re-

119. Wang Yao, *Manuscript on China's New Literary History* (1951) (Shanghai: Shanghai wenyi chubanshe, 1982), vol. 1, 225.

120. "The Dawn of Chinese Modernism: A Dialogue with the Master of New Sensationism, Shi Zhecun" (*Zhongguo xiandai zhuyi de shuguang:yu xin'ganjuepai dashi Shi Zhecun xiansheng duitan*), an interview conducted by Zheng Mingli and Lin Yaode, *Unitas* (*Lianho wenxue*) 69 (July 1990): 136.

121. Yan Jiayan, *Schools of Modern Chinese Fiction* (Beijing: Renmin wenxue chubanshe, 1989). Yang Yi, *A History of Modern Chinese Fiction,* 3 volumes totaling over two thousand pages (Beijing: Renmin wenxue chubanshe, published consecutively in 1986, 1988, 1991).

search and groundbreaking work that Shanghai modernism—the *xin'gan-juepai*—became recognized in the late 1980s as one of the most important, but forgotten, chapters of modern Chinese literary history.

Literary histories produced in the United States discouraged the use of the term "modernism" in discussions of modern Chinese fiction,[122] owing to: (1) an excessive propensity to judge Chinese literature by the "superior" and "universal" standards of Western literary criticism, rendering no Chinese text worthy of the qualifier "modernist"; (2) the lack of access to primary sources; and (3) the perception that literary histories should downplay "minor" literary movements. Of these three, the first is the most problematic and warrants some analysis. Judging modern Chinese literature against the standards of Western modernism is not equivalent to applying Western theory to Chinese texts in order to illuminate their complexity. The "Western" in the former case is constituted in a hierarchical relationship with Chinese texts. Such a practice produces statements like the following: Since James Joyce best employed the stream of consciousness technique, no Chinese writer could reach his level of aesthetic achievement, hence Chinese literature could not deserve to be called modernist. This Eurocentric stance, furthermore, found itself in curious agreement with what can be called a sinological nativism. For sinological nativists, the lack of modernism in China proved that Chinese literature was unique, so that its cultural difference could be safeguarded. Whether for the purpose of dismissal or with the more "well-intentioned" aim of safeguarding Chinese cultural difference, the result was an equal occlusion of Chinese modernism. Hence some claimed that there was no "modern" literature possible in China,[123] while others dismissed "Westernized" Chinese literature as not authentically Chinese enough. While the former position has yet to be seriously challenged—which shows how per-

122. There has been more openness in the United States to the discussion of modernist poetry from Republican China than modernist fiction. I think this fact is related to the secondary role poetry was assigned in the cultural imaginary in modern China, as opposed to fiction which became the primary genre. For discussions of Chinese modernist poetry from the Republican era, see Ping-kwan Leung, *Aesthetics of Opposition: A Study of the Modernist Generation of Chinese Poets, 1936–1949,* Ph. D. dissertation, University of California, San Diego, 1984; Gregory Lee, *Dai Wangshu: The Life and Poetry of a Chinese Modernist* (Hong Kong: Chinese University Press, 1989); Wai-lim Yip, *Lyrics from Shelters;* and Zhang Zao, "Development and Continuity of Modernism in Chinese Poetry Since 1917," in *Inside Out: Modernism and Postmodernism in Chinese Literary Culture,* ed. Wendy Larson and Anne Wedell-Wedellsborg (Aarhus, Denmark: Aarhus University Press, 1993).

123. W. J. F. Jenner asks the question, "Is modern Chinese literature possible?" and answers with a resounding "No." Jenner concludes that Chinese literature in the twentieth century is not "modern" because it does not belong "fully to the modern world," by which is meant that Chinese writers did not understand the modern "sense of abyss where earlier thinkers had seen firm ground." "Is a Modern Chinese Literature Possible?" in *Essays in Modern Chinese Literature and Literary Criticism,* ed. Wolfgang Kubin and Rudolf G. Wagner (Bochum: Studienberlag Brockmeyer, 1982), 192–230, quotations from 194–195.

sistent the practice of evaluating modern Chinese literature by Eurocentric criteria is—the latter position has been eloquently criticized by Rey Chow in her passionate argument for recognizing the "givenness" of Westernized Chinese-ness as a historical reality in modern China.[124]

This collusion between Eurocentricism and sinological nativism, along with the political nativism of the Chinese communist party, prevented a sustained inquiry into Chinese modernism from theoretical, historical, or textual perspectives. To sum up, modernism from the Republican era was criticized alternately as morally corrupt, decadent and escapist, unfit and useless for the Chinese, a degenerate version and unworthy imitator of Western modernism, shallow and unsophisticated, or inauthentically Chinese because of its Western affinities. Context-based arguments against the existence of modernism were easy to win: since all literary movements spring from a specific set of local conditions, and the conditions that made modernism possible in the West were not present in China, modernism in China was a theoretical impossibility. These arguments, complicit with the Eurocentric historiography of Western modernism that emphasized its particularity beneath the apparent rhetoric of internationalism, have had the effect of *absenting* modern Chinese modernism from literary history once and for all.

Only when it became clear that Western modernist "influence" was undeniable—such as in the 1960s modernist movement in Taiwan, and in the flourishing of conspicuously Western modernist-inspired writing in 1980s China, culminating in the eruption of the controversial 1982–1983 debate on a "Marxist modernism"—did native modernism became a legitimate topic of literary history.[125] Studying modernism from Republican China, however, necessitates nothing less than a new paradigm for the study of modern Chinese literature, requiring not only a rethinking of literary history, but also of historiography. Historiography as a narrative construction overdetermined by the ideological imperatives of given contexts underlies the production of literary history. To write about Republican modernism is first to write against the language of state-sponsored Marxist literary history from China, which organized modern Chinese cultural history in order to legitimize communist insurgency and delegitimize bourgeois sensibilities. Second, it is to write against the language of Eurocentric and nativist paradigms through contextualizing Chinese modernism in modern Chinese history and culture, and

124. Rey Chow, "Preface," in *Woman and Chinese Modernity: The Politics of Reading Between West and East* (Minnesota: University of Minnesota Press, 1991), xi–xvii. Also see her criticism of Orientalism in Chinese Studies in *Writing Diaspora*, 1–26.

125. See Sung-sheng Yvonne Chang's *Modernism and the Nativist Resistance: Contemporary Chinese Fiction from Taiwan* (Durham: Duke University Press, 1993); Wendy Larson, "Realism, Modernism, and the Anti-'Spiritual Pollution' Campaign in China," *Modern China* 15:1 (January 1989): 37–71; and Larson and Wedell-Wedellsborg, *Inside Out: Modernism and Postmodernism in Chinese Literary Culture*.

reconstructing its connections and negotiations with other histories and other cultures.

Marxist ideology and Eurocentricism aside, however, we may still legitimately ask why we should insist on "modernism" when identifying and discussing certain literary texts from the Republican era. Might the desire to retain the term "modernism" be just another projection of Eurocentric universalism? By way of an answer, we may posit modernism as a *problematic* that demands investigation, precisely because the absenting of modernism in literary history betrays anxiety about the term. This anxiety itself indicates the limits of the hegemonic critical language of realism, and to a lesser extent romanticism, in modern Chinese literary studies. Modernism, in this sense, is strictly the means by which we name those literary experiments that simultaneously exceed the referential demands and formal constraints of realism, and refrain from the heroic and emotional exuberance of romanticism, whether revolutionary or bourgeois.[126]

An alternative answer lies by way of another question: If we have deployed the discourse of modernity and modernization in the Chinese context and claimed the experience of modernization as having universal valence, then why not "modernism"? What this rejoinder asks is, again, not whether modernism is a legitimate category, but what gets legitimized by the absenting of modernism. If modernization theories have time and again helped prove the "backwardness" of China, the absenting of the concurrent cultural practice of modernism in China consolidates the West as the sole proprietor of modern culture, with China relegated to the realm of the premodern. "China" once again remains securely the object of either positivistic study or Orientalist fantasy.[127]

More importantly, however, there is a historical rationale for the use of "modernism" that attends to the specific discursive formations of modern China in the context of semicolonialism. As the following chapters will show, many fiction writers since the May Fourth era self-consciously appropriated Western and Japanese modernist techniques, forms, and sentiments. They imported and translated Western and Japanese modernist writing, wrote about the manner in which they understood it, posited a theory of Chinese modernism (though in a fragmentary manner), and further put this theory into productive practice. The corpus of this writing is significant, as many writers who earlier might have been romanticists went through a "modernist

---

126. For realism in China, see Marston Anderson, *The Limits of Realism* (Berkeley: University of California Press, 1990), and David Der-wei Wang, *Fictional Realism in Twentieth Century China: Mao Dun, Lao She, Shen Congwen* (New York: Columbia University Press, 1992). For romanticism, see Leo Ou-fan Lee, *The Romantic Generation of Modern Chinese Writers* (Cambridge: Harvard University Press, 1973).

127. See Chow, *Writing Diaspora* and *Woman and Chinese Modernity,* both cited above.

phase" and later became realists or naturalists.[128] This trajectory of passing through romanticism, modernism, and realism/naturalism is found in several major writers of modern Chinese literature, including Yu Dafu and Guo Moruo. Even Lu Xun worked extensively with modernist forms and techniques. By the late 1920s, a distinct modernist literary movement had formed in Shanghai and, amidst the growing division between Beijing and Shanghai, divergent modernist inscriptions of Beijing and Shanghai cultures also emerged.

Cultural productions of the Republican era—fanned by the massive reorientation which was "stimulated" (in both the positive and negative senses of "willingly inspired" or "forced to confront") by knowledge of more "advanced" Western culture—were compelled to "negotiate" (again in both the positive and negative senses of "incorporating" or "resisting") with that knowledge.[129] What has not been shown is the complex nature and politics of such negotiation as executed in modernist writing. As a form of writing that often self-consciously borrowed early-twentieth-century Western and Japanese modernist manners, forms, and techniques—considered the least "belated," most contemporaneous way of acquiring cultural modernity—modernism in Republican China was undoubtedly one of the most important sites of such negotiation. Furthermore, the complex modes of negotiation can be informative, if not paradigmatic, of similar negotiations with other "borrowed" discourses from the West and Japan, whether philosophical, cultural, or even political. Due to its proximity in time to that of Western and Japanese modernism (in the language of teleological history), Chinese modernism perhaps embodies the most intense search for cultural modernity, and thereby becomes the site where manifestations of cultural politics in the pursuit of modernity are most revealing.

128. I think it is generally indicative of the ambiguous and unsettled nature of cultural discourses in modern China that many writers went through various phases that may ordinarily appear contradictory. For instance, Lu Xun can be called a realist, a modernist, or a symbolist, depending on the texts being considered. Arif Dirlik makes a similar observation about Chinese political thinkers: many Marxists and members of the Nationalist Party, although they are ideologically opposed to each other, went through a similar anarchist phase. See Arif Dirlik, *Anarchism in the Chinese Revolution* (Berkeley: University of California Press, 1991).

129. Here, I am appropriating the concept of "negotiation" from Gayatri Spivak, who emphasizes the importance of negotiating with Western theory as a postcolonial critic: neither ignoring it nor excusing its inadequacies. See *Outside in the Teaching Machine* (New York: Routledge, 1993), 128.

PART ONE

Desiring the Modern

May Fourth Occidentalism and Japanism

CHAPTER 1

Time, Modernism, and Cultural Power
Local Constructions

*The difference between the East and the West lies in nothing but time. . . . It is the
difference between slow and fast, and not anything essential.*
                    QU QIUBAI (1923)

Like the phoenix from the fire, they can only attain rebirth after self-immolation.
                    CHEN SIHE (1990)

Time, rather than space, was the crucial category in the radical rethinking
of Chinese culture and literature during the May Fourth era (1917–1927).
That is, the quintessential embodiment of the May Fourth zeitgeist was the
desire to leap into the time of the modern. This modern time was perceived
as the property of the West and Westernized Japan, but nonetheless universally available to those behind in the trajectory who wanted to catch up. For
instance, Guo Moruo's much celebrated "Phoenix Nirvana" (*Fenghuang
niepan*, 1920), the poem said to have captured the essence of the May Fourth
spirit, charts the phoenix's radical transformation into a new being. The linear procession of death and rebirth served as a perfect metaphor, for the
now-totalized Chinese "tradition" had to be slain if May Fourth intellectuals
were to be reborn in the new, modern time. The death of tradition was the
premise for a magical leap into modern time, for only by killing off tradition could a new youthful self of "freshness," "sweetness," "radiance," "passion," and "love" be born out of its ashes.[1]

But for the magical leap to be possible, modern time had to be a concrete
and measurable entity with a universal standard that could be accessed with
due effort. This measurable time was the Darwinian time of linear development, the Hegelian time of World History, and modern Western calendri-
cal time that allowed the emergence of a global consciousness. In this chapter, I investigate the question of May Fourth subjectivity by analyzing the
ideology of linear temporality underlying May Fourth enlightenment discourse on cultural differences between China and the West—particularly fo-

---

1. Guo Moruo, "Phoenix Nirvana," in *Goddess* (*Nüshen*) (Beijing: Renmin wenxue chubanshe, 1957), 30–42.

cusing on the discourse of "neoromanticism" (*xin langman zhuyi* or *xin luoman zhuyi*, a May Fourth neologism borrowed from Japan for the yet-to-be-codified "modernism"), and the translation of Western modernist philosophical discourses (Nietzsche, Bergson, and Freud). I do not attempt to provide an exhaustive inquiry into or definition of May Fourth constructions of modernity and modern subjectivity—there were multiple, competing constructions—but instead focus on the dominant strand of May Fourth subjectivity that privileged temporal over spatial modes of thinking.

I argue that the linear, temporal mode of thinking, in the *local* discursive context, was used to legitimize such major May Fourth enlightenment agendas as antitraditionalism and cosmopolitanism, of which modernism was one important literary expression. This legitimation was useful in several ways. First, it allowed intellectuals to repudiate the cyclical, dynastic mode of traditional time as repetitive and stagnant, and to sharpen the iconoclastic image of May Fourth intellectuals and their antitraditionalism. Second, by constructing China as the past of the West, intellectuals could invent a cosmopolitan subjectivity that did not take the nation-state or the ethnos as the sole boundary marker of identity, and they could establish a transnationally mediated identity in the global terrain. Third, this transnationally mediated cosmopolitan subjectivity naturally carried esteem and cultural power within the domestic terrain, creating a new form of cultural capital available only to the "enlightened" few. These legitimations were the expression of May Fourth agency in the *local* discursive field.

In the *global,* cross-cultural discursive context, however, the incorporation of linear temporality meant subjecting the Chinese past to a Hegelian critique that disrupted the notion of Chinese subjectivity as a continuum from the past to the present. Hence there emerged a dichotomous, discontinuous, and oppositional vision of tradition (as Chinese and particular) versus modernity (as Western and universal). The ideology of linear temporality produced, so to speak, "tradition" in order to repudiate it as old and outdated, and celebrated "modernity" as discontinuity from the past, in order to create a new subjectivity that prioritized the present and the future.[2]

One distinct purpose this ideology served was to allow May Fourth intellectuals to harbor a fantasy of equality with the West. If time was the only measure of difference between China and the West, China could become an equal partner in a world dominated by the West by simply catching up as fast as it could. Disregarding the reified hierarchy embedded in the Western conception of linear temporality—which measured the West's superiority through its canonization of such dichotomies as "advanced" versus

2. I am suggesting that the binary categories of tradition and modernity evident in the scholarship on modern China are actually a legacy of May Fourth enlightenment discourse. See below.

"backward," freezing the Third World in the eternal past[3]—May Fourth intellectuals professed an optimism toward the possibility of becoming "contemporary" or coterminous with the West, as the quote from one May Fourth
leader Qu Qiubai (1899–1935) at the beginning of this chapter illustrates.
The contradictory relationships between the local and the global implications of May Fourth subjectivity therefore troubled its cosmopolitanism from
the very start. I analyze this global context in greater detail in chapter 5.

In the West, modern subjectivity, which premised itself on the discontinuity between past and present, was also seen as the subjectivity of national
temporality. In Benedict Anderson's well-known characterization, the time
of the modern nation-state was that of progressive temporality, a narrative
separating the present from the past, and shifting progress from the past toward the future. National temporality reorganized time into the standardized, unified, homogenous units of clock and calendar time, so that time
steadily moved forward in a chronological fashion and became simultaneous across space. This allowed for a new conception of time that could be
shared by a multitude of people across a wide geographical space as contemporaries of each other, allowing these people to imagine the community
or collectivity as a nation.[4] In this view, linear temporality, by standardizing
time as a forward-moving engine that could be objectively measured, made
possible the constitution of a modern, national subject. While this model of
inquiry is limited in its applicability, as critics of Anderson's thesis have
pointed out,[5] it in large part parallels the May Fourth process of incorporating linear temporality, although they did so for a different purpose. By
adopting linear temporality, May Fourth intellectuals imagined becoming
contemporaries with the West in the expanded, larger community of the
world, wherein China, like other countries, could be a member of modernity. If, in the West, linear temporality helped inspire national consciousness,
in May Fourth China it heralded the emergence of transnational or global
consciousness.

In the case of May Fourth China, furthermore, the entry into modern linear temporality cannot be seen as just another break of the present from the
past, as it was for Western nations. This is because the break in China was ef-
fected by a belated incorporation of a Western notion of time, made com-

3. Hegelian World History is a good example of how progressivist theories can work to denigrate "backward" nations in Asia as unfree and unenlightened, and portray the West as the unchallenged goal of History. See Georg W. F. Hegel, *The Philosophy of History*, trans. J. Sibree (New
York: Dover Publications, 1956), Part I, "The Oriental World," 111–222.

4. See Benedict Anderson, *Imagined Communities* (London: Verso, 1992), 22–36.

5. See for instance E. J. Hobsbawm, *Nations and Nationalism Since 1780* (Cambridge: Cambridge University Press, 1990), who criticizes Anderson's model as limited in its rush to impose
closure on many otherwise indeterminate and ambivalent entities, such as print capitalism, ethnicity, and language, which function in the formation of national consciousness.

pelling due to the experience of Western imperialism.[6] The May Fourth advocacy of discontinuity with tradition was conceived in much more radical and totalistic terms than in the West, since the necessity for a discourse of discontinuity did not arise so much from internally developed notions of modernity as from the horizontally transplanted modernity of the West, made powerful and convincing by the West's proven superiority. A useful analogy to illustrate this point can be found in Hegel's discussion of the symbolism of the phoenix for the Asian and the Westerner. While the Chinese phoenix had to die to be reborn a totally new being (as in Guo Moruo's poem mentioned earlier), the Western phoenix, in Hegel's conception, draws strength from its previous incarnation to engender a new form. In a characteristic movement of Hegelian dialectics, the sublation of the previous form allows the phoenix, the embodiment of Hegelian Spirit, to emerge "exalted and transfigured"; however, instead of negating the past self, the Spirit "reworks that existence, so that whatever went before is the material for what comes after, as its labor elevates it into a new form." Thus, its changes are "*elaborations* of its own self" (emphasis mine) rather than negations of its past self.[7] Unlike the Hegelian phoenix, the May Fourth phoenix did not elaborate upon its past self but simply repudiated it; there was no luxury of continuity in sublation. It is ironic that what Hegel articulated about a century before the May Fourth era, in his characteristic Eurocentric vein, concerning the different uses of the phoenix metaphor by the Westerner and the Asian, rang true for the May Fourth intellectuals. In their haste to negate tradition for the many legitimations such negation served, May Fourth intellectuals unwittingly proved and substantiated Hegel's remark about the Asiatic phoenix. This irony reveals more than anything else the prevailing Hegelian perspective in May Fourth thinking about modernity.

6. Various Western theorizations of modernity as a disjuncture from the past in order to construct a new present are available from Michel Foucault and Marshall Berman, to name two representative theorists. Dennis Washburn likewise defines modernity in Japan as a moment of discontinuity. My argument, however, is aimed not at refuting their theses, but at urging a consideration of the different *cause* and *nature* of this discontinuity in China. That is to say, modernity as discontinuity in the Chinese context (and for the Meiji Japan that Washburn studies, for that matter) was much more of a necessity due to Japanese and Western imperialisms. What Chinese modernity rejected—Chinese tradition—was also by nature divergent from that which Western modernity resisted. Questions of problematic agency and the loss of indigenous tradition therefore need to be attended to in this particular Third World construct. See Marshall Berman, *All That Is Solid Melts Into Air: The Experience of Modernity* (New York: Penguin Books, 1988); Dennis Washburn, *The Dilemma of the Modern in Japanese Fiction* (New Haven: Yale University Press, 1995); and any of Foucault's works.

7. Georg W. F. Hegel, *Introduction to the Philosophy of History*, trans. Leo Rauch (Indianapolis: Hackett Publishing Company, 1988), 76–77.

TIME AND CULTURAL DIFFERENCE

The radical debunking of Chinese tradition entailed an unambiguous construction of Chinese tradition and Western modernity as oppositional dichotomies in cultural terms. These dichotomies undergirded much of May Fourth enlightenment discourse in the "East-West culture debate" (*dongxi wenhua lunzhan*), and placed the locus of the new, modern subjectivity in the midst of Hegelian World History. In the writings of enlightenment intellectuals such as Chen Duxiu (1879–1942), Li Dazhao (1889–1927), Qu Qiubai, and others, the series of dichotomies employed can be roughly drawn as follows:

China	*The West*
old	new
ancient/past	modern/present
traditional	modern
spiritual	material
mental	physical
feudal	constitutional
agricultural	industrial
pacifist	militarist
family-based	individualistic
emotional	ruled by law
calm	active
intuitive	rational
pessimistic	optimistic
fatalistic	creative-progressivist
dependent	independent[8]

In these dichotomies, a temporal value was attached to each pair of contrasting properties, so that all the properties of the West corresponded to the new and modern, while those of China corresponded to the old and traditional. Time became the final measure of difference between the two cultures, hence China needed only to overcome its outdatedness and belatedness to become modern.

Such dichotomous thinking was not only prevalent among antitraditionalists, but also, significantly, among those who opposed May Fourth antitraditionalism and adhered to milder positions such as syncretism (the so-called

---

8. See, for instance, the articles collected in Chen Song, ed., *Collected Essays from the Debate on the Question of Eastern and Western Culture During the May Fourth Period* (*Wusi qianhou dongxi wenhua wenti lunzhan wenxuan*) (Beijing: Zhongguo shehui kexue chubanshe, 1989). The "Introduction" (1–33) by Chen Song provides a good summary of major positions on cultural difference.

zhezhongpai). Du Yaquan (1873–1933), the editor of *Eastern Magazine* (*Dong-fang zazhi*), opposed "calm" Chinese culture to "active" Western culture,[9] and Chang Naide (1898–1947) echoed the dichotomies set up by the iconoclasts as follows:

Eastern Civilization emphasizes:	*Western Civilization emphasizes:*
the past	the present
hierarchy	equality
conservatism	progressivism
meditation	pragmatism
religion	science
withdrawal	competition
nature	human effort
disengagement	engagement
from human affairs	with human affairs[10]

As one can see, the categories "calm" versus "active," "pacifist" versus "militaristic," and "spiritual" versus "material" could serve both antitraditonalists and traditionalists in their denigration of China *or* the West, as either pole can be endowed with essentially negative or positive connotations. For a nation at the mercy of Western guns, "militarism" could become an important goal (as it did for late-Qing reformers of the *Yangwu* school), and could become problematic for the traditionalists who preferred the pacifist retreat into harmony and nonviolence. What they all shared, however, was their haste in essentializing cultural difference between China and the West and then giving that difference a temporal value. The theoretical connection between such binary thinking and the Eurocentric, imperialist thinking in the West—which persistently employed a linear, temporal metaphor to relegate the non-West to the realm of the past and denied the non-West a coterminous temporality—is easily recognizable.[11]

Though troubling to latter-day cultural historians, the linear, developmental conception of history and culture was the most salient characteristic of the particular May Fourth understanding of modernity.[12] Space was

9. Cang Fu (Du Yaquan), "Calm Culture and Active Culture" (*Jing de wenming yu dong de wenming*, 1916), in ibid., 23–31.

10. Chang Naide, "Eastern Civilization and Western Civilization" (*Dongfang wenming yu xifang wenming*, 1920), in ibid., 287.

11. See Ashis Nandy's delineation of this imperialist practice in his "The Savage Freud," a talk given at the University of California, Los Angeles, April 25, 1995. See as well his *The Savage Freud and Other Essays on Possible and Retrievable Selves* (Princeton: Princeton University Press, 1995).

12. Leo Ou-fan Lee traces the origin and development of this new historical consciousness in "In Search of Modernity: Some Reflections on a New Mode of Consciousness in Twentieth-

persistently contained in the category of time, understood in temporal terms, or translated into temporal equivalents. A temporal notion of modernity, whether based on the ideologies of capitalism (Hu Shi) or socialism (Qu Qiubai and Chen Duxiu), dominated May Fourth enlightenment discourses on culture. This teleology in turn became the justification for determining the "inferiority" of Chinese culture: thus Wu Zhihui's (1865–1953) extremist assertion that Chinese national treasures (*guocui*) should all be thrown into the toilet,[13] and the May Fourth dictum that China should undergo "complete Westernization" (*quanpan xihua*).

Examples that illustrate this haste to Westernize are numerous. Literary journals published during this era bore titles suggesting the dawning of a *new era* of modernity—such as *New Youth* (*Xin qingnian*), *New Tide* (*Xin chao*), *Creation* (*Chuangzao*), *The Dawn* (*Shuguang*), etc.[14] The concept of "*wenxue shi*" (literary history), furthermore, was codified as a means to delineate the temporal difference in literature between the past and the present as a way to chart the new path to literary modernity. By 1933, more than a dozen comprehensive histories of Chinese literature were published.[15] Another significant, and perhaps somewhat humorous, phenomenon was that of Chinese writers adopting Darwinist names: Yang Tianze ("Natural-selection Yang"), Sun Jingcun ("Struggle-for-existence Sun"), Zhang Jingsheng ("Struggle-for-life Zhang"), and Hu Shi ("The fit Hu," from the Chinese phrase for "survival of the fittest," *shizhe shengcun*).[16] There could not have been a more ironic example of the Confucian practice of the "rectification of names." No longer to exalt morality, it was now deployed to reflect the inscription of Darwinian teleology.

TIME AND NEOROMANTICISM

The earnestness with which Chinese intellectuals incorporated the ideology of linear temporality was equally pronounced in the protomodernist

---

Century Chinese History and Literature," in Paul A. Cohen and Merle Goldman, eds., *Ideas Across Cultures* (Cambridge: Council on East Asian Studies, Harvard University, 1990), 109–135.

13. Quoted in Hu Shi, "Cultural Conflicts" (*Wenhua chongtu*, 1929), in Luo Rongju, ed., *From "Westernization" to Modernization* (*Cong xihua dao xiandaihua*) (Beijing: Beijing daxue chubanshe, 1990), 365.

14. For the obsession with the "new" in May Fourth culture, see also Lee, "In Search of Modernity."

15. For instance, Hu Shi, *A History of Vernacular Literature* (*Baihua wenxue shi*); Tan Zhengbi, *The Evolutionary History of Chinese Literature* (*Zhongguo wenxue jinhua shi*); Zheng Zhenduo, *Illustrated History of Chinese Literature* (*Chatu ben Zhongguo wenxue shi*); Gu Shi, *Outlines of Chinese Literary History* (*Zhongguo wenxue shi da gang*).

16. I added to the examples found in Jerome B. Grieder's *Hu Shih and the Chinese Renaissance* (Cambridge: Harvard University Press, 1970), 27.

discourse of neoromanticism.[17] For some Chinese writers and critics, ne-oromanticism in the 1910s and 1920s embodied the *latest* development in literature, and hence the most advanced and the most modern. Writ-ers and critics saw the contemporary trend of modernist writing as signi-fying the ultimate stage of progress, the knowledge and adoption of which would herald the achievement of their own literary modernity. Leading literary magazines published the works of major philosophers and thinkers whose ideas had laid the foundations of Western modernism, which in-cluded, most notably, Nietzschean existentialism, Henri Bergson's theory of time and philosophy of life, Havelock Ellis's sexual psychology, and Sig-mund Freud's psychoanalytic theory. Selective translations of early West-ern modernist literature of the late-nineteenth and early-twentieth cen-turies were also published alongside the philosophical essays. The earliest use of the specific term "modernism" was probably the 1921 article (trans-lated from the Japanese) by the then well-known Japanese literary histo-rian, Noboru Shōmu (1878–1958), in which the English term "mod-ernism" was cited and translated as *modanpai*, literally the "modern school" in Chinese, and was used interchangeably with "neoromanticism." In this article, Noboru argued that Russian decadent symbolism of the 1890s and after was heavily indebted to Western modernism, as it espoused Nietz-schean individualism, French symbolism, and Ibsenism. Writers such as Fyódor Sologúb, Valéry Bryúsov, Aleksándr Blok, and Leoníd Andréev were considered representatives of the group.[18] Besides marking probably the first time the term "modernism" was used in China, the article is significant because the writers Noboru mentioned were already translated into Chi-nese and played important roles in the formative phase of Chinese mod-ernist writing, exemplified by the work of the "father of modern Chinese literature," Lu Xun.

Modernism was predictably articulated in temporalized rather than spa-tialized terms. The use of linear temporal categories here is not unlike that within the cultural debate, but I discern a specific rationalization here hav-ing to do with the "importability" of Western literature onto Chinese soil. By substituting temporal difference for the geographical difference between

---

17. There is no consensus among Western critics and literary historians regarding the defini-tion of "neoromanticism," but their use of the term fundamentally differs from Japanese and Chinese uses. Bernarda C. Broers used the term to designate the Pre-Raphaelites in his *Mysti-cism in the Neo-Romantics* (Amsterdam: H. J. Paris, 1923), and Paul Volsik described it as a reac-tion against modernism in the 1930s and up to the 1950s in his "Neo-Romanticism and the Poetry of Dylan Thomas," *Études Anglaises* 42:1 (1989): 39–54. The only overlap between the Chinese conception and Broers's seems to be the emphasis on mysticism.

18. Noboru Shōmu, "Main Literary Trends in Contemporary Russia" (*Jindai Eluosi wenyi de zhuchao*), trans. Chen Wangdao, *Short Story Monthly* (*Xiaoshuo yuebao*) 12, special issue on Rus-sian literature (September 1921): 1–20.

China and the West, Western modernism could be claimed as the future of Chinese literature, hence the destination of literary teleology. Chinese literature is departicularized, and the importation of Western literature naturalized. In such a spirit, Yu Dafu argued that modern Chinese literature belonged to the European literary lineage, not the native one.[19] Japan-educated Tian Han's (1889–1968) long essay "Neoromanticism and Others" (*Xin langman zhuyi ji qita*, 1920), perhaps the most important Chinese-authored treatise on neoromanticism from the May Fourth era, is representative in viewing modernism in temporal terms.

As literary modernity was conceived as the cultural equivalent to social modernity, a discussion of neoromanticism often entailed what one would ordinarily consider such extraliterary issues as the Chinese national character. Neoromanticism served as a discourse with which to criticize Chinese national character, to ascribe gender and age value to the Chinese self, and to serve as the destination of literary teleology. Tian Han argued that one of the major reasons for the literary achievements of Russia was its harsh natural environment, which bred in writers a sense of struggle and a strong desire for human achievement. The Chinese national character lacked this sense of struggle and thus the Chinese tended to become slaves to nature. The masculinity required for the struggle with hostile nature, in other words, was a goal to be attained by the Chinese, and this masculinity was embodied in the hard, scientific proclivities of naturalism. For the Chinese national character to acquire the masculinity of naturalism was to enhance the survival of the Chinese in evolutionary struggles. Conflating the discourses of biological evolutionism, literary movements, and the Chinese national character, Tian Han placed heavy emphasis on the necessity of naturalism, as the passageway to arrive at the ultimate destination of neoromanticism.

So what was neoromanticism, the latest stage of literary development that would embody the best of everything? Tian Han contended that neoromanticism was the offspring of romanticism (the mother) and naturalism (the father), hence it contained both feminine and masculine characteristics. Romanticism embodied the passion of Lord Byron, and naturalism advocated calm reason like the "limpidity of still water." Neoromanticism benefited from both characteristics by maintaining romanticism's mystical tendencies and tempering it with naturalism's rationality. Borrowing the analogy of life stages used by Kuriyagawa Hakuson (1880–1923), a famous Japanese literary theorist and professor at Kyoto University who had close contacts with Chinese students in Japan and whose work was popular in China

19. From Yu Dafu's "On Fiction" (*Xiaoshuo lun*) and "The Road Modern Fiction Took" (*Xiandai xiaoshuo suo jingguo de lu*), as mentioned in Yan Jiayan, *Schools of Modern Chinese Fiction* (*Zhongguo xiandai xiaoshuo liupai shi*) (Beijing: Renmin wenxue chubanshe, 1989), 16, 28.

at the time, Tian Han further attributed age value to these three literary movements and charted neoromanticism as the age of maturity:

Romanticism: the passionate age, around twenty.

Naturalism: the perturbed and frustrated age, around thirty.

Neoromanticism: the mature age, around forty.

Notwithstanding that the generation of May Fourth intellectuals, including
Tian Han himself, was at this time in their early twenties and thus could not
be middle-aged neoromantics, in the logic of the temporal leap that they
advocated, the moment of neoromanticism embodied the "paradise" that
Tian Han "diligently longed for."[20] This longing and desire for a modernist
paradise, reflective of their belief in linear temporality, would manifest itself
as the organizing principle for May Fourth writers' and critics' interpretation of Western modernist thought, as I analyze in the next section.

TIME AND TRANSLATED MODERNIST PHILOSOPHIES

Although discussions of literary modernism were few in May Fourth writing,
Western modernist thought received a much more extensive treatment. The
introduction, translation, and critical evaluation of Western modernist
thought attended to such important and specific issues as individualism (via
Nietzsche), vitalism (via Bergson), psychological interiority (via Freud), and
sexuality (via Freud, Havelock Ellis, and Kuriyagawa Hakuson), and they complicated a simple notion of linear temporality. Nietzschean existentialism was
imported into China as early as 1902, and met with immense popularity during the May Fourth decade. At least three different translations of *Thus Spake
Zarathustra* were available, two of them partial translations and one complete,
done by three writers who came close to monopolizing the May Fourth literary scene: Mao Dun (1896–1981), Lu Xun, and Guo Moruo. There was
even a Chinese counterpart to Nietzsche's text, Zhang Shuiqi's (n.d.) "So-
liloquies of Amen" (*Amen duyu*), serialized in *General* (*yiban*) magazine in 1926
and 1927, which borrowed from *Zarathustra* the parable form and much of
its content. Interpreted primarily as the prototypical rebel fighting against
tradition and established convention, Nietzsche embodied the May Fourth
spirit of iconoclasm. For the May Fourth intellectuals, he was the "destroyer

20. Tian Han, "Neoromanticism and Others," *Young China* (*Qingnian Zhongguo*) 1:12 (June
1920): 24–52. In another article by Tian Han entitled "Poor Lüliyan—*Pauvre Lelian*," he characterized the French symbolist poet Verlaine as a "decadent modernist" (*Creation Quarterly*
[*Chuangzao jikan*] 1:2 [August 1922]: 3). For another important May Fourth treatise on neoromanticism, see Tang Heyi, "The Rise of Neoromanticism" (*Xinlangman zhuyi wenyi de boxing*),
Sixth Anniversary Issue of Chenbao (*Chenbao liuzhounian jinian zengkan*) (December 1, 1924):
229–251.

of idols," the one who advocated the "transvaluation of all values," who called for the Superman of the future, and who opposed "slave morality."[21] Nietzsche's assertion of the "transvaluation of all values" would even seduce the moderate liberal Hu Shi who, in an uncharacteristic Nietzschean vein, advocated the importance of a critical attitude.[22] Other existential philosophers such as Kierkegaard and Schopenhauer, however, gained much less exposure and were discussed only in very generalized terms.[23]

An exaltation of the individual and an optimism about the future as embodied in the Superman together explain much of May Fourth intellectuals' fascination with Nietzsche. As Zhang Yuhong explains:

> The "Superman" as conceived during the May Fourth era mainly refers to Chen Duxiu's description [in his manifesto for *Youth Magazine* (*Qingnian zazhi*) in 1915] of a man with aristocratic morality and not slave morality, a man whose character is liberated, who does not follow blindly, who respects individual will, and who has the strength of a powerful man.[24]

"Slave mentality" (*nuxing*) was taken to be the worst national characteristic, and Nietzschean anticonventionalism was conscripted to deal a fatal blow to that "feudal remnant" (*fengjian yidu*). Lu Xun, in his pre–May Fourth writings on Nietzsche, had regarded the individual intellectual as the "great man and genius" (*dashi tiancai*) who could enlighten society while the "stupid masses" (*yuzhong*) could only lead society into degradation and therefore should be detested as if they were "snakes and scorpions."[25]

When he expressed these views in 1908, Lu Xun was writing specifically against the utilitarian, technologically driven reform movement of the late Qing, attacking it as too tepid to bring about a thorough "cultural revolution"; hence his ideas had taken on a radical cast, and the elitism embedded in Nietzsche's thought suited Lu Xun's discursive purposes. But by the May Fourth period, such elitism could not be voiced publicly. May Fourth agendas of enlightenment and national salvation elevated the masses to the ob-

---

21. Xie Zhixi, *Existentialism and Modern Chinese Literature* (*Cunzai zhuyi yu Zhongguo xiandai wenxue*) (Taipei: Zhiyan chubanshe, 1990), 75. So far, this book offers the most comprehensive and in-depth analysis of the reception of existentialism in Republican China, particularly as manifested in literary texts.

22. Grieder, *Hu Shih and the Chinese Renaissance*, 110.

23. See chapter 1 of Xie Zhixi's *Existentialism and Modern Chinese Literature*, 73–116, for an account of the transmission and reception of existentialism in philosophical and literary circles in May Fourth era China.

24. Zhang Yuhong, "The Infiltration and Transformation of Modernist Thought" [*Xiandai zhuyi sichao de shentou yu xingbian*], in Yue Daiyun and Wang Ning, eds., *Western Literary Thought and Twentieth Century Chinese Literature* (*Xifang wenyi sichao yu ershi shiji Zhongguo wenxue*) (Beijing: Zhongguo shehui kexue chubanshe, 1990), 134.

25. Lu Xun, "On Cultural Extremities" (*Wenhua pianzhi lun*, 1908), in *The Complete Works of Lu Xun* (*Lu Xun quanji*, hereafter *LXQJ*) (Beijing: Renmin wenxue chubanshe, 1981), 1:52.

jects of reform. By 1919, Lu Xun's occasional mentioning of Nietzsche had become devoid of any trace of elitism, and instead Nietzsche's anticonventionalism was championed as the path to a new progressive future for all. Nietzsche now was seen as supporting the May Fourth dictum of "overthrow the idols" (*dadao ouxiang*).[26] I analyze the relationship between these two different uses of Nietzsche in greater detail in the next chapter, devoted to Lu Xun. I argue that instead of tension, these two uses of Nietzsche underlie Lu Xun's particular understanding of humanism. Hence we have, on the one hand, such heavily existentialist prose poems as "Wild Grass" (*Yecao*, 1927), in which a Nietzschean inquiry into the nature of existence is conducted in dense and often grotesque language and imagery. On the other hand, we have the madman figure in "The Diary of a Madman" (*Kuangren riji*, 1918), who is presented as a prophet with the foresight of Zarathustra, warning the not-yet-true humans of their impending doom. Zarathustra's work, whether as an individual embroiled in existential anguish or as a socially conscious, anticonventional enlightener, remains a humanist endeavor of bettering both the individual and the collective.

We may still raise the questions, however, of whether the elitism embedded in Nietzschean existentialism could have been transformed through discursive transplantation and traveling or if it had to remain as an integral part of that discourse, and whether Lu Xun's original use of Nietzsche, as a discourse of the Superman who denigrated the masses, could readily be replaced by a discourse of collective hope. The answer to these questions is perhaps clear in the case of Lu Xun: to import Western discourse and appropriate it for local use was not an act of complete reappropriation, as the internal mechanisms of that discourse exercised discursive constrictions in the appropriation and the characteristic marks of that discourse indelibly lingered in the uses of its borrowing agent. Lu Xun's pre–May Fourth elitist thinking was predisposed to a Nietzschean elitism (note also how this elitism closely traces the Confucian *junzi/xiaoren* [gentleman/small man] divide). It was not so much that he jettisoned elitism as that he rationalized it via a particular understanding of humanism (the collective can only improve when the individual has), so that elitism became compatible with enlightenment agendas aimed at the collective.

The May Fourth use of Henri Bergson was, on the other hand, explicitly in the service of the rationalist paradigm of scientific progress which, one could argue, was exactly what Bergson wrote *against* in his emphasis on intuition (over reason) and duration (over linear time). Chinese intellectuals reinterpreted Bergson in a manner that undermined the possible contradictions between his philosophy and its applicability in China. Fang Xun's

---

26. See, for instance, Lu Xun, "Random Thought 46" (*Suiganlu 46*, 1919), in *LXQJ* 1:332–333.

"Bergson's *Philosophy of Life*" (*Bogesen Sheng zhi Zhexue,* 1919) and Feng Youlan's "Bergson's Philosophical Method" (*Bogesen de zhexue fangfa,* 1920) are characteristic of such an attempt. Fang Xun's article provides a clear example of how the May Fourth ideology of progress must misread Bergson. He begins the article by explaining the two reasons why Bergson's philosophy is appropriate for study in China. One, since knowledge is universal, he explains, the fact that Bergson is French should not discourage the Chinese from studying and learning from his philosophy. Two, Bergson's philosophy is not only influential, but at present also functions as an important impetus for human progress. If universalism and progress initially justify the need to know Bergson's philosophy, the specific conditions in China are what made that knowing important. Fang Xun lays out the problems of China throughout history as a lack of a spirit of struggle and creative ability, the blind following of ancestors' ways, no liveliness, no important scientific inventions, no equality between the sexes, no human justice and happiness, no individuality, and an inability to escape from the constrictions of conventional morality, all of which add up to a "corrupt life" in which individual freedom is repressed and society is blocked from evolution. How then can Bergson's philosophy rectify this? By helping the Chinese exercise instrumental intellect and intuition for the benefit of social evolution. Fang Xun explains Bergson's notion of time in terms of evolutionary linearity, and sees historical force in terms of forward-moving action. In this "flow of time," the intellect serves as the tool of creation, specifically the creation of machines such as the airplane, seaplane, railroad, steamship, and submarine. Intuition, on the other hand, is a philosophical tool that allows one to understand the truth of life. It allows for individuality and freedom, and it opposes customary morality. It cultivates the creative spirit that is required for human progress. In this way, intuition integrates knowledge and life. Intellect and intuition both serve the agenda of collective progress.[27]

Feng Youlan, later associated with new traditionalism and one of the most important Chinese philosophers of the twentieth century, wrote extensively on Bergson at this time and generally followed Fang Xun in his assessment of Bergson, albeit with more scholarly acumen. In his "On Bergson's *Mind-Energy*" (*Ping Bogesen de Xinli,* 1922), he concluded that the vital life force innate in human beings has always struggled with the material world to express itself through creation, and the release of this life force motivates the creative evolution of the human species.[28] In his "Bergson's Philosophical Method," he attributed Bergson's theory to evolutionism and argued that his theory of intuition was scientific, not mystical. Feng took great pains to

27. In *Young China* (*Qingnian Zhongguo*) 1:7 (1919): 3–7.
28. In *Scholarly Essays from Three Pine Studio* (*Sansongtang xueshu wenji*) (Beijing: Beijing daxue chubanshe, 1984), 17–22.

explain how intuition is a necessary part of scientific process and that Bergson is not opposed to science.[29]

The picture that emerges from these accounts of Bergson is a distinctly utilitarian one, which shows more about the Chinese philosophers' "use" of Bergson in the context of Chinese society than about Bergson's actual ideas. Bergson's philosophy of life and mind-energy was seen as useful in arousing people's dormant creative power so that Chinese society would quickly develop; intuition, along with knowledge and concepts, were useful tools in scientific and other projects designed to improve people's lives. Not heeding the historical fact that Bergson's philosophy arose as a reaction against nineteenth-century positivism, these writers chose to emphasize the positivistic aspect of Bergson's writing.[30] It was from a similar motivation that they exaggerated the social function of Nietzsche as the prophet who spoke for a better future. These uses are diametrically opposed to the way Nietzsche and Bergson were used in Western modernism. Sanford Schwartz has shown, for instance, how Nietzsche and Bergson laid the philosophical foundation for important aspects of Western modernist poetics through their emphasis on recovering the flux of concrete sensations, in their theories of the "chaos of sensations" and "real duration," respectively, which they posed against the tyranny of conventions in order to recover immediate experience.[31] Leo Lee has also pointed out how the progressive orientation of the Chinese conception of modernity starkly contradicted Western modernists' distrust of scientific modernism.[32]

When properly historicized, however, the difference between the Western modernist use of this body of philosophy and the May Fourth use becomes more easily understandable. May Fourth China was at the threshold of entering the Western narrative of modernity and modernization, and its

29. In ibid., 1–10. Another example showing Feng's endorsement of Hegelian unilinear history underlined by progress and development is discussed by He Lin, his contemporary and a philosopher, in his *Chinese Philosophy in the Last Fifty Years* (*Wushi nianlai de Zhongguo zhexue,* 1945) (Shenyang: Liaoning jiaoyu chubanshe, 1989), 21. The fact that Feng is sometimes associated with New Confucianism is because of his post-1940s writings.

30. Jerome Ch'en, in his impressive, though heavily modernization theory–based book *China and the West: Society and Culture 1815–1937* (Bloomington: Indiana University Press, 1979), 186–188, notes that Bergson's influence continued for about a quarter of a century in various forms and that those who came under his influence were various, including politicians. Bergson's thought was popular among philosophers such as Li Shicen, Carsun Chang (Zhang Junmai), and Zhang Dongsun, and even Liang Shu-ming, who especially attempted to link Bergson with Chinese philosophy. In the hands of Nationalist Party followers such as Chen Lifu, the integration of Bergson and Confucius helped create a Chinese vitalism—*weisheng lun* (the "life only" theory)—as opposed to idealism (*weixin lun*) and materialism (*weiwu lun*).

31. See Sanford Schwartz, *The Matrix of Modernism: Pound, Eliot, and Early Twentieth-Century Thought* (Princeton: Princeton Univ. Press, 1985), 19–31.

32. Leo Lee, "In Search of Modernity."

temper was more akin to the Western early-modernist celebration of technology and science, and diametrically divergent from the so-called high-modernist distrust of them. In the West, the early modernist culture of the late nineteenth century and the first decade of the twentieth century included an obsession with speed in the technological sphere, and a proliferation of science fiction and the founding of futurism in the artistic sphere. Stephen Kern, in his *The Culture of Time and Space, 1880–1918,* illustrates this view with meticulous documentation covering science, technology, art, literature, and philosophy.[33] The "time lag" between the Western early-modernist celebration of speed and progress and its May Fourth replication further indicates the conditions of China's participation in "universal" modernity as always already "late"; the desire of Chinese intellectuals to become "contemporary" with the West therefore could only remain a fantasy. The ideology of linear temporality would disenable, rather than enable, the realization of this fantasy of contemporaneity.

More than existentialism and Bergson's philosophy, psychoanalysis was welcome not only in literary circles but also in scholarly circles, triggering the publication of a large number of articles and studies.[34] And this is where the May Fourth ideology of collective progress did not appear to fit seamlessly. Freudian psychoanalysis did signify a new, progressive front in science, and provided a general celebration of individualism (the basis of May Fourth iconoclasm). But beyond that, psychoanalysis did not appear to have any greater collective significance. It did not readily promise a better future, nor did it open itself easily to instrumentalization for the immediate improvement of the society. Instead, psychoanalysis could justifiably be designated as a philosophy of the past in its heavy reliance on memory. Freud's theories regarding various mental disorders uniformly locate the source of the disorder in the patient's past, be it infantile sexuality, childhood traumatic experiences, or tribulations from a more recent past. The main operation of psychoanalysis is to probe the patient's desires and knowledge, repressed in the unconscious, in order to provide explanations for abnormal tendencies in the present. So psychoanalysis is in fact a mode of interpreting the past so as to understand and deal with the present. Instead of looking forward, it looks backward and inward. Instead of searching for concrete

33. Stephen Kern, *The Culture of Time and Space, 1880–1918* (Cambridge: Harvard University Press, 1983).

34. At least forty-eight articles and books were published on the subject between 1919 and 1927. The authors of these works range from writers and critics (Chen Duxiu, Zhu Guangqian, Zhou Zuoren, Shen Yanbing [Mao Dun], Zheng Zhenduo), to scholars and psychologists (Gao Juefu, Zhang Dongsun, Pan Guangdan, Wang Pingling), to laymen. See Zhang Jingyuan's *Psychoanalysis in China: Literary Transformations, 1919–1949* (Ithaca: Cornell East Asia Series, 1992). However, the earliest introduction of Freud can be dated to 1914. See Qian Zhixiu's "Study of Dreams" (*Meng zhi yanjiu*), in *Eastern Magazine (Dongfang zazhi)* 10:11 (May 1914): 7–8.

progress on the outside, it delves into the depths of the unconscious. In the process, the linearity of time is disrupted; time is made to jump back and forth, to slow down or reverse, and to be spatialized for purposes of careful scrutiny.

Zhu Guangqian's (1897–1986) "Freud's Theory of the Unconscious and Psychoanalysis" (*Fulude de yinyishi shuo yu xinli fenxi,* 1921) provides an interesting illustration of how psychoanalysis could be rendered to support May Fourth teleology despite its apparent incompatibility. An extremely erudite scholar, Zhu would later become one of the most important thinkers of modern China, known for his synthesis of Western and Chinese thought (see chapter 6). In this early article, we already see traces of such an integration when he readily draws from classical Chinese sources to explain psychoanalysis. Zhu provides a succinct summary of Freud's notion of the unconscious in relation to dream psychology, myth, psychotherapy, art, religion, psychoanalysis, and most interestingly education. He consistently notes that psychoanalysis and psychotherapy are scientific methods, and it is in his unorthodox theorization of the role of the unconsicou in education that we can locate how his functionalistic interpretation of Freud fits the May Fourth teleology. Zhu describes the unconscious as a stream of water that needs the right "conduit" (*guidao*) of "expression/flow" (*liulu*) so as not to become the source of madness, hysteria, or other psychological problems. He explains that autocratic societies place individual lives under great external pressure, forcing them to obey social norms and "striking down all individuality to the eighteenth level of hell," thereby crowding the individual unconscious with repressions. Conversely, in a society where freedom is respected and no senseless bondage is imposed on the individual, the individual will suffer from less repression. Chinese society clearly falls into the first category and reform needs to be conducted through the education of children. Zhu notes that Chinese children are not allowed to explore their desires, hence their morality and intellect are blocked from developing according to the natural order. Schools and families, he argues, should instead encourage children to have freedom of thought, and allow them to nurture their independence and self-respect so that they can judge matters by themselves. This would prevent the children from having "bad desires" that need to be repressed, and their potential could then be fully "released" (*faxie*). If desires are not allowed release, the unconscious would "overflow and run wildly" (*fanlan hengliu*), resulting in pathological conditions. He therefore advises parents, brothers, teachers, and educators to become enlightened about this matter as quickly as possible and to allow children to "walk on the necessary path of natural development."[35] Psychoanalysis here is promoted as the justification for a

---

35. Zhu Guangqian, "Freud's Theory of the Unconscious and Psychoanalysis," *Eastern Magazine* 18:14 (1921): 41–51.

new educational method that will encourage a "natural" and "less repressed" acknowledgment of one's desires.

In the May Fourth context, such a call for allowing children to be "natural" echoes the madman's famous plea to "Save the children! Save the children!" at the end of Lu Xun's "The Diary of a Madman." If the present society is permeated by a total and inhumane corruption, approaching a state of cannibalism, as Lu Xun's story suggests, children are the only site of innocence not contaminated by social degradation, and hence the only hope for a better, nobler future. Zhu Guangqian's appeal to allow children to grow naturally does not explicitly spell out a teleological notion of psychoanalysis, but his pragmatic, socially constructive application to children's education encompasses a future-oriented, instrumentalist perspective. Psychoanalysis, in short, served progress by liberating individuals from repression.

As a form of social criticism, psychoanalysis was also used by May Fourth intellectuals as a theoretical basis for denouncing what they called feudal sexual morality, and for celebrating erotic sexuality. Lu Xun's brother Zhou Zuoren (1885–1967), at the time supportive of the May Fourth enlightenment agenda, denounced the so-called moralists who upheld traditional sexual ethics as perverts whose inability to control their own sexual desires required them to proscribe behavioral excesses: their asceticism paradoxically exposed their perverse and licentious sexual appetites.[36] Guo Moruo also did not hesitate to use the hyperbole that "China, which has been proud of her feudal ethics for thousands of years, is in fact nothing but an oversized hospital full of sexual perverts!"[37] Almost as soon as psychoanalysis was introduced to May Fourth intellectual circles, it became another powerful instrument in the service of antitraditionalism.

As can be seen in Zhu Guangqian's discussion of psychoanalysis, sexual well-being, seen from the point of view of emotional and physical health, increasingly became a justification for open discussions of sexuality, licensed by the promotion of psychoanalysis as a "science." Zhou Zuoren, an avid reader of the English psychologist Havelock Ellis (1859–1939),[38] was also a champion of this cause and came to the defense of younger writers such as Guo Moruo and Yu Dafu whose work had explicit sexual content. He further advocated collecting erotic stories and songs, saying that they provided a healthy release from the dissatisfactions arising from male-female sexual

36. Zhou Zuoren, "To Come Back Again" (*Chong lai*, 1923), in *About Tigers*, 109–112.

37. "An Aesthetic Critique of *The Story of the Western Chamber* and the Personality of the Author" (*Xixiangji yishu shang de pipan yu qi zuozhe xingge*, 1921), in *Complete Works of Guo Moruo* (*Guo Moruo quanji*) (Beijing: Renmin wenxue chubanshe, 1985), 15:322–323.

38. Havelock Ellis was famous for his studies of sexual psychology deemed "scandalous" by some of his contemporaries. His *Psychology of Sex* was translated by Pan Guangdan and published in 1946. Understandably, the book was basically ignored after 1949 until it was reprinted in the 1980s. *Xing xinlixue* (Beijing: Sanlian shudian, 1987).

relationships, and went so far as to imply that erotic sex was actually a mark of high civilization.[39] Gao Juefu's 1925 translation of Freud's 1910 Clark University lectures, "The Origin and Development of Psychoanalysis," introduced such concepts as sexual repression, sublimation, dream analysis, the subconscious, and free association.[40] The application of these concepts could be readily discerned in the works of Guo Moruo, Lu Xun, and Yu Dafu, all of whom studied medicine in Japan. May Fourth intellectuals "cashed in" on this opportunity to explore the various implications of sexuality: two full-length studies of abnormal psychology and sexuality were published in the mid-1920s, and selected Japanese fiction that had sexuality as its theme (such as fiction by Nagai Kafū and Satō Haruo) was also translated.[41]

Beyond flaunting the naturalness of sexuality, intellectuals also considered the relationship between sexuality and culture. The translated works of U.S.-educated Kuriyagawa Hakuson were most influential in this regard. Three translations of his *Symbols of Mental Anguish* (*Kumon no sōchō*, 1923) were published, among which Lu Xun's 1924 translation was the most popular. Lu Xun's preface to his translation succinctly pointed out the main theme of the book as a Freudian discourse on the origin of literature as a form of sublimation: "bitterness and frustration arising from the repression of the life force is the basis of literature and art; the way this bitterness and frustration gets expressed is symbolism in the general sense."[42] Here, Kuriyagawa integrated the Bergsonian notion of life force and the Freudian notion of culture as sublimated libido to lay out a theory of art and literature. Lu Xun advises Chinese readers to read the book two or three times, for it could help reinvigorate the "apathetic and occluded" spirit (read: repressed sexuality) of China. Lu Xun's own application of this theory is found in "Mending Heaven" (*Butian*, 1922), where artistic creation is explained as the result of an original sexual longing by the mythical figure Nü Wa.

If literature is sublimated libido, aberrant sexuality must be conducive to art. Kuriyagawa offered a popular version of sexual psychology in two articles on abnormal sexuality, which were translated and published in the prestigious *Short Story Monthly* (*Xiaoshuo yuebao*). He observed that all artistic geniuses were mentally disturbed and sexually deviant and that all art was the

39. Qian Liqun, *A Biography of Zhou Zuoren* (*Zhou Zuoren zhuan*) (Beijing: Shiyue wenyi chubanshe, 1990), 34.

40. Included in *Gao Juefu's Essays on Psychology* (*Gao Juefu xinlixue wenxuan*) (Shanghai: Jiangsu jiaoyu chubanshe, 1986), 168–203.

41. See both Wu Lichang's *Psychoanalysis and Sino-Western Literature* (*Jingshen fenxi yu Zhong xi wenxue*) (Shanghai: Xuelin chubanshe, 1987), 145–149, and Yu Fenggao's *Psychoanalysis and Modern Chinese Fiction* (*Xinli fenxi yu Zhongguo xiandai xiaoshuo*) (Beijing: Zhongguo shehui kexue chubanshe, 1987), 42–71.

42. Lu Xun, "Preface" (*Yinyan*), to *Symbols of Mental Anguish* (*Kumen de xiangzheng*, 1924) (Beijing: Renmin wenxue chubanshe, 1988), 4.

product of sexual desire. Since he saw sexuality as an ambiguous affair—every person combined both masculine and feminine sexual attributes to different degrees—he considered sexual "abnormalities" such as lesbianism, male homosexuality, bisexuality, and necrophilia, as well as masochism and sadism, to be perfectly normal for art and artists.[43] The prevalence of stories dealing with these themes during the May Fourth era—for example Ye Dingluo's (b. 1900) and Lu Yin's (1899–1934) stories of homosexuality, and Yu Dafu's stories of repressed sexuality, fetishism, and autoeroticism—was an expression of this larger fascination with newly discovered territory.

This is not to say that traditional Chinese literature lacked works of erotica. But psychoanalysis legitimated the discussion of sexuality as a scientific and therefore distinctively "modern" act, which could readily circumvent issues of sexual propriety defined by conventional sexual ethics. Ultimately, psychoanalysis, along with Nietzschean existentialism and Bergsonian vitalism, were justified by their May Fourth users as promising modernity, the longing for which underlay May Fourth teleology. Yet, as I suggested earlier, neither psychoanalysis nor Nietzschean existentialism merely served teleological modernity: the former also foregrounded a non-unilinear interiority while the latter recorded the existential anguish of an individual. May Fourth modernism as a literary expression registers a deep fissure between a teleological modernity and an introspective aesthetics that did not seem to serve any teleology. It was caught in a dilemma: on the one hand, it promised a shortcut to modernity (since it embodied the most modern and current of all literary movements in the West, and hence served as the cultural equivalent to social modernity); on the other hand, it emphasized formal experimentation and psychological introspection, which recorded a personal confrontation with the modern that was fraught with anxiety and frustration. In contrast to Western modernism—which is predominantly perceived as antimodern because it self-consciously critiqued technological modernity as having dehumanized mankind—May Fourth modernism splits right at the moment when promodern teleology and psychological introspection diverge. While we cannot fail to note the rhetorical similarity between the Italian futurists' *antipassatismo* ("Down with the past") movement and May Fourth antitraditionalism,[44] we must also recognize the deployment of modernist narrative frameworks that engage the modern in nonteleological ways.

In modernist practice, then, the tension between teleology and interiority became apparent: the former sanctioned the ideology of progress, na-

43. "Abnormal Sexual Desire and Literature" (*Bing de xingyu yu wenxue*) and "Art and Sexual Desire" (*Wenyi yu xingyu*), both translated by Fan Zhongyun, *Short Story Monthly* 16:5 (May 1925): 1–9; *Short Story Monthly* 16:7 (July 1925): 1–4.

44. For "*antipassatismo*," see Renalto Poggioli, *The Theory of the Avant-Garde*, trans. Gerald Fitzgerald (Cambridge: Harvard University Press, Belknap Press, 1968), 54.

tional development, and the didactic impulse, but the latter foregrounded psychological introspection, lyrical impulse, and the spatialization of consciousness. Modernity in the specific context of May Fourth modernist writing was both its justification and its nemesis. In the use of Western modernist techniques via various routes of mediation, didactic and lyrical impulses, national and private desires, would clash in a way that fractured the May Fourth project of literary modernity. In the works of Lu Xun, Guo Moruo, Tao Jingsun (1897–1952), Yu Dafu, and others, which I examine in chapters 2 to 4, we witness how these fractures become manifest in the modernist practices of formal experimentation, psychoanalytic interiority, and decadence.

LANGUAGE, MODERNITY, AND CULTURAL POWER

Whether Western modernist thought was deployed to champion collective or individual causes, an unspoken, underlying reason for its appropriation was access to what Pierre Bourdieu calls the "cultural capital" available to the educated elite. This cultural capital was often converted into economic capital: many May Fourth enlightenment writers and thinkers, particularly those who had acquired advanced degrees from either the West or Japan, took prestigious academic jobs or worked for notable literary journals as editors or contributors, and these journals paid their editors, writers, and translators handsome remunerations. Fame also followed, which accorded them further "symbolic capital," providing them with prestige and honor.[45] To these forms of capital which knowledge of modern Western and Japanese culture afforded to May Fourth writers, one must also add the "linguistic capital" acquired and asserted through their advocacy of a linguistic revolution.

As concerted attempt to dislodge tradition, the linguistic revolution heralded during the May Fourth era sanctioned the substitution of the traditional literary language (*wenyan*) with the modern vernacular (*baihua*) as the language of modern writing. The vernacular was a tool to debilitate the highly stylized classical written language, symbolically subverting the hierarchy and authority of the classical literary tradition, and, at least theoretically, debunking the elitism associated with it by recuperating the common language spoken by the masses. Almost everyone active in the May Fourth scene took up the vernacular, and virulent attacks on the "ornateness" and "decadence" of *wenyan* were voiced, most notably by Chen Duxiu and oth-

---

45. John B. Thompson provides a succinct definition of Bourdieu's "cultural capital" as "knowledge, skills and other cultural acquisitions, as exemplified by educational or technical qualifications," "economic capital" as "material wealth," and "symbolic capital" as "accumulated prestige or honor." See his "Editor's Introduction" to Pierre Bourdieu's *Language and Symbolic Power,* trans. Gino Raymond and Matthew Adamson (Cambridge: Harvard University Press, 1991), 14. See also Bourdieu, *The Logic of Practice,* trans. Richard Nice (Stanford: Stanford University Press, 1990), 124–125.

ers. Hu Shi's famous "Eight Don'ts" should be remembered foremost as the manifesto of a new stylistics of language that sought to dethrone the rhetorical conventions of the past.[46] Such syntactic and semantic changes at the same time portended a grave transformation of the Chinese vernacular, and in fact almost all aspects of the language went through realignment in this period, which Edward Gunn illustrates copiously in his *Rewriting Chinese*. Besides the free use of "Japanized" and Europeanized words and writing styles, the application of disjunctive techniques, such as stream-of-consciousness writing and interior monologues, further enforced a radical breakdown of sentence cohesion and coherence.[47] If Western modernism is defined, following Fredric Jameson, as the moment when the separation between sign and referent became ineluctable,[48] the May Fourth linguistic revolution registered even more extravagant changes on the signifying structure of language. Ironically, then, May Fourth China was especially ripe for modernism due to its radical antitraditionalism. By disrupting reigning authoritarian discourses—specifically, by subverting the law of syntax, which according to Julia Kristeva signifies the subversion of the Law of the Father—a radical social change could be imagined.[49] Linguistic revolution was a synecdoche for social revolution. This is why Meng Yue and Dai Jinhua, using a psychoanalytic language similar to that of Julia Kristeva, also describe the May Fourth moment as the "epoch of patricide" (*shifu shidai*) in their book *Surfacing from History*.[50]

The social-revolutionary potential and democratic implications of the vernacular movement are due to the necessity of standardized vernacular for the constitution of the modern nation-state and the mass appeal of a vernacular for socialism. Karatani Kōjin's discussion of the relationship between the vernacular and the nation-state is illuminating here. Using Benedict Anderson's commonly cited thesis that the development of the vernacular was indispensable to the formation of the modern nation-state, and Michel Foucault's short discussion on the standardization of literature as linked to the

46. See Chen Duxiu, "On Literary Revolution" (*Wenxue geming lun*), and Hu Shi, "Tentative Proposals for Literary Reform" (*Wenxue gailiang chuyi*), both collected in *Materials on the History of New Chinese Literary Movement* (*Zhongguo xinwenxue yundongshi ziliao*), ed. Zhang Ruoying (Shanghai: Guangming shuju, 1934), 40–44 and 27–39. An extreme expression of the linguistic revolution took place in 1918 and 1919, when *New Youth* magazine advocated a romanization system or Esperanto to replace the Chinese vernacular altogether.

47. Edward Gunn, *Rewriting Chinese: Style and Innovation in Twentieth-Century Chinese Prose* (Stanford: Stanford University Press, 1991), 12–36.

48. Fredric Jameson, "Literary Innovation and Modes of Production: A Commentary," *Modern Chinese Literature* 1:1 (September 1984): 67–77.

49. See Julia Kristeva, *Revolution in Poetic Language*, trans. Margaret Waller (New York: Columbia University Press, 1984), especially the chapter on Mallarmé.

50. Meng Yue and Dai Jinhua, *Surfacing from History* (*Fuchu lishi dibiao*) (Kaifeng: Henan renmin chubanshe, 1989).

establishment of the nation-state, Karatani argues that the vernacular novel in Meiji Japan had a similar function of providing the cultural basis for the formation of the nation-state. The *genbun itchi* movement (the drive to bring writing closer to the vernacular), he continues, occurred in every non-Western society impacted by Western imperialism (and, in the case of China, by Japanese imperialism as well).[51] The synchronicity between the May Fourth drive to promote the use of modern vernacular and the anti-imperialist demonstrations suggests the interrelatedness of the vernacular and the nation-state. Furthermore, the fact that leading socialist thinkers such as Chen Duxiu himself were outspoken instigators of the linguistic revolution bespeaks the agenda of the "massification" of language. The institution of the vernacular was therefore a direct expression of the May Fourth agenda of "Mr. De" (democracy).

The democratic potentialities of the vernacular movement, however, were effectively undercut by the specific form the revolution was to take, namely the Westernization of the Chinese language, which assured that the vernacular thus recuperated was distanced from the vernacular spoken by the masses. There are numerous aspects of Chinese vernacular's Westernization. First, foreign words were often borrowed and used alongside Chinese: turning the pages of *Short Story Monthly* is enough to impress upon the reader the profuse use of English, French, German, Russian, and Japanese words embedded in original Chinese texts. Second, newly translated foreign terms, or loan words, were created almost every day. Particularly convenient in this regard were loan words from the Japanese *kanji* translations of Western terminology, since *kanji* could be directly used as Chinese without the labor of translation. In the discourse of psychoanalysis alone, for instance, words such as "consciousness" (*yishi*), "the unconscious" (*wuyishi* or *yinyishi*), "the subconscious" (*qianyishi*), and "neurasthenia" (*jingshen shuairuo*) were imported from the Japanese, as was the translation for "psychoanalysis" (*jingshen fenxi*) itself. Third, the Chinese vernacular went through a radical transformation when such adjectival and adverbial auxiliaries of "*de*" (的), "*di*" (底), and "*di*" (地) became commonly used to incorporate Western syntax and connote a sense of modernity in Chinese texts, and when the "more scientific" gendering of the third person pronoun into "*ta*" (他) and "*ta*" (她) was instituted (thanks to the French-educated phonologist and poet Liu Bannong [1891–1934]). Even though some of these terms, especially the third type, would soon acquire wide circulation and acceptance, they nevertheless effectively alienated the masses from accessing the newly established canon of *xinwenxue*, the "new literature" of modern China. *Xinwenxue* became the hallmark of the linguistic capital accessible only when one acquired

---

51. Karatani Kōjin, "Afterword to the English Edition," in *Origins of Modern Japanese Literature*, trans. Brett de Bary (Durham: Duke University Press, 1993), 193–195.

enough training in the new educational system, and of course this linguistic capital was most readily available to those educated in the West or Japan.

The massive importation of Euro-Japanese syntax and semantics meant that the May Fourth writer writing in the vernacular was not someone who collected the "words from the street corners and alleyways" (*jietou xiangyu*), as in the *xiaoshuo* tradition, but rather was more of a *double translator*, translating Chinese vernacular into a more scientific and "modern" language while translating Western and Japanese languages into Chinese. His or her heavily Europeanized and Japanized (i.e., translated) vernacular might in effect be as alien to the ordinary reader as *wenyan*. Translation, in both of these senses, provided immediate access to cultural and symbolic capital. The May Fourth writer derived much of his/her power of persuasion from his/her knowledge of Euro-Japanese literature. Reading Lu Xun's ironic and self-conscious story "Lamenting Loss" (*Shangshi*) as an allegory shows how this power of persuasion was actually a power over life and death. In the story, a young woman aspiring to learn new ideas of the West, Zijun, falls helplessly in love with the first-person male narrator who functions as the transmitter of Western feminist ideas via Ibsen's plays. She accepts him as her self-ordained enlightener, and becomes thoroughly interpellated by the values he acquired from reading Western literature. Upon his advice, she leaves her family to prove her dedication to free love and rebellion against patriarchy. But she withers away in a doomed relationship with the narrator, who turns out to be a hypocrite and a coward, and she dies in the end. The male narrator as the translator of Western ideas is here presented unambiguously, albeit allegorically, as a murderer.

As Prasenjit Duara has noted, the discourse of modernity in modern China was undoubtedly one of power, since its enunciator could oppress others in its name or enjoy the benefits of becoming a cultural leader.[52] In the specific cultural context of May Fourth China, the practitioners of cultural translation were positioned in an ambivalent relationship with the "masses," an ideological category that did not readily coincide with the actual masses themselves. Rather, the ideological production of the "masses" in the new literature was more alienating to the masses than accommodating of them. If we see this production of "the masses" as a rhetorical trope in the service of May Fourth antitraditionalism, it becomes clear that this trope did not necessarily need physical embodiments. Furthermore, the struggle for cultural leadership within the cultural arena also meant a radical challenge to those intellectuals who could be readily designated as "backward" and "unenlightened," as "cherishing the outmoded and preserving the outworn"

52. Prasenjit Duara, "Knowledge and Power in the Discourse of Modernity: The Campaigns Against Popular Religion in Early Twentieth-Century China," *Journal of Asian Studies* 50:1 (February 1991): 67–83.

(*baocan shouque,* a phrase commonly used by May Fourth intellectuals in their attack on those who advocated the preservation of national treasures, *guocuipai*). This suggests that the translation of Western modernity itself was a marker of difference from and a challenge to other intellectual formations of the time, as much as it was another production of culture that differentiated the elites from the masses.

To sum up, a continguity of relationships can be located between the vernacular, the nation-state, and translation, all of which can be seen as different expressions of the will to power. The modern vernacular situates itself in opposition to the classical tradition, the nation-state against imperialism, and the translator against the culturally inferior and the parochial pedant. These expressions of power reveal the transformation of the structuration of power dictated by the teleology of Western modernity as legitimized by the ideology of linear temporality. The ideology of modernity allowed nothing less than a "reorganization of power" in the domestic context.[53] As I have argued earlier, however, this domestic context is never independent of the implications of the same practice in the global context. I analyze the implications of May Fourth intellectual subjectivity in the global context in chapter 5.

53. Ibid., 77.

CHAPTER 2

Evolutionism and Experimentalism
Lu Xun and Tao Jingsun

Now survey China: Where are the warriors of the spirit? Is there a genuine voice to lead us to goodness, beauty and rigor? Is there a warm voice to deliver us from this barren winter?

LU XUN, "ON THE POWER OF MARA POETRY" (1908)

Drive my dead thoughts over the universe
Like withered bodies to quicken a new birth!
And, by the incantation of this verse,
Scatter, as from an unextinguished hearth
Ashes and sparks, my words among mankind!
Be through my lips to unawakened earth
The trumpet of a prophecy! O Wind,
If Winter comes, can spring be far behind?

P. B. SHELLEY, "ODE TO THE WEST WIND,"
AS QUOTED IN KURIYAGAWA HAKUSON'S *SYMBOLS OF MENTAL ANGUISH*,
TRANSLATED INTO CHINESE BY LU XUN (1925)

It is better to admire Darwin and Ibsen rather than Confucius and Guan Yu; it is better to be sacrificed to Apollo rather than to the General of the Plague and the God of Five Spheres.

LU XUN, "ESSAY NUMBER 46" (1919)
("APOLLO" IN ENGLISH IN THE ORIGINAL)

When Lu Xun (1881–1936), the anointed "Father of Modern Chinese Literature," was eighteen years old, he reputedly read Yan Fu's translation of Thomas E. Huxley's *Evolution and Ethics* with great passion, to the point of committing the entire text to memory. This episode was recounted again and again in various essays he wrote later, and constituted one of the most memorable experiences of his student years at the Jiangnan Naval Academy during the waning years of the Qing dynasty (1898–1902). From the naval academy in

Nanjing, he would go on to study in Japan for seven long years (1902–1909), and return to China to emerge as a scholar, educator, essayist, and formidable fiction writer. I am evoking this anecdote of Lu Xun reading Huxley as a paradigmatic entryway to the thought of Lu Xun through the Japan years and up to the late 1920s when he stopped writing fiction and turned to Marxism. In light of my discussion in chapter 1 of the ideology of evolution, the discourse of progress, and the modernist writing in the May Fourth movement, this chapter will argue that a fundamentally evolutionary mode of thinking underlies much of Lu Xun's thought and literary practice until the late 1920s, and that there is a surprising coherence in the complex structure of his thought when viewed from the lens of evolutionism. One might even argue that since Marxism was itself premised on a teleological conception of history, Lu Xun never really strayed far from his own particular evolutionary mode of thinking when he turned to Marxism. Concentrating on Lu Xun's work from the pre-Marxist phase, this chapter's central task is to establish the metonymic continuity among several important vectors of his thought, namely evolutionism, science, individualism, and humanism. I will argue that these vectors are organically connected and are contiguous with each other, and literature is situated within this continuity, not apart from it. His penchant for narratological experimentation, which is where I locate his modernist tendencies, must therefore be examined in light of this continuity.

This chapter begins with an analysis of the above-mentioned vectors of his thought, then examines his self-conscious deployment of experimental narrative techniques. I argue that his particular use of modernist form remains instrumental, which is why his work could so easily be taken up by Fredric Jameson as a perfect example of Third World national allegory.[1] Jameson needed a Third World representative, and literary historians of China readily provided him with Lu Xun. This need for a representative reduces the Chinese literary field to an externally imposed coherence that violently disregards multiple and contradictory developments within the field. Hence, this chapter transitions to the unapologetic technical experimentalism of Tao Jingsun, also Japan-educated, whose writing prefigured the work of the Shanghai new sensationists many years later. His stories will show how the best refutation of Jameson's theory is the multiplicity and complexity of Third World writing itself.

LU XUN AS EVOLUTIONARY THINKER

Generally speaking, Darwinian evolutionism theorized that progress was part of the inevitable natural process of human development, and science was progress's facilitating agent. Lu Xun's first chosen vocations were natural sci-

---

1. Fredric Jameson, "Third-World Literature in the Era of Multinational Capital," *Social Text* 15 (Fall 1986): 65–88.

ence (mineralogy) and then biological science (medicine). Among his earliest writings are an essay on Madame Curie's discovery of uranium, published one year after his arrival in Japan, and a long Darwinian essay entitled "The History of Men" (*Ren zhi lishi*), published in 1907. He also extensively researched the mineral products and deposits of China, which culminated in *A Record of China's Mineral Products* (*Zhongguo kuangcan zhi*, 1906) and a companion map book, *The Complete Map of Chinese Mineral Products* (*Zhongguo kuangcan quan tu*).

A slightly later essay on the history of science, "Notes on the History of Science" (*Kexue shi jiao pian*), published in 1908, is notable for laying out his evolutionary notion of science and for prefiguring how he would later arrive at his conception of the function and role of literature in relation to science. He begins the essay by remarking how the advance of science has helped conquer Nature, and by describing science as a torrent that started in the West and is rushing toward China. In a panegyric to science, Lu Xun traces its development from ancient Greece to the mid-nineteenth century in broad generalizations, and concludes that science is "the holy light that illuminates the world." The metaphor of light is particularly important for Lu Xun due to its close association with the ideals of the enlightenment, and it will be repeatedly, almost obsessively, deployed by Lu Xun in many of his essays and stories, as I will examine in closer detail later in relation to Lu Xun's own self-designated role as the light-bearer.

At the close of this essay, however, Lu Xun notes the limits of science and brings into focus the necessity of culture:

> If the whole world respects only knowledge, life will return to dry stillness. If this [situation] continues, emotions of beauty will become thin, radiant and sensitive thoughts will be lost, and the so-called science will be as good as nonexistent. Hence what people hope for is not just Newton, but also a poet like Shakespeare; not just Boyle, but also a painter like Raphael. Since there is Kant, there is also the composer Beethoven; since there is Darwin, there is also the writer Carlyle.[2]

Here humanistic endeavors are seen as complementary to the pursuits of knowledge in the scientific realm, and as the other half of what constitutes "life" as a holistic experience. Lu Xun's theorization of the relationship between evolutionary science and art would later change, as he tried to rationalize his literary pursuit not as complementary to science but as itself the instigator of evolution. But what remained consistent was his view that evolution, science, and art are intimately connected.

Another attempt Lu Xun made to bridge literature and science was through the translation of science fiction. By the time Lu Xun arrived in

---

2. Lu Xun, "Notes on the History of Science" (*Kexue shi jiao pian*), in *Complete Works of Lu Xun* (*Lu Xun quanji*, hereafter *LXQJ*) (Beijing: Renmin wenxue chubanshe, 1981), 1:35.

Japan in 1902, numerous translations of Western science fiction already existed. Even by 1884, many of Jules Verne's (1828–1905) novels had already been translated into Japanese, and science fiction was one of the most popular genres during the late Meiji era.[3] Liang Qichao translated *20,000 Leagues Under the Sea* (*Vingt mille lieues sous les mers*) into Chinese in 1902 while in exile in Japan, and Lu Xun eagerly followed suit, translating three of Verne's novels based on Japanese translations: *From the Earth to the Moon* (*De la terre à la lune*) in 1903, *Journey to the Center of the Earth* (*Voyage au centre de la terre*) in 1906, and an unpublished manuscript translation of *An Antarctic Mystery* (*Les Anglais au pole nord*) around the same time. Through these translations, Lu Xun sought to popularize science for the purpose of social evolution. As he explained in the preface to his translation of *From the Earth to the Moon,* his aim was to make science less boring for the average reader, who, through an enjoyable reading experience, would attain scientific knowledge unawares. As a result, "inherited superstition can be destroyed, thought can be reformed, . . . civilization can be bolstered," and the "ignoble *yellow race* [the Chinese] can rise up" ("yellow race" in English in the original).[4]

This last statement about the Chinese as the "*yellow race*" marks a moment of racialized self-consciousness that many Chinese students who went to study in Japan had felt keenly,[5] and such self-consciousness of racial inferiority provoked a passionate discourse on the national character and its transformation through science and other means. Lu Xun had personally encountered incidents of Japanese racism against the Chinese, several times being the target of racial taunts and slurs that the Chinese are "slaves with tails" for wearing their long queues (braids). In 1905, when he was studying at the Sendai Medical School, Lu Xun was accused by his Japanese classmates of cheating on the final exam in anatomy, the reason being that it was impossible for a Chinese student to pass the difficult test when many native students had not. It was a clear incidence of racist scapegoating. Furthermore, Japanese newspapers and magazines carried various racist commentaries on the Chinese; notions of the yellow peril were rearticulated by some Japanese who claimed the Japanese were Aryans to differentiate them from the yellow Chinese; and one Japanese reputedly suggested that the Chinese should be displayed as savages with tails in the 1903 Osaka World's Fair. Incensed, Lu Xun cut off his queue, believing that it symbolized the slave-like status of the Chinese in the eyes of the

---

3. Cheng Ma, *Communication and Renewal: Exploring the Relationship between Lu Xun and Japanese Literature* (*Goutong yu gengxin: Lu Xun yu Riben wenxue guanxi fawei*) (Beijing: Zhongguo shehui kexue chubanshe, 1990), 7–18.

4. "Preface" (*Bianyan*), *LXQ J* 10:151–53.

5. See chapter 4 for my discussion of the case of Yu Dafu.

Japanese, because it suggested to him the enslavement of the Han Chinese by the Manchurians.[6]

Personal anger aside, Lu Xun's reaction did not dispute the accusations, since he implicitly agreed with their validity. Using the term *"yellow race"* in the passage quoted above to refer only to the Chinese was to agree with the Japanese othering of the Chinese as inferior, and cutting off his queue was to take heed of the Japanese slur that the Chinese are slaves with tails. This latter event was commemorated by a photo of himself without the queue, which he saw as the record of his symbolic act of severance from Qing China. Zhou Zuoren wrote in his dairy about this act as the firm establishment of Lu Xun's revolutionary thought to overthrow the Manchurians and to reinstate the Han nation. Furthermore, from 1906 on, Lu Xun chose to wear Japanese kimonos instead of the long gowns that were current in the Qing, saying that kimonos were more Chinese since they had the flavor of the Han and Tang dynasties, while long gowns were barbaric and were symbols of enslavement.[7] Lu Xun would also grow a moustache in the style that was then fashionable in Japan, a practice memorialized in a satiric essay he wrote about Chinese people accusing him of looking un-Chinese during one of his return trips to China.[8] Maintaining a Japanese appearance (in hairstyle, dress, and moustache), though Lu Xun articulated this choice in terms of anti-Manchu sentiments, was also a means to repress or suppress his Chinese-ness as defined by Japanese racist discourses and representations. His strategy was not to refute these essentialist representations but to redefine them as Manchurian. Hence he preferred to be called a *Shinajin* ("Chinaman"), even though it was just as derogatory a term, rather than a *Qingguoren* ("man of the Qing nation"). One could argue that this was a classic case of Japanese racism internalized and expressed as self-hatred. But the object of the self-hatred, in this case, could be readily compartmentalized as Manchurian qualities, not Han Chinese qualities. In light of this, it is interesting to reconsider Lu Xun's famous Ah Q, with "Q" standing for the queue, as the representative of Qing national character, not the Han-Chinese national character per se. However, it is perhaps the tension between the possibility and impossibility of exorcising Manchurian qualities from the Chinese national character that underlies Lu Xun's meditation on the issue of national character in general, hence the instability between Qing-ness and Han-ness in Ah Q.

It appears that his experiences in Japan fueled his Han nationalism against the Qing—it was the Qing dynasty's enslavement of the Han Chinese that

---

6. Cheng Ma, *A History of Lu Xun's Studies in Japan* (*Lu Xun liuxue Riben shi*) (Xi'an: Shanxi renmin chubanshe, 1985), 20, 109–44.

7. Ibid., 19–34, 170.

8. "On the Moustache" (*Lun huxu,* 1924), *LXQJ* 1:174–178. The main thrust of the essay is to critique the cultural essentialism of Chinese conservatives who said that wearing a Japanese-style mustache is betraying China.

had led the Chinese to their present sorry state. Lu Xun had taken Japanese accusations to heart, not so much to contest them, but to use them as guidelines for how to improve the Chinese national character. (This of course echoes Xia Mianzun's much later approval of Akutagawa's disparaging portrayal of the Chinese that I related in my introduction, which shows a surprising consistency in the way Occidentalized and Japanized semicolonial intellectuals looked at China and its people.) It was this obsession with national character that motivated Lu Xun's change of careers from medicine to literature. As he later disclosed in his famous account of the traumatic slide incident,[9] his experience in Japan led him to the conclusion that medicine can only cure the body, but literature is the medium for curing the spirit and improving the character.

This of course did not mean that science was to be simply replaced by literature. Lu Xun continued to defend science, and saw it as necessary for the improvement of the national character.[10] As he moved closer to literature, however, he viewed the problem of national character from a different perspective, and this is where the issue of individualism, largely in the elitist sense of a superior being who can lead the masses with flawed characters into enlightenment, became important for him. The most crucial mediator in Lu Xun's thinking on individualism was Nietzsche. Lu Xun's mentor Zhang Taiyan had himself written in 1907 about Nietzsche's Superman as the embodiment of high morality and unconventionality who can promise "hope for China's future,"[11] and in Lu Xun's two most widely read and cited essays from the Japan period, "On Cultural Extremism" (*Wenhua pianzhi lun*) and "On the Power of Mara Poetry" (*Moluo shili shuo*), both published in Japan in 1908, Nietzsche was represented as having the final word on evolutionism and individualism (*geren zhuyi*).

In "On Cultural Extremism," German idealist philosophy as represented by Nietzsche was the major theoretical support for his advocacy of individualism, in which the self is situated against the masses, the individual against the collective ("Trust the individual and reject the collective," Lu Xun urged). The masses constitute the realm of conformity, vulgarity, and corrupt materialism, against which the individual must rebel. The successful rebel embodies the "dignity of the human character and the value of the human

---

9. At Sendai Medical School, Lu Xun one day saw news slides about Japanese war efforts in China. A Chinese man was being executed by the Japanese and a group of Chinese onlookers witnessed the spectacle in apathy. This incident convinced Lu Xun that he had to cure the spirit, not the body, of the Chinese, hence the move from medicine to literature as his life's vocation. Numerous interpretations of this incident are available; for representative ones, see Leo Lee, *Voices from the Iron House* (Bloomington and Indianapolis: Indiana University Press, 1987), 17–19, and Lydia Liu, *Translingual Practice*, 62–64.

10. See essays number 33 and 38, *LXQ J* 1:298, 313.

11. Quoted in Cheng Ma, *A History of Lu Xun's Studies in Japan*, 61.

species." Like a Nietzschean Superman, he "abhors" the "stupid masses" as if they were "snakes and scorpions." Lu Xun continued: "He [Nietzsche] means that [if] the world is left to the masses to govern, the vigor of society will be destroyed. It is better to sacrifice the stupid masses in hope for the birth of one or two geniuses." The genius or the "man of the greatest will" will then enlighten and transform the masses and turn the Chinese nation into a "nation of human beings," resulting in the ascent of the Chinese nation.[12] If natural science earlier constituted the means of evolution, now it was culture, particularly mediated by Nietzschean existentialism, that underlay an instrumental conception of individualism as the means to propel the evolution of the Chinese national character from barbarism to humanity.

"The Power of Mara Poetry" presents an even more explicitly evolutionary mode of thinking coupled with Nietzschean individualism. Lu Xun notes that "Nietzsche was not hostile to primitives; his claim that they embody new forces is irrefutable. A savage wilderness incubates the coming civilization; in primitives' teeming forms the light of day is immanent. Civilization is like the flower, savagery the bud, civilization the fruit, savagery the flower. Herein lies progress and hope as well."[13] Using evolution to explain Nietzsche's notion of the barbaric (which I would argue is in fact more closely associated with Nietzsche's reversal of values than with evolution), the Nietzschean man of the greatest will in Lu Xun's earlier essay is now specifically located in the figure of the poet-prophet of European romanticism, "who is committed to resistance, whose purpose is action." Militant, rebellious, iconoclastic, the poet-prophet's poetry "disturbs people's minds," "breaches the stagnant peace," and "enables humanity to emerge, evolve, advance, and scale the heights of the possible." Without a poet-prophet such as the first-person speaker in Shelley's "Ode to the West Wind," the Chinese will continue to spiral backward to "reptilian decline," and run "counter to the reality of human evolution."[14] Specifically, holding onto Chinese traditional practices such as polygamy and footbinding are examples of reverse evolution.[15] If the current course is not reversed, Lu Xun argues in another essay, there will not only be manlike apes in the world, but also apelike men devolved from humans.[16]

Literature therefore has an important responsibility. As Lu Xun puts it: "The effect of literature has educational value, which is how it enriches life;

12. "On Cultural Extremism," *LXQJ* 1:44–57.

13. "On the Power of Mara Poetry," trans. Shu-ying Tsau and Donald Holock, in *Modern Chinese Literary Thought*, ed. Kirk A. Denton (Stanford: Stanford University Press, 1996), 98. The translation quoted here is slightly modified.

14. Ibid., 99–102. Translation slightly modified.

15. "What Kind of Fathers Should We Be?" (*Women xianzai zenyang zuo fuqin*, 1919), *LXQJ* 1:129–140.

16. Essay number 41, *LXQJ* 1:325.

unlike ordinary education, it shows concretely a sense of self, valor, and a drive toward progress. The decline and fall of a state has always begun with its refusal to heed such teaching."[17] The writer is then naturally the person responsible for the enlightenment of the masses; he is the man of great will, or his synonymous variations as the "awakened" (*juexing de ren*), the "fierce rebel" (*yongmeng de chuangjiang*), and the "warrior" (*zhanshi*), whose exemplary individualism manifested as expressive literature can lead evolution.[18] The ultimate goal is to turn China into a nation of individual human beings, wherein lies Lu Xun's particular kind of humanism articulated through what appears to be elitist individualism. This is a humanism that is based on the individual, whose individualism is not so much about rescuing the oppressed people of China from imperialism, but about the edification of the Chinese character so as to embody human dignity and values, with the ultimate goal of creating a humane nation. This humanism is very similar in conception to Zhou Zuoren's notion of "humane literature" (*ren de wenxue*) which takes as its basis human morality and a humane life, with the "I," the individual, as its unit and humanity as its sum total.[19] Lu Xun explained years later that he started writing fiction for the goal of enlightenment, believing that humanity could be improved, so "he focused on the unfortunate characters in a diseased society as a means to expose sickness and bitterness and to arouse attention for cure."[20] From medicine as bodily cure, to medicine as metaphor for curing the ills of Chinese national character, there is a consistent train of thought grounded in what may be called evolutionary humanism.

As the mediator of enlightenment humanism, the writer or the awakened man is the bearer of light, for example in Lu Xun's poignant and oft-cited iron house metaphor. But according to him, the bearer of light does not exist of and for himself, as the Nietzschean Superman may seem to; rather, he anticipates and makes possible stronger forms of light: torches and the sun.[21] Lu Xun repeatedly claims that in his role as a writer he is "caught between darkness and light," and that his function is that of a medium or a bridge so that a greater light can be hoped for. In a later es-

---

17. "On the Power of Mara Poetry," 106–107.

18. For early Western modernists as well, the obsession with progress was often expressed through the metaphors of darkness and light, as well as awakening from a long sleep. See Frederick R. Karl, *Modern and Modernism: The Sovereignty of the Artist 1885–1925* (New York: Atheneum, 1983), 9. Karl also notes that the continuity between romanticism and modernism lies in the profound sense of the artist as "legislator and prophet, as elitist" (23).

19. Zhou Zuoren, "Humane Literature" (1918), trans. Ernst Wolff, in Denton, *Modern Chinese Literary Thought*, 151–61.

20. Lu Xun, "How I Started Writing Fiction" (*Wo zenyang zuoqi xiaoshuo lai*, 1933), *LXQJ* 4:511–514.

21. Essay number 41 (1919), *LXQJ* 1:325.

say reflecting on the May Fourth movement, he explained this role using clearly evolutionary terms:

> Perhaps because I am lazy, I rationalized for myself that there are always transitions in the transformation of all things. Between animals and plants, between spineless and those with spinal chords, there are [life forms] in between. Or perhaps we can say that in the chain of evolution, every life form is in transition. When we started literary reform, there were of course writers of dubious convictions, which was inevitable and also a necessity. Their duty, being more aware, was to shout out a new voice. Since they came from the old dust, they could see the situation more clearly; so their sword slashing back was a fatal blow to the resilient enemy. But they should still fade with time and gradually disappear, at most serving as a log or a stone in a bridge, not a goal or model with a future [of its own]. What will come after them shall be different. Even though it may not be extraordinarily superior, and even though old habits will not have been all dispelled, there has to be a newer situation.[22]

Lu Xun is clearly making allusions to his own circumstances, as someone coming from "the old dust" (the Qing), modestly rendered as having "dubious convictions." Having fulfilled the function of a transitional figure from the late Qing to the May Fourth period, he refused to view his role as an end in itself, so that evolution, the search for the ever new and newer, could be continuous. He had earlier likened this role to that of a father who, "carrying the burden of convention on his back, blocks the gate of darkness, so that [the children] can be liberated to the space of expansive brightness."[23] Lu Xun's use of the parental metaphor, as well as viewing himself as a transitional figure, is important—not because he was about ten years older than most of the May Fourth iconoclasts, but because it is indicative of his profound humanism. Seemingly elitist in his characteristic sarcasm as well as in his unrelentingly dark portrayals of human nature, his chief sentiments remain humanist insofar as darkness, seen from the perspective of evolution, is the harbinger of the light to come. This is the light that will shine on the then much evolved and improved collective.

Lu Xun therefore establishes, in the works discussed above, a metonymic relationship among evolutionism, science, individualism, the discourse of national character, and literature. These relationships can also be seen in his evaluations and translations of three Japanese writers: the U.S.-educated literary critic Kuriyagawa Hakuson and the writers Arishima Takeo (1877–1923) and Mushakōji Saneatsu (1885–1976) of the Shirakaba ("white birch") School. In April 1924, Lu Xun purchased Kuriyagawa's *Symbols of Mental Anguish* (*Kumon no shōchō*), and he began translating it in September. The translation was completed within twenty days and was published in December. Lu

22. "Postscript to *Grave*" (*Xiezai Wen houmian*, 1926), *LXQJ* 1:285–286.
23. "What Kind of Fathers Should We Be?" *LXQJ* 1:130.

Xun viewed Kuriyagawa's literary thought as a synthesis of Bergson, Freud, and Nietzsche, as manifested in three interrelated ideas: vital life force as the basis of human life (Bergson); the origin of literature as anguish from repressed libido (Freud); and the writer as the poet-prophet (Nietzsche).[24] In Kuriyagawa's book, a clear evolutionary mode of thinking also connects these three ideas. Bergsonian creative energy is that which propels evolution; literature abolishes the slave mentality and liberates men from all obstacles and constrictions, and it is also the "geyser," embodying the power of individualism, erupting from the ground. But what is striking about this book is its clearly antinaturalist orientation: its voicing of the modernist sentiment that literature is expression and creation, not the representation of nature or mimesis. Kuriyagawa sees Freud's notion of *Darstellung*, which describes the representation of experience in the dream, as equivalent to the literary representation of experience: both are always mediated by distortions, subjectivism, and repressions, use various expressive strategies, and have strong imagistic tendencies. The realm of literature, like Nietzschean reversal of values, is thus a realm of inversion.[25] Contemporary literary historian Cheng Ma notes that Kuriyagawa's text was written during the Taishō era in the aftermath of World War I, when Japanese literature increasingly turned inward to expressionism, the I-novel, and psychological fiction,[26] and this helps explain the modernist tendency in the text.

A year later, in Lu Xun's postscript to his translation of Kuriyagawa's posthumously published *Outside the Ivory Tower* (*Zōge no tō o dete*), Lu Xun focused on Kuriyagawa's critique of the Japanese national character as applicable to the Chinese, saying that his diagnosis is the first step towards a cure: "If quinine can cure malaria in Japanese people, it can also cure the Chinese."[27] Lu Xun zeroed in on the issue of national character despite the fact that it was merely one of many topics dealt with in the essay collection.

Lu Xun's affinity with the Shirakaba writers Mushakōji and Arishima, whose stories he translated into Chinese, can be located in their shared humanist orientations. Mushakōji upheld a humanist ideal, and sought after self-realization for himself and others through his social experimentation with righteous communities called "new villages." Arishima, on the other hand, was strongly influenced by Bergsonian philosophy. He leaned toward the ideological left, and was especially remembered for giving away his prop-

---

24. See Lu Xun's "Preface" (*yinyan*) and chapter 2 of Lu Xun's translation of *Symbols of Mental Anguish*, in *"Symbols of Mental Anguish" and "Outside the Ivory Tower"* (*Kumen de xiangzheng; Chule xiangya zhi ta*) (Beijing: Renmin wenxue chubanshe, 1988), 3–10.

25. *"Symbols of Mental Anguish" and "Outside the Ivory Tower,"* 13–35.

26. Cheng Ma, *Communication and Renewal*, 203–230.

27. Lu Xun, "Postscript" (*Houji*), in *"Symbols of Mental Anguish" and "Outside the Ivory Tower,"* 281–287.

erty to the poor.[28] In both of their cases, we see a complementary relationship between individualism and humanism. Lu Xun lauded Arishima as "awakened,"[29] wrote approvingly of Mushakōji's goal of "awakening the masses,"[30] and would himself gradually lean toward Marxism in the ensuing years. This later turn to Marxism could not have been easily anticipated from Lu Xun's earlier stance vis-à-vis Japanese literature when he and his brother Zhou Zuoren translated Japanese short stories in their *Collection of Modern Japanese Stories* (*Xiandai Riben xiaoshuo ji*, 1923). They included mostly modernist writers (Natsume Sōseki, Mori Ōgai, Akutagawa Ryūnosuke, and Kikuchi Kan) and Arishima's work was explained not in terms of his humanism and altruism but in terms of "loneliness," "love," "erotic desire," and "self-transformation." The only socialist writer included, Eguchi Kan, received only a two-line treatment in their otherwise lengthy introduction to the writers in the anthology.[31]

Lu Xun's Marxist turn would prompt later literary and cultural historians to interpret all of Lu Xun's work from a Marxist point of view, viewing his early Darwinian evolutionism positively, as the basis of his later materialist ideology, and criticizing the individualistic tendencies in his use of Nietzsche. Such an oppositional view of ideology and art has affected evaluations of Lu Xun's creative work as an interplay or tension between collectivism and individualism. In light of my discussion of humanism (as a form of hope for the collective) and the individual (as leader in humanist pursuits), we will need to reinterpret the relationship between the collective and the individual not as contradictory but as complementary.[32] There is a procedural nature to this relationship, as I explained above: the writer as individual criticizes the stupidity of the masses in order to expose their illness and devise ways for cure, the end of which is to turn the masses into individuals. The methods of exposé and criticism that Lu Xun utilized are relentlessly sharp, his sentiments dark, yet his disparaging of the masses fundamentally rested on a hope for the future.

But this hope for the future, articulated in terms of biological, cultural, and humanist evolutionism, was premised on a translocal, universalistic notion of modernity that was a Japan-mediated Western product, and herein

28. Donald Keene, *Dawn to the West: Japanese Literature in the Modern Era* (New York: Henry Holt and Company, 1984), 441–505.

29. Lu Xun, essay number 63, *LXQJ* 1:363.

30. "Translator's Preface" (*Yizhe xu*, 1919), *LXQJ* 10:192.

31. Lu Xun, "About the Writers" (*Guan yu zuozhe de shuoming*), *LXQJ* 10:216–22.

32. Both Lin Yü-sheng and Leo O. Lee have pointed out the existence of two personas in his work—a public Lu Xun and the private Lu Xun—and how they are in tension with each other. See Lin Yü-sheng, *The Crisis of Chinese Consciousness* (Madison: University of Wisconsin Press, 1979), and Leo O. Lee, *Voices from the Iron House: A Study of Lu Xun* (Bloomington: Indiana University Press, 1987).

lies Lu Xun's distinctly May Fourth orientation. In various essays, Lu Xun
articulated his notion of modernity as (1) the abolition of cultural syncretism,
and (2) a critique of Western Orientalism. Calling the notion that Chinese
society is the site of coexistence of past and present a form of "dual thinking," Lu Xun repeatedly emphasized the need to uproot and discard such
thinking for the sake of progress.[33] The targets of his attack were consistently
the late-Qing reformers who could not entirely forsake Chinese tradition or
wholeheartedly accept Western culture, as emblematized in Zhang Zhidong's
syncretism.[34] Lu Xun's own recommendation was to never read Chinese
books, to emulate Western modernity through Japan, and to seek a universal culture of progress and evolution so that the Chinese people would become "global humans" (*shijie ren*), not just Chinese.[35] Hence when Western
travelers marveled about the beauty of ancient China, he saw in such Orientalist tendencies a desire to have Chinese preserve their barbarism and to
prevent them from evolving into a modern civilization.[36] Orientalists oppose
the Europeanization of Chinese culture, he said, because they want to enhance
the pleasures and exoticism of travel. To Lu Xun, this amounted to not only
encouraging cannibalistic barbarism but also participating in it.[37] This critique
of Orientalism far surpasses even Edward Said's in its sharpness.

Although a constructive side effect of Lu Xun's cultural universalism is
the critique of Western Orientalism, he does not exalt hybridity but rather
attributes universal qualities to Western culture. This view distinguishes him
from later anti-Orientalist critiques in Western academia, and marks him as
a May Fourth intellectual. When Western philosophers were criticizing the
bankruptcy of European culture in the post–World War I context, therefore,
Lu Xun defended Western culture, saying that their very self-critique was a
catalyst for their further progress and therefore promised everlasting hope.[38]
Lu Xun's Occidentalism was complete. Accordingly, he rejected Indian, He-
braic, Egyptian, Iranian, and other non-Hellenic cultures as having taken a
path the Chinese had to avoid if they wanted to follow the road to progress.[39]
And he embraced Japan, whose shallowly rooted traditions made it easy to
adopt Western ways and thus become fit for survival, as a model and mediator of Western culture.[40]

---

33. Essay number 54, *LXQ J* 1:344–45.

34. Essay numbers 38 and 48, *LXQ J* 1:311–14 and 336–37; "On the Power of Mara Poetry," 105; "Notes on the History of Science," *LXQ J* 1:26.

35. The term "*shijie ren*" appears in essay number 36, *LXQ J* 1:307.

36. Essay number 42, *LXQ J* 1:327–28.

37. "Random Notes under the Lamp" (*Dengxia manbi*, 1925), *LXQ J* 1:216.

38. Essay number 61, *LXQ J* 1:358–59.

39. "Notes on the History of Science," *LXQ J* 1:27; "On the Power of Mara Poetry," 97.

40. "Postscript," *"Symbols of Mental Anguish" and "Outside the Ivory Tower,"* 284.

LU XUN AS AN EXPERIMENTAL WRITER

To analyze Lu Xun's literary experimentalism, we may first identify three different yet interrelated strands of experimentalism in May Fourth China: the scientific experimentalism of Chen Duxiu's "Mr. Science," John Dewey's philosophical experimentalism as popularized by Hu Shi and captured in Hu's famous axiom "Make hypotheses boldly, but seek proof carefully," and literary experimentalism as practiced by writers, especially those belonging to the Creation Society. It was peculiar to the May Fourth era that these three strands were not clearly divided into the hard/soft categories of science and humanities, but rather constituted a general experimental temper within cultural discourse, as Lu Xun's case clearly shows. This was because "Mr. Science" in the May Fourth imaginary was not so much a system of knowledge for the study of physics, biology, or technology, as an ideology promising a new theory and praxis of culture. His presence was thus most strongly felt not in laboratories, but in the studies of society, politics, ethics, and morality (for Chen Duxiu), and in humanistic studies such as literary, historical, and philosophical research (for Hu Shi).[41] Science was a *cultural ideology* necessary for the enlightenment of the mind, while a broad understanding of the experimental method as a daringness to rebel against the old and to try something new was applied to all realms of cultural practice and discourse. Literary experimentalism, as part of this new cultural ideology, was therefore an expedient means of inscribing modernity onto the text.

In 1923, upon reading Lu Xun's *Call to Arms* (*Nahan*), Mao Dun wrote that "In China's new literary arena, Lu Xun is often at the vanguard of creating 'new forms'; almost every one of the ten or so short stories in *Call to Arms* has a new form. These new forms are bound to be greatly influential among young writers who will surely follow Lu Xun in experimentation."[42] The key words here, "new forms" and "experimentation," appropriately describe the nature and spirit of the May Fourth literary revolution in general, of which Lu Xun was a leading voice even though he was of an older generation. Lu Xun's "The Diary of a Madman" (1918) is considered the first "modern" Chinese short story ever published.[43] As was also characteristic in his essays discussed above, his literary practice here is premised on an Oc-

41. Wang Hui, "The Fate of 'Mr. Science' in China: The Concept of Science and Its Application in Modern Chinese Thought," trans. Howard Y. F. Choy, *positions* 3:1 (Spring 1995): 1–68.

42. Quoted in Wang Yao, *Collected Essays on Lu Xun's Works* (*Lu Xun zuopin lunji*) (Beijing: Renmin wenxue chubanshe, 1984), 65.

43. Not that China did not have its own forms of short vernacular fiction (*xiaoshuo*), but the modern short story form, as it has been used since the May Fourth period, was modeled explicitly after its Western counterpart, where more emphasis is given to the economy of plot and character conflict, and where supposedly "modern" issues are dealt with.

cidentalist universalism, which in literary practice is crystallized in his notion of "grabbism," defined as borrowing from other countries with confidence, like a master who chooses freely according to his needs and not like a neurotic who fears the loss of indigenous tradition or enslavement by what is borrowed.[44] Lu Xun himself openly acknowledged direct intertextual debts to foreign writers without feeling uneasy. This confidence of the individual writer as a global citizen who can freely borrow without the anxiety of cultural contamination or subjugation is what grounds Lu Xun's resolute search for new techniques. Utilizing various fictional techniques and modes as well as his knowledge of such diverse disciplines as medicine, psychoanalysis, history, myth, and art, Lu Xun presented himself as a self-conscious writer much like the Western modernists. His formal experimentation can be said to reveal a consciousness of the crisis of old forms of writing and an iconoclastic stance in the valorization of the new. Furthermore, Lu Xun's penchant for the new and the experimental, like the Western modernists', was always in the process of becoming, as it replaced the old and in turn became outdated itself to be replaced by the still newer. The conception of the new again echoes his notion of evolution as a process and as constituted by transitions and his description of himself as a transitional figure. Reading Lu Xun's short stories is like reading his performance of new narrative techniques.

Lu Xun's first short story, "Remembering the Past" (*Huaijiu*, 1912), though written in classical Chinese and on the surface appearing "premodern," already contained a conscious manipulation of the ironic distance between the narrator and the narrated event by means of different narrative voices and points of view, and a self-reflexive meditation on the fictionality of fiction. There are two narrators in the story, an adult and a child, to mark the temporal distance between the adult self and the child self of the same person and to distinguish the two different moments of narration. The adult narrator comments on a past event with an ironic bent: he recounts the false alarm created by a supposed invasion of bandits, and the different reactions it aroused in a hypocritical schoolteacher and in an old man named Wang, thereby exposing the folly of Confucian ethics. But the child narrator, a participant in the event, only sees it through his innocent eyes, and is unable to interpret its larger meaning. Carefully delineating the two voices and points of view, Lu Xun foregrounds the distance and difference between the two temporal points of narration, thus dramatizing the relationship between experience, time, memory, and writing.[45] The distance between the time of experience and the time of retelling necessitates two different voices and points

44. "Upon Seeing a Mirror" (*Kanjing yougan*, 1925), *LXQJ* 1:198.
45. "Remembering the Past (*Huaijiu*)," *LXQJ* 7:215–223. Lu Xun's other stories, such as "In the Wineshop" (*Zai jiulou shang*) and "Hometown" (*Guxiang*), deal with similar issues.

of view, as the present voice cannot but become colored by a selective memory of the experience and its present environment. The language of the present as it is used by the adult narrator further mediates the presentation of past experience, so that representation is many times removed from the real event by multiple mediations of time, memory, and language. Using formal devices to present a central theme of the story—the mediation of reality through narration—Lu Xun suggests fictionality is embedded in the very definition of writing.

The same theme is emphasized again in another story recounted by old Wang, who, like the adult narrator, cannot accurately recapture the past. When old Wang cuts short his monologue due to a sudden downpour, the pause is given a metanarratological comment by the narrator: "As is the case with most fiction, immediately after suspenseful descriptions there is usually a pause, and one has to wait for the next chapter to know what happens, so that one is always eager to read on to the next chapter and on forwards until the whole book is read."[46] The real experience of old Wang, when told in recollection, becomes endowed with a fictional quality. Old Wang's story thus calls attention to its own fictionality, while at the same time reinforcing the fictionality of the frame story told by the adult narrator.

Call to Arms (1923), Lu Xun's first collection of stories, is a showcase of a wide range of new techniques and forms. "The Diary of a Madman," even more than "Remembering the Past," presents a form-content coherence very much characteristic of the Western modernist notion that form is as important in engendering meaning as content, with both operating in a complementary, organic fashion. The fragmented form of the story befits the outbursts of thoughts and feelings of a madman suffering from persecution complex and paranoia. We again have two narrators: the person who writes the preface and the madman who writes the diary. The narrative distance between the author and the narrated event is carefully maintained through these two narrative mediations, one of them provided by a mentally ill, thus unreliable, narrator, the other spoken in the language of outmoded *wenyan*. Again, the view of fiction as a self-conscious artifact removed from reality marks the story's departure from realism.

In addition to the *mise-en-scène* of fictionality, the predominantly surrealistic and grotesque imagery in the story distances it from traditional realism. Lu Xun mentioned elsewhere that the "grotesk" (his own word) was the most fitting mode of description in a country like China, ridden by grotesqueness, and so overstatement and exaggeration were entirely appropriate for Chinese writing.[47] With a madman as the focalizing narrator, the reader is forced to view things through a distorted lens, as in a Nietzschean reversal. When

46. *LXQJ* 7:222.
47. "How *The True Story of Ah Q* Was Written" (*Ah Q Zhengzhuan de chengyin*, 1926), *LXQJ* 3:380.

the madman's attention is directed toward human behavior, history, literature, and language, his perceptions and observations take on surrealistic and
grotesque overtones that disrupt and play with the boundaries between representation and reality. For instance, when the madman reads a history book,
he finds that all the words are repetitions of the same two characters, *chiren*
("man-eating" or "cannibalize"). He perceives in literal terms what a normal
reader would recognize as a metaphor: to say that history only records the
words "man-eating" is to imply that the Confucian ethics inscribed in history books like the one he is reading are cruel and inhumane. His literal-
ization is the reader's metaphor. What is even more complex here, however,
is that this involves a (mis)recognition of Chinese written characters, hence
even the literal is restricted to the realm of representation, that is, the realm
of language. The madman's perception of violence through his inverted lens
is therefore also a commentary on the close relationship among the reality
of violence, the representation of violence, and the violence of representation. In a different incident, when he hears a woman on the street shouting to her son "I have to take a few bites of you to vent my anger towards
you," he takes the figurative expression literally and relates it to his own paranoia over cannibalism. Here metaphorical violence is again rendered as literal, but it is no longer restricted to the realm of representation; rather, it
produces in the madman a palpable fear of physical violence. From metaphorical to literal representation and then to their interconnectedness with physical reality, these incidents capture Lu Xun's experimental temper, which challenges the boundedness of the realms of reality and representation and
straddles them through the narrative deployment of a mad narrator.

By presenting a madman's perspective on history and language, Lu Xun
dislodges clichéd meanings, and forces the reader to question habitual responses to language. The story thus marks an important moment in modern Chinese literature where the conventional relationship between sign and
referent within a metaphor is subverted and the possibility of multiple
signification, as many significations as there are perspectives, is inaugurated.[48]
Perspectivism now entered the literary scene, its relativism allowing for the
recording of more subjective and personal experiences, and endorsing the
use of monologues (interior or exterior) in fiction, which was soon to become a fashionable technique. By literalizing metaphors, furthermore, Lu
Xun revealed the arbitrary nature of language as a construct bound by societal conventions, and opened up the path to a radical subversion of common assumptions of linguistic communication.

---

48. Fredric Jameson also notes that in semiotic terms the moment of separation between
sign and referent marked the onset of modernism in the West. See his "Literary Innovation and
Modes of Production: A Commentary," *Modern Chinese Literature* 1:1 (September 1984): 75.

Madness was used not only as a strategic device for debunking the conventions of language, however, but also as his favorite tool to represent the inverted, "true" reality behind the veneer of convention. In this light, we can read "The Diary of a Madman" as a morality tale about the violence of Chinese society and historiography. In "White Light" (*Baiguang*, 1922), Chen Shicheng the protagonist has failed the civil service examinations sixteen times, and after the last of these examinations he becomes deluded and starts seeing visions and hearing voices. He digs up a skull from under the floor of his room and, to his horror, witnesses the skull moving its jaws to speak to him. The talking skull may be taken as a metaphor for the decayed Confucian worldview, which, though dead, retains the power of speech and continues to hold sway over him. The fact that the obsession to achieve success in the Confucian universe through passing the examinations produced madness could not be a more fatal criticism of the Confucian system. Madness is here wedded to an anti-Confucian critique. "The Lamp that Was Kept Alight" (*Changming deng*, 1925), from his second collection of short stories *Hesitations* (*Panghuang*, 1926), depicts a madman obsessed with snuffing out a temple lamp whose flame is considered by the ignorant and superstitious villagers to be the source of the village's well-being. They believe that if the lamp goes out, a flood will engulf them and they will be turned into loaches, so they lock up the madman to prevent him from extinguishing the flame. Chen Shicheng's madness implicates the folly of the exam system, while the madman in the second story is paradoxically the only "sane" person who perceives the foolishness of superstition and wants to quell it by extinguishing the flame. Lu Xun again makes the madman literally and physically act out the metaphorical meanings he wants to communicate to his readers. These madmen challenge not so much the actual practice as the symbolic realm of state and religious institutions.

The grotesque image of the speaking skull in "White Light" points even more forcefully to Lu Xun's desire to go beyond realism. A similar image can be found in a scene from "Remembering the Past," where bandits throw the bloody, torsoless head of master Zhao into the arms of an old servant. The culmination of the grotesque imagery of the severed head can be found in "Forging Swords" (*Zhujian*, 1927), in which severed heads swim around and bite each other in a cauldron of boiling water. Surrealistic images also prevail in his prose poetry collection, *Wild Grass* (*Yecao*, 1927), which contains such images as a man gnawing on his own heart, a naked woman trembling in the wilderness with her arms outstretched toward the sky, a corpse speaking from the grave, and two naked figures in a frozen pose, each with a dagger pointed at the other.

The justification for the use of these grotesque images can in part be located in Lu Xun's interest in Freudian psychology, which endorsed dream visions as having significant value for understanding reality. In more explicitly

Freudian terms, Lu Xun explored the realm of libidinal desire and its relationship to artistic creation and character psychology. For instance, in *Wild
Grass,* we see Eros and Thanatos, the two fundamental libidinal drives in the
Freudian scheme, encounter each other at close quarters. With "Mending
Heaven" (*Butian,* 1922), the first story in the *Old Stories Retold* (*Gushi xinbian*)
collection, Lu Xun also meant to explain how the "primordial incipience of
the sexual urge resulted in creation and death."[49] Much of the Freudian content in Lu Xun's work echoes Kuriyagawa Hakuson, in whose conception
the repression of desire and life force in the libido produces anguish, and
the expression of this anguish in symbolic form is art. Lu Xun's three studies of madness discussed above can be interpreted as the release of unconscious fears and desires in the form of grotesque images, as making manifest the latent content of Chinese society. Madness becomes the manifestation
and embodiment of anguish, and ultimately the channel with which to convey, symbolically, a Nietzschean reversal of existing values. In the case of "The
Diary of a Madman," the madman's seemingly illogical utterances upset the
conventions of language, which then serves as a synecdoche for a project
against the larger conventions of society.

As in Lu Xun's essays discussed earlier, his creative works are also un-
derlied by an evolutionary, future-oriented perspective, and herein again
lies Lu Xun's peculiar blending of humanism, evolutionism, and individualism. In *Wild Grass,* for instance, although the prevailing mood seems pessimistic, hope is ultimately sustained through relentless struggle against the
pessimism engendered by both social corruption and individual existential
anguish. The decision of the traveller in "The Passerby" (*Guoke,* 1925) to
walk resolutely down the road of life, even though he knows that death awaits
him at the end, is a powerful expression of an uncompromising spirit in the
face of certain destruction. This traveler takes a fundamentally different path
than the one taken by Albert Camus's protagonist in *The Stranger.* As late as
in a 1932 essay, Lu Xun confessed that he was a firm believer in evolutionism during the 1920s, convinced that the future would be better than the
past, and that the young would be better than the old.[50] He had faith that
"there would be humans more noble and closer to perfection in the future."[51] Writing upon the publication of his other brother Zhou Jianren's
translation of a treatise on evolutionism, he further emphasized his belief
in the importance of studying evolutionism to fathom the future fate of the
Chinese people.[52]

49. Lu Xun's own words, in his "How I Started Writing Fiction" (*Wo zenme zuoqi xiaoshuo lai,*
1933), *LXQJ* 4:513.
50. "Preface" (*Xuyan*), *LXQJ* 4:5.
51. "Random Thought 41" (*Suiganlu 41,* 1919), *LXQJ* 1:325.
52. "A Short Introduction to *Evolution and Regression*" (*Jinhua he tuihua xiaoyin,* 1930),
LXQJ 4:250.

Again and again, Lu Xun worked on integrating evolutionism, Nietz-schean individualism, and humanism (as I defined it earlier). Expressed in literary endeavors, such integration meant that experimental form, to a large extent, is subsumed by the symbolic content, which is in some sense prede-termined by these three vectors of his thought. Here again, we can see how the transitional role Lu Xun carved out for himself affects his literary ex-perimentalism, yoking it to social and symbolic anticonventionalism, so that form becomes more instrumental than autonomous. His experimentation with narrative techniques could serve social progress by virtue of its artisti-cally progressive nature and expedient conveying of social messages. In this view, the modernist form, as deployed by Lu Xun, is both the marker of the modern in and of itself, and the instrument to bring about social modernity through its effective embodiment of socially critical content. In instrumen-talizing the modernist form, Lu Xun in some sense became the quintessential Third World writer of national allegories—little wonder that, as mentioned above, Fredric Jameson's prime example in proving his national allegory the-ory is Lu Xun. A First World theorist choosing a representative Third World writer is a highly reductionist act, and yet the easiest way to dispute Jame-son's totalizing, some would say condescending, theory is not necessarily to reread Lu Xun, but rather to show how so many Chinese modernists *after* Lu Xun wrote differently.

AFTER LU XUN: TAO JINGSUN'S EXPERIMENTALISM

For the generation that came of age during the May Fourth period, espe-cially for those involved in the Creation Society, formal experimentalism was no longer necessarily a vehicle for social messages. When Tao Jingsun started writing in Japan in the early 1920s, he had already been running a diasporic Chinese literary journal with Guo Moruo called *Green* (original English ti-tle) in Kyūshū. This was also the time when the Japanese *shinkankakuha* or new sensationist writings of Yokomitsu Riichi and others (such as the early Kawabata Yasunari) were being introduced to a welcoming readership in Japan. Their aesthetics were inspired by Western avant-garde movements such as dadaism and futurism, and in their practice they favored the writing tech-niques of Joyce and Proust.[53] A Chinese counterpart to this Japanese literary movement, which I examine in Part Three, was inaugurated a few years later in Shanghai, but Tao was the first self-conscious Chinese writer who wielded the seductive wand of new perception and sensationism in his writing.

Having gone to Japan at age nine and received virtually all his education there, Tao not only knew many foreign languages, including German, En-

---

53. See Donald Keene, *Dawn to the West: Japanese Literature in the Modern Era* (New York: Henry Holt and Company, 1984), chapter 19: "Modernism and Foreign Influences," 629–719.

glish, French, and of course Japanese, but was also very well informed about current Japanese literary trends. First a student of medicine, then a student of the physiology of acoustics (*yinxiang shengli xue*) and the conductor of the school orchestra, Tao Jingsun was urbane and "modern" in ways that Lu Xun never was. His modernist experiments were more suggestive of the simultaneity of literary movements in an age of frequent travel facilitated both by technological advances and cultural imperialism. One might therefore see in his work a particular manifestation of the "Japanized modern," constituted by his transnational upbringing, cosmopolitan tastes, and interlingual writing practices.

Characteristically, Tao engaged in formal experimentation without the burden of commitment to social evolution that Lu Xun was obsessed with. Fluent in Japanese, he wrote many of his stories in Japanese and then translated them into Chinese, which are also often dotted with English and French. The creative writer in this case was literally a translator who transplanted Japanized expressions and syntax (which were earlier Europeanized in the Japanese context) into Chinese. Intermingled with Japanized and Europeanized diction and syntax were also unmediated foreign words, especially French and English. This juxtapositional use of several languages and the foreign-sounding syntax and diction gave his work an exotic ambience. Fittingly, his stories were either set in the foreign concessions of Shanghai or in Japan.

Following is an excerpt from Tao's "Advertisement for *Café Pipeau*" (*Café Pipeau de guanggao*), from his collection *Concert Ditties* (*Yinyuehui xiaoqu*, 1927). Words appearing in original English and French are in italics:

> *Modern girl* and *boy*! We are washing cups and brewing coffee waiting for your arrival.
>> See our coffee,—*Mocca, Java, Brazil*
>> In this gray city, have you never seen the black color of our coffee?
>> *Custard pudding, Neapolitan Ice cream*
>>> *Minted lime, Mince pie*
>>>> *Ecrier, Zinger,*
>>>> All of which our boss
>>>> learned at
>>>>> the *Stove* of *Café Atlier,*
>> And WINE, WINE, WINE, WINE,
>>> Goblet stems should be tall, colors bright and shiny,
>>>> *Cocktail, Cocktail, COCKTAIL*
>>>> *Rose, Violet, Rose,*
>> Our boss is a musician, how can he not give you a treat of music?—
>>> So we have a phonograph inviting you to listen to—
>>>> *Classic, moderne, violon, orchestra,*
>>>>> And he is also putting together "*Orchestra Pipeau.*"
>
> . . .

Our boss and kitchen staff and waitresses have brewed the coffee and are
waiting for you.   *PIPEAU!*
PIPEAU!
PIPEAU!!
PIPEAU!!![54]

The linguistic and typographic features here are semantically and visually
striking. The profuse use of foreign words and their juxtaposition with Chinese create a powerful visual effect, while at the same time suggesting an urban, cosmopolitan context. The incremental enlargement of the words
"wine" (*jiu*) and "Pipeau" shows a painterly sensitivity for size and spatial
arrangement to capture the viewer's attention. The line breaks are that of
poetry, and the text in actuality hybridizes the forms of fiction, poetry, and
advertisement. For the first time in modern Chinese literature, language
is explicitly used for its visual quality, and, also for the first time, the semantics here denotes the culture of a hybridized urban space with colonial
implications.

"Advertisement for *Café Pipeau*" does have a narrative. The narrator tells,
in the form of a dramatic monologue, of how a young man from southern
China comes to be a cafe owner in Shanghai. He is a country man sent to
Japan for education, where he spends a lot of his time deeply nostalgic for
the Chinese countryside dotted with stone bridges, willow trees, boats, and
grass hills. But the impact and temptation of Japan's urban culture—"rushing cars, fragrant faces, ladies' mature bare arms and long legs flying into
his face, the *Modern girl* in a cafe making his stomach burst"[55]—changes him
into a city man. So now he runs a cafe in Shanghai. In less than four pages,
the story captures the owner's transition from a country man to an urban
man in economic language fraught with syntactic and semantic oddities that
suggest the urban exotic. Even the line above, "the *Modern girl* in a cafe making his stomach burst" (咖啡店里的 *Modern girl* 要涨破他的肚皮), suggests
the intensity of his excitement and attraction when he encounters modern
girls in cafes.[56] The name of his cafe, "Pipeau," has a double meaning: it is
a French word meaning a reed or shepherd's pipe, used here to represent
the owner's nostalgia for the countryside, but it is also transliterated into the
Chinese *piaobo*, meaning "wandering." The sense of wandering in a foreign
country is the experience the owner provides his customers with his exotic
foods and ambience, similar to what Tao provides to his readers with his exotic semantics and distorted syntax.

Trained in music, Tao often made use of this talent; the impact of music
is especially notable in his particular choice of syntactic and semantic struc-

54. Tao Jingsun, *Concert Ditties* (Shanghai: Chuangzao she, 1927), 151–153.
55. Ibid., 151.
56. For an analysis of the "modern girl" issue in the Chinese context, see chapter 11.

tures. As in the above example, the listing of nouns, the increase of emphasis leading to crescendo, and the alternating rhythm of longer and shorter
phrases and sentences all foreground the author's attention to the musical-
ity of language. Music and concerts are as well often the content and context for Tao's stories, such as the collection's title story, "Concert Ditties,"
and "Two Scenes" (*Liang qingjing*). The latter juxtaposes the scenes of two
concerts: a traditional Japanese concert and a Western one. The language
of the first scene mimics the grace, purity, and unhurriedness of the Japanese musicians and their music, while the language of the second scene repli-
cates the vibrant, sensual atmosphere at the Western concert. A Caucasian
woman at the Western concert, surnamed Bob, is described this way:

> As for [Miss] *Bob*, she held a rose in her hand, waving, waving, waving, that
> rose like her lips, red, red, red, red, red like her half wet lips, but what she was
> waving was a rose, waving, waving, waving.
>
> Now, the rose suddenly left her hand, flew high in the air, then dropped
> down, down to the group of flower-like Westerners and beautiful Japanese
> ladies—fell into a young Western man's hand. Miss *Bob* looked down, and the
> rose, you see, was still on her red lips.[57] (original English in italics)

The image of the rose is first used as a simile for the redness of Miss Bob's
lips and a metaphor for her sensuality, but then it becomes a metonymy for
her lips when it lands on the man's hand signifying a flirtatious encounter.
Mme. Schuman's singing on the stage, the repetition of Miss Bob's hand waving the red rose, and the rhythmic movement of language in these passages
harmonize to create a concert of sound, movement, image, and language.

In "Three Short Chapters" (*Duanpian sanzhang*, 1925), Tao describes the
succession of images in the way one would perceive them from a particular
perspective, as in Guo Moruo's "Sunny Spring Farewell" (*Yangchun bie*) discussed in the next chapter. Here the perceiving subject is himself in motion,
rolling down a hill: "He fell. This side of the cliff had grass, and they rolled
down the grass on the slope. Sky, grass, pine tree, pine tree, grass, sky, grass,
pine tree, blue sky, blue sky, blue sky, tender grass, blue sky, tips of pine trees;
and also—his, and her, white feet."[58] The act of perception itself is foregrounded much more assuredly than in Guo Moruo's story. Tao, more than
any other writer in this period, rewrote the Chinese language, extending its
capacity through linguistic experimentation, exploring the connection of
visuality and music to language, and concretizing the effects perception and
other sensual experiences have on linguistic expression.

What most clearly emerges in a comparison between the experimentalisms
of Lu Xun and Tao Jingsun is the marked absence of social instrumentality

57. Tao Jingsun, *Concert Ditties*, 26.
58. "Three Short Chapters" (*Duanpian sanzhang*), in ibid., 138.

in the latter. In their difference, we can identify the two divergent modes of May Fourth experimentation: experimentalism wedded to the project of *social* modernity on the one hand, experimentalism standing alone as a marker of *cultural* modernity on the other. These two forms of modernity are intimately linked, but their linkages are not of mutual implications only, since the cosmopolitan production of literature as a transnational act of creation in many languages, as Tao's case exemplifies, will also have to be contextualized by way of political and cultural imperialisms. If the urban setting is exotic in nature, that fact is due to the presence of colonial concessions; if exoticism is a precondition for urban cosmopolitanism, that urban cosmopolitanism has to be a form of cultural identity rooted in the semicolonial condition; if urbanism and exoticism are conducive to formal experimentation because they provide naturally powerful stimuli, then formal experimentalism as a technique or methodology cannot be extricated from the history of semicolonialism.

CHAPTER 3

Psychoanalysis and Cosmopolitanism

The Work of Guo Moruo

"Individualized individuals" do not exist by nature: they are created through the conflictual (dis)integration of primary memberships, i.e., when individuals can view the superior community as a liberating agency, which frees them from belonging to one single group, or possessing a single, undifferentiated, massive identity.

ETIENNE BALIBAR (1995)

What happens to Freudian psychoanalysis in the Chinese context, or rather, what happens to Chinese literature when it confronts psychoanalysis, especially in the context of the May Fourth valorization of teleological modernity? How does the construction of a landscape of desire that must self-consciously conform to psychoanalytic frameworks become possible and necessary? As an imported discourse, how did psychoanalysis speak to the needs and agendas of modern Chinese intellectuals? Finally, what are the multiple implications of using psychoanalysis in local and global contexts? This chapter is an attempt to answer these questions through an analysis of the fictional and critical works of Guo Moruo (1892–1978) written before his mid-1920s conversion to Marxism. I examine the intersection between the desire for the modern and forms of modern desire, as they converge in texts that experiment with psychoanalysis. In general, psychoanalysis first had to be seen as having universal value in order to justify its use in the Chinese context, since psychoanalysis dictated desiring in very specific ways. Representing desire in the mode of psychoanalysis therefore necessitated a calculated process of objectification: breaking the theory down to its usable parts and in turn applying them.[1]

---

1. Jingyuan Zhang underlines this point when she argues that Chinese writers selectively appropriated Freudian psychoanalysis, and especially prioritized three of its aspects: theories of artistic creativity, the Oedipus complex, and the interpretation of dreams. See her *Psychoanalysis in China: Literary Transformations, 1919–1949* (Ithaca: Cornell East Asia Series, 1992), 3.

Simultaneously, this chapter interrogates what is often described as modern Chinese cosmopolitanism by querying the premises upon which it is established. I argue that the application of the term "cosmopolitanism" is by definition asymmetrical, depending on the position of the subjects in question. When applied to Third World intellectuals, "cosmopolitanism" implies that these individuals have an expansive knowledge constituted primarily by their understanding of the world (read: the West), but when applied to metropolitan Western intellectuals there is a conspicuous absence of the demand to know the non-West. This "asymmetrical cosmopolitanism" is another manifestation of a Western-dominated world view. My interest in this chapter is to trace how this asymmetrical cosmopolitanism becomes embedded in May Fourth thinking, using Guo Moruo's psychoanalytic stories and critical essays as an example. There exists an intimate relationship between psychoanalysis and cosmopolitanism, since both assume a universalism (of mind and culture, respectively), even though this universalism is Eurocentric in nature.

The specific connections between psychoanalysis and cosmopolitanism goes beyond their shared universalistic assumptions. First, Freudian psychoanalysis was seen as endorsing sexual emancipation; it also became one of the major modes of legitimizing individualism, constitutive of the "modern-ness" of the individual who enjoys the freedom of sexuality beyond the dictates of traditional morality. Second, in an era when Occidentalism was the discourse of cultural power, psychoanalysis also allowed its users to emerge as cosmopolitans with additional cultural capital. Especially since it was considered esoteric by the general readership, psychoanalysis was an even more authentic example of one's cosmopolitanism, marking the greatest difference between the intellectual and the masses. But before we trace the necessarily spurious process of acquiring "modern" ways of desiring through psychoanalysis and its implications, first we need to engage with literary history and excavate the site where Guo's fictional work is buried.

GUO MORUO AS FICTION WRITER

Partly because he is known primarily as a poet in the Whitmannian vein who captured the romantic outbursts of the May Fourth spirit, Guo Moruo's experimental endeavors in the narrative form have received scant attention. Guo is recalled mainly as the poet who cried out for the need to attain metaphorical rebirth upon the ashes of the past (using the metaphor of the phoenix discussed in chapter 1), and who therefore embodied the May Fourth spirit of iconoclasm and antitraditionalism. Furthermore, critics and historians have commonly linked the radical vanguard spirit of Guo Moruo's romantic poetry with his political activities from the mid-1920s and after, the former interpreted as a literary exemplification of the latter. This kind of interpretation willfully dismisses the fact of Guo Moruo's gradual ideological and aesthetic transformation from a romantic iconoclast to a Marxist, and instead constructs a consistent chronology of Guo Moruo's work as serving Marxist ideology throughout. A much respected dictionary of modern Chinese literary figures offers a summation of Guo's life and work typical of the kind of Marxist literary history authorized by the Chinese Communist Party: "Supreme proletarian cultural warrior, an unremitting revolutionary, an outstanding writer, poet, and dramatist, a Marxist historian and philologist."[2] Guo's celebrity status as a poet, a dramatist, a scholar, and above all a Marxist cultural leader (elected as president of the prestigious National Literary Association in 1949) overshadowed his narrative work and critical essays, which could be understood neither from a perspective of historical presentism (the view that the narrative of the past should be established in terms of the results in the present), nor by a gapless, linear chronocentrism (the view that what Guo was before was a precursor of all that he later became). The pitfalls of historical presentism or linear chronocentrism are obvious, as they violently excise elements that do not fit into their narratives: it is telling that in the summation of Guo's achievements quoted above, there is no specific reference to his fictional endeavors. Guo's psychoanalytic fiction was one of the excesses that got conveniently dropped from the picture.

It is little wonder that Guo's psychoanalytic stories, such as those he wrote in his early years between 1919 and 1925 with the exploration of sexual drives as their main theme, were perceived to be incompatible with the honored political image of the cultural ideologue. Guo in fact produced three volumes of fiction before and during his gradual conversion to Marxism in the mid-1920s. If the sheer quantity of narrative creation alone is impressive—Lu Xun, the "father" of modern Chinese fiction, only published three slim volumes of fiction—so too are his unique perceptions of the traditions of China and the West, expounded in his various critical essays and exemplified in his fictional work. The early cosmopolitan Guo Moruo—the aesthetic vanguardist, the pantheist, the champion of art for art's sake—was perhaps matched by the later Marxist Guo Moruo only in the degree of radicalism.

As noted earlier, in order to justify the use of psychoanalysis there had to first be an assumption of cultural universalism. In four important essays written in 1922 and 1923, Guo expounds his belief in universalism on the twin grounds of pantheism and what he calls the "supranational" (*chao guojia*). In the first of these essays, "Preface to *The Sorrows of Young Werther*" (*Shaonian Weite zhi fannao xuyin*, 1922), Guo attributes Goethe's emphasis on emotion,

2. Yan Cunde et al., eds., *Dictionary of Chinese Literary Figures* (*Zhongguo wenxuejia cidian*) (Chengdu: Sichuan renmin chubanshe, 1979), 1:469.

the individual, self-expression, love of nature, and so on to pantheism. In his view, the individual under pantheism considers himself to be one of the gods. Since God is within the self, the universal will is embodied in the self, hence subjective emotionalism is to be celebrated. One can clearly see how the Guo who translated the Goethe novel and the Guo who wrote poetry in the explosive, cosmic language reminiscent of Walt Whitman merge here. But this pantheism that endorses individualism is rooted not merely in that portion of Western culture that appealed to him, but also in the fundamental philosophical orientations of Chinese culture: Taoism and Confucianism. In the 1923 essay entitled "The Traditional Spirit of Chinese Culture" (*Zhongguo wenhua de chuantong jingshen*), for instance, he presents both Lao-tze and Confucius as harbingers of such pantheistic notions as individualism, free thought, and self-control. Faulting post-Qin exegesis as having misrepresented their philosophies, Guo Moruo asserts that Lao-tze and Confucius continued the pre-Qin Chinese pantheism of the *Documents Classic* (*Shangshu*), the *Liezi*, and the thought of Shennong, in which nature, men, and gods were integrated into one. Lao-tze's "revolutionary thought" advocated purposelessness, which was a kind of "free thought" and a movement toward rejuvenation. Confucius, on the other hand, had been most grossly misunderstood, Guo laments. Citing various passages from the *Analects*, Guo concludes that Confucius revived the pantheistic view of the universe by recognizing the god-in-the-self.

Pantheism further went hand in hand with what Guo called the supranational in an essay entitled "The National and the Supranational" (*Guojia de yu chao guojia de*, 1923). As the nation-state has increasingly become a form of imprisonment for the individual, Guo reasons, we need to turn to the supranational, which guarantees humanism, harmony, and peace among nations by erasing the boundaries of the nation-states. Commenting on Henri Barbusse's (1873–1935) realistic novel about the absurdity of World War I, *La Clarté* (1919), Guo notes how the nation-state's proclivity to war destroys individual freedom. Guo then concludes that for the Chinese, who have traditionally had little conception of the importance of the "nation-state" (rendered in its specific modern neologism "*guojia*"),[3] the supranational has been the norm rather than the aberration, because the ultimate goal of the traditional Chinese spirit is peace for all human kind, not the governing of a

3. In this regard it is important to note the differing implications here of *tianxia* (world)— the word used by the Chinese to designate China during the imperial period—and *guojia* (nation-state). Joseph Levenson argues that the modern term "nation-state" (*guojia*) is a form of voluntarily destroying Sinocentrism, as opposed to the old term "world" (*tianxia*), which assumed that China *was* the world. The intellectual history of modern China, Levenson further comments, has therefore been "the process of making *guojia* of *tianxia*." See Joseph Levenson, *Confucian China and Its Modern Fate* (Berkeley and Los Angeles: University of California Press, 1958), 99–103.

nation-state. Supranationalism therefore unquestionably resides in the traditional Chinese spirit.[4]

Guo's next move required him to equate Chinese culture with Greek culture, which he considered the source of modern Western culture, in order to do away with geocultural boundaries between China and the West. In a 1923 letter to Zong Baihua (1897–1986), a renowned philosopher of aesthetics, Guo argues that among four cultural types in the world, which are Indian, Hebrew, Chinese, and Greek, Chinese culture comes closest to Greek culture and Germanic culture (which Guo considers an offshoot of Greek culture). Citing references to astrology in the *Book of Poetry*, physics in the *Mozi*, and deductionism in the philosophical method of Zou Yan, Guo argues that the authentic, pre-Qin Chinese culture was active, progressive, scientific, and rational like Greek culture. Furthermore, the philosophy of Laotze is akin to Nietzsche's: they share an opposition to deities, rebellion against conventional morality, and emphasis on the individual as the basis for progressive development. Even their shortcomings are the same: both are self-centered and not altruistic.[5]

In these four texts, Guo achieves his justifications for the supranational by two procedures: inquiring into the ontological cultural similarities between Chinese and metropolitan Western culture (Greek culture being perceived as the origin of metropolitan Western cultures), and locating the "modern" (Western) elements in traditional Chinese culture. Guo appears to blur geocultural boundaries between China and the West—hence the early "cosmopolitan" Guo Moruo—but the blurring is conducted within a field of hierarchies. Just as Greek culture *must be* identified as China's kindred culture, Indian and Hebrew cultures have to be decisively estranged from this particular kinship structure. Universalism thus favors the Hellenic metropolitan West as the ground of comparison and similarity.

It is not an exaggeration to say that Guo's interpretation of the supranational "traditional Chinese spirit" diverges widely from conventional perceptions. To be sure, this interpretation has its immediate political and cultural exigency within the context of May Fourth China. For instance, it can be partially construed as strategic rhetoric endorsing the iconoclastic call for openness to Western import—justified by the reasoning that it has always been part of Chinese culture. Lu Xun's grabbism discussed in chapter 2 stands as another example of this reasoning. As with Lu Xun's design,

4. These three essays can be found in Wang Xunzhao et al., eds., *Research Materials on Guo Moruo* (*Guo Moruo yanjiu ziliao*) (Beijing: Zhongguo shehui kexue chubanshe, 1986), 1:147–155, 172–178, and 192–194.

5. "On Chinese and German Cultures: A Letter to Zong Baihua" (*Lun Zhong De wenhua shu: zhi Zong Baihua*), in *Collected Essays from the Debate on the Question of Eastern and Western Culture During the May Fourth Period* (*Wusi qianhou dongxi wenhua wenti lunzhan wenxuan*), ed. Chen Song (Beijing: Zhongguo shehui kexue chubanshe, 1989), 582–589.

objections to Guo's cosmopolitanism could be easily dismissed as insecurity, paranoia, and provincialism.[6] Guo and Lu Xun advocate that modern China should without hesitation adopt a cosmopolitan open-mindedness and accept what is being offered by the West. Lu Xun even went so far as to say that none of the Chinese classics are worth reading by the Chinese youth: they should only read foreign books, although not, he hastened to add, books from India, which again hierarchicalizes what constitutes the correct "foreign."[7] To both Guo and Lu Xun, seeking modernity in the West (and the honorary West, Japan) meant simultaneously the exclusion of the other non-West (India) and of the Other within the West (Hebraism); the supranational relationship is limited to only that between China and the Hellenic West. This West remains the sole proprietor of modernity qualified to enter into a supranational relationship with China; hence this supranationalism reveals its cosmopolitan outlook to be based not on a horizontal, egalitarian conception, but on one with reified hierarchies which reiterate the geography of political and cultural power distribution in its historical moment.

The asymmetry or hierarchy inherent in Guo's conception of cosmopolitanism is further enmeshed within the teleological conception of modernity. First, even as Guo seems to deny teleological thinking, the legitimation of Chinese culture that Guo engages in is primarily conducted within the terms set by the Western teleology of modernity. Hence it is important for him to seek similarities between the modern (Nietzsche) and the traditional (Lao-tze), using their similarities to justify universal modernity: the teleology of modernity is implicit in such a search for similarity. Here the search for similarity posits Nietzsche as the point of departure and Lao-tze as the comparison, rather than the other way around. So Nietzsche remains the frame of reference and the criterion to which Lao-tze can be compared, evaluated, and judged equal. Second, the need to equate Chinese culture with Western culture requires an exclusionary definition of what the former entails: overemphasizing the active, the progressive, and the rational, while undervaluing everything which goes against such an emphasis but which is nonetheless integral to the complex tapestry of Chinese culture. This exclusivity is again dictated by a desire to be like the West in terms of the enlightenment ideology of progress and reason. The cognitive categories with which Guo analyzes Chinese culture

---

6. Lu Xun, "Upon Seeing a Mirror," in *Complete Works of Lu Xun* (*Lu Xun quanji*, hereafter *LXQJ*) (Beijing: Renmin wenxue chubanshe, 1981), 1:197–200. The continued currency of this kind of argument can be glimpsed in the way the cultural craze discourse (*wenhua re*) in 1980s China was steeped in nostalgia for the Han and Tang dynasties as the golden age of Chinese culture. Note for instance the "River Elegy" (*Heshang*) television series.

7. Lu Xun, "Books that Should be Read by Youth" (*Qingnian bi du shu*, 1925), *LXQJ* 3:12.

are undoubtedly borrowed from the West, and in Guo's fiction psycho-analysis would become a set of cognitive as well as emotive categories applied to the Chinese context.

In Guo Moruo's supranational scheme, where what the modern West has to offer was already embedded in the best of Chinese culture, to become "Westernized" was equivalent to becoming more authentically Chinese. Guo acknowledged no distinction between the ancient and the modern, the Chinese and the foreign. Within his pantheistic supranationalism, contradictions and differences could be reconciled and integrated, and everyone could be humanized. In terms of literature, his chosen metaphors are understandably those of cosmic mingling and union: the new literature "should take in the rain and dew from the sky, absorb the spring water from the earth, dissolve all that is from the outside within one's self to make it become one's own blood that gushes forth to express one's complete self."[8] All that belongs to the outside (rain, dew, spring water) is imbibed and becomes an organic part of one's self (blood). The liquid nature of water and blood make possible a complete fusion between self and Other, dissolving all distinctions. In celebrating the borderless self and the limitless world (albeit an implicitly hierarchized one) in a constant state of mutual permeation and flux, Guo's nature metaphors promise a utopian identity politics beyond the confines of the nation-state or national culture.

Supraspatial and supratemporal, psychoanalysis can thus be applied to the work of the thirteenth-century writer Wang Shifu. In a 1921 essay called "An Aesthetic Critique of the *Story of the Western Chamber* and Its Author's Personality" (*Xixiangji yishu shang de pipan yu qi zuozhe xingge*), Guo contends that the *Story of the Western Chamber* is the product of psychological trauma and repressed sexual desire. Lauding Wang Shifu's masterpiece as a song of the triumph of human sexual nature over stultifying convention, Guo analyzes the sexual drive behind Wang Shifu's writing as foot fetishism, explaining that the practice of foot-binding in China stimulated foot fetishism in the male and masochism in the female.[9] Ironically, then, just as the best of Chinese culture—Taoism and Confucianism—supranationally echoed that of the West, the worst of Chinese culture—foot-binding—made psychoanalysis possible in the Chinese context.

But it is in the ostensive *traces* in the application of psychoanalysis to the Chinese condition that we can detect the mechanical and artificial nature of its presence. Psychoanalysis was a *method*, a style, that for Guo meant chiefly an exploration of the connection between sexuality and dreams. The very

8. Guo Moruo, "Our New Literature Movement" (*Women de xinwenxue yundong*, 1923), in *Research Materials on Guo Moruo*, 180.

9. For a discussion of Guo's essay, see Wu Lichang, *Psychoanalysis and Sino-Western Literature* (*Jingshen fenxi yu Zhong xi wenxue*) (Shanghai: Xuelin chubanshe, 1987), 170–172.

first story he wrote, "The Sad Tale of a Shepherd" (*Muyang aihua*, 1919), already utilized a dream to convey the horror the protagonist feels upon hearing a tragic love story during the day. And his most intensely psychoanalytic tale was "Late Spring" (*Canchun*, 1922), which Guo not only wrote following a calculated psychoanalytic schema, but which he later offered psychoanalytic guidelines for deciphering, out of fear that the story would not be understood.

Written while Guo was in Japan, the story is also set there. Aimou, the Chinese protagonist, is a medical student like Guo Moruo himself, and is married with two children. He receives a Chinese visitor one day, Mr. Baiyang, who tells him that their mutual friend Mr. He has become insane and attempted to kill himself on his way home to China by jumping off the boat after loudly shouting "Bonzai!" (*wansui*) three times. Aimou thinks to himself that there must have been an invisible being calling Mr. He into the ocean, just as Odysseus was seduced by the sirens' songs in Homer's *Odyssey*. At Baiyang's request, Aimou goes to visit the bedridden Mr. He in a small hospital, where Aimou meets a beautiful Japanese nurse and promptly becomes infatuated with her. Miss S., as the nurse is called, was born in San Francisco where her parents both died of tuberculosis when she was only three, and she herself now exhibits early symptoms of the same disease. Her pale beauty (due to her sickly physique), exotic flavor (being U.S.-born Japanese, and simply being Japanese), and vulnerability trigger his love and protective instincts and legitimize his masculinity. His desire for her is heightened when the unsuspecting Baiyang reveals that he is in love with her too, since desire works most powerfully, as René Girard has argued, in a triangulated relationship.[10] But as a married man with a wife and children, Aimou feels guilty about his emotional disloyalty. That night, he dreams about a rendevous with the nurse on a mountain called Mt. Fudetate (*bilishan*, literally meaning "tall, erect mountain"), with the moon right above it. He describes the image of the moon above the mountain as an inverted exclamation mark (¡), an obvious phallic symbol. Aimou and S. have a conversation regarding her fear of having contracted tuberculosis, and he comforts her with a doctor-to-be's air of expertise and authority. She then asks him to diagnose her, and bares her upper body: her shoulders like "peeled lychees" and her breasts like "rosebuds not yet in bloom." Just as he is about to touch her breasts, Baiyang arrives at the scene with the news that Aimou's wife has killed their two sons and gone insane. He rushes home to find his sons dead, stabbed in the chest. Naked from the waists up, their breasts are covered with blood. His wife stabs him too and he falls, dying. The next morning, after he wakes up, he hurries home, finds his family safe and sound, and tells the

10. René Girard, *Deceit, Desire, and the Novel*, trans. Yvonne Freccero (Baltimore: Johns Hopkins University Press, 1965).

dream to his wife, who teases him that he had such a bad dream because he felt guilty.[11]

The dream is contrived in many aspects: the association of the rosebuds not yet in bloom with the nurse's breasts will later appear in the text as a symbolic foreshadowing of the fate of the nurse herself whose sickly body augurs a short life. Aimou buys roses for her the next morning and those roses also wither faster than normal; the petals fall before the buds fully bloom. Her breasts as rosebuds, herself as a yet-to-bloom rose, and the roses that he buys for her—these metonymies have been carefully strung together. Other echoing images include the breasts of Miss S. as the locus of his desire and the breasts of his children where they are stabbed—the site of desire transferring to the site of dread. But the complexity of the design is far from being revealed in the reading of a few images from the dream. It is thus useful to examine Guo Moruo's own explanation of the major architectural design of the dream, which serves as further indication to the manufactured nature of the story's psychoanalytic framework:

> The protagonist Aimou fell in love with Miss S. but he is a married man and of course his love cannot be fulfilled. Therefore, he has unwittingly repressed the desire into the subconscious. This is the major motivation that has caused the dream. In the dream, Aimou and S. meet on Mt. Fudetate. This is the unfulfilled desire of the day expressed in the dream. When Aimou is about to diagnose her, which means the contact between the two bodies, his friend Baiyang suddenly appears with the bad news. This is Aimou's thought during the day that Baiyang was his obstacle, realized in the dream—Baiyang comes to separate him and S. The biggest obstacle he felt during the day [his wife and two sons] is removed in the dream by having her kill the sons and go insane. Then the dream moves from Mr. He's madness to his wife's madness, the description of evening cloud as blood-like to the two children bleeding, from the association of sirens to the tragedy of Medea (both from Greek tragedy), and then I used the tragedy of Medea as a model for the dream.[12]

Guo here carefully manipulated the dream within a Freudian frame: the dream is Aimou's daytime wish fulfilled, while it is also an anxiety dream with a sexual content. The death of his wife, sons, and himself can further be interpreted as the materialization of his guilt, as well as as a wish for punishment; thus the dream can also be seen as a punishment dream.[13] Instead of S's breasts, he gets his sons' bloody breasts—his desire is rewarded with horror through substitution. The use of the subtext of a Greek mythology in the

---

11. "Late Spring" (*Canchun*, 1922), in *Complete Works of Guo Moruo* (*Guo Moruo quanji*) (Beijing: Renmin wenxue chubanshe, 1985), 9:20–35.

12. "Criticism and Dreams" (*Piping yu meng*, 1923), in *Research Materials on Guo Moruo*, 1:169.

13. On wish-fulfillment, anxiety, and punishment dreams, see Sigmund Freud, *The Interpretation of Dreams*, trans. James Strachey (New York: Avon Books, 1965), 155–166, 195 and 596, respectively.

dream—the allusion to Medea's killing her two children in order to avenge her husband Jason's disloyalty—also mimics Freud's own penchant for using Greek mythology as illustration for many of his key ideas. With these similarities in place, we can see that the use of a psychoanalytic dream in a Chinese text by all means required careful design. If dream materials with sexual content are natural to the Jewish psyche in Freud's Victorian-era Vienna, these materials in their specific form needed to be imported and acquired painstakingly by the Chinese writer who is experimenting with psychoanalytic tales. The fact that Sigmund Freud happened to be a Jew and his theory happened to be thoroughly conditioned by his own Jewishness[14] is an irony that Guo, who deemed Hebrew culture unworthy of his supranationalism, did not address.

"Late Spring" perhaps also marks the very first time the stream-of-consciousness interior monologue appears in Chinese fiction. On the train to visit his friend, Aimou's random thoughts shift from a concern for his family he just left behind to fearing his friend's death, to philosophizing about kinds of deaths and their meanings, and then to his children and their loneliness without him. These thoughts simply flow in a disjunctive fashion without logical cohesion. But here too, the *traces* of the design for a stream-of-consciousness narrative are exposed, precisely because the narrative is so self-consciously experimental and the technique so unprecedented in Chinese literature. It is the author's cognitive manipulation of psychoanalysis and its literary translation into the technique of the interior monologue that lurks most decisively behind the depiction of psychological realities. The interiority thus constructed is mediated by an intellectual, cognitive knowledge of psychoanalysis.

Similarly, "Sunny Spring Farewell" (*Yangchun bie,* 1924) renders an ocean liner's ticket office in a rhythmic flow of images sifted through the subjective consciousness of the viewer:

> The ringing of the telephone, the ringing of the bell, the sound of the typewriter, the sound of fountain pens racing over paper, incessantly play out the march of modern civilization. The eyes eyes eyes of maroon cats, facial muscles are caterpillars in spasm, . . . following the music of the march, incessantly jumping forward, jumping forward, jumping forward. The air is boiling, red-headed policemen, Western women, magnolia magnolia perfume fragrance, plump shins of Japanese women revealed between the folds of their dresses. . . . Men are floating waterdrops in boiling water.[15]

The paragraph effectively describes the sounds, movements, colors, and smells through a dramatized juxtaposition of various images, similes, and

---

14. See Sander L. Gilman, *The Case of Sigmund Freud* (Baltimore: Johns Hopkins University Press, 1993).

15. "Sunny Spring Farewell" (*Yangchun bie,* 1924), in *Complete Works of Guo Moruo,* 9:163.

metaphors, in broken syntax and jumping, staccato rhythm, all of which combine to produce poetic effects. It dynamically captures the perceiver's moment-to-moment registering of images in the order they strike him. The images, along with similes and metaphors, combine to produce an oppressive atmosphere ruled by noise, bustle, crowdedness, and heat. It brings into sharp relief the image of the lone young man—pale, commonly dressed, and with disheveled hair—as he is described in the following paragraph. The scene brings out the incongruity of the young man's presence, while at the same time concretizing his sense of suffocation.

Interior landscape is also externalized through perceived images in carefully delineated psychoanalytic terms in yet another story, this one tinged with lyricism. The 1925 story "Donna Carméla" (*Ke'er meiluo guniang*), like "Late Spring," deals with the motif of a married man's psychological tribulations as a result of being captivated by a young Japanese lady whom he nicknames Donna Carméla. He lives a double life, entertains a double personality, feels out of control, and daydreams about his union with her. A wish-fulfillment dream he has depicts Donna Carméla confessing her love to him, but then committing suicide by jumping off a cliff. In waking life, the Chinese protagonist pines away for this Japanese beauty, whose image in his mind is decorated with his literary and poetic imagination. She is an exotic Spanish princess who would satisfy his masochistic fantasy: lashing his body with her whip until his flesh tore. But she is also a pale, tubercular beauty, an orphan exploited by her adoptive parents, and a beautiful woman stricken by poverty, attributes that stir in him the masculine desire to rescue and protect. When it becomes clear that his one-sided love will never be reciprocated, he attempts suicide by jumping into the ocean, gets rescued, but resolves to kill himself again, this time with a pistol.[16] The story is over thirty pages long, written in the form of a letter by the protagonist to a friend, describing his mental landscape through interior monologues. It gives a detailed description of his shifting mental states, much like Yu Dafu's stories discussed in chapter 4. References to Western literature and mythology dot the story throughout (allusions to Blasco Ibáñez's *La Moja Desnuda*, Goethe's *Faust*, Shakespeare's *Macbeth*, Greek mythology, and other sources, as well as the frequent use of German, Japanese, Spanish, and other languages), which required the author to footnote his allusions. The extended description of an interior landscape, then, is also an exhibition of Guo's erudition in Western humanities; it is an interiority which, more than anything else, is textually and intertextually constructed. This Chinese mental picture, that is to say, has a heavy exotic and foreign tone to it, except in one instance.

The one irreducibly Chinese element of this story, as it were, is the ethnicity of the protagonist, marked by the difference between him and the Japa-

16. "Donna Carméla," in *Complete Works of Guo Moruo*, 9:205–238.

nese woman. The fact that the protagonist is Chinese is repressed throughout the story as he himself tries to hide it from other people, except in one
instance when he decides not to send a love letter to his beloved for fear that
his Chinese-ness will be discovered. He remarks: "At one time I did write a
letter and it was almost delivered to her hand, but I retrieved it. I was afraid
that she would find out I was Chinese and then I would lose even the little
bit of love she has for me at present. This is something I could not endure,
and I will protect [this little bit of love] at the risk of my life."[17] In this passage, the association between Chinese-ness and inadequacy of language—
due to his ethnic/racial difference from the woman—forces him deeper into
the world of desire and interiority, and even farther from the expression and
fulfillment of love. Love is overdetermined by race and can only remain forever unrequited. While unrequited love can be said to be necessary for the
emplotment of a tragic story, the factor of ethnicity/race in this instance
evokes issues of history and national/racial identity.

Anxiety over ethnic/racial difference thereby further reinforces the
Freudian trajectory of repressed sexuality and desire. One can attribute this
to the unequal status of Japan and China at the time: Japan as the successfully modernized, politically powerful, culturally more "civilized" nation, and
China as the defeated, the conquered, and the backward. Here, Karatani Kōjin's discussion of interiority in Meiji-era Japanese literature presents significant parallels to the case at hand. Analyzing how Meiji literature made
the turn to interiority, Karatani argues that "It was in the face of the overwhelming dominance of the West that the establishment of both the modern state and interiority in the third decade of Meiji became ineluctable."[18]
Just as, in the West, confessional narratives were initially written in the condition of being "subject to the Lord," so too in Meiji literature it is the defeated, hence the powerless, who confess, thus carving out an elaborate landscape of interiority. For modern Chinese literature as well, the May Fourth
writers of interior landscapes were long-time residents or students in Japan,
living in a day-to-day state of psychological disequilibrium caused by the perceived inferiority of the Chinese nation and culture vis-à-vis Japan.

To consider the problem of interiority in terms of the confessional genre
is further illuminating. If the popular confessional genre arose in Japan due
to the forced interiorization caused by Western domination, as Karatani argues, then the confessional mode of writing in the form of psychoanalytic
tales such as Guo Moruo's can be seen as both the result of a simple case of
borrowing a genre from Japanese literature, and as a complex case of multilayered domination by both the West and Japan. To borrow an argument

17. Ibid., 230.
18. Karatani Kōjin, *Origins of Modern Japanese Literature,* trans. Brett de Bary (Durham: Duke
University Press, 1993), 95.

from Gilles Deleuze and Félix Guattari, one could further say that if psychoanalysis works in non-European cultures, it is not because of the universalism of the categories of mind but because of colonial history, which has imposed Western structures on native minds.[19] The cognitive and psychological categories of psychoanalysis are hence readily accepted, and in this case eagerly sought after, by the colonized. Psychoanalysis, as a discourse borrowed from the hegemonic West via Japan, is simultaneously the *agent* and *effect* of domination and repression.

Ultimately, psychoanalysis was a multivalent discourse in May Fourth China. When situated internally alongside the May Fourth rebellion against feudal morality, psychoanalysis offered a vocabulary for registering and naming ideas of repression and sexual anxiety; when situated vis-à-vis the West and Japan, psychoanalysis was both the agent and effect of imposing cognitive and psychological structures on the dominated. In each case, psychoanalysis remained firmly a discourse of subjecthood. In the former context, the "new" and "modern" vision of sexual psychology and psychoanalysis offered the May Fourth intellectual the mark of his individualism and "modern-ness" as a subject over both feudal traditions and the common populace. In the words of Etienne Balibar quoted at the beginning of this chapter, the ability to identify with the "superior" community of the West and Japan frees the person from "belonging to a single group" (Guo's supranationalism is an exemplary theoretical construct in this regard), and allows him to possess a differentiated, individualized identity (his knowledge of psychoanalysis puts him above the unknowing, largely uneducated masses).[20]

In the latter context, the dominated attain subjecthood through being subjected to the powerful, because subjection is constitutive of subjecthood, and because subjection also evokes a will to power and control over one's subject status. This argument can be made through a chain of analogies between Guo, Freud, and psychoanalysis. If, as Sander Gilman argues, Freud's work on the problems of women is a projection of his own anxiety of being a Jew (since both women and Jews are cultural "inferiors" and share an analogous status),[21] psychoanalysis is the expression of the weak in the constitution of subjecthood. By naturalizing female subordination through his biological determinism,[22] psychoanalysis also naturalizes subjugation. But to the extent Freud painstakingly constructs a masculinism upon the basis of fe-

---

19. As summarized by Robert Young, *White Mythologies* (New York: Routledge, 1990), 144.

20. Etienne Balibar, "Ambiguous Universality," *differences* 7:1 (Spring 1995): 48–74, quotation from 60–61.

21. Sander Gilman, *Freud, Race, and Gender* (Princeton: Princeton University Press, 1993), 7.

22. This part of the argument is Gayle Rubin's. See her "The Traffic in Women: Notes on the 'Political Economy of Sex,'" in *Feminist Frameworks*, ed. Alison M. Jagger and Paula S. Rothenberg (New York, McGraw-Hill Book Co., 1984), 167.

male subordination, we see the will to power and control over one's subject status, even though this masculinism may still be the kind of defensive "hypermasculinity" that Ashis Nandy attributes to the effect of colonialism on the colonized male.[23] Analogously, Guo's use of psychoanalysis implicates him in this complex process of subject formation. The "particular," degraded Chinese culture (except that of the pre-Qin period) needed to be overcome in order to participate in the "universal modernity" through acquiring "universal" cognitive and psychological categories. In Guo's scheme, this subjection to Western discourse is therefore a necessary condition of modern Chinese subjectivity, not solely because of the historical experiences of imperialism, but more importantly because of his willfully utopian cosmopolitanism that elides its asymmetrical and hierarchical constructions in an attempt to access modernity.

23. Ashis Nandy, *The Intimate Enemy* (Delhi: Oxford University Press, 1983), 21–22.

CHAPTER 4

The Libidinal and the National

The Morality of Decadence in
Yu Dafu, Teng Gu, and Others

Now I can understand the meaning of the word death. Death is pleasurable, death is grand. Justice for the oppressed lies in the word death. When I die, I return this entirely unfree soul to its original state of freedom.

GU ZONGQI (1923)

Life is but the crystalization of sadness and bitterness. I do not believe that happiness exists. People accuse me of being a decadent, a hedonist, but they do not know the reasons behind my pursuit of wine and sex. Ah, waking up from deep drinking on a clear night, looking at the money-bought body sleeping near my chest, my melancholy and my laments are many times deeper and more painful than those of the self-appointed moralists.

YU DAFU (1923)

I wanted to make another confession before dying of starvation and repeating Goethe's dying words: "Mehr Licht! . . . Mehr Licht!"

YU DAFU (1931)

In 1923, Yu Dafu (1896–1945) wrote approvingly of the phenomenon of premature death among British decadent writers as a symbol of their thorough rebellion against a civilization built upon notions of conventional morality. He noted that the decadent illustrator Aubrey Beardsley (1872–1898) was consumed by tuberculosis at age twenty-six; Ernest Dowson (1867–1900) died of alcohol abuse at thirty-three; and John Davidson (1857–1909) committed suicide.[1] Little did he realize at the time that several Chinese writers who embraced the decadent style in writing, sometimes

1. "Writers Gathered around *The Yellow Book*" (*Jizhong yu Huangmianzhi de renwu*), in *Collected Writings of Yu Dafu* (*Yu Dafu wenji*) (Hong Kong: Sanlian shudian, 1983), 5:169–188.

under the influence of Yu himself, would also entertain death as a relief from painful existence. Born about two decades later than the British decadents, Bai Cai (1894–1926) attempted several suicides without success and finally died of illness at age thirty-two; Gao Changhong (1898–1949) collapsed after a mental breakdown; Wang Yiren (1902–1926) committed suicide by jumping off a boat at the tender age of twenty-four; and Gu Zongqi (1903–1929), from whose last letter comes the first quotation above,[2] committed suicide at age twenty-six. Yu Dafu himself contemplated suicide several times,[3] had signs of tuberculosis infection, and finally met a tragic death, assassinated by the Japanese military, in 1945.[4] This chapter seeks to understand the sudden prominence and notoriety the decadent aesthetic garnered in the 1920s by examining the treatment of sexuality and death as presented in the stories of Yu Dafu, Teng Gu (1901–1941), and others. A close examination of the libidinal in their narratives shows that it often operates as a metaphor for the national and the social. The tension between cosmopolitanism and nationalism is played out in the realm of erotic desire.

"DECADENCE" REDEFINED

Decadence or *tuifei* as a literary term has conventionally been associated with immorality in modern Chinese literary criticism ever since the term's wide circulation in the 1920s. Post-1949 orthodox Marxist critics, and sometimes even revisionist critics, have tended to use the term in a pejorative sense, asserting that a decadent aesthetic is an automatic indication of the questionable moral fiber of its practitioner. This claim is more or less based on the old assumption that "literature is a reflection of the author's character" (*wen ru qiren*): if a writer writes about sexual perversity, then he must be a pervert himself. This moralist argument used by Marxist critics is a convenient, camouflaged ideological critique of the Nationalist era: to see personal decadence as a function of moral decay is an efficient means for attacking the Nationalist government whose tolerance of "corrupt," bourgeois-capitalist leanings is said to have allowed the literature of decadence to come into prominence. The result of such ideological critique has been a complete erasure of the language of decadence in Chinese literary criticism and history;

2. Gu Zongqi, "The Last Letter" (*Zuihou yifeng xin*), *Short Story Monthly* 14:8 (1923): 16.

3. See his own account of contemplating suicide in "After Finishing the Last Story of the Cypress Vine Collection" (*Xiewan le Niaoluoji de zuihou yipian*), in *The Complete Short Stories of Yu Dafu* (*Yu Dafu xiaoshuo quanbian*) (Hangzhou: Zhejiang wenyi chubanshe, 1991), 818–819.

4. An essay by Zeng Zhuowen notes that Yu was assassinated while in exile in Indonesia after the Japanese surrender because the Japanese military feared that he knew too many secrets. At the time Yu disguised himself and worked as an interpreter. See Zeng Zhuowen, "The Death of Yu Dafu and a Lost Poem" (*Yu Dafu zhi si yu yishou yishi*), *Ming Pao Monthly* (September 1995): 57–59.

more neutral terms such as "romanticism" and "lyricism" were employed instead when outright condemnation was withheld.[5] "Aestheticist decadence" (*weimei tuifeizhuyi*) had been a "public secret" in China, as Xie Zhixi puts it, until his book length study was published in 1997.[6]

A recuperative discussion of the role of decadence in modern Chinese literature was earlier launched by Leo Ou-fan Lee in a long essay published in Taiwan in 1994. Richly documented and illustrated (in a mode reminiscent of the practice of Chinese decadent writers themselves), Lee's essay traces the history of decadence from the 1920s to the 1930s and reconstructs its links to the Western decadent movements of French symbolism and British aestheticism. Lee explains that the Chinese readiness to embrace decadence in the 1920s may be associated with the erotic consciousness in *The Dream of the Red Chamber,* thus suggesting the possibility that indigenous Chinese culture might have played a role in the popular incorporation of decadence. Lee also (after Matei Calinescu) delineates the nature of Western decadence as a critique of the "bourgeois modernity" which overemphasized technology and rationality and resulted in stultifying middle-class conventions and commercialism; Lee makes the important point that, in contrast, Chinese decadence lacked a critical evaluation of bourgeois modernity and instead flaunted it.[7] This divergence from Western decadence exemplifies how May Fourth decadence did not dichotomize the two forms of modernity—bourgeois and cultural—but rather saw these two forms of modernity as implying each other.

This is not to say that the decadents lacked critical sensibilities, but rather that, in keeping with May Fourth antitraditionalism, the object of their critique was not modernity in its various forms but that which obstructed modernity: traditional morality and the backwardness of the nation. The intimate connection between the decadent aesthetic and social criticism is indeed another site of tension between aesthetics and teleology, similar to the contradictory impulses in Lu Xun's work. Specifically contextualized in the May Fourth cultural and social formation, aestheticism itself was first of all a radical gesture against the social co-optation of literature. Thematically, furthermore, decadent stories are often veiled expressions of social criticism and discontent, where the libidinal economy operates as metaphor for political and social economy. The quote from Gu Zongqi above, where he at-

5. See for instance the most comprehensive *A History of Modern Chinese Fiction* (*Zhongguo xiandai xiaoshuoshi*), vol. 1, written by Yang Yi (Beijing: Renmin wenxue chubanshe, 1986).

6. Xie Zhixi, *The Extremities of Beauty: A Study of Modern Chinese Literary Aestheticist Decadence* (*Mei de pianzhi: Zhongguo xiandai weimei tuifeizhuyi wenxue sichao yanjiu*) (Shanghai: Shanghai wenyi chubanshe, 1997), 7.

7. Leo Ou-fan Lee, "'Decadence' in Modern Chinese Literature and Its Writers" (*Zhongguo xiandai wenxue zhong de 'tuifei' ji qi zuojia*), *Con-Temporary* (*Dangdai*) 93 (January 1, 1994): 22–47. The quotation is from page 42.

tributes the decadent celebration of death to social oppression, is a clear illustration of what I mean by the social meaning of decadence.

Here I am following the literary critic Tang Heyi's 1924 thesis that decadent literature was an expression of the hypersensitive moderns' pursuit of sensual stimulation, which was a form of escape from *but also* a kind of protest against the world, toward which they harbored profound sadness and disappointment.[8] In this specific historical moment, even escape could be construed as a form of protest, since alienation from society often indicated the individual's sense of nihilism toward desired social transformation. In keeping with the May Fourth "spirit of feeling for the time and worrying for the country" (*ganshi youguo de jingshen*),[9] the so-called decadent writers were most often socially engaged critics who protested against the conventional "morality" of society which allowed injustice, inhumanity, and other perversions to exist. Zhou Quanping (1902–1983), a member of the Creation Society and the editor of *Flood* (*Hongshui*) magazine, saw exposing immorality and corruption as the natural mission of the decadents, as can be seen in the following declaration: "A beautiful black screen is spread over the present world, like a gorgeous peel covering a rotten fruit. People know only to hold their noses and praise the lusciousness of the peel, but we want to prick the peel and expose the stinking flesh inside."[10] Through playing with the unseemly and the improper, writers like Zhou Quanping and Yu Dafu attempted to unveil the reality beneath the garb of customary morality. They consciously sought to be modern day "Satans," evil and destructive in the eyes of smug moralists, but whose job it was to disrobe the latter's cloak of pretension.[11] The generalization that the Creationists, many of whom practiced a decadent style, were interested in nothing but "art for art's sake" aestheticism is in fact a broad misconception. Their aestheticism was never detached from a strong sense of social injustice, and many of them would later turn to the political left and write stories with proletarian themes.[12] In some of their early writings, where the oppressed, be they prostitutes or the poor, are sympa-

8. Tang Heyi, "The Rise of Neoromanticism" (*Xin langman zhuyi de boxing*, 1923), *Sixth Anniversary Issue of Chenbao* (*Chenbao liu zhounian jinian zeng kan*) (December 1, 1924): 229–251, especially 236 and 245.

9. The phrase comes from C. T. Hsia's article, "The Spirit of Feeling for the Time and Worrying for the Country in Modern Chinese Literature" (*Xiandai Zhongguo wenxue ganshi youguo de jingshen*), in his *Love, Society, and the Novel* (*Aiqing, shehui, xiaoshuo*) (Taipei: Cunwenxue chubanshe, 1970), 79–106.

10. "We Shout in Unison" (*Women tongsheng jiaohan*, 1925), in *Materials on the Creation Society* (*Chuangzao she ziliao*), ed. Rao Hongjing et al. (Fuzhou: Fujian renmin chubanshe, 1985), 499.

11. Zhou Quanping, "Satan's Work" (*Sadan de gongcheng*, 1924), in ibid., 495.

12. Here one has to note the difference between the early decadence of the May Fourth period and the Shanghai decadence of the late 1920s, which became one of the defining features of urban modernism and was more purely aesthetic and escapist.

thetically represented, we can easily find in embryonic form a proletarian thrust. The move from decadence to leftist ideology marked two of the successive stages in the development of many of these writers.[13] For instance, Yu Dafu wrote compassionately about the social underclass, attempted to join revolutionary movements in Guangzhou, and even wrote what he himself called stories with "socialist color" (*shehuizhuyi secai*).[14]

Support for decadence in May Fourth China came also from such prominent literary figures as Zhou Zuoren, Yu Dafu's fellow Creationist Guo Moruo, and the famous Marxist writer Qian Xingcun (A Ying, 1900–1977). In 1922, Zhou wrote an article in defense of Yu Dafu's story "Sinking" (*Chenlun*) after it received widespread condemnation on the grounds of immorality. In this article, titled after the story, Zhou tried to make two arguments. First, he argued that the story's eroticism has an artistic purpose and is aimed at attacking established morality. In this regard, it is different from pornography. Second, the eroticism is theoretically justified by Freudian psychoanalysis, which sees sexuality as the center of human activity. In this regard, Zhou went on to say that the story is a groundbreaking attempt to acknowledge sadism, masochism, exhibitionism, voyeurism, and so on, as natural instincts.[15] Guo Moruo, a kindred spirit, also wrote years later (even after he had already becoame a staunch Marxist) that Yu's work exposed the hypocrisy of Chinese society: "His bold self-exposure is a stormy, thundering attack on the hypocrisy of the literati deeply hidden under a shell for thousands of years. It surprised the pseudo-moralists and pseudo-literati so much that they were made violently angry."[16] In like manner, Qian Xingcun defended Yu Dafu in a 1933 article claiming that sexual repression in Yu's stories is an index to both economic and social repression, and that the embrace of decadence expresses a profound sense of alienation and superfluousness taking hold of the modern individual.[17]

The works of Western decadents, the British (Oscar Wilde, Ernest Dowson, Arthur Symons, Max Beerbohm, and Aubrey Beardsley) more than the French (Charles Baudelaire, Paul Verlaine, Arthur Rimbaud, and Stéphane

---

13. Guo Moruo and Yu Dafu are two prominent examples. A writer's move from avant-gardism to political radicalism was a common phenomenon in many countries at this time. For instance, Japanese writer Kataoka Teppei, originally a new sensationist writer, turned to proletarian literature later, and the Russian decadent, Valeri Bryusov, became a communist.

14. "Preface to *Collected Writings of Dafu Chosen by the Author*" (*Dafu zixuan ji xu*), in *The Complete Short Stories of Yu Dafu*, 835.

15. Zong Mi (Zhou Zuoren), "Sinking" (*Chenlun*, 1922), in Chen Zishan and Wang Zili, eds., *Research Materials on Yu Dafu* (*Yu Dafu yanjiu ziliao*) (Hong Kong: Sanlian shudian, 1986), 1–5.

16. Guo Moruo, "On Yu Dafu" (*Lun Yu Dafu*), in ibid., 86.

17. Qian Xingcun, "Yu Dafu" (1933), in *The Grand Collection of China's New Literature: 1927–1937* (*Zhongguo xinwenxue daxi*), ed. Zhao Jiabi (Shanghai: Shanghai wenyi chubanshe, 1987), 1:629–649.

Mallarmé), served to a significant degree as inspirations for their Chinese counterparts, especially in terms of aesthetics. *The Yellow Book,* a magazine which served as the main stage for many English decadents between 1894 and 1897, found its counterpart in the various magazines published by the Creation Society: *Creation Quarterly* (*Chuangzao jikan,* 1922–1924), *Creation Weekly* (*Chuangzao zhoubao,* 1923–1924), and *Flood* (1924–1927). Yu Dafu's long essay on the writers of *The Yellow Book* was published in *Creation Weekly* in 1923.[18] The first issue of *Creation Quarterly* carried Yu's translation of Wilde's *The Picture of Dorian Gray* practically functioning as its manifesto, along with Guo Moruo's poem "The Creator" (*Chuangzao zhe*), in which Guo equated literary creation with the ultimate act of creating life: giving birth. Priority was given to the creative act itself, the meaning of creation, and the power of the created object. The editors of these magazines also attempted to make the magazines themselves works of art by carefully choosing cover designs and creative page layouts. Most importantly, they inaugurated horizontal, left-to-right printing in China after the convention of English and other European languages.

This aestheticism, however, was itself an aspect of their socially critical orientation. By redefining artistic morality as that which transcended established morality, they voiced their dissatisfaction with both aesthetic and moral conformity. Yu Dafu cited, for instance, Rémy de Gourmont's book *Decadence and Other Essays on the Culture of Ideas,* which defined decadence as concomitant to an aesthetics of innovation and originality as opposed to imitation.[19] This search for nonconformity in aesthetics is organically linked to the writers' criticism of social conformity. In reading Yu Dafu's stories it becomes obvious that the sexual or the libidinal never exists in separation from the national; rather, in a time of national and cultural crisis, it is the nation which ineluctably dictates the specific formation of sexual desire. The tension between the libidinal and the national spells out the tensions between the individual and the collective, between aesthetics and teleology, and between modernity as a cultural project and a social project, all of which further illustrate the contradictions within the May Fourth modernity project itself.

SEXUALITY AND THE NATION: YU DAFU

Yu Dafu was the earliest and most influential figure to adopt the decadent style. For a time, his short stories made the term "decadence"—*tuifei* or

---

18. Yu Dafu, "Writers Gathered around *The Yellow Book,*" op. cit.

19. Rémy de Gourmont, *Decadence and Other Essays on the Culture of Ideas,* trans. William A. Bradley (New York: Harcourt, Brace and Company, 1921); see especially "Stéphane Mallarmé and the Idea of Decadence," 139–155. Yu's reference to the book appears in a short story entitled "Emptiness" (*Kongxu,* 1922), in *The Complete Short Stories of Yu Dafu,* 156.

dikadan, and later *tuijiadang*[20]—a popular word.[21] For clarity of discussion, it is important from the outset to delineate two different contexts of meaning in his work depending on the setting of the stories (Japan or China), which in turn produce two different structures of signification. While the shared thematic of all of his stories can be described as the intersection between the aesthetic/sexual and the social/national, those about the Chinese experience in Japan play out the theme in different ways from those set in China. In China stories, bold descriptions of sexual frustration can be largely interpreted as a cry against the strict moral codes that suppress individual sexuality, and the ever-strong sense of alienation can be seen as a function of society's exclusion of nonprivileged people such as displaced youth and the social underclass. But in Japan stories, sexual frustration becomes encoded as the direct, unambiguous result of national weakness: Yu's male protagonists represent the "inferior" China whom the "superior" Japanese despise. National weakness conditions a symbolic castration of the Chinese male. The Chinese youth in Japan cannot even acquire some measure of comfort from prostitutes, whom, he suspects, do not respect him as a "man" because he is a *Zhinaren.*[22] The desire of the Chinese youth operates like the desire of the colonized: there was actually a Chinese student in Japan, named Huang Qiu, who committed suicide out of unrequited love for a Japanese nurse.[23]

Yu Dafu went to Japan in 1913 at the age of seventeen and did not return to China until nine years later. Most of his Japan stories were written there during the last two years of his stay, 1921 and 1922. Sexual repression, or in Freudian terms the "surplus of unutilized libido,"[24] is an important theme in these stories, and its referent is invariably the ailing nation, China itself. The protagonist in "Sinking" (1921), who may be seen as the prototype of all the pale wane youths in Yu's stories, admits that he suffers from hypochondria, and contemplates suicide as a direct result of the psychological and sexual traumas experienced as the citizen of an inferior nation. A student in a Japanese college, the unnamed protagonist is stricken by a severe case of neu-

20. The first term is a translation of the word "decadence"; the second is a May Fourth transliteration; the third is a more clever 1930s transliteration made current by the Shanghai decadents, which means "decadent and licentious." For a brief discussion of the 1930s trend, see chapter 10; for a more thorough treatment, see Xie Zhixi, *The Extremities of Beauty,* chapter 4, 224–255.

21. Yu's own reference to the term attributed to him, for instance, can be seen in his "Preface to *Chicken Rib Stories*" (*Jileji tici,* 1927), in *The Complete Short Stories of Yu Dafu,* 821.

22. "*Shinajin*" in Japanese: a derogatory term for "Chinese." See the discussion of this term in Chapter 1.

23. Zhou Zuoren, "The Worsening of Anti-Japanese Sentiments" (*Pai Ri de ehua,* 1920), in *About Tigers* (*Tan hu ji*) (Shanghai: Beixin shuju, 1936), 17–18.

24. Sigmund Freud, *Inhibitions, Symptoms, and Anxiety* (1926), trans. Alix Strachey (New York: W. W. Norton, 1989), xxix.

rosis rising from what may be called a national inferiority complex. He feels that all his Japanese schoolmates despise him, and are talking about him behind his back. One day, when he is walking down the street, a separate party of three male Japanese students are walking the same way. They all come across two female students, and the male Japanese students start flirting with them. Although he is not a part of the conversation, he feels extremely self-conscious, as if he were the one talking to the girls, so he runs back to his room. Talking to himself in the security of his room, he calls himself a coward for not having the courage to go up and talk to the girls, and then thinks to himself that the girls were only sending smiles to the Japanese students and none to himself. He thinks that they must have known that he was a *Zhinaren,* since they did not even care to throw him a glance. He writes in his diary that night:

> Why did I come to Japan? Why do I need to pursue knowledge? Being here, I am nothing but despised by the Japanese. Oh China, China, why can't you become rich and strong? I can't stand it anymore. . . . Oh heaven, heaven, I do not want knowledge, I do not want fame or that useless money. If you could bestow me with an "Eve" from the Garden of Eden and allow me to possess all of her body and mind, I would be most satisfied.[25]

The desire to "possess" a woman reflects his inability to do so in the present context of Japan, and the intensity of that desire paradoxically exposes his current state of sexual repression. Sexual repression, or the inability to assert his manhood, is directly attributed to the Japanese ascendancy in China as an imperialist power. On the one hand, repressing his desire can be justified by patriotism, since the object of his desire remains Japanese women. On the other hand, he feels that he is despised by all Japanese women, even prostitutes, so repression becomes an existential condition. His sexual desire is caught in the crossroads of patriotism and imperialism. In consideration of physical health, he despises himself for his frequent acts of autoeroticism; unable to release his unutilized libido, he voyeuristically spies on the innkeeper's daughter in the bath. Finally conjuring up enough courage, he visits a Japanese prostitute, only to be overwhelmed by his sense of shame:

> The way the Japanese despise the Chinese is like the way we despise pigs and dogs. The Japanese call the Chinese "*Zhinaren,*" which in Japan is more derogatory than "base thief," the phrase we use to curse people. In front of this beautiful young woman, he could not but admit: "I am a *Zhinaren.*"[26]

The main obstruction to the fulfillment of his desire is literally the nation. Unable to deal with his overwhelming humiliation and frustration, he de-

---

25. *The Complete Short Stories of Yu Dafu,* 23–24.
26. Ibid., 46.

cides to commit suicide. But before he throws himself into the ocean, he shouts out: "My country, my country, you have caused my death!"[27]

In other less known but equally intense stories, Yu Dafu further depicts the sexual landscape of the Chinese male whose object of desire, the Japanese woman, constantly eludes him, and whose manhood becomes symbolically emasculated when the same Japanese woman is immediately claimed by and succumbs to another Japanese male. "Silver Grey Death" (*Yinhuise de si*, 1921), though written with faint echoes of the life of the British decadent Ernest Dowson, still uses the disillusioned romantic encounter between the Chinese protagonist and a Japanese restaurant owner's daughter as the main catalyst for the protagonist's mental and emotional breakdown, and ultimate death. The woman is claimed by a crude-looking, undereducated Japanese man, whose national purity, so to speak, gives him the right of priority over our sensitive, intellectual, emaciated Chinese protagonist. In "Stomach Illness" (*Weibing*, 1921), the protagonist's friend "W." becomes infatuated with a young Japanese girl, then has an anxiety dream several days later in which she tells him: "Although I do love you, you are the citizen of a nation soon to be vanquished. Go away and don't try to seduce me anymore."[28] This utterance captures the essence of the doomed romantic encounters between Yu's Chinese male protagonists and their beloved Japanese women.

The most excruciating, perhaps because it is the most detailed, description of such a relationship is the story entitled "Emptiness" (*Kongxu*, 1922). Set in a hot springs hotel outside Tokyo, the protagonist, named Yu Zhifu (notice the similarity to the name of the author), finds to his great surprise a young Japanese woman intruding uninvited into his room one evening. She claims that she is afraid of the thunder outside and cannot sleep alone in her room. She begs his forgiveness but needs company desperately. They talk happily, until she asks about him: "Zhifu's face flushed as she asked him where he was from. Chinese in Japan, like the Jews in Europe, are despised by the Japanese everywhere."[29] Cleverly, though, instead of admitting that he is a *Zhinaren*, he points to his Japanese high school uniform, thereby asserting his cultural pedigree as well as ducking the question of his national identity. She falls innocently asleep in his room, inciting in him the most painful erotic fantasy. Fantasizing about her naked body under her clothes, he feels as if "his eyes would spout fire"; he feels excited like a "caterpillar in fire" but is also utterly in agony; the fragrance emanating from her body "cuts into his heart like a knife or a sword"; and his general mental and physical state is described as if he were being "interrogated with instruments of torture." When he *is* able to see her naked body at the hot springs bathhouse

27. Ibid., 50.
28. Ibid., 58.
29. Ibid., 149.

the next day, he devours the sight like "a hungry wolf having just seen a plump sheep." Thus excited, he painfully witnesses his fantasy love snatched away by a handsome, tall, Tokyo Imperial University student, her cousin, who comes to see her. He has a revenge dream that night:

> A short while after being in his room, he felt that he was sleepy. As he fell asleep on his bedding, he heard the girl sliding the rice-paper door and entering his room. Zhifu was so upset that he would not turn his body to her direction to talk to her. She walked step by step near to him, sat down on the floor cushion, set her gentle and soft hand on his waist, and asked him with a seductive voice:
> "Are you angry with me?"
> Zhifu turned over after he heard what she said and looked at her. As he did so, he noticed that her cousin was also sitting there with her. Zhifu was so furious that he picked up the knife placed on a cushion and swung it. Striking her arm with a "swish" sound, one of her slender hands was cut off and lay on the cushion in a pool of fresh blood.[30]

He never actually revealed his love, due to his national inferiority complex, hence the assumption that she knows of his jealousy is itself but wishful thinking. His violent assertion of masculinity in the dream is actually built upon nothing but a figment of his imagination from beginning to end.

Even when the Chinese protagonist's dream of a Japanese woman's love is not merely a figment of his imagination, emasculation is inevitable. "Moving South" (*Nanqian*, 1921) describes how a Japanese innkeeper readily offers herself to the Chinese protagonist, Yiren, leading him to believe that she loves him, only to have him suffer the excruciating pain of later having to listen to the sounds of this woman making love to a crude Japanese man, since she did not even care enough to hide it from Yiren. Listening to every sound that comes out from her room makes Yiren utterly miserable. His reaction to her betrayal, however, is a passive retreat into melancholy: "He did not dare to make a noise or move his body. Bitterness and regret swelled in his heart like a storm, and two streams of tears flowed from the corners of his eyes to his earlobes and then dropped from his earlobes onto the pillow."[31] Her betrayal, which he feels as a direct experience of emasculation, further generates in him suicidal thoughts, and he starts having physical symptoms of cold sweating, lack of appetite, and general weakness. Later, encountering a beautiful Japanese woman in the countryside outside Tokyo, Yiren becomes infatuated with her, and becomes seriously ill with a high fever, nearing death when the story ends. The bitterness of being the despised Chinese in Japan causes severe physical symptoms as well as emotional trauma.

30. Ibid., 154.
31. Ibid., 95.

A passage written by Yu Dafu years later in 1931 about his Japanese experience fittingly analyzes his subject position in Japan as a feminine one:

> My lyrical periods were spent on the debauched and cruel island governed by a military authority. Seeing my old country being degraded and enduring shame and humiliation in a foreign country, everything I felt, thought, and experienced was nothing but disappointment and sadness. I was like a newly widowed young woman with no energy or courage, grieving and grieving, lamenting and lamenting. It was out of my wailing that the widely criticized stories collected in *Sinking* were produced.[32]

Indeed, in every one of the Japan stories written during 1921 and 1922, Yu's Chinese protagonists were victims of Japanese imperialism's subjugation of China. But it is in the particular sexualization of this victimhood through narratives of emasculation that the trauma of imperialism is played out. The simile of a young, widowed woman in the above passage is, in this context, historically appropriate. If we assume that the founding of the Chinese Republic in 1911 was a moment of victory for patriarchal nationalism, the inability of the newly established nation-state to ward off foreign aggression metaphorically indicates the emasculation of the patriarchal state. Yu Dafu's stories exemplify an individual experience of such feminization through stories of sexual emasculation at the hands of Japanese women and men. Hypochondria, melancholy, anxiety neurosis, voyeurism, and inferiority complexes, all with sexual origins or consequences, are then manifestations of imperialist emasculation.

In stories set in China, aberrant sexuality becomes if anything even more pronounced. Here, although China is still the main referent to which an individual's sexuality is intimately situated, the difference in national context has largely changed the target of attack. In Yu Dafu's stories after his return to China, sexual predilections such as homosexuality, bisexuality, masochism, foot fetishism, and frequent sexual encounters with prostitutes are described as a means of debunking conventional morality *within* China. The national inferiority complex that obsesses the protagonists in his Japan stories is here replaced by a deep-seated anger at the condition of Chinese society. In "Boundless Night" (*Mang mang ye*, 1922), Zhifu, the same protagonist as in "Emptiness," finds himself slowly turning into a "zombie" in a China "filled with the air of epileptic hospitals."[33] Literal and metaphorical descriptions of sickness abound in these stories. His protagonists, embodiments of their sick nation, tend to be sickly in physique—thin, tall, with deeply set eyes and high, protruding cheekbones—and mentally unstable. Their living quarters are usually dimly lit, unheated, small rooms, in which they are secluded and

32. "Confessional Monologue" (*Chanyu dubai*), in ibid., 832.
33. *The Complete Short Stories of Yu Dafu*, 138 and 118.

alienated from other human beings. Most of them are depicted either as physical or as spiritual exiles, forever wandering on the margins of society, even though they move within the boundary of their own nation. They walk the streets for long hours, especially at night, to seek solace for their mental unease in the enveloping darkness, to escape from people's hostile glares, or simply to waste away lives already too broken to mend. The mind wandering in the darkness is well described in the following passage from "The Nostalgic Man" (*Huaixiang bing zhe*), written in 1922, the year Yu Dafu returned to China:

> At the moment sunlight and evening darkness meet, in the boundless wilderness, with his head towards the primordial expanse of the sky, he walks forward, step by step. He doesn't know who he is, what he should do, nor does he know where he is going. He just feels that his feet are compelled to move forward, step by step—this is Yu Zhifu's psychological state at present.
>
> In his half-awake, half-asleep consciousness, he only knows vaguely that the world will become dark from now on, the dry earth in the wilderness will gradually turn into watery swamp, and, with every approaching moment, his feet will lose freedom of movement. But he doesn't want to change directions; with his head facing the deep and dark sky, he continues walking forward, step by step.[34]

In the space of darkness, literally and symbolically, is where Yu's character Yu Zhifu—again a thinly disguised autobiographical figure—roams like a ghost. This space of darkness is also where the underworld of prostitutes is situated. Many of Yu's protagonists are especially sympathetic with or fond of these women who are, like themselves, creatures of the night. For instance, the protagonist in "Autumn Willow" (*Qiuliu*, 1924) financially supports an ugly, undesirable prostitute, and "Prayer" (*Qiyuan*, 1927) shows a prostitute's capacity for love which even shames the protagonist.

Reflected in the formal aspects of his writing, physical and spiritual wandering translates into an aesthetics of wandering, which can be discerned in a deliberate lack of emplotment. Yu saw the act of roaming, the German *Wanderlust*, as one of the conditions for innovative writing.[35] He concretized this roaming by dissolving plot within the meandering reflections, impressions, and sensations of his main characters. Instead of plot-oriented narration, he opted for what he called "direct narration" (*zhijie miaoxie*) of characters, where the focus is on psychological analysis.[36] His characters are usually torn emotionally, mentally, and oftentimes physically, causing their perceptions to fragment accordingly. Memories, dreams, and fantasies are important el-

34. Ibid., 139.
35. Ibid., 831.
36. "On Fiction," (*Xiaoshuo lun*, 1926), in *Collected Writings of Yu Dafu*, 5:28–29.

ements in their meandering thoughts, so narrative time proceeds in un-predictable fits and starts, sudden accelerations and decelerations. Yu favored using flashbacks to embed past events or thoughts between two present moments. Many of his stories are therefore composed of small sections. Decadence thus not only dictated the socially subversive content of his stories, it also endorsed the use of unconventional formal techniques in terms of characterization, setting, narrative structure, and time. It can be said that Yu formulated an aesthetics of decadence in which all the elements function organically to present a strongly charged voice of morality.

In other stories written in China such as "Blue Mist" (*Qingyan*, 1923), however, Yu shifts the locus of his social protest from an individual's sexuality, illness, and death to signs and issues from observable social reality itself. By doing so, Yu gradually moved from the decadent style to writing in the mode of "problem fiction" (*wenti xiaoshuo*), typical of May Fourth realist fiction. He was now living in China and located problems in his immediate experiences, which seemed to have caused a shift in his writing style. His most artistically audacious and decadent stories were written in Japan; the spatial distance between writing in Japan about China and writing in China about China engendered two different narrative necessities. The individual, away from China, easily becomes its embodiment by association in the stories written in Japan, while later stories set in China can more easily establish the immanent reality of China as the target of attack and thus distance the individual from that reality. Instead of inscribing the theme of social protest in the very texture of the narrative, then, the China stories present blunt social criticism. For instance, an arranged marriage is named the culprit in "Wisteria and Dodder" (*Niaoluo xing*, 1923); poverty and lack of recognition for a poor writer in "The Night When the Spring Breeze Was Intoxicating" (*Chunfeng chenzui de wanshang*, 1923); the exploitation of the underdog in "Meager Sacrifice" (*Bodian*, 1924); and so on. By 1927, Yu Dafu declared that he had become a leftist, and officially ended his "era of 'Sinking'" (*Chenlun shidai*).[37] His post-1927 stories were largely direct social commentaries, some with strong anti-Japanese sentiments.

Yu never denied the significance of decadence, however. What earlier was a mutually reinforcing relationship between the aesthetic and the political became a contradictory relationship in his later writings, as he was intensely involved in the self-appointed task of awakening people's political consciousness through literature, yet unable to ignore his aesthetic concerns. In his 1931 story "Mirage" (*Shenlou*), for example, his protagonist ponders the incompatibility between decadence and Chinese reality as follows:

37. Mentioned in Qian Xingcun, "Yu Dafu."

My whole life is but a meaningless tragedy caused by a prank of the times . . . My first mistake was being Chinese yet receiving some half-baked education from the European fin-de-siècle. The result of putting new wine in an old bottle was the common ruin of both. The fin-de-siècle thinkers say: You have to first discover your self and then faithfully guard this self, thoroughly asserting and expanding it. If the environment comes to obstruct it, you should surge forward and fight for it as if your life depended on it. . . . But in Chinese society, you, the only discoverer of this self, cannot but bump into walls everywhere. If you really have courage as well as a persistence more tenacious than Napoleon's, then maybe you can be a hero and change the world. But the Chinese have been fettered by three thousand years of traditional ethics and have followed the sly Doctrine of the Mean handed down from emperors Yao, Shun, Yu, Tang, Wen, Wu, the duke of Zhou, and Confucius. It takes at least ten or twenty Napoleons to fight the battle.[38]

Here decadence is clearly identified with the West and the new, and China is equated with stultifying tradition and the old. The donning of the decadent style was not itself a mistake, but the conditions in China prevented the pursuit of such a self-oriented philosophy and aesthetics. Here, the accusing finger is by no means pointed at decadence, but rather at the obstinate, unchanging, and fettering culture that is China. To combat this culture, he claims, necessitates the gathered rebellious spirit of ten or twenty Napoleons—many, many more decadents. In 1935, Yu Dafu again wrote a defense of decadence as a necessary and universal condition for an individual struggling against the bondage of tradition in an age of rapidly developing material civilization.[39] During the height of the May Fourth period in the early 1920s Yu Dafu exercised a decadent aesthetic to debunk conventional morality and aesthetics, but in 1935 he still remained an intellectual within the May Fourth spirit, by continuing to assert the importance of decadence as a counterdiscourse to tradition.

OTHER DECADENTS

Decadence was a contagious fashion during the May Fourth era, and Yu Dafu easily found kindred spirits, many of whom were Japan-educated like himself. Three writers—the Creation Society members Zhou Quanping and Ni Yide (1901–1970), and especially Teng Gu—are worthy of mention. In Zhou Quanping's work, decadent aestheticism as a form of social criticism is clearly apparent. His stories are invariably attacks on social ills, specifically the disparity between haves and have-nots and the oppression of material culture

38. *The Complete Short Stories of Yu Dafu,* 594–595.
39. "What is 'Fin-de-siècle Literature'?" (*Zenyang jiaozuo shijimo wenxue*), in *Collected Writings of Yu Dafu,* 6:287–289.

on the poor. His characters fit the decadent prototypes of Yu's fiction: blood-shot, listless eyes set in deep sockets, thin and pale, suffering from neuroses and poverty. Instead of prostitutes, Zhou enlists the poor as representative outsiders.[40] The continuity between this form of decadent writing and pro-letarian writing is obvious, although Zhou was a truant on the so-called "rev-olutionary path" of socialism.

Ni Yide, on the other hand, deserves more attention, if only because he would become one of the most important and famous modernist painters in Shanghai in the early 1930s. In 1931, he organized the Stormy Billows Society (*juelanshe*) with other artists such as Pang Xunqin (1906–1985), dis-seminating the artistic theories and practices of fauvism, cubism, dadaism, and surrealism. In the stories he wrote in the early 1920s before traveling to Japan in 1927 to further his study of art, decadence was articulated as a form of visual lyricism. In an autumn-time reverie recalling the beauty of a lake in spring, the protagonist of "Autumn at Xuanwu Lake" (1923) sighs at the desolate scene: "Today I come to visit and see only a few surviving lotus leaves, against the willows on the embankment; they exist in silence and express a decadent poetic beauty."[41] Being a painter, the protagonist's perceptions are naturally laden with a rich, visual texture, but just when the visual reverie seems to suggest freedom of aesthetic perception, society exercises its polic-ing. Due to his aesthetic indulgence in the beauty of his female students, the protagonist is denounced as immoral and fired from his job as an art teacher. What better illustrates how art affects life than the fact that Ni Yide would himself be fired from his job as an art teacher because he dared to publish such a story! Disillusioned, Ni Yide proclaimed:

> If the world of reality is a prison from which one cannot fly away and a devil's cave that imprisons one's thoughts, the world of art must allow for individual freedom. All citizens of the universe can enter this world [of art] and fly around at will and rejoice to the heart's content. Who would have thought that when it [the world of art] enters Chinese society with its ten thousand evils, even this little bit of freedom has to be restrained! Even this little bit of pleasure has to be destroyed! What else is there to say?[42]

Using the language of universalism (notice the phrase "citizens of the uni-verse"), Ni laments the social pressure placed on decadent aestheticism, thereby directly criticizing China as the aberrant, the evil, and thus the em-bodiment of particularism.

40. See for instance the stories collected in his *Bitter Laughter* (*Kuxiao*) (Shanghai: Guanghua shuju, 1927).

41. Ni Yide, *Autumn at Xuanwu Lake* (*Xuanwuhu zhi qiu*) (Shanghai: Taidong tushuju, 1924), 1.

42. Ni Yide, "Evening Rain at the Qin Huai River" (*Qinhuai muyu*), in *Autumn at Xuanwu Lake*, 21.

Unlike Zhou Quanping or Ni Yide, Teng Gu's contribution to May Fourth decadent literature was emotionally more powerful and aesthetically more sophisticated, though he never reached the kind of popularity Yu Dafu enjoyed. Not a Creationist by affiliation, Teng published most of his stories in *Short Story Monthly*, as well as some in *Creation Weekly*. Categorized as a "decadent modernist" in 1925 by Tang Heyi (who used the phrase in English), Teng was described as an avid reader of Oscar Wilde, Arthur Symons, and Théophile Gautier.[43] His Japanese reading list also heavily emphasized Japan's decadent writers such as Tanizaki Jun'ichirō. More than any other writer of this period, he explored sexuality's preeminent role in shaping and determining one's destiny and illustrated the strangulation of the natural man by a sex-scared society in many crushing stories of suicide and death.

Teng Gu graduated from the Shanghai Academy of Art and, like Ni Yide, went to Japan in 1921 to further his study, later becoming a prominent writer, literary critic, and art historian. In 1930, he went to Germany to study art history, and returned with a doctorate degree from Berlin University. As with Yu Dafu, it was during his Japan years (1921–1924) that Teng's most representative fictional pieces were written, although he continued writing fiction for another decade after his return, published the first book-length study of Western aestheticism in China, *Literature of Aestheticism* (*Weimeipai de wenxue*), in 1927, and continued to publish books on art history until his untimely death in 1941 at the age of 40. Like Yu Dafu, he wrote about the emasculation of the Chinese male who desires Japanese women, but the national symbolism is not given exclusive dominance. Instead, the sexual is rendered mainly in mental and physical terms as the fundamental driving force of artistic creation, much in the Freudian vein that Kuriyagawa Hakuson made known in China.

An article written later by Zhang Kebiao (b. 1903), an associate of Teng Gu and another much-unappreciated decadent, illustrates the main concerns of the decadent writers around Teng Gu. In 1924, Teng and Zhang had organized a literary society called Sphinx (*shihoushe*—literally the Society of the Lion's Roar, but also a clever transliteration of "Sphinx"). In this post-1949 reminiscence, meant to be self-critical of decadent practices as merely fashionable artifice, Zhang Kebiao unambiguously points out the social meaning of decadence:

> We were all a bit "crazy," indulging in aestheticism, which was one of the most fashionable literary and artistic movements at the time. It emphasized the strange, the grotesque, the self-contradictory, and transcendence from social

43. Reference from Yang Yi, *A History of Modern Chinese Fiction*, 1:625. Yang Yi's three-volume literary history of Chinese fiction is by far the most comprehensive of all literary histories published in China, and his is the only literary history so far that has discussed Teng Gu, Zhou Quanping, and Ni Yide at all.

and human conventions. Such socially disruptive style was what was encouraged and advocated by the Western European writers Baudelaire, Verlaine, Wilde, and Maeterlinck.

Out of curiosity and fashion-pursuit, we pretended to talk about transforming the rotten and the moribund into the new and the strange, about flowers of ugliness, flowers of evil, the beauty and happiness of death, etc. We drew extremities together, and synthesized contradictory languages . . . admiring the new and the strange, loving the grotesque, advocating ugliness, evil, rottenness, and darkness, while denigrating brightness, glory, and wealth, opposing gaudy splendor, and denouncing masters of high position and handsome salary.[44]

It is important to bear in mind that even though socialist ideology dictates much of the above passage, Zhang's unapologetic nostalgia towards the Sphinx group nevertheless comes through. While the statement may not appropriately describe all those who exercised a decadent aestheticism, it echoes Zhou Quanping's statement of decadence in *Flood* magazine, and describes the work of Teng Gu to the extent that his obsessive themes are time and again sex, death, and artistic creation.

Teng Gu was a prolific writer but his most intensely decadent-aesthetic stories were written in his Japan years and included in a 1927 collection called *Labyrinth* (*Migong*). While in Yu Dafu's Japan stories the libidinal inscribed by the national cannot find proper sublimation and hence the national becomes the most important progenitor of meaning, in Teng Gu's Japan stories the libidinal repression of the Chinese male is described as having a direct consequence in the protagonists' inability to produce artistic work. Again, it is Japanese womanhood that frustrates the protagonists' desires, but instead of concentrating on the causes of this frustration Teng Gu focuses on its result. In his most well-known story, "Mural" (*Bihua,* 1922), the sexually repressed art student Cui Taishi sublimates his repression into a masterpiece that costs him his life, an art work made in the medium of his own blood:

> T. [Cui Taishi's friend] notices many blood stains on the white wool cover of the sofa. On the wall beside the sofa is painted a rough, wild painting, where one can vaguely discern the figure of a man lying stiff on the ground, with a woman dancing on his belly. On the painting are written the words "Cui Taishi's Graduation Piece."[45]

The mural renders in graphic detail the death of a man succumbing to sexuality: the woman, figure of the conqueror, celebrates her victory by dancing on the corpse of the man. In this imaginary blood painting, Teng Gu

44. Quoted from Leo Ou-fan Lee, "'Decadence' in Modern Chinese Literature and Its Writers," 36.

45. Teng Gu, "Mural" (*Bihua*), *Creation Quarterly* 1:3 (October 1922): 54.

projects a powerful relationship between sex, death, and art, portraying both the creative and destructive power of the libido as interlocked with each other in a dance of death. Lu Xun treated the same theme in "Mending Heaven," written in the same year as "Mural," showing that men were created by the primordial sexual urges of Nü Wa, which resulted in the death of the creator herself. But more than an exposition of the origin of artistic creation, Teng Gu's story should be analyzed like Yu Dafu's Japan stories. We can read the entire story as an allegory of the interpenetrating relationship between the libidinal, the national, and the artistic: the Chinese protagonist, like many of his contemporaries, has to go to Japan in order to learn about Western avant-garde art, but, ironically, the condition of existence in Japan as a sexually repressed Chinese crowds his libido to the extent that its sublimation, as required by art, is inevitable, but the price he pays is the destruction of his body..

Awakening to sexuality proves to be *the* destiny for an ascetic man studying Christianity in a seminary in Teng's "The Resurrection of the Stone Sculpture" (*Shixiang de fuhuo,* 1923). Again set in Japan, the Chinese protagonist visits a sculpture exhibition one day and becomes unsettled by the images he sees there, especially one of a nude woman. The sculpture reminds him of a mute Japanese girl, his previous landlord's daughter, and he becomes consumed by a desire for her: the muteness of both the sculpture and the girl appears to him to be the ultimate emblem of the deepest love, a love beyond verbal expression. Substituting the nude sculpture for the girl, he dreams about the sculpture coming alive and embracing him. But as she falls upon him, she turns back into a sculpture and breaks into pieces. The next day, he is a changed man, obsessed with love and gradually losing his grounding in reality. He finally has to be incarcerated in an insane asylum. Here again, the sculpture as an artistic creation becomes interlinked with the libidinal and the national. Art, in this case, cannot provide respite from the sexual repression the Chinese protagonist feels; rather, by kindling the sexual urge, it brings about the destruction of the Chinese man.

Teng Gu's other Japan stories similarly deal with the relationship between Eros and Thanatos and their intimate connection to artistic creation. All three realms, however, remain bound up with the inscription of the national, as the condition of Japanese imperialism is also a sexual condition. It is this ineluctable inscription of the national in the context of imperialism that gives even the most decadent fiction a moral form.

CHAPTER 5

Loving the Other

May Fourth Occidentalism in the Global Context

*For symbolic power is that invisible power which can be exercised only with the com-
plicity of those who do not want to know that they are subject to it or even that they
themselves exercise it.*

PIERRE BOURDIEU (1983)

*Oh, East is East and West is West,
And never the Twain shall meet,
Till Earth and Sky stand presently
At God's great judgement seat,
But there is neither East nor West,
Border, nor Breed nor Birth,
When two strong men stand face to face
Tho' they come from the ends of the Earth.*

RUDYARD KIPLING, QUOTED BY LI DAZHAO (1918)

The May Fourth construction of "the West" as embodiment of modernity
and object of emulation had multiple, often contradictory, implications. I
have delineated the local implications of this Occidentalism (the use of the
West for specific discursive purposes, mainly as a means to produce symbolic
power) in chapter 1, and in this chapter I will delineate its global implications. By asking questions of cultural agency from a different angle, I will examine how Occidentalism has contributed to the constitution of the symbolic power of the West. This attention to the global discursive context is
where I depart from earlier discussions of Chinese Occidentalism. It is only
through examining the multiple situatedness of Chinese Occidentalists vis-
à-vis different Others that the complexity of their cultural agency becomes
apparent. Hence, I argue against the problematic conflation of Chinese Occidentalism with Western Orientalism, and emphasize the asymmetry between these two constructs. As I will show below, "the West" was not merely

an external discourse strategically deployed by the Chinese, but had become a psychological category as well, as can be seen in the profusion of narratives of anxiety and melancholy during the May Fourth period. I also depart from earlier framings of Occidentalism as a binary relationship between China and the West, and analyze the role played by Japan as the immediate mediator and intermediary in the trajectory of the West into China. Then I conclude with a discussion of the May Fourth legacy in the cosmopolitan imaginary of modern China.

RETHINKING OCCIDENTALISM AS GLOBAL

As a category in China's cultural imaginary, "the West" gained far more symbolic power during the May Fourth period than ever before. A rudimentary comparison between late-Qing and May Fourth uses of the West foregrounds the change in cultural agency that occurred in the interim. Both the historian Lin Yü-sheng and literary critic Zhang Yuhong locate the loss of the traditional self in the May Fourth period, even though Chinese intellectuals had heard the cannons of Western imperialism over half a century earlier. Lin Yü-sheng argues that members of what he calls the "first generation of the Chinese intelligentsia," a social group formed after the traumatic 1894–1895 Sino-Japanese War, remained within the "traditional socio-political and cultural moral orders," and that it was the May Fourth generation that broke away from those orders in their totalistic antitraditionalism.[1] Zhang Yuhong further offers a useful distinction between late-Qing uses of Western culture as "*wohua*" ("I transform/appropriate [Western culture]") and May Fourth uses as "*huawo*" ("[Western culture] transforms me"),[2] not only pointing out the gradual decrease of agency in the Chinese confrontation with Western culture, but also emphasizing the May Fourth earnestness in reinventing the self on totally new (i.e., Western) grounds. For the May Fourth intellectuals, the locus of cultural power was no longer the self who could use Western culture as it saw fit (cf. the famous formulation of the late-Qing reformer Zhang Zhidong: "Chinese learning as essence, Western learning as method" [*zhongxue wei ti, xixue wei yong*]); the locus of cultural

1. Lin Yü-sheng, *The Crisis of Chinese Consciousness* (Madison: University of Wisconsin Press, 1979), 26–29. Lin observes that by 1911 and 1912, the "framework of the Chinese tradition collapsed" (29). Also note Paul A. Cohen's observation in a similar vein: "All the justifications for reform [in the late Qing] were aimed at maintaining the Confucian order intact. None affirmed the possibility—certainly not the desirability—of a fundamental change of this order." *Discovering History in China* (New York: Columbia University Press, 1984), 31.

2. Zhang Yuhong, "The Infiltration and Transformation of Modernist Thought" (*Xiandai zhuyi sichao de shentou yu xingbian*), in *Western Literary Thought and Twentieth-Century Chinese Literature* (*Xifang wenyi sichao yu ershi shiji Zhongguo wenxue*), ed. Yue Daiyun and Wang Ning (Beijing: Zhongguo shehui kexue chubanshe, 1990), 155.

power was instead an alien Other that was to be welcomed with open arms to replace the old self and usher in its rebirth. "Western learning" was no longer an external category, but was incorporated for the "enlightenment" of the self, becoming an internal category. As an internal category, "the West" enjoyed much greater prestige, not only in cognitive but also in emotive universes. Therefore, proximity to "the West" and its honorary intermediary "Japan" became the measure of desirability, and that which did not belong to this particular logic of desire was virulently denounced. David Wang argues, in this regard, that the May Fourth cultural movement effectively silenced the multiple negotiations with "the West" in the late Qing period.[3]

To mark their difference from late-Qing reformers, and others opposed to total Westernization, May Fourth iconoclasts charged their antagonists with all manner of evils. Lu Xun, for instance, criticized the late-Qing reformers as entertaining dual systems of thought (*er chong sixiang*), as unable to forsake the old even as they received the new, and hence as obstructing the development of progress.[4] Those who did not approve of the May Fourth cultural agenda of Westernization were accused of "Europeanization phobia" (*Ouhua kongjubing*, the poet Wen Yiduo's term), or of "embracing the leftover and guarding the flawed" (*baocan shouque*, a commonly used term), since according to someone like Wu Zhihui Euro-American material culture was not "Western" but "new," and therefore universal. Lu Xun further advocated reading no Chinese books and "grabbing" freely from the West; Hu Shi championed wholesale Westernization even well after the May Fourth period; and Qian Xuantong (1887–1939) argued for eliminating the Chinese writing system altogether. Poised to discourage and dismiss any conservative rebuttal, May Fourth Occidentalism effectively inserted the West into the Chinese cultural imaginary as the arbiter of cultural capital, and ultimately of symbolic power.

For the West to become the embodiment of the cultural capital that provides access to symbolic power, a systematic denunciation of "China" had to proceed simultaneously. As I have illustrated in chapter 1, this denunciation of China was conducted through constructing China as the past of the West using a conception of history based on a teleological notion of temporality and modernity. Added to this temporal denunciation was a denunciation of the Chinese national character that appeared frequently on the pages of *New Youth* (*Xin Qingnian*). Reading through the journal, Pang Pu gathered the following descriptions of the Chinese national character by May Fourth intellectuals: "negligent, stealthy, incompetent people"; "base and shameless,

---

3. David Der-wei Wang, *Fin-de-siècle Splendor: Repressed Modernities of Late Qing Fiction, 1849–1911* (Stanford: Stanford University Press, 1997).

4. Lu Xun, "Random Thought 54" (*Suiganlu wushisi*, 1919), in *Complete Works of Lu Xun* (*Lu Xun quanji*) (Beijing: Renmin wenxue chubanshe, 1981), 1:344–345.

withdrawn and timid, content with temporary ease and comfort, deceitful and cunning, slick and sly"; "low-grade ethnic group that loves peace and desires leisure and grace"; "half-civilized"; "people who are like pigs' tails, barbaric, illiterate and without economic ability"; "proto-dogs and proto-pigs," to list a few.[5] Lu Xun's famous Ah-Qism—which inadvertently made the "Ah-Q spirit" (*Ah Q jingshen*) of slave mentality and vain egomania synonymous with the Chinese national character—should also be understood in this context of the eager denunciation of all that was "Chinese" and represented "Chinese-ness."

The essentialization and reification of the so-called Chinese national character through neatly summed-up, hyperbolic phrases helped constitute Chinese culture and the Chinese people as the locus of the particular, the repudiation of which was necessary for the entrance of and into the Western universal. Hence even as nationalism was part of the original motivation for May Fourth Occidentalism, the intellectuals' rhetoric was filled with the language of denationalization. Yu Dafu called nationhood a "prison";[6] Cai Yuanpei (1867–1940), the reputable educator, asserted that truth had no national boundaries;[7] and Chen Duxiu called "respecting the nation" the third most harmful practice after "respecting the saints" and "respecting the ancients."[8] Hu Shi's brand of liberalism and Guo Moruo's supranationalism are also prominent examples of this rhetoric of denationalization.

It is in this sense that I call the discourse of Occidentalism in May Fourth China a particularization of Chinese culture and a universalization of Western culture. Occidentalism, a strategy of appropriating the West, hence cannot be conflated with Orientalism, a strategy in which the supposed Western universal consolidates itself by incorporating, managing, and controlling the non-Western, particular Other.[9] I therefore disagree with Frank Dikötter's and Xiaomei Chen's recent discussions of Occidentalism in China. Frank Dikötter discusses the Occidentalism of the New Culture Movement of the May Fourth era by listing its three strategies of polarization, projection, and fragmentation. With "polarization," he describes the May Fourth construction of China (as represented by Confucianism) and the West as polar op-

5. Pang Pu, "Inheriting 'May Fourth,' Transcending 'May Fourth'" (*Jicheng wusi chaoyue wusi*), in Lin Yü-sheng et al., *May Fourth: Reflections from Multiple Perspectives* (*Wusi: duoyuan de fansi*) (Hong Kong: Sanlian shudian, 1989), 136.

6. Yu Dafu, "Art and Nation" (*Yishu yu guojia*, 1923), in *Collected Writings of Yu Dafu* (*Yu Dafu wenji*) (Hong Kong: Sanlian shudian, 1983), 5:149.

7. Mentioned in Joseph R. Levenson, "'History' and 'Value': The Tensions of Intellectual Choice in Modern China," *Studies in Chinese Thought* 55:5 (December 1953): 174.

8. Chen Duxiu, "Random Thoughts" (*Suiganlu*, 1918), in Chen Song, ed., *Collected Essays from the Debate on the Question of Eastern and Western Culture During the May Fourth Period* (*Wusi qianhou dongxi wenhua wenti lunzhan wenxuan*) (Beijing: Zhongguo shehui kexue chubanshe, 1989), 45–46.

9. See Edward Said, *Orientalism* (New York: Vantage Books, 1979).

posites, whereby the West becomes China's "alter ego." His term "projection" refers to May Fourth intellectuals seeing native ideas in the West, and using Western thought as "a cloak of authority." When talking about "fragmentation" however, Dikötter's language turns explicitly judgmental:

> Fragmentation was the third feature of Occidentalism. Chinese habits of thought often accommodated Western thought only in the most fragmentary form. The latter underwent *simplification* and *deformation*, with quotations being taken out of context. To ease assimilation, Western thought was *impoverished, dissected* or *mutilated;* it was introduced to China in the form of primers, summaries and digests.[10] (emphasis mine)

The words he uses to describe May Fourth Occidentalism unambiguously show a critical, if not condescending, attitude, according to which the Occidentalists did not properly understand Western thought. Without showing any sensitivity to the inevitable processes of negotiation and appropriation that accompany the traveling and translation of ideas (what Xiaomei Chen would emphasize as the necessary "misreading" in the act of translation), Dikötter displays a Eurocentric vision. He seems to imply that the Third World native should shoulder the burden of learning the authentic metropolitan culture as correctly as possible so as not to violate the sanctity of Western thought. His three features of Occidentalism, instead of being seen as the ineluctable results of the traveling of ideas, are used to condemn the iconoclasts for not grasping the depth and sophistication of Western thought. They are thus three "limitations." With this kind of reasoning, and since Dikötter implies in his book that the Chinese held racist ideas about other races, it comes as no surprise to read a reviewer for the *Times Literary Supplement* crowing that racism is not limited to Anglo-Saxons alone.[11]

Unfortunately, the Eurocentricism of Frank Dikötter's judgments is not unique: earlier discussions of modernism in Republican China are also filled with such statements as "the Chinese did not understand Western modernism in depth," "they can't produce as sophisticated work," "the Chinese did not and cannot produce a James Joyce," and so on. In such commentaries, we see the operation of what David Palumbo-Liu has called the "Eurocentric universal,"[12] applying Western criteria of judgment to non-Western cultural appropriations and productions. The Eurocentric universal works to consolidate its power precisely through evaluating the varying degrees of Third World natives' faithfulness to and respect of First World culture.

---

10. Frank Dikötter, *The Discourse of Race in Modern China* (Stanford: Stanford University Press, 1992), 129.

11. See the reviewer's comment on the back cover of Dikötter, *The Discourse of Race in Modern China.*

12. David Palumbo-Liu, "Universalisms and Minority Culture," *differences* 7:1 (1995): 188–208.

Xiaomei Chen's study of Occidentalism is the most comprehensive treatment of the problem to date, although her period of analysis is centered on the post-Mao era (post-1976). Her conclusions bear implications for the May Fourth case, however, because the issues are arguably very similar. She defines Occidentalism in post-Mao China as "a discursive practice that, by constructing its Western Other, has allowed the Orient to participate actively and with indigenous creativity in the process of self-appropriation, even after being appropriated and constructed by Western others."[13] Giving full agency to the Chinese Occidentalists, she argues that Occidentalism was a discourse used within the context of domestic politics in post-Mao China as a "strategy of liberation" and a counterdiscourse to the government's ideological domination (what she calls "anti-official Occidentalism"), even as the government itself evoked the West to support a repressive nationalism ("official Occidentalism"). The Chinese Occidentalists were constantly "revising and manipulating" Western theories and discourses, with the power of selection and incorporation thoroughly on their side. They imagined the questions, looked for answers from Western culture, and came up with "misreadings" as solutions to their questions.[14] Chen defines her notion of "misreading" as a "sociological," not "epistemological," conception, and one which does not assume the preexistence of an epistemologically grounded "proper" and "correct" understanding.[15] This sensitivity to the complexity of the cultural translation process is exactly what Dikötter so glaringly lacks.

Chen and Dikötter come from drastically different positions of enunciation. Chen is dissatisfied with the valorization of the West as the ultimate frame of reference in current theories of culture, hence she asserts the need to attend to the domestic context in which "the West" as a discursive entity was produced, while Dikötter seems to embrace a kind of repetitious Orientalism, whereby studying the problematic Orient enables the West to feel good about itself. In both cases, however, full agency is attributed to the Chinese Occidentalists, even though Dikötter does so to criticize them, while Chen does so to recuperate their subject position. In Chen's paradigm, since the Chinese can manipulate and exploit "the West" in the discourse of Occidentalism (just as Western Orientalism did with "the Orient"), one should not flatly criticize Orientalism as a strategy of domination and control, or, in Chen's words, as only "negative and sinister."[16] That Chen equates Chinese Occidentalism with Western Orientalism is problematic, however, not merely because it shifts the burden of responsibility, but also because it flattens the

13. Xiaomei Chen, *Occidentalism: A Theory of Counter-Discourse in Post-Mao China* (New York: Oxford University Press, 1995), 4–5.
14. Ibid., 5–15, 97.
15. Ibid., 85–97.
16. Ibid., 167.

historical specificities within which Occidentalism arose. That is, it ignores the very *conditions* that made Occidentalism possible or inevitable in China.

In this regard, I find it necessary to enlarge our frame of analysis from the domestic to the global context, especially to include the history of imperialism with which even post-Mao China is inescapably connected (although Chen only mentions it in passing). It is important to bear in mind that Orientalism was not merely a strategy that utilized the Orient for discursive purposes at home: it influenced and sometimes shaped specific political strategies of domination in the West's imperialist invasions of the Orient.[17] Occidentalism, on the other hand, whether in the May Fourth or post-Mao version, was never involved in any form of political domination of the West. Even as a cultural discourse, Occidentalism cannot be equated with Orientalism because it never subjugated the West for the sake of self-consolidation: the self-empowering impetus of Occidentalism came rather from the negation of the Chinese self. When the Chinese intellectuals resorted to an idealized construction of the West, they used it to debunk tradition (in the May Fourth case) or to criticize the Chinese government (in the post-Mao case). Furthermore, the cognitive justifications for appropriating the Other rest on significantly different grounds in Orientalism and Occidentalism. When the West used the Orient as self-consolidating alterity, the Orient was the particular against which the Western universal could be reaffirmed. But when Chinese Occidentalism appropriated the West, the West was seen as the universal, its prerogative of modernity the goal of universal history.

Joseph R. Levenson uses the metaphor of language to describe the unequal cultural appropriations of China and the West, and his illuminating comment is worth quoting:

> The fact is, simply, that a European who admired traditional Chinese achievements remained just a European with cosmopolitan tastes, not the synthetic Sino-European whom [Cai Yuanpei] envisaged; while the Chinese who admired Western achievements might pass through cosmopolitanism and synthesis together and become a Western convert. It is a matter of difference of tone. When Toulouse-Lautrec or Gauguin made a painting in an oriental vein, it was pastiche, a foreign-dialect story. But when a painter who signs himself Zao Wou-ki [Zhau Wuji, b. 1920] paints a Paul Klee, it is a token of serious commitment, a story in a foreign language. . . . [W]hat the West has probably done to China is change the latter's language—what China has done to the West is to enlarge the latter's vocabulary.[18]

There is a glaring asymmetry between the Western cosmopolitan whose cultural materials are expanded with the inclusion of Chinese materials and the

---

17. See Said, *Orientalism* and *Culture and Imperialism* (New York: Alfred A. Knopf, 1993).

18. Joseph R. Levenson, *Confucian China and Its Modern Fate* (Berkeley: University of California Press, 1958), 113, 157.

Chinese intellectual who becomes a Western convert by fundamentally transforming his/her culture. This asymmetry also informs the unequal politics of Orientalism and Occidentalism, for both see the universal as remaining steadfastly the property of the West.

Another useful way to illustrate the asymmetry of Orientalism and Occidentalism is by way of Hegelian dialectical recognition. Briefly, in Hegel's unabashedly classist and elitist paradigm, the lord/master is distinguished from the bondsman/slave because the former is the subject whose essential, independent consciousness utilizes the unessential, dependent consciousness of the bondsman-object to recognize his own independence, while the latter has neither the power nor the ability to do the reverse. Hegel takes this inequality as a matter of fact and explains it this way: the lord is a consciousness that exists for itself, and although he uses the bondsman as the negative Other for the achievement of his consciousness, he exercises his power over the bondsman and rightfully holds the bondsman in bondage and subjection. The bondsman also relates negatively to the lord, but this negation "cannot go the length of being altogether done with it to the point of annihilation," hence the bondsman can only "work" on the sublation but not achieve any power over the lord.[19] This unequal dialectic between the lord and the bondsman parallels the unequal dialectic in the use of the Other in Orientalism and in Occidentalism: the Western Orientalist negates the Orient and confirms his position as the lord; the Chinese Occidentalist can never negate the Occident, and thus reveals his own state of subjection to the Occident.

The problem of Chinese agency in Occidentalism is further compounded by scholars' contradictory appraisals. In Xiaomei Chen's formulation, post-Mao Occidentalism is a strategy of liberation, but May Fourth Occidentalism, which she interprets in a feminist vein, was "another way in which Western fathers subjugated and colonized non-Western women" since it was employed by Chinese males for their own political agendas.[20] Tani Barlow, in contrast, argues that it is the post-Mao discourse of cultural Westernization that is a form of "self-colonization," while the May Fourth discourse of cultural Westernization is a successful example of "localization," by which she means that "signs enter and circulate within specific, autonomous, local political contexts."[21] In their opposing arguments, we witness the inevitable difficulty of making clear-cut statements about Chinese agency in the cross-cultural context.

19. G. W. F. Hegel, *The Phenomenology of Spirit,* trans. A. V. Miller (New York: Oxford University Press, 1977), 111–119.

20. Xiaomei Chen, *Occidentalism,* 138.

21. Tani Barlow, "*Zhishifenzi* [Chinese Intellectuals] and Power," *Dialectical Anthropology* 16 (1991): 211.

My argument builds upon these opposing observations to emphasize the importance of mapping the interrelatedness of the local and the global. These dual contexts have simultaneously informed the production and operation of Occidentalism in May Fourth China, though the specific weight of each context will differ from utterance to utterance. When the idea of "the West" traveled from the metropole to China, its original meaning was never entirely reinscribed or its power neutralized; hence we need to ask questions regarding the conditions of traveling and appropriation. Occidentalism is therefore both the project of strategic appropriation of the West on the local level and the site of cultural colonization on the global level. But the local was never innocent of the global, and the latter most often dictated the production of the West in the local context, as the question of universalism and particularism I delineated above indicates.

Even within the domestic context, Occidentalism was more than a simple counterdiscourse against a clear target. Here, Tani Barlow's argument that the discourse of Occidentalism is a discourse of power within China is useful. The May Fourth Occidentalists might have experienced racism in Japan and Euro-America, but at home they wielded the cultural power of Western knowledge over the unenlightened masses and the "corrupt" Confucian paragons of society. To use Barlow's language, the self-appointed enlightenment intellectuals exercised Occidentalism as a strategy of power in four ways: (1) by being "the agent of universal knowledge"; (2) by making "native Tradition an internal other"; (3) by constructing themselves as heroic polyglot subjects; and (4) by demonizing the past as "regressive and infectious." In these ways, they justified their "cultural critique" as necessary political intervention and as a form of national salvation.[22] Occidentalism was also class politics. If we assume that agency inevitably circulates in the process of discursive traveling and localization, its circulation within China was defined by class and other factors. From the global to the local, the process of mediation instituted a hierarchical layering of power, to which only the enlightened few had access.

THE WEST AS PSYCHOLOGICAL CATEGORY

Although Chinese intellectuals strategically localized Western discourses, these uses were at the same time indexes to the imposition of Western modernity, which partially dictated how the semicolonial elites were to organize their social and libidinal desires. That the West was also a psychological category is where the global implications of Occidentalism become apparent. In the literary works that most ostensibly appropriate Western modernist tropes, techniques, and modes, the tension resulting from such multiple sit-

22. Ibid., 212–213.

uatedness is manifested as textual expressions of melancholia and anxiety neurosis. Li Dazhao's quotation from Kipling cited at the beginning of this chapter implies one of those imposed mandates of desire: an explicit valorization of the masculinity of the "strong man," through whom, the poem implies, the difference between the West and the East can be bridged. Through Indian scholar Ashis Nandy's discussion of Kipling as an Indian-born British poet who tried at every turn to assert the colonizer's superiority, one can correlate Kipling's endorsement of masculinity with British colonialism's pressure of hypermasculinity among the colonial elites in India.[23] When repeated by a Chinese intellectual, especially one of the founders of the Chinese Communist Party, the quotation from Kipling implies both masculinist nationalism and a kind of colonial globalism at the same time. Most important to my purposes here, it shows how a potent Third World nationalism is underlaid by an internalized ideology of masculinity.

Paradoxically, however, colonialism both upholds the ideal of masculinity and withholds it from the colonized in order to maintain its own power and position. Since sexuality is a vital aspect of the social realm that needs to be incorporated into the structure of domination, masculinity is held up as a trope of power. Sexual and political domination accompany each other in many colonial situations. Ashis Nandy argues that there is a homology between sexual and political domination, because colonialism is congruent with the "existing Western sexual stereotypes" which produced the cultural consensus that political and socioeconomic dominance symbolize the dominance of men and masculinity over women and femininity.[24] Hence colonial domination is imbued with sexual connotations. The stories by Guo Moruo, Yu Dafu, Teng Gu, and others which I analyzed in the preceding chapters clearly thematize the threat of emasculation posed by the masculinist imperialist power of Japan. Masculinity as a trope of political power and a trope of sexual power become conflated.

It is in this particular context that I would like to invoke Freud's notion of "anxiety neurosis." Anxiety and sexuality, according to Freud, are closely linked in anxiety neurosis: "The psyche is overtaken by the affect of anxiety if it notices that it is incapable of allaying a [sexual] excitation that has arisen from within. Thus it behaves as though it were projecting this excitation to the outside." In the generating of anxiety, therefore, what is discharged is the "surplus of unutilized libido."[25] Anxiety neurosis as a psychological condition resulting from sexual frustration parallels the condition of the colonized man

23. Ashis Nandy, *The Intimate Enemy: Loss and Recovery of Self Under Colonialism* (Delhi: Oxford University Press, 1983).

24. Ibid., 4.

25. James Strachey, "Editor's Introduction," in Sigmund Freud, *Inhibitions, Symptoms, and Anxiety* (1926), trans. Alix Strachey (New York: W. W. Norton, 1989), xxviii–xxix.

who occupies a feminine role because of colonial domination. This parallel is more than incidental; the two conditions are consequential to each other.

As I argued in chapter 4, the sexual is also closely related to the national and the racial/ethnic. Their interrelatedness is further intertwined with specific historical conditions. As the racial/ethnic and national Other, the male Chinese intellectual in Japan suffers from sexual alienation and exhibits his frustration through a kind of anxiety neurosis, becoming hypersensitive, introverted, self-denigrating, and self-denying to the point of suicide. A series of causes result in the psychological condition of anxiety neurosis in the May Fourth intellectual: national subordination, racial/ethnic inferiority, and sexual emasculation. In such a situation, as I discussed in the preceding chapters, the national, racial, and sexual do not merely imply each other but rather constitute a triple force of emasculation, whose traumatizing effects can be glimpsed in the narratives of self-destruction and suicide prevalent in May Fourth modernist fiction. These narratives of anxiety neurosis are expressions of a larger cultural neurosis which occurred when the self willingly adopted Western ways (most often via Japanese mediation—more about this later), and was confronted with the threat of losing cultural agency. To revise a phrase of the famous contemporary Chinese dissident Su Xiaokang, one can describe this as the "latecomer's anxiety toward modernity":[26] the subject in question desires modernity but is unable to mediate the violence such desiring commits against the self. This anxiety is thereby expressed not through aggression against the supposed "enemies," but in a form of self-aggression, hence the prevalence of decadent indulgence in the forms of debauchery, masochism, and suicide.

This self-aggression can also be explained by the total denunciation of Chinese tradition, upon which the self had been nurtured until the recognition of Western superiority. Hao Chang aptly describes this:

> The scope of their [May Fourth zealots'] moral iconoclasm is perhaps unique in the modern world; no other historical civilization outside the West undergoing modern transformation has witnessed such a phoenixlike impulse to see its own cultural tradition so completely negated. This radical iconoclasm, which created in its train a widespread sense of moral disorientation, naturally produced anxieties of the acutest kind.[27]

Joseph R. Levenson also observed, in 1953, that the May Fourth alienation from tradition had caused a "malaise" in the iconoclasts, who found no "psychological peace."[28]

---

26. Su Xiaokang, "The Excitement and Confusion of Identity" (*Rentong de hangfen yu miluan*), *China Daily News* (*Shijie ribao*), November 12, 1995, p. A4. My use of the term is a slight revision of Su's "latecomer's anxiety toward modernization" (*xiandaihua houlaizhe de jiaolü*).

27. Hao Chang, "New Confucianism and the Intellectual Crisis of Contemporary China," in Charlotte Furth, ed., *Limits of Change* (Cambridge: Harvard University Press, 1976), 281.

28. Levenson, "'History' and 'Value,'" 150.

Freud's definition of melancholia is useful to our analysis of the mode of operation of the psychology of loss here:

> We have discovered that the self-reproaches, with which these melancholic patients torment themselves in the most merciless fashion, in fact apply to another person, the sexual object which they have lost or which has become valueless to them through its own fault. From this we can conclude that the melancholic has, it is true, withdrawn its libido from the object, but that, by a process which we must call "narcissistic identification," the object has been set up in the ego itself, has been, as it were, projected onto the ego. . . . The subject's own ego is then treated like the object that has been abandoned, and it is subjected to all the acts of aggression and expressions of vengefulness which have been aimed at the object. A melancholic's propensity to suicide is also made more intelligible if we consider that the patient's embitterment strikes with a single blow at his own ego and at the loved and hated object.[29]

The analogy here is as follows: if tradition constituted the implicit object of desire for May Fourth intellectuals (who were also scholars of the Chinese cultural tradition), then the May Fourth repudiation of tradition, due to the tradition's essential faults, results in the condition of melancholia. Projecting the object onto his ego, the melancholic expresses resentment toward the loss through forms of self-aggression. As a narcissistic disorder, melancholia can be seen as the symptom of a cultural narcissism that becomes a pathological condition when it is fundamentally challenged by the invading cultures of the West. The West, so to speak, has supplanted tradition and has become the object of desire. As Wu Xiaoming describes it, when Sinocentric cultural narcissism was destabilized in modern China, it was forcibly replaced by the "master narrative" of modernity and progress, within which China was no longer the narrator but the narratee, no longer the master but the slave, no longer the superior but the inferior race and culture. The shock of such self-discovery through the willing assumption of Western perspectives then resulted in the image of the self as stealthy, base, and shameless (in the Chinese national character discourse) and even as cannibalistic (as in Lu Xun's "The Diary of a Madman," discussed in chapter 2). The emotional and psychological responses to this trauma of self-recognition were then expressed as symptoms of melancholia (Yu Dafu) and madness (Lu Xun).[30]

Wu Xiaoming makes another important point, describing the result of this trauma as narcissism (*zilian*) giving way to "loving the Other" (*talian*). This description parallels Zhang Yuhong's conception of the May Fourth mo-

29. Sigmund Freud, *Introductory Lectures on Psychoanalysis*, trans. James Strachey (New York: W. W. Norton and Company, 1966), 427.

30. Wu Xiaoming, "The Self-Consciousness of Chinese Culture in Facing the West in the Twentieth Century" (*Ershi shiji Zhongguo wenhua zai xifang mianqian de ziwo yishi*), *Twenty-First Century (Ershi yi shiji)* 14 (December 1992): 102–112.

ment as the moment when "the Other transforms me" (*huawo*), not the late-Qing moment when "I transform the Other" (*wohua*). The West has now become a psychological category: it transforms the self and demands love from the self such that the landscape of the self's libido becomes structured in its image.

LOVING THE OTHER VIA JAPAN

One of the most fascinating questions regarding May Fourth Occidentalist modernism concerns the Japanese mediation of the May Fourth modernists' construction of the West. All the modernists whom I examined in the previous chapters were Japan-educated. When the Creation Society was active with its three publications—*Creation Quarterly, Creation Weekly,* and *Creation Daily*—its chief members, Guo Moruo, Yu Dafu, Tian Han, and Tao Jingsun, were traveling frequently between China and Japan. They often used Japan as their base and mailed their contributions to China for publication. Guo Moruo, furthermore, married a Japanese woman, and repeatedly noted in his memoirs that he was always in a better and more productive mode when he was in Japan,[31] which is where he wrote almost all of his psychoanalytic stories. Yu Dafu and Tao Jingsun's most experimental stories were also written in Japan. Apparently, writing in Japan provoked an avant-garde tendency in these writers, while writing in China predominantly inspired realism, as Yu Dafu's China stories discussed in chapter 4 exemplify. It was in the mid-1920s, when the Creation Society merged with a Euro-American educated group, the Pacific Society (*taipingyang she*)—including such writers as Hu Shi and Xu Zhimo (1986–1931)—that the Creation Society slowly disintegrated. The members' shared Japanese connection was an organic element in the society's constitution. Thus this particular production of Occidentalist modernism was intricately connected to the condition of Chinese students in Japan. What then was this condition?

From Guo Moruo's detailed writing about the establishment and dissolution of the Creation Society in the years between 1918 and 1926, we know of the general patriotic tenor of Chinese students in Japan on the one hand, and their profound interest in the Japanese literary scene on the other. Students there responded passionately to political questions in China, and there were waves of returnees when such political movements as the May Fourth movement began. They also maintained relationships with such prominent Japanese critics and writers as Kuriyagawa Hakuson and Satō Haruo. A strong tension existed between the students' patriotic fervor (illustrated by the pres-

---

31. Guo Moruo, *The Complete Works of Guo Moruo* (*Guo Moruo quanji*) (Beijing: Renmin wenxue chubanshe, 1985), vol. 12 (which is vol. 2 of the *Autobiography of Moruo* [*Moruo zizhuan*]).

sure Chinese students imposed on those who married Japanese women, sometimes even forcing them to divorce)[32] and a cosmopolitan appreciation of modern Japanese culture. This tension required intellectuals to adopt the strategy of bifurcation (colonial Japan versus metropolitan Japan) which I examined in my introduction, and which undergirded the contradiction between the agendas of nationalism and enlightenment.

In the 1920s, when the Creation Society was active in Shanghai, the Japanese population there outnumbered all other foreign nationalities, and the Uchiyama Bookstore, opened in 1917 and run by Uchiyama Kanzō (1885–1959), was the premiere center for Sino-Japanese literary encounters. Lu Xun, who spoke impeccable Japanese, formed such a close bond with Uchiyama that sometimes Chinese writers had to go through Uchiyama for appointments with Lu Xun. Guo Moruo and Yu Dafu were also closely involved with the bookstore. Various Japanese literary personalities were visitors to the bookstore, the list of them reading "like a prewar *Who's Who*": novelists Tanizaki Jun'ichirō and Satō Haruo, the poet Noguchi Yonejirō, the famed sinologist Takeuchi Yoshimi, and so on. When Tanizaki visited in 1926, Uchiyama arranged a party for Chinese writers to meet with him, and a later party organized by Guo Moruo for Tanizaki drew together over ninety cultural personalities in Shanghai.[33] The Uchiyama Bookstore was also the space where Japanese mediation of Western culture was encapsulated in physical form: it carried the largest collection of Japanese books in China, and had in stock almost all the extant Chinese translations of Japanese works. Chinese writers, especially the Japan-educated Creationists, flocked there, and continued their learning of the West through Japanese books. As Tanizaki noted in his travelogue, "new learning in China is largely obtained from Japanese books and also from Western books translated into Japanese," to which the Uchiyama Bookstore contributed most significantly.[34] The episode I described in my introduction, concerning Xia Mianzun's willing capitulation to Akutagawa's denigration of China in a travelogue recommended by Uchiyama Kanzō, also illustrates how this particular Japan connection helped constitute the Chinese writers' cosmopolitanism, which was expressed as a willingness to be self-critical on the one hand, and the desire to associate with Japan culturally, not politically, on the other.

One of the most crucial elements in the particular formation of Occidentalist modernism in the May Fourth era, however, can be located in the

32. See Guo Moruo's response to the opposition to his Japanese wife in *The Complete Works of Guo Moruo*, 12:39–40.

33. Paul D. Scott, "Introduction" to a translation of Tanizaki Jun'ichirō's "Shanghai Friends" (*Shanhai kōyū ki*, 1926), *Chinese Studies in History*, 30:4 (Summer 1997): 56–70. The short quotation is on p. 62.

34. Tanizaki Jun'ichirō, "Shanghai Friends," trans. Paul D. Scott, *Chinese Studies in History* 30:4 (Summer 1997): 72.

similarity between Chinese Occidentalist ideology and Meiji era Japanese Occidentalist ideology. My contention is that, as an expression of May Fourth faith in linear temporality and teleological modernity, the Chinese students in Japan perceived that the Taishō Japan (1912–1926) that they witnessed and admired was the logical consequence of its Meiji antecedent (1868–1912), when a cultural enlightenment movement similar to that of the May Fourth era had occurred. There were, indeed, many similarities between the Meiji and May Fourth enlightenment projects. Not only was the term "enlightenment" borrowed by the Chinese from Meiji intellectuals, but the Meiji agenda was also predominantly geared toward Westernization at the expense of native tradition. According to Dennis Washburn, both *kindai* and *gendai* in Japanese parlance indicate that "the modern is defined by the process of Westernization, which involved a set of social or ethical values extrinsic to native culture," and the institution of this modernity began in the Meiji period with the government's official sanction: "The official sanctioning of modernization . . . represented a deliberate acceptance of cultural discontinuity, an acceptance that brought with it a simultaneous sense of liberation and loss. The sanctioning of the modern, even when there was no universally accepted understanding of its meaning, threatened a break in cultural memory."[35]

What Washburn says about Meiji literature is unsettlingly apt for May Fourth writing, especially when he notes that the literature of the Meiji period is marked by an "extremely strong sense of discontinuity and a near-obsession with the modern." The Meiji Japanese writers, like their May Fourth counterparts, restated what constituted tradition so as to more clearly define or locate the modern, and tried to reform the Japanese language, e.g. by creating a new literary language (one extreme proposal included the replacement of all Japanese, whether *kanji* or *kana*, by a romanized script, just as Qian Xuantong later proposed for Chinese).[36] That is, the Meiji obsession with the modern also instituted Japanese culture as the particular and Western culture as the universal. Meiji writers, furthermore, linked their self-identity to the modernization of literary practice, created through experimentation with narrative voice and perspective just as the May Fourth writers did. But the resulting cultural discontinuity heightened a sense of

---

35. Dennis Washburn, *The Dilemma of the Modern in Japanese Fiction* (New Haven: Yale University Press, 1995), 57.

36. Ibid., 78–80. Also see Qian Xuantong, "The Problem of Language in China's Future" (*Zhongguo jinhou zhi wenzi wenti*, 1918), in Cai Shangsi, ed., *Collected Materials of the Modern Chinese History of Ideas* (*Zhongguo xiandai sixiangshi ziliao jianbian*) (Hangzhou: Zhejiang renmin chubanshe, 1982), 1:416–421. In this article, Qian makes the point that the elimination of the Chinese written language is the ultimate goal. If more moderate reforms are temporarily necessary, then the Chinese should at least follow what the Japanese had done in their linguistic reform and curb the use of Chinese characters.

self-awareness during the late Meiji period and narrative perspective began to turn inward, resulting in the proliferation of confessional writing. On the one hand, the confessional writing was virtually synonymous with the "creation of a new cultural identity," because the writers continued to desire to be cut off from the past.[37] On the other hand, the turn to interiority was made inevitable by the "overwhelming dominance of the West," since it is the defeated who confess, not those in positions of power.[38] Kenneth Pyle's characterization of Meiji intellectuals is also worth quoting:

> For many Japanese in this period of intense national consciousness, alienation from their own cultural tradition posed perplexing dilemmas. Building a powerful nation required supplanting much of Japanese tradition with techniques and practices borrowed from the West. Young Japanese were troubled by the implications of this process, for the very modernity they sought had in some sense to be regarded as alien in origin.[39]

It is not surprising that there were abundant cultural similarities between Meiji literature and May Fourth literature: the advocacy of Westernization in all areas of society, the construction of modernity as a Western import necessitating the repudiation of tradition, and the writers' turn to interiority due to a crisis of cultural identity.

These similarities need to be analyzed on two levels. First, in terms of the specific relationship between Chinese students in Japan and May Fourth culture, I suspect a lateral, horizontal transference of Meiji enthusiasm about Westernization from Japan to China by Japan-educated students. Precisely because Taishō Japan was more modernized, it was seen as the roadmap for the Chinese attainment of modernity. Second, the similar paths toward Westernization that Meiji Japan and May Fourth China took indicates how a teleological, evolutionary perception of historical development played a role in both. Because modernization is perceived to occur in stages, May Fourth China had to be similar to Meiji Japan—May Fourth China was at the stage of development at which Meiji Japan had been half a century earlier.

Although Japan acting as a mediator to China's Westernization constituted a triangular relationship among Japan, China, and the West, this love story is actually a linear story of who arrived at modernity sooner or later, and who is thereby worthy of affection. The one who arrived first became the ultimate object of love, the second to arrive became the more immediate object of love or the intermediary to reach the ultimate object, and the last to

---

37. Washburn, *The Dilemma of the Modern in Japanese Fiction*, 162.

38. Karatani Kōjin, *Origins of Modern Japanese Literature*, trans. Brett de Bary (Durham: Duke University Press, 1993), 95 and 86.

39. Kenneth Pyle, *The New Generation in Meiji Japan: Problems of Cultural Identity* (Stanford: Stanford University Press, 1969), 4.

arrive had the responsibility of loving, rather than being loved. Because love for the ultimate object is mediated through the intermediary, Japan, which also loves the ultimate object, that love is made even more powerful and the object even more desirable. To become deserving of the love of the West and Japan, then, meant to catch up with modernity as soon as possible. To catch up, geopolitical differences were displaced by temporal difference, so that the fulfillment of love was possible. Once such a linear, temporal view of historical development was adopted, May Fourth China had to go through exactly what Meiji Japan went through, perhaps faster, to facilitate the leap into modernity. The crucial issue here was the compression of time, as May Fourth China was engaged in the job of catching up. What took Meiji Japan fifty years might take only ten years in May Fourth China.

By the end of the May Fourth decade, it became clear that the cultural Westernization campaign via Japanese mediation was not to be realized. In a 1933 lecture delivered at the University of Chicago, Hu Shi finally retrieved notions of geopolitical difference to explain why the campaign was unsuccessful. He named three reasons why the Chinese could not become as well Westernized as the Japanese: (1) the total absence of a powerful ruling class to effectively lead and implement policies; (2) the lack of interest in military affairs and the low social status of the military; and (3) the lamentable failure of China in establishing a stable government as the controlling center in its modernization work.[40] Hu Shi makes clear that even while the Chinese consciously imitated the Japanese, the Chinese did not have the right social and political conditions for successful Westernization.

Hu Shi's emphasis on these differences between the Japanese and Chinese Westernization projects returns us to the question of spatial, geopolitical difference, and suggests that, seen with historical hindsight, the May Fourth optimism of displacing spatial categories of difference with temporal categories is idealistic at best. We might, therefore, infer that it is precisely this idealistic incorporation of linear temporality that forestalled a close attention to local conditions, which had to be rigorously attended to if a project of Westernization as the Chinese envisioned were to become possible. Ironically, it is the ideology of linear temporality that disenabled a cultural Westernization campaign from arriving at modernity.

THE MAY FOURTH LEGACY

Anthony Giddens, like many other Western scholars of modernity, argues that modernity has been a Western project. The nation-state and systematic capitalist production, which he calls the "organizational complexes of moder-

---

40. Hu Shih [Hu Shi], *The Chinese Renaissance: The Haskell Lectures, 1933* (Chicago: University of Chicago Press, 1934), Lecture One.

nity," arose in the West and spread throughout the world because of the power they have generated. No traditional social forms have been able to contest the power of modernity and maintain complete autonomy from its trends and consequences.[41] In contrast, Taiwanese scholar Ping-hui Liao expands Foucault's notion of modernity and self-invention and argues that modernity is not a cultural event unique to the West, but rather the product of the hybrid, uneven structure of the colonial encounter: recognizing the self in the Other.[42] Certainly, modernity as a social formation in the West could not have been possible without the colonial structure, or the appropriation of the non-Western alterity.

To combine the insights of both Giddens and Liao, modernity as a Western project should be seen as both the source and product of the domination which subjugated the non-West and helped consolidate the West's modern identity. While the West is able to discover and reinvent itself through its domination of the non-West, the non-West is forced into a soul-searching self-examination and reinvention of the self as it becomes overwhelmed by the West. In terms of identity formation, then, the West and the non-West are in a grossly unequal relationship. For the non-West, modernity is the condition of a forcible repudiation of the self and the often self-imposed internalization of a new identity structured in the image of the West. Hence modernity for the non-West is not merely the site of geopolitical, cultural, and psychological trauma, but also the site of an identity crisis. May Fourth modernist writing's demonstrative expressions of madness, anxiety, and melancholia indicate the depth of this identity crisis.

The attempt to resolve the identity crisis took two different routes by the mid- and late-1920s. One was a cultural recuperation of Chinese tradition as inherently modern. Around Beijing, for example, *jingpai* philosophers and writers sought to locate convergences and compatibilities between Chinese and Western cultures (see Part Two). The other approach was an ideological turn to the left as a way to salvage nationalism from the denationalized Westernization campaign. Around Shanghai, numerous intellectuals were swept up by Marxism, which they felt had direct applicability to China. Several of the May Fourth modernists turned to the ideological left, which allowed them to integrate anti-imperialism into their cultural agenda and made the bifurcation of Western/Japanese metropolitan and colonial cultures irrelevant. Yu Dafu was assassinated by the Japanese police for his patriotic activities, Guo Moruo became a known socialist fighter, and Lu Xun helped establish the League of Left-Wing Writers (*zuolian*) and became the guru

41. Anthony Giddens, *The Consequences of Modernity* (Stanford: Stanford University Press, 1990), 174–175.

42. Ping-hui Liao, "Hope, Recollection, Repetition: Turandot Revisited," *Musical Quarterly* 77:1 (Spring 1993): 67–80.

figure of the leftist literary scene in the 1930s. To use Joseph Levenson's formulation, Marxism allowed the May Fourth intellectuals to be iconoclastic and nationalistic at the same time. For the emotionally "wracked" May Fourth iconoclast, such a solution was ideal, Levenson concludes.[43] The dominance of Marxist ideology in the cultural arena was the context in which Shanghai modernists had to struggle for artistic autonomy, even while they professed leftist leanings (see Part Three).

In criticizing the May Fourth cultural enlightenment project, the *jingpai* philosophers and writers and the Marxists chose their issues very differently. While *jingpai* philosophers and writers attacked the May Fourth agenda for its unwarranted denigration of tradition, the leftists accused it of being dictated by foreign imperialism: the Cultural Criticism Society (*wenhua pinglun she*) led by Hu Qiuyuan (b. 1910), for example, charged that May Fourth intellectuals were, whether consciously or unconsciously, spokespersons of Western imperialism.[44] But post–May Fourth leftist reflection on the May Fourth era, though critical of the inscription of imperialist culture, nonetheless acknowledged the May Fourth legacy of science or scientific method as a positive agenda to be further developed to end feudalism.[45] May Fourth antitraditionalism was renamed "antifeudalism," even while May Fourth Occidentalism, excluding its valorization of science, was repudiated as imperialist. However, this selective endorsement and criticism of the May Fourth legacy was itself predicated upon the shared assumptions, in both Marxist and May Fourth ideology, of linear temporality and teleological history, which repudiated the Chinese past as feudal. As Arif Dirlik has pointed out, Chinese Marxism was influenced by the Marxist globalized historical consciousness, so it took unilinear European history as the model and sought China's admission into universal history.[46] In the end, Hegelian historical teleology underlay both the May Fourth enlightenment campaign and Chinese Marxism.

A less widespread, but equally critical, perspective on the May Fourth campaign was later articulated by the right-wing nationalists. A particularly illuminating text in this regard is the 1943 article by the U.S.- and German-educated Sichuanese writer Chen Quan (b. 1905), editor of the Chongqing-based *National Literature* (*Minzu wenxue*, 1943–1944), which served as the fo-

43. Levenson, "'History' and 'Value,'" 180–181.

44. "The Truth's Call to Arms" (*Zhenli zhi xi*), by the Cultural Criticism Society, originally published in the inaugural issue of *Cultural Criticism*, and then included in Du Heng [as Su Wen], ed., *Debates on Literary Freedom* (*Wenyi ziyou lunbian ji*) (Shanghai: Xiandai shuju, 1933), 302–307.

45. Ibid., 302.

46. Arif Dirlik, "Marxism and Chinese History: The Globalization of Marxist Historical Discourse and the Problem of Hegemony in Marxism," *Journal of Third World Studies* 4:1 (1987): 151–164.

rum for a group of writers called Strategies of the Warring States (*zhanguoce*). Many May Fourth intellectuals held the notion that the May Fourth movement was similar to the *Sturm und Drang* movement of Goethe's Germany, for both marked the historical transition from a feudal society to a new society.[47] Chen Quan refutes this equation, however, and says that the May Fourth movement did not achieve what *Sturm und Drang* achieved for Germany.

Chen Quan enumerates three reasons for the failure of the May Fourth movement. First, the intellectuals mistook what was a "Warring States" period (*zhanguo shidai*) for a "Spring and Autumn" period (*chunqiu shidai*). During a Warring States period, military organization and operation are necessary; during a Spring and Autumn period, alliance and negotiation are necessary. While the problems facing May Fourth China should have been solved through military means, Chinese intellectuals advocated international peace, the reduction of arms, and an idealistic cultural campaign, influenced by the war-weariness of the post–World War I milieu in the West. This approach diminished nationalist consciousness and bred war-weariness in the people. Second, they mistook the May Fourth era as an age of individualism while it had actually been an age of collectivism. Thus May Fourth leaders advocated the reverse of what was necessary, namely individualistic rebellions of son against father, wife against husband, student against teacher, and subordinate against officer, which caused a dissolution of order and organization, a dearth of patriotic spirit, and an absence of military will. Third, they mistook the May Fourth era as an age of rationalism, when it had actually been an age of irrationalism. Addressing the evolution of European thought from the enlightenment (*guangming yundong*) to the modern period, Chen Quan argues that irrationality was the main agenda in the work of Nietzsche, Schopenhauer, Hegel, and Bergson, and in such cultural phenomena as psychoanalysis, literary expressionism, and futurism. The May Fourth agenda of enlightenment mimicked the rationality of the Western enlightenment as its philosophical foundation and advocated science and rationality, and so they were two centuries behind the West. Chen Quan concludes that this last mistake had to do with the rational paradigm in Confucian thought, noting that Western enlightenment intellectuals were actually admirers of Confucius. That is, the May Fourth leaders, though advocating anti-Confucianism, paradoxically embraced the Confucian paradigm. Since nationalism is not a logic, but an emotion and a will, the rational enlightenment discourse could not serve up the nationalism that China desperately needed. He then concludes that the May Fourth movement was wrong

47. Guo Moruo, "Postscript to the Translation of Part II of *Faust*" (*Fushide dierbu yihou ji*), in *Guo Moruo on Writing* (*Guo Moruo lun chuangzuo*), ed. Zhang Chenghuan (Shanghai: Shanghai wenyi chubanshe, 1982), 657.

for its times. Its leaders understood neither the West nor China deeply enough, and hence they could not correctly introduce the West or overthrow Chinese tradition.[48]

To be sure, Chen Quan was writing at the height of nationalist zeal during the Sino-Japanese War, but his appraisal of the May Fourth movement reveals some important concerns of post–May Fourth intellectuals. The prioritizing of enlightenment over nationalism was clearly considered a mistake that had resulted in confusion, despondence, dissolution of energy, and depression in the Chinese cultural milieu. The increasingly interiorized landscape in modernist writing evidences this state of confusion and despondence. As an ideology that combines nationalism with enlightenment ideals of progress and modernity, it is little wonder that Marxism was able to bring disparate groups of intellectuals together into its fold. So, when the next generation of Shanghai modernist writers tried to write, publish, and form a salon, they had to devise ways to deal with the constant attacks by leftists. The dominance of nationalist intellectuals associated with the left generally made the ideological milieu in the next decade much more volatile for the modernists who wanted to assert the autonomy of literature.

48. Chen Quan, "The May Fourth Movement and the *Sturm und Drang*" (*Wusi yundong yu kuangbiao yundong*), *National Literature* (*Minzu wenxue*) 1:3 (September 1943): 1–6.

PART TWO

Rethinking the Modern
The Beijing School

CHAPTER 6

Modernity without Rupture

Proposals for a New Global Culture

The task to be accomplished is not the conservation of the past, but the redemption of the hopes of the past.

MAX HORKHEIMER AND THEODOR W. ADORNO (1944)

The horizon open to the future, which is determined by expectations in the present, guides our access to the past. Inasmuch as we appropriate past experiences with an orientation to the future, the authentic present is preserved as the locus of continuing tradition and innovation at once . . . .

JÜRGEN HABERMAS (1987)

Foreign influence and native style are not contradictions in opposition. The determining element of native style is language.

WANG ZENGQI (1988)

To many contemporary Western thinkers, Jürgen Habermas's 1980 lecture "Modernity—An Incomplete Project" mapped a curious intellectual constellation where those who are commonly considered radicals, such as postmodernists, were cast as conservatives, and the enlightenment ideals of rationality and modernity were once again, though in revised forms, declared to be paramount virtues. For Habermas, the problems of contemporary Western societies did not arise due to the damage wrecked by modernity and rationality, as claimed by such postmodernists as George Bataille, Michel Foucault, and Jacques Derrida, but rather due to the incompleteness of modernity and an insufficiency of rationality. Rationality and modernity, if developed more completely to their professed goals, could have built and still promise to build a world of "communicative rationality" which would integrate the lifeworld (society) with culture (art and morality), overcoming present alienation. Habermas calls postmodernists "young conservatives" who are very much the descendents of aesthetic modernism in their critique of humanism, rationality, and modernity, and also calls those who advocate a withdrawal into the culture prior to modernity "old conservatives," and those who welcome modernity in science and technology but oppose its incursion into the realms of culture and morality "neoconservatives." In this typology, the postmodernists, premodernists, and cultural antimodernists are thrown together into what to many is an awkward alliance against modernity.[1]

What interests me first of all in this diatribe, mainly directed at the French postmodern theory known as poststructuralism/postmodernism,[2] is how the definitions of cultural radicalism and conservatism fluctuate in relation to a given enunciative position, and how this inevitably undercuts their critical potential as modes of recognition and ways of categorizing cultural positions. Habermas's reversal of more familiar usages of conservatism and radicalism is illuminating, therefore, in aiding our rethinking of the role of so-called "conservatism"[3] in modern Chinese cultural history. Long dominated by the May Fourth perspective on modernity as a rupture of Chinese history and discontinuity from Chinese tradition—that is, modernity as a Western property obliging the Chinese both to emulate it belatedly and to reject tradition wholeheartedly—evaluations of anti–May Fourth positions have facilely dismissed them all as "conservatism."

This chapter aims to reinvestigate the immediate post–May Fourth cultural formation that negated May Fourth iconoclasm, as a way to contextualize the rise of *jingpai* writing—the writing of the Beijing school. I seek to understand how a mode of writing that did not base itself on a teleological conception of history and culture arose in the post–May Fourth era, how its nonteleological position marked a particular form of modernity and modernism (in this sense closer to Western aesthetic modernism than the May Fourth modernism discussed in Part One was), and how this modernism the-

---

1. Jürgen Habermas, "Modernity—An Incomplete Project," in *The Anti-Aesthetic: Essays on Postmodern Culture,* ed. Hal Foster (Seattle: Bay Press, 1983), 3–15. Another contemporary thinker taking a similar position to Habermas is Marshall Berman. See his influential book *All That Is Solid Melts Into Air* (New York: Penguin Books, 1988), in which he professes faith in the promise of modernity within which human subjects struggle, and through struggle define themselves to be subjects of history. The ability to become agents of history is a great concern in the work of both the *Critical Review* group and New Confucianists.

2. Habermas provides a more sustained criticism of poststructuralism in his *The Philosophical Discourse of Modernity,* trans. Frederick G. Lawrence (Cambridge: MIT Press, 1987).

3. Charlotte Furth has edited the only volume on the so-called "conservative" cultural formation in modern China: *Limits of Change: Essays on Conservative Alternatives in Republican China* (Cambridge: Harvard University Press, 1976). The lack of books in the United States on this vast cultural formation is indicative of the hegemony of the May Fourth perspective of modernity defined exclusively in evolutionary terms as a rejection of tradition as the property of the past. The same hegemony operated to repress discussions on New Confucianism and the thinkers associated with the *Critical Review* in China until the 1990s, when a form of cultural nationalism began to try to resist the onslaught of Western commercialism.

orized space, place, and locality in their connections to culture in the global context.

Second, Habermas's insistent modernity-oriented perspective, though harboring a telling neglect of the non-Western world, curiously parallels that of many anti–May Fourth thinkers in modern China. These thinkers, the *Critical Review* (*Xueheng*) group and the New Confucianists (*xin rujia*), rejected Western imperialism and the May Fourth discourse of total Westernization (what I call Occidentalism in chapter 5), but nevertheless professed a commitment to modernity. Like Habermas, they rescued modernity from evolutionary progressivism and developmentalism, and reevaluated it in terms of intersubjective, or rather intercultural, communication and rationality. These Chinese intellectuals in their own manner saw intersubjectivity, taken as an integration of the cultural systems of China and the West, as the basis for what they considered to be a true universality or globality, and not the Eurocentric universality endorsed by May Fourth iconoclasts. As I argue below, the atrocities of World War I shocked Westerners and Chinese alike into seeing the West's experience of modernity as a particular one arising from a specific sociocultural context, and not universally beneficial to mankind; hence there was a compelling reason and need to redefine the universal: to rescue the universal from Western claims.

Within this context, the neotraditional aspects of *jingpai* thought involved a reaffirmation of Chinese tradition and its validity in the modern world as another particularity like Western culture, with equal claims to universality since universality was now up for grabs. This reaffirmation was, however, not nativist in nature, since it did not repudiate Western modernity on nationalist grounds. Rather, it was often cast in Western conceptual frameworks, and asserted the need to integrate Western modernity into Chinese culture even as it criticized the excessive materialism and militarism of Western modernity. In other words, it sought to *extend the scope of what constituted modernity* rather than reject modernity per se. What vindicated Chinese tradition in *jingpai* thought was therefore not its essentialized particularities, but its perceived universal qualities which could be shared by both China and the West. The intellectuals involved were opposed to the May Fourth Occidentalism according to which being modern means negating all that is Chinese — but they were not antimodern. I suspect, however, that such a fundamental commitment to modernity betrays their unintended affinity to an enlightenment vision, like that of Habermas, and thus in reality they were closer to their May Fourth compatriots than they thought.

The parallels between Habermas and these anti–May Fourth Chinese thinkers are intellectual in nature, and not historical. A closer historical analysis reveals that these Chinese intellectuals incorporated many of the critiques of modernity voiced by their contemporaries in the West, the same thinkers who were in turn criticized by Habermas decades later. This was an eclectic selection of Western philosophers such as Henri Bergson, Rudolph Eucken (1846–1926), Bertrand Russell, and Irving Babbitt (1865–1933), with whom several of the Chinese neotraditionalists studied or had personal contact. This odd configuration—Chinese intellectuals deploying Western antimodern thought to support a qualified critique and yet fundamental commitment to modernity—is crucial to our understanding of these neotraditional cultural figures as revisionist moderns. Evidence shows that for the neotraditionalists to launch a critique of Western modernity, it was first necessary for the West to have done so itself; the modernity-critique of the Western philosophers named above served as the theoretical justification for their own project. While this shows the neotraditionalists' nonparochial approach to Chinese tradition, the necessity of the Western gaze in their revalidation of Chinese tradition also poses the thorny question of derivative agency.

First sporadically then more systematically, as early as the turn of the century and then especially in the post–World War I intellectual milieu, indeed throughout the interwar years up to the post–World War II 1950s, there was a soul-searching rethinking of Western civilization in the West. One re-members G. Lowes Dickinson's famous "Letters from John Chinaman" (1901), which posed a dichotomous vision of China and the West and insisted on the need to temper the West's instrumentalism, capitalism, and imperialism with China's morality and ethics. One also remembers the crucial role played by Ernest Fenollosa (1853–1908) in the creation of Western modernist poetics through his endorsement of Chinese aesthetics, as well as his argument, in *East and West* (1893), for fusing feminine Eastern culture and masculine Western culture.[4] Around World War I, the idealist philosophy of Emile Boutroux (1845–1921) and Henri Bergson (who was Boutroux's disciple) in France, Rudolph Eucken and his disciple Hans Driesch (1867–1941) in Germany (the latter of whom visited China as an invitee of Liang Qichao's Peking Lecture Association [*jiangxueshe*] for almost a year during 1922–1923), and the American New Humanism of Irving Babbitt became leading dissenting voices against Hegelianism and called for a fundamental rethinking of the value of Western civilization. Especially by the close of World War I, and particularly in the 1920s, the relation between the Eastern and Western worlds "was the topic of the day," with "countless lectures, articles, and books on the problem, most of them in a vein of optimism concerning the final harmonization to arrive between East and West," as the Europe-educated Chinese-Indonesian philosopher Tjan Tjoe Som tells us.[5] A civilizational discourse, or what later became known as the "civilizational

4. G. Lowes Dickinson, *Letters from John Chinaman and Other Essays,* with an introduction by E. M. Forster (London: George Allen and Unwin Ltd., 1946), 11–44. Ernest Fenollosa, *East and West* (New York: Crowell and Company, 1893).

5. Tjan Tjoe Som, "The Meeting of East and West: The Oriental View," in *Eastern and Western*

project" seeking to reinvigorate the now bankrupt Western culture through its synthesis with Eastern culture,[6] became a popular intellectual discourse.[7] This is the context in which someone like Rabindranath Tagore, and to a lesser extent Liang Qichao, could become ambassadors of Eastern culture and be told again and again that they should disseminate superior Eastern culture in their journeys to the West.

Commenting on this frenzy of civilizational discourse, which on the surface exhibits an unprecedented humility of Western intellectuals towards the teachings of the East, Tjan Tjoe Som makes the critical observation that the meetings between East and West proselytized by this discourse were premised on a general, arbitrary, and "romantic division between East and West." This discourse produced "the East" in order to project the Western self into "some object and to try to discover itself in the contemplation of the object." Hence "[b]y the posing of the problem of the meeting of the East and the West, the West tried to discover the nature of its being."[8] Furthermore, "It is typical again of the West that it now worries about its crisis, and has been ignorant of the fact that the East has since centuries been living in one crisis after the other. But Eastern crises have hitherto not very much affected the West, whereas a crisis in the West would immediately be of influence on the world as a whole."[9] Som shows not only that the cultural synthesis thesis is legitimized by a Hegelian procedure whose goal it is to rejuvenate the Western self, but also that this procedure solipsistically serves the West and hides within itself a hierarchy of importance between West and East.

Som's view of the West's perception of crisis and resulting call for East-West synthesis translates, to a certain extent, into what Stephen N. Hay has called the "Western encouragements for the message of the East" in his brilliant *Asian Ideas of East and West.* Although Hay's main example is Tagore, it is illuminating to think about *jingpai* thought in light of his arguments, since the Chinese neotraditionalists also received such encouragements. Hay's

---

World, conference proceedings organized by Netherlands Universities Foundation for International Co-operation (Hague: W. Van Hoeve Ltd., 1953), 13–23.

6. See for instance A. Abdel-Malek, ed., *The Civilizational Project: The Visions of the Orient,* proceedings of the Thirtieth International Congress of Human Sciences in Asia and North Africa (Mexico City: El Colegio de México, 1981).

7. Examples for this popular civilizational discourse are numerous. See for instance René Guénon, *East and West,* trans. William Massey (London: Luzac and Co., 1941), in which he criticizes the superiority complex of Western Civilization (with a capital "C") in its blind belief in progress and science and urges the necessity of learning from the Orient: "the first step towards rousing western intellectuality from its slumber must be the study of the doctrines of the East" (227). See also Maurice Parmelee, *Oriental and Occidental Culture* (New York and London: The Century Co., 1928).

8. Som, "The Meeting of East and West," 22–23.

9. Ibid., 23.

main thesis regarding Western encouragements in his analysis of Tagore's thinking is that Tagore's ideas on Asian civilization "cannot be understood apart from the effects of European Orientalist scholarship and Indophilia on nineteenth century Hindu thought," as well as the many actual encouragements Tagore received from his Euro-American friends and admirers, especially his winning the Nobel Price in 1913 and the resounding welcome he received in his numerous trips to the West throughout his career.[10] Hay goes on to note that Asian intellectuals, particularly those interested in revitalizing their native culture ("revitalists"), were most often educated or spent a number of years in the West, and were thus susceptible to the encouragement of the Orientophiles.[11]

Thus contextualized in the West's encouragement of Eastern intellectuals to revitalize their traditions, as well as in the uneven relationship between the East and the West in the synthesis-driven civilizational discourse, the agency of Chinese neotraditionalists becomes more ambiguous. Although they flaunted a global vision, it was one that was mediated by the Western confirmation that Chinese culture could finally claim to enter the global, a confirmation with Orientalist strings attached. The apparent similarity between their position and Habermas's, both claiming that Western modernity could be recuperated, thus suggests a deeper affinity between Habermas's Western-oriented and the neotraditionalists' Western-endorsed worldviews.

This ambiguous agency, then, is equally a product of the bifurcation of metropolitan and colonial Western cultures in the imagination of *jingpai* thinkers. The metropolitan modernity-critique and "encouragement" became the justification for the recuperation of Chinese tradition, on the one hand, while on the other hand colonial epistemology was neither refuted nor even challenged in a sustained fashion. This was substantially unlike the kind of cultural revisionism more common in thoroughly colonized countries such as India, the object of much postcolonial theoretical inquiry, and this again recalls crucial differences between semicolonial and colonial formations of culture. Prasenjit Duara has pointed out that modern India witnessed a "greater prominence of critiques of modernity" than China because such critiques were precipitated by a close encounter with colonial ideology, which necessitated the generation of psychologically valid alternatives to modernity. In China, however, due to the absence of institutionalized colonialism in most parts of the country, "colonial ideology was not entrenched among both colonizer and colonized in the same way as it was in India and

10. Steven N. Hay, *Asian Ideas of East and West: Tagore and His Critics in Japan, China, and India* (Cambridge: Harvard University Press, 1970), chapter 4, 124–145. The quote is from 135–136.

11. Ibid., 314–315.

other directly colonized countries."[12] Hence there was no "thorough-going" critique of modernity, but rather a persistent commitment to modernity.

Ashis Nandy, moreover, notes that there was a strong presence of "non-modern" thinkers in India who refused altogether to comply with colonial categories, and opted to operate *outside* modernity.[13] This nonmodern India is described by Nandy as "the India which has survived the Western onslaught. It coexists with the India of the modernists, whose attempts to identify with the colonial aggressors has produced the pathetic copies of the Western man in the subcontinent, but it rejects most versions of Indian nationalism as bound irrevocably to the West—in reaction, jealousy, hatred, fear and counterphobia."[14] This nonmodern awareness provides neither a radical critique of the West nor an aggressive affirmation of Indianness. Because this position is premised on not binding itself in any form of organic cultural relationship with the West—be it the resistance of natives or the emulation of colonial modernists—it is also the strongest enemy of modernity.[15] Negating both the ideology of progress and European science, Gandhi was thus the leader of nonmodern India who based his main thoughts outside the parameters of the "modern civilization" produced by the West.[16]

It will be clear from the following exegesis that the Chinese neotraditionalists took neither the thoroughgoing antimodern position nor the transcendent nonmodern position, and this points to semicolonialism as a cultural condition that, though seemingly farther from the sphere of Western colonial domination, ironically absorbed Western modernity more thoroughly. The absence of high-handed intervention by colonial powers in local culture made Western modernity less an object of resistance. Via the strategy of bifurcation, the neotraditionalists chose, so to speak, a different set of metropolitan Western justifications for their thought than the Occidentalists. Their cultural attitude, often criticized as conservative, therefore was not nativist in temperament, but rather exemplified an investment in modernity perhaps best defined as a *critical modernity* that critically examined but also simultaneously affirmed the constitutive elements of Western modernity. Modernity was criticized as the engine of greed and destruction for its aggressive manifestations in war and economic conquest, but, at its best,

12. Prasenjit Duara, *Rescuing History From the Nation: Questioning Narratives of Modern China* (Chicago: University of Chicago Press, 1995), 221–224.

13. See Ashis Nandy, *The Intimate Enemy: Loss and Recovery of Self Under Colonialism* (Delhi: Oxford University Press, 1983) and *The Savage Freud and Other Essays on Possible and Retrievable Selves* (Princeton: Princeton University Press, 1995).

14. Nandy, *The Intimate Enemy,* 74.

15. See especially the chapter entitled "The Uncolonized Mind" in *The Intimate Enemy,* 64–111.

16. Partha Chatterjee, *Nationalist Thought and the Colonial World: A Derivative Discourse* (Minneapolis: University of Minnesota Press, 1993), 85–91.

modernity promised rationality without the progress-oriented craze for competition, a rationality which could be productively applied to Chinese culture to create a new global culture. This critical modernity, in the local context, constituted their grounds of opposition to May Fourth Occidentalism; in the global context, it was subjected to a Eurocentric civilizational discourse that sought to absorb Eastern culture to cure its own ills. The neotraditional subjectivities are located in the interaction and tension between these two contexts. Revitalist and yet cosmopolitan and bicultural, these are subjectivities produced through processes similar to those of the Occidentalists in the semicolonial condition.

The neotraditionalist project, then, was as intimately connected to Western thought as May Fourth Occidentalism had been. The difference lay in their appropriation of opposing Western thought systems—idealism, vitalism, and New Humanism for the former, Hegelian progressivism for the latter—and of course in their diametrically opposed attitude to tradition. Another crucial difference lay in their assumption of a different audience for their projects. The Occidentalists wanted to create for China and the Chinese audience conditions hospitable to the total absorption of Western modernity, by emptying out what constituted the particularities of China in order to graft the Western universal onto this newly blank slate—I described this process in chapter 5 as the particularization of Chinese culture and universalization of Western culture. But the neotraditionalists saw their interlocutors as both the local audience and the imagined audience "out there" in the West, which meant that their incorporation of Western modernity had to be critical since the voice of modernity-critique was already popular in the West. In this sense, the neotraditionalists were paradoxically more global and cosmopolitan in their recuperation of locality, while the Occidentalists were more local in their negligence of the global implications of their articulation. This global vision, as I will argue in the following sections, is itself acquired through the process of particularizing Western culture and universalizing aspects of Chinese culture. How this process came about, and what the neotraditionalists' project entailed on both philosophical and literary fronts, is the subject of the narrative that follows.

Walter Benjamin's angel of history was derived from his meditation on a Paul Klee painting; Benjamin saw Klee's angel—eyes staring, mouth open, and wings spread—as being turned towards the past, blown irresistibly forward into the future by the storm of progress. The angel of history was Hegelian in its movement towards a telos propelled by progress and development.[17] When the neotraditionalists rejected this unilinear Hegelian telos, they helped transfix the angel of history in the conjuncture between the

---

17. Walter Benjamin, "Theses on the Philosophy of History," in *Illuminations*, ed. Hannah Arendt, trans. Harry Zohn (New York: Shocken Books, 1969), 257–258.

past, present, and future as a kind of simultaneous coexistence. Space, rather than time, was a prominent feature of their cross-cultural theorization, but due to their immersion in Western philosophy and aesthetics, space was never reified: it was seen as an interactive arena for East-West encounters. In this sense, the constructive, productive relationship they built between space and modernity may remain their most significant contribution to the ongoing debates about cultural identity and modernity in the Third World.

CULTURAL DISCOURSE: LOOKING BACKWARDS TO THE FUTURE

The narrative of post–May Fourth neotraditionalism must trace its trajectory to several groups of intellectuals who shared a disenchantment with May Fourth Occidentalism. At the core of this disenchantment was their resentment toward the Occidentalists' totalistic rejection of tradition and assertion of complete Westernization, and the perceived threat of an accompanying loss of cultural agency and identity. By equating tradition and everything prior to the modern with conformity, the Occidentalists considered their antitraditionalism a means to push China into the temporality of modern nation-states. The May Fourth choice was to fully incorporate Western cultural ideologies to replace native ones, which naturally often undermined any nationalist intent, as I discussed earlier. This May Fourth perspective has been so dominant that forms of cultural nativism or neotraditionalism were generally considered ineffectual articulations, not engaging with the modern world and therefore useless or irrelevant to China's critical situation. Joseph R. Levenson's declaration—"[m]odern Chinese traditionalists have been, not political manipulators in a smoke-filled room, but self-persuading devotees of a culture drying up" [18]—vividly repeats such dismissals, and assumes, like the May Fourth Occidentalists, that "traditional Chinese culture" has lost its validity and anyone who advocates its revival is engaged in a losing battle. The general assumption had been that the "drying up" of this culture was a *fait accompli*, and the production of modern Chinese culture had to be, by definition, in opposition to traditional Chinese culture. For the neotraditionalists, however, modernity was not based on such a bipolar construction, but rather on a critical appreciation and incorporation of both.

The post–May Fourth neotraditional cultural formation, then, consisted of a distinct contingency of intellectuals with diverse cultural and intellectual positions, loosely unified through their shared opposition to Occidentalist ideology. If we see late-Qing reformer Yan Fu, translator Lin Shu, and the National Essence School as precursors to this post–May Fourth neotraditionalism, it would mostly be in the sense that they were all critical of May

18. Joseph R. Levenson, *Confucian China and Its Modern Fate* (Berkeley: University of California Press, 1958), 129.

Fourth Occidentalism, not because they shared similar intellectual orientations. Though a reformer radical in his day, Yan Fu reputedly lost his faith in Western culture due to the devastation of World War I, became critical of Occidentalism, and advocated a return to traditional ethics and culture. Lin Shu, on the other hand, had seen a deep affinity between Western culture and Confucian ethics, and in one illuminating comment criticized the Occidentalists this way: "Seeing that the young child was thin, weak, and fatigued, they did not seek the advice of a good doctor, but instead looked to see if the child's parents had any hidden illness, thinking that if they expelled this hidden illness in the parents, the child would soon become plump and radiant."[19] With the young child as a metaphor for modern China and the parents representing Chinese tradition, Lin Shu here pointedly criticizes May Fourth antitraditionalism as misdirected and devoid of rational and scientific (medical) basis. The metaphor is ironically apt, since the Occidentalists also saw themselves as the youthful contingency against a superannuated, fossilized tradition, and often exploited the metaphor of youth and vitality to their advantage in their iconoclastic pronouncements.

The one late-Qing reformer who played a key role in the emergence of neotraditionalism was Liang Qichao (1873–1929). Liang, like Yan Fu, became disillusioned with Western culture after witnessing the ravages of the First World War, and his work was widely influential in the post–May Fourth era. In February 1919, three months before the May Fourth incident, he left China for a protracted tour of postwar Europe, traversing France, England, Belgium, Holland, Switzerland, Italy, and Germany, before returning to China in March 1920. The result of this tour was the classic *Impressions of Travels in Europe* (*Ouyou xinying lu*, 1920). Seeing devastation-ridden Europe, Liang delved deeper into his recent conviction that China should not blindly follow the West but rather resurrect its traditional culture[20] by finding evidence of the corruption of the West, which had pursued the Enlightenment ideals of progress and reason at great costs. He noted that Western thought of the nineteenth century had encouraged excessive materialism, militarism, scientism, and individualism, and he labelled these trends as the roots of war:

> In the mid-nineteenth century, two extremely persuasive schools of thought generated the flourishing of economic liberalism and industrialism: one was biological evolutionism and the other was individualism. . . . [Darwin's survival

---

19. Quoted in Shen Songqiao, *The Critical Review Group: A Conservative Alternative to the New Culture Movement in the May Fourth Era* (*Xuehengpai yu wusi shiqi de fan xinwenhua yundong*) (Taipei: Guoli Taiwan daxue chuban weiyuanhui, 1984), 37.

20. Liang Qichao's conviction before his European tour can be seen in his "On National Character" (*Guoxing lun*, 1912), mentioned in Guy Alitto, *The Last Confucian: Liang Shu-ming and the Chinese Dilemma of Modernity* (Berkeley: University of California Press, 1979), 47.

of the fittest] doctrine, along with [John Stuart] Mill's utilitarianism and [Jeremy] Bentham's happiness principle, became the conerstones of English thought. In the meantime, Max Stirner and Søren Kierkegaard advocated individualism, their problematic theory extending to Nietzsche who saw altruism as slave mentality and saw the defeat of the weak to be the mandate of the strong and a necessity for social evolution. These strange theories were based on Darwinian biology and catered to the psychology of contemporary people. Therefore, on the individual level, it came to be considered natural for people to worship power and money; on the national level, the most fashionable policy became militarism and imperialism. The source of this current world war lies in this, and it is also the source of future class wars in nations.[21]

This critical assessment of Darwinian evolutionism and Nietzschean individualism is diametrically opposed to their celebration by the Occidentalists, but it parallels similar critiques by such Western thinkers as Bergson and Eucken, with whom Liang Qichao personally met and conferred. Recall that the Occidentalists in China reshaped Bergson's theory so as to fit a conception of teleological modernity (as discussed in chapter 1), but Liang offers an interpretation closer to Bergson's original intention. Bergson's theory of intuitive evolution, notes Liang, sees the universe as constituted by the flow of consciousness resulting from the generation of free human will, hence human beings can daily engage in creative evolution. Liang argues that both Bergson and Eucken see the limits of materialism and advocate the need to integrate and harmonize spiritualism and materialism, which Chan Buddhism had successfully accomplished centuries ago. Confucianism, Taoism, and Mohism likewise sought to unify ideals (spiritualism) and pragmatics (materialism), and, says Liang, they have much to offer the modern world.

During his trip, Liang had many encounters with Western intellectuals and journalists who urged him to promote Chinese culture as an antidote to a now-bankrupt Western civilization.[22] The prevailing pessimism towards Western civilization in postwar Europe professed a new politics of the Other: instead of repudiating the Other, it was eager to absorb the culture of the Other as a resource and corrective to its internal problems. As I have suggested, the convergence of this new politics of the Other and the neotraditionalist revival in China was a matter of great historical importance, since without the former, the latter might not have found its theoretical justification. The Chinese neotraditionalists time and again corroborated their agenda by invoking this new politics of the Other in the West. When

21. Liang Qichao, excerpts from *Impressions of Travels in Europe,* in Chen Song, ed., *Collected Essays from the Debate on the Question of Eastern and Western Culture During the May Fourth Period* (*Wusi qianhou dongxi wenhua wenti lunzhan wenxuan*), (Beijing: Zhongguo shehui kexue chubanshe, 1989), 359.

22. Ibid., 349–390.

Liang Shuming noted that the new trend in current Western philosophy was "Eastern in color" (*dongfang secai*),[23] he voiced a shared perception of many of his contemporaries.

The crisis of legitimation of Western culture created by the world war then inadvertently revealed "the regional nature of the modern historical imagination" of the West for the Chinese observer, as Xiaobing Tang has argued, and allowed Liang a critical distance from which to reconceptualize the question of modernity and culture in China.[24] More specifically, the world war *particularized* Western culture as arising from what Liang calls a specific *shidai beijing* ("epochal context"), and exposed its assumption of universality to be false. If modern Western culture is itself merely a particular culture, whose overwhelming problems in the present moment can be plainly seen and criticized, then where does the non-Western thinker look for universality? Liang's solution was to re-examine Chinese culture—which, no longer considered inferior to Western culture (especially by the Westerners), was simply another particular entity as legitimate as the latter—and to construct a new global culture out of a creative integration of the two. This was clearly in step with Bergson's and Eucken's critiques of Enlightenment rationality and modernity.

Liang differentiated himself from both the nativists and the Occidentalists—those who asserted that China has had always had everything the West has had, and those who considered everything Western to be superior to everything from China—and instead affirmed the need to borrow from the West to bring Chinese culture into full play, that is, to use Western research methodology to analyze and organize Chinese culture.[25] He outlined four

23. Liang Shuming, *Eastern and Western Cultures and Their Philosophies* (*Dongxi wenhua ji qi zhexue,* 1921) (Taipei: Liren shuju, 1983), 209.

24. Xiaobing Tang, *Writing a History of Modernity: A Study of the Historical Consciousness of Liang Ch'i-ch'ao* (Ph.D. dissertation, Duke University, 1991), 287. This dissertation is available in a revised book form: *Global Space and the Nationalist Discourse of Modernity: The Historical Thinking of Liang Qichao* (Stanford: Stanford University Press, 1996).

25. Note that this advocacy of using Western methodology to organize Chinese tradition diverges from that of the "Organization of National Treasures" (*zhengli guogu*) movement led by Hu Shi and Gu Jiegang. Liang worked under the assumption that Chinese tradition had much to offer the modern world, and hence needed to be reframed or reinvigorated for modern use. Hu and Gu saw the organization of Chinese tradition as a project of demythification, to show that it contained nothing but "rotten trash" (*liushui lanzhang,* Hu Shi's phrase). For Hu, the organization of national treasures was a way of "assaulting ghosts" and "catching the evil" of Chinese tradition, and was an extension of the Nietzschean "transvaluation of all values" (*chongxin guding yiqie jiazhi*) in May Fourth antitraditionalism. See Hu Shi, "The Organization of National Treasures and 'Assaulting Ghosts'" (*Zhengli guogu yu dagui,* 1927), in *Collected Materials of the Modern Chinese History of Ideas* (*Zhongguo xiandai sixiangshi ziliao jianbian*), ed. Cai Shangsi (Hangzhou: Zhejiang renmin chubanshe, 1983), 2:123–126. For the New Confucianists' disagreement with such views, see Hao Chang, "New Confucianism and the Intellectual Crisis of Contemporary China," in Furth, *Limits of Change,* 286; see also Shen Songqiao, *The Critical Review Group,* 202–203.

steps for the committed youth to follow, which are also steps to the production of a new global culture and of China as a "globalist nation" (*shijie zhuyi de guojia*):

> I wish for our beloved youth to take [these steps]. First, everyone has to maintain a sincere attitude of respect towards and protection of native culture. Second, use Western research methodology to study it so as to discover its true nature. Third, synthesize it and combine it with Western culture to cause a chemical reaction and produce a new cultural system. Fourth, disseminate and expand this new system so that all of humanity will benefit from it.[26]

The assertion of the importance of native culture, as is made clear here, is not based on a nativist rejection of Western culture, but premised on a vision of global magnitude and aims to benefit all mankind. But this global vision first requires, as Liang's particular ordering of the four steps reveals, a fundamental confidence in Chinese culture. By prioritizing cultural confidence, Liang in fact indicates its palpable absence given the strength of May Fourth Occidentalist discourse, and shows his foremost agenda to be a kind of decolonization of consciousness,[27] thereby indirectly implying that the Occidentalists' lack of cultural confidence in China is a form of colonized consciousness.

But in his recommendation of Western research methods to discover the "true nature" of Chinese culture, there appears the nagging question of the relationship between method and content. If Chinese culture is to be examined and categorized according to Western conceptual frameworks, does that change the content of the Chinese culture thus represented? What this recommendation evinces is Liang's essentially non-nativist and nondefensive position, and a kind of cosmopolitanism (though different in cultural orientation from the Occidentalists') that flaunts a bicultural stance, all of which was "encouraged" by the Westerners he encountered. Liang says that it is due to the urging of Europeans that he saw the necessity of advancing Chinese culture: he notes again and again how the many thoughtful Europeans he encountered all exalted the virtue of Chinese culture and in one case even reprimanded him for not sharing Chinese cultural "treasures" with the West. He claims further that Chinese culture has been misunderstood

---

26. Liang Qichao, *Impressions of Travels in Europe*, 390.

27. Zhang Junmai (Carlson Chang), one of the three chief New Confucianists of the 1920s and 1930s, also emphasized the retrieval of cultural confidence: "For all aspects of culture from now on, such as reform in politics and scholarship, the fundamental issue is national confidence. When a nation has confidence, although it is inferior to others in the present moment, it can gradually devise remedial measures. A nation without confidence may become successful for a brief time, but it will eventually decline and then fall." "Tomorrow's Chinese Culture" (*Mingri zhi Zhongguo wenhua*), in *Collected Works of Zhang Junmai (Zhang Junmai ji)*, ed. Huang Kejian (Beijing: Qunyan chubanshe, 1993), 177.

even by the Chinese themselves, and Western methodology must be employed to better understand it. Otherwise, how can the Chinese have been reading Confucius and Li Bai for centuries and yet not have benefited from them?

Liang's conception of the new globalized Chinese culture, then, is based on a simultaneous critical evaluation of both Chinese and Western cultures with each serving as correctives to the other. While criticizing the excess induced by evolutionism and individualism in Western societies, he observes that this excess is being reconsidered and recontained by the philosophies of Bergson, Eucken, and William James (1842–1910), all of whom emphasize individuality as the basis of creative evolution without taking either evolutionism or individualism to materialist extremes.[28] He also uses the Confucian notion of "the exhaustive exercise of one's nature" (*jinxing zhuyi*) as justification for the necessity of developing individualism. Rather than refuting modernity, Liang seeks to revise it. Even his view of these Euro-American philosophers as revisionist modern thinkers rather than anti-moderns points to Liang's fundamental commitment to modernity. This modernity-critique then, is not at all similar to the Western postmodernist rejection of modernity as the oppressive agent of humanity, but rather continues to endorse Western modernity.[29]

Liang's timely trip and publication of *Impressions of Travels in Europe* spoke to a generation of intellectuals dissatisfied with May Fourth Occidentalism. With an awareness of and as a response to the prevailing pessimism towards Western civilization in Western intellectual circles, the neotraditionalist agenda was also given a boost when Liang invited John Dewey (who stayed in China for two years, 1919–1921) and Bertrand Russell (one year in China, 1920–1921) to visit and lecture. Though coming from different philosophical persuasions, Dewey and Russell expressed a shared view in regard to the question of Eastern and Western cultures—that the two should not be hierarchized and should instead be given equal respect and combined to produce a higher form of culture than what the world has known. Dewey was Hu Shi's mentor and therefore his pragmatist thought was often presented by Hu Shi in such a way as to foreground scientism and scientific methodology; still, Dewey's lectures on the syncretism of Eastern and Western cultures were also widely influential. Furthermore, having themselves been educated in the West in the postwar intellectual atmosphere, the returned neotraditionalist intellectuals were steeped in the West's self-critique of its industrial civilization and were thus armed with theoretical knowledge

28. Liang Qichao, *Impressions of Travels in Europe*, 349–390.

29. See the works of Michel Foucault, Jean-François Lyotard, Herbert Marcuse, Jacques Derrida, and others for the insistent postmodern criticism of modernity (rationality, the ideology of progress, and humanism).

of this critique. These several factors contributed to a sustained anti-Occidentalist conceptualization of the role and function of Chinese culture from Beijing to Nanjing, in which milieu the critical and creative writings of Zhu Guangqian (1897–1986), Zhou Zuoren, Fei Ming, Ling Shuhua, and Lin Huiyin—what by 1934 is called *jingpai* writing—emerged.

Among the three major New Confucianists in the 1920s, Liang Shuming's work was probably most controversial, not only because of its immense influence but also because of its inner contradictions. Guy Alitto's study shows how Liang criticized modernization and yet embraced it, and how he defied linear, evolutionary history in the manner of Bergson but then reconfirmed a new teleology of culture and history conceived in terms of development and destination. My own reading of Liang's seminal *Eastern and Western Cultures and their Philosophies* (1921), however, considers what Alitto sees as contradiction as instead one of the modes of the *critical modernity* mentioned above. Instead of considering Liang's thought in terms of a nativism/syncretism problematic, for which ultimate analysis is confined to the task of identifying whether he is asserting a nativist/essentialist or a syncretist position (for these categories are at once too broad and too essentialist in themselves, and Liang himself ostensibly opposed syncretism for its lack of critical spirit),[30] it is more useful to analyze how Liang works out a unique notion of modernity, given that Westernization had already begun in China and could not be reversed. Liang was not antimodern when he condemned technological modernity as the agent which has dehumanized and mechanized life, and which endorsed economic competition and the survival of the fittest mentality so as to objectify people and turn the world into a place of unrest. He was, rather, intent on exposing modernity's limits. And when Liang advocated total Westernization in the same book, he was not contradicting himself, because he asserted the importance of a careful and "fundamental transformation" (*genben gaiguo*) of Western culture. Equally, he asserted the need to critically examine and revive aspects of Chinese culture, again from a nonnativist standpoint. Such a construction of critical modernity was considered conservative or nativist only because it did not endorse the all-out Occidentalist position of the May Fourth movement; in the atmosphere of May Fourth discursive hegemony, to assert native cultural confidence at all was to be dismissed as reactionary.

Liang Shuming's critical thinking on modernity incorporated the philosophies of Bergson and insights from Freudian psychoanalysis and

---

30. Liang Shuming criticized both the essentialist/binary and the syncretic conceptions of Eastern and Western culture in *Eastern and Western Cultures and Their Philosophies*, 21–64. He put Liang Qichao, John Dewey, and Bertrand Russell, essentialist Japanese cultural discourse, and missionary narratives such as George William Knox's *The Spirit of the Orient* in the same category: all had uncritically endorsed essentialism or syncretism.

tried to find parallels between them and Confucianism in what he considered to be their shared celebration of intuition (*zhijue*) over instrumental intellect (*gainian*). He refuted evolutionary, unilinear conceptions of history and cultural development by asserting a multidirectional or multilinear history:

> It is not that the Chinese are walking on the same path as the Westerners, have been slow in their walking, and hence lag behind the West for several tens of *li.* If they are on the same path, then even if one walks slowly, one will surely catch up in the future; but if they are walking on different paths in different directions, then no matter how far the Chinese walk, they will never end up where the Westerners are! For China, this is the case.[31]

It is important to note that neither of Liang's assertions—similarity in Western and Chinese philosophies and the divergent paths of their cultures—are assertions of cultural or historical essentialism, but rather of conjunction and multiplicity. Conjunction insofar as the West would ultimately choose to take the path that China had taken (since there is growing affinity between contemporary Western philosophy and traditional Chinese philosophy); multiplicity insofar as he was able to reinforce the need to rescue the framing of China's problems from terms set solely by the West. Together, these two notions posited the Chinese as subjects of history who must critically evaluate both Chinese and Western cultures without having to borrow blindly those Western frameworks dictated by a problematic modernity. The result would be a reconsidered, critical modernity which accepts the hybridization of modern Chinese culture as a given, but draws a global vision in imagining a new cultural formation through the process of decolonization, empowerment, and active construction. This was later evidenced in his dedication to rural reconstruction projects in the decades after 1921.

Bergson's and Eucken's thought exercised formative influence on Japan- and German-educated Zhang Junmai (Carlson Chang, 1887–1969), who had earlier accompanied Liang Qichao in his travels through Europe. First educated in Waseda University in Japan and exposed to German idealist philosophy there, Zhang studied with Eucken during his first period of study in Germany (1920–1921), and served as interpreter and host when Eucken's disciple Hans Driesch visited China upon Liang's invitation. Eucken, the 1908 Nobel Prize winner, reputedly advised Zhang that German idealism was the Western tradition which could best exert "a fruitful and beneficial effect" on China, for it could strengthen the Confucian tradition of ethical idealism.[32] Zhang was taken with not only German idealist philosophy, of

---

31. Liang Shuming, *Eastern and Western Cultures and Their Philosophies*, 77.
32. Quoted in Hay, *Asian Ideas of East and West*, 141.

which Eucken and Driesch were major proponents, but also German socialism, and even German sinology.[33]

In his 1922 essay entitled "The European Cultural Crisis and the Direction of China's New Culture," Zhang notes the Bergsonian philosophy of
change and Eucken's anti-intellectualism as the new currents in the West
which have replaced Kantian pure rationalism and Darwinian scientism. He
then lays out what he calls a "Chinese cultural policy" (*Zhongguo wenhua
fangzhen*) consisting of four points: (1) The Chinese should achieve cultural
self-determination by not becoming puppets of Western culture, but instead
by autonomously determining what Chinese culture needs. (2) Old Chinese
culture is thoroughly corrupt and is in need of "transfusion," i.e., individualism, democracy, and scientific experimentalism from the West. (3) The importation of Western culture should be critically conducted in the same way
that Chinese culture should be critically evaluated. (4) Differences between
Western and Chinese cultures should be laid out and examined in detail,
and should be allowed to contest each other. What emerges as the winner
will be the "new Chinese culture" (*xin Zhongguo wenhua*).[34] Although there
may be slight differences between Zhang and Liang Shuming in deciding what
of Western culture should be critically incorporated, the basic position—dual
critical evaluation of both Western and Chinese cultures—is shared.

Again like Liang Shuming, Zhang disapproved of the conception of evolutionist, linear history, although his model for this historical perception was
Marxism, with which Liang was somewhat sympathetic as evidenced in his
friendship and a degree of ideological affinity with Li Dazhao. Zhang noted
that the main problem of Marxist materialist dialectics is that it mistakes temporal differences between past and present, and spatial differences and coexistence, as contradictions. He thus considered dialectics to be a unilinear
process that entails contradiction and synthesis, and criticized its evolutionist
assumptions of history; instead, he asserted spatial difference and coexistence
as a different mode of history, which suggests a multilinear and multiple existence and a simultaneous temporality. This spatial multiplicity and temporal
simultaneity is anti-Marxist in nature, and it allows for the affirmation of cultural specificity, difference, and multiplicity. Hence locality is not dismissed
but is seen as organically connected to culture.[35]

33. See two books by Roger B. Jeans, Jr., for a fuller examination of Zhang's intellectual
and political ideas: *Syncreticism in Defense of Confucianism: An Intellectual and Political Biography of
the Early Years of Chang Chün-mai, 1887–1923* (Ph.D. dissertation, George Washington University, 1974), and *Democracy and Socialism in Republican China: The Politics of Zhang Junmai,
1906–1941* (New York: Roman and Littlefield, 1997).

34. Zhang Junmai, "The European Cultural Crisis and the Direction of China's New Culture"
(*Ouzhou wenhua zhi weiji ji Zhongguo xinwenhua zhi chuxiang*), in Chen Song, *Collected Essays*, 452–461.

35. Zhang Junmai, "The Philosophical Background of Our Thought" (*Woren sixiang zhi
zhexue beijing*, 1938), in Cai Shangsi, *Collected Materials*, 4:125–145.

Finally, like Liang Qichao, Zhang also asserted the need to acquire cultural confidence as a necessary corrective to the Occidentalist tendency to destroy all that is Chinese. He condemned both Occidentalists and Marxists as advocating a narrowly defined, superficial scientism,[36] as applying wrong medicine to the symptoms, as forgetting their roots, and as undermining Chinese self-confidence in their earnestness to gain notoriety, all of which are self-destructive and are forms of self-loss.[37] Yet again, this assertion of cultural confidence is couched in a global perspective: "We are a member of this world, and cannot afford not to adopt another's strengths to mend our own shortcomings."[38] Xiong Shili would similarly criticize May Fourth Occidentalism as a series of short-lived, superficial fads produced by a fragmented approach to Western learning, and as an ill-founded denunciation of traditional Chinese culture. Like Liang Shuming, Xiong devoted himself to the creative reformulation of Confucianism, asserting that it is only with a high level of self-knowledge and self-determination that Western culture can be appropriated.[39]

Although these three main figures of New Confucianism diverged on other issues, they shared a conviction in a modernity that examined both Western and Chinese cultures from critical perspectives. The constructive work based on this critical sensibility would be the revival of Confucianism, redefining its relevance and value in all areas of experience, whether social reconstruction, political ideology, moral and ethical values, or metaphysics, and rescuing it from the damage wrecked by the Occidentalists' "toppling of the Confucian hall" (*dadao Kongjia dian*). This new imagining of Confucianism presents it as transcultural and transnational, and according to philosopher He Lin, one of the earliest scholars to study New Confucianism as a school of thought, it revives universal Lu-Wang Confucian values of intuitionism and self-consciousness. These anti-utilitarian and nondivisive values were seen as correctives to the excessive materialism in the West. Hence He Lin notes that the revival of Lu-Wang Confucianism was a result of a comprehensive examination of global cultural changes and transformations.[40] Throughout, however, the New Confucianists advocated Western science (they only criticized the superficial scientism of the May Fourth and the development of weapons, not science per se)[41] and democracy, rescuing these

36. Zhang Junmai, "Science and Philosophy Hold Hands" (*Kexue yu zhexue zhi xishou*, 1933), in Cai Shangsi, *Collected Materials*, 3:602–610.

37. Zhang Junmai, "Tomorrow's Chinese Culture," in *Collected Works of Zhang Junmai*, 197–198.

38. Ibid., 199.

39. Tu Wei-ming, "Hsiung Shih-li's Quest for Authentic Experience," in Furth, *Limits of Change*, 242–275.

40. He Lin, *Chinese Philosophy of the Last Fifty Years* (*Wushi nian lian de Zhongguo zhexue*, 1945), expanded version (Shenyang: Liaoning jiaoyu chubanshe, 1989), 1–23.

41. Hao Chang notes that the New Confucianists revolted against scientism (as a mode of thinking or as the only valid view of reality), but not science (as a useful method for under-

two ideological slogans from the dictates of May Fourth Occidentalism. It is clear, then, that rather than being diametrically opposed to May Fourth Occidentalists, the New Confucianists shared much in common with them, except that their discourse was underscored by "rational" philosophical negotiations in which the May Fourth iconoclasts, in their zeal for the total revolution of culture, were unable to engage. The New Confucianists were as erudite in Western learning as the Occidentalists, if not more so, and their revival of Confucianism was itself filtered through their incorporation of Western methodologies and their knowledge of how Western philosophers perceived its merit.

Similarities between the May Fourth Occidentalists and the *Critical Review* circle are also easy to locate, and this again forces us to rethink the epithet "conservatism" in characterizing this group. Harvard-educated Mei Guangdi (1890–1945) was a friend of Hu Shi's before the latter became famous as an iconoclast in the May Fourth scene: both were educated in the U.S. and both saw the need to reconsider the Chinese tradition from Western perspectives. Hu Shi would advocate the total overthrow of Chinese tradition and Mei would emphasize the revival of Confucianism from the perspective of New Humanism. They shared the conviction that China needed the West: their differences lay in different conceptions of *what* features of the West China needed. It was the content and attitude of the Occidentalists' Westernization campaign, not Westernization itself, that was criticized when they were accused of advocating "fake Europeanization" (*wei Ouhua*).

Mei Guangdi, another Harvard-educated thinker Wu Mi (1894–1978), and a few other intellectuals in the *Critical Review* circle attacked the May Fourth Occidentalists, using language that was as polemical as the Occidentalists' own. In a 1922 article, Wu Mi accused the Occidentalists of propagating what in the West was considered "dregs and poison," comparing them to a long-sick person believing no one but a quack and taking arsenic every day. In their rejection of tradition, the Occidentalists were likened to someone who "throws out the baby along with the bathwater," quoting a common Western saying. Asserting instead that the best of Western culture (Greco-Roman philosophy) is compatible with the best of Chinese culture (Confucianism and Buddhism), Wu Mi maintained that Europeanization does not require the destruction of national treasures.[42] Mei Guangdi used similar phrases in attacking the Occidentalists as imitators of the West, taking only the "dregs" of Western culture, hence their importation of Europeanization was actually a form of "slander" of European culture. The other three points

---

standing the objective world). See his "New Confucianism and the Intellectual Crisis in Contemporary China," 283–285.

42. Wu Mi, "On the New Cultural Movement" (*Lun xinwenhua yundong*, 1922), in Chen Song, *Collected Essays*, 555–569.

of attack included the following: (1) The Occidentalists are not thinkers but sophists who misrepresent information. This can be seen in their espousal of evolutionism, which has already been rejected by the West, and in their oppositional construction of the relationship between the vernacular and the literary language, when in fact the difference between the two is stylistic, not essential. (2) They are not scholars but fame-seekers who are motivated by the desire for self-advancement, which is merely a new version of "the dream of success at the civil service examinations" (*keju meng*). (3) They are not educators but politicians, manipulating mass psychology and exploiting the mass's weakness and lack of knowledge in order to satisfy their own ambition for fame and advancement.[43]

The *Critical Review* group's agenda involved two main thrusts: disseminating traditional learning and importing Western learning. To do either, one must critically and rationally evaluate and incorporate those aspects that are not essentially Eastern or Western, old or new, but trans-East/West, universal, and not bound to specific contexts. The universal expressions of Chinese culture can be found chiefly in Confucianism, and those of Western culture can be found, in their view, in New Humanism, Hellenism (Greek and Roman philosophy), and classical Western literature (Dante, Shakespeare, Hugo, etc.).[44] Rejecting an essentialist, oppositional construction of East/West cultures, they sought instead to see the cultural encounter between the East and the West, facilitated by modern technology such as the postal system, as an opportunity to be "celebrated" and taken advantage of, so that through "thorough research, precise criticism, and exact procedures" a new global culture could be produced and disseminated.[45]

Along with Confucianism, New Humanism constituted the epistemological foundation of the *Critical Review* group. In the United States, New Humanism was a minor philosophical movement that opposed Darwinism, Marxism, pragmatism, materialism (scientism), and literary romanticism and naturalism, and advocated the recovery of the human law, self-discipline, traditional moral and spiritual values, and a return to classics.[46] Mei and Wu were both disciples of the chief proponent of New Humanism at Harvard University, Irving Babbitt, and saw in New Humanism the validation of Confucianism, for Babbitt himself had high regard for Confucianism as sanctioning a humanist set of values. In some ways, what New Humanism opposed was more revealing than what it advocated—evolutionism, instrumental sci-

---

43. Mei Guangdi, "A Critique of the New Culture Promoters" (*Ping tichang xinwenhua zhe*, 1922), in Cai Shangsi, *Collected Materials*, 2:232–238.

44. For a thorough analysis of the *Critical Review* circle and their work, see Shen Songqiao, *The Critical Review Group*, 202–234.

45. Mei Guangdi, "A Critique of the New Culture Promoters," 238.

46. J. David Hoeveler, Jr., *The New Humanism: A Critique of Modern America, 1900–1940* (Charlottesville: University Press of Virginia, 1977), 3–27.

entism, mass democracy, and extreme individualism—and these oppositions found contextual resonances in China because of the Occidentalists' advocacy of these exact same ideologies. This fact proved to the *Critical Review* group that New Humanism had universal value and could serve a critical function.

While New Confucianism found its intellectual endorsement in the continental philosophy of Bergson and Eucken, the *Critical Review* group found it in American New Humanism, and the divergence in their agendas probably results from different intellectual heritages. But where the two groups converged was with the perception that Western culture was in the process of decline and Chinese culture needed to be revitalized, and this revitalization was seen to be of global significance. In the radically antitraditional atmosphere of the May Fourth era, it was therefore important to them as a first step to assert confidence in traditional culture, which readily gave the Occidentalists a reason to conflate them with the National Essence thinkers of the late Qing period and brand them as conservatives. This confidence in traditional culture begins on the local level and extends to the global level—hence the emphasis is on the universal, the transnational, and their corresponding elements in the best of Western culture. The aesthetics of the Beijing school was in no measure a call to "return to tradition," but a conscious rethinking of the properties of May Fourth modernity to construct a new, universal modernity out of materials both from China and the West. In this sense, we may say that the difference between May Fourth Occidentalism and *jingpai* philosophy and aesthetics is a difference in the conception of globalism: for the former, to be global means to become as Westernized as possible; for the latter, it means to be Chinese and Western at the same time.

Critics have sometimes challenged the elitist assumptions of the *Critical Review* group as undemocratic, and the philosophical musings of New Confucianism as obscure, irrelevant, or simply a repeat of old syncretist arguments. In the profuse attacks on Liang Shuming in the aftermath of the publication of his *Eastern and Western Cultures and their Philosophies,* development, progress, and evolutionism were reasserted time and again.[47] Hu Shi, for instance, warned the youth in 1930 that they should not be deceived by the neotraditionalists and follow their "propensity for self-aggrandizement."[48] A book on the neotraditionalists appeared in Taiwan as part of the series on modern Chinese literature as late as 1980, and it was tellingly entitled *Ob-*

47. The publication of *Eastern and Western Cultures and Their Philosophies* was responded to widely by the Occidentalists, in contrast to what Guy Alitto takes to be simple dismissal without engaged criticism. These responses were written by Hu Shi, Li Shicen, Zhang Dongsun, and others.

48. Hu Shi, "Introducing My Own Thought" (*Jieshao woziji de sixiang,* 1930), in *Which Path Should We Take?* (*Women zou natiaolu*) (Taipei: Yuanliu chubanshe, 1986), 227–245.

stacles to the New Literature Movement (Xinwenxue yundong de zuli).[49] The Chinese Communist Party repressed the memory of neotraditionalism for decades until the 1990s. And of course the discourse on Chinese neotraditionalism in the U.S. has also considered it mainly as a form of cultural conservatism, an anomaly in the May Fourth–oriented telling of modern Chinese history. It is May Fourth hegemony in the writing of modern Chinese cultural history, which was instituted persistently by the Communist Party in China and sporadically by the Nationalist Party in Taiwan for different ideological purposes, that has resulted in this facile dismissal. Lung-kee Sun captured well the operation of May Fourth hegemony in post-1949 China when he noted that the "reapotheosis of May Fourth" was fundamental to the victory of communism in China, for the latter shared the former's evolutionary paradigm of history.[50] For the Nationalist Party, the negation and endorsement of neotraditionalism, especially New Confucianism, served two divergent but equally instrumental purposes: to be modern meant to adopt the May Fourth project of enlightenment, but to assert cultural authenticity as a basis for political nationalism meant to project the Nationalist Party's image as the capitalist Confucian, spokesperson of both modernization and cultural nationalism. And judging from the revival of Confucianism in the 1990s, in increasingly capitalist China as well as in other successful capitalist Confucian economies such as Singapore, an intimate linkage exists between Confucianism and capitalism in that Confucian rationality and ethics is considered conducive to economic development. This is indeed an ironic historical development for New Confucianism, which originally set out to critique excessive materialism in the capitalist societies of the West.

In the typical "Eastern" nationalist imagination, the endorsement of Enlightenment progress contradicted the need to assert cultural distinctiveness, but the Chinese neotraditionalism of the *Critical Review* group and New Confucianism neither adopted such a nationalist stance[51] nor desired to stand altogether outside the thematic of Western modernity, as Gandhi did in India. Instead, modernity was a fact to be reckoned with, to be debated, to be better defined and delineated, all with an eye towards the native cultural tra-

49. Chen Jingzhi, *Obstacles to the New Literature Movement* (Taipei: Chengwen Chubanshe, 1980).

50. Lung-kee Sun, "Historian's Warp: Problems in Textualizing the Intellectual History of Modern China," *positions* 2:2 (Fall 1994): 366–367.

51. Both John Plamenatz and Horace B. Davis see the "Eastern type of nationalism" as "disturbed and ambivalent," due to its dilemma of (1) having to imitate the West in order to try to be consistent with the conditions of historical progress (which undermines their cultural specificity), while (2) having to reject the West in order to assert its national identity. This economy of imitation and rejection of the imitated object makes the Eastern type of nationalism a site of struggle, and in the end the modernizing attitude always wins over and tradition is forsaken. Cited in Chatterjee, *Nationalist Thought and the Colonial World*, 2–18.

dition, so that modernity would no longer remain the sole property of the West, but would rather be hybridized, revised, and rewritten, and able to be claimed by the Chinese as well without their losing a fundamental sense of cultural confidence. The Chinese tradition was to be handled similarly, with an eye towards Western cultural traditions so that it would no longer remain the sole property of China but rather be hybridized, revised, and rewritten for larger purposes extending to the world. In such imagining, the tradition/ modernity and China/West dyads become irrelevant, because what is local becomes at the same time global and vice versa.

The cultural agency implicated in this globalist thinking, however, was not possible without endorsement by contemporary philosophical trends in the West, and this also returns us to the question of derivation that South Asian historian Partha Chatterjee has so eloquently analyzed vis-à-vis Indian nationalism. For one, it was the explanatory power of Western philosophical shifts to anti-Enlightenment ideas in the form of vitalism, anti-intellectualism, and New Humanism which helped justify the neotraditionalist agenda in China. Secondly, by the early twentieth century, both the anti-Confucian and pro-Confucian arguments had been made in Western missionary or diplomatic narratives of China, of which there were many.[52] Linkages between May Fourth discourse and the anti-Confucian missionary narratives, or between neotraditionalism and pro-Confucian missionary narratives, cannot yet be directly established except that these narratives were occasionally brought up in the writings of both camps, while the linkages with Western philosophical currents were made forcefully by both camps to mark their cultural legitimacy. Based on these linkages, can we say that Chinese neotraditionalism was also derivative?

In Chatterjee's consideration of nationalism as a derivative discourse, he is mainly interested in delineating the indebtedness of Indian nationalism to Enlightenment reason, to which India had no previous historical linkage; for Chinese neotraditionalism, in contrast, the Western philosophical discourse of which they were derivative actually included a compelling consideration of Chinese tradition itself. In other words, a cultural explanation can be found for the historical conjunction between Chinese neotraditionalism and anti-Enlightenment Western philosophy: for the Chinese neotraditionalists to borrow arguments from anti-Enlightenment Western philosophy was a way of validating the Chinese tradition itself. This then poses a different set of problems than Chatterjee's Indian nationalism, where nationalism and native culture necessarily contradicted each other because the former was

---

52. For two anti-Confucian positions see Arthur Smith, *Chinese Characteristics* (Shanghai: North-China Herald, 1890), and Chester Holcombe, *The Real Chinese Question* (New York: Dodd, Mead and Company, 1900); for a pro-Confucian position, see George William Knox, *The Spirit of the Orient* (New York: Thomas Y. Crowell & Co., 1906).

a discourse borrowed from the colonizer and the latter was a means of resistance to the colonizer. If we say that the West used the Chinese tradition as a counterdiscourse to Enlightenment ideology, in a characteristic incorporation of non-Western material for Eurocentric purposes,[53] this recognition or endorsement meant to the neotraditionalists that the Chinese tradition as such could harmoniously coexist with modernity, and that they could be Chinese and Western at the same time. This conscious desire to be both is perhaps a more egalitarian form of cosmopolitanism than the exclusively Westernized vision of the May Fourth intellectual who conflated cosmopolitanism with Occidentalism.

This cosmopolitanism of the neotraditionalists had its limits, however, as I have suggested earlier in the chapter. Other limitations I have not yet mentioned include the following: like their May Fourth counterparts (be they liberal or Marxist), the neotraditionalists ascribed to "India" all those elements which comprise the undesirable "East," and they also preferred Hellenism over Hebraism. Recall Hu Shi's assertion that everything that went wrong in Chinese culture was caused by the importation of Indian Buddhism, Chen Duxiu's characterization of Indian culture as the most regressive of all, and Liang Shuming's contention that China needed to reject the "Indian attitude" (defined as otherworldly and backward-looking).[54] On Hebraism, the *Critical Review* group followed Matthew Arnold's position in his famous *Culture and Anarchy* (1869), denouncing it and embracing Hellenism as the best of Western civilization. Liang Shuming saw Hebraism as being just as otherworldly as Indian Buddhism and hence irrelevant to current Chinese needs. Recall too how Guo Moruo eulogized Greek mythology as a celebration of cosmic masculinity, power, persistence, and so on.

In all these modern Chinese forms of cosmopolitanism, then—whether asymmetrical Occidentalism, internationalized socialism, or a more egalitarian neotraditionalism—we find gradated procedures of Othering. Japan needed China to be its backward Other when it sought to represent itself as the Westernized modernizer in Asia, and China needed India to be its Other when it sought to emerge as a modern nation. In a different context, as I will make clear in chapters 7 and 8, "woman" in this neotraditionalist cosmopolitanism was a theoretical, not a social, category. A recuperative neotraditonalism did not challenge, and perhaps could not have challenged, Confucian and Taoist gender cosmologies and the social relations they engendered.

53. See my introduction for a discussion of Western aesthetic modernist appropriation of Chinese material.

54. The comment by Hu Shi is mentioned in Tu Wei-ming, "Hsiung Shih-li's Quest for Authentic Experience," 251. Chen Duxiu's remark is from "Tagore and Eastern Culture" (*Taige'er yu dongfang wenhua*, 1924), in Chen Song, *Collected Essays*, 625–627. Liang Shuming's phrase is in *Eastern and Western Cultures and Their Philosophies*, 239.

Another, more crucial problem plaguing the neotraditionalist conception of culture has to do with what constitutes "Chinese culture." Although the neotraditionalists conceived of the China-West cultural relationship in nonessentialist terms, with equal participants in overlapping and complementary dialogues with each other, they could not avoid totalizing "Chinese culture" as such. By prioritizing Confucianism over Buddhism, Taoism, and other popular forms of culture for that matter, they downplayed the inherent diversity of Chinese culture itself in order to locate those particular elements of Chinese culture allegedly endowed with the capacity to become universal. In this particular sense, they are very much counterparts to their May Fourth colleagues. In trying to solve questions of Chinese culture, they made totalistic judgments and evaluations of what "Chinese culture" ought to have been and ought to be.

AESTHETIC DISCOURSE: THE PRODUCTION OF THE LOCAL

In the aftermath of May Fourth iconoclasm, neotraditionalist cultural formation was extensive, and it included a significant literary component. With the exception of the *Critical Review* group, which mainly operated out of Nanjing due to its members' appointments at Southeastern University (*Dongnan daxue*), most of the New Confucianists, critics, and writers who contributed to the neotraditionalist formation were gathered in Beijing. A group of literary theorists and writers later known as the Beijing School started a sustained critique of the May Fourth legacy from a position similar to the neotraditional philosophers.[55] In synergic conjunction with the philosophical-cultural discourses of New Confucianism and the *Critical Review,* they brought similar concerns to the aesthetic and formal dimensions of literary writing. Soon "Beijing" would take on the status of a cultural sign or attitude, set up in opposition to the highly Westernized sign that "Shanghai" came to represent. Starting as a symbol of locality, "Beijing" became significant as the symbol of a *jingpai* culture which simultaneously opposed both May Fourth Occidentalism and the commercialism of the Shanghai School, *haipai.*

The geopolitical situation in Beijing was partially accountable for the rise of *jingpai,* and this suggests how "locality" as a cultural and theoretical conception in *jingpai* writing was also geopolitically grounded. Even though *jing-*

---

55. A noteworthy example is Xiao Qian's (b. 1910) comment that May Fourth writers were "prisoners newly released from prison." He describes the cultural and literary arena of the May Fourth as "a bustling bird market, a madhouse. When they were irritated, they screamed their lungs out; when they got hysterical, they let loose with shrill laughter. The poor jumped to their feet and shouted out their demands; the sexually frustrated went so far as to strip themselves naked in public." See his "Ideals and the Future" (*Lixiang yu chulu,* 1935), in *Selected Writings of Xiao Qian* (*Xiao Qian xuanji*) (Chengdu: Sichuan renmin chubanshe, 1983), 4:35.

pai writers evoked various sites of locality besides Beijing (Zhou Zuoren's Shaoxing, Fei Ming's Huangmei county in Hunan), Beijing was the prototypical locality in which most of them wrote, published, and in which their conception of locality became increasingly integral to their aesthetic theories. In the spring of 1926 the Beijing government of warlord Duan Qirui, in a sweeping move to quell dissent, sent out warrants for the arrest of fifty radical intellectuals and college professors, including such celebrities as Lu Xun and Zhou Zuoren. This purge followed on the heels of a bloody massacre of unarmed protesters in the March 18 demonstrations earlier that year. Coupled with a fiscal crisis which forced teachers to go for months without pay at the nine universities in Beijing, this purge caused an exodus of intellectuals and writers from Beijing to the south, most notably to Shanghai. By 1927, Shanghai was considered to have eclipsed Beijing as the cultural center of China, and Beijing was also soon to be deprived of its centuries-old political importance when the Nationalist government established Nanjing as the new Chinese capital in 1928 and renamed Beijing "Beiping." With the departure of many of the May Fourth cultural and literary leaders and having lost its political status (which also formed the basis for much of its economic livelihood), Beijing became, for the intellectuals who stayed, a time and space much altered from being the fervid center of May Fourth controversy. On the one hand, the corruption and violence of warlord politics discouraged intellectuals from engagement with politically sensitive issues, thus sequestering the city from the kind of volatile political and ideological debates prevalent in Shanghai. On the other hand, the powerful invasion of Western technological culture did not engulf Beijing as it did Shanghai, prompting David Strand to call Beijing a "twentieth century walled city" whose mode of economic operation was largely preindustrial and whose transportation was for the most part conducted by rickshaws rather than streetcars.[56]

To emphasize the geopolitical locality of Beijing in the constitution of *jingpai* is not, however, to reduce the conception of *jingpai* into essentialist categories or qualities associated with the city of Beijing alone. Others have pointed out that Beijing represented the *xiangtu Zhongguo* (rural China) sensibility, for which the critique of capitalist/materialist culture was a given (especially in reference to the 1934–1935 debate between the *jingpai* and the *haipai*).[57] A nonutilitarian aesthetics of restraint, concision, leisure, mildness, traditionalism, and lyricism was said to be the natural consequence of this

56. David Strand also notes that the introduction of the streetcar caused an unprecedented riot in 1929 when the rickshawmen nearly destroyed the streetcar system, which suggests the persistence of the preindustrial economic system as ingrained in Beijing's economy and culture. See his *Rickshaw Beijing: City People and Politics in the 1920s* (Berkeley: University of California Press, 1989).

57. In 1934, Shen Congwen, at the time editor of the literary supplement to *Dagong Daily* (*Dagong bao*) in Tianjin, wrote an article called "On the Shanghai School" (*Lun haipai*) criti-

sensibility.[58] Setting *jingpai* against *haipai*, studies have constructed reified and essentialized categories of opposition and concluded that *jingpai* represents the rural Chinese perspective, and *haipai* the *yangchang,* "foreign-city" Chinese.[59] Hence the general perception that *jingpai* is more "Chinese" than *haipai,* while *haipai* is more "Western," as if what constituted "Chinese-ness" were a set of unchanging characteristics beyond which lay that which is non-Chinese. Granted that geopolitical context affects culture, the sum total of culture cannot be reduced to geopolitical attributes alone.

The dichotomous reading of *jingpai* and *haipai* tends to reduce the question of Chinese modernity to a set of reified, simplistic, outdated categories of cultural identification, and cannot articulate the complexities and challenges the two groups pose for the cultural historian, since what differentiates the two groups in cultural terms is much less obvious than previously construed. They could be said to have represented two distinct ways of imagining Chinese modernity, but they were all committed cosmopolitans, even though their approaches to cosmopolitanism were different. Here, my main divergence from previous discussions of *jingpai* and *haipai* is to extricate the discussion from a nationalist politics of culture. My reading of the works of Zhou Zuoren and Zhu Guangqian, the two most prominent theorists of *jingpai,* will show that their conception of neotraditionalist aesthetics, much like the New Confucianists' and the *Critical Review* group's, was not a nativist "return" to an essentialized Chinese tradition, but in effect a valorization of locality based on a new conception of the relationship between the local and

<hr />

cizing the commercial orientation of certain writers, although not merely those from Shanghai. Contrary to Shen's intention, the ensuing responses and criticism polarized the Shanghai School and the Beijing School, making them literary adversaries. The term "Shanghai School" came to have a strong pejorative sense, connoting selling out to commercial culture, kowtowing to the government, and resorting to gossip and plagiarism for fame and profit. These writers were mostly associated with the earlier Mandarin Ducks and Butterflies school, but the term "Shanghai School" was sometimes mistakenly used to designate all Shanghai writers, which was the reason for the heated debate. For some of the important essays in the debate, see Shen's "About the Shanghai School" (*Guanyu haipai*), in *Collected Works of Shen Congwen* (*Shen Congwen wenji*) (Hong Kong and Guangzhou: Sanlian shudian and Huacheng chubanshe, 1985), 12:158–162, 162–165. See also Du Heng [as Su Wen], "Writers in Shanghai" (*Wenren zai Shanghai*), *Les Contemporaines* 4:2 (December 1933): 281–282.

58. See such studies on the *jingpai* as Wu Fuhui, "A Comparative Study of the Beijing and Shanghai Schools of Fiction" (*Jingpai haipai xiaoshuo bijiao yanjiu*), *Studies of Modern and Contemporary Chinese Literature* (*Zhongguo xiandai dangdai wenxue yanjiu*) (October 1987): 199–204, and Yang Yi, "The Cultural Causes and Aesthetic Attitudes of the Beijing and Shanghai Schools of Fiction" (*Jingpai he haipai de wenhua yinyuan ji shenmei xingtai*), *Research on Modern and Contemporary Chinese Literature* (*Zhongguo xiandai dangdai wenxue yanjiu*) 6 (1996): 83–93.

59. The word *yangchang* was commonly used to refer to Shanghai and evoked associations of commercialism and foreignness, with a possible implication of decadence and immorality. This dichotomy of rural versus *yangchang* was set up by Yang Yi.

the global in nonessentialist, noncontradictory terms. If for the New Confucianists and the *Critical Review* group the local was emblematized by Confucianism, for *jingpai* critics and writers the local was a spatialized conception of the culture of a given locality that in its particularity equally has claims to the universal.

The impetus for the valorization of the local in this context poses important questions of cultural modernity. I have mentioned earlier how Liang Qichao's travelogue marked the moment when the Eurocentric universal was challenged and the "West" as such was constructed as another particularity (just as Chinese culture had been seen during the May Fourth era). This recognition of both Chinese and Western cultures as particularities promised the possible recognition of universality in either or both. That is to say, if all cultures are particular, then claims to the universal can be made by all cultures on behalf of those elements in their domain that best serve the world and thus have universal applicabilities. This was the argument for the global significance of Confucianism made by New Confucianism and the *Critical Review* group. When the universal is released from the grip of the West, it is open to inclusions from the non-West. In this conception, then, the local is not opposed to the global, but becomes the site of potential for the universal.

Such a production of the local is profusely illustrated by the critical works of Zhou Zuoren and Zhu Guangqian. As early as 1922, Zhou Zuoren advocated the notion of "Ancient/modern/Chinese/foreign school" (*gujin zhongwai pai*) as exemplifying an ideology of "tolerance" (his own English word).[60] By the time he decided to stay in Beijing and not follow the exodus of intellectuals to the south, he was already in the process of formulating a theory of aesthetics that would depart substantially from his May Fourth advocacy of an evolutionist conception of humanism. Most critics, steeped in May Fourth language, have seen this shift in Zhou as the transformation of a cultural vanguard to a conservative, a rebel to a hermit, without seriously questioning their own assumptions about what radicalism and conservatism entail.[61] They emphasize Beijing's isolation from the rest of the country to explain Zhou's turn to more "hermetic," aestheticist views.

But Beijing in the 1920s and 1930s was by no means a cultural backwater disassociated from the rest of China. Preeminent literary journals such as *Literature Magazine* (*Wenxue zazhi*, May–August 1937 and June 1947–November 1948), *Literary Supplement to the Dagong Daily* (*Dagongbao*

---

60. Zhou Zuoren, "Ancient/modern/Chinese/foreign school" (*Gujin Zhongwai pai*, 1922), in *Representative Works of Zhou Zuoren* (*Zhou Zuoren daibiaozuo*), ed. Zhang Juxiang (Zhengzhou: Huanghe wenyi chubanshe, 1987), 58.

61. See for instance David E. Pollard, "Chou Tso-jen [Zhou Zuoren]: A Scholar Who Withdrew," in Furth, *Limits of Change*, 332–356, and his *A Chinese Look at Literature: The Literary Values of Chou Tso-jen [Zhou Zuoren] in Relation to Tradition* (Berkeley: University of California Press, 1973).

wenyi fukan, 1941–1944), *Xuewen Monthly* (*Xuewen yuekan*, May 1934–?), *Literature Quarterly* (*Wenxue jikan*, January 1934–December 1935), *Thread of Talk* (*Yusi*, November 1924–October 1927 in Beijing; December 1927–March 1930 in Shanghai), *Contemporary Review* (*Xiandai pinglun*, December 1924–December 1928), *Water Star* (*Shuixing*, October 1934–June 1935), *Camel Grass* (*Luotuocao*, May 1930–November 1930), and many other journals were based in Beijing. The Shanghai-based magazine *Crescent Moon* (*Xinyue*) had close associations with the Beijing circle, and the Nanjing-based *Critical Review* of course shared many views in common with them. There were also concerted efforts to create a community of writers and scholars in Beijing: a "salon culture" (*shalong wenhua*) emerged through Zhu Guangqian's poetry reading meetings at his house (themselves a continuation of Wen Yiduo's 1920s Picai alley salon in Xidan), Lin Huiyin's famous "Madam's Salon" (*taitai keting*), and the monthly gatherings organized by Xiao Qian at the Laijinyu Studio Teahouse located in the southwest corner of the Central Park.[62]

Susan Daruvala's research on Zhou Zuoren's work has shown that Zhou by no means became a cultural nativist in these post–May Fourth years, but instead imagined a nonnationalist localism. Daruvala points out that like the Japanese philosopher Watsuji Tetsurō (1886–1960), whose *Fūdo* (*Climate and Culture*) was a classic localist text in Japan, Zhou was interested in finding a third option besides a "suspect Euro-universalism and a narrow nationalism." Based on his readings of Heidegger, Watsuji sought to make up "the lack in Western philosophy of a spatial basis for man's self-identification, in addition to time," and this spatial basis is the sum total of the environment, or the climate.[63] Similarly, Zhou sought to deliver literature from both universalist and nationalist confines. Zhou's main discontent with May Fourth literature, he revealed later, was its instrumentalist conception of literature in general and the literature's proximity to nationalist politics in particular. Taking a pluralistic approach, Zhou emphasized the diversity of localities and thereby wrested culture away from the narrative of unilinear cultural development. Here the cultural imagination takes a spatial turn rather than a tem-

---

62. Yang Yi, "Cultural Causes and Aesthetic Attitudes," 83. Also see Yan Jiayan, *Schools of Modern Chinese Fiction* (*Zhongguo xiandai xiaoshuo liupai shi*) (Beijing: Renmin wenxue chubanshe, 1989), 205–248.

63. According to Daruvala's summary, the monsoon type of climate includes Japan and China, where unrelenting humidity and terrifying natural disasters such as typhoons and floods on the one hand and life-giving vegetation on the other induce a resigned and passive attitude; the desert type induces aggressiveness as survivors also need to submit to the power of the group for their survival; the meadow type includes Europe, where good weather induces the development of reason. This typology of culture determined by climate is in some ways reminiscent of Liang Shuming's typology. Susan Daruvala, *Zhou Zuoren and the Alternative Chinese Response to Modernity* (Ph.D. dissertation, University of Chicago, 1993), 86–89.

poral one: multiplicity of localities in their simultaneity and difference undermine the unilinearity and uniformity of time.

Zhou's localism, in this context, was a buffer against "the ideological demands of the nation," which dictated a vision of native culture as a unified whole within the nation-state. Hence it constituted a refusal of both the nationalist and the Occidentalist prescription that Chinese culture must serve as the "essentialized civilizational 'other' to the West,"[64] a refusal of both the Eurocentric universal and the analogous universalism underpinning May Fourth Occidentalism. Commenting on May Fourth writing, Zhou notes that "It was too abstract, universalistic, prescriptive, and unable to express individuality truthfully or powerfully. The result was of course monotony. Our hope is to abandon these self-imposed shackles and to freely express the individuality which has grown from the soil."[65] Contrary to its professed commitment to individualism, Zhou points out that the May Fourth universalistic agenda actually undermined precisely what it set out to promote. The romantic exploration of subjectivity in May Fourth discourse to a large extent dictated that individualism be diametrically opposed to anything Chinese. Zhou Zuoren argued instead that choosing a traditional lineage to one's cultural position should itself be construed as an act of individualism, and that the legitimacy of that individualism should not be circumscribed by Western standards. Hence the spatialized particularity of a given locale should also constitute a legitimate site of individualism—the "individuality that has grown from the soil." May Fourth discourse, temporalizing individualism as a quality of the modern West that needed to be incorporated fully by the Chinese at the expense of their own tradition, is here replaced by Zhou's spatialized imagination, in which a multiplicity of localities and particularities better enunciate the spirit of individualism as the basic respect of individual choice and inclination.

If nationalism as an imagined community required a linear imagining of time as a homogeneous entity,[66] then the spatialized, heterogeneous time of multifarious localities resists the nationalist imagination bound to the nation-state. Daruvala cogently illustrates this fact when she compares the different ways in which Zhou Zuoren and his famous brother Lu Xun construct the locality of Shaoxing. In Lu Xun's work, Shaoxing is the embodiment of the past, where the modern intellectual returns only to find despair and alienation, while for Zhou Zuoren it is never evoked as the site of the past, but rather as the site of a distinct local culture that in its particularity speaks vol-

---

64. Daruvala, *Zhou Zuoren and the Alternative Chinese Response*, 20–33, 289–310.

65. Zhou Zuoren, "Locality and Literature" (*Difang yu wenyi*, 1923), in *About Dragons* (*Tan long ji*) (Shanghai: kaiming shudian, 1930), 12. The translation here is largely based on that of Susan Daruvala, *Zhou Zuoren and the Alternative Chinese Response*, 199.

66. See Benedict Anderson, *Imagined Communities* (London: Verso, 1992).

umes about cultural diversity, difference, and multiplicity. There is a conti-
guity of relationships among nationalism, linear temporality, and antitraditionalism for the Third World nation, and Zhou's post–May Fourth stance
is to reject all three.

Zhou's critique of the May Fourth universalistic assertion of linear temporality, along with his emphasis on locality, is also manifest in his assertion
of cyclical time. Criticizing linear temporality, he notes:

> Shallow scholars have tried to periodize time either in terms of the twentieth
> century, the successful completion of the Northern Expedition, or peasant mil-
> itary uprisings, saying that a new world is immanent and there will be great
> changes, that this new world will be absolutely different from the past. It is as
> if all preexisting human beings have suddenly become extinct and new human
> beings are either falling from the sky, emerging from the earth, or jumping
> out from parachutes, as if these are two species of human beings. This is the
> problem of shallow learning.[67]

While New Confucianists repudiated linear temporality on philosophical
grounds, Zhou Zuoren here does so by appealing to a sense of continuity
and repetition. In his seminal *The Origin of Modern Chinese Literature* (*Zhongguo xinwenxue de yuanliu,* 1932), he would expound his notion of cyclical literary history as a way to link the present with various moments in the past.
History is here experienced as variety in repetition or repetition in variety,
with each historical moment marking its difference as well as its inevitable
link to the past. He accomplished this by providing a typology of Chinese
literature as having two divergent emphases throughout history—there are
works which remain constant and defy the passage of time, and others which
retain the imprints of time. He argued that the history of Chinese literature is the fluctuation between these two poles of aesthetic and pragmatic/
instrumentalist works. Whenever political power is decentered, the aesthetic,
what he calls the "literature of self-expression" (*shi yan zhi*), flourishes; whenever the central government has the empire under effective control, the pragmatic agenda of "literature as carrier of the Way" (*wen yi zai dao*) predomi-
nates. These two trends alternately dominated the literary scene throughout
Chinese history.

Thus modern Chinese literature, in its emphasis on individual expression,
was in fact a repetition of and tribute to the late-Ming literary formation of
the Gong'an and Jingling schools of writing. Zhou contended that the tenets
of Gong'an writers were very similar to those of Hu Shi (minus Western
thought): Hu Shi's "Eight Don'ts," for example, could find their antecedents
in Gong'an writers' advocacy of "direct expression of the soul without the

---

67. Zhou Zuoren, "On Reading Behind Closed Doors" (*Bimen dushu lun,* 1928), in *Collected
Essays of Zhou Zhoren* (*Zhitang wenji*) (Shanghai: Tianma shudian, 1933), 32.

restraints of formality" (*du shu xingling bu ju getao*).[68] Furthermore, both the late-Ming trend and modern Chinese literature rejected "imitational classicism" and supported "spontaneity, idiosyncrasy, contemporariness, truthfulness to one's own expression and understanding . . . , and belief in continuity in literature (even if it manifests itself in reaction against, not conformity with)."[69] The late-Ming trend also extolled a fresh formalism that emphasized craftsmanship and concision of expression, against the archaism of the Former and Latter Seven Masters, and Zhou himself would theorize modern literature in these terms, attributing these qualities most prominently to the *jingpai* writer Fei Ming. Here, Zhou is claiming the legitimacy of *jingpai* aesthetics in terms of the late-Ming trend, and simultaneously claiming *jingpai* aesthetics as the true embodiment of the modern spirit. By defining the modernity of Chinese literature in terms of the late-Ming trend, and by finding its prime example in *jingpai* writing, Zhou's endeavor is nothing less than redefining what is most authentically "modern."

This authentic modernity, for Zhou Zuoren, involves both a sustained theoretical inquiry into the concept of locality, and a set of formal and aesthetic characteristics. First of all, a poetics of locality, where locality is seen as the sum total of social customs and native conditions, would emphasize *bense* (native hue) and *quwei* (flavor). In talking about Zhejiang province, he notes how its culture acquired a unique individuality from its environment (*fengtu*), which in turn engendered the two strands of culture that are prominent in Zhejiang—the lofty aesthetics of Ming-dynasty painter Xu Wei, and the sarcastic essays of Qing-dynasty scholar-poet Mao Xihe.[70] A piece of writing marked by locality is also less transparent in meaning, which satisfies the requirement of opaqueness in good writing. Opaqueness refers to the qualities of *kuse* (bitterness and astringency), where *se* refers to the stylistic "preference for the rough or rasping over the smooth, the opaque over the clear, the implicit over the explicit, the dense over the thin."[71] In describing Fei Ming's stylistic tendencies, Zhou uses such aesthetic qualifiers as *qipi* (rare and peculiar), *shengla* (raw and spicy), and *huise* (obscure and astringent).[72] While the terms he evokes can be traced to traditional poetic criticism, they also correspond to the Western modernist predilection for formal constraint and obscurity in content. It therefore comes as no surprise when Zhou evokes Charles Baudelaire to support his aesthetic views:

68. Zhou Zuoren, *The Origin of Modern Chinese Literature* (Beiping: Renwen shudian, 1934).

69. Pollard, *A Chinese Look at Literature*, 163.

70. Zhou Zuoren, "Locality and Literature," 11–16.

71. Pollard, *A Chinese Look At Literature*, 103–104.

72. Zhou Zhoren, "Preface to *Dates* and *Bridge*" (*Zao he Qiao de xu*), in Fei Ming's *Bridge* (*Qiao*) (Shanghai: Kaiming shuju, 1936), 1–6.

There is a French poet whose poetry is very difficult to decipher. According to him, reading poetry is not so different from children's guessing games. In the beginning one cannot know a poem fully and can only understand three or four tenths of it. Extending and adding to this three or four tenths, one gains the pleasure of creation. As one understands the poem more and more, there is more pleasure.[73]

Zhou here argues for the hermeneutical pleasure resulting from the act of interpretating a "difficult text," very much like both Baudelaire and the French structuralist Roland Barthes. In Barthes's conception, a "writerly text" discomforts and unsettles the reader's assumptions of transparent meaning and the facile decipherability of a "readerly text," and thereby provides the reader with the greatest hermeneutic "bliss."[74] Zhou likewise praises the lack of transparency in the work of Fei Ming as a creative challenge to the reader. Zhou's aesthetic views, despite their "classical"-sounding terminology, therefore exemplify the conjunction between classical aesthetics and Western modernism.

Zhu Guangqian, on the other hand, was a phenomenally erudite scholar, educated in classical Chinese learning and diverse Western subjects such as literature, psychology, philosophy, art history, and aesthetics in England, France, and Germany. In a manifesto printed in the inaugural issue of *Literature Magazine* (*Wenxue zazhi*), which he edited, Zhu brought his broad knowledge to bear in calling for a nonpartisan, open-minded reception of different literary endeavors, a gesture diametrically opposed to the May Fourth penchant for extremism. He attacked the slogans "literature for the masses," "literature for revolution," and "literature for national defense," which were being loudly voiced in Shanghai at the time, accusing their enunciators of imposing a harmful unification of thought. He advocated "free growth and free discussion," with "eyes aimed afar and feet firm and steady," to "explore, experiment, and prevent any one particular literary interest or style from becoming 'orthodox.'"[75]

Zhu's influential views on literature and aesthetics can be generally characterized as a critical syncretism, what he would call a "harmonious middle way" (*tiaohe zhezhong de lu*), premised on a rational investigation of various aesthetic traditions and an organic conception of art as an integration of the aesthetic, moral, ethical, and scientific realms.[76] In terms of the language deemed appropriate for modern literature, he disavowed the May Fourth valorization of the vernacular (*baihua*) over the classical literary language

73. Zhou Zuoren, *The Origin of Modern Chinese Literature,* 11–12.

74. See Roland Barthes, *The Pleasure of the Text,* trans. Richard Miller (New York: Hill and Wang, 1975).

75. *Literature Magazine* (*Wenxue zazhi*) 1:1 (May 1937): 1–10.

76. Zhu Guangqian, "The Author's Confession" (*Zuozhe zibai*), a preface to his *Psychology of Literature and Art* (*Wenyi xinlixue,* 1936), included in *Complete Works of Zhu Guangqian* (*Zhu Guangqian quanji*) (Hefei: Anhui jiaoyu chubanshe, 1987), 1:198.

(*wenyan*). Zhu instead analyzed the strengths and weaknesses of the two languages and disputed the conception that it is easier to write well in the vernacular than in *wenyan*. He admitted that the vernacular does have the advantage of easy decipherability for the reader. However, the boundary between the vernacular and *wenyan* is at best blurry, since the vernacular cannot exist without words and phrases borrowed from the classical language. Here, Zhu made the significant observation that the capacity of the modern vernacular can be developed to its fullest only if it makes use of the rich vocabulary from *wenyan*. This desire to retain and retrieve *wenyan*, though, was not a return to nativist conservatism, as he at the same time advocated the use of European grammatical syntax.[77] He noted that the Europeanization of the vernacular is an unalterable fact, just as the vernacular's inherent connection to *wenyan* cannot be denied: it is not possible to willfully separate the three since the impurity of modern Chinese language is a necessary historical fact.[78]

The debate between the Creation Society and the Literary Research Society over the function of literature during the previous decade again saw a more rational synthesis in Zhu's theory of aesthetics. In his 1936 *Psychology of Literature and Art* (*Wenyi xinlixue*), Zhu devotes an entire chapter to a synopsis and critique of the Italian philosopher Benedetto Croce's aesthetic theory. While he more or less agrees with Croce's aestheticist emphasis on the intuitive nature of art, he also points out the limitations of Croce's pure formalism, concluding that the assertion of absolute artistic autonomy excludes the multiplicity of elements necessarily involved in aesthetic experience.[79] Zhu reiterates this point in the preface, noting that he held an organic view of life in which no absolute separation can be made between the scientific, ethical, aesthetic, and other aspects.[80] In another chapter devoted entirely to the question of art and morality, he emphasizes that art should not be censored by morality, but that it is also not independent of morality.[81] He also holds a middle ground regarding the relationship between subject and object in the artistic process: when the distance between subject and object is too far or too close, art results in the extreme forms of idealism and real-

77. Zhu Guangqian, "How I Studied Chinese Literature" (*Cong wo zenyang xue guowen shuo qi*), originally published in *The Writings of Mengshi* (*Mengshi wenchao*) (Shanghai: Liangyou tushu gongsi, 1936), later collected in *Me, Literature, and Others* (*Wo yu wenxue ji qita*) (Shanghai: Kaiming shudian, 1943), 178–180.

78. See Zhu Guangqian, *On Literature* (*Tan wenxue*) (Hong Kong: Wenyi chubanshe, 1961), 107–119.

79. Zhu Guangqian, *Me, Literature, and Others*, 353–367. Note that this was a revised stance from his earlier more purely formalistic, aestheticist position. He talks about his conversion from Kantian-Crocean aesthetician to eclectic synthesist in "The Author's Confession," op. cit.

80. *Complete Works of Zhu Guangqian*, 1:198.

81. Ibid., 310–325.

ism, both equally flawed. Instead there should be a dialectical relationship between subject and object.[82]

Zhu was to suffer for his views during the Cultural Revolution decades later, sent to do demeaning labor in the cow shed and subjected to continuous criticisms, but he would insist on the integration between the subjective and objective (*zhu ke guan tongyi*) and not be swayed by the emphasis on objectivism dictated by state Marxism in communist China. As late as 1983, he finished the translation of Italian philosopher Giambattista Vico's (1668–1744) *Scienza Nuova* (*New Science*), once again to illustrate that recognition occurs when the subjective and objective interact with each other. Through all of this, we can see Zhu's unflinching dedication to rational scholarship above and beyond ideological determinations by the state.

His most important contribution to *jingpai* aesthetics was perhaps his construction of what may be called an "aesthetics of correspondence" between traditional Chinese aesthetics and Western modernism, to which Zhou Zuoren also contributed as I discussed earlier. Characteristically, he retheorized aspects of traditional Chinese aesthetics using modern Western aesthetic concepts and juxtaposed them in creative tension with each other. In an article entitled "Defending Chinese Art from the Perspective of the Theory of 'Distance'" (*Cong "juli" shuo bianhu Zhongguo yishu*), Zhu cited the Western modernist painting theories of cubism and postimpressionism as well as Greek drama to defend the lack of realism and the conscious maintaining of aesthetic distance in traditional Chinese painting and drama.[83] In "The Beauty of Wordlessness" (*Wuyan zhi mei*), he pointed out that the traditional notion of *hanxu* (suggestiveness; understatement) is similar to ambiguity in modern art: what is left unsaid becomes a space for the reader/spectator to fill in.[84] Drawing upon the newest physiological theory of literature from the West, he explained the traditional poetic concepts of *qishi* (momentum) and *shenyun* (charm) as two different affective powers of literature, one active the other meditative.[85] Through his editorship of *Literature Magazine*, furthermore, Zhu gave a prominent place to writers and poets who experimented with traditional literary theories and motifs which reinforced, rather than detracted from, the modernistic orientation of their works. The poetry of Bian Zhilin (b. 1910) and Dai Wangshu (1905–1950) and the fiction of Fei Ming are enthusiastic expressions of an experimental language that sought to synthesize Chinese

---

82. Ibid., 216–229.

83. Zhu Guangqian, *Me, Literature, and Others*, 67–79.

84. Ibid., 66.

85. "On 'Momentum' and 'Charm' in Poetry From the Perspective of Physiology" (*Cong shenglixue guandian tan shi de qishi yu shenyun*), in *Me, Literature, and Others*, 51–60.

traditional poetic syntax and semantics, modern vernacular, and Europeanized syntax.[86]

With Zhu Guangqian, these writers shared the desire to dissolve the binaries between China and the West, tradition and modernity. Zhu achieved this further by repudiating the modernity-as-rupture thesis of May Fourth discourse, and saw tradition in terms of historical continuity. Zhu suggested that tradition should be one of the resources available for writers to draw from, noting that "a total destruction of indigenous tradition is not allowed by virtue of history's continuity."[87] Zhu reiterated this view in 1948, reflecting upon the historical continuity between modern and traditional Chinese literature:

> Literature is the expression of the life of an entire people. Life grows gradually, so there has to be historical continuity. Historical continuity refers to the succession of lives, the pushing of waves by those in back, and a former cause resulting in a later effect. Even when the later generation rebels against the former generation, it is still the descendent of the former generation.[88]

What Zhu pronounced here anticipated the contention of Renalto Poggioli, Italian theorist of the avant-garde, that "the reaction of modernism to tradition is one more bond, *sui generis,* to that very tradition."[89]

Another theoretician of *jingpai* and a regular contributor to *Literature Magazine,* Ye Gongchao (1904–1981), would cite T. S. Eliot's "Tradition and the Individual Talent" (1917) to argue for the inseparable relationship between traditional and modern poetry.[90] Bian Zhilin had earlier translated this essay into Chinese in the other important forum of *jingpai* writing, the *Xuewen Monthly.*[91] The *jingpai* writers were probably most impressed by Eliot's notion of the "historical sense":

> [Tradition] cannot be inherited, and if you want it you must obtain it by great labor. It involves, in the first place, the historical sense . . . [which] compels a man to write not merely with his own generation in his own bones, but with a feeling that the whole of the literature of Europe from Homer and within it the whole of literature of his own country has a simultaneous existence and

86. For a discussion of the authors' modernism, see Michelle Yeh, *Modern Chinese Poetry: Theory and Practice Since 1917* (New Haven: Yale University Press, 1991), 119–129, and Gregory Lee, *Dai Wangshu: The Life and Poetry of a Chinese Modernist* (Hong Kong: Chinese University Press, 1989).

87. Zhu Guangqian, "Editor's Note" (*Bianji houji*), *Literature Magazine* 1:1 (May 1937): 221.

88. Zhu Guangqian, "Modern Chinese Literature" (*Xiandai Zhongguo wenxue*), *Literature Magazine* 2:8 (January 1948): 17.

89. Renalto Poggioli, *The Theory of the Avant-Garde,* trans. Gerald Fitzgerald (Cambridge: Harvard University Press, Belknap Press, 1968), 178.

90. Ye Gongchao, "On New Poetry" (*Lun xinshi*), *Literature Magazine* 1:1 (May 1937): 11–31.

91. Bian Zhilin's translation appeared in the first issue. *Xuewen Monthly* (*Xuewen yuekan*) 1:1 (May 1934): 87–98.

composes a simultaneous order. This historical sense . . . is what makes a writer traditional. And it is at the same time what makes a writer most acutely conscious of his place in time, of his own contemporaneity.[92]

In Eliot's conception, the historical sense is necessary so that the modern writer can gauge not so much whether he can inherit tradition and use it, but rather how he stands vis-à-vis tradition, that is, how he differs from it. In other words, what makes the writer "traditional" is not what he draws from traditional literature but how he stands within a lineage of writers. The emphasis is on the method of evoking tradition and the nature of the relationship to the past, not on the content of what constitutes tradition or that content's relevance in the present. Hence the writer needs to place all past writers in a simultaneous order to become acutely aware "of his place in time, of his own contemporaneity."

It is in this sense—an awareness of tradition as the basis for the awareness of one's contemporaneity—that "Tradition and the Individual Talent" has become a modernist classic in the West, functioning almost like a modernist manifesto. But when the *jingpai* writers translated and cited Eliot's essay to justify their argument that the traditional and the modern are not contradictory but constitute a relationship of continuity, at least two problems manifested themselves. First, their use of Eliot revealed how their conception of tradition fundamentally differed from the Western modernist conception, for theirs flaunted an integrated content and formal linkages to selected traditional writings. Second, it suggested their eagerness to garner the support of Western modernism, even though the Eurocentric conception of modernism that Eliot propounded had little relevance to the Chinese context.

This second point also pertains to the important question of the role Western modernism played in *jingpai* writing. Even when not ostensibly referred to, Western modernism seems to have been the subtext of many of the experiments in which *jingpai* writers were engaged. In Fei Ming's work, for instance, we see a syncretic mixture of Western stream-of-consciousness techniques and the paratactic linguistic structure of classical Chinese poetry, while Lin Huiyin's use of the episodic narrative structure of traditional vernacular fiction smacks of Joycean literary montage. Although we may find their characters mostly in traditional social contexts (e.g., members of extended families, poor lower-class and country folk), these authors' styles were not at all innocent of the knowledge of what was happening in the Western modernist literary scene. It is no accident that Zhu Guangqian was educated at Edinburgh University and the Universities of London, Paris, and Strasbourg, Zhou Zuoren in Japan, Fei Ming at the English Department of Beijing University, Lin Huiyin (Phyllis Lin) at the University of Pennsylvania and Yale

92. T. S. Eliot, "Tradition and the Individual Talent," in *The Sacred Wood* (London: Metheun & Co. Ltd., 1960), 49.

University, and Ling Shuhua at the English Department of Yanjing University. It is also no accident that the Crescent Moon Society, of which Ling Shuhua and Lin Huiyin were members, mainly consisted of graduates of Euro-American universities, and its publication, the *Crescent Moon,* featured prominently the modernist writings of Virginia Woolf, Katherine Mansfield, Joseph Conrad, and Eugene O'Neill. Their valorization of aspects of traditional aesthetics, then, was mediated through their knowledge of Western modernist and other literary trends.

This returns us to the crucial question of their localism and traditionalism in relation to globalism. As example after example has shown, the local, or that which is evoked as the traditional, is not construed in a nativist fashion, but is filtered through a bicultural and multilingual awareness of Chinese tradition and Western modernism. Zhou Zuoren's contention that the "globality" or "universality" of a piece of literature demands a strong suggestion of local color [93] spells out the logic of the relationship between the local and the global here. As the local itself was never essentially separated from the global (the aesthetics of correspondence is an eloquent example), the local actually becomes the site of potential for the universal. Imitating the West is slavish and will result in a hackneyed pattern, becoming a "Western eight-legged essay" (*yang bagu*),[94] since the West as such is merely another locality or particularity. True globalism finds correspondences among various cultural traditions and accepts promising elements from other cultures, thus making up the stuff of a true universalism.

In the following two chapters, I offer a reading of three *jingpai* writers, Fei Ming, Lin Huiyin, and Ling Shuhua, who have largely been ignored in standard literary histories in China and the U.S. The study of the *jingpai* that I am presenting here does not presume to be comprehensive, but is meant to be illustrative of their efforts in the coproduction of modernity between China and the West. Shen Congwen is arguably one of the most prominent members of the *jingpai,* because of the strong presence of localism (western Hunan) in his work and his personal involvement in the *jingpai-haipai* debate, but, with rare exceptions, he is more strictly a regional writer with less of an interest in formal innovations, and so he does not readily fall under the modernist framework that this book is grappling with. In the 1940s, he did write a short story entitled "Watching Rainbows" (*Kan hong lu*) that

93. Mentioned in Yan Jiayan, *Schools of Modern Chinese Fiction,* 45. Zhou Zuoren's remark appears in his preface to Liu Dabai's *Old Dreams* (*Jiumeng*), entitled "Old Dreams," in *Representative Works of Zhou Zuoren* (*Zhou Zuoren daibiao zuo*), ed. Zhang Juxiang (Zhengzhou: Huanghe wenyi chubanshe, 1987), 91–93.

94. Zhou's remark related in Qian Liqun, *A Biography of Zhou Zuoren* (*Zhou Zuoren zhuan*) (Beijing: Shiyue wenyi chubanshe, 1990), 407–408.

seemed more *haipai* than *jingpai* in its depiction of an erotic fantasy.[95] Most of his writings, however, fall more fittingly within the category of realism, and three extensive studies on the life and work of Shen Congwen have already appeared in English.[96] As for Wang Zengqi (1920–1998), the 1940s student of Shen Congwen at Southwestern United University in Kunming and perhaps the most self-conscious modernist of the *jingpai* school in his Joycean and Woolfian manipulation of language and form with intertextual evocations of traditional Chinese aesthetics, I will return to his work in my appendix, where I summarize the modernist developments in the 1940s and beyond.

95. For an analysis of this story, see Yan Jiayan, *"Jingpai* Fiction and Modernism" (*Jingpai xiaoshuo yu xiandai zhuyi*), unpublished paper.

96. See David Der-wei Wang, *Fictional Realism in Twentieth-Century China: Mao Dun, Lao She, Shen Congwen* (New York: Columbia University Press, 1992); Jeffrey Kinkley, *The Odyssey of Shen Congwen* (Stanford: Stanford University Press, 1987); and Hsiao-yen Peng, *Antithesis Overcome: Shen Congwen's Avant-gardism and Primitivism* (Taipei: Institute of Chinese Literature and Philosophy, Academica Sinica, 1994).

CHAPTER 7

Writing English with a Chinese Brush
The Work of Fei Ming

Fei Ming is an eccentric talent, his looks "strange and peculiar" (Zhou Zuoren's words), his face thin and eyes clear, ears large and mouth broad, hair in the "monk" style (but not shaved), clothes in disarray, looking a bit like a vagrant monk, with a hoarse voice and heavy rural flavor. When I first entered Beijing University, among my schoolmates there circulated the story that he wrote English exams with a Chinese brush.

BIAN ZHILIN (1984)

In the immediate post–May Fourth years between 1922 and 1929, there emerged in the hotbed of May Fourth iconoclasm at Beijing University a student in the English department, Feng Wenbing (1901–1967), who would soon become a key figure in *jingpai* writing. Thin and bespectacled, he dressed himself in a manner self-consciously contrary to the image of a Westernized May Fourth enlightenment intellectual, preferring to wear the classic Chinese intellectual's long gown and write with a Chinese calligraphy brush. In 1926, he "abolished" his name Feng Wenbing and started calling himself "Abolishing Names" (Fei Ming), a moniker with strong Taoist overtones. He later practiced Chan Buddhist meditation, taught Confucius's *Analects* and other Chinese classics both as a college and a secondary school teacher, wrote commentaries on Buddhist scriptures, and throughout tried to integrate Buddhist, Taoist, and Confucian cultural traditions in his own thinking and writing.[1]

The traditionalist Fei Ming, however, constituted only part of who Fei Ming actually was; depending on the particular selection of details, Fei Ming could emerge as a diametrically different figure. There was also the Fei Ming who avidly read French symbolist poetry (Charles Baudelaire) and fiction (Gus-

1. This biographical information is taken from Bian Zhilin, "Preface to *Collected Writings of Feng Wenbing*" (*Feng Wenbing xuanji xu*), *Historical Materials on New Literature* (*Xinwenxue shiliao*) (February 1984): 113–119.

tave Flaubert), British drama (William Shakespeare) and realist novels (George Eliot, Thomas Hardy), as well as the Spanish classic *Don Quixote*, who claimed that he had learned how to write from reading Western literature and that Chinese classics were devoid of life, and was himself often compared to such Western writers as Marcel Proust and Virginia Woolf by Zhu Guangqian and others.[2] What is the nature of the relationship between these two seemingly incompatible Fei Mings?[3] What is it about this relationship that characterizes his particular expression of *jingpai* sensibility?

Without falling into the essentialist task of trying to identify which Fei Ming was the true or real one or which Fei Ming took precedence—especially since Fei Ming himself distrusted authenticity, as evidenced by his new name—the question to consider is rather the particular, contingent nature of his traditionalism as well as his modernism, which in the end thoroughly unsettles the binary. Merely for the sake of discussion, then, I would make the following references to Fei Ming's unique evocation of traditionalism in the Chinese cultural context. First, Fei Ming's traditionalism is a particular selection of tradition and a particular interpretation of that tradition; second, his particular selection and interpretation was itself *mediated* by his knowledge of Western literature. For instance, he equated simple, unquestioned clinging to the traditional as a form of plagiarism, which could stifle true genius and originality;[4] he satirized the illusive world of antiquated Confucian values with the figure of a Chinese Don Quixote in his novel *The Biography of Mr. Neverwas* (*Moxuyou xiansheng zhuan*, 1932). Works he referred to include Six-dynasty essays, late-Tang poetry, and Jin Shengtan's (1610–1661) fiction criticism, as well as his own peculiar interpretations of Buddhist, Taoist, and Confucian classics (the Taoist *Zhuangzi* read as exquisite depictions of natural phenomena; Confucius's *Analects* read as a school diary). As to the mediation of tradition by Western literature, he was not at all ambiguous when he made such pronouncements as these: "I started reading Chinese works after I had read Western literature . . . and I realized that the Chinese language could actually be used to write a lot of beautiful things";[5] "Western literature first initiated my writing techniques

2. For Zhu Guangqian's comment, see his "*Bridge*" (*Qiao*), *Literature Magazine* (*Wenxue zazhi*) 1:3 (July 1937): 183–189.

3. As a poet, Fei Ming wrote Chan poems and city poems. The first were inspired by Chan Buddhism and incorporated notions of "sudden enlightenment" (*dunwu*), while the second were a distinct form of modernist poetry in the style of his compatriot symbolists Bian Zhilin, Li Jinfa, and Dai Wangshu.

4. Fei Ming, "On Modern Poetry," in *Modern Chinese Poetry*, trans. by Harold Acton and Ch'en Shih-hsiang (London: Duckworth, 1936), 41.

5. Fei Ming, "Chinese Writing" (*Zhongguo wenzhang*, 1936), in *Collected Writings of Feng Wenbing* (*Feng Wenbing xuanji*) (Beijing: Beijing renmin wenxue chubanshe, 1985), 345.

and then I turned to native forms."[6] But if his access to traditional Chinese literature was mediated by Western literature, as he clearly claims here, his practice of Western modernist techniques such as stream of consciousness was more informed by his engagement with the peculiar properties of the Chinese poetic language than by Western modernist writing itself. The question here is that of *mutual mediation* or *mutual implication,* not a traceable influence or cause-and-effect relationship between what may be tenuously delineated as essentially either Chinese or Western.

"Mutual implication" is one of the ways in which *jingpai* writers negotiated their aesthetics, an aesthetics which subverted binary and essentialist conceptions of cultural difference. For Fei Ming, both modernity-in-tradition and tradition-in-modernity informed his writings; that which was reified as the modern (read: Western) in May Fourth discourse is made part of tradition and vice versa, as their boundaries are considered uncertain and perhaps even nonexistent. Modernity and tradition work through their mutual implication and correspondence, such that the attempt to delineate their separate properties (as in the May Fourth project) becomes a futile, simplistic, essentialist undertaking that is ultimately but a reactive response to the imposition of metropolitan modernity within the semicolonial cultural formation of modern China. If metropolitan modernity is constitutive of that which is considered traditional, again, its colonial implications are displaced, and a form of agency can emerge for the cultural worker who is at ease with both cultures. The emergence of this agency is premised on an assumed complementarity and correspondence between what many considered to be two disparate cultural systems. What appears as creative renderings of Taoist, Buddhist, and Confucian notions of art and reality, as well as classical lyrical tropes and techniques, therefore manifests itself as recognizable qualities in Western modernism. As part of the larger anti-Occidentalist cultural formation, Fei Ming's writing reinvented the relationship between the particular and the universal. As his poet friend Bian Zhilin noted, the zeitgeist of the 1930s, in which Fei Ming came into prominence, was "nondistinction between the East and the West."[7]

AN AESTHETICS OF MUTUAL IMPLICATION

Fei Ming is a master of appropriation in his self-conscious parody and mediation of literary traditions, tropes, and conventions from China and the

---

6. Quoted in Feng Jiannan, "Fei Ming—Outstanding Essayist" (*Fei Ming: jiechu de sanwenjia*), in *Studies of Modern and Contemporary Chinese Literature* (*Zhongguo xiandai dangdai wenxue yanjiu*) (August 1988): 238.

7. Bian Zhilin, "Preface" (*Xu*) to *Records of Insect Carvings* (*Diaochong jili*) (Hong Kong: Sanlian shudian, 1982), 3.

West. His masterpiece *Bridge* (1932), an almost plotless serialized novel, makes parodic references to traditional vernacular storytelling conventions, and appropriates classical Chinese poetic syntax and semantics, while flaunting a modernist style that is disjunctive, free-associational, and yet stoically nonurban in content. An unfinished novel which he nonetheless took six years to write, it is a simple triangular love story between Xiao Lin, his fiancée Qinzi, and her female cousin Xizhu, with the bulk of the narrative consisting of descriptions of natural and mental landscapes.[8] In its valorization of the rural, it is reminiscent of the pastoral lyricism of Thomas Hardy and George Eliot, whose pessimistic fatalism deeply impressed Fei Ming, while he also saw similar qualities in the poetry of Yu Xin (513–581), Tao Yuanming (363–424), and others. His choice of children as protagonists in *Bridge* echoes that of George Eliot's *The Mill on the Floss* (1860),[9] and reverberates strongly with the "green plum blossom and bamboo horse" (*qingmei zhuma*) motif—the innocent affection between a girl and a boy in their childhood—that one finds, for instance, in Li Bai's long poem "Chang'gan Xing" and Cao Xueqin's novel *Dream of the Red Chamber*. This mutual mediation on the level of subject matter is further accompanied by various stylistic experiments that commingle the supposed aesthetic qualities of China and the West.

Although he claimed that he had not read Virginia Woolf or James Joyce while he was actively writing his stories in the late 1920s and early 1930s, his texts often depict the interior thoughts of his characters in a manner similar to the Western stream-of-consciousness narrative. This, as he himself later explains and many other critics have pointed out, has to do with his self-conscious appropriation of classical poetic syntax and diction, which foregrounds a kind of semantic and syntactic disjunction. An early example can be found in his 1927 story "Peach Garden" (*Taoyuan*), in a passage that depicts the girl Ahmao's moment-to-moment reflections:

> Ahmao had caressed these many trees with her little hands. No, each and every tree here grew in Ahmao's embrace! Did Father grow them to be so big by irrigating them? She remembered the mountain outside the town, a mountain full of graves, her mother had one there too. Isn't Mother's grave here in the garden? Why does Father quarrel with Mother? Once a whole basket of

8. The 1932 publication of *Bridge* was, according to Fei Ming, only half of the projected novel. He later published a few other episodes in different magazines. They include: "On Water" (*Shuishang*) and "Key" (*Yaoshi*), *Crescent Moon* (*Xinyue*) 4:5 (November 1932): 1–17; "Window" (*Chuang*), *Crescent Moon* 4:7 (June 1933): 1–7; "Lotus Leaves" (*Heye*) and "Untitled" (*Wuti*), *Xuewen Monthly* (*Xuewen yuekan*) 1:2 (June 1934): 27–41; "Light of Fireflies" (*Yinghuo*), *Literature Magazine* 1:3 (July 1937): 45–57; and "Morning Glory" (*Qianniuhua*), *Literature Magazine* 1:4 (August 1937): 117–129.

9. Fei Ming noted that reading *The Mill on the Floss* made him realize that children's lives can be the subject matter of fiction. See Feng Jiannan, "About Fei Ming's Life" (*Shuo Fei Ming de shengping*), *Historical Materials on New Literature* (February 1984): 106–112.

peaches was kicked over and Ahmao had to pick them up one by one and put them back into the basket! What should I do if the Heavenly Dog [the constellation Aries] really swallows up the sun? . . . Ahmao thought of the nun. She didn't know which temple the nun belonged to; she remembered the nun's face, then the nun walked into her garden![10]

Moving from third-person narration to Ahmao's shifting thoughts, the passage shows a few linguistic features peculiar to the Chinese language in general and the poetic language in particular that allow for the rendering of mental and physical gaps in time and space. The lack of tense markers in the more paradigmatically inclined Chinese language makes the time frame of events ambiguous: the expression "Why does Father quarrel with Mother?" can also be rendered "Why did Father quarrel with Mother?" The former better conveys the sick child Ahmao's confused state of mind which annihilates spatial and temporal boundaries, but the latter translation is also viable. The jumps in time and space—as in the last sentence where memory of the nun brings the experience to the present as if it were happening right at that moment—were also explained by Fei Ming as associated with such poetic practices as destroying spatial and temporal continuity and causal associational thinking. Fei Ming described Li Shangyin's (c. 813–858) poetry as "moving up to heaven and down to earth, jumping to the east and to the west" (*shangtian xiadi dongtiao xitiao*),[11] thereby prioritizing a kind of illogicality by depicting time and space in discontinuity.[12] Incoherence, abruptness, fragmentation, and illogicality are innate qualities of such poetic language, which is coincidentally akin to the language depicting the free-associational experience of the stream of consciousness.

The omission of the subject and the free-floating subject-verb-object relationship in classical poetic syntax also contribute to the sense of disjunction in Fei Ming's prose. Take this short example from "Water Chestnut Lake" (*lingdang*, 1927), which Fei Ming considered to be the beginning of his conscious attempt to write concise prose the way a Tang dynasty poet would write quatrains:[13]

Water bucket resting on the field path; Shouldering a hoe, walking along the field; Eyes seeing one eggplant after another.

水桶歇下畦径，荷锄沿畦走，眼睛看一个一个的茄子[14]

10. Fei Ming, "Peach Garden" (*Taoyuan*), in *Selected Writings of Fei Ming* (*Fei Ming xuanji*) (Sichuan: Sichuan wenyi chubanshe, 1988), 146–150.

11. Mentioned in Feng Jiannan, "On Fei Ming's Fictional Writing" (*Tan Fei Ming de xiaoshuo chuangzuo*), *Studies of Modern Chinese Literature* (*Zhongguo xiandai wenxue yanjiu congkan*) 4 (April 1985): 149.

12. Fei Ming, "Jottings" (*Suibi*), in *Literature Magazine* 1:1 (May 1937): 200–201.

13. Fei Ming, "Preface to *Selected Stories of Fei Ming*" (*Fei Ming xiaoshuoxuan xu*, 1957), in *Collected Writings of Feng Wenbing*, 394.

14. Fei Ming, "Water Chestnut Lake" (*Lingdang*, 1927), in *Selected Writings of Fei Ming*, 158.

In the first line, if the verb is read in the active voice, the grammatical subject is the water bucket, but it may also be read in the passive voice, in which case the implied subject is an unmentioned person. The necessity of choosing one voice over the other in English cannot capture the sense of the original where the ambiguity of the subject-verb-object relationship is retained. The first two phrases are suggestive of five-character regulated verse with the slight variation of six characters in the first phrase. The second phrase has a typical regulated poetic rhythm and tone and is reminiscent of Tang nature poetry. But the third phrase dramatically disrupts the seeming conformity to the old style: here is a ten-character phrase written in casual vernacular speech with the repetition of "*yige yige*" ("one after another"), breaking the taboo against repetition in conventional poetic practice. This reverberates with the practice of another of Fei Ming's favorite poets, Yu Xin, who defied the rigid formal stipulations of poetry through the exercise of wit and playfulness, especially by breaking the monotony of conventional parallelism.[15]

These two qualities in the poetry of Li Shangyin and Yu Xin—temporal and spatial flexibility, and linguistic innovation and playfulness—are noticeably displayed in *Bridge*, and Fei Ming self-consciously made the presence of classical poetry in his writing not merely a matter of syntactic appropriation but also of intertextual allusion. It is not coincidental that examples of the so-called "lyrical novel" in the West, where the novel approaches the function of a poem, foreground the psychological experiences of introspective characters.[16] Likewise, Fei Ming's peculiar borrowing of aspects of classical poetry enhances his emphasis on interiority, and characteristically, as Zhu Guangqian has pointed out, this interiority is most often triggered by natural landscape:

> One day [Xiao Lin] went out and by chance saw a white horse rolling in the green grass. His poem was finally successfully composed at this time. Great joy. "This thing is really happy!" He didn't stop walking. "I'm like a—," of course like this thing [the horse]. But a thought walks so much faster [than language] that [uttering] just these three words completes [the simile in his mind]. Ah, this "I" is the subconscious with its head buried in a woman's bosom.

> 一天外出，偶尔看见一匹白马在青草地上打滚，他的诗到这时才俨然成功了，大喜，"这个东西真快活！"并没有止步. "我好比——"当然是好比这个东西，但观念是那么的走得快，就以这三个字完了.这个 "我," 是埋头予女人的胸中呵一个潜意识[17]

15. Fei Ming, "Three Poles, Two Poles" (*Sangan lianggan*, 1936), in *Collected Writings of Feng Wenbing*, 342–343.

16. Ralph Freedman's examples of the lyrical novelists include Virginia Woolf, Hermann Hesse, and Andre Gide, all of whom emphasize interior experience. See his *The Lyrical Novel* (Princeton: Princeton University Press, 1963).

17. Fei Ming, *Bridge* (Shanghai: Kaiming shudian, 1932), 279.

As with the previous passage, this one is much harder to comprehend in Chinese than in the English translation, because translating it into English compels the translator to make the passage "make sense," adding subjects and connectives as well as punctuation, besides the explanatory words provided in brackets. Rendered in jumping rhythm and syntax, the passage makes the reader's understanding tentative and requires his/her active participation in the process of producing meaning. Nature, rather than events or narrative conflict, is here the most important object of representation and the catalyst for the production of lyrical emotion and poetic meaning.

This prominent relationship between landscape and emotion in fact echoes back to a specific kind of traditional lyricism embodying the poetic harmony between feeling (*qing*) and landscape (*jing*). Note the following passage:

> Qinzi and Xizhu left. [Xiao Lin] stayed at home. [In his imagination] the two of them seemed to be walking on an expansive prairie. Grass grew beneath their every step. But grass is grass as it is so on every road. [All the grass] together left him with the feeling of greenness, elusive, ephemeral. This was perhaps because he didn't know the road, and [Qinzi and Xizhu] of course were walking, so [his mind] roamed about freely, beauty and sweet grass.[18]

The line "grass grew beneath their every step" is an intertextual evocation of "with every step there grows a lotus blossom" (*bubu sheng lianhua*), famously used to describe the historical beauty Pan Yu'er of the Southern Qi dynasty; "beauty and sweet grass" (*meiren fangcao*) echoes the phrase "beauty and fragrant grass" (*meiren xiangcao*) from Qu Yuan's (c. 340–278 B.C.) *On Encountering Sorrow* (*Li Sao*). The scene described here exists simultaneously in nature and in Xiao Lin's imagination. It is colored by his amorous feelings towards both girls, a sense of their beauty merging with nature, where the sweet grass becomes the metonymy for the girls. Here, as in classical poetry, the feeling-landscape correspondence is predicated on a harmony between man and nature,[19] which can be seen in many other lyrical passages in the novel, such as this one:

> With grass banks on either side, a winding stream flowed under the stone bridge which transported Xizhu. And suddenly, she was standing under the flower trees on the other side of the bank. Flowers bloomed on the intertwined branches of a peach and a plum tree. The peach tree was still young. Her two hands climbed a branch of plum blossoms. She breathed fast as if she were riding a swing. This branch, as she casually reached for it with her outstretched

18. Ibid., 267.

19. The theme of harmony between man and nature that Fei Ming appropriated from classical poetry can also be seen in the titles of his books. The association of Tao Yuanming's peach blossom spring was implied in his *Peach Garden; Stories of the Bamboo Grove* evokes the Seven Sages of the Bamboo Grove; and so on.

hands, looked shorter than herself. Then she just rested, not only without any words, but closing her eyes and waving her hair. Her hair shaded her eyes. Less than two inches from her lips were branches full of peach blossoms.[20]

In this description of Xizhu in nature, Xizhu stands as the trees stand, her arms outstretched like the branches of the trees, her face covered by her hair as the treetops are covered by flowers, her silence participating in the stillness of nature. Instead of a metaphorical relationship between man and nature, where a hierarchy of importance is implied, here the trees and Xizhu are equal metonymies for each other. Nature, as in Chinese landscape paintings, is not a background for characters' actions; instead, it shares the same space and equal significance with characters. The foreground and background mingle in a way similar to the Western modernist technique of "flattening," where the mingling, as in a cubist painting, is meant to subvert and disrupt the audience's perception of what is primary and what is secondary in space.[21] While Western modernists had to strive laboriously to arrive at an intellectualized conception of spatial flattening, the nonhierarchy between foreground and background, especially between man and nature, has always been part of the very definition of the Chinese artistic tradition.

Bridge consists of a series of landscapes: almost all the chapter headings are scenes from nature, and the events depicted are the characters' movements within nature. Since there is not much plot in the novel, the characters' actions often appear to function as links or connecting threads between the different scenes they visit. The nonintrusive and quiet actions of the characters rather seem to become fragments of the landscapes with which they harmoniously merge. Each section of the novel therefore functions like a scene in a landscape painting, giving the novel what can be called a "scroll form." Turning the pages in the book can be compared to turning the scroll of a landscape painting. As one unrolls a scroll, for example the celebrated "On the River during the Qingming Festival" (*Qingming shanghetu*) where there are multiple scenes depicted in a spatial continuation, one visually travels to those scenes. Reading Fei Ming's novel, like viewing the scroll, is not merely a temporal experience; a spatialization of all the scenes in the reader/viewer's mind is also possible so that these scenes can be perceived simultaneously. Furthermore, one is allowed entry into the novel or the painting at any point, since sequentiality and plot development are of no important concern. Hence it was possible for the novel to be published fragment by fragment in a serial form—even in different magazines—with each fragment capable of standing independently as an autonomous piece of prose

20. Fei Ming, *Bridge*, 234.

21. Stephen Kern, *The Culture of Time and Space, 1880–1918* (Cambridge: Harvard University Press, 1983), 132.

writing. The modernist narrative in the West has been celebrated for its spatial form—the capacity of the text to require the reader to read and reread the novel over and over again in order to grasp its meaning in the simultaneity of time.[22] Fei Ming looked to classical nature poetry instead for his own spatial form of the novel.

Similarly, the multiple-perspectivism of Western modernism, whose counterpart in the plastic arts was cubism, finds a kindred spirit in Fei Ming, who valorized the free-floating perspective of conventional Chinese vernacular narrative. Much of the unique structure of *Bridge* derives from this self-conscious manipulation of the narratological perspective. Fei Ming later noted:

> Chinese fiction and drama are written in the style of official biographies. Like Chinese paintings, one writes from and to all directions . . . there is no consideration given to the problem of focus and perspective. The more I wrote, the more I felt that Chinese fiction and drama are more natural and more real than Western fiction and drama, the reason being that Chinese ways of expression are much freer.[23]

Instead of a focused and fixed narrative perspective, Fei Ming chose to valorize a multiplicity of free-floating perspectives that weave in and out of landscapes of nature and the mind; instead of unilinear, sequential plot development, events are loosely strung together in a spatial form. In a later essay, he described the difference between Western fiction (presumably realism) and Chinese fiction as like the difference between photography and "talk story" (*shuo gushi*): Western literature's demand for verisimilitude requires the storyteller to take up a fixed position and perspective like a photographer taking a photograph, while Chinese narrative conventions valorize the telling of good stories and the presentation of vivid characters. To succeed in telling good stories, the Chinese storyteller has to move in and out of different perspectives, never standing in one fixed spot.[24] The painting-scroll form of his novel is wedded coherently to the free-floating narrative perspective that defies verisimilitude, producing a spatial form that subverts linear temporality, and by extension the teleological modernity of the May Fourth period.

Fei Ming's parody of Chinese narrative conventions not only approaches the qualities of Western modernism on the technical level, but also on the

---

22. See Joseph Frank's classic essay, "Spatial Form in Modern Literature," *Sewanee Review* 53 (1945): 221–240, 433–456, 643–653. For recent discussions of spatial form, see Jeffrey R. Smitten and Ann Daghistany, eds., *Spatial Form in Narrative* (Ithaca: Cornell University Press, 1981).

23. A passage from an unpublished manuscript, quoted in Feng Jian'nan, "On Fei Ming's Fictional Writing," 146.

24. In his *Talking to Youth About Lu Xun* (*Gen qingnian tan Lu Xun*) (Beijing: Zhongguo qingnian chubanshe, 1956), 107.

level of the aesthetic meditation or theorization of the nature of fiction. For example, the novel is full of metafictional moments and commentaries. One of these is the presence of a narrator who calls himself the writer (*zhibiren*) and addresses the audience as "Dear Sirs" (*kanguan*), as in traditional vernacular fiction. He uses such stock expressions as "Please wait for the next chapter" and calls his chapters by the old term "*hui*," but he uses the phrase "Please wait for the next chapter" in quotation marks and as a chapter heading, instead of as the last line of the previous chapter, as it was customarily used. The first chapter tells a mirroring story that serves as a foreshadowing, comparison, and contrast to the main story, as in the "introduction" (*yinzi*) of traditional *huaben* narratives, but Fei Ming's first chapter is humorously and self-reflexively entitled "The First Chapter." The metafictional quality of *Bridge* is especially apparent in the way the narrator acknowledges the limits of his knowledge and does not assume the truthfulness of his narration. In contrast, the storyteller's voice traditionally assumes an authenticity like what one finds in historical narratives. Fei Ming takes this convention and ironically comments on it. His narrator first pretends that he is telling a true story, only to show later that certain scenes in the novel are purely imagined. The narrator also self-consciously draws attention to the narrative's fictionality by showing how the narrative depends on the characters for the events to proceed: "Grandma Shi went to town this time to be the matchmaker for the two children [Xiao Lin and Qinzi], thus I have something to write about for our story."[25] Here the narrator is conscious of the act of telling as a fictional process. At the beginning of Part Two of the novel (the novel in its published form, though incomplete, is divided into two parts), he mentions that the empty page between the two parts represents ten years. In another instance, he comments that he spent much time writing many words to describe one action, but that the action itself only took a split second to complete. What is experienced as time becomes space in writing and vice versa, and Fei Ming thereby makes a metafictional commentary on the impossibility of representing time as it is experienced.

Instead of outer reality, the novel refers to itself and the literary tradition it comes from. It is therefore self-reflexive and narcissistic.[26] In his recent reminiscence of Fei Ming, Zhu Guangqian pointed out self-reflexivity (*ziyuxing*) to be one of the major characteristics of Fei Ming's work, along with discontinuity (*fei lianxuxing*), defamiliarization (*moshenggan*), and obscurity (*menglong*).[27] The peculiarity of Fei Ming's style is such that, in Edward Gunn's

25. Fei Ming, *Bridge*, 45.

26. I am using the term from Linda Hutcheon's book *Narcissistic Narrative: The Metafictional Paradox* (New York: Metheun, 1980), where she calls metafictional narratives "narcissistic" due to their self-reflexivity.

27. Zhu Guangqian, "'I Am the Colorful Pen Transmitted in the Dream': A Brief Account of Fei Ming" (*Wo shi meng zhong chuan caibi: Fei Ming lueshi*), *Dushu* 10 (October 1990): 28–34.

words, it "leads away from the existing structures of organized narrative and intellectual discourse, and keeps on distancing itself from such expectations."[28] Narcissism therefore can be understood as a valorization of obscurity and ambiguity which distances the texts from readers' expectations. In his texts, as Fei Ming put it, "words give birth to each other, sentences grow from sentences, as ungraspable as a dream."[29]

THE REJECTION OF THE REAL

While still a college student in 1925, Fei Ming published his first collection of short stories entitled *Stories of the Bamboo Grove* (*Zhulin de gushi*), for which he used Baudelaire's prose poem "Windows" ("*Les fenêtres*") as an inscription preceding the preface:

> When a person looks through an open window, he will never see as many things as when he looks at a closed window. There is nothing more profound, more mysterious, more fecund, more dazzling than a window lit by a candle. What we can see under the sun is always less interesting than that behind the glass. In that space of darkness or light, life lives, life dreams, life suffers.[30]

Here, the real as such is seen as an impediment to poetic representation, as it is only when the real is disguised or hidden that the poetic faculty of imagination exercises itself to express a deeper reality. Without question, Fei Ming gives a prominent place to Baudelaire's symbolist/modernist repudiation of verisimilitude as an extension of his own aesthetics of mutual implication, where illogicality, nonsequentiality, and disjunction are crucial features. But how does Fei Ming achieve this repudiation of the real, and through which discursive justifications from the Chinese tradition, while also implying the symbolist aesthetic of Baudelaire? How does mutual implication work in this case?

Fei Ming draws from various Chinese sources. In this passage describing the male protagonist Xiao Lin's astonishment at seeing a wild goose flying in the sky, we see an example of how Fei Ming utilizes intertextuality (between text and text, between the real and the imaginary) to arrive at a theoretical repudiation of verisimilitude: "A wild goose flying over in this weather,—it is definitely a wild goose from 'The wild geese on the frontier /

28. Edward Gunn, *Rewriting Chinese: Style and Innovation in Twentieth-Century Chinese Prose* (Stanford: Stanford University Press, 1991), 128.

29. Fei Ming, "About Dreams" (*Shuomeng*), in *Collected Writings of Feng Wenbing*, 323.

30. My own translation of the first paragraph of the poem from Baudelaire's *Petite Poèmes en Prose*, ed. Melvin Zimmerman (Manchester: University of Manchester Press, 1968), 65. Fei Ming's Chinese translation of the whole poem is in *Stories of the Bamboo Grove* (Shanghai: Beixin shuju, 1927), 1–2. The collection of stories was originally published in Beijing by the New Tide Society (*Xinchaoshe*) in 1925.

Rouse the crows on the citadel'! So [Xiao Lin], facing the wall, wondered 'Can the golden partridges on the painted screen also be flying?'"[31] Seeing the wild goose reminds Xiao Lin of Wen Tingyun's (c. 812–870) lines in "Song of the Water Clock at Night" (*Genglouzi*): "The wild geese on the frontier / Rouse the crows on the citadel / And the golden partridges on the painted screen." In Wen's poem, there is an intersection of two different realities, the natural (the geese and the crows) and the artificial (the painted partridges). In Fei Ming's use of the poem, there are three levels of reality—the goose Xiao Lin sees with his physical eyes (the perceived real), the geese and crows from the poem (the real mediated by representation), and the painted partridges on a screen from the poem (the represented real mediated by memory)—Xiao Lin's mind and vision move fluidly across these three realms without giving hierarchy or priority to any of them, thereby deconstructing any notions of the authentic real.

The theme of the fluidity of realities, the blending of the natural and artificial, is exemplified in several other scenes in the novel. When Xiao Lin is caught stealing a peach from the ancestral altar by his sister, he defends himself by saying that he was only trying to steal one of the many painted peaches in the palm of the god of longevity in the painting hanging above the altar, not the real ones on the altar. When her sister complains to him that the rocks he painted on her fan were like real rocks, not like the rocks one finds in Chinese paintings, he replies that if she were right, the rocks he painted would weigh heavily on the fan and tear it. In a reverse manner, the natural world often takes on the static quality of paintings. One lyrical example of the merging of the actual and the imaginary concerns Qinzi and Xizhu's outing to Flower Red Mountain to pick flowers, but having forgotten why they went they come home with no flowers. Xiao Lin muses: "It is better to forget [about picking flowers]. At this flashing instant the mountain full of red flowers has not one blemish, as perfect as the other side of the bank."[32] In Xiao Lin's imagination, the mountain scene acquires the qualities of a painting, so that if flowers are picked from the scene, the painting will be lacking. The actual fact of not picking the flowers allows Xiao Lin's imaginary, painterly evocation of the scene to be complete and without blemish.

In all these examples, imagination or consciousness as a mediation between and overcoming of dualities relates to the doctrine of nonduality as expounded by *The Vimalakirti Nirdesa Sutra* (*Weimojijing*), Fei Ming's favorite Buddhist text. In this sutra's scheme of things, Dharma is the absolute state free from dualities, relativities, and contraries. According to the sutra, Dharma can be achieved when dualities such as those between subject and

31. Fei Ming, *Bridge*, 270.
32. Ibid., 272.

object, birth and death, good and evil, samsara and nirvana are *perceived* to be nonexistent. In the capacity of the mind to perceive thus lies the elimination of duality.[33]

Fei Ming's prose reverberates with Buddhist motifs, and here the return to some form of the spirituality that Western modernism and modernist philosophy have been striving towards finds a fluent, unstrained translation. The novel takes the nonduality between samsara, this mundane world of illusion, and nirvana, the ultimate, supramundane world, as one of its main themes. In the "Light of Fireflies" (*Yinghuo*) chapter, for example, we come to know the story of two young nuns, Da Qian and Xiao Qian, whose names are Buddhist terms for the numerous worlds (chiliocosms) contained in the universe—Da Qian refers to the major chiliocosm, Xiao Qian to a small chiliocosm. The triangular love story of the two sisters and Da Qian's diseased husband is a prefiguration of the love triangle between Qinzi, Xizhu, and Xiao Lin. In the first triangle, the sisters fall in love with the same man; in the second, the two cousins, Qinzi and Xizhu, who are often described as being like sisters, fall in love with Xiao Lin. Since the first triangular love story ends with tragedy (with the man's death and the two sisters renouncing the world and becoming nuns), the prefiguration implies the tragedy of love to be a perennial problem of existence in the mundane, corporeal world. Only by overcoming desire can the emotional frustrations at the root of human suffering be eliminated and can one approach the supramundane. This Buddhist penchant to find the supramundane in the mundane using love tragedy as an example of course harkens back to the *Dream of the Red Chamber*, where the Buddhist worldview likewise underscores the denouement of the narrative.

Fei Ming's use of Buddhist motifs in conjunction with his rejection of the real and his presentation of the mutability of realities is most prominently encapsulated in his images of water and mirrors, through various allusions to the Buddhist phrase "flowers in the mirror and the moon in the water" (*jinghua shuiyue*). Departing from their conventional interpretation as connoting the illusive nature of reality, Fei Ming uses them to emphasize the mutability between reflected and tangible realities. The mirror contains myriad things, just as the world does:

> Xizhu's mind is always the busiest. The reverse is also true: hers is the least busy. She is like flowing water; it is thus busy, it is thus not busy. Yes, we look at the stars in heaven, look at stones, look at mirrors, look at the clear autumn moon, look at flowers, look at old trees, each and every one of them inspires the tranquility of life. Isn't tranquility a burden? Isn't it a thought? I guess only when the water flows, the mind doesn't rush. Flowing water is also rocks, is

33. Lu K'uan Yü, trans., *The Vimalakirti Nirdesa Sutra* (Berkeley: Shambala Publications Inc., 1972), chapter 9, 92–100.

mirrors, is stars in heaven, is the moon, is flowers, is grass, is the shadow of trees on the banks.[34]

In this passage, water does not merely reflect all the natural and manmade things, it *is* and contains them. The distinction between reflected and external realities is obscured. Water here is also a metaphor for both the tranquility and the hurriedness of the mind. It contains paradoxes and opposites, as does the mirror: "There was the mirror. As it touched [Xiao Lin's] eyes, it made his heart tremble. In reality, this canvas of brightness . . . had always resided within his own secret thoughts, as if he himself had always been in this room together with the mirror. But he never thought somebody else could be seen in the mirror: himself."[35] The mirror that Xiao Lin earlier associated only with Qinzi and Xizhu, as a metonymy for female identity and beauty, surprises him with an image of himself when he walks inside the girls' room. Through its capacity to encompass them all, the mirror functions as an agent that bridges the separation between the male and the female, whereby their dualism is overcome and the self becomes immersed in the other.

In conclusion, the aesthetics of mutual implication encompasses both the cross-cultural dimension of China-West negotiation and corresponding modernist literary techniques, and the philosophical-aesthetic dimension of a theory of representation that defies realism through flattening out the difference between the real and the represented, the external and the internal, the tangible and the reflected. In this scheme of things, cultures are mutable like realities. Essentialist, hierarchical, and oppositional conceptions of cultural difference are to be thoroughly rejected, while the dichotomy between modernity and tradition is also revealed to be false and irrelevant. What in May Fourth discourse was construed as "traditional" is reinscribed with a modern as well as universal characteristic that rejects the May Fourth attempt to particularize Chinese tradition. Although Fei Ming would later become a Marxist nativist, perhaps due primarily to the pressure of history, his efforts toward an aesthetics of mutual implication made a profound impact on generations of writers contemporary to him and succeeding him: Shen Congwen (1902–1988), He Qifang (1912–1977), Bian Zhilin, Lu Fen (1910–1988), and Wang Zengqi. All of these writers have self-consciously worked with his legacy, writing a kind of modernism that escapes spatial, temporal, and most importantly cultural boundaries. The lesson they learned from Fei Ming was how to write English with a Chinese brush: how to be Chinese and Western at the same time.

34. Fei Ming, "Morning Glory," *Literature Magazine* 1:4 (August 1937): 125–126.
35. Fei Ming, *Bridge*, 269.

CHAPTER 8

Gendered Negotiations with the Local

Lin Huiyin and Ling Shuhua

The blue of the sky fell in love with the green of the earth.
The breeze between them sighs, "Alas!"
RABINDRANATH TAGORE'S POEM DESCRIBING LIN HUIYIN (1924)

I often envy you, for being in such a large wild place with a very old civilization.
VIRGINIA WOOLF, LETTER TO LING SHUHUA (APRIL 17, 1939)

The relationship between the May Fourth enlightenment project and gender has been a topic of much interest, particularly the ways in which gender is deployed as a trope or figure for the articulation of the project, instead of being a socially grounded issue in the service of women's liberation. The troping of gender is perhaps best illustrated by Lu Xun's various stories where "woman" is represented as the receptacle of tradition in need of the male modern's enlightenment, an allegory of old China's (female) need for modernity and modernization (male). It was the male voice propounding an agenda of national cultural rejuvenation that ironically displaced the feminist agenda of women's liberation as articulated by such feminist writers as Lu Yin (1898–1934).[1] Encapsulated in the genre of fiction called "problem fiction," the "problem" of the patriarchal oppression of women was displaced as the problem of "tradition," which was seen as having tyrannized men and women alike. Women's problems were merely one of the many indexes to larger problems of tradition; hence if traditional culture were eliminated, women's problems should also automatically evaporate into thin air, as the logic went.

1. See my "Female Confessional Narratives in Modern Chinese Literature" (*Zhongguo xiandai wenxue zhong de nüxing zibai xiaoshuo*), *Con-Temporary* (*Dangdai*) 95 (March 1994): 108–127, and Stephen Chan, "The Language of Despair: Ideological Representation of the 'New Woman' by May Fourth Writers," in *Gender Politics in Modern China: Writing and Feminism*, ed. Tani E. Barlow (Durham: Duke University Press, 1993), 13–32.

In the context of the Beijing School, where tradition was reinscribed as productive of global modernity, how was gender reconfigured? Did the *jingpai* advocate a simple return to traditional patriarchy, or did it propose an agenda of reinventing the cultural priorities of femininity and masculinity? As I illustrated in chapter 6, the cultural and aesthetic discourses of the *jingpai* took gender into consideration mostly in terms of the recovery of spirituality or femininity of traditional Chinese culture as a corrective to the overly masculinized militant culture of the West. Fei Ming's fiction revealed, on the other hand, an aesthetic recuperation of the feminine as necessary to the complementarity of the male in the metaphysical sense of the Taoist androgynous ideal.[2] In both cases, the feminine functions as a theoretical principle and not as a social category linked to specific women's issues. While May Fourth enlightenment discourses subsumed gender in the name of an anti-local, antitraditional ideology, the neotraditional discourse defended the local by circumscribing the question of gender within the realm of the theoretical, and thus did little to subvert the patriarchal underpinnings of the local. Despite the opposing agendas of the May Fourth and the *jingpai*, "woman" seemed to have been unquestioningly equated with the local, and was made to hide behind fervent discussions of the validity of the local within opposing definitions of and competing claims on modernity, except in the works of the two *jingpai* women writers: Lin Huiyin (1903–1955) and Ling Shuhua (1904–1990).

If it had been difficult for women to write during the May Fourth period, under the hegemonic rhetoric of antitraditionalism, one could argue that it must have been even more arduous for women writers in the *jingpai* milieu, which was predicated on an agenda of recuperating the traditional as constitutive of the modern. To be sure, the *jingpai*, especially in the literary activities of the Crescent Moon Society mainly consisting of Euro-American returnees, flaunted a new kind of biculturalist cosmopolitanism that saw the East/West divide in modern Chinese cultural constructions as artificial, but the gender divide was often left unchallenged. The questions that drive this chapter are therefore centered around the two prominent women writers whose work and life stories serve as eloquent exemplifications of women's circuitous routes to writing, representation, and modernity due to their ambivalent relationship to "tradition," being themselves participants in the modernist revalidation of tradition. The crucial question is how they negotiated with a sanctioned recuperation of the local and its subsumption of women's issues. Briefly, it can be said that a dual structure of inheritance and exclusion generally informed their re-

2. For the androgynous ideal, see Roger T. Ames, "Taoism and the Androgynous Ideal," in *Women in China*, ed. Richard W. Guisso and Stanley Johannesen (Youngstown, N.Y.: Philo Press, 1981), 21–45.

lationship with the local, while a Western-mediated feminist subjectivity challenged this exclusion.

As I will illustrate below, these negotiations with the local can be seen as *tactics* of subversion, reinscription, and production of a feminine modernism through and within the larger project of recuperating the local and the traditional.[3] Their writings show how the local itself is not unified or cohesive, as a gendered position reveals a different access to and perspective on the local, particularly in relation to so-called Chinese literary heritage. While Fei Ming could ingeniously incorporate the aesthetics of Tang nature poetry into a modernist language and syntax of disjunction and fragmentation, these two women writers' appropriations of traditional literary practices, episodic narrative, and the boudoir complaint genre necessarily involved a double gesture of incorporation and critique through parody. This double gesture arises out of the tension between their willing collaboration with the existing idioms of writing and their need to struggle against the gendered determinants of these idioms.

The question of a cosmopolitan neotraditionalism, as part of a larger semicolonial cultural formation that appropriated metropolitan Western culture without much anxiety, further complicates this double gesture of women writers. In terms of a transcultural, transnational stance that informs the neotraditionalist discourse in general, Lin Huiyin and Ling Shuhua are typical members of the *jingpai*. Their bicultural and bilingual consciousnesses, however, are also specifically gendered, and this is where their voices become internal dissenters within the neotraditionalist discourse. Access to "the West" would also serve as a kind of counterdiscourse that qualified their recuperation of the local with a gendered dimension. While I note the gendered intervention of the local, I also reveal how such intervention sometimes gets caught in a complicitous relationship with Western Orientalism in its rejection of Third World patriarchy (in the specific case of literary relations between Ling Shuhua and Virginia Woolf). Although Lin and Ling's was a distinctively gendered transnational modernity erected upon transcultural mediations, I address the politics of these mediations to reveal the specific transnational processes at work in the formation of a Chinese feminist subjectivity in the *jingpai* milieu.

A GENDERED, TRANSNATIONAL MODERNITY

The day in April 1924 when Nobel laureate Rabindranath Tagore (1861–1941) gave a lecture at Beijing University during his two-week visit to China

3. Here I am specifically invoking Michel de Certeau's notion of tactics. He notes that the "place of a tactic belongs to the other. . . . It has at its disposal no base where it can capitalize on its advantage, prepare its expansions, and secure independence with respect to circumstances. . . . It must constantly manipulate events in order to turn them into 'opportunities.'" See his *The Practice of Everyday Life*, trans. Steven Rendall (Berkeley: University of California Press, 1984), xix.

was a day of fateful encounters and celebrations. The then youthful and beautiful Lin Huiyin served as Tagore's interpreter along with the handsome and brilliant poet Xu Zhimo, with whom she had previously had an amorous relationship in England. On this day as well, Ling Shuhua met her future husband Chen Yuan (1896–1970), the ebullient twenty-eight-year-old chairman of the English Department at Beijing University, who had been educated for the most part in England. The former romance was destined not to develop as Lin Huiyin would soon leave the country for the United States and be betrothed to Liang Sicheng (1901–1972), the eldest son of Liang Qichao. The brief romance between Lin Huiyin and Xu Zhimo has since become one of the great legends of modern China. The romance between Ling and Chen, on the other hand, would soon develop into a marriage and a relationship that would nourish two productive careers—one as a cultural critic and the other as a fiction writer. The paths of Lin Huiyin and Ling Shuhua would cross time and again as they published in the same journals, socialized in the same literary salons, and through their personal relationships with many other literary figures in Beijing, especially Xu Zhimo. Before Xu Zhimo died in an airplane crash while hastening to attend a lecture on Chinese architecture to be given by Lin Huiyin in Beijing on November 19, 1931, he had entrusted his personal letters and diaries to Ling Shuhua, whom he considered a close friend. The conjecture is that Xu, being something of a romantic, was probably also attracted to Ling Shuhua, and that there might have been ambivalent feelings between Lin Huiyin and Ling Shuhua, especially since the letters Xu left behind (which later disappeared mysteriously) presumably included some private correspondences between Xu and Lin Huiyin.[4]

But these intersections should not eclipse their individual life stories, each richly textured with bicultural and bilingual upbringings, marriages between prestigious families, privileged transnational mobility, and finally the two writers' particular gendered negotiations with all these circumstances.

Lin Huiyin, known also as Phyllis Lin or Lin Whei-yin,[5] was born to father Lin Changmin (1876–1924), a graduate of Waseda University in Japan and

4. It is striking that when we think of these two women writers, we often think of the romantic lives I have just summarized. This has much to do with the tendency in modern Chinese literary histories to trivialize the importance of women writers. The implications here are multiple: women writers are often trailed by gossip about their romantic lives, and their worth is measured according to the men whom they married, not their literary output. In sum, only absolutely "extraordinary" human beings such as Lin and Ling deserve mention in literary histories at all. My summary of their romantic lives here is the basis of my subsequent critique of their elite background, as both a necessity for women's expression at the time and a constraint on the articulation of a radical antipatriarchal critique.

5. Lin Huiyin is mainly known as a poet of the Crescent Moon school, which includes such poets as Xu Zhimo and Wen Yiduo. I am concentrating on her fiction in this chapter, however, as my general focus in this book is the narrative.

a famous scholar-diplomat politically active in the first decade of the Republic; her mother bore no male heir. Even though her father later took on a concubine who bore him four sons, she was his favorite child and was early on taken to England for her education during his diplomatic posting there. She thus grew up caught between paternal love and consuming maternal jealousy and frustration about her father's polygamy, a tension which later translated into a debilitating schism in her own life, between the aspirations for the world of culture approved by her father and the frustrations of the domestic world represented by her mother.

Before she entered St. Mary's Collegiate School in London at the age of sixteen in 1920, she attended the Peihua Girl's School in China, run by British missionaries. On her way back to China from England a year later, she travelled with her father across Europe. In 1924, she left with her future husband Liang Sicheng, first to Cornell University's summer program, then entering the University of Pennsylvania in the fall of that year. There she found her aspiration for a career in architecture thwarted, since the School of Architecture did not admit female students. Undeterred, she enrolled in the School of Fine Arts and managed to take architecture classes that way. By the spring term of 1926, she was a part-time assistant to the Architectural Design Staff, and for the academic year 1926–1927 she was a part-time instructor in Architectural Design.

When she graduated in 1927, having completed the four-year coursework with flying colors in three years, she and her husband were employed as assistants to professor Paul P. Cret (1876–1945), the then-leader of the Beaux-Arts tradition of architecture in the United States. In 1927, without her fiancé, she studied stage design under the renowned George P. Baker at Yale University, joining Liang in 1928 after his year at Harvard University researching the history of Chinese architecture. Together, they travelled to Vancouver where they got married, then traversed Europe and the expanse of Siberia before arriving in China in the Fall of 1928.[6]

Assuming the position of professor of architecture at Dongbei University, where her husband was appointed the chair of the Architecture Department (the gender hierarchy is obvious here), Lin in the ensuing years worked on various architectural design and historical writing projects. She helped design the national emblem of the People's Republic of China in 1949, and wrote at least one crucial chapter for the *History of Chinese Architecture* (*Zhongguo jianzhushi*) in the 1930s, later published under her husband's name.

---

6. Information regarding Lin's schooling is derived from her friend Wilma Fairbank (the wife of the famous sinologist John K. Fairbank); see her moving account of Lin's and Lin's husband's life, *Liang and Lin: Partners in Exploring China's Architectural Past* (Philadelphia: University of Pennsylvania Press, 1994), as well as Lin Shan's lyrically written *Biography of Lin Huiyin* (*Lin Huiyin zhuan*) (Taipei: Shijie shuju, 1993).

Liang Sicheng was later to be honored with the title of "the first Chinese architectural historian," while Lin Huiyin was perceived as no more than his helper. Her contribution to her husband's work as a professional architectural historian has so far been systematically ignored, although, according to several close friends who knew her professional relationship with her husband, it was she who was the major inspiration behind what passed as Liang Sicheng's work.[7]

Besides the obvious gender inequities she must have felt when barred from the entrance to the architectural school, the minimizing of her professional contribution by patriarchal assumptions was perhaps even more difficult to bear ("I have really helped [Liang's work] in my way though no one would ever believe its truth,"[8] she said in a letter to Wilma Fairbank, the wife of the sinologist John K. Fairbank). In other letters to Wilma Fairbank, she would also write about the constrictions her gender imposed on her and the contradictory demands of work and motherhood. In a 1936 letter, Lin expressed how she felt oppressed by housework which prevented her from engaging in literary work.

> Whenever I am engaged in household chores, I feel what a waste of time it is, thinking that I am neglecting more interesting and more important people whom I do not know. So I quickly finish up the chores in order to share my thoughts with these people. If household chores cannot be finished no matter how hard I work on them, and new items continue to be added to existing ones, I become very frustrated. Hence I can never do a good job with the chores. . . . On the other hand, if I am writing something or seriously engaged in a similar activity, and housework is neglected, I do not feel at all uneasy. Frankly, I feel I am quite happy, thinking myself quite wise, being engaged in a more meaningful act. It is only when the children get sick or lose weight that I feel bad. Sometimes I chide myself in the middle of the night, feeling that I am not fair to my children.[9]

Note that these complaints were not expressed to her Chinese acquaintances but to her American friend. In this regard, an interview with Lin by a fellow American student, published in the *Montana Gazette* when Lin was at the University of Pennsylvania, is noteworthy for her opinions on modern womanhood, as represented by American flappers: "I have to admit that in the beginning I thought them very silly but now I think that when you get beneath

7. See the accounts of Wilma Fairbank, Xiao Qian (who called Lin the real "nameless hero"), and poet Bian Zhilin (who called her the "source of [Liang's] inspiration"). Wilma Fairbank, *Liang and Lin*; Xiao Qian, "The Talented Lady of a Generation, Lin Huiyin" (*Yidai cainü Lin Huiyin*), *Dushu* 10 (October 1984): 115–116; Bian Zhilin, "Inside and Outside the Window: Remembering Lin Huiyin" (*Chuangzi neiwai: yi Lin Huiyin*), in *Bian Zhilin*, ed. Zhang Manyi (Hong Kong: Sanlian shudian, 1990), 90.

8. Lin Huiyin, letter to Wilma Fairbank, in *Liang and Lin*, 92.

9. Xiao Qian, "The Talented Lady of a Generation," 115–116.

the top layer you'll find them the best companions in the world. In China a girl is worth only as much as her family stands for. Here, there is a spirit of democracy that I admire."[10] Here, the comparison between American flappers and Chinese womanhood is articulated in terms of democracy and autocracy: Lin sees the woman's worth as autonomous in America and dependent on the stature of the family in China. These examples suggest that Lin's feminist subjectivity is contingent upon Western mediation, and this is where her intervention of the local is the most clearly defined.

The question of Western mediation is crucial in a different sense. In the mid-1920s, when she was studying at the University of Pennsylvania, she was reputedly a frequent visitor to the art museum there which housed a number of Chinese art objects, particularly two reputedly very precious glazed ceramic horses from Tang dynasty royal tombs. Her biographer Lin Shan notes that encountering these two ceramic horses was for her "a sudden rediscovery of a China that had been lost."[11] This is the moment of re-cognizing oneself in another's territory, an experience shared by many *jingpai* thinkers and writers including her husband Liang Sicheng, who around this time determined to find and record the "grammar" of Chinese architecture. This is not a self-Orientalization or an emergence of cultural nationalism, but rather the discovery of the self in an alien terrain, matched by an equal identification with and alienation from the familiar terrain of China itself, thereby unsettling both the unmediated West and the pure China in their claims upon subjectivity.

The best illustration of Lin and Liang's alienation from China was the cultural shock they experienced upon returning to China in 1928, feeling, in Wilma Fairbank's words, like a "pair of Rip Van Winkles," totally lost.[12] Theirs was a biculturality in which neither culture (American or Chinese) was taken for granted or unquestioningly accepted. In one of her 1935 letters to Mrs. Fairbank, she articulated her biculturality in this way: "You see, I was biculturally brought up, and there is no denying that bicultural contact and activity is essential to me. Before you two [the Fairbanks] really came into our lives here at No. 3, I was always somewhat lost and had a sense of lack somewhere, a certain spiritual poverty that needed nourishing."[13] Liang Sicheng would characterize this biculturality, in his posthumously published *A Pictorial History of Chinese Architecture*, claiming that "there is a basic similarity between the ancient Chinese and the ultramodern."[14] This statement can be read as both the modern/Western authentication of the traditional/Chinese, and vice versa. In this scheme, modernity is not conceived in opposing cul-

10. Quoted in Fairbank, *Liang and Lin*, 27.
11. See Lin Shan, *Biography of Lin Huiyin*, 68–69.
12. Fairbank, *Liang and Lin*, 36.
13. Ibid., 91.
14. Liang Ssu-ch'eng [Liang Sicheng], *A Pictorial History of Chinese Architecture*, ed. Wilma Fairbank (Cambridge: MIT Press, 1984), 3.

tural terms, nor is it seen as the property of one given geographically bounded terrain. Rather, it is a kind of bicultural liminality made possible by the subjects' transnational movements and cosmopolitan knowledge of both cultures. This is a notion of culture which vigilantly situates itself in the global context beyond nationalist paradigms, but this globalization does not conform to the rules of cultural homogenization imposed by the colonial structures of knowledge and culture, as in other colonized states in the Third World. Semicolonial cultural formation seems to allow a kind of elite cultural production of transnational modernity.

MODERNIST MONTAGE AND EPISODIC NARRATIVE

The above account highlights two aspects of Lin Huiyin's life and work which can serve as entry points to understanding her 1934 masterpiece "In Ninety-Nine Degree Heat" (*Jiushijiudu zhong*), published in the inaugural issue of *Xuewen Monthly* (for which she also designed the cover illustration). The story was hailed by Wang Zengqi as the first Chinese piece of self-consciously Virginia Woolf–like stream-of-consciousness fiction.[15] Two facts inform the structural and thematic aspects of the story, as mentioned above. First, Lin was one of the few writers in modern China who was completely bilingual and bicultural. Second, her gender played a restrictive role in her life as a writer and an architectural historian: to call someone a "talented lady" *(cainü)* is a traditional way of relegating her to a special category outside the male-dominated literary canon.

In nine sections depicting approximately fourteen episodes and scenes, the story gives an account of more than forty characters on one particularly hot day in Beijing. The episodes appear unrelated as the omniscient narrator introduces the characters, their concerns, and their actions one after another, seemingly at random. For instance, section two ends with a delivery man's longing for cold sour-plum juice and section three begins with a rickshaw puller's thirst:

> "Since it's so hot please give us an extra tip," the delivery man pursed his dry lips, thinking about the sour-plum juice vendor in the corner of the alley, feeling the thirst in his mouth.

> It was because of this thirst in his mouth, Yang San, while pulling Second Master Lu on his rickshaw to the Western Gate of the Dongan market, thought to himself that a while ago at the front gate of Happy-something Hall he saw Wang Kang sitting on a rickshaw taking a nap. Wang Kang owed Yang San thirty-four

15. Wang Zengqi, *Evening Green Essays* (*Wancui wentan*) (Hangzhou: Zhejiang wenyi chubanshe, 1988), 41.

strings of cash since the end of last month but refused to return it and had been avoiding him.[16]

There is no apparent connection between the delivery man and the rickshaw puller Yang San. They neither know nor ever come across one another in the course of the story. The motif of thirst on a hot summer day serves as the only transition.

Lin uses several other techniques for transitions, such as geographical proximity of unrelated characters, thematic relevance, and the movement of a character's mental associations, but often she simply jumps from one scene to another without any transition. Like a camera capturing diverse scenes of life and presenting them in montages, Lin's narrative perspective moves in a fluid manner without explanatory subtitles or voice-overs. Lin captures certain images specifically using the language of film: "A woman riding a bicycle rushed past his left side. As if set in fast motion [*kuaijing*], a view of vibrant colors, feet and legs, waist and back, side of the face, eyes and hair, were all taken in by the eyes of Old Lu."[17] Another filmic analogy can be found in section four, where three characters meet in a cafe to while away the time. Appearing in the middle of the section is a seemingly irrelevant paragraph describing a couple in the cafe eating ice cream. This paragraph operates structurally like a movie camera capturing an activity other than that of the main characters, to help create the desired background atmosphere and to provide foils for the activity of the main characters.

Overlapping descriptions of a single event are given from different perspectives as the camera shifts its angle and varies the relationship between foreground and background. A quarrel between two characters, Wang Kang and Yang San, is first depicted as the main physical event in section three; section five has Mrs. Liu noticing a policeman leading them, this time identified only as two rough fellows, to the police headquarters with their arms tied tight by a white rope; their quarrel becomes a news item in the local newspaper in section eight. The sickness and death of the nameless delivery man is likewise the focus of one section of the story, mentioned only in passing in other sections. The narrative perspective moves with immense freedom, thereby cutting the story into even smaller fragments.

The fragmentary nature of the narrative harkens back to the traditional episodic narrative, where events are frequently merely juxtaposed or connected as if by coincidence and form a vast "interweaving" and "reticular" relationship rather than a linear, causal one. Some critics have related this type of narrative to the Chinese worldview that the cosmos is created not by an external force but by a "self-contained, self-generating, dynamic process,

16. Lin Huiyin, "In Ninety-Nine Degree Heat" (*Jiushijiudu zhong*), *Xuewen Monthly* (*Xuewen yuekan*) 1:1 (May 1934): 25–26.

17. Ibid., 22.

with all of its parts interacting in one harmonious, organic whole."[18] The aesthetic coherence of the Chinese episodic narrative is said to be perceived in the "interstitial, rather than the architectonic, dimension," because Chinese narrative emphasizes the "interweaving" or "dovetailing" of episodes and smaller units.[19] The plot is by definition loose, since sequentiality is not an important concern. The narrative perspective also tends to be movable rather than fixed. All these characteristics of traditional episodic narrative, such as one finds in the Qing-dynasty classic *The Scholars,* are also the structural characteristics of Lin's story.[20] By exhibiting a kind of correspondence between elements of traditional aesthetics and Western modernism, Lin's text arrives at a distinct Chinese modernism of its own. It is no wonder that the *jingpai* literary critic Li Jianwu (1906–1982) noted in 1935 that this story exhibits the "fullest modernity" (*zui fu xiandaixing*) in its structure, technique, control, and above all in its solid base in tradition—hence it is extremely traditional and extremely modern at the same time.[21]

Structural looseness aside, however, coherent thematic threads can still be detected through a strategy of spatial, simultaneous reading. The story contrasts the idle, rich leisure class and the hard-working, exploited labor class, to bring out the theme of social inequality. For example, an image of heavily sweating delivery men, clad in muddy shoes and walking with heavy loads, is counterposed with Second Master Lu comfortably sitting on a rickshaw and fretting over what to have for lunch. No didactic commentary is given, but the presentation of the contrasting images expresses a critical content. As a rich and prestigious family prepares for the old matriarch's luxurious and extravagant birthday, a poor rickshaw puller is put in jail, and a delivery man is helplessly dying of cholera, ignored by doctors. As the quarrel between Wang Kang and Yang San creates a great commotion on the street, a beautiful young woman in her wedding gown is mechanically going through the ceremony for her wedding, which she has been forced into by her family.

The young woman is Ah Shu. Although she desires a marriage of choice, her father considered her a financial burden, and put her under tremendous pressure to consent to the arranged marriage. The distance between

18. Shuen-fu Lin, "Ritual and Narrative Structure in *Ju-lin Wai-shih* [*Rulin waishi*]" in Andrew Plaks, ed., *Chinese Narrative* (Princeton: Princeton University Press, 1977), 249–250.

19. Andrew Plaks, "Towards a Critical Theory of Chinese Narrative," in Plaks, *Chinese Narrative,* 334–335.

20. Lu Xun traced the generic genealogy of the short story form to *The Scholars,* which has an episodic structure, in his *A Short History of Chinese Narrative* (*Zhongguo xiaoshuo shilue*). Mentioned in Wang Yao, "Historical Connections between Modern Chinese Literature and Classical Literature" (*Zhongguo xiandai wenxue yu gudian wenxue de lishi lianxi*), *Beijing University Journal* (*Beijing daxue xuebao*) 5 (1986): 1–14.

21. Li Jianwu, "'In Ninety-Nine Degree Heat'—Written by Madam Lin Huiyin" (*Jiushijiudu zhong—Lin Huiyin nüshi zuo*), in *A Selection of Li Jianwu's Creative and Critical Writing* (*Li Jianwu chuangzuo pinglun xuanji*) (Beijing: Renmin wenxue chubanshe, 1984), 454.

the May Fourth theory of free love that she has been inculcated with through books and magazines and the reality of arranged marriage makes her fate even more devastating. Not knowing about free love and accepting her fate is one thing; knowing the possibility of free love and then being forced into an undesirable marriage is another. In lyrical language, Lin describes Ah Shu's feelings on her wedding day:

> Theory and practice never seem to have any connection with each other. What theory says marriage should be like, Ah Shu cannot remember it now. In practice, it had only taken her one nod of her head to let a strange person of a different last name and a different sex sit in her home, even next to her, in the time that it had taken to eat a meal the problem that her parents had had for the past two or three years—perhaps five or six years—had been suddenly, and in what they considered to be a civilized way, solved. . . . That day she first saw the strange person of a different last name and a different sex, his crass looks crushed the little bit of longing she had for beauty. She was terrified. Could she seek death, commit suicide because of a bad marriage? . . . And now she bows once and then again, saying good-bye to happiness. It's already too late. . . . But Ah Shu thinks to herself, why am I still so panic-stricken? I should be like a dead person, the waves of life do not matter to me anymore. I am like one about to be executed.[22]

The repetition of "the strange person of a different last name and a different sex" underlines Ah Shu's tragic betrothal to a complete stranger, which amounts to a total negation of her self as an independent being with independent desires. In that strange person, *that* name and sex, there is no place for her person, *her own* name and sex. The May Fourth ideal of free love remains an ideal that only mocks Ah Shu. More than a decade after the May Fourth movement, Lin contemplates the tragic inadequacy of its idealism against the backdrop of an unchanged society. The ideal remains an empty slogan that only enhances the pain of gender oppression.

When she was called upon to suggest short stories for a collection published by the *Dagong Daily* of Tianjin, whose literary supplement was at the time edited by Xiao Qian, she recommended, among others, the woman writer Luo Shu's (1903–1938) "Sold Wife" (*Shengrenqi*), which dramatizes the tragic plight of a woman sold into marriage. Both her unfinished play *Meizhen and Them* (*Meizhen tong tamen*, 1937) and her short story "Wenzhen" (*Wenzhen*, 1936) deal with the issue of bonded female servants and again emphasize the contradiction between the May Fourth rhetoric of emancipation and the present reality of oppression.[23] If we would construe this as an anti–May Fourth stance, we would also have to recognize it as a specifically

22. Lin Huiyin, "In Ninety-Nine Degree Heat," 30–31.
23. The unfinished four-act play was serialized in *Literature Magazine* 1:1–3 (1937): 147–180; 111–140; 98–127. "*Wenzhen*" and two other stories by Lin Huiyin can be found in Wu Fuhui,

gendered one, built upon the need to expand and improve the May Fourth perspective on women rather than reject the May Fourth stance as a whole. This was clearly unlike the male neotraditionalists' all-out attack on May Fourth ideology.

ORIENTALISM AND FEMINISM

Ling Shuhua (Su Hua Ling Chen), like Lin Huiyin, was born to an illustrious family, with a father whose official positions during the late Qing had been equivalents of the mayor of Beijing and governor of Hebei province, and a mother (the fourth of his six wives) without a male child in an unhappy marriage of neglect and frustration. Her maternal grandfather Xie Lansheng (1760–1831) had been a famous painter-calligrapher in the literati style in Guangdong, and Ling, her father's favorite daughter, was handpicked early on to continue the legacy of this maternal grandfather and become a painter. At the tender age of seven she was sent to study in Japan for three years with her siblings, later continuing her education at the foreign language department of Yanjing University (1923–1926). After having married Chen Yuan the year she graduated, she spent a year in Japan in 1927, studying such modern Japanese writers as Kikuchi Kan, Satō Haruo, Kawabata Yasunari, Tanizaki Jun'ichirō, and Natsume Sōseki. The literary intertexts to her stories written during the late 1920s, however, were mainly from British modernism: the New Zealand–born Katherine Mansfield (1888–1923) and Virginia Woolf. Deemed the "Chinese Mansfield" by her Japanese readers for her subtle psychological portraitures, Ling Shuhua started corresponding with Virginia Woolf in the late 1930s, and in 1947 emigrated to England to join her husband, then the Chinese representative to UNESCO. There her English autobiography *Ancient Melodies,* written earlier in increments with Woolf's encouragement, was published in 1953 by the publishing house of the Bloomsbury group, Hogarth Press, with a preface by Woolf's close friend, the novelist and poet Vita Sackville-West (1892–1962). Ling's total creative output consists of three collections of stories published in China, the autobiography, two essay collections, and her paintings exhibited in England and in catalogues.

Ling Shuhua's correspondence with Virginia Woolf is important for revealing a new dimension in the relation between Chinese and Western modernisms not yet discussed in this book, particularly in terms of the question of a Third World feminism's self-positioning vis-à-vis the West. Woolf is said to have read Ling's *Ancient Melodies* chapter by chapter as Ling sent them to

---

ed., *Selected Stories of the Beijing School* (*Jingpai xiaoshuo xuan*) (Beijing: Renmin wenxue chubanshe, 1990), 203–232. Only one other story besides these is extant: "Embarrassment" (*Jiong*), *Crescent Moon* (*Xinyue*) 3:9 (n.d.): 1–21.

her through the last few years of the 1930s until Woolf's suicide in 1941, and Ling finally retrieved the manuscript for her autobiography from Woolf's study, with the help of Vita Sackville-West, before revising, expanding, and publishing it. Woolf's remarks to Ling and comments on Ling's writing, as well as Ling's responses in her own writing, reveal a complex interweaving of the ambivalent properties of Orientalism and feminism. If their mutual sympathy was largely built upon their gendered position within patriarchies, as Wu Luqin has argued,[24] this sympathy points to the translocal nature of feminism. I explore below how this translocal feminism is articulated in Ling's *Ancient Melodies,* how its representation is premised paradoxically on an overt emphasis on historical and cultural specificity of Chinese lives to the point of exoticism, and how Ling's Third World feminist position may have required a process of voluntary self-Orientalization in order to cohere with Woolf's First World feminist position.

Ling Shuhua originally decided to start corresponding with Woolf after having read *A Room of One's Own* (1929), Woolf's long feminist essay on the status of women and the difficulty of being a woman artist, and having met Woolf's nephew Julian Bell, as well as Christopher Isherwood (1904–1986) and W. H. Auden (1907–1973), who later cowrote *A Journey to a War* (1939) after witnessing the Sino-Japanese War. Julian Bell would introduce Ling to Woolf, and Isherwood once carried Ling's gifts to Woolf. In Woolf's second letter to Ling, dated April 5, 1938, she first broached the subject of Ling Shuhua writing "an account of [her] life." From Woolf's letter, it is clear that Ling had earlier written to her about the difficulties of living and working in remote Sichuan after having escaped from the war zones during the Sino-Japanese War, and in response Woolf said that her "only advice" was for Ling "to work."

What is troubling about this advice for the literary historian is that she told Ling to do this "work," that is, to write her account, in English: "At any rate please remember that I am always glad if you will write and tell me anything about yourself: or politics: and it would be a great pleasure to me to read some of your writing, and criticize it: so think of writing your life, and if you only write a few pages at a time, I could read them and we could discuss it." By this time, Ling Shuhua was already an established writer in China, and there was no particular reason why she should want to or need to write her autobiography in English. The unspoken presumption behind Woolf's suggestion seems to be a hierarchical conception of language and audience, that English, the language in which she herself wrote in, is the authentic, if not superior, language for creative endeavors, and that the Western audience is the one worth writing for. This subtle Eurocentric attitude was dis-

---

24. Wu Luqin, "Virginia Woolf and Ling Shuhua" (*Weijiniya Wuerfu yu Ling Shuhua*), in his *Writers Respect Each Other* (*Wenren xiangzhong*) (Taipei: Hongfan shudian, 1983), 5–33.

closed when she also urged Ling to write a work "of great value to other people," indirectly implying that works of great value should be written in English. Following such a suggestion, it then comes as no surprise that Woolf somewhat condescendingly commented on how Ling's English was "good enough" and that she would be happy to edit or correct Ling's English.[25]

Ling must have seen Woolf's mentorship in the writing of an autobiography in English as flattering, at a time when the adoration of metropolitan Western culture was taken for granted in semicolonial China, and when Woolf in particular had been hailed as a modernist master and widely read by Chinese writers and critics.[26] As we recall, the main agenda of *jingpai* cultural discourse was the integration of metropolitan Western culture. *Jingpai* writers therefore accepted the universality of Western modernism just as much as their May Fourth antecedents did (one remembers Xu Zhimo's meeting with Mansfield in England in the early 1920s, which was considered a "historic" event by some in modern Chinese literary history), and Woolf as the feminist practitioner of modernism was very probably someone to look up to for a protofeminist like Ling herself. Even their exchange of gifts, however—Ling sending "two little gifts" in a "lovely little box" from China on one occasion, and a red and black poster on another, while Woolf sent her eighteenth-century British novels— spells out the asymmetry in this relationship.[27] The gifts from China were not drawn from the vast heritage of Chinese literature (Ling did not at all try to impress this upon Woolf), while the gifts from England were solid exemplars of the British literary tradition. If the latter were so important that they should serve as models for Ling's prose, as Woolf suggested, the former were merely souvenirs to be displayed on Woolf's table. The imbalance of their correspondence also probably explains why Ling did not attempt to clarify how her name should be spelled, and allowed Woolf to mistakenly call her Sue Ling again and again; Woolf did not at all understand the conventions of Chinese names, nor did she try to understand them.

In a letter dated October 15, 1938, only six months after Woolf had made the suggestion that Ling write an autobiography in English, Woolf ac-

25. Letter dated April 5, 1938, in *The Letters of Virginia Woolf, vol. 6: 1936–1941*, ed. Nigel Nicolson and Joanne Trautmann (New York and London: Harcourt Brace Jovanovich, 1980), 222.

26. Virginia Woolf was widely read by Chinese writers since the 1920s. The magazine *Crescent Moon* (1928–1933) prominently represented Woolf and Mansfield through translations. There was even an imitation of Woolf's "The Mark on the Wall" (translated in a 1932 issue) called "That Hazy Spot" (*Na mengmeng longlong de yituan*) in the March 1933 issue, by a writer named Chang Feng.

27. Letter dated July 27, 1938, in *The Letters of Virginia Woolf, vol. 6, 259.

knowledges having already received the first chapter. Her comments on the chapter are worth quoting at some length:

> Now I write to say that I like it very much. I think it has a great charm. It is also of course difficult for an English person, at first, there is some incoherence, and one does not understand the different wives; who they are; which is speaking. But this becomes clear after a time; and then I feel a charm in the very unlikeness. I find the similes strange and poetical. How far it can be read by the public as it stands, I do not know. That I could only say if you would go on sending me more chapters. Then I should get the whole impression. This is only a fragment. Please go on; write freely; do not mind how directly you translate the Chinese into the English. In fact I would advise you to come as close to the Chinese both in style and in meaning as you can. Give as many natural details of the life, of the house, of the furniture as you like. And always do it as you would were you writing for the Chinese. Then if it were to some extent made easy grammatically by someone English I think it might be possible to keep the Chinese flavor and make it both understandable yet strange for the English.[28]

The semantic linkages among such words as "charm," "unlikeness," "strange," and "Chinese flavor" indicate Woolf's lack of familiarity with China on the one hand, and her desire to remain unfamiliar as the necessary condition of appreciation on the other, for the value of Ling's work lay in its strangeness and unlikeness. Hence the implication that Ling should write in as authentic a "Chinese" fashion as possible, which includes providing daily details of life, furniture, the house, and so on. Here of course the notion that Ling should write for the Chinese audience is ironic—Ling had already been doing so in dozens of stories. In those stories, Ling did not find it at all necessary to provide materials only to authenticate their "Chinese-ness" for the Western gaze, because only a nonnative audience demanded strangeness and unlikeness in the representation of one's customs and culture. To put it bluntly, Woolf was calling for Ling to exoticize herself in the gaze of the West (embodied by Woolf herself and the future Western readers of the autobiography), to present herself as the Other to the West. When Vita Sackville-West wrote the preface to *Ancient Melodies,* she noted that the book was a record of a "vanished way of life" and a "forgotten world" that was ancient and remote. *Ancient Melodies* is naturally filled with aestheticized depictions of "ancient" Chinese customs and habits (although the narrative is set in the twentieth century), with ample explanations for these strange customs, rituals, clothes, etc. for the legibility and curiosity of the Western audience.

In terms of cultural content, then, *Ancient Melodies* had to embody the exotic, antiquated Orient whose strangeness would provide charm and delight to the Western reader secure in his/her own culture of familiarity and moder-

28. *The Letters of Virginia Woolf, vol. 6,* 289–290.

nity. When the book was finally published, it was also graced with illustrations by Ling Shuhua herself depicting childhood scenes in Chinese ink—for the first time, her training in traditional literati painting and her literary work seemed to coexist harmoniously, although in another context she saw them as oppositional (more about this in the next section). Since Woolf had suggested before her death that the book be proofread or edited by an English person, it was edited by the sister of the famous historian and essayist James Strachey, Margery Strachey, and proofread by the renowned poet C. Day Lewis (1904–1972). The book received immediate acclaim with a review by the important essayist J. B. Priestly (1894–1984) who named it the "book of the year." André Malraux (1901–1976) called it "a ravishing book," and it got several rave reviews in *Times Literary Supplement, Time and Tide, New Statesman,* and elsewhere. Subsequently, the book was also read aloud on the airwaves of the BBC by Peggy Ashcroft.[29]

Reading *Ancient Melodies* in terms of gender, one is immediately struck by the explicit and direct expression of a feminist intent, in contrast to Ling's earlier stories where such intent was articulated in a complex web of negotiations with patriarchy and modernity, as my readings will show in the next section. The constrictions that her gender imposed on her are conspicuously articulated throughout *Ancient Melodies*: if it weren't for a father's friend discovering her talent in painting, she would never have been educated at all; the six wives were constantly vying for the patriarch's favor and thus struggling for power, and such struggling translated into tensions among the many half sisters and brothers; on one occasion, with the absence of the patriarch in the household for a protracted period of time, all the wives were "on better terms with each other," which clearly points at patriarchy as the controlling power that pits women against one another.

But what is most revealing is the careful account of the making of a feminist in Ling Shuhua, specifically in chapter 10, entitled "Our Great-Uncle." This chapter begins with the visit of her two male cousins, educated abroad and bringing with them tastes of the modern lifestyle in the West (telephones and motor cars), and goes on to relate the times she spent alone with her great-uncle, who brought books of traditional Chinese vernacular stories. Among these books were two that depicted heroines who disguised themselves as men and passed the Civil Service Examination. These stories were then sung by Ling's mother, while all the children, wives, and maids sat together to enjoy them. Ling notes how then and there she wanted to be like a man and pass the Civil Service Examination. The great-uncle also told the story of Empress Wu of the Tang Dynasty, noting in feminist fashion that the

29. See Wu Luqin, "Virginia Woolf and Ling Shuhua," and relevant information from the dust jacket of the American edition of Ling Shuhua [Su Hua Ling Chen], *Ancient Melodies* (New York: Universe Books, 1988).

negative accounts of her private life were expressions of men's jealousy towards her power, that these "narrow-minded people could not bear to see a woman reign over a country." His final judgment on Empress Wu was that she was "the most powerful ruler of the Tang dynasty," and ruled over China for "sixty peaceful years." Furthermore, she opened the Civil Service Examination to women, who had been heretofore barred from it, and allowed women to serve at court. He then says to Ling: "Tell your mother this story; let her cherish a hope for her daughters."[30] Empress Wu is depicted as the regal feminist, and the stories serve as inspirations for the girl to aspire to a future no longer confined to the inner chambers of a household. Here, the effeminate and aged great-uncle is somehow aligned with the women in the household, and Chinese patriarchy gets represented solely by the stubborn father who will not hear these stories, nor Ling's foreign-educated cousins' stories about the modern lifestyle. For the Western audience, this was a clear moment of emergence of a feminist sensibility, made possible through her reading of stories not sanctioned by her father, and therefore built upon a clear rebellion against the Chinese patriarchy he represents.

The representation of a Third World feminist voice rejecting native patriarchy is problematically situated vis-à-vis the West. The work on South Asian women by postcolonial critics Gayatri Spivak and Lata Mani has illustrated how fraught such representations can be in their unwitting complicity with First World domination in the form of liberal feminism.[31] Seen through such a critical lens, Ling Shuhua's feminist bildungsroman about the exotic details of her childhood is subject to the same criticism, particularly since this narrative was written under the gaze of a powerful Western feminist. This Western-mediated feminism is especially troubling when we realize that between 1905 and 1949 there were about 110 journals or newspaper supplements in China devoted to women, where myriad issues relating to women and feminism were broached. Granted that most of these were innocuous discussions of home economics and commercialism, there were also such long-running publications with clear feminist agendas as the weekly supplement to *World Daily* (*Shijie ribao*), called *Rose* (*Qiangwei*), which ran for eight years between 1926 and 1934.[32] Ling Shuhua's setting of her feminist bildungsroman in the space of a traditional household disregards this entire

30. *Ancient Melodies*, 150–151.

31. See for instance Gayatri Spivak, *Outside in the Teaching Machine* (New York: Routledge, 1993), chapters 4, 6, 7, and 8, and Lata Mani, "Contentious Traditions: The Debate on *Sati* in Colonial India," in *Recasting Women: Essays in Indian Colonial History*, ed. Kumkum Sangari and Sudesh Vaid (New Brunswick: Rutgers University Press, 1990), 88–126.

32. See Jiang Weitang et al., eds., *A Study of Beijing Women's Newspapers and Journals, 1905–1949* (*Beijing funü baokankao, 1905–1949*) (Beijing: Guangming ribao chubanshe, 1990). Feminist writers associated with this supplement included Lu Jingqing (b. 1907), Shi Pingmei (1902–1928), Lu Yin, and others.

cultural context, perhaps because it is set in an earlier period of her child-hood, but her feminist subject-formation could not have been entirely in-dependent of these women's publications.

In sum, it is important to distinguish Lin Huiyin's feminist subjectivity, mediated through her bicultural upbringing and her intimate friendship with Wilma Fairbank and other Westerners, from Ling Shuhua's, which was largely constructed on an asymmetrical relationship with Virginia Woolf in the writing of *Ancient Melodies.* Although in both cases Western mediation contributed to the formation of feminist subjectivities and their challenges to the local, the "West" as such played significantly different roles in the two cases. This suggests that the "West" mediates Chinese subject positions variously and differentially, and that there is no coherent, unified "West" which informs the Chinese subjectivity in a predictable and uniform fashion. This multi-farious mediation then fundamentally denotes a complexity of transcultural interactions that cannot be neatly summed up through such simplified and reified categories as those of domination and resistance.

PARODYING THE FEMININE

Ling Shuhua's most well-known and acclaimed works are the short stories written from the mid-1920s to the late 1930s and collected in three an-thologies (eventually appearing in the two-volume *Collected Stories of Ling Shuhua* [*Ling Shuhua xiaoshuoji*]). In these stories, she did not anticipate the gaze of the West, as was the case for *Ancient Melodies,* and she wielded a pen less anxious to please and more understated and profound. The stories ex-ude a kind of quiet intensity that disturbs her readers in ways somewhat akin to the work of Katherine Mansfield and some of Virginia Woolf's stories of domesticity and other so-called feminine subjects. She has been perceived as a "minor" writer in modern Chinese literary history due to the fact that her stories deal with seemingly trivial events surrounding women and chil-dren rather than grand social issues. Male critics of her time and after identified her as a representative writer of the so-called "New Boudoir Lady School" (*xin guixiu pai*).[33] Conflating Ling's gender with her work, these male critics applied to her writing a term used to describe a woman of good breeding. In one crude appraisal, a critic went so far as to suggest that since Ling was a beautiful woman, the feminine beauty of her writing was a reflec-

33. Yi Zhen's "A Few Contemporary Chinese Women Fiction Writers" (*Jiwei dangdai Zhong-guo nüxiaoshuojia*), in Huang Renying (Qian Xingcun), ed., *Contemporary Chinese Women Writers* (*Dangdai Zhongguo nüzuojia lun*) (Shanghai: Guanghua shuju, 1933) first used the term to de-scribe Ling's work. For a critique of the term, see Rey Chow, "Virtuous Transactions: A Read-ing of Three Stories by Ling Shuhua," in *Modern Chinese Literature* 4:1–2 (1988): 72–73. As Rey Chow puts it, the application of a term about domestic femininity as a literary critical termi-nology implies that Ling's style is romantic and lightweight.

tion of her physical beauty,[34] while another critic said that judging from her stories she must be a very "talented and intelligent woman."[35] American feminist critic Mary Ellmann once coined the term "phallic criticism" to denote the practice of male critics who treat women's books as though the books themselves were women, using such adjectives as charming and sweet, passive and confined, while at the same time concentrating obsessively on women writers' femininity.[36] Ling's Shuhua's male critics would not be exempt from being called practitioners of phallic criticism. Katherine Mansfield, with whom Ling was frequently compared, had a similar reception in the West as someone who wrote "delicate, minor, and feminine" work, and Western feminist literary historians have sought to combat this reception, dissociating the feminine from its demeaning implications and reinscribing it as a particular female aesthetics.[37] In this recuperative effort, the feminine is revalorized as a specific mode of representation which foregrounds indirection, obliquity, the trivial, the common, and the domestic, and through which deeper meanings are intimated and expressed.[38] I argue alongside these feminist perspectives, but insist on the specificity of the feminine in the Chinese literary tradition as deployed and parodied by Ling Shuhua.

The misunderstanding of Ling's works in terms of negative associations of the feminine in the specific Chinese context is in part caused by an inadequate understanding of her relationship to representation. As a female writer, her access to representation was circumscribed because there was no female tradition in Chinese literature other than that written in a feminine style. Ling was raised in a very traditional family with her main training conducted in classical studies and traditional literati painting, and her father forbade her from writing in the vernacular, not to mention writing in that most illegitimate form (from the classical point of view), fiction. Ling hid all her writings from him, and he never read or knew about her literary activities.[39] Unlike Lin Huiyin, whose modern behavior against an entrenched classical background often shocked more traditional women (including her own mother-in-law), Ling's role was to be appropriately "modern-yet-modest," to borrow Deniz Kandiyoti's succinct phrase used to describe the cir-

---

34. Chen Jingzhi, *Women Writers of Early Modern Literature* (*Xiandai wenxue zaoqi de nüzuojia*) (Taipei: Chengwen chubanshe, 1980), 79–93.

35. Yi Zhen, "A Few Contemporary Chinese Women Fiction Writers," 15.

36. Mary Ellmann, *Thinking About Women* (New York: Harcourt, Brace and World, 1968), 29.

37. Clare Hanson, "Katherine Mansfield," in Bonnie Kime Scott, ed., *The Gender of Modernism* (Bloomington: Indiana University Press, 1990), 298–305.

38. Scott, *The Gender of Modernism*, 13, 301–303, 647–649.

39. Ling Shuhua, "Postscript to the Singapore edition of *Selections of Ling Shuhua*" (*Xinjiapo ban Ling Shuhua xuanji houji*), in *Collected Stories of Ling Shuhua* (*Ling Shuhua xiaoshuoji*) (Taipei: Hongfan shudian, 1986), 2:269.

cumscribed role of Third World women as nonthreatening icons of modernity.[40] One would also need to factor in the element of her "anxiety of authorship,"[41] the feeling of inadequacy and illegitimacy that plagues a woman writer. Writing in the feminine style was, after all, "proper" and "correct" for a woman writer and could easily win her public approval because it signaled her acceptance of the marginal space reserved for women writers outside the mainstream male canon. This is what Rey Chow, in analyzing Ling's work, calls the "virtuous transaction" between a woman writer and language: she appears to abide by the contract with patriarchy and its rules of writing in order to appear nonthreatening, but then she subtly undercuts its hegemony.[42] Just when she seems to be voluntarily co-opting the patriarchal regime of writing and relegating women's writing into the realm of the feminine, she subverts the regime through parodic practices. In her work, it is common to hear the voice which voluntarily accepts her marginalized femininity ironized by another that disrupts it from within. Ling's work therefore can be called a "double-voiced discourse" where there is a clash of two voices,[43] and this clash is manifest in her prominent use of parody.

Reading "Embroidered Pillows" (*Xiuzhen*, 1925) as an allegory for a woman writer and her writing offers a way to understand how the recuperation and parody of tradition functions as a narrative and formal strategy. Written in a graceful style like many of her other stories, with sentences and phrases rich with classical aesthetic tonalities, this is the story of a young nubile woman painstakingly working in the heat of summer on a pair of extremely fine embroidered cushions, which are to be presented to a rich family as a way to present herself for a possible marriage match, as is customary for women of her breeding. Through the comments made by her admiring maid and the maid's uncouth daughter, as well as through the protagonist's own interior monologues, the reader is given a glimpse into the degree of care and pain she takes with her embroidery: she uses thirty or forty different colored threads for the embroidery of a phoenix alone; she has to embroider the crown of the green bird three times over after having used wrong colors; to bring out the liveliness of a large lotus leaf, she uses twelve different tones of green threads; for the delicate pink colors of the lotus blossom, she has to first wash her hands and put powder on them so as not to allow

40. Deniz Kandiyoti, "Identity and Its Discontents: Women and the Nation," in Patrick Williams and Laura Chrisman, eds., *Colonial Discourse and Post-colonial Theory* (New York: Columbia University Press, 1994), 379.

41. The phrase is from Sandra M. Gilbert and Susan Gubar's *The Madwoman in the Attic: The Woman Writer and the Nineteenth Century Literary Imagination* (New Haven: Yale University Press, 1984).

42. Rey Chow, "Virtuous Transactions," 85.

43. The term comes from chapter five of Mikhail Bakhtin's *Problems of Dostoevsky's Poetics*, trans. and ed. Caryl Emerson (Minneapolis: University of Minnesota Press, 1984), 181–269.

her sweat to soil the tender threads; and from working at night due to the heat of the summer in the daytime, her eyes hurt for over ten days. The pillows are, so to speak, the best exemplars of "women's work" in the patriarchal order of an elite family. Within this order, the lower class maid and her daughter are considered lowly and dirty. But later it is through the daughter's mouth that the lady hears about the fate of her cushions: vomited on by a drunken man during a party, then trampled upon, then given away to a maid, then indirectly landing in the hands of the daughter who now cuts them into pieces to be sewn onto pillow cases. Two years pass, and the nubile lady is still caught within the patriarchal order.

Ling's subtle critique of the protagonist's state of imprisonment within the patriarchal order and her willingness to abide by it (demonstrating, in Rey Chow's words, "the complete efficacy of patriarchal ideology"[44]) has both a gender and a class dimension. It reveals that her patriarchal interpellation is a classed one, to which the maid's daughter is not subjected. As an allegory for a woman artist engaged in conventional, proper, sanctioned, elite forms of writing, the story reveals how such an engagement is self-negating. Read as a metafictional commentary, the story ultimately denotes Ling's ambivalent engagement and simultaneous disengagement (through parody and irony) with the feminine tradition of writing.

This simultaneous double gesture of inheritance and parody is traceable to the feminine voice in the poetic subgenre known as the Boudoir Complaint (*guiyuanshi*), in which the most renowned classical women writers such as Li Qingzhao (1084–c. 1151) and Zhu Shuzhen (c. eleventh century) excelled. Although this subgenre was later subsumed under the larger category of *guixiu wenxue*, defined as lightweight writing by and for ladies which is suitable as bedside reading for refined women,[45] and a category to which Ling's work has been said to belong, specific motifs from the Boudoir Complaint subgenre can be traced in Ling's work. Conventionally, such poems were written either by politically marginalized male poets assuming female voices as a vehicle to relate their allegorical, often political, messages, or by female poets to convey their feminine sensibilities and longings, often melancholy and sentimental. The central figure is often a beautiful woman, left behind by her lover or husband for various reasons. Her location is inside the boudoir, and her posture is that of looking out through her window to the scene outside.[46] Ling situates many of her melancholy female char-

44. Rey Chow, "Virtuous Transactions," 79.

45. On the feminine style of *guixiu wenxue,* I am borrowing Clara Yü Cuadrado's definition. See her "Portraits by a Lady: The Fictional World of Ling Shuhua," in Angela Jung Palandri, ed., *Women Writers of Twentieth-Century China,* Asian Studies Publication Series, (Eugene: University of Oregon, 1982), 41.

46. Hans H. Frankel, *The Flowering Plum and the Palace Lady: Interpretations of Chinese Poetry* (New Haven: Yale University Press, 1976), 56–57.

acters exactly in such a space and posture, but she provides the situation with subtle twists with subversive connotations.

In many of her stories, she contrasts the stasis of a languid woman's inside space with luxurious and blossoming flowers outside, to show the inside as a place of death and imprisonment. In "Embroidered Pillows" discussed above, the "fiery red flowers of the pomegranate tree reflecting the sunlight" mock the lifeless embroiderer inside the boudoir; in "The Tea Party" (*Chicha*, 1925), "the pink roses bathed in the sun emanating exceptional brightness" ironically comment on the old-fashioned lady's false hope for matrimony; in "Spring" (*Chuntian*, 1926), a listless lady inside the boudoir looks outside and feels offended by a verdant and luxuriously flowering crabapple tree, which, surrounded by butterflies and bees, looks like a young lady adorned with tiny flowers in her hair.[47] Especially in "The Tea Party," one finds the classic case of a boudoir beauty, appropriately named Fangying ("beautiful shadow") to denote her complacent narcissism, who constantly looks at herself in the mirror and recites classical poetry about beautiful women. The only way she knows how to define herself is by following a set of outmoded standards of feminine beauty prescribed by patriarchy. Her identity is bound up with the interior space in which the discourse of the feminine beauty is the means of legitimation. Ling shows how these female characters' voluntary acceptance of the values attached to the interior space brings them a death-in-life existence, and thereby exposes the patriarchal mechanism which induces women to internalize these values. In "Spring," Ling further parodies the lady-by-the-window motif by locating the object of the woman's longing in a man other than her husband, thereby registering her transgression of the values of the inside.

Ling's other way of showing the devastating effects of the inside/outside dichotomy on women's lives is by ironically juxtaposing women who stay inside with women who venture out. The traditional ladies waiting passively for marriages to be arranged for them in "After the Tea Party" (*Chahui yihou*, c. 1926) are depicted as the exact opposites of other ladies, who are young and vivacious and who go out and seek their own marital prospects as equal partners to men. Ling mercilessly attacks the former's pathetic pretentiousness and useless pride while anticipating the fate that awaits them— to grow ungracefully into spinsters. The difference between a woman who holds her fate in her own hands and the other two traditional women in "Sending Off" (*Songche*, 1929) is unambiguous: while the modern woman enjoys a beautiful marriage, the other two are bound in marriages that are no more than financial and biological contracts.

The unquestioned acceptance of the values associated with the inside, this

47. Originally published in the collection *Temple of Flowers* (*Hua zhi si*) (Shanghai: Xinyue shudian, 1928). I am using *Collected Stories of Ling Shuhua*, 1:13, 22.

time the domestic sphere of a married woman, proves to be even more de-structive in "The Night of the Midautumn Festival" (*Zhongqiuwan*, 1925). The wife in this story is so obsessed with following the customs and rituals of the midautumn festival sanctioned by the patriarchal order that she inadvertently jeopardizes nothing less than her own marriage. Convinced that not eating the "together duck" on the eve of the festival will portend the separation of husband and wife, she forces her husband to wait for the duck and eat a bite of it before rushing out to see his dying stepsister. It turns out that he is five minutes too late and the stepsister dies without seeing him. In a bout of fury, he blames his wife for delaying him, and quarrels between the couple en-sue. A flower vase is knocked over and broken to pieces; he starts to visit other women and squanders away his money; she has two miscarriages, each of which is described in gruesome detail; finally, we see a desolate scene of the wife and her mother sitting in the house seized by debtors amid spiderwebs, moths, and bats. She is victimized by her own insistence on performing the wifely duty of preserving domestic customs. The story shows, among other things, that the inside operates according to a patriarchal logic which para-doxically victimizes those who are interpellated to perform according to its norms and who perpetuate them.

Such a logic is exposed again in "A Blessed Person" (*You fuqi de ren*, 1926). The venerable grandmother in this ironically titled story finds out, by coin-cidentally overhearing her children, that their professed love and respect to-wards her is nothing but a ploy to entice her to give them her wealth. She has done everything correctly: bearing and raising four sons and three daughters, and rightfully favoring her sons over her daughters as the patriarchal proto-col has called for. She is "blessed" when measured by the objective criteria of the traditional patriarchal society, but she discovers that her blessed state is a mere facade, hollow and false. Her lifelong endeavors in the affairs of the inside—her role as wife and mother—win her nothing but her children's hypocrisy. Female domestic identity is here exposed as a patriarchal mecha-nism that binds women under roofs, as the female protagonist in "Ennui" (*Wu-liao*, 1936) says in reference to the graphic components of the Chinese char-acter "*jia*" ("home"): "home is a cangue that yokes a pig under a roof."[48]

While choosing to write about domesticity and triviality, Ling exposes their social and ideological implications as oppressive mechanisms. In so doing, she empties out the supposed passivity and melancholy of the feminine voice associated with domesticity and triviality, and endows it with a subversive edge. Her parody of the voice is further paired with a constructive presentation of a kind of female lyricism in "Temple of Flowers" (*Huazhisi*, 1925) and "A Poet Goes Mad" (*Fengle de shiren*, 1928), through a subtle critique of the inherited

48. Ibid., 2:376.

lyricism from classical poetry that male poets comfortably claim. Youquan in the former story has a high regard for himself and spends a lot of his time reading and reciting Song-dynasty *ci* poetry, while he considers his wife Yanqian to be an ordinary housewife preoccupied with domestic affairs such as embroidery and gossiping with other women. He bemoans that the spring time is too relaxing for him to write poetry, and that his life is so well-structured and organized that he lacks the inspiration for writing. He almost drops a tear of self-pity at such thoughts. In the evening of this particular day, to his great pleasure, he receives an intensely lyrical love letter from an anonymous admirer. He goes to secretly rendezvous with her at the Temple of Flowers the next morning, only to find that the person who wrote the letter is his wife! Her mockery of his infidelity aside, the story points out the difference between his and her lyricism. In the span of the story, he recites poetic lines from Song poetry and even has the nerve to recite a line from the all-time erotic classic *The Story of the Western Chamber* to express his longing for his admirer, but he never utters a line of poetry of his own. He also compares natural scenery to the paintings he has seen, so that nature is always perceived through mediation by classical learning. Unlike his mediated, learned perception, however, her letter is teeming with a refreshing lyricism, written in the vernacular shorn of clichéd expressions and inherited metaphors.

Similarly, in "A Poet Goes Mad," the male poet Juesheng can appreciate natural beauty only through the mediation of clichéd lyrical sentiments. He is inspired to recall the poetry of Lu You (1125–1210), Wang Wei (701–761), and Tao Qian (365–427), as well as the paintings of Mi Fei (1051–1107) and other Song and Yuan dynasty literati painters, when he is confronted with awesomely grand natural landscapes on his way home. Nature for him is legible only through the lens of previous cultural expressions, and is therefore subordinate to culture, without which he would not know how to relate to it. His wife Shuangcheng, by contrast, is innately a poet in tune with nature in a personal way. She physically acts out poetic sentiments—raising flowers in the garden accompanied by birds, insects, and dogs; enjoying the beauty of the moon; making flower wreaths and fantasizing about flower gods—and she speaks in a language rich with a kind of modern lyricism. The prints from the dog's paws on her shirt, she says, are like "half-bloomed daisies"; dew is "the tears of stars"; the silkworms, when they awaken from slumber, "will put on five-colored flowering dresses and go out wandering."[49] What Juesheng can only learn from books, she embodies. In her natural state, she is declared insane, but Juesheng later realizes that she personifies what he has been striving for as a poet: to live the lyricism that for him has been mediated by written culture. Hence her name,

49. Ibid., 1:212, 218, 217.

Shuangcheng, an anagram for "double" (*chengshuang*) since her poet husband desires to become her double; hence also the story's title, "A Poet Goes Mad."

The recuperation of the feminine voice in one context parodies the lady-by-the-window motif, and in another actively seeks to define a feminine aesthetic beyond the literary tradition. This is the "virtuous transaction" between Ling Shuhua the modern vernacular writer and her inherited literary tradition, simultaneously employing and undercutting that which she is recuperating or appropriating. And significantly, it is this virtuous transaction that helped mark a hybridization of the vernacular and the classical, the modern and the traditional, so that they might become intermingled and interdependent. Zhu Guangqian remarks how Ling's writing is stylistically similar to literati painting in her economy of words/ink and the profundity of meaning/expression.[50] Clara Yü Cuadrado notes how Ling's stories are filled with the "verbal stasis of visual images" and with natural sketches given in the "vocabulary of painting," written consciously "in the format of a horizontal handscroll."[51] This kinship to the literati painting style, in which realism is persistently undercut by subjective rendering of the painter's sentiments, further points to the antirealistic aesthetic espoused by Ling Shuhua—the female poet who is either unconventional or deemed mad is a fitting metaphor for a modernism that rejects the real.

Ling's use of a genre designated feminine, then, was inevitable, an inevitability however that was also legitimated by the feminine writings of Katherine Mansfield then being translated in great quantity by Xu Zhimo, Ling's husband Chen Yuan, and Ling Shuhua herself on the pages of the *Contemporary Review* (*Xiandai pinglun*), *Crescent Moon,* and *Short Story Monthly.* Xu also published a translated collection of Mansfield's stories in 1927.[52] The feminine modernism thus created takes on a transcultural dimension in its incorporation of a Western feminine modernism: the revelation of deep meanings through "the slightest gesture" and indirection, as Mansfield professed to write.[53] Engaged in a double conversation with a Chinese feminine literary tradition and a Western feminine modernism, where the lines between the two are more than blurred, Ling Shuhua's work offers us a different way of understanding how the construction of a gendered modernity in the specific context of her times had to be parodic in style and content.

50. Zhu Guangqian, "On *Brothers*" (*Xiao ge'er liang*), in *Collected Stories of Ling Shuhua,* 2:460–462.

51. Palandri, *Women Writers of Twentieth-Century China,* 52–53.

52. Xu Zhimo, trans., *Stories of Mansfield* (*Manshufei'er xiaoshuoji*) (Shanghai: Beixin shuju, 1927).

53. Scott, *The Gender of Modernism,* 301.

PART THREE

Flaunting the Modern
Shanghai New Sensationism

CHAPTER 9

Modernism and Urban Shanghai

I think modernism *in the 1930s was not local or national but international. It was a general* tendency *in literature. In each country there was a small minority of writers [who wrote in the modernist style] . . . and all of these writers from different countries together formed a trend. Modernism was not [merely] a Euro-American phenomenon . . . it was a simultaneously shared literary trend. Modernism in the West was influenced by Eastern culture. Obvious examples include Amy Lowell and Ezra Pound, but the influence was felt in different writers. . . . I always suspected that Emily Dickinson was also influenced by Chinese poetry, because there was no American predecessor to the kind of poetry she wrote. . . . To say that I "Easternized" modernism is wrong. It is Western modernism that is Easternized, and my modernism Westernized.*

SHI ZHECUN, INTERVIEW (1990)

There is no need to analyze the ways in which [foreigners'] contempt [towards the Chinese] is shown: non-admission of Chinese even as guests to foreign clubs, extreme limitation of social intercourse (to this there are exceptions, of course), prohibition of Chinese enjoyment of parks and embankments for the upkeep of which they help to pay. It is impossible to talk to educated Chinese without becoming aware that this is a matter of which they are most bitterly conscious.

ARTHUR RANSOME, *THE CHINESE PUZZLE* (1927)

In the opposition between the two quotations above is a pronounced tension that I have explicated in terms of the strategy of bifurcation many self-styled cosmopolitan writers and intellectuals deployed: constructing *metropolitan* Western and Japanese culture as the object of desire to incorporate or become contemporaneous with, while repudiating the humiliating presence of Western and Japanese *colonial* culture. The two were rarely made to confront each other, and since the valorization of metropolitan culture necessitated the displacement of colonial culture, nationalism was often muted in the writings of self-styled moderns and cosmopolitans. As I have illustrated, in the cosmopolitan imaginary of the May Fourth period, to confront the closely intertwined relationship between the metropolitan and the colonial West/Japan would have meant facing a level of contradiction reconcilable only through a nationalistic rejection of both, which would in turn invalidate the enlightenment project itself. Out of discursive necessity, then, the May Fourth cultural enlightenment project often glided over the question of colonial domination and instead concentrated on the rejection of tradition.

When the *jingpai* modernity project reconsidered this contradiction and sought an integrated notion of modernity that was not purely metropolitan in character, it simultaneously re-evaluated the merit of aspects of traditional culture, thereby reconnecting "value" (which the May Fourth ideology construed as solely the property of Western culture) to "history," in Joseph R. Levenson's terms. But even among the *jingpai* writers, this same bifurcating tendency can be located in Zhou Zuoren's work on metropolitan Japanese culture versus his work on Japanese colonialism in China (see my introduction). In the *jingpai* discourse in general, a celebration of *selective* Western and Japanese metropolitan culture was still very much taken for granted.

For Shanghai writers and intellectuals operating in the decade leading up to the outbreak of the Sino-Japanese War (1937–1945), this strategy of bifurcation was no longer applied merely to the realm of discourse, but became an immanent necessity in their lived experience. This is because living in Shanghai provided easy access to both the metropolitan Western culture, through its communication networks, and the colonial culture of the various Western powers, for whom these networks were built in the first place. The need to delineate the two cultures therefore became even more imperative, since Shanghai as a city encouraged so many different ways of reading Western culture. Shanghai was an ostentatious visual reminder of multiple colonial presences and uneven development; it was a city with a hierarchized, multiracial social structure; it was a semicolonial city integrated with global economy and politics through the efforts of an economy-driven Euro-American imperialism and a territorially and economically ambitious Japanese imperialism; it was a city of sin, pleasure, and carnality, awash with the phantasmagoria of urban consumption and commodification; and it was also a city of fragmentary political and ideological control that provided a measure of "freedom" from strict ideological domination. Confronting all these different "Shanghais," the Shanghai modernists expressed an ambivalent, and at best oscillating, allegiance to nationalism and critique of the colonial presence, where one would have imagined a heightened awareness of colonial presence and humiliation (as Arthur Ransome points out in the passage quoted above).

This ambivalence is best exemplified by the fluidity and ambiguity with which two of the leading proponents of new sensationism—Liu Na'ou and Mu Shiying—negotiated with various ideologies: the Nationalist Party, the Chinese Communist Party, the Japanese puppet regime of Wang Jingwei, and Euro-American colonial and metropolitan cultures. Semicolonialism again sanctioned the strategy of bifurcating the metropolitan and the colonial, with these writers celebrating the metropolitan culture of the West and Japan as constitutive of their cosmopolitanism, but the bifurcation threatened to break down when they flaunted a Western-style urbanism which was largely a by-product of semicolonialism. The city's multiracial and multinational as well as colonial institutions and structures could not but be represented, even if obliquely, if one wanted to write about its urban culture. What was Shanghai's landscape of urbanism without its Western-style theatres, dance halls, cafes, racecourses, imported cars, and Hollywood films? But if there were implicit references to the semicolonial condition of social stratification along racial lines, the writers avoided representating the explicitly colonial dimensions of the urban experience, such as racism and economic exploitation. Hence the city in its full urban allure became, more than anything else, a playground of desires for the pursuit of commodities and entertainment. Shanghai was where certain "universal" urban issues of capitalist modernity, such as commodification and human alienation, became favorite subjects. The vacillation between these two forms of representating urban materiality—as only implicitly colonial but as universally capitalist—is further testimony to the unsettling challenge which the lived experience of semicolonial urbanism posed to writers keen on becoming integrated into an international modernism.

GEOCULTURAL SHANGHAI AND NATIONALISM

When the Antillean psychologist Frantz Fanon wrote about the spatial geography of colonialism in Algeria in *The Wretched of the Earth* (1961), he noted the presence of a Manichean logic governing the separation of the European quarter from that of the natives. The colonial quarter had asphalt streets, large buildings, and modern conveniences; it was an island of affluence and consumption, bounded by a system of guard barracks and police stations. The native quarter, on the other hand, was a place of ill repute, crime, poverty, hunger, overcrowding, and filth, whose residents looked at the colonial quarter with envy. Each quarter stood as the other's opposite in this entirely dichotomous colonial/colonized world, both operating under a "principle of reciprocal exclusivity."[1] For Fanon, who was a practicing psychologist in Algeria at the time, the project of Algerian independence required a complete decolonization, which meant a total destruction of all colonial structures, including the colonial quarter, so as to eliminate the dichotomization of space and unify the native people. His was an impassioned call to remove all vestiges of colonialism: "The destruction of the colonial

---

1. Frantz Fanon, *The Wretched of the Earth,* trans. Constance Farrington (New York: Grove Press, Inc., 1968), 37–46.

world is no more and no less than the abolition of one zone [the colonial quarter], its burial in the depths of the earth or its expulsion from the country."[2] In the nationalist imaginary of the Chinese Communist Party from about the 1930s until the late 1970s, the city of Shanghai likewise evoked a similar sense of disgust as a symbol of national humiliation and colonial exploitation. The Party propounded the need to eliminate all vestiges of colonialism, if not through physically tearing down colonial architectures then through the intense ideological remodeling of its populace.

Going back further in history to when Shanghai became a treaty port after China's defeat in the first Opium War in 1842, however, informs us of a more complicated view of Shanghai in the modern Chinese cultural imaginary. From 1842, Shanghai emerged as a place of the hybridization of Chinese and foreign cultures, where Euro-American (and later Japanese) colonials' consistent discouragement of nationalist outbursts was aided by the efforts of native merchants and businessmen who often opted for economic stability over political confrontation. Native merchants signed the "Southeast Protection Treaty" (*Dongnan baohu yuekuan*) and the "Procedures to Protect the Environs of Shanghai" (*Baohu Shanghai chengxiang neiwai zhangcheng*) during the Boxer Uprising (1899–1900), for example, to prevent anti-imperialist activity from spreading to Shanghai.[3] With the exception of the May Thirtieth Incident of 1925 and the resistance against Japanese bombing in 1932, both of which were immediate reactions to imperialist provocations, Shanghai's most significant political event was its participation in the nationalist revolution of 1911, which was more directly anti-Manchurian than anti-imperialist. Seen from this perspective, imperialism (as both an economic and political entity) and native protocapitalism both contributed to creating Shanghai as an economic, not a political, center. Furthermore, the ambivalent attitude towards nationalism expressed by the so-called "treaty port men"—deemed a "new kind of Chinese" who promised to act as indigenous agents for the remaking of China along Western lines[4]—was part of a Shanghai cosmopolitanism that, for the time being, bracketed and deferred nationalism for the purpose of incorporating metropolitan Western and Japanese cultures.

Shanghai's ambiguous relationship with nationalism can be further seen in the accounts of many Western historians who portrayed Shanghai as a "foreign" city, produced by imperialism and set apart from the rest of China.[5]

2. Ibid., 41.

3. Zhang Zongli, ed., *A Study of Modern Shanghai* (*Jindai Shanghai chengshi yanjiu*) (Shanghai: Shanghai renmin chubanshe, 1990), 13–14.

4. Rhoads Murphy, "The Treaty Ports and China's Modernization," in Mark Elvin and G. William Skinner, eds., *The Chinese City Between Two Worlds* (Stanford: Stanford University Press, 1974), 20–21.

5. See Murphy, "The Treaty Ports," 17–71; Marie-Claire Bergère, "'The Other China': Shang-

While such a perception lays the blame for Shanghai's problems on imperialism, it also paradoxically attributes to imperialism the "success" of Shanghai as a capitalist paradise and a modernizing agent in China—imperialism,
when seen in the world historical terms of Hegel, Weber, or Marx, in the
end brought the blessings of development. Except for the difference in the
way capitalism was evaluated, both the capitalist and communist perspectives
saw Shanghai in dualistic opposition to the "authentic China" of the rural
countryside. As the place of the foreign, Shanghai would have little claim to
nationalism, but would rather become the reminder of its failure. In Western scholarship on pre-1949 Shanghai, Shanghai appeared as "a city of sin,"
the "site of China's modernism," a "paradise of adventurers," a "capitalists'
paradise," and a city where everything was "for sale."[6] All these descriptions
of Shanghai flaunted its capitalism (if only in its distorted form, with a predominantly one-way flow of capital) and its capitalist culture of modernity,
and rarely considered nationalism one of Shanghai's characteristics.

One can trace some semblance of nationalist sentiments in the Chinese
cultural *perception* of Shanghai from the mid-nineteenth century on, but
Shanghai itself was rarely considered a center of revolutionary or nationalist activities. Xiong Yuezhi sums up the polar conceptions of the city in this
native imaginary nicely: in economic terms, Shanghai had been a "paradise
for the rich, and hell for the poor"; in colonial terms, a "paradise for foreigners, and hell for the Chinese"; and in moral-cultural terms, the "source
of evil and the source of civilization," and the "urn of black ink and the window to Western learning."[7] Shanghai was simultaneously a "city of light," with
its enlightened education, journalism, literary revolution, and social reform,
and a "city of darkness," a source of contamination, depravation, sexual
promiscuity, and moral corruption.[8] Rather than a site of anticolonial nationalism, Shanghai was perceived to be a necessary evil whose advances would
eventually be extended to the rest of China. While the imperialists and colonials saw Shanghai as the "cork of a vast bottle containing the major share of
a great nation's vital life," the Chinese employed similar metaphors to describe
Shanghai as producing the "milk of civilization" that could "irrigate the en-

---

hai from 1919 to 1949," in Christopher Howe, ed., *Shanghai: Revolution and Development in an
Asian Metropolis* (New York: Cambridge University Press, 1981), 1–34; Harriet Sergeant, *Shanghai* (London: Jonathan Cape, 1991).

6. See for instance Hendrik De Leuuw's *Cities of Sin* (1933), Ernest Hauser's *Shanghai: City
for Sale* (1940, translated into Chinese in 1941), G. E. Miller's *Shanghai: Paradise of Adventurers*
(1937), and *All About Shanghai: A Standard Guidebook* (1934–1935).

7. Xiong Yuezhi, "On Shanghai's Image in History" (*Lishi shang de Shanghai xingxiang sanlun*), *History Forest* (*Shilin*) 3 (1996): 139–153.

8. Yingjin Zhang, *The City in Modern Chinese Literature and Film* (Stanford: Stanford University Press, 1996), 9–13.

tire nation."[9] Evoking the Yangtze River, each side utilized a liquid metaphor appropriate to its own imagination. For both, Shanghai is the source, but each sees the city's bounty as flowing in opposite directions. To protect the source, however, there was a curious consensus in the way Shanghai was perceived by both imperialists and natives alike: Shanghai was a site that could be absolved of the pressure of nationalist imperatives. The imperialists repressed nationalism to protect their interests, and the Chinese strategically exempted Shanghai of nationalist burdens to make it serve as the modernizing agent for China.

The geopolitical Shanghai of the 1920s and 1930s—spatially divided, with about half of its twenty-five square miles taken up by the French Concession and the International Settlement (as well as an informal Japanese district in Hongkou [Hongkew]),[10] and with separate legal jurisdictions—encourages the conclusion that the city was literally, geographically semi-colonial: half owned by the imperialists and half by the Chinese. Through these divisions, the colonials enjoyed extraterritorial rights, modern conveniences, and capitalist power, while the colonized had restricted access to both modernity and power. Spatial arrangements aside, however, the situation was probably much less clear-cut: the population of about two million in Shanghai represented forty-eight nationalities, according to a 1930 census,[11] whose varying, multiple, and overlapping subject positions formed a spectrum of power that was arguably much less reified than the usual Manichean, neatly racially configured hierarchy of power in other colonial cities, such as those in India or Africa. The fact that the majority of the foreigners were Japanese also disrupted a colonial hierarchy established exclusively along racial lines, and the low economic position of white Russian refugees in the city was another factor that disrupted a racialized marking of power.

For the eighty percent of the Chinese population in Shanghai who were immigrants from the vast Chinese interior, and whose identities were far from unified,[12] the pressing issue was not anti-imperialism but rather economic livelihood. Shanghai's economy improved steadily in the 1930s, despite the Great Depression elsewhere in the world, boosting the growth rate of the

9. The first quotation is from *All About Shanghai: A Standard Guidebook* (Shanghai: University Press,1934–35; rpt., Hong Kong: Oxford University Press, 1983), 27; the second and third quotations are from Xiong Yuezhi, quoting a 1904 newspaper article called "New Shanghai," in his "On Shanghai's Image in History," 146.

10. Sergeant, *Shanghai*, 11.

11. *All About Shanghai: A Standard Guidebook* , 35–37.

12. Zhang , *A Study of Modern Shanghai City*, 25; also see Wen-hsin Yeh and Frederic Wakeman, "Introduction," in Yeh and Wakeman, eds., *Shanghai Sojourners* (Berkeley: Institute of East Asian Studies, 1992), 1–14. Yeh and Wakeman refer to various types of sojourners in Shanghai, such as urban youths, petty urbanites, compadore elites, and nationalist compadores.

Chinese economy to 6.7 percent every year between 1931 and 1936.[13] The fifth-largest city in the world by 1933, Shanghai was also one of the main manufacturing centers in China, providing opportunities of employment for the new immigrants. As one of the most important shipping centers, it provided easy access to the rest of the world from China.[14] By 1927, China was also more or less under the control of the Nationalist government, which increasingly sought more political and legal representation in Shanghai's foreign courts. Shanghai's foreign powers gradually learned to accede to the demands of the Chinese capitalists and the Nationalist government.

This picture of a flexible Shanghai with significant Chinese representation should not mask our perception of inequalities in a city marked along various lines of nationality, race, gender, and class, even though some of these boundaries were not entirely codified and hence permeable and porous. This again suggests the existence of a space not exclusively defined by the demands of nationalism or imperialism, where we can chart the emergence of a Shanghai cosmopolitanism that straddled the multiple demands of ideology (from the Nationalist government and the League of Left-Wing Writers), the seductions by and abhorrence towards the semicolonial city, and an avowed celebration of metropolitan Western and Japanese literary cultures.

This cosmopolitanism was nowhere as explicit as in the work of the self-styled modernists and decadentists who, refusing to be dictated to by the ideological left or right, opted to be "Third Category Men" (*disanzhongren*).[15] If the 1927 purge of communists in Shanghai by the Nationalist government had served as the catalyst for an outpouring of empathy towards the left among Chinese intellectuals, the demagogic dicta of the League of Left-Wing Writers turned away even its "fellow travellers" (*tongluren*) by the early 1930s. As Wen-hsin Yeh has argued, Shanghai's cultural and political life was characterized by strife rather than consensus because of the fluidity of norms, statuses, and languages.[16] For the writers who lived in the midst of such a

13. *The Cambridge History of Republican China (Jianqiao Zhonghua minguo shi)* (Beijing: Zhongguo sheke chubanshe, 1993), 175–182.

14. H.J. Lethbridge, "Introduction" to *All About Shanghai: A Standard Guidebook*, vii–x.

15. For an account of the "Third Category Men" debate of 1932 between the non-League Marxist Hu Qiuyuan, the modernist Du Heng (Su Wen), and the League member Qu Qiubai, see Leo Ou-fan Lee, "Literary Trends: The Road to Revolution 1927–1949," in *The Cambridge History of China*, vol. 13, ed. Denis Twitchett and John K. Fairbank (Cambridge: Cambridge University Press, 1983), 434–437. All the relevant articles of the debate are collected by Su Wen in his *Debates on Literary Freedom (Wenyi ziyou lunbianji)* (Shanghai: Xiandai shuju, 1933). Also see Wang-chi Wong, *Politics and Literature in Shanghai* (Manchester: Manchester University Press, 1991). Hu Qiuyuan and Su Wen came under fierce attack by leftist writers/critics such as Yi Jia (Qu Qiubai), Lu Xun, and Zhou Qiying (Zhou Yang), who misinterpreted their resistance to literary prescriptions from League theorists as asserting the independence of literature from politics.

16. Wen-hsin Yeh, *The Alienated Academy* (Cambridge: Council on East Asian Studies, Harvard University Press, 1990), 55.

strife-ridden cultural space, cultural fluidity created the possibility of a cosmopolitanism that deployed a strategy of selective non-engagement with the main polemics of the day. In an interview decades later, Shi Zhecun mentioned how, as chief editor of the nationally circulated *Les Contemporaines* (*Xiandai*), he had to carefully balance the left and the right to the extent that if he ran a special issue on American literature, he also had to run a special issue on Russian literature to appease the leftists.[17]

The decade 1927–1937 was dubbed the "Left League Decade" due to the prominence of the League in the cultural affairs of Shanghai. It exercised considerable influence on cultural workers in Shanghai, from the more open-minded debate on the relationship between ideology and literature in the pre-League period (1927–1929), to the League's gradual shift to a more dictatorial and exclusionist leftism in the ensuing years, which inevitably led to its demise.[18] But precisely because the League gradually increased its control over writers, there was considerable resistance from the middle-of-the-roaders, like the Third Category Men and other "fellow travellers," who considered themselves leftist but did not agree with the heavy-handed ideological containment of literature that the League propagated and increasingly policed. Mu Shiying's many run-ins with League members through the 1930s, and with other leftists in the 1940s, were rarely provoked by disagreements over ideology (Mu sometimes came across as more of a Marxist theorist than his detractors in the League), but rather over the containment of aesthetics by ideology.[19]

The Shanghai intellectuals, then, were situated within a nexus of relationships crisscrossing the spheres of domestic ideological struggle, imperialist presence, alluring urban material culture, and cultural cosmopolitanism, all of which factored into the formation of their subjectivities. This subjectivity was markedly different from the so-called "native elites," handpicked to learn the colonial ways under formal colonialism, whom Frantz Fanon identified as the ultimate proprietors of the colonized consciousness that yearns to mimic the colonizer.[20] A less structured and more fragmented colonial formation created ambivalent subject positions for native intellectuals, beyond the logic of Manichean colonial relationships. Since the mid-nineteenth-century cultural articulation of Shanghai as the site of modern civilization, we can trace the emergence of a Shanghai cosmopolitanism that could be fully explained in neither the language of compadorism nor that of nationalism. This cosmopolitanism was instrumental in the rise of a bustling literary industry in Shanghai in the 1920s and 1930s.

17. Interview with Shi Zhecun, October 22–24, 1990.

18. Wong, *Politics and Literature in Shanghai.*

19. See chapter 11 for the debates between Mu Shiying and the leftists.

20. See Fanon, *The Wretched of the Earth* and *Black Skin, White Masks*, trans. Charles Lam Markmann (New York: Grove Weidenfeld, 1967).

THE PRINT CULTURE OF MODERNISM

The Shanghai literary scene from 1927 to 1937 was a vibrant playground of creative energies, even though contentious ideological currents tried to contain these energies or rechannel them for specific propagandistic purposes. In Shanghai's numerous bookstores, one could find books from around the world.[21] Its literary landscape was populated by a diverse contingent of writers, including May Fourth veterans who had left Beijing,[22] self-styled urbanites and cosmopolitans, leftists, Nationalist-sponsored intellectuals, and many others not easily categorizable. Culturally and ideologically divergent viewpoints were heatedly debated in magazines such as the politically moderate *Les Contemporaines* and the leftist *Big Dipper* (*Beidou*), while writers associated with the decadent journals *Oazo* (*Huanzhou*) and *Gold Chamber Monthly* (*Jinwu yuekan*) fashioned an aestheticist dandyism. Most of the important Western and Japanese modernist texts could be found either in translation or in the original: James Joyce's *Ulysses* and Virginia Woolf's *A Room of One's Own*, for instance, were extensively circulated among the Shanghai literary community.[23]

As a literary concept, modernism was still often referred to as "neoromanticism" like during the May Fourth era, except that it was now a very common term, readily available and frequently used. Almost every standard European literary history compiled at this time ended with a section entitled "neoromanticism," the term employed to encompass all the major turn-of-the-century literary movements such as symbolism and aestheticism.[24] But

21. For an account of this "bookish culture" in urban Shanghai, see Leo Ou-fan Lee, *Shanghai Modern: A Study of Urban Culture and Literary Imagination in China, 1930–1945* (Cambridge: Harvard University Press, 1999), chapter 4.

22. Marie-Claire Bergère notes that in the spring of 1926 more than fifty university teachers went to Shanghai to escape the chaotic and brutal warlord regime in Beiping [Beijing], and such May Fourth luminaries as Guo Moruo, Yu Dafu, Mao Dun, Xu Zhimo, and Lu Xun were all in Shanghai as well. See "'The Other China,'" 12–13.

23. There was also a full-length study of Joyce translated from the Japanese, and scholarly treatments of both Joyce and Woolf. Feng Cixing, trans., *James Joyce* (*Zhanmushi Zhushi*), by Doi Kōchi (Shanghai: Xiandai shuju, 1934); Fei Jianzhao, "The Irish Writer Joyce" (*Ai'erlan zuojia Qiao'ousi*), *Literature Monthly* (*Wenyi yuekan*) 3:7 (January 1933): 351–353. Virginia Woolf's *Flush* (1933) was translated by Shi Pu as *Folaxi* only two years later (Shanghai: Commercial Press, 1935). Other scattered translations of individual stories and articles can be found in the literary magazines of the time. Ye Lingfeng also writes, in his remembrances of the Shanghai years, about how his copy of Joyce's *Ulysses* was circulated among friends. See Ye Lingfeng, "On Joyce" (*Qiaoyisi jiahua*), in *Jottings from Reading* (*Dushu suibi*) (Beijing: Sanlian shudian, 1988), 1:115–117.

24. See for instance Lu Tianshi, *Modern Literary Movements in Europe* (*Ouzhou jindai wenyi sichao*) (Shanghai: Commercial Press, 1931); Xia Yande, *Comprehensive Study of Literature* (*Wenyi tonglun*) (Shanghai: Kaiming shudian, 1933); Zeng Zhongming, *Essays on French Literature* (*Faguo wenxue lunji*) (Shanghai: Liming shuju, 1932); Liu Dajie, *Introduction to German Literature* (*Deguo wenxue gailun*) (Shanghai: Beixin shuju, 1928). Each book includes a chapter on neoromanticism.

the more precise terms of *xiandaizhuyi, jindaizhuyi,* and *xiandaipai* (all meaning "modernism") were now frequently employed, and words such as *xiandai* or *jindai* ("modern"), *xiandaixing* ("modernity"), and *xiandaizhuyi de* ("modernist") formed part of the acknowledged literary lexicon of the time.[25] Western magazines and newspapers such as *Vanity Fair, Harper's, The Dial, Le Monde,* and *Lettre Française* were also readily available.[26] There were roughly thirty publishing houses, the most prestigious of which included the Commercial Press (*Shangwu yinshuguan*), the Xiandai Bookstore (*Xiandai shuju*), and the Zhonghua Publishing Co. They published translations of Western literary history and criticism, and almost every Chinese writer in Shanghai was engaged in either compiling or translating these works.

Many of these publishing houses sponsored literary magazines, and altogether over one hundred literary journals were published in Shanghai during this decade. The ABC Series Bookstore (*ABC congshushe*) published introductory textbooks on Western literary history and individual Western writers, all of which included "ABC" in their titles (*English Literature ABC, German Literature ABC,* and so on), popularizing knowledge about Western literature and making it accessible to the average reader. An anthology of short essays entitled *One Hundred Questions about Literature* (*Wenxue baiti*), edited by Fu Donghua and Zheng Zhenduo, was a cooperative work of the leading writers and critics of the time, including such illustrious contributors as Yu Dafu on fin-de-siècle literature, Mu Mutian on symbolism, and Li Jianwu on dadaism.[27] The speed and eagerness with which foreign literature was read and disseminated can be witnessed in Zhao Jingshen's *World Literature in 1929* (*Yijiu'erjiu nian de shijie wenxue*) and *World Literature in 1930* (*Yijiusanling nian de shijie wenxue*), published in 1930 and 1931 respectively, which kept avid readers abreast of current literary events outside China.[28]

Similar reports on current trends in literature abroad were fixtures in most

25. In Gao Ming's translation of Abe Tojimi's "The New Poetic Schools in England and America" (*Yingmei xinxing shipai*), *Les Contemporaines* 2:4 (February 1933): 550–566, "modernist" is used as a label for Eliot, Stein, Cummings, etc. Zhao Jiabi's "From the Crosscutting Novel to John Dos Passos" (see note 45 below) and Lu Tianshi's *Modern Literary Movements in Europe* (cited above) also use the English term "modernist." Examples of other texts that use "modernism" are Xu Xiacun, "Italian Literature of the Past Twenty Years" (*Ershinian lai de Yidali wenxue*), and "Spanish Literature of the Past Twenty Years" (*Ershinian lai de Xibanya wenxue*), *Short Story Monthly* 20:7 (July 1929): 1101–10 and 1111–18.

26. See Leo Ou-fan Lee, "In Search of Modernity: Some Reflections on a New Mode of Consciousness in Twentieth-Century Chinese History and Literature," in Paul A. Cohen and Merle Goldman, eds., *Ideas Across Cultures* (Cambridge: Council on East Asian Studies, Harvard University, 1990), 109–135, especially 128–129.

27. Fu Donghua and Zheng Zhenduo, eds., *One Hundred Questions About Literature* (*Wenxue baiti*) (Shanghai: Shenghuo shudian, 1935).

28. Zhao Jingshen, *World Literature in 1929* and *World Literature in 1930* (Shanghai: Shenzhou guoguangshe, 1930 and 1931).

of the leading journals, which all published translations or discussions of Western and Japanese modernists. Table 9.1 illustrates the availability of and particular interest writers and readers had toward modernist literature from abroad. Note that Japanese writers were as widely translated and read as Western writers. The writer most frequently translated was, for instance, the Japanese new sensationist writer Yokomitsu Riichi (1898–1947); also note the translation of two volumes of stories and a novel by the early Japanese modernist Satō Haruo (1892–1964).[29] Both of these writers visited China several times and were acquainted with many Chinese writers, and several Chinese writers from Shanghai either visited or studied in Japan. The imaginary traffic among these literatures then also materialized as actual transnational crossings, the implications of which I will examine in regard to Japanese new sensationism later in this chapter and in chapter 12.

The first five magazines in Table 9.1, *Les Contemporaines, Literary Landscape, La Nouvelle Littérature, Trackless Train,* and *Literary Vignettes,* either had the same editor, Shi Zhecun, or were associated with each other by virtue of their common coterie of writers, most notably Shi Zhecun, Liu Na'ou, Mu Shiying, and the poet Dai Wangshu. These were the arenas where new sensationism prominently showcased its new style and attracted a wide audience. The next four, *Gold Chamber Monthly, Oazo, Modern Fiction,* and *New North,* shared a decadent outlook, and their contributors were mainly Francophiles. The three magazines following were publications of the Literary Research Society, which, though ordinarily known as advocating "literature for life," also contributed to disseminating Western and Japanese modernist writing.

A brief summary of the publication activities of these modernist journals reveals the particular focus and direction of Shanghai modernists' translation and creative work. *Trackless Train,* edited by Liu Na'ou and published with his own personal funds, was the first magazine that self-consciously promoted modernist literature in the Franco-Japanese mode. On the pages of this magazine, Liu advanced new sensationism with his mesmerizingly unique language, technique, and form, in conjunction with translations of Japanese and French new sensationist works, as well as introducing an aestheticized form of leftist ideology. The first issue published in September 1928 began with Liu Na'ou's pathbreaking story "Games" (*Youxi*), which for the first time experimented with the production of a new language that could relate the sensations of living in the urban city—the tempo of the cabaret, the dance hall, and other arenas of fast life; the loneliness of the urban man;

---

29. Satō Haruo, *Melancholy of the City* (*Duhui de youyu*), trans. Zha Shiyuan (Shanghai: Huatong shuju, 1931); *Stories by Satō Haruo* (*Zuoteng Chunfu ji*), trans. Gao Ming (Shanghai: Xiandai shuju, 1933); *Regeneration* (*Gengsheng ji*), trans. Zha Shiyuan (Shanghai: Zhonghua shuju, 1935).

TABLE 9.1

Literary Magazine	Editor(s)	Western and Japanese Modernist Writers Translated or Discussed
Trackless Train (Wugui lieche, 1928)	Liu Na'ou	Paul Valéry, Paul Morand, Paul Fort, Azorín (José Martínez Ruiz)
La Nouvelle Littérature (Xinwenyi, 1929–1930)	Liu Na'ou, Shi Zhecun, Du Heng [Su Wen], and others	Francis Jammes, James Joyce, Stéphane Mallarmé, Colette, Azorín, Kataoka Teppei, Arthur Schnitzler, Tanizaki Jun'ichirō, Ernest Dowson, etc.
Les Contemporaines (Xiandai, 1932–1935)	Shi Zhecun, Du Heng, Wang Fuquan	Guillaume Apollinaire, Amy Lowell, H. D., T. S. Eliot, Gertrude Stein, Jean Cocteau, Raymond Radiguet, Marino Moretti, Yokomitsu Riichi, John Dos Passos, W. B. Yeats, D. H. Lawrence, Azorín, Rémy de Gourmont, E. E. Cummings, Richard Aldington, William Faulkner, Federico García Lorca, etc.
Literary Landscape (Wenyi fengjing, 1934)	Shi Zhecun	Stein
Literary Vignettes (Wenfan xiaopin, 1935)	Kang Siqun	Luigi Pirandello, Lorca, Akutagawa Ryūnosuke, Nagai Kafū, Lawrence, Yeats
Oazo (Huanzhou, 1926–1928)	Ye Lingfeng, Pan Hannian	Aubrey Beardsley, Oscar Wilde
Modern Fiction (Xiandai xiaoshuo, 1928–1930)	Ye Lingfeng, Pan Hannian	Edgar Allan Poe, Dowson, Wilde, Schnitzler
Gold Chamber Monthly (Jinwu yuekan, 1929–1930)	Shao Xunmei, Zhang Kebiao	Tanizaki, Beardsley, Wilde, Natsume Sōseki
New North (Beixin, 1926–1930)	Sun Fuxi	Paul Verlaine, Dowson, Poe, Jun'ichirō
Short Story Monthly (Xiaoshuo yuebao, 1921–1931)	Mao Dun, Ye Shengtao, Zheng Zhenduo	Joyce, Virginia Woolf, Mori Ōgai, Yokomitsu, Sōseki, Verlaine, Schnitzler

Publication	Editor/Society	Authors
Literature Weekly (*Wenxue zhoubao*), Literature Biweekly (*Wenxue xunkan*), Literature (*Wenxue*) (1921–1929) Literature (*Wenxue*, 1933–1937)	Zheng Zhenduo and others	Wilde, Poe, Yokomitsu, etc.
	Shanghai Literature Society	Lawrence, Joseph Conrad, Stein, Ernest Hemingway, Thomas Mann, Eugene O'Neill, Charles Baudelaire, Yokomitsu, Joyce, Dos Passos
Modern Literature (*Xiandai wenxue*, 1930)	Zhao Jingshen	Lawrence, Yokomitsu, Filippo Marinetti, Baudelaire
General Magazine (*Yiban*, 1926–1929)	Xia Mianzun, Fang Guangshou	Akutagawa
Chinese Literature (*Zhongguo wenxue*, 1934)	Zhao Jingshen and others	Yokomitsu, Hemingway, Joyce
New Fiction (*Xin xiaoshuo*, 1935)	Zheng Boqi	Sherwood Anderson, Pirandello
Rushing Stream (*Benliu*, 1928–1929)	Lu Xun, Yu Dafu	Dowson, Fort, Apollinaire

the moral abandon of urban existence—through the techniques of repetition, interior monologue, filmic montage, anthropomorphizing urban objects, etc. This inaugural story largely defined the characteristics of what was later called Chinese new sensationism, and did not escape the attention of critics at the time who saw a certain similarity between this story and Japanese new sensationism. In the same issue, an article on Paul Valéry by L. Galantiére was translated into Chinese by Xu Xiacun, one of the minor writers in the new sensationist movement, followed by poems by Dai Wangshu, the most important symbolist-modernist poet in modern China.[30] A story entitled "Metropolis" (*Daduhui*) by L. Sosnovsky and translated by Hua Shi (Feng Xuefeng, 1903–1976) also appeared, which found the urban spirit in the working-class crowd who claimed the streets. From the very beginning, new sensationism claimed the two fronts of urbanism and socialism, their relationship appearing at times complementary and other times contradictory. On the pages of *Trackless Train*, these two fronts were negotiated as both representing the vanguard—the artistic vanguard and the ideological vanguard.

An article in the second issue of *Trackless Train* by Feng Xuefeng, who would later become the official spokesman of the League of Left-Wing Writers during the Third Category Men debate, further suggests this openness in the late 1920s (before the League became dictatorial) to ideological difference in the cultural sphere. Entitled "Revolution and the Intellectual Class" (*Geming yu zhishi jieji*), the article is important for Feng's categorization, from the Marxist point of view, of three possible modes of relating to leftist revolution. The first kind of intellectual renounces individualism and elitism completely and becomes a socialist; the second kind desires revolution but is hesitant and unwilling to renounce his privileges, which makes him feel guilty; the third kind is an opportunistic intellectual who shifts according to the direction of the wind. Feng asserts that the left should tolerate the second kind of intellectual, allowing them to articulate their decadent inner torments as historical monuments, truthful records of the mental states of those situated at the very transition from capitalism to socialism.[31] Note that the second kind of intellectual in this typology generally foreshadows what would later be denounced as the Third Category Men. What Feng's article suggests to the cultural historian is that, in the late 1920s, the left-leaning bourgeois intellectual was not repudiated outright by the left, and that it was possible for a staunch socialist such as Feng to work closely with the likes of cosmopolitan new sensationists, as evinced by his close engagement with *Trackless Train*.

30. For a study of Dai Wangshu as a modernist see Gregory Lee, *Dai Wangshu: The Life and Poetry of a Chinese Modernist* (Hong Kong: Chinese University Press, 1989).

31. Hua Shi (Feng Xuefeng), "Revolution and the Intellectual Class," *Trackless Train* (*Wugui lieche*) 2 (September 25, 1928): 43–50.

Leftist sentiments were prominent in *Trackless Train,* thanks to Feng's articles, translations of Russian and American literature, and stories by Kataoka Teppei (1894–1944), the Japanese new sensationist who turned to the proletarian literature movement in 1927. A story by Kataoka translated in *Trackless Train,* entitled "An Experience" (*Yige jingyan*), depicts a young factory worker's struggle against the forces of capitalism,[32] and another story that appeared in *La Nouvelle Littérature* (published by Liu Na'ou after *Trackless Train* was banned), entitled "The Poverty of Art" (*yishu de pinkun*), can be read as Kataoka's manifesto in which he shed the garb of new sensationism and donned that of the proletarian fighter. The artist-protagonist in the latter story exhausts his energy trying to satisfy his femme-fatale girlfriend (explicitly referred to as "the modern girl") and maintain his decadent lifestyle— a situation found in many new sensationist stories—but eventually finds liberation from lust and commercialism through participation in the proletarian movement.[33] Shi Zhecun also experimented with the leftist genre, publishing one story entitled "Chase" (*Zhui*) in *Trackless Train.* The young and talented Mu Shiying would soon publish an entire volume of leftist stories about the lumpen proletariat, his influential *Poles Apart* (*Nanbeiji*).

Issue number four of *Trackless Train* was devoted to the French writer Paul Morand (1888–1976), an important inspiration to the Japanese new sensationists and their Chinese counterparts alike, and this is where we find the valorization of new language, technique, form, and urbanism most prominently displayed. Many of the leftist writings published in *Trackless Train* to a certain extent simplified the art of writing to mere mimeticism of revolutionary spirit, but writing about and by Paul Morand foregrounded the aesthetics of writing and the depiction of urban sentiments. This was in spirit closer to the Japanese new sensationists such as Yokomitsu and the early Kawabata, for whom Paul Morand was also an inspiration. Although Morand is not remembered as a great writer now, he was famous in Europe in the 1920s and 1930s: Marcel Proust wrote a preface to Morand's *Fancy Goods* (*Tendres Stocks,* 1921), and Ezra Pound translated both *Fancy Goods* and *Open All Night* (*Ouvert la Nuit,* 1922). To mark the occasion of Morand's visit to China in 1928, this special issue of *Trackless Train* published a long translated article on Morand by Benjamin Crémieux and two stories by Morand.[34]

32. Kataoka Teppei, "An Experience" (*Yige jingyan*), trans. Ge Momei, *Trackless Train* 7 (December 1928): 376–381.

33. Kataoka Teppei, "The Poverty of Art" (*Yishu de pinkun*), trans. Guo Jianying, *La Nouvelle Littérature* 1:1 (September 1929): 105–143.

34. *Trackless Train* 4 (October 1928). The two stories by Paul Morand, "Laziness" (*Landuo*) and "New Friends" (*Xinpengyou*), both translated by Dai Wangshu, appear on 160–162 and 163–175. Later Liu Na'ou edited a volume called *Paul Morand ABC* (*Bao'er Muhang ABC*), with appended stories translated by Dai. I discuss the article by Crémieux and its relationship to Liu Na'ou's writing in chapter 11.

Whereas Kataoka depicted the modern girl as the embodiment of capitalist commodification, Morand in these earlier stories had her represent exotic sensuality, mystery, and coarseness, thus squarely situating himself in the exoticist tradition of French literature made prominent by Gustave Flaubert.[35] The difference here captures the ambiguous stance of the journal: simultaneously fascinated by a leftist critique of capitalist decadence and fetishizing that decadence itself. *Trackless Train* thereby typified the second kind of subjectivity defined by Feng Xuefeng, ambiguously situated vis-à-vis socialism (sympathetic but not willing to be dogmatic) and capitalism (critical but not willing to reject its urban lures). Translated into literary terms, this subjectivity has leftist leanings but is attracted to pure aesthetic formalism and refuses strict leftist prescriptions; it is critical of capitalism, but delights in its pleasures. For this subject position, the city oscillates between a site of the Benjaminian eruption of the crowd (the potential arena of collective rebellion by the urban masses) and a site of sheer pleasure, speed, and "carnal intoxication" (Liu Na'ou's words).

This divided subject position, while emblematic of the ambivalent experience of modernity in the semicolonial city, would by the late 1930s and early 1940s become impossible in an atmosphere of either-or identity politics: by then one had to be either a socialist nationalist or a capitalist collaborator; there was little space in between. This polarization had devastating consequences: Liu Na'ou and Mu Shiying later worked for the Japanese puppet regime of Wang Jingwei, were denounced as traitors, and were assassinated. The inflexible division carried consequences even farther into the post-1949 years: even though Shi Zhecun tried to maneuver himself into a more moderate ideological position "in the middle with a twist to the left" (*zhongjian pianzuo*),[36] he could not escape persecution during the Cultural Revolution.

Liu Na'ou's Waterfoam Bookstore (*Shuimo shudian* in Chinese; *Librarie Sue Mo* in French), located in the two-story building on North Sichuan Road where Liu Na'ou, Dai Wangshu, and Shi Zhecun lived together for a while, published the literary monthly *La Nouvelle Littérature* immediately after *Trackless Train* was banned by the Nationalist government for its allegedly leftist orientation.[37] It too had a short duration (only eight issues), but during its lifetime it continued where *Trackless Train* left off and succeeded in

35. See chapter 11 for an extended discussion of the figure of the modern girl.

36. Interview with Shi Zhecun.

37. An official circular promulgated by the Shanghai Provisional Court in January 1929 explained why *Trackless Train* was banned. It allegedly "contains suggestions to raise the standard of equality, thereby inciting laborers to make trouble. This is evidently printed matter made by the Communists. It should be strictly prohibited so as to put a stop to its troublesome beginnings." Shanghai Municipal Police File, reel 1, D-39, under the heading "Communist Literature," February 18, 1929.

enhancing the double vanguard efforts of experimenting with pure literary form and propagating socialist ideology. Literary experimentation was represented by the stories of Shi Zhecun, Liu Na'ou, and others, as well as translations of Japanese new sensationism and French and other Euro-American literary avant-garde writings. Leftist ideology, on the other hand, was less prominently displayed, except in the last two issues published in 1930, when the literary arena in Shanghai became predominantly leftist with the establishment of the League of Left-Wing Writers in March of that year. Previously, the Waterfoam Bookstore had compensated for this lack by publishing book series such as the "Newly Emergent Literature Series" (*xinxing wenxue congshu,* which included the works of John Reed and Upton Sinclair) and the "Scientific Theories of Art Series" (*kexue de yishulun congshu,* which included the theoretical works of Georgy Plekhanov and Anatoly Lunarcharsky).

The formalist sentiment predominated in *La Nouvelle Littérature,* however. The first issue included the first of Shi Zhecun's four psychoanalytic studies of eroticism,"Kumarajiva" (*Jiumo luoshi*); Liu Na'ou's equally erotic "Etiquette and Hygiene" (*Liyi yu weisheng*); an article on the relationship between syphilis and art; stories by Kataoka and Colette; and poetry by Francis Jammes. Other minor modernists such as Xu Xiacun, Guo Jianying, and Du Heng also contributed either stories or translations over the life of the journal. As a journal run mainly by a group of like-minded "colleagues" (*tongren*), like *Trackless Train,* it concentrated its efforts on propagating a distinctly modernist style of writing. The bookstore also published Guo Jianying's 1929 translation of Yokomitsu Riichi's collection of stories, *The Sensations of the Bridegroom* (*Xinlang de ganxiang*), and reprinted Liu Na'ou's 1928 translation of modern Japanese stories *Erotic Culture* (*Seqing wenhua*), whose title comes from a story by Kataoka. The journal ceased publication in April 1930 due to various reasons, chief among which was the drastic transformation of the journal into a completely leftist one since the March issue, in response to the changing demands of the literary milieu under the sway of the League. The editor and his friends made a final defiant gesture by calling their last issue the "Abolishing the Magazine Issue" (*feikanhao*), although they left it ambiguous as to at whom this gesture was targeted.[38] At the time, Dai Wangshu and Du Heng both attended the inaugural meeting of the League of Left-Wing Writers, which had already started to exclude many middle-of-the-roaders, and the ensuing 1932 Third Category Men debate as well as other acrimonious confrontations increasingly soured the relationship between the League members and the modernists.

One notable development from *Trackless Train* was the expanded view of the global cultural context in *La Nouvelle Littérature.* From the former's some-

---

38. Editorial Committee, "Words from the Editors" (*Bianji de hua*), *La Nouvelle Littérature* (*Xin wenyi*) 2:2 (April 1930): 399–400.

what narrowly focused selection of Franco-Japanese modernist and leftist works, the latter, averaging over 150 pages per issue, had more space to include American, British, Italian, Spanish, and German literature. This sensitivity to an expanded global context and the role of Chinese culture in it is illustrated in one important book review by Bo Zi (most probably a penname), about a collection of modern Chinese stories published in Paris, *Anthologie des Conteurs Chinois Moderne,* edited and translated by Jing Yinyu. The reviewer disparages the inadequate job Jing has done with the anthology, not only in terms of the biased selection of stories but also the problematic representation of China in Jing's preface. The review notes how Jing chose to emphasize the antiquated China of Lao-tze and Zhuangzi, the "ghostly China that could arouse the curiosity of the Europeans." It quotes from Jing's preface:

> But China is so mysterious and simplistic! There are complacent, quiet and yet profound people in the world, and the Chinese are such a people. They do not show their strong points but hide them deeply through honesty and humility. They are intuitive. Their "logic" is primitive. The intuitive truths that are sudden, short, and unrelated to other things, are something to be captured immediately, for they will disappear soon without returning again. It is difficult to say what these truths are. . . . [39]

The review argues that instead of demystifying China and Chinese culture for the French readership, Jing opted to further the disassociation of China with modernity by deepening the mystification of the Chinese as the unknowable, intuitive, and primitive, which is complicitous with the European prejudice that sees China as "an ancient antique." In contemporary postcolonial terms, Bo Zi is charting the complicity between Jing's self-Orientalization and the Western Orientalism which represents China as the primitive, mystical Other. The refutation of this complicity again evinces the desire for "coevalness"[40] with the West on the part of the Chinese intellectuals. But this desire for coevalness is qualitatively different from the May Fourth desire to catch up with the West, as it did not imply the "behind-ness" of Chinese culture. For Shi Zhecun to name his journal *Les Contemporaines* suggests that coevalness was taken as a statement of fact rather than a future goal. Hence it was possible to criticize Jing Yinyu's representation of China in anti-Orientalist terms.

After *La Nouvelle Littérature* ceased publication, the Waterfoam Bookstore lingered on for about a year, publishing a few books here and there. When

---

39. Bo Zi, "Jing Yinyu's *Anthology of Modern Chinese Short Stories*" (*Jing Yinyu de Zhongguo xiandai duanpian xiaoshuoji*), *La Nouvelle Littérature* 1:1 (September 1929): 171–175.

40. The term "coevalness" comes from Johannes Fabian's famed analysis of Western anthropology as tending to imprison its ethnographic objects in the time of the past, hence denying their contemporaneity, or coevalness, with the West. See his *Time and the Other: How Anthropology Makes Its Object* (New York: Columbia University Press, 1983).

the bookstore was damaged during the Japanese bombing of Shanghai in January 1932, Liu Na'ou took stock of the situation and decided that his losses (estimated at ten thousand yuan)[41] were too great for him to continue. As a result, the core group of modernists who edited the above two journals dissolved: Liu Na'ou turned to film and by all accounts ceased writing stories; Dai Wangshu returned to his hometown and made preparations to leave for France; Du Heng retreated behind closed doors and concentrated on translation work; Xu Xiacun went to Beijing; and Shi Zhecun returned to Songjiang to continue teaching in a middle school.[42] As Shi Zhecun remembers, the bombing of Shanghai virtually stopped all literary publication, since many publishing houses were destroyed during the bombing.

But in fact the Shanghai literary scene picked up again soon after the bombing, and the most memorable event after the bombing in terms of Chinese modernism was the swift formation and publication of *Les Contemporaines* (first issue: May 1932). Shi Zhecun was brought back from Songjiang by the publishers of the Xiandai Bookstore to be its chief editor, and was entrusted with running a large-scale, non-*tong'ren,* and ideologically neutral literary magazine. From the publisher's perspective, it was designed to be a commercial success, and from Shi's perspective he would be able to resort to the "value of literature itself" as the standard of judgment, independent of ideological dictates.[43] Averaging about 7,000 copies per issue, *Les Contemporaines* was arguably the most important literary forum in all of China for a long time—at its height it sold 10,000 copies when a prestigious national newspaper such as *Shenbao* sold a maximum of only 15,000 copies.[44]

Shi Zhecun was a remnant of the earlier group surrounding Liu Na'ou; his friends Du Heng and Dai Wangshu remained intimately connected to the current magazine, and he published the work of Mu Shiying who clearly wrote in a style akin to Liu Na'ou's, so obviously Shi's penchant for modernism was not going to be completely displaced in this journal which professed to appeal to a larger, nonsectarian readership. Besides publishing Mu

41. Another estimate suggests that Liu lost a total of thirty thousand yuan from his publishing venture. See Yi Tong, "Remembering Liu Na'ou" (*Ji Liu Na'ou*), in Yang Zhihua, ed., *Historical Materials on the Literary Arena* (*Wentan shiliao*) (Shanghai: Zhonghua ribaoshe, 1944), 233–234. Whether ten thousand or thirty thousand, the amount was significant. The average cotton mill worker's monthly salary (working over ten hours a day) was at the time around fourteen yuan, so ten thousand yuan would equal roughly the salary of an average worker for sixty years. Information regarding worker's monthly salary comes from C.C.F., "Shanghai's Standard of Living," *The Chinese Nation* 1:51 (June 3, 1931): 1439, 1442–1443.

42. Shi Zhecun, "We Ran Three Bookstores" (*Women jingying guo sange shudian*), *Historical Materials on New Literature* (*Xinwenxue shiliao*) (January 1985): 190.

43. From Shi Zhecun's "Inaugural Manifesto" (*Chuangkan xuanyan*), *Les Contemporaines* 1:1 (May 1932): 2.

44. Shi Zhecun, "Miscellaneous Remembrances of *Les Contemporaines* (3)" (*Xiandai zayi*), *Historical Materials on New Literature* (March 1981): 221.

Shiying's many stories, *Les Contemporaines* also prominently published the entire earlier coterie of writers: Liu Na'ou contributed a rare translation or two after he departed for Japan for a visit in 1932; Du Heng worked closely with Shi and later became the coeditor of the journal, sparking the heated Third Category Men debate on the pages of *Les Contemporaines* using the penname Su Wen; most importantly, Dai Wangshu served as the journal's French correspondent and a frequent contributor. Dai systematically translated French postsymbolist poetry such as Rémy de Gourmont's and prose works by Raymond Radiguet and others, wrote on French literary currents, and published his own symbolist-modernist poetry.

Besides the coterie of writers still active on the pages of *Les Contemporaines*, two important critics stand out for their contributions to the magazine's modernist outlook: Zhao Jiabi (b. 1908), an eminent literary critic and scholar of Anglo-American literature, and Gao Ming, scholar and translator of Japanese literature. Perhaps the most learned, if not the most important, scholar of Anglo-American literature in China, Zhao Jiabi played a seminal role in the literary scene of the 1930s as the editor and publisher of various books such as the *Compendium of Modern Chinese Literature* (*Zhongguo xinwenxue daxi*). His two articles on John Dos Passos, one published here and the other in *Writers* (*Zuojia*), again illustrate the twin literary and ideological concerns of the time and show how it was possible for a writer to satisfy both his revolutionary and his modernist proclivities. According to Zhao, Dos Passos is a "communist writer" who uses new forms to depict a new social structure, and at the same time is a modernist like James Joyce. Zhao highlights the modernist techniques Dos Passos uses to present the complex images of life in capitalist America, such as spatial discontinuity (which Zhao calls "crosscutting," *hengduan*), newsreels, and camera-eye perspectives.[45] Gao Ming continued where Liu Na'ou, Guo Jianying, and others had left off, and translated the Japanese new sensationist writings of Yokomitsu and Iketani Shinzaburō, wrote on the modern Japanese literary scene, and translated essays on Euro-American literature from the Japanese. His stature as a Japan scholar was perhaps second only to Xie Liuyi (1898–1945), who wrote extensively on Japanese literary history.[46]

45. Zhao Jiabi, "Passos" (*Pasuosi*), *Les Contemporaines* 4:1 (November 1933): 220–229; "From the Crosscutting Novel to John Dos Passos" (*Cong hengduan xiaoshuo dao Dusi Pasuosi*), *Writers* 2:1 (October 1936): 179–192. Many of his other articles on modern American literature feature Dos Passos as a central figure; see, e.g., "The Growth of American Fiction" (*Meiguo xiaoshuo zhi chengzhang*), *Les Contemporaines* 5:6 (October 1934): 839–859. Zhao Jiabi's other important contributions to the literary scene at this time included a book-length translation of critical articles taken from *The Fortnightly Review* under the general heading "Tendencies of the Modern Novel," and collected as *Tendencies of the Modern Euro-American Novel* (*Jinri Oumei xiaoshuo zhi dongxiang*) (Shanghai: Liangyou tushu gongsi, 1935).

46. Xie was a member of the Literary Research Society and an editor at the Commercial Press. Educated in Japan, he wrote and translated about thirty books on Japanese literature by

Despite the professed heterogeneous outlook of *Les Contemporaines,* a discernible modernist school of poetry formed on its pages. This was related to the fact that poetry was a genre less affected by political and ideological contention since the May Fourth era, perhaps due to its professed personal and lyrical nature with no pretension to social significance. Dai Wangshu's poetry stands out as a modernist watershed, as do his influential poetry remarks entitled "Wangshu on Poetry" (*Wangshu shilun*).[47] Shi Zhecun, as a critic, theoretician, translator, fiction writer, and poet was also instrumental in fomenting the modernist temper. "Wangshu on Poetry," for instance, was put together by Shi from Dai's notes as Dai was then busy preparing himself for the long journey to France to be commenced in October 1932. Shi coined the term "*yixiang,*" his translation of "image" from Euro-American imagist poetry, and described in his editorial notes what he called a "purely modern poetry that captures the modern sentiments of the modern man in modern life, written in a modern language and modern form."[48] This short editorial note in which the word "modern" (*xiandai*) is repeated five times soon became canonized as the manifesto of modernist poetry (*xiandaipai shi*) in China. Shi further explained modernity in the following oft-quoted passage from the editorial:

> The so-called modern life includes various idiosyncratic forms: harbors lined with large steamers, factories clamoring with noise, mines burrowing deep into the earth, dancing floors playing jazz music, sky-scraping department stores, air battles, spacious race courses. . . . Even the natural scenery is different from that of earlier periods. How can the emotion such a life inspires in the poet be the same as those of the previous generation?[49]

Li Jinfa, Xu Chi, Luyishi, and others helped consolidate this temper into a poetic movement. By 1935, the poetry published in *Les Contemporaines* was heralded as the poetry of the modernists (*xiandaipai*).[50] As new sensation-

---

1933. His important literary history, *A History of Japanese Literature* (*Riben wenxueshi*) (Shanghai: Beixin shuju, 1929) in two volumes, is still a standard textbook in contemporary China. His other major contributions include editing and translating a thirteen-volume mega-treatise on world literature with Wang Fuquan, entitled *Lectures on World Literature* (*Shijie wenxue jiangzuo*) (Shanghai: Beixin shuju, n.d.). He was also an important figure in the promulgation of erotic literature as high literature.

47. Dai Wangshu, "Wangshu on Poetry," *Les Contemporaines* 2:1 (November 1932): 92–94.

48. Shi Zhecun, "Again About the Poetry in Our Magazine" (*You guanyu benkan de shi*), *Les Contemporaines* 4:1 (November 1933): 6.

49. Ibid., 6–7. My translation is partially based on that of Yomi Braester, from his "Shanghai's Economy of the Spectacle: The Shanghai Race Club in Liu Na'ou's and Mu Shiying's Stories," *Modern Chinese Literature* 9:1 (Spring 1995): 42.

50. In the 1930s, the "modernist school" of poetry was already the object of scholarly scrutiny as an important poetic movement. See Sun Zuoyun, "On 'Modernist School' Poetry" (*Lun xiandaipai shi*), *Qinghua Weekly* (*Qinghua zhoukan*) (March 1935): 56–65. Shi Zhecun also notes that *xiandaipai* became synonymous with modernism in poetry. See his "Miscellaneous

ism was to fiction, *xiandaipai* was to poetry; both were specific nomenclatures for the modernist movement in Shanghai.

A note should be made about *Les Contemporaines* within the context of Shanghai as a favorite destination of Euro-American and Japanese writers. In the early 1930s Shanghai received such celebrities as George Bernard Shaw, Langston Hughes, and Paul Vaillant-Couturier. The journal's connection with the European mainland was also maintained through Dai Wangshu's personal association with the French writers André Malraux, André Breton, Max Jacob, Etiemble, and others.[51] Together with the Xiandai Bookstore's comprehensive publication of books on all manner of Euro-American and Japanese literature, literary criticism, and literary theory, the activities of *Les Contemporaines* in the years between 1932 and 1934 contributed to invigorating the literary community.

One of the most notable events in Shanghai's literary arena in 1934 was the appearance of the journal's October issue, especially devoted to modern American literature. The issue began with introductory essays by the major Chinese literary critics of the time, and included articles on and translations of all the major American writers: William Faulkner, Ezra Pound, John Dos Passos, Eugene O'Neill, Gertrude Stein, and many others. The issue ran over 400 pages in length, and was unprecedented in its systematic, comprehensive effort to cover American literature, which until that time was seen as inferior and secondary to European literature due to its short history. Shi Zhecun and Du Heng provided a succinct justification for their choosing American literature as the first in a series of special issues they were planning to run on other, more well-known literatures, a justification with three parts: modernity, creativity, and liberalism. First, they noted that besides the Soviet Union, America is the only country deserving the moniker "modern," because unlike other countries still bound by tradition and unable to "enter into the stage of modernity," America has shaken off the shackles of England and has become the model site for the development of an independent national literature. For this reason, American literature stands as a powerful example and comrade for modern Chinese literature, which has also eagerly cut all ties with an old-world tradition of its own. Second, American literature is creative because it was nurtured in the context of the new culture of films, jazz music, skyscrapers, radio, and all the other achievements and evils of the modern world. This new context called for a self-conscious creation of Americanism, and one can see the effects of Americanism in the way American literature has increasingly come to influence other Western literature (Edgar Allan Poe's influence on French symbolism, Walt Whit-

---

Remembrances of *Les Contemporaines* (1)" (*Xiandai zayi*), *Historical Materials on New Literature* (January 1981): 219.

51. See Gregory Lee, *Dai Wangshu*, 31 ff.

man's on the radical poetry in the Soviet Union, etc.). Third, unlike other literatures produced under despotic regimes, American literature is created in the context of liberal debate, where different opinions are allowed free expression. Since liberalism is "the absolute and the only safeguard for the development of literature," it should also serve as a model for the development of new culture in China.[52]

The essay by Zhao Jiabi following this introduction again emphasized that American literature is the prime example of a previously colonized, slavish literature that proclaimed its independence.[53] This identification of the unique characteristics of modern American literature was revealing of the general outlook of *Les Contemporaines* under the editorship of Shi and Du, who valorized the modern, creative, liberal, and independent, for which the struggle of American literature served as an allegorical precedent. The inspiration from American literature as a role model covered the whole spectrum of literary activity, from reflecting the modernity of everyday life, to rejecting the ideological containment by the League, to creating a new, independent national literature which was nonetheless a part of the international community, and fostering liberal discussions and freedom of expression.

Months later in early 1935, however, it became clear with the death of the publisher that the Xiandai Bookstore had financial problems, and Shi and Du left the journal. By this time, their close associates Liu Na'ou and Mu Shiying were working for the Nationalist government, and Shi became unwillingly embroiled in an acrimonious debate with the sharp-tongued Lu Xun over whether the youth should read the Taoist classic *Zhuangzi* or not, all of which soured the modernists' public image.[54]

A separate, more radical movement was being formed concurrently with the efforts of *Trackless Train*, *La Nouvelle Littérature*, and *Les Contemporaines*. On the pages of *Gold Chamber Monthly*, *Oazo*, *Modern Fiction*, and a few other journals, a stylishly rebellious voice was gathering momentum, its avowed aim being the subversion of every convention through the celebration of decadence and eroticism. The self-proclaimed fin-de-siècle writer and Francophile Shao Xunmei founded the *Gold Chamber Monthly*, imitating in style and design the *Yellow Book* of the English decadents.[55] Shao and his friends,

52. Shi Zhecun and Du Heng, "Introduction to the Special Issue on Modern American Literature" (*Xiandai Meiguo wenxue zhuanhao daoyan*), *Les Contemporaines* 5:6 (October 1934): 834–838.

53. Zhao Jiabi, "The Growth of American Fiction."

54. Shi Zhecun, "Miscellaneous Reminiscences of *Les Contemporaines* (1)," 214.

55. Shao Xunmei wrote a book of poems entitled *Flower-Like Evil* (*Hua yiban de zui'e*, 1928) after Baudelaire's *Les Fleurs du Mal*. He was a fashionable dandy who built himself a marble house, acquired an American mistress (reporter Emily Hahn), and smoked opium. See Heinrich O. Freuhauf, *Urban Exoticism in Modern Chinese Literature, 1910–1933* (Ph.D. dissertation, University of Chicago, 1990), 227–230. For a portrait of Shao and an analysis of his works, see also Leo Lee, *Shanghai Modern*, chapter 7.

as well as a group gathered around *Oazo* and *Modern Fiction*, headed by Ye Lingfeng, picked up where the May Fourth decadents had left off (see chapter 4). Both the translations and the original texts in the *Gold Chamber Monthly* maintained a consistently aestheticized outlook. Tanizaki Jun'ichirō, Oscar Wilde, George Moore, and Walter Pater were their favorite writers whose works appeared in translation. Chinese writers such as Zhang Kebiao (a coeditor of the journal and a much underappreciated but important fiction writer), Teng Gu (a decadent writer active since the May Fourth), and Xu Xiacun contributed creative works to the magazine. In their manifesto, the editors propounded a nonutilitarian and universalist view of literature and art, defying politics and all time-bound literary ideas, and holding the ultimate expression of art in utmost esteem.[56] A peculiarly urgent tone colored their work, perhaps because of the chaotic political climate of the time; their indulgence in decadence matched the intense ideological tenor of the times.

Zhang Kebiao's lyrical piece entitled "Come, Let Us Soundly Sleep by the Crater of the Volcano and Rejoice in Our Dreams" portrayed decadence as the unfettered eruption of passion that one experiences at the moment of death:

> If we sleep by the crater of the volcano, we will feel the burning of the passion underground, its rushing, surging, torrid, hot blood. For this reason alone, we should willingly sleep by the crater of the volcano, and we can even dream our dreams there.
>
> If we sleep and dream by the crater of the volcano, the dream we dream will be like this.
>
> The volcano erupts and fulfills our desired dream vision. It blasts us into flying dust, our blood splattering like rain, our flesh flying through the sky like flower petals, our bones falling to the ground like hailstones. Then we will know that our bones are still hard, our flesh still strong, and our hearts not yet withered by death.
>
> With our flesh and blood a beautiful world of myriad shiny lights will be created. Our fragments engendering more fragments, which will spread all over the ground, and create a very bright and shiny world.
>
> This is because if the volcano erupts, all the filth and ugliness of the world will disappear. . . . [57]

What "we" seek is to "dream" in a world of impending doom and to dream about the beauty of destruction and death. Before the unavoidable destruction occurs and an imaginary utopia emerges, "we" will revel in the thrill of danger. As another instance of decadence, Shao Xunmei's stories that are written in the form of interior monologues, such as "Gambling" (*Du*) and

56. Shao Xunmei and Zhang Kebiao, "Colors and Flags" (*Secai yu qizhi*), *Gold Chamber Monthly* (*Jinwu yuekan*) 1:1 (January 1929): 1–6.

57. Zhang Kebiao, "Come, Let Us Soundly Sleep by the Crater of the Volcano and Rejoice in Our Dreams" (*Lai ba rang women chenshui zai penhuokou shang huanmeng*), *Gold Chamber Monthly* 1:2 (February 1929): 4.

"After the Gambler Left the Casino" (*Duqianren li le duchang*), muse upon gambling as an art form. He defended the erotic art of Chang Yu by comparing it to the paintings of Matisse and Picasso,[58] and edited a collection of drawings and poetry by Aubrey Beardsley (1872–1898),[59] the arch-decadent artist of late-nineteenth-century England.

Ye Lingfeng edited two consecutive journals, *Oazo* and *Modern Fiction*, both of which were sumptuously illustrated by Ye himself with his Beardsley-inspired fin-de-siècle–style drawings. The journals were horizontally printed and beautifully bound, with an almost absolute aestheticist orientation and an unapologetic hedonism. Many of the writers in his group were originally associated with the Creation Society, but they took Guo Moruo's "explosion of the self" and Yu Dafu's self-indulgence to an extreme, aggrandizing the self in defiance of all constrictive norms and celebrating sexuality without the kind of anxiety that had troubled their May Fourth predecessors. *Oazo* was an especially decadent and rebellious journal, at least on the rhetorical level, providing the ground for a sweeping subversion of the status quo. Every issue of the journal is divided into two parts, "The Ivory Tower" (*xiangya zhi ta*) and "The Crossroads" (*shizi jietou*), the former edited by Ye Lingfeng and containing mainly literary work, while the latter, edited by Pan Hannian, explored the "crossroads" of society, i.e., social issues.[60] Ye Lingfeng declared the journal "decadent" and "sentimental" (his own English words), intending to create an artificial "*oazo*" (Esperanto for "oasis") of art and literature in a land forsaken by both Satan and Jesus.[61]

Pan Hannian, on the other hand, advocated what he called "New Hooliganism" (*xin liumang zhuyi*), blaming the so-called "righteous men, *junzi*, gentlemen and scholars" for having caused the demise of China. He entreated young people to stand up and rebel: "We believe that all of those youths who feel fettered, oppressed, fooled and bullied . . . must believe in New Hooliganism in order to rebel against everything. New Hooliganism has no slogans, no creeds. The most important thing is to rebel with utmost effort when one feels dissatisfied."[62] A prominent aspect of this New

58. Shao published these stories under the pseudonym Hao Wen, in *Gold Chamber Monthly* 1:3 (March 1929): 45–50 and 1:5 (May 1929): 40–43, respectively. [Shao]Xunmei, "Treasures of the Contemporary Art Scene" (*Jindai yishujie zhong de baobei*), *Gold Chamber Monthly* 1:3 (March 1929): 82–86.

59. Shao Xunmei, again under the pseudonym Hao Wen, *Poems and Drawings of Beardsley* (*Piyacilü shihuaji*) (Shanghai: Gold Chamber Bookstore, 1929).

60. Leo Lee notes that these two section headings are direct references to Kuriyagawa Hakuson, the former to his *Out of the Ivory Tower* (*Chule xiangya zhi ta*), translated into Chinese by Lu Xun, and the latter to an essay characterizing the modern mind as "wandering at the crossroads." See Leo Lee, *Shanghai Modern*, chapter 7.

61. See Ye Lingfeng, "Inside the Ivory Tower" (*Xiangyata zhong*) and "On Editing the Journal" (*Bianhou suibi*), *Oazo* (*Huanzhou*) 1:1 (October 1926): 1–3 and 55–58.

62. Ya Ling (Pan Hannian) "New Hooliganism" (1), *Oazo* 1:1 (October 1926): 7.

Hooliganism was the release of sexual inhibition. Numbers four and seven of volume one were special issues devoted to "Soul and Flesh," and Pan Hannian explained the motivation behind the first of these special issues as follows:

> Our "Soul and Flesh Issue" launches a sincere and wholehearted attack on a fundamental defect of the society, that is, the slave-like position of women. We hope to arouse and awaken those female comrades who have the spirit of New Hooliganism so they may stand up to evil powers and struggle against the old society in order to reach the grand goal of male and female sexual freedom.[63]

Issues such as prostitution, free sex, women's right to inheritance, eugenics, women's education, and the physical abuse of women are raised and discussed in heated, often graphic language. The two most outspoken advocates of sexual freedom and eugenics education—the notorious "Dr. Sex," Zhang Jingsheng (1888–1969), who was also the editor of *New Culture* (*Xinwenhua*), and Jianbo (Lu Jianbo), editor of *New Woman* (*Xin nüxing*)—were also published prominently. Ye Lingfeng, an incredibly prolific writer, published a story in almost every issue, many of them erotically charged, dealing with such themes as autoeroticism, homosexuality, and incest. Along with his other works published in *Modern Fiction, Les Contemporaines,* and other journals, these stories were later collected into four volumes of stories published as part of the Oazo Series (*huanzhou congshu*).

Though intent on making a lofty social and artistic statement by advocating decadence and eroticism, the editors of *Oazo* were nonetheless fully aware of the market value of their journal. It sold about 4,000 copies each issue. *Oazo* therefore attests to the Shanghai phenomenon of a "high" cultural scene permeated by commercialism, or an eye towards the market. *Les Contemporaines,* for instance, was purely a commercial venture from the point of view of the owner of Xiandai Bookstore, who bet on the conviction that "high literature" could have a market. That this estimation of the market proved correct explains the flourishing of a publishing industry on a scale never before seen in China as a whole, let alone within one single city. Shi Zhecun mentioned decades later that if the Sino-Japanese War had not interfered, the modern Chinese literature that was so vibrant during the Nanjing decade would have had more time to mature and develop, and a new chapter of modern Chinese literary history would have been written.[64] The onslaught of war shifted the focus of most of the writers from art to society and politics. Debates on National Form (*minzu xingshi*), Defense Literature (*guofang wenxue*), Mass Language (*dazhongyu*), and so on took center stage beginning in the late 1930s, but none of them attracted the kind of large-scale

---

63. "New Hooliganism" (5), *Oazo* 1:6 (December 1926): 263.
64. Interview with Shi Zhecun.

participation of writers from across the spectrum as did *Les Contemporaines,* nor could they form a literary movement of any kind that sought to define literature anew.

The geocultural landscape of Shanghai as described above, with its fragmentary colonial presence, urbanism, bustling publishing industry, and ideological strife, comprised the immediate local conditions in which Shanghai modernism arose. One may say that these were modernism's extrinsic conditions. Before charting the interrelatedness between these extrinsic conditions and the intrinsic aspects of writing style, particularly in terms of the stylistic and aesthetic propensities of Japanese new sensationism as mediated by Shanghai modernists, a brief introduction to Japanese new sensationism is in order.

New sensationist writing in Japan was a short-lived (1924–1930), distinctly modernist movement that began around a coterie magazine called *Literary Age* (*Bungei jidai,* 1924–1927), with such participants as Kawabata Yasunari, Kataoka Teppei, and, most importantly, Yokomitsu Riichi. Arising after the earthquake in the Kantō area on September 1, 1923, the literary movement sought to create a language that could account for the new sensations of modernity in the now-transformed modern metropolis of Tokyo. Yokomitsu's later recollection of the impact of the earthquake on new sensationism, which is reminiscent of what Shi Zhecun said of the materials of modernist poetry (quoted above), illustrates this point:

> My prior faith in beauty was entirely destroyed by this tragedy [the earthquake]. The period that people have labelled new sensationism began at this time. The great metropolis had been unbelievably reduced to burnt-out fields before our eyes; in the midst of this, the manifestation of speed called the automobile began to crisscross the city for the first time, and soon after the strange mutation of sound called radio appeared, and then the artificial birds called airplanes began to fill the skies as machines of practical use. All of these material embodiments of modern science first appeared in our country following the earthquake. The sensations of a youth, faced with the appearance of these materializations of modern science in the midst of the burnt-out fields, could not help but be transformed.[65]

The destruction of the old by the earthquake left room for the unobstructed entrance of modern technology, which fundamentally transfigured social re-

---

65. Yokomitsu Riichi, translated in Seiji Lippit, *Japanese Modernism and the Destruction of Literary Form: The Writings of Akutagawa, Yokomitsu, and Kawabata* (Ph.D. dissertation, Columbia University, 1997), 5–6.

ality, triggered new sensory responses, and demanded new modes of perception, experience, and feeling.

As avowed formalists, Yokomitsu and his compatriots invented a new language that could relate this new experience through fiction, theoretical essays, and film, all of which are by now classics of Japanese modernism. Kawabata wrote the screenplay of the only new sensationist film, *A Page of Madness* (*Kurutta ichipeiji*, 1926), rendering in visual terms the premises of new sensationism; his 1930 novel *Asakusa Kurenaidan* is the perfect illustration of this new mode in its embodiment of the speed, sight, and sensation of modern urban life, and in its incorporation of mass culture such as film, radio, journalism, and (in the words of renowned Japanese critic Maeda Ai) "the syncopation of jazz."[66] This type of Japanese modernism was "an attempt to construct a language capable of representing the rapidly transforming urban environment."[67]

But what was the nature of this language and how did it capture the new sensations of modernity? As Seiji Lippit explains, the answer lies in this language's unmediated registration of sensations themselves, instead of depicting experience as objective events (as in naturalism) or narrating the subjective interior reaction to experience (as in the so-called I-novel [*watakushi sōsetsu*]).The new sensationists self-consciously positioned themselves against both of these models, projecting subjective consciousness and individual sensations onto the empirical world of material objects by reducing language into "raw sense-data," and thus turning the sensations themselves into material artifacts.[68] Yokomitsu defined what he called the new sensation in "On New Sensations" (*Shinkankakuron*, 1925): "Sensation is an intuitive explosion of subjectivity that rips off the external aspects of nature to give direct access to the thing in itself. . . . The new sensationalist [i.e., new sensationist] method . . . gives a more material representation of an emotional apprehension."[69] Yokomitsu presents the author's subjectivity as splitting into "limitless fragments," leaping into all objects and setting them in motion, rejecting the symbiotic relationship between subjectivity and interiority, and instead exteriorizing subjectivity by casting its fragments into the material world of objects. Language, or the written word, then becomes part of the dynamic material world, its own materiality the best exemplification of literature's capacity to be part of that world.[70]

In concrete terms, this style is marked by short sentences, often following each other with no apparent logical connection; personification (as a

---

66. Lippit, *Japanese Modernism and the Destruction of Literary Form*, 200–255.

67. Ibid., 223.

68. Ibid., 200–255.

69. Translated and quoted in Dennis Keene, *Yokomitsu Riichi: Modernist* (New York: Columbia University Press, 1980), 79–80.

70. See Lippit, *Japanese Modernism and the Destruction of Literary Form*, 55–59.

way to lodge subjectivity in the material object); profuse images without intrusive commentary; montage and collage; third-person narrative perspective; and the violation of normal grammatical principles of language.[71] The avant-garde European movements kindred to Japanese new sensationism have been identified as futurism, cubism, expressionism, symbolism, dadaism, and Russian constructivism. The Western figure most influential for Japanese new sensationists, like for the Chinese new sensationists, was Paul Morand, some of whose stories were translated into Japanese by Horiguchi Daigaku, and were seen as operating through a "logic of sensation" in the way his narratives move through various countries, customs, and sexual encounters.[72]

New sensationism in Japan did have actual relationships with China and the Chinese new sensationists. As I discussed in chapter 2, Tao Jingsun started writing in the new sensationist mode as early as fall 1925, which was contemporaneous with the height of Japanese new sensationist writing. The Shanghai modernists began writing in the new sensationist mode in 1928, with the publication of *Trackless Train*, and again the proximity in time and space between the two movements is significant, attesting to the rapid flow of information and the immediacy of the cultural encounter between the two nations. As was the case with most literary encounters between China and the rest of the world, however, the flow was one-sided, and the relationship between the two sides hierarchical. The Japanese new sensationists did not learn of the similar endeavors of their Chinese counterparts until much later, nor were they interested in cultural encounters with China on equal terms. Just as Japanese writers who travelled to China in the early years of the Republic predominantly portrayed China as a negative example of what not to emulate for Japan,[73] Japanese new sensationists revealed no particular knowledge or interest in China per se except as a specimen of degradation at the hands of Western imperialism, whose fate Japan needed to avoid at all costs.

Yokomitsu's novel *Shanghai*, for instance, like Akutagawa's travelogue, largely fit into an existing Japanese subgenre which depicted Shanghai as embodying the grotesque, the morally corrupt, and the filthy.[74] By the early 1940s, Yokomitsu, along with the now-reconverted Kataoka (part of the *tenkō* phenomenon—converting from the left to the right), became staunch supporters of Japanese imperialism. Kataoka wrote an essay admonishing the Chinese writer most friendly to Japanese culture, none other than Zhou

---

71. Donald Keene, *Dawn to the West: Japanese Literature in the Modern Era* (New York: Henry Holt and Company, 1984), 630–653.

72. Dennis Keene, *Yokomitsu Riichi*, 76–77.

73. See Joshua Fogel, *The Literature of Travel in the Japanese Rediscovery of China, 1862–1945* (Stanford: Stanford University Press, 1996), 129–275.

74. These two works are discussed in more detail in my introduction.

Zuoren himself, for not being cooperative enough with the Japanese occupation forces in Beijing, explaining that the conquered Chinese must be absolutely submissive to the conqueror.[75] When Mu Shiying was assassinated while working for the Japanese puppet regime of Wang Jingwei in Shanghai, Kataoka and Yokomitsu wrote elegies for Mu, recalling him as compatriot in the service of Japanese imperialism (see chapter 11).[76] Not surprisingly, Yokomitsu was later accused of bearing responsibility for the war. The political position of these new sensationists is a testimony to how an avowedly apolitical and aestheticist stance could become complicit with Japanese imperialism.

Generally unaware of the orientation of Japanese new sensationists towards China and the Chinese, the Chinese new sensationists took it upon themselves to incorporate this metropolitan Japanese cultural practice. In the only extant record of a conversation between Mu Shiying and Yokomitsu (Mu visited Japan at least twice in the 1930s), we hear Mu lament the demise of Japanese new sensationism as a result of its turn to nationalism and abandonment of aesthetic ideals.[77] Ironically, it was the Chinese new sensationist in this case who had remained staunchly committed when his Japanese predecessors had already given up their avant-gardism in favor of nationalistic imperialism. If we recall that there was constant warfare between the Chinese and the Japanese during much of the 1930s (the Manchurian incident, the bombing of Shanghai, the Nanjing Massacre), and that by 1937 Shanghai was literally Japan's colony except for the foreign concessions (which later also fell into Japanese hands during the Pacific War), it is revealing that Mu would accuse the Japanese new sensationists of nationalism. The Chinese writer's strategy of bifurcating the metropolitan and the colonial could no longer be legitimized when the metropolitan Japanese culture of new sensationism itself became increasingly integrated into the anti-Chinese imperialist endeavors of the Japanese state. Recognizing the complicity between the metropolitan and the colonial cultures of the imperialist state, though, Mu could only deplore it in terms of the Japanese writers' renunciation of aesthetic ideals.

The Chinese incorporation of Japanese new sensationism in the late 1920s and early 1930s went through the familiar routes of translation and criticism, innocent of the kind of charge Mu made in the late 1930s. Liu Na'ou's 1928 translation of *Erotic Culture* included Kataoka's "Erotic Culture," Yokomitsu's

75. Qian Liqun, *A Biography of Zhou Zuoren* (*Zhou Zuoren zhuan*) (Beijing: Shiyue wenyi chubanshe, 1990), 471.

76. These essays were published in *Literary World* (*Bungakukai*) 7 (September 1940). *Literary World* was the forum where the "overcoming modernity" debate was later conducted in 1942. See chapter 12 for a more detailed discussion of these articles about Mu upon his death.

77. Yokomitsu Riichi, "The Death of Mr. Mu Shiying" (*Mu Shiying shi no shi*), *Literary World* 7 (September 1940): 174–175.

"Activities of the Seventh Floor" (*Qilou de yundong*), and Iketani Shinz-aburo's "Bridge" (*Qiao*). In his introduction to the collection, Liu writes that new sensationism is a symbolic form of writing, best suited to depicting the "color of the times" (*shidai secai*) in modern Japan. It exudes "the aura of importation" (*pailai de qiwei*) and does not seem very "Japanese," but that this is precisely where its uniqueness lies. It does have a clear ideological content, according to Liu, in that it exposes the corruption of Japan's cap-italist society, while providing a prophetic vision of the coming proletarian society.[78] The recipe for new sensationism as laid out by Liu is a combina-tion of (symbolic) modernism, (anticapitalist) socialism, and (imported) exoticism.

Another story of Yokomitsu's translated by Guo Jianying, "The Lit Ciga-rette" (*Dianle huo de zhiyan*),[79] presents some of the themes later populating Mu Shiying's stories. Here the love story involves a self-reflexive commen-tary on the male writer as being attractive to his female readers, and is punc-tuated by exotic-sounding cigarette brand names given in their original lan-guages. (See also Kataoka's "The Poverty of Art," discussed earlier in this chapter.) An early 1931 lecture at Fudan University given by the famed scholar of Japanese literature Xie Liuyi further shows the Chinese adulation of the technical endeavors of new sensationism. Xie Liuyi notes that new sen-sationism is a cure for imitationism and clichéd expressions through a novel "arrangement of sensations" (*ganjue de zhuangzhi*) and new expressive tech-niques. Emphasizing the technical aspects of writing, he notes how emotions can be externalized through an act or an image (somewhat akin to T. S. Eliot's notion of objective correlatives), rather than being described or given names as such, and an ordinary event such as walking can be viewed from the per-spective of the legs as active agents in and of themselves, or through the per-sonification of material objects around the legs, thereby injecting the ob-server's subjectivity into material objects.[80] This inventory of the techniques of new sensationism is clearly evocative of the writings of Yokomitsu and oth-ers on the new sensationist method.

In sum, Japanese new sensationism as it was translated and discussed was primarily a formalist experiment (though sometimes with a Marxist bent) that sought to capture the new sensations of modern urban life through the use of exotic and unfamiliar motifs and avant-garde techniques. Among the Japanese new sensationists, it was Kataoka who clearly advocated a Marxist position for a few years until he shifted again to the right, while Yokomitsu

78. "Translator's Note" (*Yizhe tiji*), in Liu Na'ou, ed. and trans., *Erotic Culture* (*Seqing wen-hua*) (Shanghai: Diyixian shudian, 1928).

79. Yokomitsu Riichi, "The Lit Cigarette" (*Dianle huo de zhiyan*), in *The Sensations of the Bride-groom* (*Xinlang de ganxiang*), trans. Guo Jianying (Shanghai: n.p., 1930), 67–121.

80. Xie Liuyi, "New Sensationism" (*Xin'ganjuepai*), *Modern Literary Criticism* (*Xiandai wenxue pinglun*) 1:1 (April 1931): 1–10.

and Kawabata remained true to their aesthetic formalism until their turn to a nationalist aesthetic in the late 1930s. The debate between the Japanese modernists and the Marxists in the late 1920s over form, in which the modernists sympathetic to Marxism insisted on a formalist theory and resisted the dictation of form by ideological content, thus prefigured the 1932 Third Category Men debate in China.[81]

If earlier literary movements in the May Fourth era, such as realism, decadence, and early modernism, looked directly to the West for inspiration and used the Japanese translation of Western literature as a means of access to the West, in Shanghai modernism Japanese literature no longer played merely a mediating role. Here, Japanese literature became an agent in its own right and took on an importance relatively independent of its borrowed power from the West. Even though Japanese modernism also incorporated Western avant-garde elements, the particular translation of these elements in the context of post-earthquake Tokyo is what provided an aesthetic attractive to Chinese writers. The perception of Japanese modernism as independent of the Euro-American avant-garde partly reflected the increasing presence of metropolitan Japanese culture in Shanghai—frequent visits by Japanese writers, Japan-educated Chinese returning to the city, and the esteemed activities of the Uchiyama Bookstore. It also reflected Japan's increasingly self-assured perception of itself as a modern cultural player. Earlier Chinese writers who went to Japan mainly studied Western literature in Japanese translation, but the generation of Liu Na'ou and his friends took Japanese literature seriously in its own right.

Like its Japanese counterpart, Shanghai modernism was a product of the urban milieu. In 1926, Liu Na'ou wrote a letter to Dai Wangshu in which he established the connection between the city, urban sensations, and modernism:

> To us moderns, *Romance* cannot but be distant. . . . The streetcars are too noisy, the sky that was once blue is blackened by factory soot, and the songs of the skylarks are mute. Muses, their harp strings broken, have flown away to who knows where. Does this mean that there is no beauty in modern life? No, there is, except its form has changed. We don't have *Romance,* no trumpets sounding from castles, but we have *thrill* and *carnal intoxication.* This is what I mean by modernism [*jindaizhuyi*].[82] (author's original English in italics)

This passage predates Shi Zhecun's manifesto of modernist poetics in *Les Contemporaines,* but similarly asserts that modern writers must come to terms with the new sensibility and corporeal/sensory experience created by the transformed technological landscape of modern life. In a letter to Zhao Jingshen,

81. Lippit, *Japanese Modernism and the Destruction of Literary Form,* 60–66.

82. Liu Na'ou, letter to Dai Wangshu, November 10, 1926, collected in Kong Lingjing, ed., *Letters of Modern Chinese Writers* (*Xiandai Zhongguo zuojia shuxin*) (Hong Kong: Yixin shudian, 1971), 266–267.

Xu Xiacun claimed "urbanism" and "modernism" were synonymous;[83] as early as 1927 the city was perceived as the precondition for modern art;[84] and in stories by Liu Na'ou and Mu Shiying we often find an inventory of urban material artifacts—cars, jazz, Hollywood films, dance halls, racecourses, etc.—fetishized as embodiments of exoticism and providers of "carnal intoxication."

Two stanzas from a poem by Shao Xunmei, "The Soul of Shanghai" (*Shanghai de linghun*), present a similar inventory of urban Shanghai:

> Ah, I stand atop the seven-story building,
> Above is the unreachable sky,
> Below are cars, electric wires, horse races,
>
> Front doors to stages, backs of prostitutes;
> Ah, this is the spirit of the city:
> Ah, this is the soul of Shanghai.[85]

The aerial view of the city made possible by the tall modern building presents a panoramic vision of the urban landscape, populated by objects and personalities unique to the city. The aerial view mimics that of the airplane, and the panoramic vision of the city mimics that of the cinema. If these two stanzas remind one of the famous Tang poem by Chen Zi'ang (661– 702) on the occasion of his ascending the Youzhou pagoda—"I see no ancients in front / No followers in back / Thinking about the eternity of heaven and earth / I alone cry in desolation"—it is the jarring incongruity between the two that leaves the greater impression. Ascending the pagoda inspired a cosmic, philosophical meditation, while for Shao the vision of urban artifacts and allures appears devoid of spirituality. But it is the city's very material manifestations that Shao perceives as making up its "spirit" and "soul."

In the following passage from Mu Shiying's later work, "Pierrot" (1934), we see how an urban culture constituted by materialism also considered "modernism" itself a material artifact to be found in a Shanghai literary salon:

> A not so large study is furnished with a bust of Tolstoy, a small transistor radio playing "Spring River Flowery Moon Evening," Pu'er tea, banana skins, cigarettes and cigarette smoke, laughter, materialism, American culture, an eight-inch-high full-body photo of Greta Garbo, walls of books, modernism

83. In ibid., 78–79.

84. Fu Yanchang, "Standards of Art," in Fu, et al., *Three Views on Art* (*Yishu sanjiayan*), mentioned in Freuhauf, *Urban Exoticism in Modern Chinese Literature*, 203.

85. Shao Xunmei, *Flower-Like Evil* (*Hua yiban de zui'e*) (Shanghai: Jinwu shudian, 1928), 47.

[*xiandaizhuyi*], a sofa, and the patrons of the Chinese literary scene, Pan Heling and a group of friends, whose fingers and nerves have both been stained yellow.[86]

In this odd juxtaposition, "modernism" participates in the materiality of urban culture, claiming a space for itself in the fashionable literary salon like a sofa or a pack of cigarettes.

As a material thing like food and cigarettes, modernism is also integrated with the common appetites and popular culture. The "modernist writer" (*xiandaizhuyi zuojia*), a character in this story, makes the following connection between popular culture, eroticism, and modernity: "The loveliness of modern girls lies largely in the huskiness of their voices. A husky voice hints at an over-active sexual appetite, and sexual appetite is the most developed and most important aspect of modern life. Isn't that why the husky-voiced Garbo is admired by the masses?"[87] Greta Garbo is attractive because she is sexy, and this sexiness is a mark of modernity for the modernist writer. In many of Liu's and Mu's stories, it is precisely this Hollywood-style eroticism of their female characters that gets flaunted as one of the key signatures of new sensationism. No wonder that the Chinese label *xin'ganjuepai* was soon applied liberally to other forms of popular culture. Zhang Ruogu used it to name one of the columns on modern female fashion in the journal *Women's Pictorial* (*Furen huabao*),[88] and the *xin'ganjuepai* style of writing became popular, with numerous imitators.[89] For a time, new sensationism was in vogue along with other popular cultural forms such as cinema and fashion. The fact that Liu Na'ou and Mu Shiying later both wrote extensively on popular cinema is another indication of the proximity of new sensationism to popular culture.

The left naturally felt threatened, and was prompted to write scathing criticisms of new sensationism such as Shen Qiyu's (1903–1970) 1931 article "The So-Called New Sensationism." This article by the Japan-educated Marxist translator, critic, and writer was published in the leftist journal *Big Dipper* a few months after Xie Liuyi delivered his famous lecture on new sensationism at Fudan University. Shen targeted new sensationism in hyperbolic terms as a foreign import, just as bad as the forced importation of "armaments, opium, and morphine" by the imperialists. Quoting from Xie Liuyi's lecture, he noted how the valorization of the new sensationist technique overlooked its ideological and other defects. Shen cited theoretical works by Kawa-

86. Mu Shiying, "Pierrot," in *Platinum Statue of a Female Nude* (*Baijin de nüti suxiang*) (Shanghai: Xiandai shuju, 1934), 199.

87. Ibid., 200–201.

88. See Freuhauf, *Urban Exoticism in Modern Chinese Literature*, 256–257.

89. See Ye Lingfeng's 1935 letter to Mu Shiying, in which he notes: "There are so many imitators of new sensationism recently that they are neither donkeys nor horses but tigers painted as dogs." Included in Kong, *Letters of Modern Chinese Writers*, 227.

bata, Kataoka, and Yokomitsu to illustrate how new sensationism was a strictly subjectivist, symbolist form of literature with only a pretentious co-option of simplistic notions of Marxist materialism and dialectics. He then deplored the current situation in Shanghai where Japanese new sensationism was touted as a literary treasure, with the readership all drugged by "opium, morphine, and anesthesia" from Japan.[90] Its polemical tone aside, this article at least shows the extent to which new sensationism captured the attention of the general public, and the weight of its presence in both the high and popular cultural imaginaries at the time. In the 1980s, the prominent leftist critic Lou Shiyi, who had written a much-cited criticism of Shi Zhecun's new sensationism as decadent and corrupt in the 1930s, confessed that he had been pressured into writing the critical essay and that at the time anyone who wrote outside the leftist cause had been branded *xin'ganjuepai*.[91]

The new sensationists were so influential in their creation of the subgenre of urban fiction (*dushi xiaoshuo* or *duhui xiaoshuo*) that 1932 was declared the year of the "literature of urbanism" (*duhuizhuyi wenxue*) by the editors of the 1932 *Yearbook of Chinese Literature* (*Zhongguo wenyi nianjian*), who attributed the initiation of this trend to Liu Na'ou, followed by Ye Lingfeng and Mu Shiying.[92] Translations of urban fiction criticism on it from Japan also accompanied this trend. The 1928 translation of Katagami Noboru's "City Life and Modern Literature" (*Duhui shenghuo yu xiandai wenxue*), for instance, proclaimed city life as the most "human," most favorable, desirable, intense, magical, and passionate, and the city as a place of sensual stimulation and refinement. The literature produced from such a setting is necessarily decadent, and such is the "true" and "new" modern literature.[93]

In the profuse urban fiction written about Shanghai, the city became not merely the setting, but the subject. Many of these writers were neither associated with nor sympathetic to the new sensationist camp, but nonetheless appropriated many of the new sensationist techniques. Representative works include such works as Lou Shiyi's "Shanghai Rhapsodies" (*Shanghai kuangxiangqu*), Peng Zi's "Urban Sonata" (*Dushi Sonata*), Zhang Ruogu's *Urban Symphony* (*Duhui jiaoxiangqu*), Li Qingya's *Shanghai*, Xu Weinan's *Urban*

90. Shen Qiyu, "The So-Called New Sensationism" (*Suowei xin'ganjuepai zhe*), *Beidou* 1:4 (December 1931): 65–70.

91. Interview with Yan Jiayan, Los Angeles, California, June 1997. I treat Lou's article in detail in chapter 13.

92. Mentioned in Xia Yuanwen, "A Preliminary Discussion of Urban Fiction" (*Duhui zhuyi xiaoshuo culun*), *Suzhou University Journal* (*Suzhou daxue xuebao*) (January 1990): 79.

93. Translated by (Han) Shiheng, in *Beixin* 2:20 (September 1928): 39–43. Note that Satō Haruo's *Melancholy of the City* and Hiyashi Fusao's *The Double Curved Lines of the City* (*Duhui shuang qu xian*), two important works of urban fiction from Japan, were also translated at this time. *Melancholy in the City*, op. cit.; *The Double Curved Lines of the City*, trans. Shi'er (Shanghai: Shenzhou guoguang she, 1932).

Men and Women (*Dushi de nannü*), and Huang Zhenxia's *The Destruction of Metropolitan Shanghai* (*Da Shanghai de huimie*). Eager to depict the pace and rhythm of the city, they borrowed metaphors from music and dance just as in new sensationist fiction. A major structural feature of many of these works is the use of counterpoint, in music the technique of adding a countertheme to an already existing melody, used frequently in fiction by Mu Shiying, such as in his "Shanghai Foxtrot" (see chapter 11). In these stories of Shanghai, the given melody is normally the fast-paced city and its pleasure-seeking inhabitants, while the counterpoint is often the city's underclass, juxtaposed to project a social commentary. This is best illustrated by Huang Zhenxia's *The Destruction of Metropolitan Shanghai*, in which alternating chapters contrast soldiers dying as they fight the Japanese with the decadent urban reality where pleasure is the sole pursuit. The counterpoint allowed a measure of expression of anticolonial sentiments, but the fetishization of urban entertainment and consumption often undermined those very same sentiments.

The profusion of sites, avenues, and methods of decadence and erotic pleasure in the city provided another important connection among new sensationism, popular culture, urbanism, and eroticism. This is also the point where new sensationism overlapped with the Francophile decadence of Shao Xunmei, Zhang Ruogu, and others, who sought the immediate gratifications of the new, the extraordinary, the sensual, the mysterious, and the artificial.[94] Stories of erotic pleasure set in a city populated by young Chinese men and exotic women with unclear "national" or "ethnic" features proliferated in new sensationism, as did stories involving prostitutes. Recall that during the May Fourth period, there was already a body of literature dealing with sexual themes,[95] and at that time a relatively mild discourse on sexuality by someone like Yu Dafu was considered sensational enough to bring him immediate notoriety. In later Shanghai, sexuality and eroticism no longer served predominantly as counterdiscourses to tradition; rather, they were recognized as part and parcel of the urban condition, and thus this era witnessed a much more extensive treatment of erotic themes in both creative and critical works.[96] In addition to Freud, Havelock Ellis's sexual psychology was also

94. See Lu Tianshi's definition of decadence in his *Modern Literary Movements in Europe*, 158–159, and Wu Yun's in his *Modern Literature ABC* (*Jindai wenxue ABC*) (Shanghai: Shijie shuju, 1928), 89–90.

95. Zhao Jingshen provides numerous examples in his "Modern Chinese Literature and Abnormal Sexuality" (*Zhongguo xinwenyi yu biantai xingyu*), *Yiban* 4:1 (January 1928): 204–208. The themes of abnormal sexuality listed were incest, autoeroticism, homosexuality, Oedipal complex, masochism, and sadism, which appear in stories such as Lu Yin's "Lishi's Diary" (*Lishi de riji*) and Tian Han's "Spring Dream by the Lakeside" (*Hubian chunmeng*). See also chapter 4, on May Fourth decadence.

96. See for instance Matsumura Takeo's *Literature and Erotic Love* (*Wenyi yu xing'ai*), trans. Xie Liuyi (Shanghai: Kaiming shudian, n.d.), and Albert Mordell's 1919 text *The Erotic Motive*

widely read. But practical sexual guidebooks such as Marie Stopes's *Married Love* and Edward Carpenter's *Love's Coming of Age,* two Shanghai best-sellers, were more popular. Notoriety therefore necessitated a more extreme and graphic eroticism.

The commercial appeal of eroticism was naturally not ignored either. Unlike in the May Fourth era, literary developments in 1930s Shanghai were closely linked to the rise of the literary industry. Without the capital provided by the affluent Liu Na'ou, Shao Xunmei, the Xiandai Bookstore, and many other popular publishers, there may not have been a Shanghai literary renaissance at all. The modernist writing produced in such a context was necessarily affected by the commercialized operations of the literary industry, a fact observed by writers such as Du Heng, who commented in 1933 that "Shanghai flavor" was concomitant with "urban flavor," and that commercialization could not but affect literary writing.[97] Even the Japanese Marxist critic Hirabayashi Hatsunosuke's article "Commodified Modern Fiction" (*Shangpinhua de jindai xiaoshuo*), the translation of which appeared in 1930, recognized the market value of literature.[98] The overriding concern about sales volume was readily apparent: numerous advertisements for literary texts can be found in magazines of the time, side by side with advertisements for cigarettes and perfumes and often sharing similar tantalizing language. And nothing tantalized quite like eroticism. Even the "high" modernists allowed commercialism to permeate their writing to the extent that kitsch was promoted as serious art—this is another instance of high literature becoming integrated with (or, some might say, degraded by) popular culture. Many of Ye Lingfeng's stories sought to combine the commercial appeal of eroticism with modernist techniques.

Less commercialized, however, were the erotic stories of Shi Zhecun and a serious academic discourse on psychoanalysis then circulating. In Shi's work, eroticism aimed less to tantalize than to explicate the Freudian notion of the libido, while the academic writings on psychoanalysis investigated various available theories on sexuality. This academic wing of psychoanalysis can be seen in the scholarly works of Zhu Guangqian, Pan Guangdan, and translations from Lefcadio Hearn's (1850–1904) literary criticism.[99] Zhu's *Schools of Abnormal Psychology* (*Biantai xinlixue paibie*) and Pan's translation of Ellis's

---

in Literature (*Jindai wenxue yu xing'ai*), trans. Zhong Ziyan and Wang Wenchuan (Shanghai: Kaiming shudian, 1931). The novels and stories of Tanizaki and D. H. Lawrence were also readily available in several translations.

97. Du Heng [Su Wen], "Writers in Shanghai" (*Wenren zai Shanghai*), *Les Contemporaines* 4:2 (December 1933): 281–282.

98. Hirabayashi Hatsunosuke, "Commodified Modern Fiction" (*Shangpinhua de jindai xiaoshuo*), trans. Qian Gechuan, *Beixin* 4:16 (August 1930): 49–55.

99. Lefcadio Hearn was known to Chinese readers by his Japanese name of Koizumi Yakumo (*Xiaoquan Bayun*).

one volume edition of *The Psychology of Sex,* as well as Wang Wenchuan's translation of Albert Mordell's *The Erotic Motive in Literature* were important contributions. Particularly noticeable was a newfound interest in sadism and masochism, as evidenced by Shi Zhecun's fiction and such scholarly articles as Hong Suye's "Sadism and Masochism in Literature" (*Wenxue shang zhi yinnuekuang yu shounuekuang*).[100] A certain blend of the erotic with the grotesque, similar to the Japanese style of "*ero-guro-nonsensu*" ("erotic-grotesque-nonsense"), became a subtrend of Chinese new sensationism in the historical fiction of Shi Zhecun (see chapter 12).

VISUALITY, COMMODITY, AND SEMICOLONIAL SUBJECTIVITY

The engagement with and incorporation of mass culture most clearly distinguish Shanghai modernism from its Japanese and Western counterparts.[101] As illustrated earlier, Shanghai modernism was intently interested in the erotic, exotic, urban, material, and decadent, and often approximated in content mass cultural forms such as cinema and popular magazines. In form as well, the visual and technical qualities of cinema and illustrated magazines were frequently exploited, either through the use of cinematic perspective, montage, a structure of erotic gaze, or pictorial illustrations, or through the incorporation of the technical language of film production. In Ye Lingfeng's story "Flu" (*Liuxingxing ganmao*, 1933), for instance, the erotic gaze of the male narrator combines his fascination with a modern girl and his fascination with a new-model sportscar, the two objects becoming similes for each other:

Sleek body
V-shaped radiator
Buoyant chassis
Water-compression shock absorbers
Five-speed gear shift

She, like a new 1933 car, in the orange-tinted air of May, on the asphalt pavement, glides through the crowd like an eel. . . .

The gear shifts from fourth to fifth. Heading into the wind, a sculpted handsome beauty of 1933: V-shaped radiator, two half-moon lights, Isadora Duncan–style short, flying hair.[102]

100. Hong Suye, "Sadism and Masochism in Literature" (*Wenxue shang zhi yinnuekuang yu shounuekuang), Literature Monthly (Wenxue zazhi)* 7:1 (January 1935): 96–106.

101. For an analysis of Western high modernism's rejection of mass culture, see Andreas Huyssen, "Mass Culture as Woman," in his *After the Great Divide* (Bloomington: Indiana University Press, 1986), 44–62.

102. Ye Lingfeng, "Flu" (*Liuxingxing ganmao), Les Contemporaines* 3:5 (September 1933): 653–654.

Later in the story, Ye grafts the technical language of a screenplay onto the story:

> *D.:* Dark atmosphere, the tail of a comet sweeping across like lightning.
>
> *D. I.:* Gradually appearing in the light is Zhenzi's face.
>
> *Close-up:* Zhenzi's eyes, from the eyes extend octopus-like tentacles, the captured animal, struggle. (*F. O.*)
>
> *Subtitle:* Although I am not "her," I think there is a possibility that I may love you.
>
> *F. I.:* Myself holding a photograph of "her." Zhenzi standing beside me, grinning. Putting down the photo, laughs, walks over to the camera.
>
> *Close-up:* Surprised but at the same time happy face of Zhenzi.
>
> *Long Shot:* Street in spring. Flowers. Sparrows. Trembling laughter. A thermometer with a high mercury level.
>
> *Close Shot:* Race track. Two contestants at the end of their fierce competition.
>
> *Close-up:* Score board: My name, his name.
>
> *Insertion:* Prize for losing: a necktie.
>
> *Subtitle:* Because I disliked that tie of yours, I thought of buying one like that for him.
>
> *Close-up:* The sad face of the loser holding the prize.
>
> *Close-up:* Zhenzi's face.
>
> *D. I.:* Dissolves into "her" face.
>
> *D. I.:* Then dissolves gradually into Zhenzi's face approaching. . . . [103]

Ye mixes screenplay and short story, while creating a filmic structure of gaze and gazed-at, all the while making specific references to Hollywood films and film stars. (Joan Crawford, Greta Garbo, Clara Bow, and Norma Shearer were some of the most frequently evoked names in new sensationist stories.) The gaze of the narrator at the object of his desire, be it a young woman in fashionable attire, a Hollywood actress on the screen, the latest model sports car, or a soaring, phallic skyscraper, depicts the visual sense in a heightened state of stimulation.

The question remains why such mass cultural forms were so intimately integrated into Shanghai's literary modernism in both form and content. In the popular imaginary of foreigners and Shanghai modernist depictions, there seemed to be a certain consensus in the perception of Shanghai as a city of sin and easy pleasure. The "Entertainment" chapter of *All About Shanghai: A Standard Guidebook* (1934–1935) compiles an array of enjoyments so rich and varied that a reader may indeed believe Shanghai to be a city of pure pleasure and sin, where "wine, women and song" was the standard fare.[104] Jerome Ch'en notes how moral degeneration characterized the for-

---

103. Ibid., 658; the abbreviations "D." ("dissolve"), "F. O." ("fade-out"), and "F. I." ("fade-in"), as well as the other headings, are in English in the original.

104. *All About Shanghai*, 73.

eign communities in Shanghai to a significant extent because many of the expatriates were "trash" elements who committed all manner of crimes with impunity due to extraterritoriality.[105] The rampant prostitution in Shanghai has also been well-documented in the work of Gail Hershatter.[106] So Shanghai *was* a decadent city, where foreign opportunists, travellers, and merchants sought excitement, pleasure, and easy money; where the reigning culture was that of commodity consumption and entertainment. Prostitutes and dance girls were for sale, their value hierarchized according to their racial identity, exemplifying the infiltration of commodity logic in human relationships. Other residents of Shanghai, those who had the means to afford it, partook in the urban consumptive culture of fancy goods, dance halls, jazz, liquor, cinemas, and gambling.

This consumption-oriented culture with its commodity fetishism was only available within the boundaries of Shanghai: one cannot imagine latest-model sportscars zipping around China in the mid-1930s—for one thing, outside of Shanghai gas stations were not readily available.[107] The boundedness of this consumptive culture clearly marks it as a particular Shanghai culture, and underscores Shanghai's condition as a quintessential semicolonial city. The commodity fetishism prominent in Shanghai modernism was itself reflective of the semicolonial city as a playground of erotic and decadent desires, consumptive rather than productive in nature. Because these commodities were foreign and unavailable in the rest of China, they exuded a refreshing and exotic flavor; because the entertainment options that Shanghai provided were equally foreign, they triggered feelings of profound decadence—the characters in new sensationist stories do not drink Chinese wines but Western whiskey, and they dance to the rhythms of jazz, the foxtrot, or the waltz, not to Chinese tunes.

The logic of consumption involves a powerful visual dimension, because the desiring medium of commodity fetishism is triggered by vision: seeing a commodity gives one the illusive promise that one may own it. Seeing it and yet unable to possess it, one desires it even more. Raymond Williams discusses how Western modernism was produced by immigrants from the countryside whose encounters with the urban center were characterized by an experience of visual strangeness.[108] Shanghai modernism's chief proponents were all emigrés as well—Liu Na'ou from colonial Taiwan via Japan, Mu Shiying and Du Heng from Zhejiang province, Shi Zhecun from

---

105. Jerome Ch'en, *China and the West: Society and Culture 1815–1937* (Bloomington: Indiana University Press, 1979), 213–216.

106. See for instance Gail Hershatter, "The Hierarchy of Shanghai Prostitution, 1870–1949," *Modern China* 15:4 (1989): 463–98.

107. I thank Yibing Huang for this observation in his "Reading Between Western Modernism and Chinese Modernism," unpublished manuscript, 1995.

108. Raymond Williams, *The Politics of Modernism* (London: Verso, 1989), 34.

Song jiang, Hei Ying from Indonesia, and so on—and the sense of visual strangeness must have been even more intense for these writers than it was for Western modernists, because what they saw had little connection with the indigenous "place" of China itself. The Shanghai that they saw was a *space* where modern institutions were transplanted from foreign countries, not a *place* connected to the indigenous idea of locale or local culture. As Anthony Giddens has argued, modernity in the West caused the separation of space from place, as time became standardized and modern institutions became easily "disembedded" from their social contexts and infinitely transplantable. Space became more easily controllable from afar, and thus place, as locales and the "physical settings of social activity as situated geographically," became increasingly "penetrated by and shaped in terms of social influences quite distant from [it]." To infuse Giddens's useful point with a colonial dimension, Chinese semicolonialism as a product of the imperialism of Western modernity displaced the local place of Shanghai with the colonial space of modern technology and institutions. Thus, to borrow from Giddens, the place of Shanghai became increasingly "phantasmagoric," where what "structures the locale [the place] is not simply that which is present on the scene."[109] In this particular sense, then, the urban phantasmagoria of Shanghai as a "fantastic sequence of haphazardly associative imagery"[110] assaults and seduces the new arrival, and turns him into a voyeur of the stimulating, exciting, yet confusing city. In the semicolonial city, vision was at the front line of confrontation and negotiation between the Chinese subject and the spectacle of the city, and therefore it was the dominant mode of experience of the urban phantasmagoria.[111] The emigré writers, with the exception of Liu Na'ou, were for the most part too poor to own the commodities they viewed. Phantasmagoria subjected the viewer to a promise of consumption, and then, breaking that promise, led the viewer to loss and dejection. Desire thus aroused in a structure of seduction and inevitable unreachability is then confined to the realm of vision. As scopophilia or as a form of "ocular desire" invested with anxiety, vision itself becomes the most heightened sense exposed to the force of eroticization.[112] This may account for why the prime objects of desire in new sensationist fiction, Westernized modern girls, are always presented as the objects of an erotic gaze, always beyond the grasp of the male protagonists (see chapter 10).

109. Anthony Giddens, *The Consequences of Modernity* (Stanford: Stanford University Press, 1990), 18–19.

110. This definition of phantasmagoria is taken from *The American Heritage College Dictionary*.

111. Ying jin Zhang also notes the dominance of vision in the experience of Shanghai; see his *The City in Modern Chinese Literature and Film*, 141.

112. I borrow the concept of "ocular desire" (St. Augustine's term) from Rosalind Krauss, "The Im/pulse to See," in Hal Foster, ed., *Vision and Visuality* (Seattle: Bay Press, 1988) 51–75.

The predominance of vision and the sense of unreality in the experience of Shanghai is also intimately connected to the experience of cinema. Nineteen twenty-six, the year Liu Na'ou came to Shanghai from Japan, saw the arrival of sound and color in Shanghai cinemas. Statistics show that in the year 1935 alone, 378 foreign films were shown in Shanghai's thirty-seven cinemas, 332 of them American.[113] The fetishization of foreign films reached almost religious fervor in a short essay published in *Trackless Train* in October 1928. I quote it here in its entirety:

> Tired from work I enter the cinema to enjoy one or two hours of *devotion.* I want to *worship,* I want to *rejoice.*
> The white canvas in front of me encompasses the entire world from the Eastern hemisphere to the Western hemisphere, from the outside to the inside — one's heart—all represented on this white canvas. Here one can see freezing cold Russia, the decadent city of Paris, merry and carefree American women, the unfathomable mountains and rivers of Africa. One can see Arabians riding on camels, southern natives eating betel nuts. One can see the behind-the-scenes evil of the city, a man and a woman making love under the moonlight . . . And all other views [that the cinema provides] expand one's mind and put one's spirit at ease, while giving the eyes too much to consume. One ought not forget all these *endowments of grace* by the silver screen.[114] (emphasis mine)

Here the cinema is glorified as a sacred place, where simulated experiences of adventure, exploration, and romance in exotic settings, in the absence of such experiences in reality, become possible through visual consumption. In another short piece on the relationship between cinema and women's beauty, the sense of simulation is even more pronounced:

> There are many reasons to go to the cinema. Some go for the purpose of watching a romantic story, some to enjoy the pleasant excitement with one's lover in the cozy darkness. However, the most seductive figures in the cinema are the beautiful women's images intermittently shining on the silver screen. Melancholy eyes, smiling eyes, angry eyebrows, speaking lips, wind-blown hair, necks bitten by pearl necklaces, protruding breasts hiding tenderness, slender waists, round abdomens, a body with a feeling as soft as rose petals in its movements, feet clad in dove-like high heel shoes—the silver screen is the discoverer of women's beauty, the platform for the dissection of women's beauty. On the silver screen we can see the beauties of the Caucasus converse about elegant matters with Parisian women, dance the passionate tango with Spanish women, and strut along paved roads with the American *modern girl.* If Hungary holds natural beauties, the silver screen discovers them. If a portion of Italian women's bodies is especially lovely, the silver screen dissects it. Women all over the world should be grateful to the grace of the silver screen, because it allows

113. Ch'en, *China and the West*, 219–220.
114. Meng Zhou, "Devotion of the Silver Screen" (*Yinmu de gongxian*), *Trackless Train* 4 (October 10, 1928): 208.

their formerly hidden beauty—beauty of the body, of the spirit, of tranquility, and of athletic physicality—to express itself before the people in the world.[115] (original English in italics)

This short article reveals how the pleasure of the cinema lies in its capacity to allow for a simulated experience of desire and conquest: European and American women are exhibited and dissected for the visual consumption of the Chinese male viewer. It is the structure of visual pleasure that turns the woman into the gazed-at and the viewer-man into the gazer.

There is, however, a profound ambiguity in the relationship of power between the two, and Laura Mulvey's classic formulation of cinematic visual pleasure as generated for the sole enjoyment of the male viewer, who turns the woman on the screen into the gazed-at object of desire,[116] needs revision in the context of the racialized male viewer of European women on the screen. The fascination European women held for the Chinese male viewer was largely built upon the impossibility of its fulfillment, hence the male gaze was not the active agent and the gazed-at not the passive party, nor was the male subjectivity constituted through the assumption of power as a gazer. Agency is distributed ambiguously, and can even be said to be reversed, as the male subjectivity thus construed was a simulation or imitation of the European male subjectivity constituted by the cinematic structure of visual pleasure. To identify with the camera's gaze, which most often represented the European male gaze in the eroticization of the European female—in other words, for the film to be pleasurable—the Chinese male viewer had to temporarily suspend his ethnicity by taking on·the position of the European male.

The cinema was a world of simulacra that extended to the lived experience of Shanghai cosmopolitans and modernists. As they simulated the subjectivity of the European male viewer, they also demanded that their women imitate European actresses on the screen. It is due to the translation or imposition of simulacra onto reality—what I call "dissimulation," i.e., life imitating representational art—that many female characters in new sensationist fiction, the modern girls in particular, seem so foreign and exotic. This sense of living in, or representing, a world of simulacra can be gleaned in an essay by the decadent writer Zhang Kebiao and in Shen Congwen's critique of Mu Shiying's work, respectively. In an essay entitled "On Mirages" (*Guanyu shenlou*), Zhang Kebiao sees unreality as the stuff that makes up modern existence:

As for mirages, I have never seen them nor have I ever thought about them. But is not all that we experience, hear, and see but mirages? As for us, yes us,

115. Ge Momei, "Cinema and Women's Beauty" (*Dianying yu nüxingmei*), *Trackless Train* 4 (October 10, 1928): 207. Leo Lee conjectures that Ge Momei may be a pseudonym used by Liu Na'ou: see his *Shanghai Modern*, chapter 3.

116. Laura Mulvey, *Visual and Other Pleasures* (Bloomington: Indiana University Press, 1989), 14–26.

what are we? Who understands who one is? Isn't our daily life like a dream? It doesn't have to be an imagined love affair, an unseen beauty, or a crazy wish—an ordinary thing from everyday life is fantastic enough to be a mirage.[117]

Although life as a dream is a clichéd metaphor, the above passage takes on historical significance and added meaning in the context of Shanghai's phantasmagoric reality. Shen Congwen emphasized this sense of unreality when he criticized Mu Shiying as follows: "Most of [Mu's] works are like temporary ceremonial archways, background screens made of fabric in a photography shop, paper-maché humans and horses in a funereal store. . . . All are essentially fake."[118] Liu Na'ou was also criticized for depicting Shanghai as if it were Tokyo, incongruously transplanting the latter's mores into Shanghai. In sum, the dissimulated quality of Shanghai new sensationism, populated by the sentiments, behaviors, and appearances of the cinema, may be historically analyzed as the condition of Chinese subjectivity in a world of colonial simulacra and unobtainable objects of desire.

This sense of living in a simulated reality in which the Chinese could not fully participate was potentially the site of colonial humiliation and anti-colonial critique, but new sensationism, with its penchant for cultural cosmopolitanism, instead grounded its sense of simulacra *within* the capitalist culture of consumption, desire, and commodification. In a few urban stories by Mu Shiying and Du Heng, vague nationalist, anti-imperialist sentiments can be detected, but they were more often than not displaced by a more generalized critique of industrial capitalism as the source of human alienation and corruption.[119] This generalized critique is part of the premise upon which the new sensationists' cultural cosmopolitanism was constructed. Refusing to allow nationalism to dictate cultural production, their cultural cosmopolitanism flaunted itself with passion and gusto. Bertrand Russell noted in the 1920s that the generation of young intellectuals under thirty in 1922, whom he designated the "young China," were more confident and energetic than those in their thirties and forties. They had come into contact with Western ideas at a sufficiently early age, and were usually taught

117. Zhang Kebiao, "On Mirages," *Gold Chamber Monthly* 1:9–10 (June 1930): 325–338. The quote is from 332.

118. Quoted in Wu Fuhui, "The Rise and Fall of Chinese New Sensationism and Japanese Literature" (*Zhongguo xin'ganjuepai de chenfu he Riben wenxue*), *Japanese Literature* (*Riben wenxue*) 2 (1986): 231–244.

119. Here I draw from Gregory Lee's comments on Chinese modernism: "What distinguished modernism in China from the other modern literary modes was its ambivalence towards the modernizing, industrializing, materialist road to national salvation or regeneration which constituted the dominant narrative of progress for most patriotic Chinese intellectuals and producers of culture; an anti-imperialist narrative which can so easily become confused with national chauvinism. Modernists in general, while rejecting much of the cultural past, were not chauvinists; they were also resistant to the utopian realism being promoted by the communist-

these ideas by Chinese teachers; therefore, they could acquire Western knowledge without being torn by spiritual conflicts.[120]

Any consideration of cultural cosmopolitanism must return to the historical context of semicolonialism. A helpful way of conceiving semicolonialism is to see its structure in terms of the separation of dominance and hegemony. On the one hand, when semicolonialism exercised dominance through political and military means, its cultural hegemony was by no means complete, seamless, or thorough. Due to the fragmentary nature of its dominance, there was always room for the Chinese to exercise options in the production and critique of culture. On the other hand, when semicolonialism operated in conjunction with effective policies of cultural imperialism emanating from metropolitan centers, it was able to construct a symbolic hegemony of Euro-American culture over native culture, and this hegemony was supported by the culturally colonized native elites. In this latter mode, semicolonialism was akin to neocolonialism in the way it instituted metropolitan cultural hegemony without direct aid from the military and political control of the territory of China.

I would argue that these two modes of control—dominance without hegemony and hegemony without dominance—formed a dialectic relationship in the semicolonial condition in China and affected various intellectuals to different degrees. In both of these modes, neither nationalism nor resistance was the necessary or given response to semicolonialism, and there were perceived spaces of freedom for the production of a cosmopolitan culture that could choose to engage or not to engage with imperialist presence. In concrete historical terms, the confusion over overlapping, fragmentary colonial control and the tug-of-war between the leftists and rightists were the immediate conditions in which cosmopolitans celebrated metropolitan cultures of the West and Japan and shied away from nationalist politics. With his distaste for cultural syncretism, Joseph R. Levenson once criticized Shanghai cosmopolitanism as "imperialist-puppet," "rootless," and "denationalized," satirizing it as nurturing an "admirable cosmopolitan simplicity" and having no concern for the people.[121] Such a criticism would have benefited from a more complex understanding of the cultural options and limitations for Chinese cultural workers under semicolonialism.

---

dominated left." Quoted from his *Troubadours, Trumpeters, and Troubled Makers: Lyricism, Nationalism, and Hybridity in China and Its Others* (Durham: Duke University Press, 1996) 72.

120. Bertrand Russell, *The Problem of China* (New York: The Century Co., 1922), 78.

121. Joseph R. Levenson, *Revolution and Cosmopolitanism: The Western Stages and the Chinese Stages* (Berkeley: University of California Press, 1971), 34–38. Frederick Wakeman, Jr.'s "Foreword" notes that Levenson personally resisted assimilation into a neutral cosmopolitan identity and had a distaste for cultural syncretism (xviii), which explains his value judgment of the Chinese cosmopolitans.

CHAPTER 10

Gender, Race, and Semicolonialism
Liu Na'ou's Urban Shanghai Landscape

Mr. Na'ou is a sensitive urban man. With his special talent, he wields a sharp scalpel to dissect airplanes, movies, jazz, skyscrapers, eroticism, the high speed of long-bodied cars, and the mass production of modern life. . . . We especially recommend Mr. Liu Na'ou's style. The freshness of his style is unprecedented and best reflects our times. From him we can learn new literary techniques, new artistic forms, new tunes, as well as disjointed and tortuous syntax.

ADVERTISEMENT FOR LIU NA'OU'S *SCÈNE* (1930)

In 1924 a Taiwan-born and Japan-educated man travelled from Japan to Shanghai to study French at the Jesuit Aurora University.[1] He was young, flamboyant, and rich, and eventually used his own personal funds to found two bookstores and three journals in Shanghai. Despite his ambiguous cultural identity and lack of formal Chinese education, he became the founder of the Shanghai modernist literary movement new sensationism (*xin'ganjuepai*), earned substantial notoriety, and attracted a host of followers. Murdered by an unidentified assassin in 1939, Liu Na'ou (1900–1939) in his short life mirrored the literary movement which he created and which died with him, but not before he had published an intriguing collection of short stories entitled *Scène* (his own French title for *Dushi Fengjing xian*, 1930). This collection was in large measure to define what urban writing meant

---

1. Although Liu Na'ou's descendents claim that Liu was purely ethnic Chinese, Liu's friends and various scholars suspect that Liu had Japanese blood. Ye Lingfeng, a close associate, for instance, noted in 1972 while being interviewed in Hong Kong: "Up until now we are not very clear as to Liu Na'ou's birthplace and identity, whether he is from Amoy, Taiwan, or an overseas Chinese with Japanese blood. But he himself said that he was Chinese." Interview of Ye Lingfeng entitled "A Comet in the 1930s Literary Arena: Ye Lingfeng talks about Mu Shiying" (*Sanshi niandai wentan shang de yike huixing: Ye Lingfeng xiansheng tan Mu Shiying*), *Four Seasons* (*Siji*) 1 (November 1972): 27–28. After Liu died, various newspaper articles accusing him of being a traitor also attributed his collaboration with the Japanese puppet regime of Wang Jingwei to the fact that he was half-Japanese. See also note 14 below.

for Chinese writers in Shanghai during the Nanjing decade, as the quotation above suggests.[2]

In this chapter I ask questions regarding cultural constructions of gender, race, and cultural identity in relation to semicolonialism in Liu Na'ou's work by examining the specific representations of the Westernized "modern girl," whose Chinese incarnation embodies elements of exotic women from both Franco-Japanese literary sources and Hollywood icons. I begin with a brief discussion of gender and racial politics in the postcolonial theory that deals with the representation of Westernized women, in order to contrast its politics with the semicolonial politics of gender and race in Shanghai in general, and Liu Na'ou's representation of these issues in particular. I point out the tendency in postcolonial theory to link discussions of gender and racial politics in the colonial setting with nationalism, often exclusively, and propose a reconsideration of this link in the semicolonial context of Shanghai by questioning the given-ness of nationalism. The partial, multiple, and fragmentary domination of semicolonialism and its colonial racism is often displaced in the putatively cosmopolitan imagining of Shanghai. As I have shown, this cosmopolitan imaginary sanctioned a strategy of displacement which bifurcated the metropolitan (writings about modernity and race in reference to discourses in the metropolitan West and its honorary member, Japan) and the colonial (modernity and racism as colonial constructs). In this bifurcation, nationalism did not necessarily undergird cultural articulations. This bifurcation was a useful strategy that helped legitimate the cosmopolitan ideology so that the search for "civilization" in the Western mode[3] need not be totalistically constricted or defined by the existence of Western imperialism in China. With this ambivalent location of nationalism, the semicolonial formulation of gender and race in Shanghai as seen in Liu's work did not characteristically endorse patriarchy, nor did it ostensibly repudiate racism; instead, it saw the Westernized "modern girl" as a desirable embodiment of antipatriarchal, autonomous, urban, and hybrid modernity.

Following this discussion of semicolonial politics of race and gender, I provide a short genealogy of Liu Na'ou's life and work in relation to Japanese new sensationism and French exoticist literature. I then examine in detail the decoupling of nationalism from the politics of gender and race in Liu Na'ou's work. I argue that the alienated urban man in Liu's writing has a contradictory relationship with the semicolonial city—the embodiment of

2. Advertisement for Liu Na'ou's *Scène* (*Dushi fengjingxian*) appearing on the inside cover of *La Nouvelle Littérature* 2:1 (March 1930).

3. For a discussion of the pursuit of "Civilization" in the Western mode by Shanghai exoticist writers and artists such as Shao Xunmei and Zhu Yingpeng, see Heinrich Freuhauf, "Urban Exoticism in Modern and Contemporary Chinese Literature," in Ellen Widmer and David Der-wei Wang, eds., *From May Fourth to June Fourth: Fiction and Film in Twentieth Century China* (Cambridge: Harvard University Press, 1993), 133–164.

the materiality of colonialism—which destabilizes his subjectivity by both seducing and rejecting him, and that Liu's response to such rejection lacked
nationalist overtones. Here, urban reality begins to filter into a new construction of modernity: the physical settings of the city such as the cabaret,
the theatre, and the racetrack are the sites of action and narration. Liu's
innovative language and syntax grace these sites with a sensuous and seductive allure, self-consciously creating a myriad of new sensations that Liu
would characterize as distinct experiences of the urban—hence the name
new sensationism.

I then conclude this chapter with a sustained examination of the osmosis between the city and the modern girl in Liu's fiction. I argue that the
modern girl's excessive materiality unsettles the bifurcation between the metropolitan (predominantly construed in discursive terms) and the colonial
(predominantly construed in material terms). This shows how Shanghai cosmopolitanism, unlike its May Fourth antecedent, acknowledged urban materiality as part of the constitution of modernity. But the modern girl's illu-
siveness, being herself a dissimulated image from Franco-Japanese literary
sources and Hollywood cinema, again illustrates how she is inevitably construed as part of the phantasmagoric reality of Shanghai, to which the Chinese subject has dubious access.[4] She is in this sense represented predominantly as an unreacheable object of desire, a constitutive element within the
two-dimensional urban canvas that one can gaze at from a distance, as one
looks at a store display window or the image on a screen.

THE COLONIAL AND SEMICOLONIAL POLITICS OF GENDER AND RACE

Scholarship on China during the Cold War era insisted that China was a "non-
colonial" nation, thereby "displacing" the need to examine colonialism,
whereas recent scholarship has aimed first to introduce colonialism as an
important category of analysis and then to define semicolonialism as a colonial formation specific to the Chinese situation.[5] For the few scholars engaged in this effort, theories of colonialism and postcolonialism based on

4. Leo Ou-fan Lee, in chapter 9 of the manuscript version of *Shanghai Modern*, notes how
such a modern girl could not have been realistic: "In the early 1930s, such a modern woman . . .
was just emerging on the Shanghai urban scene as a new 'media image' in film and popular
journalism before she assumed presence in real life in the 1940s. . . . [These] women figures
[—]who pick up men at horse races, ride on fast cars, dance madly in nightclubs, or administer cocktail recipes to the awe-stricken male narrator—are all so beyond the pale of plausibil-
ity that they have become, in a way, floating signifiers or 'figures' rather than human characters." This passage is not included in the printed version, *Shanghai Modern: A Study of Urban
Culture and Literary Imagination in China, 1930–1945* (Cambridge: Harvard University Press,
1999).

5. Tani Barlow, editor's introduction and "Colonialism's Career in Postwar China Studies,"
positions 1:1 (Spring 1993): v–vii and 224–67.

South Asian, African, and Caribbean experiences have been influential but of limited applicability to the Chinese context. In this effort, Gail Hershatter's rethinking of Southeast Asian postcolonial theory, particularly the concept of the "subaltern," in light of the specific condition of semicolonialism in China, is most noteworthy.[6] I continue this rethinking of postcolonial theory by examining semicolonial gender and racial politics, providing important contextual information and analytical tools for reading Liu Na'ou's work, and at the same time "provincializing" postcolonial theory, much as it has already proposed "provincializing" Europe's hegemonic discourse of history and modernity.[7]

I find that much postcolonial theory acknowledges three general assumptions about gender and racial relations in colonial situations: (1) the fact of racialized colonial domination and the resulting confused condition of cultural and racial identity for the colonized subject who must resist colonial racism; (2) the gender implications of colonialism as the emasculation of the colonized male, hence the tendency to counter such emasculating force by constructing an equally, if not more, masculinist nationalism, as in the famous conception of "hypermasculinity";[8] (3) the tendency to deploy "women" as signifiers of nationhood, as "victims of social backwardness, icons of modernity or privileged bearers of cultural authenticity," which further subjects women to the patriarchal nationalist imaginary.[9] In these assumptions, the conflict between the colonizer and the colonized is chiefly seen as the struggle of men against men; women either serve that struggle or are left out entirely. On the one hand, if the colonial struggle is troped as a "heterosexual" conquest of feminized native men by masculine colonizers, colonized native women become an irrelevant third term in the struggle. On the other hand, the persistent patriarchal representation of women in the service of the nationalist imaginary also discounts the actual varied experiences of women under colonialism. In general, in the name of nationalism, patriarchal dictates absorb discussions of race and gender politics under colonialism.

Two brief but representative examples that specifically deal with Westernized native women in the nationalist imaginary of the colonized will suffice to illustrate how the above assumptions about gender and race operate. Frantz

6. Gail Hershatter, "The Subaltern Talks Back: Reflections on Subaltern Theory and Chinese History," *positions* 1:1 (Spring 1993): 103–130.

7. Dipesh Chakrabarty, "Postcoloniality and the Artifice of History: Who Speaks for 'Indian' Pasts?" *Representations* 37 (Winter 1992): 1–26.

8. Ashis Nandy, *The Intimate Enemy: Loss and Recovery of Self Under Colonialism.* (Delhi: Oxford University Press, 1983), 1–63.

9. Deniz Kandiyoti, "Identity and Its Discontents: Women and the Nation," in Patrick Williams and Laura Chrisman, eds., *Colonial Discourse and Post-colonial Theory* (New York: Columbia University Press, 1994), 378.

Fanon's seminal text *Black Skin, White Masks* (1952), extremely influential for postcolonial theorists, well illustrates the subsumption of women's issues by the nationalist patriarchy. In this text, Fanon works with an implicit masculinist supposition that denigrates Westernized native women in the Antilles as complicit with colonialism in doubling the emasculation of the native male. He does this by way of analyzing the desire of Westernized native women to be wooed by and eventually to marry white men, and their rejection of black men as potential marriage partners. Fanon describes this process of gaining white acceptance as "bleaching" and "lactation," finding it a "nauseating phenomenon," especially when the subjects are educated, Westernized, black or mulatto women.[10] Unlike his in-depth analysis of a similar desire for white acceptance among black men as the result of the psychosocial effects of colonialism, which represents black men as wronged but nevertheless sovereign national subjects, his value-ridden, accusatory treatment of Westernized native women is strikingly unequivocal. Obsessed with the question of manhood under colonialism, Fanon considers black women to be traitors, furthering the oppression of black men. In so doing, Fanon exposes the patriarchal underpinning of his own anticolonial discourse.[11]

Partha Chatterjee's typology of three kinds of women in nineteenth-century Indian nationalist discourse offers further insight into the procedures by which Westernized women are denigrated. In nationalist discourse, the lowest rung in the hierarchy was occupied by the "common women": the maidservants, washer women, barbers, prostitutes, and other such women who were considered "coarse, vulgar, quarrelsome, devoid of superior moral sense," and "sexually promiscuous"; on the next rung were the "Westernized women" (the *memsaheb*), who came from wealthy parvenu families with colonial connections and who were seen as "brazen, avaricious, irreligious," and "sexually promiscuous," like the common women; on the highest rung were the "new women" (the new *bhadramahila*), a nationalist construction, closely monitored by the new native patriarchy and hence, although educated in Western knowledge, maintaining all the feminine virtues and barred from becoming "essentially Westernized." Such distinctions among types of women, Chatterjee argues, were due to the fact that nationalist ideology dichotomized the "home" (the uncolonized, the spiritual) and the "world" (the colonized, the material). It was crucial to define "new women" who were worthy proprietors of the spiritual domain of the "home," and to guard the home against "common women" and "Westernized women" in the "world," who were vulgar and immoral manifestations of Western material-

10. Frantz Fanon, *Black Skin, White Masks*, trans. Charles Lam Markmann (New York: Grove Weidenfeld, 1967), chapter 2.

11. Rey Chow, "The Politics of Admittance: Female Sexual Agency, Miscegenation and the Formation of Community in Frantz Fanon," *UTS Review* 1:1 (1995): 5–29.

ism and colonialism.[12] Like educated Westernized black women in Fanon's Antilles, "Westernized women" in Bengal, by their transgressive behavior and unacceptable outlook on life, embodied a threat to native identity, the threat of men losing control of the domestic realm, and above all the threat of native men seeing in them a double of themselves (Chatterjee notes that men were forced to become Westernized and materialistic in order to cope with the "world"). The native male's fear of becoming too Westernized was displaced as the rejection of Westernized women, and as the passion to maintain in "new women" the embodiment of Indian spirituality.

In formally colonized sites such as the Antilles and India, then, Westernized women represented in the discourse of the native intelligentsia both the invasion of colonial ideology into the domestic sphere and the threat to native manhood and identity. The Westernized woman's transgressive behavior, predominantly troped as her sexual promiscuity, threatened to destroy the boundaries which the native men policed: their property, their possessions, and their rights as men (especially the right to possess native women's sexuality). Ultimately, then, the Westernized woman was accused of complicity with the colonial regime's emasculation of native manhood. But the charge against her was not at all in proportion to the crime itself (the male intelligentsia were as guilty of the crime of being Westernized as the women); rather, it was merely indicative of the nationalist patriarchy's monopolization of discursive power within the colonized domain. In sum, the coupling of anticolonial nationalism and gender politics persistently inscribed Westernized women as transgressors of racial and sexual boundaries, and thereby the agents of crimes against the nation.[13]

Reflecting on the above assumptions of gender and racial politics in postcolonial theory leads to the following considerations. (1) Semicolonialism as a different mode of colonial control operates through fragmented, multiple, or multilayered forms of domination. Hence the strategies used to deal with colonial culture and colonial racism are quite different, and the positions of the subject within this fragmentary, multilayered colonial structure cannot be characterized in any Manichean fashion. (2) The complex trajectory of Liu Na'ou's identity—was he Taiwanese? Japanese? half-Japanese and half-Taiwanese?[14]—opens up the question of cultural, na-

12. Partha Chatterjee, *The Nation and Its Fragments: Colonial and Postcolonial Histories* (Princeton: Princeton University Press, 1993), 116–157.

13. From a different angle, feminist scholars have critiqued the masculinist assumptions of nationalism as a "fraternity of men" (Benedict Anderson's term) and its subjugation of women. See for instance, Andrew Parker et al., eds. *Nationalisms and Sexualities* (New York: Routledge, 1992), especially the "Introduction," 1–18.

14. Peng Xiaoyen summarizes the various contentions regarding Liu Na'ou's national and cultural identity and concludes that Liu was a thorough Taiwanese in her essay "Wandering in the World: The 1927 Diaries of Liu Na'ou" (*Langdang tianya: Liu Na'ou 1927 nian de riji*),

tional, and racial/ethnic identity and how it operated within the semi-colonial setting. (3) Liu's ambivalent identity also challenges the undisputed presence of a masculinist nationalist imagination, and raises instead the prospect of an antipodal relationship between modernism—as the literary product of immigrants with little territorial allegiance[15]—and nationalism. (4) Finally, if the absence of a masculinist nationalist imagination is part of what constitutes semicolonial cultural politics, what does "woman," in this case the "modern girl," signify? These questions not only problematize the postcolonial paradigms of racial and gender politics outlined above, but also undermine a homogeneous reading of modernity in different Third World locations as a predictable set of reactive and "reactional" responses to colonization.

As I illustrated in the introduction to this book, "semicolonialism" refers to the state of *multiple* and *multilayered* colonization of China by competing foreign powers. These various powers vying for more and more influence and profit at once performed an arbitrary form of domination exascerbating the fragmentation of Chinese reality and stability, and at the same time paradoxically afforded Chinese intellectuals ideological, political, and cultural options beyond the typical Manichean choices of anticolonial nationalism or antinationalist collaboration. As a discursive context, semicolonialism designates both (1) the multiple intellectual positions made available by a fragmented colonial structure and by the urgent task of antitraditional, pro-Western cultural criticism, and (2) how these multiple positions are all in tension with the material existence of multilayered colonial domination.

Within this context, the new sensationist school of writing proposed to write in a mode that celebrated writing for its own sake. In the self-conception of these writers, it was possible to be a writer without a stable ideological, cultural, or even national identity. The city of Shanghai was a place of relative cultural flexibility, and indeed fragmentation: the fragmentation of both colonial control and the authority of the Nationalist government was literally visible in the division of Shanghai into three independent jurisdictions, whose different levels of tolerance formed sanctuaries from unitary ideological control and where a "strategic use of law"[16] was possible. However, this state of affairs should by no means be extolled as benevolent imperial powers bestowing cultural "freedom" to the Chinese, but rather should be seen as the paradoxical emergence of culture

---

Chinese Literature and Philosophy Studies Quarterly (Zhongguo wenzhe yanjiu jikan), forthcoming. See also note 1 above.

15. See Raymond Williams, *The Politics of Modernism* (London: Verso, 1989), 31–35.

16. Tahirih V. Lee, "Introduction" to "Coping with Shanghai: Means to Survival and Success in the Early Twentieth Century—A Symposium," *Journal of Asian Studies* 54:1 (1995): 5.

in the fissures between different agents of control whose authority did not overlap.[17]

Another argument against celebrating the "freedom" of Shanghai's semicolonial cultural context is the disjuncture between the discursive construction of the liberating potential of Occidentalism (the emulation of the metropolitan West and Japan; see chapter 5) and the actual material condition of the city. Since the May Fourth movement, the presence of "the West" in the enlightenment imaginary was largely "positive"—it was embraced as a corrective to the supposed inadequacy of Chinese tradition in the modern world—but the West's material presence in Shanghai was embodied in the colonizers and the exploitative industrial culture they produced. The materiality of this colonial West was obvious in the racial hierarchization of the city,[18] the modern conveniences built exclusively for the colonizers, and the cordoning off of spaces to prevent Chinese entry.[19] Everyday life in Shanghai, as Wen-hsin Yeh and Frederic Wakeman note, was "suffused with ambivalence" for the Chinese intelligentsia, who daily experienced both an adoration of Western culture and a loathing of the foreign imperialists.[20]

Colonial racism was part and parcel of the political and material construction of foreign Shanghai. Racism against the Chinese was endorsed by a series of unequal treaties and arbitrary laws since the Treaty of Nanjing

17. Poshek Fu also writes about Shanghai's paradoxical experience of modernity. "Republican Shanghai's experience with modernity was full of ambiguity: it represented a new commodity culture offering rich possibilities for individual development on the one hand and an imperialist regime of terror and exploitation on the other." Poshek Fu, *Passivity, Resistance, and Collaboration: Intellectual Choices in Occupied Shanghai, 1937–1945* (Stanford: Stanford University Press, 1993), 165.

18. One event which threatened to destabilize the racial hierarchy in Shanghai was the entrance of white, Russian women, who served both Western and Chinese clients, into the thriving prostitution industry (there were about 48,000 prostitutes within the 12.5 square miles of the settlements in 1929). By 1935, 25,000 Russian women were living in Shanghai. See Jerome Ch'en, *China and the West: Society and Culture 1815–1937* (Bloomington: Indiana University Press, 1979), 213–216, and Gail Hershatter, "The Hierarchy of Shanghai Prostitution, 1870–1949," *Modern China* 15:4 (1989): 463–98.

19. Editorials in *The Chinese Nation*, an English weekly published in Shanghai, frequently note various cases of inequality. They note for instance how the hospital and educational facilities for the Chinese residents in the International Settlement were incredibly inadequate, unlike the situation for foreigners, although the Chinese formed the largest contributors to its treasury. In another instance, the reader is told that no Chinese person has any legal rights to own or purchase land in the International Settlement. The discussions of inequality are most often rendered in racial terms, with the "whites" dominating the Chinese. Many foreign clubs, the weekly also notes, prohibit Chinese entry, and even after the prohibition is removed the foreigners prefer not to mix with the Chinese and ostracize them. See issues of *The Chinese Nation* throughout 1930 and 1931, for instance Maxwell S. Stewart, "What Is Wrong with Shanghai," *Chinese Nation* 1:8 (August 6, 1930): 119–120 and 133.

20. Wen-hsin Yeh and Frederic Wakeman, "Introduction," in *Shanghai Sojourners* (Berkeley: Institute of East Asian Studies, University of California, Berkeley, 1992) 1–14.

was signed in 1842. It was probably most strongly felt and most commonly exercised, however, on the level of day-to-day contact, or lack thereof, between Chinese and Shanghailanders (foreign residents of Shanghai). As Marie-Claire Bergère points out, "humiliation showed up at every crossroad" for the Chinese residents of the city, in the "brutality of a policeman" or the "grimace of a blond child."[21] Many of these Shanghailanders were criminals and undesirables, such as opium traffickers, gamblers, prostitutes, and quack-evangelists who committed crimes such as petty larceny, terror, murder, fraud, and vagrancy.[22] According to two separate accounts, this foreign community was not intellectual, was not interested in culture, and considered it a "sin" to be friendly with a Chinese and "utterly ridiculous" to marry one. In foreign commercial buildings, the Chinese were forced to use a separate elevator; on French-controlled trams, they were not allowed to ride in the first-class compartments; no Chinese were admitted to foreign clubs except as guests of foreigners; and, except for domestic servants and city employees, the Chinese were barred from entering the Public Garden (Huangpu Park) and other recreational grounds, the upkeep for which the Chinese helped to pay.[23] Nicholas Clifford notes that Chinese contributed fifty-five percent of all taxes and fees in the International Settlement, but were barred from using the most modern and best equipped hospitals, and were given very little voice in the Settlement's governance. Clifford therefore notes that foreign Shanghai looked like "parasites on the body of China" that only took without giving, serving only as "channels through which the country's wealth passed on its way to enrich London and Tokyo, New York, and Paris."[24]

Although colonial racism, as part of the material reality of the semicolonial city, infused one's daily life as a visual, physical, and psychological experience, the Chinese discourse of race studies, eugenics, which was mainly centered in Shanghai in the 1930s, did not seemed to take colonial racism into consideration in any integrated way. Instead, the perception of the white race in that discourse was more often than not as the pure race which nat-

21. Marie-Claire Bergère, "'The Other China': Shanghai from 1919 to 1949," in Christopher Howe, ed., *Shanghai: Revolution and Development in an Asian Metropolis* (Cambridge: Cambridge University Press, 1981), 13.

22. Ch'en, *China and the West*, 213–216.

23. Arthur Ransome, *The Chinese Puzzle* (Boston and New York: Houghton Mifflin, 1927), 142–149; Ch'en, *China and the West*, 232–233. Citing Betty Pei-t'i Wei's *Old Shanghai* (Hong Kong: Oxford University Press, 1993), Leo Lee notes, however, that the public gardens were opened to the Chinese by 1928. But he also notes that the Shanghai racetrack had a racially divided seating arrangement, with the Chinese allowed to occupy only the lower viewing platforms and the upper stands reserved for foreigners. See *Shanghai Modern*, chapter 3, especially footnote 94.

24. Nicholas Clifford, *Spoilt Children of Empire: Westerners in Shanghai and the Chinese Revolution of the 1920s* (Middlebury, Vt.: Middlebury College Press, 1991), 25–27.

urally commanded superiority. Some said that the Chinese were like the white race in that they were pure; others said that the original Chinese, the Xia, were actually similar to Caucasians in physical features; while there were still others who responded to Western racist anthropology and contested white superiority.[25] Despite their differences, these treatments of race ignored the concrete manifestations of colonial racism and instead adopted eugenics as a Western discourse potentially beneficial to China, again continuing the May Fourth valorization of the discursively constructed metropolitan West while displacing the materially constructed colonial West.

The bifurcation of the metropolitan and colonial contexts of race and racism was a crucial characteristic of semicolonial cultural politics. The intellectual could actually ignore the existence of racism if he/she so chose (and not simply because racism was fairly contained within the concessions), while at the same time engaging in a discourse of race heavily indebted to racial theories from the West. Fragmented Shanghai, then, kept colonial racism from becoming hegemonic to the extent of thoroughly oppressing the Chinese intellectual, and racism could be displaced by a cosmopolitan celebration of the culture of the metropolitan West and Japan and a fascination with urban modernity. Hence, ironically, racial hierarchy often remains either unproblematized or merely replicated in Liu Na'ou's stories, and the material culture of the West, as it is present in Shanghai, becomes transformed into an alluring urban modernity embodied in the figure of the modern girl.

THE ALIENATED INDIVIDUAL IN THE SEMICOLONIAL CITY

The Shanghai in which Liu Na'ou arrived in 1924 was inhabited mainly by immigrants from other parts of the country.[26] Born of Taiwanese parents and raised in Japan, Liu Na'ou was well-versed in both modern Japanese and French literature, and spoke the fluent Japanese of the Tokyoites, but his Chinese was heavily accented. After completing his university education at Keiō University in Japan, he arrived in Shanghai to attend the special two-year French program at the French Jesuit Aurora University. Among his classmates were Dai Wangshu, Shi Zhecun, and Du Heng, with whom he would later initiate new sensationism. At the time, his written Chinese was reportedly rather awkward, prompting Shi Zhecun to note decades later that Liu initially wrote Chinese as if he were writing Japanese.[27] Leftist literary crit-

25. Frank Dikötter, *The Discourse of Race in Modern China* (Stanford: Stanford University Press, 1992), 132–190.
26. Yeh and Wakeman, "Introduction."
27. Shi Zhecun, "Two Years at Aurora University" (*Zhendan ernian*), *Historical Materials on New Literature* (*Xinwenxue shiliao*) (April 1984): 51–54.

ics from the 1930s on would seize upon the "un-Chinese" quality of Liu's writing to delegitimize modernist writing in general, although native-born Mu Shiying, who followed Liu's style, came under the same kind of attacks. But this departure from authentic "Chinese-ness" itself had been part of the aesthetic agenda of Shanghai modernist fiction from its inception. As a cosmopolitan literary project drawing heavily from French and Japanese antecedents, Shanghai modernism prided itself on writing fiction that interweaved urban, exotic, and erotic motifs in an experimental style and form that supposedly knew no national boundaries.

After a visit to Japan in 1926, Liu returned to Shanghai in 1928 with a library of books, including stories by Kawabata Yasunari, Yokomitsu Riichi, and Tanizaki Jun'ichirō. With his own funds and with the help of his classmates, he immediately opened a publishing house called Frontline Bookstore (*Diyixian shudian*), which published such works as *Erotic Culture*, a translated collection of Japanese new sensationist works (see chapter 9). When the bookstore was banned by the Nationalist government for allegedly promoting left-leaning publications, Liu moved his publishing activities first to the International Settlement and then to the French Concession. There he started the Waterfoam Bookstore, which again published the works of, among others, Japanese new sensationists, most notably a collection of Yokomitsu's stories entitled *The Sensations of the Bridegroom*. During this time, he also financed and edited two influential literary journals, *Trackless Train* and *La Nouvelle Littérature* (see chapter 9), wrote his famous collection of short stories, *Scène,* and translated the works of Japanese new sensationism and French writer Paul Morand. Later he turned to writing film scripts, ran a journal called *Modern Cinema* (*Xiandai dianying*), and even produced a film version of *La Dame aux Camélias* at the Guangming studio in 1938, a year before his assassination. It is not known exactly who sent the assassin, and varying conjectures point to such diametrically opposed parties as the Nationalist Party (for Liu's alleged sympathy for leftist causes in his previous publication activities, although he was at the time working for the Nationalist Party paper *Wenhui Daily*), the Chinese Communist Party (for working for the Nationalist Party), and the Green Gang (for his connection with the underground and related to his decadent life style). If anything, the disagreement over the identity of his killer points to Liu's own fundamental ideological ambiguity and instability.

Ideological ambiguity and instability were also characteristic of the Japanese new sensationists whom Liu so ardently admired. Many of Liu's short stories, eight collected in *Scène* and two uncollected ones, "A Lady to Keep You Company" (his own English title) and "Below the Equator" (*Chidao xia*), do not appear to have overt political references at all; rather, a profound ideological ambiguity enshrouds them. The so-called "depravity of capitalist culture" becomes the locus of allure and eroticization, thereby reducing the supposed socialist thrust to a kind of empty, perhaps fashionable, gesture. His other literary activities in the late 1920s also illustrate his ambivalence. On the one hand he admired and translated the Marxist classic *The Sociology of Art*, by the Soviet literary theoretician Vladimir M. Friche (1926; Liu's translation, 1930),[28] while on the other he affected the writing style of the French aesthete Paul Morand, without noting the potential ideological contradiction between the two. In terms of the publication activities of his bookstores as well, he and his fellow modernists were chiefly interested in two kinds of literature: "newly emergent literature" (*xinxing wenxue*), i.e., literature emerging from post–October Revolution Soviet Union, and "avant-garde literature" (*jianduan wenxue*) with a high aesthetic and often decadent thrust, such as psychoanalytic fiction.[29] The affinity in meaning and implication between the Chinese terms—*xinxing* and *jianduan*—helps explain why these two kinds of literature were not considered contradictory: both foregrounded the sense of the new and the vanguard. The Marxian notion of the political vanguard was wedded harmoniously with avant-garde aesthetic radicalism, and it was therefore considered possible for Chinese modernists to be anticapitalist (not necessarily nationalist) and yet write in a modernist form where "technique is of foremost importance," as one critic said of Liu Na'ou's style.[30]

Despite Liu's critique of city culture as an immoral capitalist product, he was at the same time profoundly fascinated by it. The exotic setting of the partially colonized city of Shanghai afforded an occasion for him to use techniques that mimic the smells, sounds, images, and speed of the city. Liu clearly took great pleasure in describing city scenes, eroticizing them as the objects of his gaze. In almost every one of Liu's stories, extended passages in metaphoric language depict aspects of city life and its material culture. Even the moral degradation of the city becomes seductive in such linguistic feasts. The city may be anthropomorphized into a horrifying monster—it "swallows up" people; its elevators and buildings "vomit" people out into the streets[31]— but the thrill the author suggests in describing such horror as a new mode of urban experience goes against his supposed critical intent.

The urban setting in the first story in *Scène*, "Games" (*Youxi*), allows Liu to experiment with unprecedented ways of capturing new sensations. With-

28. Liu Na'ou, trans., *The Sociology of Art* (*Yishu shehuixue*), by Vladimir M. Friche (Shanghai: Shuimo shudian, 1930).

29. Shi Zhecun, "We Ran Three Bookstores" (*Women jingying guo sange shudian*), *Historical Materials on New Literature* (*Xinwenxue shiliao*) (January 1985): 184–90.

30. Yi Tong, "Remembering Liu Na'ou" (*Ji Liu Na'ou*), in Yang Zhihua, ed., *Historical Materials on the Literary Arena* (*Wentan shiliao*) (Shanghai: Zhonghua ribao she, 1944), 233.

31. These two anthropomorphic images were used frequently by Liu Na'ou and later by Mu Shiying and others who imitated his style.

out the nightclubs of Shanghai, there could not have been a description such as this:

> Everything in this "Tango Palace" is in melodious motion—male and female bodies, multicolored lights, shining wine goblets, red, green liquid and slender fingers, garnet lips, burning eyes. In the center is a smooth and shiny floor reflecting tables and chairs around it and the scene of people mixed together, making one feel as if one had entered a magic palace, where one's mind and spirit are both under the control of magical powers. Amidst all this the most delicate and nimble are the movements of the waiters clad in white. Vivaciously, like butterflies among flowers, they fly from here to there, then from there to another place, without a trace of rudeness.
>
> The air is heavy with a mixture of alcohol, sweat, and oil, encouraging all to indulge in the high level of excitement. There is a middle-aged man laughing heartily with his teeth showing, a young lady speaking endearingly while her arms make charming, affected gestures. Over there, the one with his hands supporting his chin, staring at a bottle of beer on the table in front of him and always silent, is a lone man. Finding the couple sitting at a table by the window in this merry crowd is not so easy.
>
> ——Ha, ha, ha, ha.
>
> ——What's so funny?
>
> ——You look so funny, look, your eyes are filled with tears!
>
> . . . Suddenly the air begins to stir and a blast of music vigilantly cries out. The musician in the middle of the band holds a *saxophone*, the demon of *jazz*, and blows wildly at the people. Then the cymbals, the drums, the organ and the strings start to howl madly. This is like a memory of African blacks, the sacrifice before the hunt, the pumping of blood in the veins, the discovery of primitive sexuality, the cymbals, drum, organ, strings, boom boom boom.[32] (original English in italics)

The narrative angle moves like a film camera, capturing a large scene in a third-person, objective tone, then zooming in on a couple sitting by the window and pausing with them for a short while before moving onto the jazz band. Along the way, the nightclub affords the author the opportunity to describe the sights, sounds, colors, tastes, smells, and tempo of the place, in a technique that may be called "synaesthetic listing," in which a string of sense-crossing images follows one after another.[33] This is a classic new sensationist technique, often utilized later by many writers who wrote about the city, which has its source not only in the Japanese new sensationists but also in the "grandfather" of both Japanese and Chinese new sensationists, Paul Morand. In his article on Morand (translated by Liu), Benjamin Crémieux

32. Liu Na'ou, *Scène* (*Dushi fengjingxian*) (Shanghai: Shuimo shudian, 1930), 3–6.

33. On synaesthesia in new sensationist writing, see also Yan Jiayan, *Schools of Modern Chinese Fiction* (*Zhongguo xiandai xiaoshuo liupaishi*) (Beijing: Renmin wenxue chubanshe, 1989), 125–74.

lists the repertoire of Morand's favorite techniques, many of which are dutifully employed by our Chinese Morand: the flash method of films, ellipsis, listing, roundabout description, irony, and so on.[34] But what is also notable in the above passage is that the urbanism of the scene is not presented without racial stereotyping: jazz is the music of African blacks and an expression of their "primitive sexuality."[35] Such stereotyping will appear time and again in Liu's other stories, and I will come back to this point later.

In the above passage, the tempo of the city as embodied in the constant darting of the narrative angle is a quick-time staccato, mimicking the wild trembling movements of the bodies dancing to the fast rhythms of the music. The speed of the city is also captured through flashing images. The male protagonist Buqing, the man who has tears in his eyes in the passage above, suddenly sees a tiger leaping, only to realize that it is a fur stole draped over a woman's shoulders. His perception is the camera capturing a sudden image as an illusion and later focusing it into a clear picture. Indirect descriptions abound: "Waves rose on the snow-white sheets" describes lovemaking; "he found by his lips a row of teeth not his own," describes a kiss.[36] The rhetoric has a persistent cinematic quality, using suggestive euphemisms coupled with imagistic, visual details. The lights of the city are as pale as "the faces of tuberculosis-stricken patients"; as noted earlier, the metropolis is a "hungry monster" that engulfs people.[37]

Because of the hubbub and moral corruption of the city, Buqing becomes an alienated, disillusioned individual, the classic protagonist of modernist literature. Whereas Western modernism saw human alienation as brought on by the overdevelopment of dehumanizing technology, Buqing's alienation in Shanghai is caused by his inability to come up to "speed," so to speak, with the urbanized city. He loves his urban girlfriend, appropriately named Yiguang ("moving light"), but she leaves him for a richer Chinese man with a Charlie Chaplin–like moustache who will provide her with a Hollywood-style romance and a racy red sports car, complete with two "black-faced chauffeurs." When as a parting gift she voluntarily offers Buqing her virginity, his outdated patriarchal moral sensibilities prevent him from experiencing any pleasure in the act. He only feels sorry for her future husband, who has lost his right to her virginity. After finally parting with her, the city becomes a

---

34. Liu Na'ou, trans., "On Paul Morand" (*Bao'er Muhang lun*), by Benjamin Crémieux. *Trackless Train* 4 (October 1928): 147–60.

35. Here it is informative to consider Frantz Fanon's discussion of colonial sexual psychology, where he notes that black men are made to represent primitive sexual instincts in the colonialist thinking as a way to vilify them as less than human. See chapter 6 of *Black Skin, White Masks*. Also note the mistaken attribution of jazz to Africans rather than to the African diaspora in the United States.

36. Liu Na'ou, *Scène*, 14.

37. Ibid., 9, 17.

spiritual "desert" in Buqing's eyes, a degenerate place of abandon and immorality. He embodies the residual values of chastity, morality, and faithfulness, and therefore is all the more hopelessly alienated. With its anthropomorphic power, the city plays colossal jokes on him (Liu calls this "urban humor"), and eventually swallows him up. He is a modern man lost in the city whose speed he cannot keep up with, dragging along his traditional sense of propriety (including his male chauvinism) and trudging toward his inevitable doom. This discrepancy between the speed of the city and the character's slowness indicates on the one hand how the urban is experienced in mainly temporal terms,[38] and on the other hand how the unevenness of the temporal experience implies the semicolonial subtext of urban modernity.

The semicolonial subtext is especially visible when we note the stereotypical and hierarchical representation of race, as in the "black-faced chauffeurs." Similarly, in Liu's "Etiquette and Hygiene" (*Liyi he weisheng*), the narrator records the male protagonist Qiming's visual experience of race as he travels from the bund along the Huangpu River to the Chinese city:

> The streets around the Huangpu bund before *rush hour* seemed to be occupied by Western women shopping. Their high heels stepped on tender sunlight, emitting light quick sounds on the wooden pavement. A *blonde* walked out from a flower shop holding an armful of tulips. A car arrived in a hurry and parked on the side of the street, spitting out a woman in a light coat with the scent of green grass and her little daughter. A big Indian guy raised his short baton, so Qiming crossed the track following the vehicles, and entered a large drugstore. His nose immediately detected a meal of fancy fragrant dishes.
>
> ——How can I help you, sir? a Slavic woman asked, raising a face with only lips and eyes.
>
> ——*Sana* . . . Do you have the German make?
>
> —— *Sana? Sana?* . . . Of course, you mean . . .
>
> She replaced the rest of the sentence with a smile and, after throwing him a knowing glance, went into the back of the store.
>
> . . . Slavic women are not bad either. Their primitive flavor like barbecued lamb from the Caucasus is worth tasting. Since their race has only relatively recently received the baptism of technology, they at least have less technological coldness than other nationalities. After having left their country, haven't they built an oasis along Avenue Joffre to humidify this desert-like Shanghai?
>
> . . . Only a distance of two or three blocks and the scenery changed as if having crossed a huge ocean. The colorful store signs protruding from the shops made the area above the head a danger zone. From inside stores which never received the grace of sunlight spewed a cold ghastly stench. The mixture of oil, sweat, and dust pierced directly through the nose and into the lungs.

38. For an analysis of the urban temporal experience in modern Chinese literature, see Yingjin Zhang, *The City in Modern Chinese Literature and Film* (Stanford: Stanford University Press, 1996).

Health had fled to a remote place. Even the "cu cu" sound of a hooker soliciting customers had the pungent odor of ammonia from the alley. A boiling
teahouse opened its gigantic tiger mouth and sucked in the prostitutes and all
other conspiracies, business plots, and machinations.[39] (original English in
italics)

Reading the different women described in this passage from the perspective
of racial economy, the white women are the high-class consumers in the most
trendy area of the city, the Slavic clerk is the capitalist mediator between
commodity (prostituted bodies) and consumer through her sale of aphro-
disiacs, the Russian prostitutes are the providers of exotic sexuality, and the
Chinese prostitutes are the least expensive commodities, lowest in the hierarchy. The narrative focalizer of this passage, Qiming, is an elite lawyer who,
known in the city as one who works for women's rights, is ironically on his
way to visit a Chinese prostitute in the Chinese city. Along the way, he records
what to him is just the common visual reality where racial hierarchy is assumed, and further consolidated through his own participation, not interrogated. His perception of the Chinese quarter in the last paragraph quoted
above, as laden with associations of filth and illegality, would also easily pass
as that of a racist Shanghailander. Furthermore, the hierarchically constituted racial structure of the city parallels its stratified spatial structure. The
lawyer moves from the bund to the Chinese city, from affluence to squalor,
from the smell of "green grass" to "ammonia," marking the spatial disjunc-
tures between modernity and underdevelopment as the very condition of
possibility for the semicolonial city. If Shanghai is a metropolis, the passage
implicitly makes clear, it is a distinctly Third World metropolis created by a
semicoloniality that sanctions extremely uneven development.

Just as in Japanese new sensationist writing, so too would the "aura of importation" or exoticism, which the semicolonial city of Shanghai abundantly
provided, be a necessary ingredient in the Chinese brand of new sensationism that Liu created. The specific historical conditions of Shanghai ironically rendered it the perfect site for the creation of this modernist, new sensationist writing. Chinese writers did not have to travel far to find materials
to write in such a mode; even foreign writers could easily write about Shanghai as the perfect object of modernist representation—Yokomitsu's novel
Shanghai being one example. This immigrants' city, in which there were very
few "native" residents, did not discriminate against Liu Na'ou or prevent him
from creating a new school of modern Chinese writing. The ambiguity surrounding his national and cultural identity merely dissipated into a sea of
ambiguities that comprised the everyday existence of the urban man living
in a fragmented city. His characters' alienation from the city results both from
the city's fast-paced modernity and from the characters' inability to identify

39. Liu Na'ou, *Scène*, 111–114.

with the large Chinese populace whom they too denigrate. In the concessions, the intellectual protagonist in "Games" feels alienated; in the Chinese city, the lawyer from "Etiquette and Hygiene" willfully alienates himself from the Chinese throng to assert his superiority and his purchasing power.

THE CITY AND THE MODERN GIRL

The male protagonist in "Games" observes a curious osmosis between the city and the modern girl, who is also a "product of modernity" (*jindai de chanwu*). She has round, thick lips, protruding breasts, a body soft and smooth like an eel, and dangling jade earrings (references to her sexuality and seductiveness); she has a "rational" forehead, short hair, and a Greek nose (references to her Western appearance). She seeks pleasure, speed (she loves the 1928 Viper sports car), and money; she is attractive, precocious, and, most importantly, unfaithful. In this story, Liu Na'ou creates a prototype of the modern Shanghai femme fatale who will populate many stories written in this era. Lodged in her are the characteristics of the urban culture of the semicolonial city and its seductions of speed, commodity culture, exoticism, and eroticism. Hence the emotions she stimulates in the male protagonist—helpless infatuation and hopeless betrayal—replicate the attraction and alienation he feels towards the city.

The origin of this modern girl can be traced partly to Franco-Japanese sources. A short genealogy here is useful to show how Liu adopts and yet subverts the figure in terms of the cross-cultural politics of gender and race. The images of exotic women in Paul Morand's influential short story collections *Fancy Goods* (*Tendres Stocks*, 1921) and *Open All Night* (*Ouvert la Nuit*, 1922) are descended from an exotic tradition in French literature traceable to Gustave Flaubert. In one of Flaubert's famous travel notes, he depicts an encounter with an Egyptian dancer, Kuchuk Hanem, who becomes the embodiment of the "Oriental": carnality and animality. Edward Said has shown how this figure of the Oriental woman provided an occasion for Flaubert to muse upon his own thoughts: she is passive, silent, gazed at, studied, and represented. Said therefore sees this as an example of Orientalism, a form of cultural domination exercised by Westerners to relegate the Orient to the status of the subhuman Other.[40] The novels of Pierre Loti (1850–1925) reproduce this classic Orientalist exoticism even more blatantly. In 1885, Loti went to Japan and was reputedly horrified by the ugliness and shabiness of the Japanese, whom he considered to be a "species of human hedgehog." In his autobiographical novel *Madame Chrysanthème* (1888), set in Japan and later translated into Chinese by Xu Xiacun, a Japanese woman is, in one

---

40. Edward Said, *Orientalism* (New York: Vintage Books, 1979), 184–190.

critic's words, the protagonist's "inanimate exotic object," strange and therefore attractive, mysterious, and inaccessible.[41]

This lineage is then taken up by Paul Morand, many of whose stories have exotic, foreign women as protagonists. These women are wild, undisciplined, sentimental, and, of course, carefully studied by the male narrators as objects of erotic reveries. In *Fancy Goods,* Morand chronicles the lives of three young women adrift in wartime London, and in his most popular book, *Open All Night,* he centers the narrative around six women. In Ezra Pound's translation, one of these women is described as follows:

> Perfect body. The back muscles moved like ivory balls under the sunburnt skin, stretched, a tissue solid and precious as silk for airships; one could pick out the muscles as easily as on an anatomic chart, where their rubicund arborescence is shown covering our organs; the bent flanks are flush with the water, the prowlike breasts, the long legs striped of all the weight by her dancing, slender at the ankles, hollow inside the thigh, filled amply over the knees.[42]

This microscopic, anatomic look at the beautiful woman who is eroticized through the male gaze is characteristic of Morand's descriptions of young women.

When this figure traveled to Japan, the Occident's Oriental woman became the Orient's Occidental woman. The "modern girl" or "*modan gāru*" (*moga* for short), as she was called in one of the variations in Japan, had Westernized, if not Eurasian, looks. Tanizaki Jun'ichirō's Naomi in his novel *A Fool's Love* (*Chijin no ai,* 1925), for example, wears bobbed hair, sheer stockings, high heels, and often a brightly colored one-piece dress in the fashion of American film idols such as Clara Bow, Pola Negri, Mary Pickford, and Gloria Swanson.[43] The modern girl is a "glittering, decadent, middle-class consumer who, through her clothing, smoking, and drinking, flaunts tradition in the urban playgrounds of the late 1920s,"[44] and she traveled to China on her own sometimes, appearing as the Japanese modern girl in Xu Xiacun's story "Modern Girl" (Xu's English title; 1929). The first mention of a Chinese "modern girl" (in her English appellation) is in a story by May Fourth writer Tao Jingsun (discussed in chapter 2), collected in *Concert Ditties* (*Yinyuehui xiaoqu,* 1927). When her image traveled to China through both

41. Michael G. Lerner, *Pierre Loti* (New York: Twayne Publishers, 1974), 69–72. Xu Xiacun's translation of Pierre Loti was published in 1929. Xu Xiacun, trans., *Mme. Chrysanthème* (*Juzi furen*), by Pierre Loti (Shanghai: Shangwu yinshuguan, 1929).

42. Paul Morand, *Fancy Goods & Open All Night,* trans. Ezra Pound, ed. Breon Mitchell (New York: New Directions, 1984), 50.

43. Barbara Hamill Sato, "The *Moga* Sensation: Perceptions of the *Modan Gāru* in Japanese Intellectual Circles during the 1920s," *Gender and History* 5:3 (1993): 363–81.

44. Miriam Silverberg, "The Modern Girl as Militant," in Gail Lee Berstein, ed., *Recreating Japanese Women, 1600–1945* (Berkeley: University of California Press, 1991), 239.

American films and Japanese literature, she also took on the characteristics of a typical Chinese flapper—that product of the Jazz Age. In a news item in the *North China Herald* in January 1928, she is defined as a young woman "usually dressed in semi-foreign style with bobbed hair . . . short skirt . . . and powdered face. She attends movies regularly and expects to be courted in screen lover fashion. . . . [She leads] a wholesome outdoor life and thrive[s] on it." The newspaper then announces: "The Chinese flapper has come to stay."[45]

In the web of signs in which she is produced within Liu Na'ou's fiction, however, the modern girl becomes a reciprocal metaphor of the city. The city is eroticized as the girl is eroticized; the girl is gazed at as the city is observed. Erotic intimacy and ineluctable separation—the latter could be said to enhance the former since desire operates through lack—characterize the male protagonist's relationship with both the city and the modern girl. After the modern girl has dumped the protagonist in "Games," Liu makes an explicit connection between the modern girl and the city in terms of their joint betrayal of the protagonist:

> She was gone, gone on a path he did not know. He followed the crowd rolling out of the station. Walking, he thought to himself: . . . What is this? . . . Is this a joke played on me by the city? Ha, ha. . . . A spasm of bitter laughter rolled from his stomach. Feet, feet, feet, feet on the pavement. . . . In a moment, he was in the midst of a crowd, and the city, like a hungry ghost, swallowed him up.[46]

The speed of the city is paralleled by the speed with which the modern girl changes boyfriends and by the modern girl's love of speedy sports cars: transitory scenes and transitory romances, a city of fast cars and brief encounters.

Similarly, the modern girl in "Two Men Out of Tune with Time" (*Liang ge shijian de buganzhengzhe*) seduces several men around her, and then promptly and skillfully jilts all of them. She appears at a horse race like a puff of wind, bearing the fragrance of "Cyclamen" perfume:

> When *H.* turned his head he saw the image of a *sportive,* modern girl. Under transparent, glossy French silk were elastic muscles trembling as if engaged in a slight exercise. When his eyes focused, he saw the small cherry break open and a smile protruding from the green lake. He felt that he could not remove his eyes from the pair of white knees slightly covered by the *opera bag* and peering out through the grey-black stockings.[47] (original English in italics)

As luck would have it, the protagonist H. wins a large sum at the racetrack, is soon approached by the modern girl who unabashedly offers him a date, and goes with her to an American cafe. From the racetrack to the cafe, and

45. Harriet Sergeant, *Shanghai* (London: Jonathan Cape, 1991), 271.
46. Liu Na'ou, *Scène,* 17.
47. Ibid., 93.

then while promenading on busy commercial streets, urban lures such as a "Fontegnac 1929" automobile attract his attention, and he prides himself for being in tune with the urban tempo. But soon, they run into a dapper young man named "T.," who says that he has a date with this modern girl. The two men, now rivals, go to a dance hall together with her, at her suggestion. After T. and the girl dance to the blues (*bolusi*), H. gets to dance a waltz (*hua'erzi*) with her, during which she abruptly tells him that his time is up. She lets fly the following remark at H., who is still in shock:

> ——Ah, you are just a child. Who told you to be so clumsy and slow with your hands and feet? What's with eating ice cream and taking a walk, what a bunch of nonsense! Don't you know that *lovemaking* should be done in a car amidst the wind? There is green shade outside the city [to park the car under]. I have never spent more than three hours with one *gentleman*. This was already an exception![48] (original English in italics)

She soon leaves both of them for another date, and upon leaving recommends to them that they pick up some "taxi dancers" instead (special dancers hired to dance with clients as though they were taxis for hire). Although H. believed himself in tune with the urban tempo, he abruptly discovers that he is lagging far behind the pace of the modern girl.

In "Landscape" (*Fengjing*), a chance encounter between a city man and the modern girl leads to a sexual frenzy in which the girl takes the initiative. The girl "smells of Brazilian coffee"; has "boyish short hair," "firm muscles," and a "rational, straight nose"; wears a "European-style short dress"; and speaks in a metallic voice. When they first meet on a train (riding which is described as "sitting on speed"), the male protagonist, Ranqing, barely begins to muse upon the beauty of the female passenger sitting opposite him before she stares back at him and aggressively eroticizes him with her own "oppressive gaze." She then takes the lead by telling him that he has a "cute male face." Shocked by her directness, he gingerly begins to converse with her. At her suggestion they get off at a station and check into a hotel. But she is not to be constrained by the hotel room, and runs out into a field, stripping her clothes off as she goes. The "green grass" becomes their "bedsheets."[49] In the end, however, she belongs to someone else, or to no one in particular, so his desire for her can never take the traditional form of "possessing" her sexuality. Similarly, when the male protagonist in "Below the Equator" takes his wife to a tropical island to separate her from her numerous male admirers in the city, he finds that even there she is unfaithful to him. His fantasy to maintain patriarchal authority, to be able to "order her

48. Ibid., 104.
49. Ibid., 24, 32.

to laugh, to cry, and even to beat her when necessary," ultimately to possess her fully, simply eludes him.[50]

Departing from the genealogy of exotic women from which she came, the modern girl in Liu Na'ou's fiction is no longer the passive object of erotic gaze, but the one who returns the gaze. Also, contrary to the ways in which the representations of the modern girl in Japanese intellectual discourse are made to displace the actual militancy of modern Japanese women,[51] the particular "modernity"—or, shall we say, "semicolonial modernity"—of Liu's modern girl affords her a surprising degree of autonomy and agency. It is patriarchal sexual morality—in the form of the ideology of female chastity ("Games"), marriage as convenient sexual contract ("Etiquette and Hygiene"), and the male possession of women ("Below the Equator")—that is treated ironically and subtly criticized throughout these stories, not the transgressive behavior of the modern girl.

The main female character in "Flow," for instance, is a "modern, masculine woman" (*jindai de nanxinghua le de nüzi*) who transgresses the boundaries of gender and class, and who fights the imperialists through her involvement in the labor movement. Furthermore, in the ironically entitled "The Passionate Man" (*Reqing zhi gu*) and in "Etiquette and Hygiene," a modern girl who defies Orientalism appears. In the first story, a Frenchman named Pierre comes to the Orient in search of exotica. A self-styled Pierre Loti, as he himself puts it, he dreams of meeting his own Madame Chrysanthemum, as in Loti's novel of the same name. One day at a flower shop, amid the fragrance of chrysanthemums and marigolds, he discovers his "Chrysanthemum," his "mermaid," a "spring goddess from the flower garden." She promptly becomes the repository of Oriental exotica for him:

> He could not believe that such a charming lovely Chrysanthemum could be so close at hand. He thought about her and felt that every point on her body from head to toe was lovely. Those black eyes seemed to hide in their depths the passion of the Orient, those two pearl-colored ears were the shells in the ocean from which Venus was born. The subtle movements around her waist carried with them a mystery that those Near Eastern women in Hugo's poetry do not have. Slender delicate eyebrows, Ah! Those small feet that cannot bear a squeeze! Compared to the animal-like Western European women, how fragile and sweet she is![52]

He goes about colonizing her materially, so to speak: buying her things, bringing her chocolates from Marseilles, and taking her out to the theater and ball games. The shroud of mystery surrounding her background, like her "mysterious black eyes," only enhances her seductiveness. However, in what

---

50. "Below the Equator" (*Chidao xia*), *Les Contemporaines* 2:1 (November 1932): 166–174.
51. Silverberg, "The Modern Girl as Militant," 239–255.
52. Liu Na'ou, *Scène*, 76.

to him is an unbelievable anticlimax, at the crucial moment when he, mumbling "Ma chérie" and entirely engrossed, bears down upon her "fragile body" that seems to crush beneath his weight, she suddenly says, "Will you give me five hundred yuan?" She plummets from goddess to prostitute in his eyes, and, his exoticist imagination completely shattered, he turns away in disgust. Far from being the passive receptacle for his fantasies, she rebukes him in a letter that he receives the next morning:

> Do you think I am too materialistic [for having asked you for money]? But when all abstract things such as justice and morality can be bought with money in this economic age, why do you demand that I not exchange my chastity for some urgently needed cash? . . . Are you saying that I should not have requested it at that moment? I have never been a woman with constraints. I speak when I want to, and I cannot comprehend those people who cannot express their thoughts as they come to them. I think it is good to be as *materielle* as I am.
>
> Whenever you speak, you write poetry like a poet. But the kind of poetry you demand is nowhere to be found in this age. The content of the poem has changed. Even if there is poetry in front of your eyes, I am afraid you won't see it. That's all. You may go back to dream those old dreams of your past.[53] (original French in italics)

Demanding money from him is, from her point of view, in keeping with his own method of seducing her through material gifts. She therefore exposes the snobbishness of his exoticism: it is created purely out of his imagination and will, and it refuses to allow for the existence of anything that runs counter to his carefully constructed illusion. Within this manufactured Orientalist dream or poetic fantasy, he can shower her with material goods, but she may not request them. Her demand for money therefore unsettles this unequal colonial relationship, where the colonizer is invariably constructed as the giver or benefactor and the colonized as the passive recipient of the colonial gift. With her demand, she consciously shatters Pierre's exotic fantasy and sabotages his Orientalism. Most significantly, this sabotage occurs through a strategic self-commodification. Her unabashed materiality is the marker of her anti-Orientalist agency; her materiality is the gaze back at the Orientalist imagination by refusing to conform to the latter's rules.

"Etiquette and Hygiene," from which I earlier quoted the passage about Qiming the lawyer traveling from the bund to the Chinese quarters, further dramatizes a subversion of Orientalism, but in this story a Frenchman's Orientalist fantasy is thwarted at the same time Qiming's patriarchal authority is repudiated. Using the exact same words that Pierre used in "The Passionate Man" to describe his Oriental beauty, the Frenchman Pouillet notes that Keqiong, Qiming's wife and the object of his desire, is not animalistic like West-

---

53. Ibid., 86.

ern women, her black eyes "hide the secret of the East," and her ears are "as lovely as the seashells brought from the depth of the ocean." He calls his infatuation with Keqiong part of his "intoxication with the East" (*dongfang zui*), which includes a passion for Chinese antiques and art objects. An erstwhile Beijing-based diplomat who became a seller of Chinese antiques to Westerners in Shanghai, Pouillet decides to pursue his Orientalist dream by "purchasing" Keqiong from her husband Qiming. He offers Qiming his antique shop and all its contents in exchange for a couple of years of "seductive bliss" (*yanfu*). As a patriarchal and unfaithful husband, Qiming ironically sees Pouillet's Orientalism as an expression of true love, although he neither accepts nor rejects Pouillet's offer but instead rushes home. There he finds that Keqiong has disappeared; a note informs him that she has left with her new lover whom she calls her "Pekinese." Keqiong thereby refuses to play either the role of an erotic objet d'art for Pouillet, or the faithful wife for a husband who frequents prostitutes, but instead becomes an active agent in pursuit of her own pleasure. She leaves her mute sister with her husband because, as she explains in the note, what her husband needs and wants is not so much a woman as a female body. She further explains that she is leaving her sister with him to prevent his contracting sexual diseases from visiting prostitutes. Finally, she taunts him by saying, "the easy to get are not always the most hygienic"—hence the ironic title, "Etiquette and Hygiene."

The modern girl who gazes back and resists both Western Orientalism and Chinese patriarchy is able to do so precisely because of an ambivalent identity that is no longer "essentially" Chinese, but rather has attributes of both the Hollywood actress and the Westernized *moga* from Japan. She communicates signs of Western material culture through her paraphernalia (clothing, handbag, cosmetics), her sexual promiscuity, her mannish Western looks (high nose, slender body, short hair, often muscular arms and legs), and her unrestrained behavior. She is in this sense a dissimulation of the images of Hollywood actresses and the *moga*, which allows her to exude an exotic imported air. But in the intimate cofiguration of her and the city of Shanghai, we see how her excessive materiality simultaneously implies the semicolonial condition. Both a discursively constructed (borrowed, dissimulated from metropolitan Western/Japanese culture) and a materially contextualized figure (who roams the urban spaces of the semicolonial city), she unsettles the bifurcation of the metropolitan and the colonial. By so doing, she disrupts the intellectual conception of modernity as the property of the metropolitan West which can be learned only belatedly by the Chinese, and instead pushes it into an impure realm where "contamination" from semicolonial culture cannot be entirely prevented. She is therefore the object on which, to borrow Leo Lee's phrases from a slightly different context, an "urban imagination of Chinese modernity" is focused and where the "modernity of the everyday life" is envisioned and materialized.[54] Liu Na'ou's cosmopolitanism, then, departs from that of the May Fourth intellectuals in its incorporation of semicolonial urbanity. This explains why Liu's vision of modernity appeared decadent and corrupt to nationalist intellectuals associated with the League of Left-Wing Writers or the Nationalist Party. It is no longer merely a projection of an ideal based on a discursive emulation of the metropolitan West, but also a willing engagement with the materiality of the West in its "corrupted" form of urban culture.

DESIRE AND URBAN MODERNITY

In the absence of a securely positioned nationalist imaginary, as in Frantz Fanon's Antilles or nineteenth-century Indian nationalist discourse as presented by Partha Chatterjee, the Westernized modern girl in Liu Na'ou's work comes to represent not the object of repudiation but the object of desire. Departing from the representation of Westernized women in the nationalist imaginary, the modern girl's sexual promiscuity, rather than being condemned on patriarchal moral grounds, becomes the mark of her free will to pursue her own desires. Her materiality is not condemned as vulgar and corrupt, but rather becomes the sign of her ability to adapt to the modern world; her materiality is a metonymic extension of the inescapable materiality of modernity. Rather than posing a threat of double emasculation to the native male, she embodies the speed of modernity that demands pursuit. Instead of being a threatening double to the male intellectual, she subverts tradition in a way that the male intellectual himself might have liked to do.

In these ways, she plays the mediating role between Western material culture and the male intellectual, as she stands at the vanguard in the pursuit of urban modernity. This icon of modernity threatens Liu's male characters' sense of masculinity, but since that masculinity is not undergirded by nationalism, the usual union between nationalism and patriarchy is sundered. This absence of nationalism in the patriarchal imagination may be due to Liu's own ambivalent cultural identity, but it reveals, in large measure, the agenda of a cosmopolitan project whose categories are conceived in terms other than the nation. When nationalism no longer operates to subsume and subjugate issues regarding women, a radical subversion of patriarchy becomes securable, and a more sustained gendered inquiry into male-female relationships becomes feasible, albeit mainly on the representational terrain. Indeed, as history tells us, nationalism in Third World nations has time and again served as effective ammunition for the patriarchy to assert its control

54. Leo Ou-fan Lee, "The Cultural Construction of Modernity in Early Republican China: Some Research Notes on Urban Shanghai," typescript, 1996, 23.

over women in order to displace frustration with threats of colonial, and more recently neocolonial, forces. The ironic conclusion we may derive from Liu Na'ou's work is that denationalized cosmopolitanism may be the only position from which women's emancipation from patriarchal control can be expressed.

In the modern girl's refusal to conform to the fantasies of Western Orientalism (as represented by the characters of Pierre and Pouillet), we see that her modernity does not co-opt the Western categories of gender relegated to "Oriental" women, nor does she readily accept all Western cultural values. Her rebellion is therefore two-pronged, against both the patriarchal and the Orientalist imaginaries, which raises the provocative question of whether there are structural similarities between Third World patriarchy and Orientalism in their shared desire to subjugate native women as a depository of male fantasy. When Pouillet offered to exchange his antique shop for the "ownership" of Keqiong in "Etiquette and Hygiene," Qiming's understanding of that offer as arising from love leads one to believe that the Orientalist and the patriarchal indeed can be complicit: if she had not resisted, Keqiong could have been bartered, transacted, and trafficked, to help maintain both communities of men and their *homo*geneous interests.

The modern girl's refusal to play by either set of rules distinguishes her from the myriad representations of modern women since the May Fourth era. In the trajectory of changing representation of women in modern Chinese literature, the modern girl's antecedent may be traced back to the "new woman" (*xin nüxing*) of May Fourth writing, where the new woman's emancipatory behavior was projected by a generation of male writers who could not themselves overcome existing feudal structures such as arranged marriages. The "new woman"—for example, Hu Shi's version of Ibsen's Nora, Lu Xun's Zijun, and Mao Dun's many heroines—was the courageous figure who put into practice the agenda of "total westernization" (*quanpan xihua*) and antitraditionalism, hence her failure to achieve complete liberation embodied the eventual despair of May Fourth male writers at the tenacity of feudal structures and the difficulty of completing the cultural enlightenment project.[55] So the new woman was predominantly a trope for the projection of male desire, the site where male subjectivity negotiated its changing relationship with the May Fourth dyad of tradition and modernity. The representation of the new woman was more or less subjugated by male narrative voices, which often unabashedly articulated antifeminist sentiments.[56]

55. Stephen Chan, "The Language of Despair: Ideological Representations of the 'New Woman' by May Fourth Writers," in Tani E. Barlow, ed., *Gender Politics in Modern China: Writing and Feminism* (Durham: Duke University Press, 1993), 13–32.

56. See Shu-mei Shih, "Female Confessional Narratives in Modern Chinese Literature" (*Zhongguo xiandai wenxue zhong de nüxing zibai xiaoshuo*), *Con-Temporary* (*Dangdai*) 95 (March 1994): 108–27.

The modern girl may be interpreted in terms of the question of male subjectivity as well. In her transgressiveness on the planes of gender, race, culture, and national identity, we may read a cosmopolitan male subjectivity's projection of an ideal double upon whom he lavishes desire and adoration. Neither complaining about the difficulties of achieving cultural enlightenment nor using women to criticize society, both of which are premised on a stable male identity and a sense of patriarchal right, Liu Na'ou's work instead presents a male subjectivity that questions its groundings in patriarchy, that does not assume a stable identity, and that opens the question of newly constructed gender roles in the urban context of semicolonial Shanghai. Instead of despair, then, the modern girl's relative success in attaining autonomy may indicate a certain hopefulness in Liu's vision of urban modernity.

Finally, the representation of the Westernized modern girl as absorbing the material culture of urban Shanghai unsettles the persistent bifurcation of the West in modern Chinese intellectual discourse into separate metropolitan and colonial spheres. However, as I will explain in the next two chapters, the new sensationists see this urban materiality more in capitalist terms than in semicolonial terms. It is the materiality of dance halls, racetracks, and cinemas in the foreign concessions, without explicit references to the colonial presence in these places. It is mainly the materiality of commodified culture which is deemed the quintessential urban experience, hence the urban culture is predominantly seen as capitalist, and its novelty is captured in consistently seductive language. To confront the semicolonial reality of racism, economic exploitation, political inequity, and so on, would have meant a resurrection of the nationalist sentiments that Shanghai modernism self-consciously eschewed.

The desire for the modern girl, therefore, as I will also analyze further in the next chapter, is a desire for capitalist modernity with all its seductive allures of commodification, consumption, and entertainment. Because of her overpowering seductiveness, she becomes securely lodged as a prominent figure in the landscape of the male protagonist's desire, and ineluctably becomes constitutive of what he is as a man of desire. But this landscape of desire partakes in another level of bifurcation, which I will explain in the next chapter. The work of the other two leading Shanghai modernists, Mu Shiying and Shi Zhecun, uncovers the make-up of this landscape of desire in its ever greater complexity. Eventually, however, the increasing ascendancy of the Manichean politics of nationalism after the outburst of the Sino-Japanese War would delegitimize the exploration of this landscape, and eliminate the conditions of possibility for the kind of semicolonial cultural politics we witness here.

CHAPTER 11

Performing Semicolonial Subjectivity
The Work of Mu Shiying

This chapter delineates the particular nexus of Shanghai cultural cosmopolitanism, nationalism, and semicolonialism in the work of another leading new sensationist writer, Mu Shiying (1912–1940). As a modernist in the early and mid-1930s, Mu Shiying upheld the standards of cultural cosmopolitanism, which meant freely incorporating Western and Japanese literary practices into his work and staunchly resisting nationalism as it was discursively and politically constructed by the Chinese Communist Party and the Nationalist Party. Mu considered such nationalism highly problematic, whether as a discourse of resistance against Western and Japanese imperialisms or as a discourse of legitimation for an oppressive regime, due to both organizations' chauvinistic and demagogic propensities. The incoherence of the Nationalist government's cultural policy enabled the League of Left-Wing Writers to dominate and move opinions, often forcefully constructing oppositions between friend and foe, and deploying hired hands to criticize those who opposed or were ambivalent about the League's dicta on literary production. Mu was a victim of ruthless criticism by the League, so what little allegiance he had left over from his earlier Marxist inclinations was gradually overwhelmed by anger and resentment. Mu emphasized instead an unapologetic belief in literary autonomy, exercised through various strategies that displaced nationalism and consequently the semicolonialism of which nationalism would have been the most direct form of critique.

I explore Mu Shiying's systematic displacement of colonial reality through multiple registers—gender representation, an ambiguous nationalism, a critique of capitalism (but not the semicolonial condition per se), and the practice of pure textuality—by reading his works written after his turn to new sensationist fiction around 1932. Through these readings, I demonstrate that Mu's displacement of colonial reality indicates not a failure to achieve nationalist consciousness or a capitulation to colonized consciousness, but rather a cultural choice made by the Chinese middle-class intellectual under semicolonialism. Mu retreated into pure textuality and technique as a means to claim autonomy in an age of contention among highly politicized native cultural groups, which coincided with the moment when a capitalist form of lived experience became available for a universalist critique. Semicolonialism as a reality would exist, then, only insofar as it was manifested as capitalism; to put it more precisely, a universalist critique of capitalism displaced the political and racial experience of semicolonialism. Thus, the critique of capitalism all but displaces colonial critique, aesthetic autonomy precedes nationalist consciousness, and in such circumstances gender and subjectivity are determined not so much by the parameters of the nation as by capitalist urbanism and commodification.

A generalized anxiety towards the industrialized lifestyle undergirds this critique of capitalism, which reveals that, contrary to other scholars' claims, the male subject who roams the streets of Shanghai in the work of new sensationist fiction is not a leisurely flâneur at ease with himself (taking a turtle for a walk, "botanizing on the asphalt," or window-shopping in the arcades, as presented by Charles Baudelaire and theorized by Walter Benjamin), nor a stranger who takes a blasé attitude as his defense mechanism against overwhelming urban stimuli (as in the work of sociologist Georg Simmel).[1] Rather, the new sensationist protagonist is a participant in the flow of urban experience (even though this participation takes a specific form). Receiving the effects of the dizzying (com)motions of the city on multiple sensory registers, mimicking the activities of the modern capitalist city (speeding, pulsating, buying, selling), and in the absence of a defense mechanism (such as Simmel's blasé attitude or what Benjamin calls the "protective shield"[2]), the protagonist often stumbles and falls from exhaustion. The new sensations of the city fall upon the male subject with such force that he gets lost in a world of sounds, lights, colors, and motion, and it is these powerful sensory impressions on the subject which provide the occasions for the author's

1. See Walter Benjamin, "The Flâneur," in *Charles Baudelaire: A Lyric Poet in the Era of High Capitalism,* trans. Harry Zohn (London: Verso, 1985), 35–66; Walter Benjamin, "On Some Motifs in Baudelaire," in *Illuminations,* trans. Harry Zohn, ed. Hannah Arendt (New York: Schocken Books, 1969); Georg Simmel, "The Metropolis and Mental Life" (1903), trans. Edward A. Shils, in *On Individuality and Social Forms,* ed. Donald N. Levine (University of Chicago Press, 1971), 324–339. Leo Lee, in his *Shanghai Modern: A Study of Urban Culture and Literary Imagination in China, 1930–1945* (Cambridge: Harvard University Press, 1999), chapter 1, also takes this problematic equation of the Chinese intellectual in Shanghai with the flâneur to task by noting the differences between Baudelaire's city (crowded with horse-drawn carts) and Shanghai (crowded with motorcars), and the fact that Francophiles who roamed the streets seldom did so alone but always in the company of friends.

2. Walter Benjamin appropriates Freud's notion here. See his "On Some Motifs in Baudelaire," 161.

linguistic innovation and technical experimentation. Unlike the Benjaminian, self-absorbed flâneur engaged in a study of the new urban life from a detached perspective, or Simmel's stranger aloof from the onrush of urban stimuli, Mu's male protagonist is often a tired urban man caught in the commodity logic of capitalism from which he cannot escape. As for the few protagonists who seem able to ride the speed of the city, they tend to seek exclusively the fulfillment of sexual desire, turning the city into a city of Eros and thus giving it a symbolic form detached from its immediate historical context. The city of Eros further ensnares them, however, in the commodity logic of sex, either through prostitution or chance sexual encounters.

In both of these processes (the protagonist serving as a receptacle of urban stimuli and the author giving the city a symbolic form as a city of Eros), it is capitalism's cultural economy, not semicolonialism's political or racial economy, which is targeted for investigation and critique. This persistent displacement of the colonial dimension in the lived experience of the semicolonial subject again indicates how cultural politics under semicolonialism did not operate in the Manichean fashion of colonial domination and nationalist resistance. Instead, Mu's displacement of nationalism and semicolonial reality with such registers as desire, gender, and textuality reveals to us that culture under semicolonialism was articulated from multifarious positions.

Summarizing thus far, and as will be illustrated later, the semicolonial subject position may be said to have the following two-layered structure of strategies of displacement through bifurcation:

First-level bifurcation:

Semicolonial Subject

   Metropolitan West/Japan (imaginary relation constructed through an asymmetrical cosmopolitanism)

   Colonial West/Japan (real relation of economic, racial, and political exploitations and inequities)

Second-level bifurcation:

Semicolonial Subject

   Shanghai as capitalist city (site of urban modernity and Eros)

   Shanghai as colonial city (site of imperialist exploitation and racism)

In both these levels, the first term presides over and displaces the second term. It is precisely due to the emphasis on the first terms that semicolonial subjectivity relates to reality as a form of simulacra. Toward the metropolitan West and Japan, the semicolonial subject harbors an imaginary cultural crossing over to, and one-sided interaction with, the West and Japan. Regarding the urban capitalism of Shanghai, he is inevitably reduced to being the viewer of the urban phantasmagoria and the consumer of Westernized, commodified images, goods, and places, hence his primary relation to the city is of consumption: seeing, buying, eating, playing at urban sites such as the dance hall, and so on. As a result, dissimulation (the production of reality through images in the movies or intertextual relations with other books) becomes the abiding trope of representation.

A PERFORMANCE IN CONTROVERSY

By many accounts, Mu Shiying is the major new sensationist writer: his extensive technical endeavors and prolific written work earned him the labels of "champion of Chinese new sensationist writing" (*zhongguo xin'ganjuepai de shengshou*) and "the Chinese Yokomitsu Riichi." Seasoned literary critics have applauded his audacious technical and formal experiments as surpassing those of Liu Na'ou, whom the younger Mu apparently looked up to and became close friends with. Starting to write and publish at the tender age of seventeen, Mu was extolled as a literary genius who came to his craft with surprising maturity and audacity. Women readers were infatuated with this handsome young man with a "Greek nose" and a "long face,"[3] especially after his photo was published in *Les Contemporaines,* and they flocked to the dance halls to spot this writer who reputedly frequented them in search of both writing subjects and the pleasure of dancing. Besides dance halls, he also frequented coffee shops (one of his favorites was a cafe called Renaissance), theaters, and racetracks.[4] He smoked Craven "A" brand cigarettes (like the female protagonist in his story named after the cigarette), hung out at a nightclub called Moon Palace, danced the foxtrot superbly, bet on jai alai, and later married a Cantonese dancing hostess.[5] According to one sympathetic account by a 1940s literary historian, Mu was a striking figure:

> Permed hair, a well-pressed Western suit, and the style of a modern artist, is the external appearance of Mr. Mu Shiying. A belly full of Horiguchi Daigaku–style witticisms, a Yokomitsu Riichi style of writing, a Hayashi Fusao

3. "A Comet in the 1930s Literary Arena: Ye Lingfeng Talks About Mu Shiying" (*Sanshi niandai wentan shang de yike huixing: Ye Lingfeng xiansheng tan Mu Shiying*), *Four Seasons* (*Siji*) 1 (November 1972): 30.

4. Kang Yi (Ji Kangyi), "Hearing a Flute at Shanyang: Remembering the 1930s New Sensationist Writer Mr. Mu Shiying" (*Lindi shanyang: daonian yiwei sanshi niandai xin'ganjuepai zuojia Mu Shiying xiansheng*), *Anecdotes* (*Zhanggu*) 10 (1972): 48–50.

5. Hei Ying, "The Mu Shiying I Knew" (*Wo jiandao de Mu Shiying*), *Historical Materials on Modern Chinese Literature* (February 1989): 142–145.

style of creating new narrative forms, such is the content of Mr. Mu Shiying. Because of this, he made a great contribution to the second decade of new literature in China. . . . Although Liu Na'ou introduced Japanese new sensationism first, in regards to technique, Mu is far superior.[6]

Du Heng, who by some accounts won the battle in the Third Category Men debate with the League, also credited Mu as a master of technique "forever in search of a new style," whose contribution surpassed that of Liu Na'ou.[7] These accounts of Mu describe a writer who was fashionable and modern in outward appearance, lifestyle, and writing style, attractive both to serious critics and to Shanghai's middle-class readers and urban consumers. These supporters were naturally adverse to ideological dictation in writing, and advocated literary freedom.

In many other accounts, however, Mu's work, was considered an imitative, "bastardized" version of Western literature, his lifestyle embodying the worst of semicolonialism's effects on the Chinese intellectual. He was accused of pursuing pleasure in the capitalist urban mode, lacking moral integrity, turning away from revolutionary causes and betraying the nationalist cause, possessing a colonized consciousness, "polluting the Chinese written language" by mixing it with foreign languages, and writing trash and pornography.[8] The attacks on him came not only from such neoconservatives as Shen Congwen, as I have related in chapter 9, but also by writers and critics associated with the League of Left-Wing Writers. Mu mentioned that he had been accused of being a "fence-sitter," a "red turnip with the skin peeled" (by Qu Qiubai, for allegedly pretending to be Marxist and yet in actuality being capitalist), and the "trash of society."[9] In *Modern Publishing* (*Xiandai chubanjie*), several articles appeared in 1932 explicitly criticizing Mu Shiying, against which Mu himself wrote a short defense. Leftist critics charged that Mu's work lacked social value due to its lack of realism, while Mu refuted the ideological dictates these critics were operating under.[10] As Randolph Trumbull aptly

6. Xun Si, "Mu Shiying," in Yang Zhihua, ed., *Historical Materials on the Literary Arena* (*Wentan shiliao*) (Shanghai: Zhonghua ribaoshe, 1944), 231–232.

7. Du Heng [Su Wen], "About Mu Shiying's Creative Work" (*Guanyu Mu Shiying de chuangzuo*), *Modern Publishing* (*Xiandai chubanjie*) 9 (January 1933): 10–11.

8. See Yu Qingxiang and Mao Jiaming, "Metropolis Contorting Under His Pen" (*Dadushi zai tade bixia jingruan*), in *Huazhong Normal University Journal* (*Huazhong shifan daxue xuebao*) (April 1989): 43–49; Wu Fuhui, "A Comparative Study of the Beijing and Shanghai Schools of Fiction" (*Jingpai haipai xiaoshuo bijiao yanjiu*), *Studies of Modern and Contemporary Chinese Literature* (*Zhongguo xiandai dangdai wenxue yanjiu*) (October 1987): 200–204.

9. "Self-Preface" (*Zixu*), *Public Cemetery* (*Gongmu*) (Shanghai: Xiandai shuju, 1933), 2.

10. Mu Shiying, "Words About Myself" (*Guanyu ziji de hua*), *Modern Publishing* (*Xiandai chubanjie*) 4 (August 1932): 9–10. He was responding to the charge by Shu Yue (Song Yi) who published an article criticizing Mu in the previous issue of the same journal. Also see Liu Weichen, "Mu Shiying's 'Shanghai Foxtrot'" (*Mu Shiying de "Shanghai hubuwu"*), *Modern Publishing* 7 (November 1932): 11–12.

puts it, to people like Qu Qiubai and other league members, "Mu Shiying represents the perversion of the May Fourth intellectual ethic; he is a problem local to Shanghai's capitalist environment, but dangerous in his ability to persuade Chinese readers throughout the nation to search for nothing nobler in life than material gratification."[11] Their disappointment with Mu was all the greater because they had endorsed his early work on the lumpen proletariat as a successful incorporation of mass language and proletarian consciousness. He then made, in their view, a fatal turn to new sensationism.[12]

These views of Mu diverge to such an extent that the significance of his works has been shrouded in an atmosphere of tentativeness and uncertainty. The complexity of this divergence is further compounded because Mu was not anti-Marxist per se: (1) as mentioned above, his early stories about the lumpen proletariat were groundbreaking exercises in proletarian fiction; (2) many of his views and convictions were implicitly Marxist in nature, and his city fiction clearly critiques capitalism; (3) his theoretical and popular essays on film, literature, and culture written in the mid-1930s deploy a sophisticated Marxist theoretical framework to combat the demagogic policing of the League, thereby beating the League at its own game.

How then do we negotiate such divergence in opinions, and how shall we, as literary and cultural historians, evaluate Mu and his work? For answers, it is instructive to turn to the limited biographical material we have on Mu, some revealing responses Mu wrote to his critics, and, most importantly, Mu's works themselves. Mu was born and raised in Zhejiang province and later attended college at Guanghua University in Shanghai, majoring in Chinese literature. His father had been a successful banker and later an agent in the gold speculation business until his fortunes took a drastic turn for the worse in the late 1920s. His father then became chronically ill from, more than anything else, depression and dejection. Mu writes about his melancholy visits to his father's sick bed and his old family house (which was later sold), and vividly describes these events and the moment of his father's death in his thinly disguised autobiographical stories "Father" (*Fuqin*, 1933) and "Old House" (*Jiuzhai*, 1933). Another autobiographical story, "The One Hundredth Day" (*Bairi*, 1933), depicts his mother's desolation after his father's death. These autobiographical stories reveal the melancholy side of Mu who, as the oldest son of a traditional patriarchal family, would have been pampered if his

11. Randolph Trumbull, *The Shanghai Modernists* (Ph.D. dissertation, Stanford University, 1989), 208.

12. See the inside cover page of *Les Contemporaines* 2:5 (March 1933) for across-the-board praises of Mu Shiying's *Poles Apart* by the leftist journal *Big Dipper* (*Beidou*), leftist critic Qian Xingcun, and middle-of-the-road critics Shi Zhecun, Du Heng, and Fu Donghua. The leftists, for instance, praised Mu's ability to use artistic methods to describe class difference and struggle, using a vocabulary of the masses unfamiliar to intellectuals. They saw *Poles Apart* as an outstanding exercise of proletarian fiction.

family fortunes had not changed, and who should have been responsible for the family livelihood but simply could not be at the tender age of sixteen when his father died. A mixture of guilt and regret lingers to haunt these stories.

But Mu's life took many more dramatic turns in the volatile political and cultural context of modern China and under pressures from many fronts (or rather, due to his desire to resist and fight these pressures). After publishing stories of male chivalry among the country lumpen proletariat in their fight against the corrupting forces of urban capitalism, and three tales of the capitalist machine exploiting the urban working class (collected in the 1932 first version and the 1933 expanded version of *Poles Apart* [*Nanbeiji*], respectively), Mu was hailed as the spokesperson of the proletarian consciousness. (These stories are somewhat reminiscent in style of the classical Chinese novel *Water Margin* [*Shuihu zhuan*], reputedly written by Shi Nai'an.) But around the time he wrote the last three tales, in which he moved the setting from the countryside to the city of Shanghai, Mu also started writing urban fiction in the new sensationist style.

Not soon afterwards, Mu began to be criticized by the League. Ji Kangyi, a friend of Mu, noted that Mu once told him that he turned away from the League largely because he was offended by Lu Xun's high-handed, condescending manner. When they were endorsing Mu's writing with enthusiasm, the League had arranged a meeting between Mu and Lu Xun, then the acknowledged leader of the League. Mu was taken first to Uchiyama Bookstore. Then the bookstore's proprietor Uchiyama Kanzō accompanied Mu to Lu Xun's flat nearby. Mu apparently was given no opportunity to defend himself as Lu Xun, uninterested in listening, kept admonishing him for writing fiction suitable only for the taste of the petty bourgeoisie and not for the needs of the great masses.[13] From then on, Mu became increasingly disillusioned with League politics as they fired attack after attack against him.

One can clearly see the bitterness Mu must have felt toward these attacks in some of the essays he wrote after 1934. Mu turned more and more decadent in the eyes of the leftists, especially when he took up the editorship of the literary supplement of *The Morning Post* (*Chenbao*), run by Nationalist Party official and Shanghai education bureau chief Pan Gongzhan, in 1934; when he became involved in the debate on soft-core cinema (the famed *ruanxing dianying lunzhan*) together with Liu Na'ou, vociferously attacking leftist cinema; and when, in the late 1930s, he worked first as the chief of propaganda for the Japanese puppet regime of Wang Jingwei in Nanjing and then took up the post left open by the death of Liu Na'ou: president of the National News Company (*guomin xinwen she*) and chief editor of *Wenhui Daily* (*Wenhui bao*), again controlled by Wang Jingwei. This last job he kept for only

13. Kang Yi, "Hearing a Flute at Shanyang," 49.

a few months until his assassination in June 1940, while riding a rickshaw to work, following on the heels of the assassination of Liu Na'ou.[14]

Over the course of his short lifetime, Mu seemed to have shifted from being a Marxist, to a capitalist, to a Nationalist Party supporter, to a collaborator/traitor who worked for the Japanese puppet regime, if we take his changes in employment as indicative of profound ideological shifts. His assassination, like that of Liu Na'ou, is therefore fittingly clouded in mystery, some claiming that he was murdered by the Nationalist Party because he was a traitor, others claiming that he was mistakenly killed by the Nationalist Party when he was actually a double agent working for them.

But to conclude that Mu underwent profound ideological shifts and was each time completely sure of his transformation and dismissive of previous convictions is a historical and analytical mistake. His friend Ji noted that a month before Mu's assassination, Ji, who then worked for the Nationalist government, sought out Mu in Shanghai and the two went for dinner at a restaurant serving Western food. Mu insisted on paying for the dinner, saying "I am using the Wang [Jingwei] regime's money to buy dinner for the Chongqing element, to happily see you off to Chongqing."[15] As there is no reason to doubt the truthfulness of Ji's recollection, this episode is of great significance as it shows Mu's attitude toward his own collaboration with the Wang regime. It appears that it was not ideological or political conviction that compelled him to work with the regime, since he openly remained friends with "the Chongqing element." I do not want to explain away the historical fact of his collaboration, but this episode suggests that Mu harbored an ambivalent attitude toward ideology, and these shifts may have resulted less from political conviction than from other, more tangible reasons. Mu had just spent approximately two years in Hong Kong with his wife Qiu Peipei, living in destitution (with a mattress on the floor and no other furniture), until he found a post with the Wang regime: he was in dire need of both financial resources (he writes about financial difficulty in many of his stories from this period) and a job in the Shanghai culture industry after years of being on the margins of cultural activities.

However, the most convincing, albeit perhaps the most forgiving, explanation for his shifts can be gleaned from the parallelism between his ideological and aesthetic inclinations, which shared an emphasis on multiplicity, performance, and experimentalism. If we may presume for the moment that one's aesthetic proclivities often reveal clues about one's ideological position(s), this may suggest a worthwhile inquiry.

The notion of performance in relation to Mu's work was first raised by

14. Kang Yi, "Hearing a Flute at Shanyang," 49–50. Also see Hei Ying, "The Mu Shiying I Knew," 145.

15. Kang Yi, "Hearing a Flute at Shanyang," 50.

Liu Yichang, famed Hong Kong writer and critic, in 1972. Referring to comments from the 1930s by both leftists and Mu defenders that Mu operated without a unified personality and hence easily shifted, Liu Yichang noted: "For Mu Shiying, writing fiction is not merely a form of 'expression'; it is a form of 'performance.'" Here, I want to connect Liu Yichang's notion of performance (*biaoyan*) with the notion of performance in American feminist philosopher Judith Butler's work *Gender Trouble*. Even though the historical gaps between the two notions are arguably unbridgeable, the latter's notion is useful in highlighting an important aspect of Mu's work and personality. Butler's notion of performance centers around her argument that gender identity is performative, multiple, and subversive of the heterosexual norm, which is a disciplinary regime of power dividing gender into a male-female binary that in turn generates a reified and oppressive notion of gender identity and difference.[16] Extrapolating only the part of Butler's notion of performance that describes it as disruptive and subversive of the norm, I would like to argue that Mu Shiying's performance of writing and living can be construed in similar ways.

There are many contextual and documented pieces of evidence for such an argument. Mu Shiying's several statements about his work and life offer us a clear glimpse of his performative attitude toward his craft as a writer and how this craft relates to ideology. The earliest document concerning this issue is Mu Shiying's August 1932 essay in *Modern Publishing*, entitled "Words About Myself" (*Guanyu ziji de hua*). Mu was then only twenty years old, and had just published his widely acclaimed first collection of stories, but he was already being attacked as a contradictory person with problematic ideological leanings. The article is short enough to be translated in its entirety here:

> Mr. Su Wen [Du Heng] said, "It is smart to be silent."
> But today, I cannot but say a few words.
> A year ago, I wrote "Poles Apart" [the title story of *Poles Apart*] and "Men Kept as Playthings" [*Beidangzuo xiaoqianpin de nanzi*]; recently, I wrote "Public Cemetery" [the title story of *Public Cemetery* (*Gongmu*)] and "The Baker Who Stole Bread" [*Tou mianbao de mianbaoshi*]. Writing two completely different styles of work as a writer is considered a mystery, a contradiction, which even I myself do not understand the cause of and just laugh about. Many friends and strangers, using either written or spoken words, criticize and admonish me from different positions. But I have never expressed an opinion in response, considering myself a smart person.
> But, today, I feel like a fool because of the article "Social Trash, Lumpen Proletariat, and Mu Shiying's Work."
> Literature is the transmission and affectation of emotion. I think that the form and content of each work is indivisible, each is synthesized rather than

16. Judith Butler, *Gender Trouble: Feminism and the Subversion of Identity* (New York and London: Routledge, 1990), especially chapters 1 and 3.

simply mixed together. To have a unified literary style and a correct consciousness, one must have a unified life and a correct life. To have a unified, correct life, the precondition is that the person have a firm belief. As for belief, it is not an emotional adoration of a certain thought or "ism," but a rational exploration that is the number one [requirement]. Rational understanding is number two. Emotion is a dangerous thing, and is connected to rashness. Only rationality is firm, and is connected to will and persistence.

Up until now, I have been rationally exploring various "isms" and the unsightly things hiding behind those "isms," hence I have not made efforts toward one life or one ism.

I am still young and there will yet be time for me to unify myself, and there will yet be time for me to develop a belief—there will yet be time to provide answers to critics and readers.

This may be considered a confession.[17]

The twenty-year-old Mu was clearly not a sophisticated theorist, nor could he offer a satisfactory answer to his critics. One point that this essay highlights, and which became increasingly important to him as a writer, however, is the notion of the writer's responsibility to his story's organic relationship between form and content, and his lack of obligation to stick to any one style of writing. A story will determine its particular form and content, but the writer is not constricted to writing in one signature style. Using his youth as a defense ("there will yet be time for me to unify myself") while subtly criticizing the hypocrisy of various "isms" ("the unsightly things hiding behind those 'isms'"), Mu further establishes a correlation between unity (a unified self with a unified lifestyle, writing style, and belief) and hypocrisy, suggesting that a firm belief in one "ism" requires emotion not rationality, and hence is irrational. Although his critics simply did not understand his position and dismissed his ideas as mere playfulness, the new rationality he constructs in this essay, against fixed belief and a unified self, should be considered more than audacious in a politically charged atmosphere where most people did not dare to be different.

This challenge to unified self and belief was more clearly articulated in an essay he wrote five months later and published in the January 1933 issue of *Modern Publishing* along with Du Heng's defense of Mu. In the same month, he also penned a preface to the revised edition of *Poles Apart*, in which he made further clarifications. Du Heng's defense was the famous essay in which he first coined the term "dual personality" (*shuangchong renge*) to describe Mu's work:

Clearly, irrefutably, and indisputably, Shiying is following two absolutely oppositional paths in his writing. His work can be naturally divided into two styles: the one in "Poles Apart," the other in "Public Cemetery," with the two of them forming two poles in themselves. . . .

17. Mu Shiying, "Words About Myself," 9–10.

This expression of dual personality has become the root cause of all the condemnations of Shiying.

But let's think more scrupulously. Dual personality is not something to be condemned in this age, as it is actually a stage in the constitution of [our] history. Almost every writer we know is an embodiment of dual personality; even those who study oracle bones or remain silent, we can say that these are indirect expressions of dual personality. The only difference among writers is whether they want to conceal or are good at concealing such self-contradictions. Critics should point out both the expression and concealment of dual personality and explain the reasons why. Those critics condemning a writer for expressing his dual personality are in fact forcing the writer to become hypocritical.[18]

Here, Du Heng makes a point about unified personality as a form of hypocrisy similar to Mu's in the earlier essay, and strikingly argues that dual personality is a historically rooted personality form for his time. Judging from Du Heng's persistent criticism of League politics, he is most likely implying here that it is the League's hegemony which has driven writers into solitary studies of antiquity or self-imposed silence to avoid ideological sanctioning.

Mu Shiying's essay, following Du Heng's defense of dual personality, provides another explanation of how this dual personality is historically rooted. Expanding the notion of duality to multiplicity, Mu starts the essay by pronouncing that he is living a "dual, even triple, quadruple . . . infinitely layered life." "I as a writer, I as a college student, I as the child disciplined by a mother, I as the wanderer in the dance hall, I as the teacher of village elementary school—all these complex personalities cannot be analyzed or comprehended even by me," he writes. He further illustrates the multiple roles and identities he lives with by noting that the names people use to call him differ drastically. Taking this sense of multiplicity to a philosophical level, he points out:

I am very young, I love the sun, I love fire, I love roses, I love everything that is bright and lively; I will never be disappointed, tired, or pessimistic. To everything in the world I open my curious, sympathetic eyes. But at the same time, in the depth of my heart, I have a loneliness as deep as the ocean, a loneliness that cannot be washed away with tears or sighs, a loneliness that cannot be comforted by friends or lovers. At such moments I can only pull my hair and sit silently, because I have an old heart. I try with all my might to pursue stimulation and newness to help me forget this loneliness, but can I? No! Suddenly, sometimes, I have an unspeakable hatred, a universal hatred toward all living beings and nonbeings. I don't want to say a word, see a thing, but I also don't want to commit suicide—not because I am a coward, but because I also love this world dearly. I am positive, I am also negative; I am yes, I am no; I am a man of no equilibrium, no middle ground.[19]

18. Du Heng, "About Mu Shiying's Creative Work," 10.
19. *Modern Publishing* (*Xiandai chubanjie*) 9 (January 1933): 12–13.

Mu takes multiplicity and self-contradiction as an existential condition here, but the comparison he makes between his two lifestyles helps root his multiplicity or duality in a historical experience: the division between the rural and the urban. As an elementary schoolteacher in the rural environment, he says that he went to classes, played basketball, rode horses, visited traditional tea houses, and took walks in the countryside, occasionally visiting parents of schoolchildren; but on weekends he came to Shanghai and lived the fast life of cinema, restaurants, and dance halls. In this opposition between the rural and the urban, we note that the historical nature of this dual personality reflects differing lifestyles defined by the rural and the urban: the two lifestyles suggest two temporal and spatial experiences conditioned by semicolonialism, and provide the grounds for a personality formation split along their dualism.

Mu's refusal of unified personality and his cognizance of multiple and contradictory forms of identity are also reflected in his restless search for new techniques and his resistance to forming a unified, signature style. Du Heng discerns a connection between dual personality and Mu's incessant search for new techniques, noting how the fresh techniques Mu uses have become seductive in and of themselves, hence the willed absence of a unified writing style.[20] In Mu's preface to the revised edition of *Poles Apart*, he himself enunciates his conviction about the primacy of technique:

> I wrote the stories in this collection with the purpose of experimenting and exercising my techniques—this is still what I hold to be the aim for my writing. As to what I write, I do not care nor have I ever cared; what I care about is the question of "how I write." After publishing these stories, I have thankfully received critics' advice that I should learn from life and overcome the incorrect elements in my consciousness. But the people to whom I am most grateful, from the depths of my heart, are those who can advise me on the shortcomings of my techniques.[21]

In the context of competing ideological indoctrinations by different political camps, this gesture of celebrating the primacy of technique takes on a certain poignancy; as a resistance to forces of indoctrination, it reveals both the indoctrinating force and the receiving force as partners in a game of hypocritical adherence to a false unity of belief. Declining to be a hypocrite who chooses a party alliance out of convenience or from an absence of rational investigation, Mu turns his multifarious experiments and performances in style and technique into a statement on literary and ideological autonomy. If his life choices, ideological shifts, and assertions about the primacy of technique can be seen as performative enactments of his principled resistance

20. Du Heng, "About Mu Shiying's Creative Work," 11.

21. "Preface to the Revised Edition" (*Gaidingben tiji*), *Poles Apart* (Shanghai: Xiandai shuju, 1933), 1–2; previously published in *Modern Publishing* 9 (January 1933): 13.

to unity, his death was the final payment he had to make for his love of contradictions, inconsistencies, and multiplicities.

His proclivity toward multiplicity, contradiction, and disunity is nowhere more pronounced as in his fictional works themselves. In almost every aspect of his writing—whether subject matter, style, form, content, semantics, or syntax—he moved in multiple directions. Although my textual analyses that follow this section concentrate more on his work associated with new sensationism—the three collections of stories he published after *Poles Apart*— a short summary of the range of his works can serve as proof of their multiplicity. As early as 1930, when Mu was eighteen, he had already published a novel called *Interflow* (*Jiaoliu*, 1930) and a few short stories, which he never mentioned later, probably due to their being early exercises in his craft.[22] A few years later, Mu would become a famous writer with stories published in *Short Story Monthly, Les Contemporaines,* and other prestigious literary journals. He quickly came out with two collections of stories, *Poles Apart* (1932; 1933) and *Public Cemetery* (1933), followed by two more, *Platinum Statue of a Female Nude* (*Baijin de nüti suxiang,* 1934) and *Saint Virgin's Love* (*Sheng chunü de ganqing,* 1935).

Poles Apart, as the title suggests, recounts the immense disparity between the haves and the have-nots as the result of the urban-rural dichotomy. The first five stories, published in the 1932 collection, are written in the first-person, gritty slang of the lumpen proletariat, and celebrate the rural ethos of morality, loyalty, and male chivalry. The first of these stories, "Black Whirlwind" (*Hei xuanfeng*), makes allusions to the rebel sentiment from the heroic tradition of *Water Margin,* and reproduces that novel's story of Pan Jinlian's adultery in a modern setting. Mu's modern day Pan Jinlian is a country girl seduced by dazzling city culture, embodied in a male college student from Shanghai. A cause-effect relationship is constructed between her betrayal of the rural ethos and the oppression of the rural underclass. The same causal relationship also appears in the title story, "Poles Apart," in which a poor country boy is betrayed by his childhood sweetheart when she leaves him for the allure of the city. Mu's representative of the rural male underclass sees himself as cast off by his woman, who opts for modernity and the city, the double source of his oppression. To resist this oppression, Mu's protagonists in *Poles Apart* flaunt extreme masculine notions of male chivalry and brotherhood, making the critique of capitalist seduction and corruption a hypermasculinist enterprise. Through their skillful allusions to *Water Margin,* these stories successfully nativize the Marxist critique of urban capitalism.

22. Yan Jiayan rediscovered the novel and the stories, and later even located other works by Mu unknown to historians. See Yan Jiayan, "Tracking Down Mu Shiying's Novels" (*Mu Shiying changpian xiaoshuo zhuizongji*), preface to *Complete Works of Mu Shiying* (*Mu Shiying quanji*) (Guangzhou: Huacheng chubanshe, forthcoming).

Three stories were added to the revised addition of *Poles Apart,* published in 1933: "The Baker Who Stole Bread" (*Tou le mianbao de mianbaoshi*), "The Man Who Lost His Arm" (*Duan le tiao gebo de ren*), and "Oil Cloth" (*Youbu,* 1931), all written around the time when Mu started writing city fiction. The narrative mode of these stories is fundamentally different from the earlier five: a more detached third-person narrative is used and thus less turbulent emotions intrude upon the narrative. In "The Baker Who Stole Bread" and "The Man Who Lost His Arm," the setting moves from the countryside to the city, and the protagonists change from country folk to workers exploited by the capitalist system. The alienation of the worker from the commodity he produces is the central theme of the former story, while the latter graphically describes the physical dismemberment of a worker—the loss of an arm—as an example of the capitalist dehumanization of workers by machines and those who own them. These three stories can be considered exercises in classical Marxist themes in the urban setting.

After *Poles Apart,* however, Mu's work, in three collections of stories, focused in on the city of Shanghai itself, its urban culture, and its resident personalities. The masculinist and nationalist rejection of the urban disappears, and an enchantment with new sensationist techniques and the new urban ethos and lifestyle takes over. Distinctly Marxist themes also take a back seat. These are the works that made Mu famous, and which have remained his most important work.

He wrote two other novels in addition to the above mentioned collections: *This Generation of Ours* (*Women zheyidai,* 1936) and *China March* (*Zhongguo xingjin,* 1936). The former was an incomplete novel serialized in *Times Daily* (*Shidai ribao*) between February 16 and April 23 of 1936; it describes the bombing of Shanghai by the Japanese on January 28, 1932, through the perspective of an elite, well-off, intellectual protagonist. The preface to the novel is tellingly entitled "Song of Slaves" (*Nuli zhige*); in dramatic, passionate language, it calls for the overthrow of imperialism and an end to slavery. But through the rest of the novel now extant, the nationalistic zeal of the preface is seriously undercut by the thoughts and actions of the elite protagonist who comes across as a Don Quixote figure lost in grandiose visions of chivalry. The third-person narrator's voice pokes fun at the sudden eruption of patriotism in the elite intellectual, for the protagonist fantasizes that he will be celebrated as a war hero when in reality he does not have the courage even to participate in battle. Besides using some of his famous new sensationist techniques, Mu employed the gritty language of soldiers in battle, much like his use of lumpen-proletariat slang just a year before. Mu remained fascinated by techniques such as interior monologue, using them superbly to spell out the disjunction between the reality of battle and the protagonist's grandiose illusion premised on a hypocritical patriotism.

The latter novel, *China March,* was previously named *China 1931* (*Zhong-*

guo 1931) and was supposed to offer a panoramic vision of China in 1931; the famous story "Shanghai Foxtrot" (*Shanghai de hubuwu*) was meant to be a fragment of this larger work. Although there were announcements that the novel was completed and was to be part of the Companion Literature Series (*liangyou wenxue congshu*), it was never published. Zhao Jiabi, the renowned Americanist and a college friend of Mu, replied to Yan Jiayan's inquiry regarding this novel in a letter:

> I encouraged Mu's writing of this novel earlier entitled *China, 1931.* At the time I was taken with American writer John Dos Passos's trilogy, of which there was one book entitled *1919.* Mu borrowed it from me, read it, and prepared to follow Dos Passos's methods to write about China, mingling historical background, personalities in the center of history, the author's own experience, and the narration of fictional stories into a unique novel. This novel was later called *China March....*
>
> According to my recollection, this novel did end up at the printer's. As it used words of varying typographic sizes, it left a comparatively deep impression on me. But it is true that the book was never published, and as far as I remember, its chapters were not published in any journals.[23]

If the novel had been published, it would have been the only new sensationist novel from modern China, comparable perhaps not just to Dos Passos but to Kawabata's new sensationist classic *Asakusa Kurenaidan.*

Besides three known novels, four collections of stories, a few uncollected stories, and numerous essays, Mu is supposed to have written two screenplays during his sojourn in Hong Kong: *Long Live China* (*Zhongguo wansui*) and *Fifteen Patriots* (*Shiwu yishi*), neither of which was published or made into films.[24] In sum, his writing can be described as acts of performance, forever in search of new styles, offering no comfort in conformity and unity, just as he sought for the right ideological home for his endeavors. In an era of volatile ideological contentions and nationalist zeal, such performance was a rebellion against the multiple pressures besetting the writer and a courageous assertion of literary autonomy. But it was also fated to be a performance in controversy, one that played with fire and resulted in the tragic finale of his assassination.

DISPLACING THE NATION WITH GENDER

Like Liu Na'ou, who depicted the modern girl as the embodiment of urban capitalist modernity, Mu Shiying turned to gender as a way to sort out the complexities of modern urban experience in his new sensationist stories. In

---

23. Quoted in ibid.
24. Huang Jundong, "Mu Shiying and His Work" (*Mu Shiying yu ta de zuopin*), *Four Seasons* (*Siji*) 1 (November 1972): 40.

Mu's work, gender displays and sometimes questions the properties of the modern and the urban, but it is not the national or the colonial per se that is either propounded or repudiated. As the modern girl is heavily Westernized and her character subverts the notion of a quintessential Chinese-ness, the division between the colonial (as Western) and the colonized (as Chinese) is blurred and interrupted, and the grounds for establishing a solid notion of the national are made unstable. Unlike typical nationalist narratives, which either deploy women as the symbol of colonial oppression or the bulwark of traditional virtue, here the modern girl displaces the nation and becomes a figure entrenched in a universal capitalism that transcends national boundaries.

A typology of Mu's female protagonists would reflect their wide range of classes, ages, and social status, but his most important figure is still the modern girl. Unlike Liu Na'ou's modern girl, however, Mu's modern girl is a cross between the urban femme fatale, the prostitute, the dancing hostess, and the withered beauty. On the surface, she flaunts her emotional and physical audacity, and emasculates men, but at the core she is vulnerable to criticism and contempt, often concealing a tragic experience. Mu's only modern girls in the Liu Na'ou mode, fearlessly defending their emotional and physical autonomy, are Rongzi in "Men Kept as Playthings," Cai Peipei in "May" (*Wuyue*), and the beautiful protagonist in "Red Diana" (*Hongse nülieshen*). In "Men Kept as Playthings," which is most akin to Liu Na'ou in both style and content, Rongzi is an aggregation of the appropriate signs of the modern girl: her face masculine, her waist slender, her body snake-like, and her long legs built for dancing, she has "modern" eyes that can seduce and deceive; dressed in a sexy red *chongsam* with high slits and red satin high-heeled shoes, she wears red Tangee lipstick, speaks in "stimulating" and "fresh" sentences, and writes as if she were Clara Bow; in all, she is a mixture of "jazz, machines, speed, urban culture, American flavor, and modern beauty," as the narrator tells us.[25] Like Liu Na'ou as well, Mu provides an ironic account of one man's hopeless infatuation with her; but unlike Liu, whose male protagonists simply lose the game, Mu elaborates on the male protagonist's futile construction of defense mechanisms against her allure. Obviously phallic and masculinist, these defence tactics include smoking to resist the seduction of the modern girl, nurturing misogyny to fight her seduction, and finally buying a walking cane to fill the absence of a girl walking next to him. Mu Shiying pokes fun at the emasculated young man, who drums up masculinist defense tactics to conceal a deep sense of loss and the feeling that he cannot catch up with her or keep her. Like Liu Na'ou's modern girls, Rongzi, as the embodiment of urban modernity, provides the Chinese male protagonist an opportunity to experience a simulated urban romance in Hollywood style, but

25. Mu Shiying, *Public Cemetery*, 18.

he finds himself emasculated in the process. She is part of Shanghai's urban phantasmagoria, filled more with material surfaces and less with substance and depth, strong in visual and erotic allure and weak in executing a full and lived romantic experience. The ironic tone Mu employs in describing the male protagonist's masculinist defenses parallels the extent to which nationalism, as the other half of masculinism, is made noncompelling.

Mu frequently represents a more complex figure of the modern girl—a mixture of the Liu Na'ou–style modern girl, the dancing hostess, the prostitute, and the exhausted, waning beauty. While also bearing signs of Hollywood beauties (frequent references to Clara Bow, Norma Shearer, and others), she has experienced a tragedy of some kind, is exhausted by the modern lifestyle, and is not an emasculating agent but an object of sympathy to the male protagonists. In some ways, this is a modern girl who has aged since Liu Na'ou's time of the late 1920s; with her youth faded and beauty withered, she can no longer remain the confident and fearless urban femme fatale. Like Ibsen's Nora, who would most likely have become degraded by circumstances after she had left home (as Lu Xun predicted during the May Fourth), she is as much, if not more, oppressed by the speedy passing of time as the male protagonists, since her worth is premised on her youthful beauty. Furthermore, this modern girl is also an economical and social being, having to confront her economic needs and low social status. She gets ensnared in the commodity logic of capitalism in three different but interrelated ways: her youthful beauty is attached with value, hence the waning of her youth and beauty is literally the loss of value; her status as a modern girl is premised on her role as an object of visual consumption by male consumers; and her facile offer of free sex further compromises her as if she were a prostitute. Commodity logic—her desirability and purchasability, or lack thereof, and these features' quantification—conditions her relation with the many men around her. In the pursuit of urban thrills, she is often the victim, not the perpetrator.

Craven "A," named thus because she smokes Craven "A" cigarettes, is a representative figure in this regard. Initially, this girl with a Parisian face, who dances the rhumba like an African native and imitates Norma Shearer in her facial expressions, is presented as a classic urban femme fatale whose erotic allure mesmerizes the male protagonist into a prolonged journey of gazing over her body. The long passage describing his gaze is a new sensationist feat of technique, sensuality, and intense eroticism, objectifying the female body into a terrain of nature:

> Examining her carefully—that's my hobby. A person's face is a map. If one studies its terrain, mountain ranges, rivers, climate, rainfall, one can immediately realize the customs, habits and ways of thinking of that place. In front of me is an outstanding national map:
>
> On the northern frontier is a black pine forest, its border marked by a white

silk band, like a wisp of white cloud in the black sky filled with soot. The black
pine forest is where fragrances are produced. South of it is a plain, a white marble plain—the origin of intelligent and witty people. Below is a verdant plateau,
on its sides are two long and slender grasslands. Legend says that here are the
nests of ancient sorceresses. Next to the grasslands are two lakes, where reside
two kinds of people: typically pessimistic Northerners and optimistic South-
erners. The weather there is fickle, sometimes below zero, sometimes above
the boiling point, with some torrid seasonal winds but very little rain. At the
southern end of the plateau is a volcano, its top slightly open, emitting the fragrance of Craven "A." Peering inside the volcano, one can see the neatly
arranged beige-colored lava. In the center of the lava is pulsating fire. This volcano suggests that passion is stored underground. People in this region are
still very primitive, offering men as sacrifices during yearly volcano rituals. For
travelers, this nation is not a very safe place. Passing the volcano one then
reaches a cape.

The map below is covered under a black and white checkerboard-design
of plain, light clouds! But its topography can still be seen. Inland past the cape
is a fertile plain. Judging from the height, windiness, elasticity, and fullness of
the horizon, there is a deep layer of clay here. The climate is mild, always around
seventy-five degrees, just enough rainfall, and the land is moist and rich. Twin
hills resolutely stand on the plain, their purple peaks seem to want to protrude
from the clouds. This must be a scenic spot. I playfully thought about the inscriptions of words and poems on the peaks, and considered the sequence of
my future trip there. But the defense of that nation is too weak, there is not
even a defense post on the cape. If one sneaks in, one can occupy this verdant
plain and its scenic spots within an hour. Further south, one can see the plain
becoming a slope, evenly pared—the map below is obstructed by a table in the
middle!

The south has more intoxicating spring winds than the north, more fertile
land, more beautiful lakes, more mysterious valleys, and lovelier landscapes!

As I longed for it, I lowered my head and saw two dikes through the netted
stockings. I saw a land that looks like salmon in white sauce. At the end of the
dikes sleep two slender, black-beaked, white sea gulls, deeply engrossed in their
early summer dreams beside a secluded beach.

Between the two dikes, judging from its topography, is a triangular alluvial
plain. Near the ocean there must be an important port, a large commercial
center. Otherwise why should such delicate dikes be built? The night scene of
the metropolis is lovely—just think about the sunset glow, the sound of waves
at the seaport, the majestic posture of the large steamboat coming into port,
the spindrifts by the bow of the boat, and the tall buildings by the bank![26]

In no other new sensationist story can one find such a sustained use of simile, nor such an intense eroticization and objectification of the female body in
seductive, voyeuristic language. While dangerous ("offering men as sacri-

26. Ibid., 108–110.

fices"), she is easily conquered ("one can occupy this verdant plain and its scenic spots within an hour"), unlike Liu Na'ou's modern girls. We soon find out that Craven "A" is treated by the men and women around her as a tramp, has no power over men, and actually harbors the tragic experience of being raped at the age of seventeen. This modern girl is a woman with a past and a foreseeably tragic future. The protagonist notes how many of his friends "had all traveled to that nation because transportation is easy and it takes only one or two days to travel through the entire nation," and "had all considered it a great site for a short trip," but none had considered remaining faithful to her or maintaining a steady relationship with her.[27] The male protagonist sympathizes with her as an unfortunate woman despised and "squeezed by society," and feels empathy with her existential loneliness, but he too considers her nothing more than a fragrant harbor (the author jestingly uses the city name of Hong Kong, which literally means "fragrant harbor") for temporary travel and respite. His gender superiority and economic status (as an elite lawyer) secure his relationship with Craven "A" as but a harmless escapade, replete with voyeuristic and sexual pleasures and without the need to assume any responsibilities. He remains the voyeur and the gazer, for which he even gets compensated by her voluntary offer of sex and confidentiality.

In the last paragraph in the passage quoted above, a playful simile is constructed comparing Craven "A"'s vagina and a seaport, which seems to suggest Shanghai as the seaport—a metropolis and a commercial center with tall buildings on the bund ("the bank"). The "majestic" steamboat coming into port is obviously a metaphor for sexual intercourse. The question here is whether this passage can be read allegorically—whether the several references to the body of Craven "A" as a nation or a national map refer specifically to Shanghai and China. But given the use of the metaphor of Hong Kong as another indication for her easy conquest, the borrowing of the Shanghai seaport metaphor seems to be devoid of historical or allegorical intentions. Given that the steamboat image projects specifically Chinese masculinity, not Japanese or Euro-American masculinity (there is no indication in the story that Craven "A" also goes out with non-Chinese men), the metaphor is clearly not meant to be extended to the dimension of interracial gender inequality or the colonial implications of sexuality. Likewise, the reference to her body as a nation is not at all inscribed with the national/cultural characteristics of a known nation, but instead with natural characteristics, described thus to cohere with the metaphor of conquest as territorial domination. Where there is ample opportunity for Mu Shiying to make allegorical links between the modern girl and Shanghai's semicolonial condition, he simply chooses to disengage from questions of the national in political terms.

27. Ibid., 112–113.

Instead, Mu's consistent frame of reference is universalistic capitalism as the fountainhead of urban culture, a capitalism that dictates human relationships through a form of commodity logic. Along with aggregating urban material cultural artifacts and signs in his stories, Mu also shows how this commodity logic infiltrates gender relations and gender identity. Besides commodifying the modern girl's youthful beauty by giving it calculable value, commodity logic also renders the modern girl as an inanimate object like a mannequin in storefront display windows. Note this passage describing Craven "A," further into the story:

> Lying on my bed is a plaster mannequin like the one displayed in the window of a women's merchandise store. . . . Is this an organism or a non-organism? At night the plaster mannequin is also naked. . . . Is this an organism or a non-organism? This is not a plaster mannequin, not a marble statue, not a snow-person. It is some flowing lines transplanted from a painting and some *cream*, forming a painting of a human figure under my sheets.[28] (original English in italics)

Also note the title story of Mu's collection *Platinum Statue of a Female Nude*, in which a male doctor, who embodies the classic new sensationist male voyeuristic gaze, examines a newlywed woman's naked body. His vision of her, conveyed through interior monologues and third-person narration, conveys a picture of inanimateness. She looks "emotionless," wears "black jewel-stone earrings," has a "bloodless face," and is depicted as a "platinum statue":

> Using slender ankles as the foundation, one leg standing erect and the other bent, is a platinum statue of a female nude. She stands there, an inorganic statue with no shame, no moral concepts or human desires. She is so metallic and sleek that his gaze swiftly glides over the lines of the body. This feelingless, emotionless statue stands there waiting for his order.[29]

What augments her inanimate state is the reverse anthropomorphizing of inorganic things, such as her black undergarment, which "languidly climbs her pale shoulders," and the straps of her slip, which "yawn" when she moves. She is appropriately not the owner of her body: she talks about it as if she were talking about a stranger. She has no resistance, and passively awaits his orders. Her existence matters only insofar as she triggers a repressed sexual longing in him. It is only natural, therefore, that at the end of the story he quickly finds a wife who will satisfy his sexual desires, to complete his list of possessions, which already includes his car, his dog, his coffee, and his cigarettes. Woman is but one material possession among an array of material objects in his life.

28. Ibid., 127.
29. Mu Shiying, *Platinum Statue of a Female Nude*, 13.

This metallic, lifeless, and machine-like modern girl and the "marble statue–like" Black Peony in "Black Peony" (*Hei mudan*) are analogous to automobiles in their being at the forefront of technological modernity and in their possessing commodity value. Images of the inorganic, the mechanical, and the lifeless combine to project these modern girls as if they are mechanical dolls or automatons, joining the material world of commodities as members. As commodity-like beings, these modern girls are subjected to a commodity regime similar to that of the prostitutes. Susan Buck-Morss, a feminist critic of Walter Benjamin's work, has noted that within the free sexuality of prostitution, "sex has a machine-like character and attraction a commodity-like one" and sexual desire, without the "distances within desire that were the source of the 'aura' of love," becomes cathected solely to commodities, demanding immediate possession.[30] The brief sexual encounters between the modern girls and the male protagonists in Mu's stories come without strings attached and are just as devoid of love as prostitution. Sexual desire, like a commodity, demands instant purchase. It is the "victory of the inorganic over the organic"[31] which the commodity regime of capitalism has ushered in.

At this juncture, it is instructive to note that this seductive figure of the modern girl is constructed differently in new sensationist fiction than in nationalist narratives from colonial India. In talking about what he calls the "woman-and-gold" figure, the Indian materialistic seductress similar to Chinese modern girls, Partha Chatterjee notes that she is the object *against* whom Indian-ness gets constructed. This figure represented

> the sign of the economic and political subordination of the respectable male householder in colonial Calcutta. It connoted humiliation and fear, the constant troubles and anxieties of maintaining a life of respectability and dignity, the sense of intellectual confusion and spiritual crisis. . . . The sign, therefore, was located with negative meanings: greed, venality, deception, immorality, aggression, violence. . . . From this signification stemmed a strategy of survival, of the stoical defense of the autonomy of the weak. . . . It involved, as we have seen, an essentialization of the "inner" self of the man-in-the-world and an essentialization of womanhood in the protective and nurturing figure of the mother. This inner sanctum was to be valorized as a haven of mental peace, spiritual security, and emotional comfort: woman as mother, safe, comforting, indulgent, playful, and man as child, innocent, vulnerable, ever in need of care and protection.[32]

If, as Chatterjee notes, in the Indian context of colonialism, the woman-and-gold figure is vilified and a coping strategy develops which enshrines the

30. Susan Buck-Morss, "The Flâneur, the Sandwichman and the Whore: The Politics of Loitering," *New German Critique* 39 (Fall 1986): 99–139.

31. Ibid.

32. Partha Chatterjee, *The Nation and Its Fragments* (Princeton: Princeton University Press, 1993), 68–69.

mother-son relationship and Indian spirituality, the moralist repudiation of this female figure is also conveniently justified as anticolonial, and therefore her dismissal is more righteous and more decisive. But in Mu Shiying's work, the modern girl is never repudiated on moralist, anticolonial, or spiritual grounds; rather, she is often a compatriot with the male protagonist, sharing the alienating experience of living in a fast, inorganic modern world. If nationalism allows for the rejection of the woman-and-gold figure on the grounds of anticolonialism and patriarchal morality, the absence of such grounds in Mu's representation of the modern girl indicates the author's ambivalent positioning vis-à-vis nationalism and patriarchy.

THE SEMICOLONIAL SUBJECT IN THE SPINNING CITY

No new sensationist fiction is complete without technically superb renderings of the urban setting which houses both the modern girls and their male gazers. In Mu's work, the city itself often takes on a life of its own, becoming the prime locus where capitalism has realized itself and where the characters experience the thrill and alienation of capitalist modernity. Many of Mu's stories can be said to be "synoptic" studies of the city in which the city itself becomes the main character, with no main protagonist but with many characters and scenes juxtaposed to convey the complex pattern of city life.[33] Shanghai existed as a cultural semiotic with images of flow and fluidity—as the word "*hai*" ("sea") in "Shanghai" connotes—ever since it became a treaty port in the mid-nineteenth century,[34] but the particular Shanghai of the early 1930s in Mu's fiction is chiefly the site of urban capitalism, a cluster of irritable nervous energies obsessed with consumption, speed, and carnal thrill. Mu's representation of time and space in the city appropriately exhibits such irritable energies.

"Five People in a Nightclub," written in fragmentary form, is a good ex-

33. Blanche H. Gelfant's definition of the synoptic novel is applied here to Mu's short stories. Gelfant defines it this way: "The synoptic novel makes the city itself protagonist. It is an inclusive form that presents the complex pattern of city life—its contrasting and contiguous social worlds (the ironic union of gold coast and slum, of gangland and bohemia, of Harlem and Chinatown), its multifarious scenes, its rapid tempos and changing seasons, its tenuous system of social relationships, meetings, and separations, and its total impact as a place and atmosphere upon the modern sensibility. . . . Unless the separate scenes and incidents of the synoptic novel are also integrated within a clearly defined formal frame, the novel will collapse into a loose series of incidents." She also argues that Dos Passos's novels are the representative synoptic novels. See her *The American City Novel* (Norman: University of Oklahoma Press, 1954), 14. As Mu's "Shanghai Foxtrot" was originally meant to be a section of the long novel *China 1931*, modeled on John Dos Passos's *1919*, the borrowing of the term "synoptic" is certainly appropriate.

34. See Yingjin Zhang, *The City in Modern Chinese Literature and Film* (Stanford: Stanford University Press, 1996), 117–129.

ample of a work of sypnotic fiction. It begins with a depiction of five people at five different places at one given time, Saturday afternoon, April 6, 1932. A tycoon who speculates in gold loses his entire fortune due to the plummeting of gold prices; a college student is broken-hearted; a socialite modern girl is reminded of her fading beauty by the malicious gossip of passersby; an intellectual solemnly ponders the question of identity in his room; and a government clerk is suddenly fired from work. About fifteen other characters, named and nameless, appear in the course of the story. Depicting simultaneous temporality in different spaces, Mu spatializes time not to prolong it so much as to convey the compression of a multitude of events into one single moment, using a "latitude" instead of a "longitude" method to depict time and space.[35] This of course is also the method of montage, juxtaposing seemingly irrelevant events occurring at the same time for a combined, associational effect. At the moment, however, the reader is not given many clues as to how these montaged scenes relate to each other.

The next section of the story, entitled "Saturday Night," has no characters and no plot, but is instead a long discourse on what a Saturday night in the city means. An overdose of images—ice cream, nightclubs, chicken à la king, cafe noir, jazz, kissproof lipstick, neon lights, whiskey, chocolates, and so on—are juxtaposed with newspaper headlines in John Dos Passos's style:

> (Universal Benefit Realty accrued net annual interest totalling one-third of its capital investment
>   100,000 taels
> Did the northeastern provinces fall
> No   the northeastern provincial militia are still fighting a last-ditch battle against the Japs
> Countrymen quickly come join the Monthly Donation Society
> *Continental News* already sold fifty thousand copies
> 1933 Bartok
>   cafeteria line)[36]

Typographically adventurous, daring in its direct excerpting of newspaper headlines, this passage also functions as a montage, compressing into a single moment a multitude of events occurring over an expansive spread of space. Although the passage alludes to the Sino-Japanese War, it is the technical experimentation that is foregrounded, not the historical events per se.

Mu's linguistic adventure is especially notable for creating, in very short, condensed passages, an almost fantastic vision of the cityscape:

35. Mu refers to this "latitude method" in a later essay on cinema, "'Licentious' and Dogmatic Pseudo-Realist" (*"Baiwu jinji" yu shuojiaoshi de ni xianshi zhuyi zhe*), *Morning Post* (*Chenbao*), May 5, 1935.

36. Mu Shiying, *Public Cemetery*, 72.

"Dawan Evening Paper!" The newspaper boy opens his blue mouth, inside which are blue teeth and a blue tongue. The neon high-heel shoe in front of him points its toe directly at his mouth.

"Dawan Evening Paper!" Suddenly he has a red mouth again, from which his tongue sticks out. The enormous neon wine bottle in front of him spills wine into his mouth.

Red streets, green streets, blue streets, purple streets . . . a city adorned with vibrant colors! Dancing neon lights—multicolored light waves, fluctuating light waves, colorless light waves—a sky flooded by light waves. Now there are wine, cigarettes, high-heel shoes, and also clocks in the sky. . . . [37]

Neon lights, the symbol of city nightlife, overwhelm the scene to such a degree that even the sky becomes artificial. The gigantic neon wine bottle spilling wine into the mouth of the newspaper boy demonstrates the unreal atmosphere of the city at night.

The next section, entitled "Five Happy People," depicts the five people encountering each other at the Empress Nightclub, all indulging in wild abandon. The perspective of the section mimics the circular motion of the revolving door of the nightclub, moving from person to person without premeditated order, while the section's language aptly captures the confusion of people in syncopated rhythm and disconnected images. The rhythm accelerates as time runs out for these people, and at the end we see the gold tycoon shooting himself in the head, and the other people standing around and gazing at his corpse in silence. The last section then depicts the four people attending the tycoon's funeral procession.

An important aspect of city life, Mu points out in this story, is the unalterable linearity of time. Saturday afternoon leads to Saturday night and then to Sunday morning—no one can alter the forward march of time. It is time that is the prime oppressor for his urban characters: when the night runs out, they all have to face an even deeper disillusionment than they had faced the day before. The coward kills himself, but the ones who continue living are not heroes either. Time, as symbolized by the flow of cars and the rushing of trains, is the rival with whom they have to compete. Those who can't are squeezed out from the pace of the city; they "fall from life." [38]

"Shanghai Foxtrot," perhaps Mu's most famous story, presents the city as protagonist even more self-consciously, beginning and ending with evocations of Shanghai as a "paradise built in hell," and anthropomorphizing the city into a living being with pulsating heartbeats. Again, there is no conventional plot or characterization in the story, but a series of scenes loosely juxtaposed in a cinematic montage. A massive number of characters roam the narrative, ranging from a gigolo, a jewelry merchant, a concubine, and a rich

37. Ibid., 72–73.
38. Mu Shiying, "Self-Preface" (*Zixu*), in *Public Cemetery*, 3.

capitalist to gangsters and laborers, and the perspective of the story registers this roaming with the fluid movement of a film camera. As the story begins, a long shot of the city zooms into a close-up of Lincoln Boulevard, where a nameless man is assassinated by three anonymous contract killers clad in long black robes. The next shot swings from a roaring train to a car waiting for the train to pass, then follows the car through the streets to a house. The view from the moving car is a new experience of speed and visuality:

> The painted, white legs of trees on the street, the legs of electric poles, the legs of all inanimate objects . . . like a military *revue,* young girls extending their crossed legs fully powdered . . . a row of painted white legs. Along that quiet road, through the curtained windows of the residential area, red, purple, and green virgin lights stealthily sneak out as if they were the eyeballs of the city.[39]

A man, who bears the ironic first name of Youde ("having morality"), gets out of the car and enters his house. He is met by his young wife who demands money from him. They exchange a few words. The man's son enters, whose first name Xiaode ("small morality") is equally ironic, and he also asks for money from his father. Then, the wife and son go out together in their brand new 1932 Studebaker, passing through the same street scene, which is now rendered in an exact repetition of the passage quoted above. The car rushes forward, passes billboards, almost runs over a man, then continues past Morton Church and the Great World department store, and arrives at a nightclub. The scene cuts to the inside of the nightclub, the whirling dancers and laughing people depicted in rhythmic language:

> An azure dusk envelopes the entire place. A *saxophone* extends its neck, its mouth gaping open, and shouts at the people. In the center of that smooth dancing floor are floating skirts and floating corners of jackets, delicate heels, heels, heels, heels, heels. Undisciplined hair and men's faces. Men's white shirt collars and women's smiling faces. Extended arms, jade earrings touching shoulders. Round tables are in an orderly row, but the chairs are disorderly. In dark corners stand waiters clad in white. The smell of alcohol, the smell of perfume, the smell of English ham, the smell of cigarettes . . . A confirmed bachelor sits in the corner drinking black coffee to stimulate his nerves.[40] (original English in italics)

As the stepmother and son dance with other people in the nightclub, the atmosphere becomes increasingly charged with moral abandon, adultery, and lies. The narrative camera then pans the scene again except in reverse order to vividly present the sensation of movement in the nightclub as swirlingly dizzy and exciting:

39. Mu Shiying, *Public Cemetery,* 197. Italicized word in French in the original.
40. Ibid., 202.

A confirmed bachelor sits in the corner and uses black coffee to stimulate his nerves. The smell of alcohol, the smell of perfume, the smell of English ham, the smell of cigarettes. . . . In the dark corners stand waiters clad in white. The chairs are disorderly, but round tables are in an orderly row. Jade earrings touching shoulders, extended arms. Women's smiling faces and men's white shirt collars. Men's faces and undisciplined hair. Delicate heels, heels, heels, heels, heels. Floating corners of jackets, floating skirts. In the center is the smooth floor. It shouts at people, that *saxophone*, with its neck extended and mouth gaping open. An azure dusk envelopes the entire place.[41] (original English in italics)

Next scene: outside the nightclub, a rickshaw puller in between the Studebakers and Fords, and a pan-shot of people in the city engaged in pleasure and deceit contrasted immediately with the death of a laborer at a construction site. The narrative camera then moves to the Huadong Hotel, rising from one floor to the next until Mr. Liu Youde is caught in the viewfinder. But the camera does not dwell here and returns down to the street, this time to hawkers among whom stands a writer observing them in order to write the stories that will make him famous. The camera pauses a while here, letting this particular episode develop a bit: the writer is approached by an old woman asking for his help to read a letter. With curiosity he follows her, thinking there may be material for a story, only to find that she is prostituting her daughter-in-law for food. The camera moves away again to the street, where the young wife is with a Belgian jewelry merchant who pretends to be French. A series of images moves them from outside the Cathay Hotel to the bedroom:

> On the goblets, Mrs. Liu's two eyeballs are smiling.
> Inside the Studebaker, those two eyeballs soaked in cocktails are smiling between the leather collar of her jacket.
> Inside the Cathay Hotel, those two eyeballs soaked in cocktails are smiling beside the loosely fallen hair.
> In the elevator, those two eyeballs are smiling under purple eyelids.
> Inside a room atop the seventh floor of the Cathay Hotel, those two eyeballs are smiling on the crimson red cheeks.
> The jewelry merchant finds the pair of eyeballs under his own nose.
> Smiling eyeballs!
> White sheets!
> Panting. . . .
> Lying motionless on the bed, panting.[42]

Here, the montage is organized around the central image of her eyeballs. One can visualize the smiling eyes staying still while the backgrounds dis-

41. Ibid., 203–204.
42. Ibid., 211.

solve into different settings. Outside again: a sailor does not pay the fare to a rickshaw puller who can do nothing but sulk away. The camera then illuminates more scenes of the city under moonlight, which gives way to the rays of the rising sun. The camera sweeps in a panoramic shot of Shanghai, just like in the beginning of the narrative. The camera's swift, disjointed movements and Mu Shiying's highly innovative language dance the foxtrot along with the characters. Refrains, repetitions, anagrams, and listings of images provide variations in speed and motion. "Shanghai Foxtrot" is therefore not merely dancing the foxtrot *in* Shanghai, but depicts the rhythm of the city *as* a wild foxtrot (*hubuwu*) under the arched street lights (*hu deng*) of the city.

Both "Five People in a Nightclub" and "Shanghai Foxtrot" depict the dazzling speed of city life in such images as rushing trains, tirelessly twinkling neon lights, fast cars, revolving doors, and elevators, all monuments of modern technology. Scattered among these monuments are personalities whose features merge with each other, even though they come from different social, racial, and economic strata, panting with the pulsating, nervous rhythm of the techno-city. Although narrative time is often rendered in fluid motions of circularity, repetition, condensation, and spatialization, real time rushes by in its linearity and pushes aside those who cannot run along with it, hence the many characters who are out of tune with time and can only struggle toward their doom. "Life is mechanical and rushes forward at full speed, but we are just organic beings," moans the male protagonist in "Black Peony." To this, Black Peony replies, "We will surely fall one day halfway."[43]

In the preface Mu wrote in 1934 for *Platinum Statue of a Female Nude,* he echoes a similar sentiment:

> Life is an express train. Man is not a holiday traveler who sits on the train comfortably looking out at the passing scenery but a professional traveler who is forced to chase the train, running with all his might to catch up with it. An organic man competing with an inorganic steam locomotive: he will certainly be exhausted one day and tragically fall dead by the roadside.[44]

If we agree with the notion that "there is a definite relation between the kind of space occupied by the subject and the form the subject takes,"[45] the subjectivity of the Chinese male protagonist (or the author himself as presented in the preface above) can be seen as arising from this new technologized, urbanized modernity, emblematized by the rushing express train. Transformations in real space brought by technology (transportation and communication technologies in particular) and urbanization have, as Kathleen

43. Ibid., 219.
44. Mu Shiying, "Self-Preface" (*zixu*), in *Platinum Statue of a Female Nude,* 1.
45. Kathleen M. Kirby, *Indifferent Boundaries: Spatial Concepts of Human Subjectivity* (New York and London: The Guilford Press, 1996), 7.

Kirby argues, complicated the "physics of identity" considerably, especially since geographical borders can no longer safely contain people.[46] In Wolfgang Schivelbusch's analysis of the relationship between human subjectivity and rail travel in nineteenth-century Europe, he notes that "rail travel divorced body and psyche from their customary attachment to an external geographic space" and, as an experience, it was received "as an assault on the physical and psychic body." It was only when travelers gradually became accustomed to rail travel that they developed "new forms of attention" (the panoramic vision) and "new structures of consciousness" (a durable psychic shield) to help deflect excess stimuli.[47] This notion of drumming up new defense mechanisms—the psychic shield—is very similar to what I had earlier referred to as the Benjaminian notion of "protective shield" and Simmel's notion of the blasé attitude as means of deflecting new stimuli from the new urban experience. Speaking with a certain historical hindsight well after the industrial revolution, Benjamin, Simmel, and Schivelbusch have the luxury of seeing how the assaults of technological modernity produced new defenses, reconfiguring and readjusting the relationship between people and their environment. But Mu's Shanghai is caught at the very moment of the traumatic encounter with technological modernity, which simultaneously assaults and fascinates the subject who is as yet unable to develop a psychic shield to ward off the onslaught of stimuli it brings. Hence the naked recording of the overwhelming sensory experiences of the urban spectacle, and the existential paranoia about the express train, i.e., the speed of modern life.

This modern male, faced with an industrial culture that he did not help create, neither had a chance to devise defense mechanisms against urban stimuli nor felt completely at home in the urban city—it became a space, no longer a place (in the terms set up by Anthony Giddens, which I discussed in chapter 9). He often felt at a loss. Note how this figure differs from the way Benjamin characterizes the flâneur in nineteenth-century Paris:

> The street becomes a dwelling for the flâneur; he is as much at home among the facades of houses as a citizen in his four walls. To him the shiny, enamelled signs of business are at least as good a wall ornament as an oil painting is to a bourgeois in his salon. The walls are the desk against which he presses his notebooks; news-stands are his libraries and the terraces of cafés are the balconies from which he looks down on his household after his work is done.[48]

Leisurely, nonchalant, and sagacious, the flâneur saunters the streets, taking in the urban spectacle in its full visual splendor, as lit by gas lamps. His leisurely appearance is a "protest against the division of labor which makes

---

46. Ibid., 8–16.
47. Mentioned in ibid., 74.
48. Benjamin, "The Flâneur," 37.

people into specialists," and it is also "his protest against their industrious-ness," Benjamin explains.[49] Not only does he feel at home in the streets, he has the luxury of standing aloof from the city, filled with people doing their busy, specialized jobs. This aloofness of the flâneur, furthermore, has a gen-dered dimension, in that no woman could be a flâneur (or rather, a flâneuse) because of the sexual division of labor into the public and private realms in the nineteenth century,[50] and because the flâneur is shamelessly misogynist. The flâneur condemns prostitutes as "monstrous" and "stupid," which is his way of expressing his "moral fecundity," and he reduces woman in general to a "trope of beauty" since she is nothing but what she wears—costumes and jewelry—not even a person or a being.[51]

Mu's male subject is clearly by no means a flâneur. He does not condemn prostitutes and women; rather, like Yu Dafu's nocturnal wanderers discussed in chapter 4, he empathizes and sympathizes with them. The prostitute Yandi (whose name is a homonym for "cigarette butt") in "Night" (*Ye*), the ex-hausted senorita in "Lady in a Dark Green Shirt" (*Molü shan de xiaojie*), and the dancing hostess Lin Bamei in "Story from a Batch of Discarded Manu-scripts in the Local News Editorial Office" (*Benfu xinwenlan bianjishi li yizha feigao shang de gushi*) are clearly compatriots with the male protagonists, who share with them a rejection by modernity. Furthermore, he does not enjoy the ease and luxury of strolling and observing the crowds, prostitutes, and other urban spectacles with the "immense joy" and pleasant noncha-lance of the flâneur, who acts like an "independent, passionate, impartial" "prince."[52] On the contrary, he is often dispassionate, alienated, and melan-choly, finding urban modernity seductive and destructive at the same time. This male subject does not have the luxury of a cohesive and stable person-ality, which the flâneur enjoys as a precondition for his ability to stand aloof. If the male subject finds himself alienated from urban culture, it is not be-cause he wants to stand aloof, but because he cannot be a full participant: the space of Shanghai is an unsettling meeting ground for local cultures, colonial cultures, and imported/imposed metropolitan cultures. If he some-times appears to be an onlooker of urban spectacle, it is because his partic-ipatory rights were not given full expression and he only can consume the city visually, in an elusive form of ownership, or receive its overwhelming sensory stimuli without an apt defense mechanism.

These divergences from Baudelaire/Benjamin's flâneur foreground the problematic access to autonomy, independence, self-sufficiency, and coher-

49. Ibid., 55.
50. Janet Wolff, *Feminine Sentences* (Berkeley: University of California Press, 1990), 39–47.
51. Charles Baudelaire, *The Painter of Modern Life and Other Essays*, trans. and ed. Jonathan Mayne (London: Phaidon Press, 1964), 30–37.
52. Ibid., 9.

ence of Mu's male subjects. He is the farthest cry from the Cartesian subject who undergirds the Enlightenment subject in the West: coherent, consistent, and rational within a consistent, stable, and organized environment. Kathleen Kirby points out that the Cartesian/Enlightenment subject is the premise upon which the imperialist subject, who wishes to traverse and occupy territories, emerges during the Enlightenment.[53] Diametrically opposed to this territorially ambitious subject, Mu's subject is curiously closer in temperament to the postmodern subject, whose inside and outside are mismatched, divided, and deformed, and whose personality is multiply split. This is the subject whose experience of space can be described as a form of vertigo, "a feeling as if external objects whirled around the person affected, or as if he himself had been whirled around."[54] He is, to borrow Mu's own metaphor, the dizzy dancer of the foxtrot spinning around the dance floor. This subject, akin to the postmodern subject, is the semicolonial subject, whose disequilibrium results from the fact that he did not help build urban modernity and that he can neither fully participate in it nor be confidently aloof from it—he feels its seduction yet finds its exotic simulacra an unsettling experience.

TEXTUALITY AND JAPANESE "MULTICULTURAL" IMPERIALISM

If external reality is alienating and promises no autonomy or fulfillment to the semicolonial subject, then perhaps textual autonomy can offer a semblance of fulfillment. I have discussed how Mu Shiying's staunch claim to aesthetic autonomy underscores the multiplicity of his writing styles, and here I want to focus on one other aspect of this assertion of aesthetic autonomy in relation to dissimulation as a cultural practice under semicolonialism, namely, the profuse textuality of his works. By textuality I mean the ostensive self-reflexivity or self-referentiality (the way the text refers to itself), metafictionality (the way the text comments on the writing of the text itself), and intertextuality (the way the text refers to other texts) in Mu's work, all of which construct the world of the text as an enclosed structure with its own autonomous frames of reference divorced from physical reality. Within this enclosed structure of textuality, what would normally be considered a textual event seems to affect or transform reality.

One may call this a process of *textual dissimulation*: what is textual takes on a seemingly "real" character and gets imitated in real life; instead of art imitating life, life imitates art. Examples of textual dissimulation are numerous in Mu's work. Many of Mu's characters are readers of Mu's fiction, or they walk out of works from Mu's favorite reading list. Rongzi in "Men

53. Kirby, *Indifferent Boundaries*, 38–46.
54. Ibid., 97–99.

Kept as Playthings" reads Mu Shiying's work, besides being a fervent fan of Paul Morand, Yokomitsu Riichi, Horiguchi Daigaku, Sinclair Lewis, and Liu Na'ou. One of Mu's male characters in "May" reads Liu Na'ou's stories and his translations of Japanese new sensationist fiction. The male protagonist of "Public Cemetery" gives Lingzi a book of Dai Wangshu's poetry as a gift and calls her the lilac girl from Dai Wangshu's famous poem "Rainy Alley" (*Yuxiang*). In a telling self-reflexive moment in a later story, "Diary of a Poor Man" (*Pinshi riji*), several of Mu's most famous female characters from unrelated stories appear in person to the male narrator—Craven "A," Rongzi, and Lingzi—as if these fictional characters had suddenly become alive and entered the reality of another story. Various intertextual echoes with the works of Dai Wangshu, Liu Na'ou, Iketani Shinzaburo, John Dos Passos, and Yokomitsu Riichi, among others, are also prevalent, while moments of metafiction and metacriticism abound in such stories as Mu's "Pierrot" (original French title), where the writer protagonist finds himself in the company of his literary critics. These critics have various theoretical convictions—Freudianism, Marxism, modernism, impressionism, and new sensationism—and the protagonist wonders whether these "isms" actually offer useful paradigms of interpretation and writing. In another illuminating example of metafiction from "Public Cemetery," the male protagonist philosophizes upon the compatibility between setting and character:

> Girls need to be placed in appropriate settings. If Miss Ling exists amidst linear architecture, in a dress with a combination of the violent colors silver, red, black, and white, or in jazz and *neon light,* she will lose her particular charm of gentle melancholy. Her knitted brows belong to the white marble tombstone standing erect from the ground, to the row of evergreens, to the desolation of withered flowers. Her enchanting tone and dreamy smile belong to the expanse of the field, the bright, sunny climate; and her foggy eyes always stare at the hometown far away and her lonely mother [in the grave].[55] (original English in italics)

These practices of intertextuality, metafiction, and self-reflexivity show Mu Shiying so obsessed with his craft that he would breathe life into his fictional world and willfully substitute the world of reality with that of textuality.

This emphasis on textuality—which contributes to, and is intimately linked to, the experience of urban simulacra as a series of stimulating images—can also be seen as a strategy of disengagement from the real world. One may argue that it is a way to displace naked confrontation with the reality of semicolonialism and imperialism, and to avoid questions of politics and nationalism. It therefore becomes a challenge for the literary historian to explain why, in the last five years of Mu's life, he shifted from being apolitical to be-

---

55. Mu Shiying, *Public Cemetery,* 151.

ing a Nationalist Party supporter and then to being a Japanese collaborator. In an essay written in 1935 when he was an editor for the Nationalist-controlled newspaper *Morning Post*, he criticized writers as hesitant, cowardly, and confused, which is ironically a perfect description of his own former self as a writer of new sensationist fiction:

> Toward these confusing times, [the writers] throw suspicious glances. Within kaleidoscopic, myriad phenomena, they feel dizzy and also that they are too insignificant and weak. They neither have the courage to gaze at the tragedy besetting this nation, nor do they have a firm grasp of their own thoughts when they face the world of myriad lights and colors. They feel intuitively that they are a sacrificed generation, that the pressure of misfortune presses down on their souls, ready to crush them. But upon this misfortune they can only throw uneasy glances and paralyzed sighs. There is no struggle and no outcry.[56]

Here he points out the cosmopolitan intellectuals' simultaneous feelings of seduction ("dizzy") and powerlessness ("paralyzed sighs") toward urban phantasmagoria ("myriad lights and colors"; "kaleidoscopic, myriad phenomena"), and implies that these feelings are a form of cowardice when seen from the perspective of a nationalist. For a writer who thrived on multiplicity and contradictions, such a nationalist critique perhaps comes as no surprise—Mu could take on any perspective at will. What is notable instead is that his perspective here alludes to the semicolonial cultural condition of the cosmopolitans as a state of dizzying excitement and paralyzing disillusionment, indicating that contradiction and confusion are the stuff that constitutes their existential condition.

A few years later, he would contradict himself again, going to the other extreme and becoming a collaborator with Japanese imperialism, at which point he was hailed by Japanese writers as a high-profile case of a conversion from the anti-Japanese camp, and as testimony to the moral power of Japan as the leader of Asia. This again is perhaps not surprising, considering his performative and contradictory actions in the past, but Mu's multiple conversions, like those of Liu Na'ou, point specifically to the complex cultural politics under semicolonialism when nationalism could not serve as the indisputable haven of intellectual convictions.

There is practically nothing written about Mu's relationship with the Japanese state or with Japanese writers; apologists for Mu consider Mu the victim of double espionage—believing that Mu was actually a double agent working for the Nationalist government when he was assassinated—while critics categorically accuse him of being a traitor. We know that he was assassinated by some patriotic contingent while he was working for the Wang Jing-

---

56. Mu Shiying, "The Mentality of Confusion Among Writers" (*Zuojia qun de mimang xinli*), *Morning Post*, September 13, 1935.

wei regime, and we know of his criticism of Japanese imperialism in his essays written during his Nationalist period. But what was the nature of his actual contact with metropolitan Japanese culture? How did he relate to such Japanese new sensationist writers as Yokomitsu and Kataoka? And finally, how did Japanese writers perceive him?

After Mu Shiying was assassinated in June 1940, the September issue of *Literary World* (*Bungakukai*) carried a special section commemorating Mu, with essays by such important writers as Yokomitsu and Kataoka, critic Abe Tomoji, and other less famous personalities.[57] These essays offer us a glimpse of how Mu related to many of these writers, and, most importantly, how his conversion was perceived by these Japanese writers, from which we can infer crucial information about Mu's position of collaboration. These are revealing documents also because by this time Yokomitsu and Kataoka had become supporters of Japanese imperialism, so they raise crucial questions regarding the relationship between nationalism, Japanese new sensationism, and Japanese imperialism. They attest to how the promoters of aesthetic autonomy turned to nationalism within the domestic realm of Japan, and how this nationalism manifested itself as imperialism when it expanded its eager vision to other nations in Asia.

From these articles, we can infer the general circumstances of Mu's association with Japanese writers and journalists as follows. About one week after Mu returned to China from Hong Kong in the fall of 1939, he joined the delegation of Chinese bureaucrats of the "Temporary New Government" (of Wang Jingwei) to visit Japan as their journalistic representative. The delegation visited several places, including Odawara, where elementary school children and their mothers lined the streets and hailed them with "bonzai," to which Mu waved a flag in response (we can infer that Mu waved a Japanese national flag). Mu expressed his wish to meet with Japanese writers during this trip, and wrote down in Chinese characters the ones whom he wished to meet: Yokomitsu, Kataoka, and Hayashi Fusao. Kikuchi Kan, one of the leading figures on the Japanese literary scene, organized a dinner party for him with many writers present. He impressed these writers with his beauty (almost everyone reminisced about his handsomeness), eloquence (he spoke good English compared to their broken English), and charm (they thought him a rare equal to them). According to the writer and critic Kon Hidemi (the brother of Kon Tōko, one of the original members of the *shin-kankakuha* who later discontinued his activities with the group), who was there, Mu was simply splendid and pleasant, and the party was a big success. Mu mentioned to Kon that he hadn't had such a pleasant evening before, and he felt an affinity with these authors because all authors were people

57. Citations for these articles are given in the following footnotes.

after all. Based on this pleasant experience, Mu told Kon that he wanted to work for cultural cooperation between Japan and China. After the meeting, Mu later wrote several letters to Kon Hidemi in which he repeatedly mentioned that it was the responsibility of writers to bring peace to Japan and China in the future and to deepen the understanding between the two. Around this time, Mu seemed convinced that culture could generate mutual understanding for the benefit of both nations. Perhaps his naivete, which had injected an element of idealism into his endeavor, helped him justify his conversion. This idealism also explains why he never took precautions for his personal safety while working for the Wang regime, although his Japanese friends thought he should (Kikuchi Kan was especially worried). He seemed to have truly believed in the rhetoric of East Asian solidarity constructed through cultural communication.

The following May, Mu went to Japan for a second visit, this time as a newspaper representative in a government delegation, and met with Kon Hidemi again. Kon notes that Mu seemed rather dejected and reticent this time, noting how difficult it had been for Mu to try to convince young Chinese intellectuals to be his comrades (i.e., to convert them into being friendly towards Japan). It was that night over dinner that Mu met the famous critic Abe Tomoji for the first time, and they had an extended conversation about the war, with Abe doing most of the talking and Mu responding gingerly. Mu tensed up as the topic of the Sino-Japanese War was raised. From Mu's responses, as recorded by Kon and Abe, Mu was apparently troubled by his role as a go-between for China and Japan, and his idealism seemed visibly dampened. One month later, he was assassinated.

These composite pictures of his visits to Japan and his associations with Japanese writers show that Mu was not an untroubled collaborator; rather, he was psychologically torn over his idealism and its practice in the context of the high-pitched anti-Japanese sentiments during the Sino-Japanese War. It became difficult to assume the semicolonial strategy of bifurcating metropolitan Japan and the colonial Japan in this hypernationalist era.

Mu could not have known that his Japanese associates' perception of him on these two visits were far from flattering in terms of both their evaluation of his worth as a writer, and how they explicitly voiced an imperialist perspective, some more subtly than others. In the first of these commemorative articles, Matsutani Tatsunosuke, an inspector in the Japanese government's cultural institution Kōain in Shanghai, provides a seemingly straightforward report on the death of Mu Shiying and the circumstances of his assassination. He mentions how Mu's funeral was solemnly conducted at the Whitehouse Mortuary in the Japanese police zone in Shanghai under the guard of Japanese military police and the city police, and laments Mu's untimely death. But he ends with the typical imperialist rhetoric that Mu's death can serve as an opportunity to promote cultural cooperation between China and Japan, so it was not in vain.[58] In a similar vein, the article by the poet Kusano Shinpei pays tribute to Mu's death as a sacrifice for the sake of the "New Asia."[59]

The article by Kataoka generally follows the same train of thought but notes that there would have been no need to pay so much attention to Mu, who was not even considered a first-rate writer by Chinese critics, except for the fact that Mu was significant as an "intellectual with the ability to speak equally with Japanese writers," who "switched from the anti-Japanese group to the opposite position." Through his conversion to the pro-Japanese position, Mu reflected the desires of the people and provided "ethical confidence and courage" for the people's desires, which caused the Nationalist government to fear and hence eliminate him.[60] Unambiguously implying that Mu's conversion to Japanese imperialism reflected the wish of the Chinese people, Kataoka's naked imperialist rhetoric here justifies Japanese aggression in China as a mandate from the people themselves.

Yokomitsu's article dwelled more specifically on Mu's writing, and in it one can see how Japanese imperialism resorted to a multicutural ideology to support the rhetoric of East Asian coprosperity. As Seiji Lippit observes, Yokomitsu was at this time serializing his novel *Travel Melancholy* (*Ryoshū*, 1937–1946), which explores the essence of Japanese cultural identity and propounds the cultural ideology of the "Return to Japan" (*Nihon kaiki*) and the rejection of the West. For this and other reasons, Yokomitsu was accused in the postwar era of bearing war responsibility for his support of Japanese imperialism.[61] In this article commemorating Mu, Yokomitsu writes that he read Mu's story "Black Peony" and was struck by how little a Japanese reader such as himself could understand its value, for it expresses the pain of modern China struggling with its tradition. But just as Yokomitsu's own efforts to return to tradition (for the renewal of Japanese new sensationism) are important to him, so too is Mu's reference to Chinese tradition important to Mu. Yokomitsu notes that such a return is shared by all Oriental youth and will thus consolidate East Asia as an entity. Hence the important point is to maintain particularities (each particular culture) within similarities (the shared project of returning to tradition).[62] This article presents Japanese im-

58. Masutani Tatsunosuke, "Mourning Mr. Mu Shiying" (*Mu Shiying shi tsuitō*), *Literary World* (*Bungakukai*) 7 (September 1940): 172–173.

59. Kusano Shinpei, "Regarding Mr. Mu Shiying" (*Mu Shiying shi no koto*), *Literary World* (*Bungakukai*) 7 (September 1940): 176–178.

60. Kataoka Teppei, "Melancholy and Beautiful Face" (*Yūutsu na utsukushii kao*), *Literary World* (*Bungakukai*) 7 (September 1940): 178–179.

61. Seiji Lippit, *Japanese Modernism and the Destruction of Literary Form: The Writings of Akutagawa, Yokomitsu, and Kawabata* (Ph.D. dissertation, Columbia University, 1997), 170, 267.

62. Yokomitsu Riichi, "The Death of Mr. Mu Shiying" (*Mu Shiying shi no shi*), *Literary World* (*Bungakukai*) 7 (September 1940): 174–175.

perialism as a form of tolerant multiculturalism capable of subsuming other national cultures and further encouraging their development: Chinese new sensationism, Yokomitsu implies, *should* keep its Chinese flavor. Here Yokomitsu successfully disguises an apology for his nationalist turn, which to many was a betrayal of his earlier aesthetic principles, as a benevolent multicultural imperialism endorsing other native traditions.

A longer article by critic and scholar Abe Tomoji, who was also famous in China, is much subtler in rhetoric, endorsing Sino-Japanese cooperation as a way to refute the West. Implying that Japanese aggression is deplorable, Abe suggests that the solution to overcoming such tragedies of war is for the Japanese and the Chinese "to hold hands and create a new world," and that this new world should turn to the profound philosophical teachings of Confucianism and Buddhism.[63] A seemingly sympathetic voice that did not endorse Japanese imperialism per se, Abe was, however, anticipating the rhetoric of "Overcoming Modernity" which would emerge in 1942, and which did much to promote Japanese imperialism as a savior of the East from the West.

The last of these articles, by Kon Hidemi, also argues that Mu's work was not particularly stellar, but that his role in the promotion of Sino-Japanese cooperation is crucial.[64] Kon repeatedly mentions what a gentle and handsome man Mu was, explaining thus his unbearable anger toward Mu's assassins. Here the Chinese nationalist assassination of Mu is condemned on humanist grounds—imperialism is couched in the language of humanism.

One could argue that Mu was probably politically unsophisticated, if not naive. But I want to emphasize the state of confusion and ambivalence that the Chinese cosmopolitans lived with (as Mu summarizes so well in the 1935 essay quoted earlier) as the condition of existence under semicolonialism. Without a clear enemy—there were too many potential enemies if one wanted to be hostile, but then the lines between friend and foe were also often very unclear—Chinese intellectuals lacked the option of direct nationalism. Partha Chatterjee writes that the intellectuals in colonial India had to live on a day-to-day basis with a mortal fear of the Englishman, and of the world over which he dominated, and describes how this fear was also the source of new strategies of survival and resistance. Nationalism was a natural choice in such a context.[65] But the Chinese cosmopolitan intellectuals could easily displace colonial reality, because the fragmentary nature of semicolonial domination seldom gave rise to such mortal fear in them. Further-

63. Abe Tomoji, "Recollections" (*Kaisō*), *Literary World* (*Bungakukai*) 7 (September 1940): 180–184.

64. Kon Hidemi, "The Pain of Mr. Mu's Unexpected Death" (*Mu kun no furyo no shi o itamu*), *Literary World* (*Bungakukai*) 7 (September 1940): 184–186.

65. Chatterjee, *The Nation and Its Fragments,* 57–58.

more, unwilling to kowtow to the two equally propagandistic and oftentimes simplistic ideological camps of the Nationalist Party and the Chinese Communist Party, they did not find another more convincing nationalist ideology to resort to. This, I think, is one of the most crucial differences between colonial and semicolonial cultural formations.

To reflect further upon the question of ideology and new sensationism, a comparison of the fates of Japanese new sensationism and its Chinese counterpart shows how new sensationists in the powerful imperialist nation of Japan could easily transform into imperialism's supporters: power was at hand and available to them, and they did not have much to lose. But for their Chinese counterparts to follow and become supporters of Japanese imperialism incurred devastating consequences, because it was not a resort to power but to further subjugation, which made them even more vulnerable in the context of war and unyielding animosities. In the end, the Japanese new sensationists could afford to shift while their Chinese counterparts like Mu could not, because they came from a partially colonized nation. The path from aesthetic autonomy to supporting Japanese imperialism, whether out of idealism or not, was a perilous one that led to the literal death of Chinese new sensationist writers.

CHAPTER 12

Capitalism and Interiority
Shi Zhecun's Tales of the Erotic-Grotesque

But the object of desire, in the usual sense, is either a phantasy that is in reality the support of desire, or a lure.

JACQUES LACAN (1964)

It was the return of the prodigal son.

SHI ZHECUN (1990)

In chapter 3, I discussed how Guo Moruo's use of Freudian psychoanalysis in literary criticism and creative writing manifested the May Fourth desire for a universalism and cosmopolitanism constituted asymmetrically across the China-West divide, and how his construction of an interior landscape relied heavily on an almost formulaic application of psychoanalysis. The interiority in his fiction largely conformed to the Freudian psychoanalytic schema, at the time considered so alien and novel that Guo had to write several essays explaining this schema to his readers to aid their understanding. Drawing from Karatani Kōjin's analogous argument that the interior landscape in Meiji literature resulted from an overwhelming sense of Western domination, I analyzed Guo's desire for psychoanalytic interiority similarly, as both the agent and effect of Western cultural hegemony in the specific context of May Fourth enlightenment discourse. In this chapter, I extend this argument by analyzing the explicitly *intertextual* nature of this interiority as an effect of what I called "textual dissimulation" in chapters 10 and 11.[1] Shi Zhecun's stories are eloquent illustrations of how an intertextually mediated interiority, which constitutes the "reality" within the narra-

---

1. By "intertextuality," I mean the intersection of texts within one text and the transposition of one or more systems of signs onto a text. Julia Kristeva took the term "intertextuality" from V. N. Volosinov's *Marxism and the Philosophy of Language,* and gives it a lengthy theoretical treatment in her *Desire in Language: A Semiotic Approach to Literature and Art,* ed. Leon S. Roudiez, trans. Thomas Gora et al. (New York: Columbia University Press, 1980). See chapters 2 and 3. Also see chapter 5 of Tzvetan Todorov's *Mikhail Bakhtin: The Dialogic Principle,* trans. Wlad

tive, self-reflexively subverts the real and substitutes for the real, thus fundamentally challenging the assumptions of realism. The rich intertextual tapestry in Shi's work further posits cosmopolitanism as textually mediated: Shi claimed that his knowledge of the West was that of the West in books he had read, not the West in semicolonial Shanghai. He made clear that the two "Wests" were fundamentally different, and as a writer and editor he strove to make connections with the metropolitan West he had never visited, not the colonial West he lived with. The exclusively textual, imaginary nature of this cosmopolitan longing for coevalness with the metropolitan West necessarily displaced the actual absence of coevalness between the Chinese cosmopolitan and the Westerner in semicolonial Shanghai.[2]

In relation to the cosmopolitan strategy of bifurcation, then, the question of interiority must also be broached socially and historically, for interiority must also be understood as a *social* construct. Much as the projection of a surrealistic reality organized by a disturbed interiority suggests the modernist formal practice of antirealism, it also shows that the city of Shanghai is turned inside out: the intricacy of the inner world is intimately related to the threats many of Shi's characters experience from the external world. This can be seen in the way urban life in Shi's fiction compromises the masculinity of urban Chinese men and weakens their nerves to produce hypersensitive psychological conditions.[3] Hence, I analyze interiority via-à-vis the urban man's relationship to the culture of consumption in Shanghai. Consumption as the semicolonial subject's mode of participating in the city—buying modern commodities and frequenting the quintessential urban spaces such as theatres and cafes—becomes the yardstick with which to determine the subject's masculinity and power. Shanghai's capitalist allure is presented as a phantasmagoria of consumption that, given the shortage of money of many of Shi's characters, can only be experienced visually as a form of shock, hence the predominance of vision in the experience of urban men. In Shi Zhecun's work, vision manifests its distortedness and hypersensitivity as hallucination, fantastic projection and introjection, illusion, superimposition, and distortion—what he called the "vision of fantasy" (*huanxiang de shijue*)[4] or

---

Godzich (Minneapolis: The University of Minnesota Press, 1984), for a succinct discussion of intertextuality.

2. "Coevalness" is borrowed from Johannes Fabian, who analyzes how representations of the Other in Western anthropological discourses have often denied the Other its presence in the time of the Western present, relegating it instead to the primitive past. See his *Time and the Other: How Anthropology Makes Its Object* (New York: Columbia University Press, 1983).

3. Randy Trumbull has made a similar point about how modernity "saps all sexual vitality" from the urban men in Shi's fiction. "Modernist Inscriptions of Traditional China," paper presented at the annual meeting of the Association for Asian Studies, Los Angeles, March 1993.

4. Shi Zhecun, "Li Shishi," in *Shi Xiu's Love* (*Shi Xiu zhi lian*) (Beijing: Renmin wenxue chubanshe, 1991), 285.

"visual complex" (his own English words).[5] His urban male characters are often suffering from neurasthenia-related anxieties, fears, and visual complexes which drive them into deep psychological turmoil, thus producing a space of perturbed interiority.

To the extent that desire operates through vision, and that the domain of vision is equal to the field of desire (as Jacques Lacan tells us),[6] the city becomes, as in Liu Na'ou and Mu Shiying's fiction, the city of Eros, except that here Eros often operates through nonnormative venues. As I have explained, this determination of Shanghai as the city of Eros exemplifies the cosmopolitan strategy of displacing colonial reality, and Shi's work takes displacement to such excess that he inaugurates a new subgenre of modernist fiction, what may be called the "erotic-grotesque." In the erotic-grotesque landscape of desire, fear often accompanies desire, leading to such erotic excesses as fetishism, sadomasochism, and necrophilia, often with surrealistic and supernatural overtones.

As a literary category, then, the obsessive treatment of physical landscape as the projection of a disturbed interior space allows for a clear stance against realism. As a social and historical category, this focus on interiority allows erotic fantasies unsanctioned by social norms to be represented in the erotic-grotesque genre. It shows how the world of semicolonial capitalism leads to a weakened and heightened state of nerves—neurasthenia—for the urban man whose vision is confused, whose desire is frustrated, and whose masculinity is compromised.

Shi Zhecun is, however, a writer of many styles that cannot be neatly organized into a coherent whole.[7] This chapter's focus is on his stories set in Shanghai, particularly the masterpiece collection entitled *The Evening of Spring Rain* (*Meiyu zhi xi*, 1933), with side references to other stories ranging in style from realist, to proletarian, to historical fiction. It also draws heavily on my three-day interview with Shi in 1990 in order to decipher the connection between the textual and the social in Shi's Shanghai. I conclude with a section on Shi's "return" to tradition, since this return marks the end of the modern Chinese cultural cosmopolitanism which ran from the May Fourth era to the rise of the Sino-Japanese War. If we understand Chinese modernism as the cosmopolitan expression of an interculturally and intertextually mediated cultural agency imbricated within local and global cul-

5. My interview with Shi Zhecun, October 22–24, 1990.

6. Jacques Lacan, *The Four Fundamental Concepts of Psychoanalysis*, ed. Jacques-Alain Miller, trans. Alan Sheridan (New York: W. W. Norton & Company, 1981), 85–93.

7. See my analysis of Mu Shiying's equally multistyled writing in terms of the split personality of the semicolonial subject in chapter 11. Shi himself remarked that for the ten years when he was most productive, between 1927 and 1937, his "creative path was at all times a meandering path of exploration and not stabilized." See his "Preface" (*Xu*) to *Shi Zhecun*, ed. Ying Guojing (Xianggang: Sanlian shudian, 1988), 3.

tural dynamics, Shi's "return" (much more than the assassinations of Liu Na'ou and Mu Shiying, whose deaths can be interpreted as uncompromising final defiances of the threats to literary autonomy) symbolizes the finale of cosmopolitan culture, a finale brought on by a leading modernist himself. In occupied Shanghai in the 1940s, and in the remote city of Kunming, scattered experiments with modernist writing would appear as the war dragged on, but none gathered the momentum or the magnitude of practices we witness in the 1917–1937 period charted in this book.

SHI ZHECUN AND COSMOPOLITANISM

Bertrand Russell characterized the people he considered to be the second generation of Chinese intellectuals, in their twenties in the 1920s, as those who did not have anxieties about modernization or Westernization,[8] and this would be a fitting description for the cosmopolitan Shi Zhecun, who attended a missionary high school where all the textbooks were in English, later changed colleges annually in search of a good cosmopolitan education, and finally ended up in French missionary-run Aurora University, even though as a child he was mainly educated in the Chinese classics. He was of the generation which had avidly read such May Fourth journals as *New Youth* and *New Tide* as teenagers. Inspired by the new thoughts propagated by the May Fourth enlightenment discourse, Shi formed his first literary association called the "Orchid Society" (*lanshe*), with such future modernists as Dai Wangshu and Du Heng, while still in high school.[9] His close association with these two figures, as well as with the Japan-educated Liu Na'ou and the youthful Mu Shiying, constituted the core group around which the modernist movement later formed.

One curious fact given Shi's life as a cosmopolitan was that he had never actually set foot outside of China (except Hong Kong), whereas Dai Wangshu went to France, Liu Na'ou came from Taiwan via Japan, Mu Shiying later visited Japan, and most of the May Fourth as well as *jingpai* modernists (with the exception of Fei Ming) went abroad. And yet Shi was one of the most well-informed of these figures about Western literatures, and was fully bilingual in English and Chinese. His case offers perhaps the clearest example of how modern Chinese cosmopolitanism relied heavily on an imaginary, literary relationship with the metropolitan West, which did not require actual travels there.

8. Bertrand Russell, *The Problem of China* (New York: The Century Co., 1922), 78.

9. This information is based on his autobiographical poems written in classical Chinese. Shi Zhecun, "Miscellaneous Poems of a Floating Life" (*Fusheng zayong*), *Guangming Daily* (*Guangming ribao*), serialized February 11 to November 25, 1990. There are sixty-four of them in total that I know of.

This issue of an imaginary or literary relationship with the metropolitan West forming the basis of cosmopolitanism also exemplifies the bifurcating strategy of Chinese modernists who evoked the metropolitan West in their writings while often ignoring or simply displacing semicolonial reality. Shi Zhecun himself offered the most revelatory example of this during my three-day interview with him, when he emphatically made the following remarks:

> As for myself, I was influenced by the *texts of Western culture* rather than Shanghai's colonial culture. Colonial influence was limited to those Shanghai writers who did not know Western languages; hence when they wrote modernist fiction, they often gave themselves away. They had not seen the outside world and their Frenchmen were the Frenchmen in the colonial settlements [and not those in metropolitan France]. That was a different case.[10] (emphasis mine)

The assumption here is that his French and English reading ability allowed him access to metropolitan Western culture, which produced a more authentic modernism than the one situated within and dealing directly with the colonial West in Shanghai. He makes a clear distinction between the metropolitan West and the colonial West, revealing unambiguously how his cosmopolitanism was built upon a necessary bifurcation between the two, and how it was a *textually mediated* cosmopolitanism made possible by his multilinguality.

Since its legitimation came from textual linkages to Western modernism in the metropolitan West, Shi's cosmopolitanism self-consciously sought *not* to take the colonial reality into consideration, for such would have resulted in an inferior form of modernism. When pressed about the colonial and racial situation in Shanghai, Shi made the following remarks:

> There were of course good and bad foreigners in Shanghai, but they were all the same in despising the Chinese. But those who had contacts with foreigners did not necessarily feel such discrimination, as they were the high-class Chinese [compadores] needed by foreigners to do business.
>
> The Chinese did not feel so oppressed. When workers were beaten by their manager, was it imperialist oppression or not? In Japanese factories, the Japanese managers beat the Japanese workers even more harshly. And of course there were lazybones among the workers, too. . . . League leftists chose these topics explicitly to denounce the darkness of foreign imperialism. But I think it wasn't really the case. Would those who worked in the factory resent their managers for having beaten them? Not really, since their salaries were higher than they could get elsewhere. . . . For their rice bowls, they would not have resented the beating. The communists would hate to hear what I just said, and would consider this extremely reactionary.[11]

---

10. Interview with Shi Zhecun, October 22–24, 1990.
11. Ibid.

Spoken after having suffered through the atrocities of the Cultural Revolution and the communist state's totalistic, pan-ideologized rhetoric of anti-imperialism (under whose name intellectuals like himself were persecuted), Shi's remarks here are tinged with nostalgia about the heyday of modernism in Shanghai. His description of the situation of workers uses economics (rice bowls) to downplay the political and ideological aspects (resentment) of imperialism which were the aspects emphasized by the communist state.

Granted the subjective tonality of these remarks, Shi nevertheless makes clear the general racial prejudice of foreigners toward the Chinese, although in his own creative work he chose not to engage with the question of race explicitly. Like Liu Na'ou, he expatriated the question of racial hierarchy in the city almost completely, instead inserting the theme of racial conflict into China's primitive past, as in his historical fictions "Princess Ah Lan" (*Ah Lan gongzhu*, 1931) and "The General's Head" (*Jiangjun de tou*, 1930). When Shi does refer to members of other races in contemporary Shanghai, as he does occasionally, they appear as silent, two-dimensional props in the background who do not cross the boundary into Chinese communities ("The Haunted House"). A Russian woman enters the center of narrative conflict with the Chinese rickshaw puller in "The Business of Sixi" (*Sixizi de shengyi*), but since she is a prostitute whose social status is economically rather than racially determined, the question of Westerners' racial superiority did not need to be considered. Here again, it is economics and not race that concerns Shi.

Such a cosmopolitanism built upon an imaginary and textual relationship with the metropolitan West reveals a fantasy of coevalness, so that Chinese modernism could be "contemporary" (*tongbu*, literally, "of simultaneous step" or "synchronic") with the West and not account for the uneven temporal registers—the coexistence of modernity and tradition—in colonial Shanghai. Shi discussed this issue as follows:

> Any literary tendency that walks outside the nation is *tongbu* with the outside. It is usually only a matter of two or three years for the influence to travel [from one place to another]. For us Shanghai youth in China it was a connection built through language. Those educated in Japan introduced [Western modernism] through Japanese, some of us through English, French, and German. All these put together became a *force* (*shili*).[12] (emphasis mine)

Emphasizing the function of foreign languages as tools to introduce foreign culture and translate between cultures, this passage nonetheless shows the telling absence of attention to literary traffic going the other way, that is, from China to the West or Japan. Here the cultural traffic that defines Shanghai cosmopolitanism is unidirectional, from the West via Japan to China, tracing the same trajectory of travel as both cultural and political imperialisms.

12. Ibid.

But within the immediate local context, this transcultural and translingual group of modernists constituted a "force" that brought them the heroic satisfaction of being the vanguard of the cultural scene. Ever since the May Fourth obsession with catching up with the West, modernism was to symbolize the moment of arrival at the modern time of the West, and the modernists themselves served as the harbingers of that arrival. The global and the local contexts of their modernism therefore situated them in a contradictory relationship to the Foucauldian twin of power/knowledge: in the global context, Chinese modernists may have been subjected to the power/knowledge of the West, which held the determining epistemological advantage, but in the local context they assumed the position of power/knowledge vis-à-vis their multiple others.

Still, we must necessarily come at the question of language from a different angle in order to determine the crosscultural politics of power in Chinese modernism. The Chinese language was a native construct: not just the tool of translation but also the medium in which Chinese modernism was written. Leo Lee has remarked, for instance, that modern Chinese writers never faced the threat of having to write in the colonizer's language, as some African and Indian writers did; they continued to write in Chinese, even though the syntactical structures of the modern Chinese vernacular may have been altered by translated terms and phrases.[13] Shi Zhecun makes a similar point in his characteristic cosmopolitan vein:

> There is no such thing as importation in literature. Everything that is written in Chinese by the Chinese is Chinese literature. Even when it is about foreigners it is Chinese literature. . . . The ancient Chinese said there are three kinds of "stealing" in writing poetry: stealing meaning, stealing syntax, and stealing images. Wang Wei and Du Fu all "stole" from others. The difference in talent lies in the varying ability to give what one has stolen a thorough re-writing.[14]

Further commenting that what was deemed "Chinese" vernacular fiction was originally from India, Shi refuted essentialism and emphasized the transnational nature of Chinese literature at its roots. "Chinese-ness" is always already the site of mixtures and foreign influences, but the fact that it is *written* in the Chinese language secures an unquestionable sense of identity for the users of this language. Leo Lee comments on this sense of security in his conclusion on Shanghai cosmopolitan writers: "From their works I draw the obvious conclusion that the sense of their Chinese identity was never in ques-

---

13. Leo Lee, *Shanghai Modern: A Study of Urban Culture and Literary Imagination in China, 1930–1945*, (Cambridge: Harvard University Press, 1999), chapter 9.

14. Shi Zhecun, in an interview with the author conducted by Zheng Mingli and Lin Yaode and published as "The Dawn of Chinese Modernism: A Dialogue with the Master of New Sensationism, Shi Zhecun" (*Zhongguo xiandaizhuyi de shuguang: yu xin'ganjuepai dashi Zhi Zhecun xiansheng duitan*), *Unitas* (*Lianho wenxue*) 69 (July 1990): 137.

tion *in spite of* the Western colonial presence in Shanghai. In my view it was only because of their unquestioned Chineseness that these writers were able to embrace Western modernity openly, without fear of colonization" (emphasis in the original).[15] The Chinese language, by never being discarded (although some May Fourth writers desired to do so in the Esperanto and romanization debates), thus served as the irreducible marker of cultural identity, on the basis of which the Chinese cosmopolitans could look outside their nation without anxieties and fears of the colonization of consciousness.

I would argue that the attribution of epistemological privilege to the metropolitan West occurred more readily precisely because there was an absence of concern about the colonization of consciousness. This self-imposition of epistemological inferiority, as opposed to an externally enforced colonial imposition of epistemological superiority, marks the essential difference between semicolonial and colonial cultural politics vis-à-vis the West, as I have discussed in chapter 5, and it also explains the comparative lack of critique of colonial modernity in China in general. It bears repeated emphasis that this cosmopolitan homage to the metropolitan West always occurred in an asymmetrical landscape. Although the Chinese language may mark the irreducibility of Chinese-ness, the ways in which Chinese-ness itself has undergone change (just as the language has) bear witness to the unequal cross-cultural traffic between China and the West. In the "contact zone" among cultures, intercultural relationships are most often unequal, even though they may be contemporary.[16]

In fact, the coevalness of cultures is also the "co-temporality of power structures,"[17] in the specific sense that Shi's assertion of contemporaneity situates his act historically in the context of semicolonialism and imperialism. Shi Zhecun noted in my interview with him that if he had had the opportunity to go to France, he would probably have never returned to China. This privileging of France, much as one may call it cosmopolitan openness, was also born of an absence of actual lived experience in France as the racial Other. The cosmopolitan fantasy of coevalness with the West, then, would only have been possible within the imaginary, textually mediated relationship with the metropolitan West. In another moment during the interview, Shi exhibited this fantasy of coevalness with the metropolitan West when he analyzed the French gesture of shrugging as an authentic French custom. He said that only those students trained at the high-class Aurora University picked up the habit of shrugging like the cultured French, while those who

---

15. Leo Lee, *Shanghai Modern*, 312.

16. The idea of the contact zone is derived from Mary Louis Pratt, *Imperial Eyes: Travel Writing and Transculturation* (New York: Routledge, 1992), 6–7.

17. The phrase is Rey Chow's; see her *Primitive Passions: Visuality, Sexuality, Ethnography, and Contemporary Chinese Cinema* (New York: Columbia University Press, 1995), 196.

went to missionary schools that focused on language training did not know how to shrug. While most foreign missionary schools in China taught foreign languages merely as instruments of administration and communication, to train Chinese personnel to work in the concessions, Aurora University transmitted authentic French high culture and retained some famous personalities as its teachers.[18] In other words, even the local landscape was stratified along various definitions of cultural "authenticity" in relation to one's linguistic access and cultural proximity to the metropolitan West. Shi noted that at the time there was virtually no opposition towards Europeanization because there were very few writers besides himself who were Europeanized.[19] This smallness in number cushioned their sense of heroic, righteous avant-gardism, with which they could flaunt their status as contemporary with the West and separate from the rest of the Chinese who were still mired within traditional cultural ideologies.

But local pressures were mounting. Around 1936, Shi made a complete turnabout and "returned" to tradition: he later called this the "return of the prodigal son." As the Sino-Japanese War grew imminent, the pressure to be patriotic dealt a death blow to textually mediated cosmopolitanism. In one of the rare instances where Shi asked me a question, he said: "When there is conflict between the East and the West which side will you tend towards?" I answered, "The East." And he replied, "Yes, this is always the case." Although the Sino-Japanese War did not involve the West per se, the conflict necessitated a nationalist response toward the foreign. During that interview in 1990 in China, which coincided with my nostalgic search for my cultural roots, my affirmative leaning toward the East (read: China) arose as much out of a sense of historical obligation as a personal longing. Imminent political conflicts, real and imagined, can push the limits of cosmopolitanism to the point of annihilating it—this is what had also happened to the Japanese modernists.

Before his "return," however, Shi Zhecun the cosmopolitan was an accomplished poet, fiction writer, and editor. While the totality of his poetic output numbers only around twenty-five poems, he published nine collections of short stories between 1923 and 1937, in addition to a handful of stories never gathered into anthologies. Unlike his poetry, in which a coherent imagistic style can be discerned, his narrative styles are multiple and shifting, hence very difficult to organize into neat categories or to analyze with of a few set parameters of interpretation. A few stories published in 1922 when he was seventeen, and four early collections—*Riverside Anthology* (*Jiangganji*, 1923), *Miss Juanzi* (*Juanzi guniang*, 1928), *Festival Lantern* (*Shangyuandeng*, 1929), and *Pursuit* (*Zhui*, 1929)—represent experiments with various

18. Interview with Shi Zhecun, October 22–24, 1990.
19. Ibid.

modes and techniques of writing: romance stories in the mode of Mandarin Ducks and Butterflies fiction, proletarian fiction, Edgar Allan Poe–inspired gothic fiction ("Ninong," 1928), naturalistic and psychological fiction in the style of Tayama Katai ("Miss Juanzi"), stories of abnormal sexuality ("Madame Zhou" [*Zhou furen*], 1926), and a handful of realist narratives. Shi considers most of these apprentice works and calls only *Festival Lantern* a product of serious literary effort. He even declares that the period between 1923 and 1929 was his "period of imitation" (*mofangqi*), when he grafted freely from other literary sources to exercise his literary imagination and hone his craft.[20]

Unlike most of his early stories, the ten stories in *Festival Lantern* are set in the countryside, most probably Songjiang, where the author's family moved to from his birthplace Hangzhou when he was eight. Intensely lyrical and nostalgic, these stories depict the erosion of country life due to the invasion of city culture: Shi explains that they recorded a rural perspective on the urban phenomenon.[21] At the time, Shen Chongwen praised these stories highly for their lyricism and craftsmanship, as did the poet Zhu Xiang for their intertextual echoes with the Greek pastoral tradition.[22] Like Lu Xun's classic hometown stories such as "In the Wineshop" (*Zai jiulou shang*) and "Hometown" (*Guxiang*), many of these stories relate a male narrator's pessimistic realization that one can never go home again. The spatial distance between the city and the country is also temporal: one cannot return to the past.

Shi notes that around the mid- to late 1920s, his literary model was the realism of Anton Chekhov and Guy de Maupassant.[23] By his last collection of stories, *Small Treasures* (*Xiaozhenji*, 1936), as well as in a few unanthologized stories, he returned to a predominantly realist mode of writing, although he then tempered this Western-inspired realism with a self-conscious effort at returning to traditional narrative modes. In between these realist periods, however, were the three collections of stories for which he became most famous: *The General's Head* (*Jiangjun di tou*, 1932), a collection of four historical stories retold with psychoanalytic perspectives; *The Evening of Spring Rain*, a masterful collection of stories dealing with psychoanalytic and erotic-grotesque interiority, which includes two stories published earlier in *Li Shishi* (1931); and *Biographies of Good Women* (*Shannüren xingpin*, 1933), a collection of portraits of urban women in Shanghai written predominantly in the realist mode with some gentle psychoanalytic and erotic touches, whose

20. Ibid.

21. Ibid.

22. Shen Congwen, "Shi Zhecun and Luo Heizhi" (*Shi Zhecun yu Luo Heizhi*), *Modern Student* (*Xiandai xuesheng*) 1:2 (November 1930); rpt. in Shi Zhecun, *Shi Zhecun*, 195–199. Zhu Xiang, "*Lantern Festival* and *My Memory*" (*Shangyuandeng yu Wo de jiyi*), *La Nouvelle Littérature* 1:3 (November 1929): 551–552.

23. Interview with Shi Zhecun, October 22–24, 1990.

organizing idea came from Theodore Dreiser's *A Gallery of Women*.[24] During this same period from 1932 to 1935, he was the chief editor (until joined by Du Heng) of *Les Contemporaines*. These few years marked his most intensely cosmopolitan and creative period, when striving to be *contemporaine* with the metropolitan West was accorded a central status.

CAPITALISM AND INTERIORITY

While interiority in Chinese literary modernism is intimately related to psychoanalysis, it is important, in the specific context of Shanghai, also to analyze its emergence in relation to capitalism and semicolonialism. That is to say, interiority was as much a social construct as a textual one. This necessity arises not only due to the importance of historical context in the formation of this interior landscape, but also because an organic relationship between interiority and capitalism has been previously established by Western philosophers specifically in reference to China. Therefore, I must make a short detour into the "white mythologies" of Western philosophy[25] in order to frame my discussion of psychoanalytic interiority.

Various Western philosophers such as Hegel, Weber, and Marx noted that the Chinese lacked interiority or "the inner man" and were passive followers of despotic rule. According to Hegel, without the concept of freedom, the Chinese passively obeyed the external ethics imposed by the state and were incapable of thinking and reflecting—the hallmarks of the Western subject who internalizes morality and rationality.[26] As a sociologist, Weber used the same characterization to explain why the West could develop into capitalist societies while China could not: morality in China was imposed from the outside, hence there was no self-regulated morality from the inside as is necessary for the rationalization of a capitalist society. The absence of a notion of conflict between the Chinese individual and the external world further bred a complacent attitude toward life, without the desire for conquering nature required of capitalism. Without conflicts, the Chinese remained, as it were, one-dimensional men, wanting the depth and complexity of the West-

24. Ibid. Shi had thought that Chinese women, having been subjected to the dictates of traditional ethical injunctions for centuries, could not be as passionate as Western women, such as those in Arthur Schnitzler's fiction. Hence his female characters are usually sexually repressed and do not aggressively seek outlets for their sexuality. Shi also does not delve into their psychology in depth, as he does with his male characters, for whom repressions explode into hallucinations and grotesque events. That is why I characterize these stories as having "gentle psychoanalytic and erotic touches."

25. "White mythologies" is the term used by Robert Young to characterize Eurocentric Western philosophy and history in his *White Mythologies: Writing History and the West* (New York: Routledge, 1990).

26. G. W. F. Hegel, *Introduction to the Philosophy of History*, trans. Leo Rauch (Indianapolis: Hackett Publishing Company, 1988), 74.

ern Christian subject.[27] Marx follows in Hegelian fashion, seeing Western imperialism as the beneficial harbinger of capitalism, which "batters down all Chinese walls," and "draws" China from barbarism to "civilization."[28]

To continue this line of reasoning, which has dominated Western thinking about why China could not develop an indigenous capitalism, the coming of imperialism and its "gift" of capitalism would then produce a useful tension between the Chinese individual and his/her environment, leading to the emergence of interiority. In other words, the Chinese *needed* imperialism to discover the interiority necessary for capitalist development. If we think about imperialism along racial and cultural lines, we might also add that its arrival signals other sources of conflict besides the one between the individual and the natural world. These would be such conflicts inherent in the colonial situation as those between the colonizer and the colonized (political and racial), between native tradition and Western modernity (cultural), and between agrarianism and capitalism (economic), all of which should intensify the tension necessary for the emergence of interiority.

While this perspective on conflict offers a seemingly historically rooted explanation for the emergence of interiority in Chinese modernism, I would argue that interiority should be approached from a different angle. The issue here is not whether the Chinese had no inner life until imperialism forced them to have one—which is the Eurocentric presumption of Hegel, Weber, and Marx, denying subjectivity to the Chinese as if the Chinese had not been complete or complex human beings until Westerners came to shake them up with cannons—but how the arrival of imperialism and capitalism spurred the production of a qualitatively different landscape of interiority from traditional modes.[29] Only from such a perspective can we mark the particular historicity of the interior landscape we see intertwined with Freudian psychoanalysis in the uneven capitalist context of semicolonial Shanghai, and explicate the colonial implications of this interiority.

In the previous three chapters on Shanghai, I analyzed how the Chinese semicolonial subject's relationship with the city is imbued with an ambivalence that can be understood in terms of three aspects of experience: (1) his/her particular mode of participation in the city through consumption rather than production; (2) the city as a site of simulacra that is visually overwhelming (anal-

27. Max Weber, *The Religion of China: Confucianism and Taoism,* trans. and ed. Hans H. Gerth (New York: The Free Press, 1951), especially chapter 8.

28. Karl Marx and Friedrich Engels, "Manifesto of the Communist Party," in *The Marx-Engels Reader,* ed. Robert C. Tucker (New York: W. W. Norton, 1978), 477.

29. Shi Zhecun noted in my interview that although there were no developed psychoanalytic theories in China, one could say that there were latent psychoanalytic ideas in such Confucian notions as the good and evil of human nature (Mencius and Xunzi), the erotic tradition in *chuanqi* tales such as the *Peony Pavilion,* and so on. Interview with Shi Zhecun, October 22–24, 1990.

ogous to the function of Hollywood films) and sexually enticing (embodied by the modern girl); and (3) the onslaught of urban stimuli which makes the overwhelmed subject feels enervated by the speed of urban life, hence not a Benjaminian flâneur. In Shi Zhecun's stories as well, the urban man is often neurasthenia-stricken and hypersensitive, and his responses to consumption, visual intensity, erotic allure, and excess stimuli take on psychopathological dimensions. To put it in Freudian terms, the weakened state of consciousness cannot function as a protective shield against stimuli so that the unconscious begins to leak and trouble conscious thoughts and behaviors. When consciousness cannot ward off all stimuli, mental instability forms, and the unconscious, where repressed desires are lodged, begins to break through the protective shield of consciousness to disorient the person thus affected.[30] Hence Walter Benjamin notes, "Man's inner concerns do not have their issueless private character by nature. They do so only when he is increasingly unable to assimilate the data of the world around him by way of experience."[31]

Lou Shiyi, a leftist critic and writer, perceptively pointed out the relationship between the urban culture of consumption and the urban man's sensitive nerves in 1931:

> Modernity also refers to the urban, mechanical society. It is within the urban space of consumption that theaters, cafes, and parks, etc. appear in [Shi Zhecun's] stories. It is not a coincidence that the opening scene in "Devil's Way" (Modao) is on the train. Living among the clamor of machines and the hubbub of the city, the modern men, who belong to the department of consumption [xiaofei bumen de ren], are all neurasthenic, suffering from intestinal frailness, and wearing pale faces. That describes the protagonist in "Devil's Way." Those who live the lives of consumption tend to harbor massive doses of doubt and nihilism.[32]

Lou here makes an explicit link between urban life and neurasthenia, under whose sway a tortured interior landscape harboring "doubt and nihilism" emerges. This space of interiority in Shi's fiction moves between consciousness and the unconscious, oscillating from acute fear of emasculation (or castration, in Freudian lingo) to projections and introjections of fear and desire sometimes of surrealistic proportions. The fear of emasculation is linked directly to the money economy of capitalism, and the eruption of desire is depicted as erotic perversion that threatens to break down the barrier between imagination and reality.

The most explicit connection between capitalism and interiority can be

---

30. As summarized by Walter Benjamin, "On Some Motifs in Baudelaire," in *Illuminations*, ed. Hannah Arendt, trans. Harry Zohn (New York: Schocken Books, 1969), 161.

31. Ibid., 158.

32. Lou Shiyi, "Shi Zhecun's New Sensationism" (*Shi Zhecun de xin'ganjuezhuyi*), *Literary News* (*Wenyi xinwen*) (October 26, 1931): 4.

found in Shi's attribution of urban men's emasculation to the money economy. The lack of sufficient money for consumption leads to the urban man's
sense of disempowerment as a man and drives him to troubling discom-
posure. In Shi's stories, it is not the modern girl who embodies the urban
materiality that emasculates the urban man—except in the case of one or
two stories written in the mode most evocative of Liu Na'ou and Mu Shiying, such as "Flower Dreams" (*Huameng*)—but rather a shortage of money
which prevents the one participatory relationship he might otherwise have
with the city: consumption. In many urban men's minds, manhood equals
money and vice versa, so that the lack of money suggests the diminution of
manhood.

In "At the Paris Theatre" (*Zai Bali daxiyuan*), for example, manhood is
given exact monetary value when the first-person male narrator calculates
how much more his female companion spent on expensive "circle tickets"
for the theatre than he had spent on the regular-priced tickets he had bought
for them the day before. His sense of humiliation is compounded because
she went ahead and bought tickets on her own (without passively waiting for
her male companion to buy the tickets, as should have been the case), got
expensive ones on top of that (to show her dissatisfaction at his buying
cheaper tickets the day before), and then handed them over to him to give
to the ticket collector (so he could pretend that he had bought them, showing that she knew her buying tickets was humiliating for him).

> Why did she rush over to buy tickets? This is my humiliation. Isn't this bald
> Russian staring at me? This woman has her eyes nailed to my face, yes, and this
> other man took the cigar from his mouth to stare at me. They are all looking
> at me. No mistake, I know what they mean. They despise me, no, they are mock-
> ing me. I don't understand why she would rush to buy tickets. . . . Doesn't she
> know that this would make me feel uncomfortable? I am a man, a gentleman.
> No man accompanying a woman to the theatre for a film—no matter what class
> of woman she is—should allow the woman to buy tickets. No, I have never seen
> that myself. . . . It feels hot on my face. I guess my face must be really flushed. . . .
> Why does she hand over the tickets to me?. . . . Ah, these are *circle* tickets! Why
> is she acting so rich?. . . . I understand it now, it is her way of showing me her
> dissatisfaction for my buying regular tickets the other day. This is even more
> humiliating. I can't stand this! I would rather cut off my relationship with her
> than accept these tickets and stay with her for the film. I will do nothing ever
> with her, going to the department stores, eating ice cream, never ever with
> her![33] (original English in italics)

To be sure, only in a social setting where manhood is equated with purchase
power via the possession of money would such a threat to manhood be so
powerfully felt. What is striking here is the degree of nervous sensitivity the

33. Shi Zhecun, *Shi Xiu's Love*, 255–256.

man harbors toward any potential threat to his masculinity embodied in the power to buy. While Liu Na'ou's and Mu Shiying's male characters tend to realize their emasculation after the fact, Shi's urban man anticipates and seeks legitimation of his castration anxiety.

The story goes on to show the urban man deploying a typical Freudian strategy: turning the threatening object of desire into a fetish by substitution. When the male protagonist gets his fingers sticky from the chocolate ice cream he eats during the intermission, his date notices that he has nothing to wipe his hands with and hands him her handkerchief. In the darkness of the theatre, confident that she cannot see him clearly now that the show has resumed, he brings the handkerchief to his nose:

> Ah, it is fragrant, it is indeed her scent. This must be the mixture of perfume and the aroma of her sweat. I want so much to lick it to see how this fragrance tastes. It must be exhilarating. I can pretend to use the handkerchief to wipe my mouth from the left corner of my lips to the right corner, and as the handkerchief passes I can stick out my tongue and lick it. Even if I suck at it nobody would discover me. Isn't this ingenious? Good, the lights are off and the film has resumed. This is a good opportunity, let me suck at it to my heart's content. . . . It's very salty here, it must be the taste of her sweat?. . . . But what is it here that tastes so fishy and spicy?. . . . Must be phlegm and mucus? Yes, it is indeed phlegm and mucus, sort of sticky. What a novel flavor! The tip of my tongue seems to feel an indescribable numbness and trembling. How strange, yet I feel as if I am holding her naked body.[34]

Unable to contain the threat to his manhood posed by her ability to buy, he turns her handkerchief into a fetish, a synecdochic extention of her naked body, so that possessing the handkerchief provides him with a simulated experience of erotic ecstasy.

In several other stories, economic emasculation is depicted as the general condition of urban existence. In "Wife's Birthday" (*Qi zhi shengchen*) and "Late Autumn Crescent Moon" (*Canqiu de xiaxianyue*), the male protagonists cannot provide for their families financially and be "men" in the traditional sense. In the "Business of Sixi," the male protagonist finds his power eroded because his wife also works and brings home income. He feels utterly humiliated by his wife's assertion that since he is not able to provide for her he has no right to control her. Frustrated by this financially provoked emasculation, he fantasizes about visiting a prostitute to satiate his desire and compensate for his compromised manhood. When a Russian prostitute happens to get on his rickshaw, he becomes aroused by her naked legs and attempts to rape her. He does not realize that this Caucasian woman is physically stronger than he is, and she throws him out during their jostle. Foreign policemen promptly capture him and throw him into prison. His frustration

34. Ibid., 263.

at his economic emasculation gets acted out impulsively, but the criminal of-
fense of rape, and his physical capture and imprisonment, only further his
state of deprived manhood.

In the lyrically rendered "The Evening of Spring Rain," emasculation is
again presented as the condition of existence for a married urban man without much money (he cannot afford to buy a raincoat). But he likes rainy
days, since at least he has a "superior" umbrella. One afternoon, he decides
to walk home from work in the rain. Intoxicated by the "erotic rain" (*yinyu*),
he becomes infatuated with a beautiful young woman who has no umbrella.
He comes to the rescue of this damsel in distress like a "valiant knight of the
middle ages using his umbrella as a shield to ward off the arrows of rain rushing toward them," and with "surging masculine courage," he desires to "conquer her heart."[35] An obvious phallic metaphor, the umbrella affords him a
simulated experience of being a chivalric knight, which he can only achieve
on rainy days with his umbrella (sword when folded; shield when unfolded)
at hand. If not having a raincoat compromises him (his coworkers sympa-
thize with his poverty by saying what a model man he is to not take the bus
home in order to save money), the umbrella affords a temporary flight of
erotic fantasy in masculine terms even while the ennui and bondage of marriage block his need for masculine heroism. If, through the lack of money
and the absence of buying power, his manhood has been compromised, it
is also through a material object—the umbrella—that his manhood can be
temporarily simulated in the realm of fantasy.

In the above stories, the shortage of money prevents urban men of varying classes from participating fully in the consumptive culture of the city;
the degree of their membership in this culture serves as their measure of
masculinity and manhood. Falling short of this participatory demand, they
develop an interior landscape filled with doubt, regret, guilt, and fantasy. It
is when this fantasy takes flight, so to speak, that we see how the interior landscape unveils the darkest recesses of the unconscious where repressed desires seek to break out and take over conscious lives. The eruption of the unconscious, a social category in relation to capitalism as I have just shown,
here takes an explicitly textual trajectory via the evocation of various tales
of interiority and desire, at the intersection between fiction and psychoanalysis.

INTERIORITY AS TEXTUAL DISSIMULATION

As the internalization of the relationship between the semicolonial subject
and the capitalist city produces an interiority of the consumer (interiority

35. Ibid., 246, 248.

as social construct), the man of interiority in Shi's fiction is often a reader whose reading list shapes the content of his thoughts and feelings (interiority as textual construct). This shaping is most prominently displayed in several of Shi's stories of neurasthenia-stricken urban characters encountering some kind of supernatural event: "Devil's Way," "Yaksha" (*Yecha*, a female Buddhist demon), "Inn" (*Lüshe*), and "Haunted House" (*Xiongzhai*).

In "Devil's Way," we enter the male narrator's paranoid mind, colored by his avid readings on Celtic witchcraft and sexual perversion such as *The Romance of Sorcery, The Journal of Psychology*, Sheridan Le Fanu's ghost stories, and *Files on Sexual Crimes*, as well as the Chinese classic of the *zhiguai* genre, *Strange Tales from a Leisure Studio* (*Liaozhai zhiyi*). His reading list also includes Persian religious poetry and British poetry; at one point he even compares himself to Lord Byron. The story has an uncanny plot: the reader-narrator, an urban man who suffers from neurasthenia and insomnia and has to take medication regularly, takes a weekend journey from Shanghai to the suburbs in order to calm his nerves, but ends up experiencing a series of hallucinatory visions. From the old woman sitting across him on the train, a black dot on the window, his friend's wife clad in white, a country woman, and a cafe waitress, to a disappearing black-clad woman at the Odeon Theatre back in Shanghai, he again and again sees the figures of a witch and a mummified imperial concubine, the two collapsing into a supernatural object of fear and desire. The intensity of his fear is only matched by his desire for the mummy (Shi calls this necrophilic desire a "surrealistic eroticism"). Considering his foreign-dominated reading list, the narrator's fantastic visions are appropriately exotic: the mummy with her paraphernalia of a golden casket in a catacomb, and the classic Western witch clad in black with gnarled fingers, piercing eyes, bent shoulders, evil wrinkles, and a witch's broom. The narrator's visual hallucinations, and the psychological trepidations that accompany them, are products of an imagination made hyperactive from reading foreign books, books which are now internalized as his mental landscape. Reading about ghosts, legends, and erotic escapades produces an interior landscape filled with textually dissimulated motifs, images, and psychological conditions.

Shi has said that his most important sources for this story were Irish writers Fiona McCleod (1855–1905), Sheridan Le Fanu, and Lord Dunsany (1878–1957); French writer Jules Barbey d'Aurevilly (1808–1889), especially his *Les Diaboliques* (*The She-Devils*); and the sadomasochist stories of the Marquis de Sade and Leopold von Sacher-Masoch.[36] The combined reading lists of the narrator and the author conjures up an imagined realm populated by phantasms and illusions, sometimes supernatural beings, that are sexu-

---

36. Interview with Shi Zhecun, Oct. 22–24, 1990.

ally charged. So while visual disorders break down the wall between consciousness and the unconscious, images of the supernatural manifest the repressed desires of the unconscious. In Le Fanu's stories, the supernatural is often an unconscious element in the mind that emerges when the barriers protecting the conscious ego are temporarily broken down.[37] In other words, the supernatural functions to bring out perverse desires exceeding the boundaries of normativity. To put it differently, the supernatural, since it has no pretension toward realism, allows for a fantastic legitimation of sexual perversity, which would otherwise be censored as immoral. The two reading lists, then, are sources for a specific form of interiority—the leaking of the unconscious into the conscious realm—that forcefully subverts assumptions of realism, due to its supernatural qualities and explicitly textual nature.

This breaking out of the unconscious to take on ghostly dimensions of erotic excess, grotesque imagery, and supernatural terror resembles the Japanese popular cultural genre known as the "*ero-guro-nonsensu*" ("erotic-grotesque-nonsense"). After Shi Zhecun published "At the Paris Theatre" and "Devil's Way," Lou Shiyi noted that Shi's new sensationism had a thick "*erotic* and *grotesque*" aura, with shadows of so-called "*nonsense* literature" (original English in italics).[38] And in a May 1933 entry of "Japan Correspondence" in *Les Contemporaines*, Zhu Yunying refers to the middle-of-the-road, nonideological writing popular in Japan as "erotic-grotesque-nonsense" (*seqing qiguai nangxingsi*) literature.[39] Appearing around 1930 and centrally located in Asakusa, this Japanese trend encompassed such popular genres as detective and psychological tales by Edogawa Rampo (the name is a take-off on "Edgar Allan Poe"), Hollywood erotic films, burlesque reviews, carnival sideshows, and nonsense literature (slapstick humor); such popular journals as *Grotesque* and *Criminology* (*Hanzai kagaku*); and flaunted such characters as modern girls (*moga*) and modern boys (*mobo*), and such social spaces as cabarets, cafes, and theatres.[40] Associated with Freudian psychoanalysis and Havelock Ellis's *Studies in the Psychology of Sex*, the combination of erotic-grotesque elements can be found especially in Tanizaki Jun'ichirō's stories of sadomasochism and fetishism. Its forms of expression also included erotomania, perversity, voyeurism, nonsensical humor, and monstrosity. As a social category, Miriam Silverberg notes, it could be construed as a form of anti-official popular culture challenging Western cultural hege-

37. See E. F. Bleiler, "Introduction to the Dover Edition," *Best Ghost Stories of J. S. Le Fanu* (New York: Dover Publications, Inc., 1964), viii.

38. Lou Shiyi, "Shi Zhecun's New Sensationism," 4.

39. Zhu Yunying, "Japan Correspondence" (*Riben tongxin*), *Les Contemporaines* 3:1 (May 1933): 167.

40. Seiji Lippit, *Japanese Modernism and the Destruction of the Literary Form: The Writings of Akutagawa, Yokomitsu, and Kawabata* (Ph.D. dissertation, Columbia University, 1997), 242.

mony, criticizing the colonizing expansion of Japanese imperialism, and exposing the grotesque body of the impoverished lumpen proletariat.[41]

The associations of the Japanese form with Shi Zhecun's work are rich and dense, including more than the "middle-of-the-road" epithet that aptly describes his position as one of the Third Category Men (I will return to the question of his politics later). Shi himself used the terms "erotic" and "grotesque" to describe his work in later interviews,[42] and we know of his literary apprenticeship to Edgar Allan Poe[43] and to the sexual psychology of Freud and Ellis, his treatment of urban settings and urban characters such as modern girls, and his penchant toward describing erotic excesses in the multiple ways the *ero-guro-nonsensu* genre authorized. Shi revealed during the interview one telling association: the books serving as the sources of "Devil's Way" were actually known to him through the work of Tanizaki Jun'ichirō.[44]

The erotic-grotesque interiority in "Devil's Way," then, can be said to result from multiple textual mediations with Irish, French, American, Japanese, and to a lesser extent Chinese texts. This story's particular interiority testifies to the typical routes Western and Japanese texts took in travelling to China. Read allegorically in terms of Shi's cosmopolitan search for contemporaneity, these texts *finally arrive* in China to make up the interiority of the urban Chinese man: they are now lodged within the Chinese unconscious, and there is nowhere else they can have deeper or more profound effects. The desire for coevalness that I discussed above, then, marks two moments of arrival for Chinese modernists: the desire to arrive at the moment of Western modernity through a contemporary cosmopolitanism, and the arrival of Western and Japanese texts in the Chinese cultural unconscious. The former arrival charts an asymmetrical cosmopolitanism, the latter a dissolution of the self-other dichotomy within the unconscious. These two arrivals beg questions of colonization (in the global context) and a nonessentialist openness and hybridity (in the local context). They are intimately interlinked in tension.

The three other erotic-grotesque stories that Shi wrote also define interiority in terms of reading. In "Haunted House," the foreign women who either commit suicide or are murdered read various kinds of books: a suicidal Russian woman always reads "pessimistic novels"; a young, vivacious Ro-

---

41. Miriam Silverberg, "Japanese Modern Montage: Was the *Ero Guro* Nonsense?" paper given at "Colonialism, Nationalism and Modernity in East Asia" conference, University of California, Santa Cruz, November 11–12, 1996.

42. Interview with Shi Zhecun, October 22–24, 1990; see also Leo Lee's interview with Shi as mentioned in Lee, *Shanghai Modern*, chapters 5 and 9.

43. Shi mentioned in the interview that in the 1920s and 1930s he had read almost the entirety of Poe's works, and considered Poe the origin of "grotesque literature." Interview, October 22–24, 1990. The Poe-inspired story "Ninong" was one of his first stories. For an analysis of this story, see Leo Lee, *Shanghai Modern*, 164–166.

44. Interview with Shi Zhecun, October 20–22, 1990.

manian princess reads Maurice Leblanc's detective novels, about Arsene Lupin and Edgar Wallace's crime fiction; an American wife reads Jack London. Their reading lists reflect their psychological conditions or foreshadow their impending fates.

When Shi's settings move from Shanghai to the countryside, the reading lists of the urban men who visit these country settings change to reflect local flavor. In "Yaksha," a typical neurasthenia-stricken urban man travels to Hangzhou for his grandmother's burial and happens to read legends about yakshas in that area in the local library. On one of his outings, he spots a woman in white and becomes so obsessed with her that he surmises she must be a yaksha, fearsome yet alluring. During his somber moments, he thinks his eyes are playing tricks on him, reminding him that he should go see an ophthalmologist in Shanghai, but when he encounters another woman in white during the night, he mistakes her for the yaksha in his imagination. He fantasizes about the yaksha:

> To love a yaksha, even with the realization that it may only be for a few minutes or a few hours. With my limbs cut off, I would be a victim to the cruelty of this unnatural love. But before I received such a punishment, what strange pleasure such an experience would bring! Reasoning thus, my heart suddenly burned with a grotesque desire.[45]

The mixture of desire and fear drives him to strangle her, but she turns out to be simply a dumb country woman out on a secret rendezvous with her lover in the middle of the night. The narrator, shocked out of his wits, becomes delirious and has to be hospitalized. Visual misrecognition leads to desire and fear, and also to death. The border between matter (the realm of reality) and mind (the realm of imagination) is broken down by a hyperactive visual faculty that can not distinguish between the perceived and the imaginary. Here again, vision serves as the medium that provides access to the fantastic, as well as breaking down the barrier between the unconscious and consciousness.[46]

In "Inn," another urban man suffering from neurasthenia seeks release by traveling to the "interior" (*neidi*) of China to find respite from Shanghai's high-stress lifestyle. In his spooky and dusty rented room with "mysterious" furniture such as an antiquated bed and an "untrustworthy" gas lamp instead

45. Shi Zhecun, *Shi Xiu's Love*, 331.

46. Todorov defines the fantastic as a fictional genre in which the events related in a text cannot easily be explained in supernatural or natural terms. Rather the reader and the character hesitate and feel uncertain about whether the events are supernatural or natural. When a text is neither categorizable as uncanny (explainable supernatural events) nor marvelous (unexplainable supernatural events), it is a fantastic text. Tzvetan Todorov, *The Fantastic: A Structural Approach to a Literary Genre*, trans. Richard Howard (Ithaca: Cornell University Press, 1987), 115–123.

of an electric light, he is reminded of having read such Chinese ghost stories as those in *Jottings from the Thatched Abode of Minute Observations* (*Yuewei caotang biji*), a Qing-dynasty collection of stories, many of which feature female ghosts, and *Record of Rainy Nights under the Autumn Lamp* (*Yeyu qiudeng lu*), a collection of *quanqi* tales. In his fantasies, he imagines seeing female ghosts all around his room, with one female corpse lying under his own body in a sexual pose.[47] The geographical "interior" of the countryside here is a metaphor for the psychological "interior" of the urban man whose weak nerves cannot tolerate the stress of urban living or his anxieties about primitive rural life. At the limit of Western civilization, in the country inn, are ghosts and corpses of the past. In Shi's erotic-grotestque tales as a whole, there exists, then, a neat dichotomy between the city (where Western ghosts roam) and the countryside (where Chinese ghosts roam).

If interiority in Shi's fiction is textually dissimulated through the evocation of Western and Chinese texts, as I have illustrated above, interiority as a *formal* construct is also intertextually mediated. Shi Zhecun refers to the formal practice of interior monologue and stream of consciousness by such diverse authors as Jean Cocteau, James Joyce, Colette, Raymond Radiguet, and Yokomitsu Riichi, and mentions that his work can be seen as similar to the Japanese new psychologism (*shin shinrishugi*) of Itō Sei and Hori Tatsuo as influenced by Joyce and Proust. Here, reading is not merely a way to create atmosphere or foreshadow the fate of his characters, but a means for the author to incorporate formal experiments in modernist interiority.

Shi repeatedly emphasized that the most crucial inspiration for such an interiority was Arthur Schnitzler (1862–1931), the Austrian writer from Vienna and a contemporary of Freud. Shi translated almost all of Schnitzler's major fictional works into Chinese, and noted that by translating Schnitzler, he "acquired" (*xuehui*) Schnitzler's "psychoanalytic method" and "transplanted" (*yizhi*) it into his own work.[48] In 1929, Shi published his first translation of Schnitzler, *Frau Berta Garlan* (1900), and over the next decade translated four other novels and novelettes, including Schnitzler's renowned *Leutnant Gustle*.[49] Shi saw Schnitzler's work as the fictional counterpart to

---

47. Shi Zhecun, *Shi Xiu's Love*, 294–301.

48. Interview with Shi Zhecun, October 20–22, 1990 and my correspondence with the author dated March 16, 1989. See also Shi Zhecun, "About Modernism" (*Guanyu xiandaipai yixitan*), *Wenhui Daily*, October 18, 1983, n.p.

49. *Frau Berta Garlan* (*Duoqing de guafu*), *Frau Beatrice und ihr Sohn* (*Biyateliesi ji qi zi*), and *Fräulein Else* (*Aiarsai zhi si*) were first translated as separate volumes, and were later compiled together as *Trilogy of Women's Hearts* (*Fuxin sanbuqu*) (Shanghai: Yanxingshe, 1947). Shi also translated *Theresa: The Chronicle of a Woman's Life* (*Boming de dailisha*) (Shanghai: Zhonghua shuju, 1937). *Leutnant Gustle* (*Shengsilian*) was serialized in *Eastern Magazine* (*Dongfang zashi*). Guo Shaoyu, Zhao Boyan, and others translated most of Schnitzler's other plays and stories into Chinese around this time.

Freud's studies of sexual psychology, and also as the precursor to the modernist fiction of Joyce and D. H. Lawrence:

> The theme of all [Schnitzler's] work is sexual love, because love is closely linked to all aspects of human life. . . . At the center of his analysis is sexual psychology. His success in this regard is comparable to Freud. Some say that he consciously adopted Freudian theories. However, for realizing Freudian theories in literature and thus ushering in a new era for modern European literature, later leading to such masters of psychoanalysis as Lawrence and Joyce, Schnitzler is indeed responsible. The interior monologues that Joyce uses for his *Ulysses* were in fact previously used by Schnitzler in *Fräulein Else* and *Leutnant Gustle*.[50] (original English and German words in italics)

Here Shi's emphasis is on both the content (sexual psychology) and the form (interior monologues) of psychoanalytic interiority in Schnitzler's fiction, a formula that Shi utilized successfully in such stories as "The Evening of Spring Rain" and the erotic-grotesque tales discussed above.

Shi's choice of Schnitzler's work as the main inspiration for psychoanalytic interiority, rather than the work of such modernist giants as Joyce, has interesting implications, which exemplify how psychoanalysis is situated vis-à-vis the political. According to the historian Carl E. Shorske, Schnitzler's work was written in the fin-de-siècle "social matrix" of Austria when liberalism was increasingly threatened by antiliberal mass movements and the social fabric of "moral-aesthetic culture" was disintegrating. "A despairing but committed liberal," Schnitzler paraded the psychology of the individual through an analysis of the "compulsiveness of Eros, its satisfactions, its delusions, its strange affinity to Thanatos," and "its terrible power to dissolve all social hierarchy."[51] The emergence of the "all-pervasive psychological man" in Vienna was, therefore, spurred by political frustrations at the crisis of liberal culture, requiring a new formulation of the relationship between politics and the psyche.[52] It was also due to stunted political aspirations in the rising tide of anti-Semitism that Freud "retreated into social and intellectual withdrawal" in the form of psychoanalysis, which, as an "a-historical theory of man and society," made "bearable a political world spun out of orbit and beyond control" for his fellow liberals. The realm of politics was displaced by that of the psyche, and politics was neutralized "by reducing it to psychological categories."[53]

The oppositional relationship between psychoanalysis and politics is crucial here, since the psychoanalytic interiority in Shi's work is also clearly de-

---

50. Shi Zhecun, "Translator's Preface" (*Yizhe xu*), in *Theresa: The Chronicle of a Woman's Life*, 4.
51. Carl E. Shorske, *Fin-de-Siècle Vienna: Politics and Culture* (New York: Vintage Books, 1981), 15, 11.
52. Ibid., 4–5.
53. Ibid., 181–203.

politicized. This attests to Shi's political position of trying to remain neutral and not cater to the demands of either the left or the right. The skittishness of the native political scene in Shanghai ironically helped engender a depoliticized cosmopolitanism through a proliferating tapestry of intertextual relations with the metropolitan West and Japan. We may then conclude that depoliticized psychoanalysis in particular, and literary modernism in general, served this cosmopolitanism most fittingly. The assertion of literary autonomy, in such a volatile political context, was legitimated by a sense of artistic purpose according to which art could transcend politics. Shi wrote several essays explicitly criticizing the right and implicitly criticizing the left (about whom he did not dare be explicit) for undermining the autonomy of culture.[54]

One note has to be made here regarding Shi Zhecun's name as it relates directly to his political views: the given name Zhecun is derived from a line in the *Book of Changes* that says "Dragons and snakes hibernate to protect themselves" (*longshe zhi zhe, yi cunshen ye*). "Zhe" refers to hibernation and "cun" means to protect, together suggesting the wisdom of withdrawal at times of turmoil. Although Shi would have liked to withdraw completely from politics, sometimes he could not help getting thrown into the political scene. One (in)famous incident was an unfortunate debate between Shi and Lu Xun over whether the Taoist classic *Zhuangzi* and the medieval *Anthology of Literature* (*Wenxuan*) should be read by youth or not. Lu Xun, who had by that time assumed the role of a leftist literary guru, made unnecessarily acrimonious attacks on Shi, which Shi had hardly provoked. Shi had only written an innocent article recommending that youth read these two classics.[55] But this debate put Shi on the blacklist, for which he had to pay during the Cultural Revolution: anyone who got criticized by Lu Xun was automatically an enemy of the people.

Besides writing the modern tales of the erotic-grotesque populated by neurasthenia-stricken urban men whose psychoanalytic interiorities at once register the tales' textually dissimilated nature and the author's depoliticized stance, Shi also experimented with the genre of historical fiction along erotic-grotesque lines. Since historical fiction is set in a remote past, with equally remote connections to the contemporary situation, Shi could take the

---

54. See his "Book Banning and Leftist Tendency in Thought" (*Shuji jinzhi yu sixiang zuoqing*), *Literary Landscape* (*Wenyi fengjing*) 1:1 (June 1934): 39–43, in which he condemns the Nationalist government's policy of book censorship as "word prison" (*wenziyu*). See also his translator's note to Ernest Toller's "Modern Writers and Europe of the Future" (*Xiandai zuojia yu weilai de Ouzhou*), praising Toller as one fighting for the autonomy of culture in the context of fascism, in *Literary Landscape* 1:2 (July 1934): 2–9. His supportive stance on the Third Category Men as an implicit criticism of the League can be found in his "Editor's Diary" (*Shezhong riji*) in *Les Contemporaines* 2:5 (March 1933): 768–769.

55. In *Complete Works of Lu Xun*, there are more than a dozen entries regarding Lu Xun's criticism of Shi Zhecun.

erotic-grotesque motifs to ever more excessive extremes. Without any pretention to realism and contemporary relevance, he could also deal with issues of racial and cultural conflicts that would otherwise be either too sensitive or too readily interpreted politically. At most, one could read stories about racial and national conflicts as allegories of Shanghai cosmopolitanism's ambivalent stance towards nationalism and national cultural identity. But since the stories were set in the remote past, allegorical readings were not readily assumed. To infuse documented historical figures long dead with sexual psychology was a safe design against potential charges of immorality; to deal with racial and cultural conflicts among different ethnic peoples in old China need not provoke any concerns about colonial critique in leftist circles.

History is here "modernized" and made ahistorical: when the psychoanalytic landscape of desire expands from the field of Shanghai to time immemorial, it brings the past to the present in present terms, thereby reviving the past but also negating the historicity of that past.[56] Here, the past appears in a way entirely dissimilar from Shi's later "return to the past": the past in Shi's historical fiction is molded by present concerns, not vice versa. The past, I am arguing, can appear in multifarious ways, and not all signify a return, as my analysis of *jingpai*'s use of the past in Part Two has shown. Shi instead uses historical narratives, whether fictional or nonfictional, as a testing ground for the author's psychoanalytic gaze acquired from Schnitzler's fiction and Freud's theory. As Yu Dafu noted after reading Shi's collection of historical stories in *The General's Head*, "the advantage of historical fiction is that one can transplant one's own thoughts into the brains of the ancients."[57]

The General's Head is comprised of four tales of erotic desire, all of which pair Eros with Thanatos and reveal the fragile hold of conventional morality upon the psyche even for those most determined to repress their erotic longings. "Kumarajiva" (*Jiumoluoshi*, 1929) records the gradual moral and spiritual disintegration of a noble Indian monk, due to the intensified psychological conflict between his erotic desire and the Buddhist injunction to remain desireless. A renowned historical figure, Kumarajiva (344–413) translated many important Buddhist sutras into Chinese. Historical records document an interesting genetic experiment conducted by his Chinese pa-

56. In this regard, see Andrew Jones, "The Violence of the Text: Reading Yu Hua and Shi Zhecun," *positions* 2:3 (Winter 1994): 570–602, in which he notes that Shi's story "Shi Xiu" (discussed below) "enacts a characteristic May Fourth faith in the power of representation to unproblematically transpose modernity onto Chinese soil. Ironically, however, the violence of his transfiguration of tradition is inevitably informed by the imperialist violence of China's entry into modernity" (574).

57. Yu Dafu, "Painting in the Heat Wave" (*Zai rebo li chuanxi*), *Les Contemporaines* 1:5 (September 1932): 643.

tron, who offered ten girls to Kumarajiva to assure that his brilliance be pre-
served in his descendants.[58] Taken from *Biographies of Eminent Monks (Gaoseng-zhuan)* and particularly the *History of the Jin Dynasty (Jinshu)*, Shi's story transforms this bare-bones plot into a lengthy psychoanalytic treatment of how
the experiment followed from a succession of erotic-spiritual conflicts tormenting the noble monk's psyche.

The bulk of Shi's story is rendered in indirect interior monologues, which
record in detail the psychological turmoils of the monk as he navigates between the eruption of his sexual desire (*mo*, the devil) and the self-censor-
ship arising from his religious piety (*tao*, the Way). Instead of describing the
sexual consummation between Kumarajiva and the imperial ladies given to
him by the Chinese patron as a mere genetic experiment, Shi reinterprets
it as a fundamentally human act arising from sexual desire. The story also
reveals an ironic view of religious asceticism in its interpretation of a detail
from Kumarajiva's biography: when Kumarajiva died, the only part of his body
not consumed in the cremation was said to be his tongue, symbolic of his
genius for language and translation. Shi carefully builds an erotic symbolism around the tongue in his version of the story: Kumarajiva's wife passionately held his tongue in her mouth as she was dying, and his tongue itched
every time he had an erotic thought. The tongue is ironically rendered not
as the immortal relic worshiped by Kumarajiva's religious followers, but as
the eternal emblem of desire.

The title story, "The General's Head," takes the power of erotic desire to
supernatural proportions in line with the erotic-grotesque genre. It features
the macabre image of a headless general riding on horseback to see his lover
after a bloody battle, a grotesque confirmation that even death cannot overcome the obsessive power of Eros. Taken from the *Old History of the Tang
Dynasty (Jiu Tangshu)* and Du Fu's poems about the famous general Hua
Jingding, this story presents a mental conflict different from Kumarajiva's:
here the conflict is between the racial/cultural allegiances of a half-Tibetan,
half-Chinese general (at a time when China and Tibet were at war) and his
infatuation with a Chinese woman. Just when he decides to desert his un-
ruly and immoral Chinese soldiers and defect to the Tibetans, he falls in love
with the woman. Direct and indirect interior monologues give a glimpse into
his tormented mind, for he is unable to decide whether to desert China
(hence the Chinese woman too) or to fight Tibet. His encounter with the
girl, however, is mired in further complications. It was because one of his
soldiers tried to rape her that she was brought to General Hua, to testify
against the soldier. In accordance with martial law, the soldier was beheaded. Thus, when the general later confesses his love to the girl, she wryly

---

58. See Kenneth Ch'en, *Buddhism in China* (Princeton: Princeton University Press, 1964),
81–83, and "Kumarajiva," *History of the Jin Dynasty, juan* 95, biography no. 65.

points out his self-contradiction: shouldn't his martial law apply to him as well? In jest she says that she will only accept him if he is also beheaded. The jest becomes a curse when his longing for her distracts him in the heat of battle and a Tibetan general beheads him. Holding his head under one arm, he rides back to see her, only to be met with her sneer telling him not to pretend to be alive. The story ends with his torso falling from the horse, his head caught by Tibetans, and his eyes weeping. The general's desire, which transcends racial boundaries, is his tragic flaw in a highly volatile context of ethnic rivalries.

"Princess Ah Lan," most likely based on a story recounted by the Ming Dynasty scholar-poet Yang Shen in his *Records of Yunnan* (*Dianzaiji*), is very similar in conception to "The General's Head," its main conflict being that between Eros and racial/national allegiance. The Han Chinese general Duan Gong's humiliation under Mongolian occupation during the Yuan Dynasty and his love for a Mongolian princess, Ah Lan, and Ah Lan's equally divided allegiance to her own race and the Chinese general, form the basis of the dual development of conflicts. Again, it is Eros, which transcends racial and national belonging, that leads Duan Gong and Ah Lan to their inevitable deaths.[59] A sadistic Mongolian general, driven by his love for the princess and uncontrollable jealousy of her husband Duan, harbors vengeful thoughts against Duan: "In his mind he only felt hatred and jealousy [toward Duan]. And this hatred and jealousy . . . was now sublimated into a cruel desire to kill. . . . He wanted Duan killed by princess Ah Lan, and the death had to be the most tragic and cruel death possible. When he thought about this, he felt that it would be the most beautiful and fantastic event."[60] He schemes to have princess Ah Lan administer poison to Duan. Ah Lan refuses to comply, so he has Duan fingered for treason and killed in an ambush. The anguished princess decides to kill the Mongolian general with the same poison, peacock's bile, that he had given her for Duan. But he spots her scheme and instead forces the poisoned wine down her throat:

> With the arm that lifted bronze shields, he held princess Ah Lan close to him as if clasping a minute insect, and poured the poisoned wine into her red lips. Once done, he let go of the princess and, like an old, evil owl, laughed wildly.
> The princess madly ran out. Her long, slender, white dress trailed on the ground and reflected the silver light of the moon, like a phantasmic goddess

---

59. Guo Moruo's famous historical play *Peacock Bile* (*Kongquedan*, 1943) is based on the same story. In Guo's "Postscript to *Peacock Bile*" (*Kongquedan houji*), he notes that Duan Pingzhang was a Han Chinese; *Research Materials on Guo Moruo* (*Guo Moruo yanjiu ziliao*), ed. Wang Xunzhao et al. (Beijing: Zhongguo shehui kexue chubanshe, 1986), 1:341–349. Shi told me that he suspects Guo's inspiration for the play came from Shi's own story.

60. *The General's Head*, 190.

passing through the dense forests of a mythical island. She ran towards that chilly ancient pond, and like the peacock she had seen earlier, bent her body over the white stone railing, so that the silent pond forever captured her last, beautiful reflection.[61]

In rococo language, Shi captures the sadistic pleasure the general derives from killing the object of his love who refuses to belong to him, and the tragic beauty of her death. Racially and nationally transgressive love is summarily punished, but this love also seemingly transcends death.

Sadism is most explicitly narrated in "Shi Xiu," a retelling, with a psychoanalystic twist, of an episode in the fourteenth-century novel *Water Margin*. In chapters 44 and 45 of the novel, the righteous Shi Xiu tells his sworn brother Yang Xiong of Yang's wife's adultery, which leads him to dismember his wife. Shi Zhecun follows the original plot closely, but he adds an analysis of Shi Xiu's sexual psychology in light of sadism. In Shi Zhecun's version, Shi Xiu's motivation for informing on Pan Qiaoyun's adultery is the tension between his erotic desire to possess her and his loyalty to his sworn brother. Unable to deal with this internal conflict, he substitutes his erotic feelings with sadistic fantasies, ultimately becoming inflamed with the urge to kill the object of his desire. First he kills Pan's illicit lover and finds the taste of blood scintillating. "Of all things in the world, killing is the most pleasurable," he muses.[62] Unable to fulfill his desire to sleep with her, he now finds killing her the only way to love her: "Although in the past he thought 'because I love her I have to sleep with her,' now his thought powerfully turned into 'because I love her I have to kill her.' Since Shi Xiu felt that the most pleasurable thing was to kill, sleeping with a woman was therefore absolutely not as pleasurable as killing a woman."[63] In an erotically charged passage, he fantasizes about the beauty of blood running down her naked body:

> If I pierce this sharp dagger through the naked flesh of Pan Qiaoyun, fresh red blood will drip from her delicate, white, clean, pure skin, her seductive head will twist with pain, her lustrous hair will hang down to her nipples, her even teeth will bite her crimson tongue or lower lip, her four limbs will tremble with slight but proportionate quivers. Just imagine such a scene, isn't it strikingly beautiful?[64]

Sexual urges constrained by the code of brotherhood result in a sadistic fantasy in which piercing with a phallic dagger replaces the sexual act. His fantasies are gratified when he persuades his sworn brother to kill Pan Qiaoyun

61. Ibid., 223.
62. Ibid., 157.
63. Ibid., 157.
64. Ibid., 158–159.

as punishment for her adultery. With each thrust of his sworn brother's dagger, Shi Xiu trembles with sadistic pleasure. Even the dismembered parts of Pan's body—her tongue, limbs, and breasts—are gazed at with fetishistic desire. Seeing ravens tearing at her entrails, Shi Xiu even exclaims to himself, "It must be very delicious!"[65] Fetishistic scopophilia and sadistic voyeurism, by which he deals with his castration anxiety,[66] converge in a final rampage of gruesome dismemberment.

Taken together, these four stories illustrate the compulsiveness and destructive power of Eros, resulting uniformly in death of the loved object or the self. Only in "Shi Xiu" are the conflictual allegiances tormenting the male psyche resolved, through a sadistic sublimation of erotic desire which seals Shi Xiu's brotherhood with Yang Xiong with the blood of Pan Qiaoyun. In contrast to the many emasculated and hypersensitive urban men in Shi's fiction, or the men who die for the sake of their obsessive desires in the other historical tales, Shi Xiu powerfully asserts his manhood and masculinity via physical and scopic violence imposed on the obstacle to brotherhood: women. In Shi's fictional world, such masculine assertion, with its obvious misogyny, can only occur in a remote past of no immediate consequence to the present (and a textually simulated past at that, since the story is derived from another text). The interiority in Shi's fiction, whether contemporary or historical, thus tends to be a nonideological and apolitical space of textual dissimulation and erotic-grotesque fantasies.

THE REJECTION OF THE WEST

The past would appear in a different mode and with a different relationship to the present by the time Shi's last collection of stories, *Little Treasures,* appeared in 1936. Around 1934 and 1935, a "literary purge" (*wenyi douzheng*) was launched by the League of Left-Wing Writers to put pressure on writers who did not conform to the literary guidelines dictated by the League. Shi maintained that Zhou Yang and Xia Yan even hired people to publish criticisms of nonleftist writers.[67] Under such pressures, Shi switched to writing realistic stories about how difficult survival was under capitalism in both the countryside and the city.

What distinguishes these stories from more ostensibly leftist stories endorsed by the League is Shi's deft portrayal of the effects of capitalism on the psychology of its victims. The peasants in "Milk" (*Niunai*) and "A Road

---

65. Ibid., 170.

66. Laura Mulvey describes these two methods as typical of a male viewer's ways of relating to the image of woman on the movie screen. See her "Narrative Cinema and Visual Pleasure," in *Visual and Other Pleasures* (Bloomington: Indiana University Press, 1989), 14–26.

67. Interview with Shi Zhecun, October 20–22, 1990.

for Cars" (*Qichelu*) and the urban salarymen in "Business Cards" (*Mingpian*) and "Unemployment" (*Shiye*) are examples of such victims. Curiously, however, when modern Chinese fiction picks up social issues as its main theme, its form usually retreats to a realism with little experimental flavor or technical innovation. Somehow Shi "returned" to his earliest mode of writing, that of his *Festival Lantern* days. But the term "returning" here takes on a different significance, since Shi began to self-consciously incorporate traditional *huaben* narrative conventions, such as the style of oral storytelling in "Hunting Tigers" (*Liehuji*). Shi noted in my interview that in order to balance the pressures coming from the left and the right, "returning to tradition" (*huigui chuantong*) was the only workable path; there was no future for psychoanalytic fiction. This "inevitability of returning" was also the "return of the prodigal son." "One cannot escape from one's roots," as he put it.[68]

In April of the following year, 1937, Shi theorized his "returning to tradition" in an important essay entitled "Dialogues in Fiction," published in the journal *Cosmic Wind*. Shi's essay was written upon reading Tanizaki Jun'ichirō's "Postscript to *The Portrait of Shunkin*" (*Chunqinchao houyu*) and finding a kindred spirit in Tanizaki, who was one of the chief proponents of the "Return to Japan" (*Nihon kaiki*) ideology which advocated the rejection of the West. Shi summarizes Tanizaki's ideas in this essay. Tanizaki asserts that the traditional Japanese way of presenting dialogue in fiction better conveys the beauty of the Japanese language. Using *The Tales of Genji* as an example, he notes that traditional narratives often present dialogue without quotation marks and intermingle dialogue with narration so that it is hard to tell them apart. In using Western-style dialogues, with such conventions as "he says" and "I said," Tanizaki confesses, his early work was very awkward. He argues that dialogue can be done away with altogether and replaced with traditional styles, such as the oral storytelling style (*gushiti* in Shi's Chinese translation) or jotting style (*suibiti*). Elaborate description (*miaoshu*) is also unnecessary.

Defending what critics might construe as an "archaism of narrative genre and technique," Shi notes that Tanizaki's aim is to "bring out the new in the old." Tanizaki's ideas here go against the grain of Western-oriented modern Chinese literary conventions as practiced from the May Fourth era on, Shi notes, and his views challenge the primacy of the Western fictional form, causing one to reflect upon the value of traditional narrative styles and genres— such as multichapter novels (*zhanghui xiaoshuo*), vernacular short stories (*huaben*), fantastic tales (*chuanqi*), and note-form jottings (*biji*)—which are more easily understood and better received by the Chinese readership. Shi uses the example of Cao Xueqin's depiction of Lin Daiyu in *Dream of the Red Chamber* to illustrate that, without psychoanalysis or cumbersome dialogues,

68. Ibid.

Lin's psychology was nonetheless well presented and easily decipherable by readers. Repudiating the value of psychoanalysis, which had undergirded most of his modernist fiction, Shi ends his article on the hopeful note that if modern Chinese writers reflect upon these issues, they will be able to transform modern Chinese literature into a new form and add new dimensions to the vernacular language.[69]

Many of the ideas covered in "Dialogues in Fiction" are put into practice in "Master Huangxin" (*Huangxin dashi,* 1937)—the lone literary evidence of Shi's "return" besides "Hunting Tigers." First of all, Shi limits description (*miaoshu*) to a minimum and combines narration (*xushu*) and unmediated dialogue to retell a legendary story about the Buddhist nun Master Huangxin of the Ming Dynasty. The dialogue appears without "cumbersome" tags, such as "he said" or "she said," but no confusion ensues as to the identity of the addresser or addressee. The narrator is a self-reflexive storyteller, commenting not only on the story he is telling but also on the mechanism of his telling it: how he got interested in the story of Master Huangxin, where he found her biographical materials, to what extent he agrees or disagrees with her biographers' interpretations of certain details of her life, and why he interprets those details in the way he does. The telling of her story also begins in the classic chronological manner, starting with a short biography from birth. He mixes modern vernacular with traditional storytelling expressions such as "This concerns later incidents and won't be related in detail here." The language sounds casual and conversational, and yet the story moves quickly, propelled by the many dramatic moments in the plot. Responding to criticism of the story by Xu Jie, Shi explained that he meant the story to mix the genres of traditional "commenting narrative" (*pinghua*), romance (*yanyi*), and fantastic tales. It was a conscious attempt to create "a new Chinese-style fictional genre" and "a new Chinese-style vernacular."[70] Since modern Chinese literature had merely been an "adopted son" of European literature,[71] he said, it was necessary to create a new form and a "pure" Chinese vernacular and to repudiate "Europeanized syntax."[72]

Recall that the entire modernist enterprise in modern China had focused on form, technique, and language, and one can see what a drastic deviation from that norm Shi was articulating at that moment in 1937. Such an artic-

---

69. Shi Zhecun, "Dialogues in Fiction" (*Xiaoshuo zhong de duihua*), *Cosmic Wind* (*Yuzhou feng*) 39 (April 1937): n.p. The fact that this returning was inspired by Tanizaki, a chief proponent of the "Return to Japan" ideology (*Nihon kaiki*) in the 1930s, further suggests that it was again an aspect of the intertextual dissimulation discussed above.

70. Shi Zhecun, "Some Words about 'Master Huangxin'" (*Guanyu Huangxin dashi de jijuhua*), *Chinese Literature* (*Zhongguo wenyi*) 1:2 (June 1937): n.p.

71. Shi Zhecun, "Dialogues in Fiction."

72. Shi Zhecun, "Some Words about 'Master Huangxin.'"

ulation marks the end of two decades of modernist experimentation. His emphasis on recuperating traditional narrative forms and techniques registers a complete turnabout from the May Fourth pursuit of Western modernity, in which Europeanized syntax, form, and technique automatically carried cultural value. His turnabout—not a critique of May Fourth modernity (through locating the correspondences between the Chinese and the Western in an expanded notion of modernity, as in the *jingpai* discourse), nor the imposition of modern perspectives on traditional materials (as in his own historical fiction)—was a return to what he considered to be the time prior to imperialism and Westernization. He wanted to herald a "revolution in form" (*wenti gaige*), as he put it in the interview, and to "transform the language of modern Chinese literature" by recuperating the Chinese language "before Europeanization."[73] It was a return to an essential, pure China before political and cultural colonization, so that a "national form" (*minzu xingshi*) could be reconstructed and "national affect" (*minzu ganjue*) could be vindicated.[74] A long novel in the planning, entitled *Gold-Melting Pot* (*Xiaojinguo*), aimed at presenting the social canvas of a small town in the Song dynasty undergoing the process of capitalization and urbanization, and was meant to bring such theoretical rethinking of form and language to fruition, although it never materialized due to the outbreak of the Sino-Japanese War.

Shi's return, however, portended a return to the temporal past: the space of the countryside (which always embodied the past in the modernist imaginary) or to the historical past. It was as if writing in the recuperated traditional style, form, technique, and language could only adequately deal with the antiquated experiences of the past. The obvious limitation to this return, then, would be its inability to capture experiences of modernity. Shi admitted that in practice it was difficult to use less description and indirect dialogue and to opt for narration and unmediated dialogue, as his returning called for. He could not have tread this path for long, even if the war had not broken out, and it could easily have been merely a resting place in the meandering path of his creative career, rather than his final destination. There was no essential China one could go back to.

To conclude, this return to national sentiments via a rejection of Western form and syntax finally collapsed the difference between the metropolitan West and the colonial West that modernist cosmopolitanism had tried so hard to maintain in order to legitimate its pursuit of modernity. The nationalist necessity to critique the colonial West could now be achieved: Shi rejected the metropolitan West by repudiating its literary form and syntax. The collapse of these two "Wests" required exorcising Westernized elements from

73. Interview with Shi Zhecun, October 20–22, 1990.
74. Ibid.

Chinese writing and constructing a pure, essential Chinese tradition. This construction of the past, however, could not be anything but impure: not because it was a reactive response to a now implicitly recognized cultural colonization as such, but because any construction of the past is necessarily a re-creation process, one that actively *produces* the past at the present moment for the purposes of the present. But the rhetoric of return unfortunately meant the demise of Shanghai modernism, much of whose impetus had been the seduction of metropolitan modernity.

Semicolonialism and Culture

Throughout this book I have argued that understanding modernism in Republican China necessitates multiple contextualization within the local and the global, with consideration to both the spatial and temporal dimensions of these contexts. The modernism that was formed in the changing local contexts of cultural debate, political strife, and social upheaval was also shaped by global cultural and economic flows propelled by imperialism. One most tangible manifestation of this local/global conjuncture was semicolonialism, a *political* formation of layered domination by multiple foreign powers who competed and cooperated with each other in pursuit of their own individual economic and political agendas. If for India the colonial state was structured like a "despotism, with no mediating depths, no space provided for the transactions between the will of the rulers and that of the ruled,"[1] the semicolonial formation was much less categorical. The sheer number of colonial powers in China prevented the constitution of a unified colonial state with well-coordinated policies of control, and the foreign powers were restricted geographically, mostly to the coastal areas of China, leaving the large hinterland relatively untouched. The Chinese were by no means entirely subject to the will of the colonial rulers. In addition to fissures in colonial control, the rudimentary sovereignty of the Chinese state also favored the possibility of political agency for Chinese intellectuals who debated and experimented with various political forms and ideologies, though these very debates and experiments contributed to increasing strife, atomization, and ultimately civil war. As a political formation, semicolonialism meant that local politics was largely bereft of stable organization and control, and was sub-

---

1. Ranajit Guha, *Dominance Without Hegemony: History and Power in Colonial India* (Cambridge: Harvard University Press, 1997), 65.

ject to extreme volatility, as the colonial powers exacerbated and even en-couraged internal political conflicts for their benefit. The politically motivated assassinations of three of the writers studied in this book—Liu Na'ou, Mu Shiying, and Yu Dafu—are testimony to this volatility.

Semicolonialism was more coherent in the *economic* realm, and herein lies its similarity with later neocolonialism, though this similarity is historically specific and situated of course. With the exception of Japan's territorial am-bitions and its institution of formal colonialism in Manchuria and Taiwan, the imperialist powers were more intent on economic gains, once extrater-ritorial rights were attained and relatively small pockets of China were ap-propriated for settlements. Given the many unequal treaties China was forced to sign, the Chinese losses to the imperialist powers in the economic domain were particularly profound, including payments of indemnity obligations, grants of monopolies in certain industries, and yielding control over the financial sector and customs (the latter until 1930). These losses caused the destruction of rural industries, and a serious drain on the Chinese economy in general.[2] Qi Shufen, the author of the early-1920s Marxist classic *China under Economic Invasion* (*Jingji qinlue xia zhi Zhongguo*), defined China's for-eign relations as chiefly economic:

> With the force of ten thousand charging horses, foreign capitalist imperialism has trampled upon our nation. In order to solve their problem of the market, we provided one hundred commercial ports; in order to solve their problem of investment, we absorbed over two billion yuan in capital and lost numerous benefits and rights; in order to facilitate their market and the management of their place of investment, we handed over immense transportation rights. The history of our foreign relations can thus be broadly summarized.[3]

For domestic Chinese politics, such economic imperialism had severe con-sequences. While the fragmentation of jurisdiction created through the set-tlement system made it impossible to institute a national and unified legal system, and often provided criminals sanctuary, the deepening economic cri-sis further frustrated efforts at domestic political unification.

Like neocolonialism, semicolonialism chiefly operated through economic and cultural imperialisms and not territorial occupation. As a *cultural* for-mation, it is especially productive to contrast its unique set of practices and cultural politics with those of formal colonialism. The political structure of

---

2. Jürgen Osterhammel, "Semi-colonialism and Informal Empire in Twentieth-Century China: Towards a Framework of Analysis," in Jürgen Osterhammel and Wolfgang J. Mommsen, eds., *Imperialism and After: Continuities and Discontinuities* (London: Allen and Unwin, 1986), 290–291.

3. Quoted in Liang Shuming, "Respectfully Presented for Mr. Hu Shih's Instruction" (*Jing yi qingjiao Hu Shizhi xiansheng*), in *Which Road Shall We Take?* (*Women zou natiaolu*) (Taipei: Yuan-liu chubanshe, 1986), 23.

formal colonialism which ruled by fear and force in India, tolerating less ambiguity and ambivalence, made the colonial state a ready target of cultural
articulations of resistance. This is what Ranajit Guha means by the colonial
state being an "absolute externality," whose policies of control favored coercion over persuasion and therefore provoked broad resistance. The British
colonial state was therefore nonhegemonic in the sense that it was unable
to "assimilate the civil society of the colonized to itself," hence it exercised
"dominance without hegemony."[4] Resistance was a structural possibility, and
even a natural consequence, in such a situation. This is why in India one
finds sustained critiques of Western modernity from both antimodern and
nonmodern positions.

Unlike the Indian cultural experience of formal colonialism, semicolonialism as a cultural formation was characterized by a different set of historically informed relations. First, the insufficiently formalized colonial
structure, lacking systematic institutional infrastructure, did not overtly position the colonial powers as the unequivocal targets of cultural resistance.
By the May Fourth period, Western presence in China was more or less stabilized in pockets of extraterritoriality, in effect constituting a space that was
other than China rather than one that had taken over China. This fragmented, and some may say diffused, presence made nativist aesthetics at most
an option, not a necessity, and many did not see nativism as a very attractive
option at that. Since colonial powers did not impose a colonial epistemology by force and could not contain relations of representation in the cultural arena, there was no perceived urgency to define Chinese culture as the
locus of resistance. Resistance as a category of cultural articulation was therefore not a given, as in the Indian case, and neither was collaboration. That
is to say, when representation is not a contest of power with the colonial powers, cultural judgment does not merely consist of identifying resistance and
collaboration. To borrow from Stephen Hay, "the greater the threat from
the West to [Asian intellectuals'] sense of cultural and political integrity, the
greater their psychological need to hold on to an idealized conception of
the East as a counterweight to Western power and influence."[5] The less the
perceived threat, whether illusory or not, the less they needed a nativist aesthetics, and the more open a cultural attitude they could have to the West.

Second, the perceived autonomy of representation and a favored openness to Western culture went hand in hand with a cultural attitude that can
be termed cosmopolitan. This cosmopolitanism was problematically constituted. As I have shown, it sought to locate its interlocutors in the global arena
by turning to the metropolitan West and Japan, and had to systematically

4. Guha, *Dominance Without Hegemony*, x–xii.

5. Steven N. Hay, *Asian Ideas of East and West: Tagore and His Critics in Japan, China, and India* (Cambridge: Harvard University Press, 1970), 312.

displace the semicolonial reality of Western and Japanese imperialisms which nevertheless was integral to the lived experience of cosmopolitans, particularly in urban Shanghai. This is what I have called the practice or strategy of bifurcating the "colonial West/Japan" and the "metropolitan West/Japan" in the cultural imaginary of the modernists who flaunted a cosmopolitan stance. By this strategy, the cosmopolitans chose not to engage with the racial, economic, and other hierarchies in their lived experience of foreign settlements, but instead chose to project their vision to faraway metropolitan centers where a liberal hegemony operated in the garb of civilization, persuasion, rule of law, and consent. Linking their cultural articulation to metropolitan practices, Chinese modernists "entered into" the global arena in a leap of imagination. I emphasize the imaginary nature of this dialogue, because, as I have shown, it was very much a one-sided affair, with the Chinese gesticulating energetically without really getting seen or heard. Hence my discussion of asymmetrical cosmopolitanism in chapter 5.

Related to this asymmetrical cosmopolitanism is my insistence that the cosmopolitans' Occidentalism (drawing from the West for local purposes) cannot be construed as the flipside of Orientalism. Unlike Orientalism, Chinese Occidentalism was not coupled with political ambition towards the West. Rather than being Orientalism's reverse, it was almost a copy of Orientalism in that it particularized Chinese culture as the locus of the past and endorsed the universal validity of Western culture. In a paradoxical fashion, the perception of China's cultural autonomy—purportedly defended by its linguistic autonomy—facilitated a more thoroughgoing embrace of an Occidentalism in which the West as a construct was largely the harbinger of enlightenment and progress. As I have shown, the one potential cultural nativism of *jingpai* philosophers and writers, who recuperated Confucianism, was itself mediated by a post–World War I Western endorsement of Confucianism by Western philosophers. It was still the West that determined what could be granted the virtue of universalism.

Third, such a cultural practice of Occidentalism, and the strategy of bifurcation which rationalizes it, complicate the circulation of agency. Using their Occidentalism to compete for local cultural authority appeared to endow the Chinese modernists with a measure of agency in the form of both cultural and symbolic capital. But in the global context of asymmetrical cosmopolitanism and self-particularizing Occidentalism, their agency was debatable. And when the imperialist powers deployed force to protect their economic and political interests, such openness to the West and Japan undermined cultural nation-building projects and became the locus of the willing colonization of consciousness. I have tried to illustrate the interpenetration of these two constitutions of agency—as both subjects and subjected—and the fundamental tension between them. Since power is relational, expanding the discursive contexts of Chinese modernism subjects it to an ever-extended set of relations which is not so much repetitive as over-lapping and contradictory. Empowerment in a given local context turns into disempowerment in the global discursive context, and many shades of complexity lie in between. Such was the case for May Fourth Occidentalists. Conversely, a disempowered articulation in the local context, such as the *jingpai* discourse in the context of the supremacy of May Fourth Westernization campaigns, can be construed as empowerment in the global context for its critical stance against Western modernity, albeit limited empowerment, for reasons I discussed in chapter 7.

By thus delineating contradictions of agency in different contexts, I emphasize that in semicolonial China, when colonial Manicheanisms were not readily apparent or structurally built into representational practices, agency operates in the logic of the contingent. By "the logic of the contingent" I mean how a particular alignment of factors, agents, and events in a specific context allows for a reading of agency which is applicable to that context alone. I do not mean by this an absolute fluidity of meaning or agency; I mean to foreground that cultural criticism is ineluctably an exercise in locating moments of fixity through an investigation of given contexts, and that, following Chantel Mouffe and Ernest Laclau, contingency is always constituted by its interplay with necessity.[6] I have tried to identify these moments of fixity and loci of necessity by examining the May Fourth Occidentalists, the *jingpai* philosophers and writers, and the new sensationists in their different historical and cultural contexts. It is inevitable then that their agencies were differently constituted, as they responded to their own conditions of exigency and contingency diversely within different temporalities and across local and global terrains.

A fascinating cultural comparison between formal colonialism and semicolonialism lies in language. The institution of English as the official language, and as the language that carried all possible forms of capital (economic, symbolic, and cultural), was part of the colonial cultural apparatus that the British had so successfully inculcated in their colonized subjects. The broad adoption of English as the language of education and cultural expression, even in postcolonial India, provides a strong contrast with the Chinese case, where linguistic autonomy was perceived to be more or less intact. What did happen to the Chinese language, however, was an extensive Europeanization of all of its properties. That is to say, depending on how one defines autonomy, one can also make a case for the colonization of the Chinese language. The marked difference in the two types of linguistic colonization is that a colonial apparatus instituted English in India, while the Chinese eagerly absorbed English and other powerful foreign languages

6. Ernesto Laclau and Chantel Mouffe, *Hegemony and Socialist Strategy* (London: Verso, 1985), 114.

(French and Japanese especially) due to the influence, prestige, and cultural superiority exerted directly by faraway metropolitan cultures, not colonial cultures present in China. Besides being a clear example of the Chinese practice of separating the metropolitan from the colonial, this also shows that Chinese culture under semicolonialism was more the object of metropolitan cultural imperialism than colonial cultural domination, a fact which further suggests an affinity between semicolonialism and neocolonialism.

A prevalent feature of our own postimperialist, neocolonial era is Western cultural hegemony positing itself as the ultimate arbiter of value or frame of reference. This positing must in turn be internalized by the neocolonized for cultural hegemony to be possible, the main operational mode of hegemony being the persuasion and consent of those thus hegemonized. Whether in the Occidentalist modernism of the May Fourth, the *jingpai* version of cultural universalism, or new sensationism, the metropolitan Western gaze was always anticipated. The metropolitan cultures were the imaginary interlocutors in all of the major Chinese dialogues about and practices of modernism. Even the recuperation of the Chinese past was filtered through this anticipated Western gaze to such an extent that one can argue for self-Orientalization as the meeting point between Western Orientalism and Chinese Occidentalism.

Finding validation for the revival of Chinese culture in the civilizational discourse prevalent in post–World War I Europe, *jingpai* thinkers and writers exemplify one of these meeting points. In a different, perhaps more straightforward way, the wholesale rejection of Chinese tradition by the Occidentalists can also be read as an act of Orientalism: Chinese tradition became modern China's "Orient" that needed to be denounced in order for modern China to become a worthy member in the Occidentalized world. As for the new sensationists, there was neither a passionate call to denounce tradition nor a qualified recuperation of it. One may argue that, with the exception of Shi Zhecun's writings after his modernist phase, tradition did not even constitute a problematic which one needed to take a stand on one way or the other. Capitalist modernity was the only reality to reckon with, and this reckoning became interiorized as there was no other readily available means—such as tradition and its reincarnation as nativism—with which to refute the overwhelming stimuli from its onslaught. Hence the predominance of descriptions of the psychological and physical symptoms resulting from modern stimuli in new sensationist narratives: neurasthenia, delusions, anxiety, neurosis, fatigue, libidinal pathologies, and so forth. Indeed, what we witness is the physical and psychic consequences to those who have absorbed the May Fourth ideology of total Westernization. This ideology was not realized as a social project (as had been wished), but instead manifested itself as psychological disturbance and erotic excess. When the shield of tradition as such was removed in the Chinese writers' confrontation with Western modernity, no other device was readily available to replace its media-tional function. It was with naked bodies and raw emotions that modernity as such came to be experienced in the urban playgrounds of semicolonial Shanghai.

These three modes of negotiation with the West—Occidentalists imagining equality by persuading themselves that they could catch up with the West, *jingpai* thinkers providing a qualified critique of the West based on the available Western self-critiques, and new sensationists accepting Western capitalist culture as a given, unalterable reality—constitute three important processes. If drawn and built upon, they would have grounded a more complex rethinking of China's relationship with the West in the decades that followed. However, with history's pendulum swing to communist nationalism, these earlier efforts were denounced altogether after 1949, and the swing back to liberalization in the 1980s therefore had to witness a repetition of these earlier efforts from scratch, although the repetition was strongly informed by difference. The sense of déjà vu in the 1980s and 1990s, when China again became incorporated into the global arena and reconfronted issues of modernity in a new burst of literary modernism, makes us pause and wonder what possibilities there might have been had this repetition not been necessary. Fully granting the importance of the socialist revolution but recognizing its unfortunate, ultimate failure, the cultural historian is left to ponder the given-ness of China's globalization, with its complex invocations of both the semicolonial past and the new neocolonial world order.

Later Modernisms

The War Years and Beyond

With the onset of the Sino-Japanese War in 1937, literary activities initially came to a complete halt. Beijing soon fell to the Japanese; Shanghai became an "isolated island" (*gudao*), and the foreign concessions were surrounded by the Japanese army encamped on the outskirts of the city until they too fell into Japanese hands during the Pacific War. Most writers left the two cultural centers and dispersed to Nationalist-controlled inland areas, with a small minority of writers going to Communist-controlled territory. A younger generation of writers came of age in the 1940s, however, and started publishing formally experimental stories in the few literary journals available. Other writers came into prominence in such cities as Kunming, Guangdong, Hong Kong, and Chongqing. In contrast to the previous two decades, the era from 1937 to 1949 witnessed a decentralization of culture as a result of national disintegration and the resultant dispersion of literary figures, although the occupied areas remained productive loci after the initial halt in activities. In this appendix, I provide a preliminary commentary on 1940s literary modernism and beyond, and reflect upon the larger issue of the repetitiveness of modernism as endemic to the modernity project in the Third World context.

During the war, several existing literary journals continued publication and some new ones appeared in at least five major cities, publishing some of the same writers, although these writers were now of rather different persuasions. During the Japanese occupation, both *Artistic and Literary Magazine* (*Yiwen zazhi*) headed by Zhou Zuoren in Beijing and *Wind and Rain Talks* (*Fengyutan*) in Shanghai prominently featured modern Japanese literature. This of course had much to do with the institution of a formalized Japanese colonial cultural policy in these two cities. Many writers gathered in the wartime Nationalist capital of Chongqing, and published in such magazines as *Literary and Artistic Vanguard* (*Wenyi xianfeng*), one of whose editors was the Shanghai modernist Xu Xiacun; *Time and Tide Literature and Art* (*Shi yu chao wenyi*), another modernist journal; *Central Plain* (*Zhongyuan*), edited by the Creation Society modernist Guo Moruo; and the famous *Literary Supplement to the Dagong Daily*. Other writers fled to Hong Kong for different lengths of time, and scattered literary efforts were found in Guangzhou (where Mao Dun edited *Literary and Artistic Front* [*Wenyi zhendi*], for instance) and Guilin (*Literary and Artistic Magazine* [*Wenyi zazhi*]). The end of the war in 1945 brought the revival of *Literature Magazine* (*Wenxue zazhi*) edited by Zhu Guangqian, and the publication of *Literary and Artistic Renaissance* (*Wenyi fuxing*) edited by Zheng Zhenduo and Li Jianwu, in the old cultural centers of the previous decades, Beijing and Shanghai.

Notwithstanding the upheavals brought on by the Sino-Japanese War and the subsequent civil war, this era witnessed impressive contributions to modernist literature. The experience of occupation in Beijing and Shanghai, as Edward Gunn observes, curiously "resulted in particularly important literary achievements," the most original of which, according to him, were the "antiromantic" works of Zhang Ailing (Eileen Chang), Qian Zhongshu, and Yang Jiang.[1] Besides these writers, whose antiromanticism exhibited the modernist repudiation of sentimentalism, the single most significant, and unjustly ignored, achievement were Wang Zengqi's (1920–1997) stories written in remote Kunming, site of Southwestern United University. Other writers, such as Mei Niang (b. 1920) writing in occupied Beijing, and Bi Jichu (n.d.), who became active on the pages of *Literature Magazine* revived in Beijing in 1947, were also committed to the modernist style. Given the experience of war, the ascendancy of cultural nationalism in unoccupied areas, and the strict censorship in occupied areas, such an interest in modernist experimentation was particularly poignant.

Three major features of modernism in the war years may be recognized, all registering a departure from its May Fourth and post–May Fourth predecessors. The first involves an increasing disintegration of the borders between high and low culture in Shanghai, as new sensationism broadened into a new form of writing that integrated both the Westernized/Japanized form of new sensationism and the middle-brow fiction of the Mandarin Ducks and Butterflies style. Most of Zhang Ailing's highly crafted yet infinitely readable short stories were published in popular magazines such as *Phenomena* (*Wanxiang*), which fluctuated between advocating serious and popular literatures.[2] Zhang's work harkens back to the new sensationist combination of artistic

---

1. Edward Gunn, *Unwelcome Muse: Chinese Literature in Shanghai and Peking, 1937–1945* (New York: Columbia University Press, 1980), 7–9.

2. It is important to distinguish two stages in the life of the magazine *Phenomena*. When first

sophistication with commercial appeal, but while the new sensationists celebrated and worried about the modern, urban condition, Zhang focuses on the persistence of anachronistic traditional household situations within the urban environment. Traditional human relationships and values, the hallmark of Mandarin Ducks and Butterflies romances but now out of context in modern Shanghai, often constitute the central tension and conflict in her stories. All these contributed to the famous Zhang Ailing phenomenon in 1940s Shanghai, 1960s Taipei, and 1990s Beijing, with a dedicated readership and scholars devoting their lives to the study of her work. Zhang is perhaps the only writer from modern China whose popular appeal approaches that of a movie star but whose literary output is simultaneously the object of sustained research and analysis.

At least two related explanations can be given for the Zhang Ailing phenomenon in 1940s Shanghai. During the Sino-Japanese War there was an ardent call for popularizing literature to serve anti-Japanese, propagandistic purposes. Prompted by nationalistic concerns, traditional popular forms of literature such as serialized novels, familiar essays, plays (particularly in the form of spoken dramas which incorporated many traditional theatrical conventions), and even comic books populated the literary scene. Against such a backdrop, Zhang's stories would not have seemed an anomaly, even though in content they appeared to have nothing to do with national salvation. The revival of nationalist literary values also tolerated the return of the Mandarin Ducks and Butterflies fiction that had earlier come under severe attack for being superficial. While so-called "serious" works like those written in the previous decades were subject to severe censorship in Shanghai, from either the Japanese or the nationalist and communist undergrounds, and indeed Mu Shiying and Liu Na'ou were even assassinated, the apparent lack of social consciousness in Zhang's work shielded her from political persecution by both the nationalists (whether Nationalist- or Communist-sponsored—both prone to view literature in terms of ideological utility) and the Japanese. Arguably, the popular mode was also the most innocuous to Japanese censorship.

The second explanation is related to her gender, having to do with the contradictory relationship between women and nationalism. To generalize: although women are often troped as representatives of the nation—as caregivers, mothers, wives, and embodiments of native culture and tradition—

---

published in 1941 it was under the editorship of Chen Dieyi and was intentionally directed toward popular tastes which favored Mandarin Ducks and Butterflies fiction. Even the editor's name had the word "butterfly" (*die*) in it. But in July 1943, Ke Ling took over the editorship and started publishing the work of Zhang Ailing as well as other writers like Shi Tuo, Shi Zhecun, Shen Congwen, and Li Jianwu. Until it stopped printing in 1945, the magazine mediated between serious and popular forms of literature.

they have universally suffered in their access to the nation-state and its re-sources, as a result of patriarchal domination. As has been theorized by var-ious feminist scholars, women often have greater opportunities to rise to chal-lenges and become powerful figures and creative agents in times of national crisis when the patriarchy is enervated.[3] This explanation is partially true for Zhang Ailing. In the male territory of literary activity in the previous decades, whose topography had been largely determined by May Fourth enlighten-ment discourse and Westernized literary standards, Zhang could easily have been dismissed as another Mandarin Ducks and Butterflies acolyte without serious literary appeal. But the Japanese occupation brought a temporary end to the hegemony of such a gendered territorialization of culture, and the cultural imaginary was left open for reinscription, even though this rein-scription had to accommodate Japanese meddling. The May Fourth master narratives of social revolution and national cultural rejuvenation were no longer desirable or permitted. Instead, we see Zhang exploring life's most quotidian and even banal moments with irony and pathos, subtly elaborat-ing their profound and symbolic implications.

The rise of feminist consciousness in the stories written by women writ-ers is the second important feature of modernism during the war years. In her subtle but restrained critique of marriage and sexual relations, Zhang Ailing can be said to be a nascent feminist. Mei Niang's stories, however, are a series of clearly articulated protests against male domination. In a story written in the form of a dramatic monologue entitled "Before Surgery" (*Dong shoushu zhi qian*, 1943), Mei Niang's female narrator points directly to pa-triarchy as the archvillain which has caused her wretched state. Unlike the predominantly melancholy May Fourth women's writing, in which the hero-ines are invariably enervated, tubercular, and gradually withering away (the classic examples being Ding Ling's Miss Sophie and Lu Yin's heroines), Mei Niang's protagonists claim their own fates and seek freedom from patriarchy. And unlike the *jingpai* writers Lin Huiyin and Ling Shuhua, who negotiated with patriarchy with much anxiety and hesitation, Mei Niang's stories artic-ulate explicitly feminist themes. Mei Niang was indeed a far cry from Ling Shuhua, who hid her work from her father, afraid that he would not approve. For her popularity, Mei Niang was dubbed the northern counterpart of Zhang Ailing, and the pair was nicknamed "Southern Ling and Northern Mei" (*nan Ling bei Mei*).

Such daring expression of feminist subjectivity was buttressed in scholar-ship as well. Two important articles on the relationship between women and literature, authored by Yu Dayin and published in *Time and Tide Literature and Art,* appeared in 1943 and 1944. The first posited that literature and art

---

3. A good summary of these theories can be found in Nira Yuval-Davis, *Gender & Nation* (London: Sage Publications, 1997).

are, by definition, feminine and that women have been unjustly barred from freely expressing themselves in writing. The second article categorized the three forms of women's self-expression in literature as submission to male ideology, indulging in unconstructive complaining, and direct rebellion against patriarchy.[4] May Fourth women's writing would fall into Yu's second category, and Mei Niang's into the third.

The third distinct feature of this era's modernism can be termed an aesthetics of looseness or dissolution—a writing style that dissolved narrative borders in terms of genre, style, character, and point of view. An extremely eloquent example of this aesthetic is the writing of Wang Zengqi. Wang justified his "loose" (*san*) style by way of Song-dynasty poet-scholar Su Shi's philosophy of writing—let writing flow like water, whose formlessness is its form—loosening the borders between poetry and fiction, between the popular "knight-errant" genre and the modern short story, and between self and the Other in characterization. In "Revenge" (*Fuchou,* 1944), for instance, a nameless swordsman in search of the enemy who killed his father discovers how he owes the very definition of his own existence to his enemy. The "self" is not only defined by but also dependent upon the Other.

Ultimately, this dissolution of the distinction between self and Other can be read as a metaphor for that between China and the West, for in Wang's work one can no longer delineate the elements that belong to each. The poetic density of his prose in capturing the interior thoughts of the protagonist is simultaneously the consequence of a Su Shi–esque "looseness" and a Western modernist penchant for psychological depiction. The result of such a "loose" style approaches what is now termed the postmodern. Indeed, all three of the features of modernism during the war years I have discussed—the intermixing of high and low cultural spheres, women's disruption of the male order of representation, and the breaking down of generic boundaries—show this modernism's affinities with postmodernism.

After the communist victory in the civil war in 1949, a class-conscious nationalist aesthetic that repudiated modernism and embraced realism was instituted in China. Sinologists in the U.S. noted in the 1960s and early 1970s how post-1949 literature reverted back to traditional narrative forms, and concluded that the brief flowering of Western-sounding modern literature from 1917 to 1949 was an anomaly in the development of Chinese literature. They therefore predicted that there was unlikely to be a recurrence of such literature in the future. Contrary to their prediction, the years immediately following the Cultural Revolution saw an immensely powerful revival of the May Fourth practice of importing Western literature, and saw the pro-

4. Yu Dayin, "Women and Literature" (*Funü yu wenyi*), *Time and Tide Literature and Art* (*Shi yu chao wenyi*) 2:2 (December 1943): 19–36; "Women's Self-Expression in Literature" [*Wenxue li de nüxing zi wo biaoxian*], *Time and Tide Literature and Art* 4:4 (December 1944): 42–54.

duction of a wide array of Western-inspired literature. A bricolage of modernist and postmodernist inclinations were found in the writings of Can Xue and others, while existentialism, psychoanalysis, and literary avant-gardism were "rediscovered," taking center stage in literary debates. The (post)modernism of the 1980s grew out of a different political, cultural, and social condition than the modernisms this book has discussed, but its sense of purpose was no less urgent and strong. Writing in a Western style was itself first and foremost a rebellious act against the Party's prescribed socialist realism, and thereby became an ideological statement. It was nothing less than a counterdiscourse to the narrow political prescription of literature, to Party ideology. Other aspects of 1980s (post)modernism, however—such as the rediscovery of humanism, exemplified in a celebration of romantic love—smacked of its May Fourth antecedent.

Between the years 1949 and 1976, there was another modernist movement, but not on the mainland. In the 1960s, a group of young writers who were trained in Western high modernist writing and experimented with their own modernist forms gathered in Taiwan around a magazine called *Modern Literature* (*Xiandai wenxue*). Because most literature published during the Republican era was banned in Taiwan, this group's knowledge of that literature was very limited. The only continuity was that maintained by the poet Ji Xian, who had earlier used the alias Lu Yishi when he was in Shanghai. The Taiwan group's inspiration was therefore largely derived from Western models. Newly decolonized from Japanese control and, according to some, recolonized by the retreating Nationalist army, Taiwan was the recipient of much U.S. aid as a bastion of anticommunism. This was also the era of political terrorism, when the Nationalist government punished political dissent with death and imprisonment. In this context, modernist writing that self-consciously called itself such, written largely by mainland immigrants to Taiwan, would be culturally and ideologically suspect from the perspective of the rise of Taiwanese consciousness in the 1980s. It comes as no surprise that these modernists came under fierce attack by Taiwanese nativists who equated modernism with imperialism as early as the 1970s,[5] and their cultural status continued to wane amid Taiwan's clamor to go native vis-à-vis China. The irony in all this, of course, is that the Taiwan modernists, with the exception of Bai Xianyong (whose work dwells on mainland nostalgia) and the leftist Chen Yingzhen (who maintains what to some is an outdated unification ideology), were more Occidentalist than "Chinese." Taiwan nativism, one also needs to clarify, is largely confined to articulations of Taiwanese identity against China and mainlanders in Taiwan; otherwise, Tai-

5. For a critical analysis of the positivistic modernism in Taiwan and the nativist revolt against it, see Sung-sheng Yvonne Chang, *Modernism and the Nativist Resistance: Contemporary Chinese Fiction from Taiwan* (Durham: Duke University Press, 1993).

wan's political and cultural elite uphold a cosmopolitan, global perspective and remain eager participants in global movements of capital, commodity, and culture.

In short, semicolonialism encouraged cosmopolitan modernism in Republican China, the post–Cultural Revolution "open door" policy invited this cosmopolitanism into China once again, and the "white terror" served as the backdrop to the production of a Westernized modernist literature in Taiwan. The curiously period-specific yet perennial condition of modernism in twentieth-century China and Taiwan calls for further critical engagement with the question of modernity in the Third World. It appears that the experience of modernity has involved a long, drawn-out process proceeding in fits and starts, violently swinging within a force field of opposing ideologies and different forms of colonialisms, and without a firm anchor in comfortable essentialisms or traditions. The traumatic entry of non-Western nations into colonial, postcolonial, and neocolonial relations of power, on the terms prescribed to them, has necessitated urgent reconstructions of national cultures. With historical hindsight, we can see that the optimism underlying much modernist experimentation was based on an optimistic estimation of the time it takes to become modern. Writing modernism did not guarantee the arrival of modernity. If modernity had already arrived with the first flowering of modernist writing, why have there been so many repetitive eruptions of modernist movements since? The project of modernity in the Third World context is incomplete not due to an unfulfilled promise, as Jürgen Habermas lamented in the Western context, but instead due to its being a particularly arduous, violent, repetitive, and *long* process, longer than any modernist writer could have anticipated.

SELECTED BIBLIOGRAPHY

Abdel-Malek, A., ed. *The Civilizational Project: The Visions of the Orient*. Proceedings of the Thirtieth International Congress of Human Sciences in Asia and North Africa. Mexico City: El Colegio de México, 1981.

Abe Tomoji. "The New Poetic Schools in England and America" (*Yingmei xinxing shipai*). Translated by Gao Ming. *Les Contemporaines* (*Xiandai*) 2:4 (February 1933): 550–566.

———. "Recollections" (*Kaisō*). *Literary World* (*Bungakukai*) 7 (September 1940): 180–184.

Akutagawa Ryūnosuke. *Travels in China* (*Shina yūki*). English translation: see Joshua Fogel, trans. Chinese translation: see Mianzun [Xia Mianzun], pref. and trans.

Alitto, Guy. *The Last Confucian: Liang Shu-ming and the Chinese Dilemma of Modernity*. Berkeley: University of California Press, 1979.

All About Shanghai: A Standard Guidebook. Shanghai: University Press, 1934–1935. Reprint, Hong Kong: Oxford University Press, 1983.

Ames, Roger T. "Taoism and the Androgynous Ideal." In *Women in China*, edited by Richard W. Guisso and Stanley Johannesen, 21–45. Youngstown, N.Y.: Philo Press, 1981.

Anderson, Benedict. *Imagined Communities*. London: Verso, 1992.

Anderson, Marston. "The Morality of Form: Lu Xun and the Modern Chinese Short Stories." In *Lu Xun and His Legacy*, edited by Leo Ou-fan Lee, 32–53. Berkeley: University of California Press, 1985.

———. *The Limits of Realism: Chinese Fiction in the Revolutionary Period*. Berkeley: University of California Press, 1990.

Arac, Jonathan, and Harriet Ritvo, eds. *Macropolitics of Nineteenth-Century Literature: Nationalism, Exoticism, Imperialism*. Philadelphia: University of Pennsylvania Press, 1991.

Ardis, Ann. *New Women, New Novels: Feminism and Early Modernism*. New Brunswick: Rutgers University Press, 1990.

Ayscough, Florence. *Florence Ayscough & Amy Lowell*. Chicago: University of Chicago Press, 1945.

Ayscough, Florence, and Amy Lowell, trans. *Fir-Flower Tablets*. New York: Houghton Mifflin, 1921.

Baker, Houston. *Modernism and the Harlem Renaissance*. Chicago: University of Chicago Press, 1987.

Bakhtin, Mikhail. *The Dialogic Imagination*. Edited by Michael Holquist. Translated by Caryl Emerson and Michael Holquist. Austin: University of Texas Press, 1981.

———. *Problems of Dostoevsky's Poetics*. Translated and edited by Carly Emerson. Minneapolis: University of Minnesota Press, 1984.

Balibar, Etienne. "Ambiguous Universality." *differences* 7:1 (Spring 1995): 48–74.

Balibar, Etienne, and Immanuel Wallerstein. *Race, Nation, Class: Ambiguous Identities*. Etienne Balibar translated by Chris Turner. New York: Verso, 1995.

Barlow, Tani. " *Zhishifenzi* [Chinese Intellectuals] and Power." *Dialectical Anthropology* 16 (1991): 209–32.

———. "Colonialism's Career in Postwar China Studies." *positions* 1:1 (Spring 1993): 224–67.

Barthes, Roland. *The Pleasure of the Text*. Translated by Richard Miller. New York: Hill and Wang, 1975.

Baudelaire, Charles. *The Painter of Modern Life and Other Essays*. Translated and edited by Jonathan Mayne. London: Phaidon Press, 1964.

———. *Petite Poèmes en Prose*. Edited by Melvin Zimmerman. Manchester: University of Manchester Press, 1968.

Benjamin, Walter. *Illuminations*. Edited by Hannah Arendt. Translated by Harry Zohn. New York: Shocken Books, 1969.

———. *Charles Baudelaire: A Lyric Poet in the Era of High Capitalism*. Translated by Harry Zohn. London: Verso, 1985.

Berman, Marshall. *All That Is Solid Melts Into Air: The Experience of Modernity*. New York: Penguin Books, 1988.

Bhabha, Homi. *The Location of Culture*. New York: Routledge, 1994.

———, ed. *Nation and Narration*. London: Routledge, 1990

Bian Zhilin. "Preface" (*Xu*) to *Records of Insect Carvings* (*Diaochong jili*). Hong Kong: Sanlian shudian, 1982, 1–24.

———. "Preface to *Collected Writings of Feng Wenbing*" (*Feng wenbing xuanji xu*). *Historical Materials on New Literature* (*Xinwenxue shiliao*) (February 1984): 113–119.

———. *Bian Zhilin*. Edited by Zhang Manyi. Hong Kong: Sanlian shudian, 1990.

———, trans. "Tradition and Individual Talent" (*Chuantong yu geren caineng*), by T. S. Eliot. *Xuewen Monthly* (*Xuewen yuekan*) 1:1 (May 1934): 87–98.

Bleiler, E. F., ed. *Best Ghost Stories of J. S. Le Fanu*. New York: Dover Publications, Inc., 1964.

Bo Zi. "Jing Yinyu's *Anthology of Modern Chinese Short Stories*" (*Jing Yinyu de Zhongguo xiandai duanpian xiaoshuoji*). *La Nouvelle Littérature* (*Xin wenyi*) 1:1 (September 1929): 171–175.

Bourdieu, Pierre. *The Logic of Practice*. Translated by Richard Nice. Stanford: Stanford University Press, 1990.

———. *Language and Symbolic Power*. Translated by Gino Raymond and Matthew Adamson. Cambridge: Harvard University Press, 1991.

Bradbury, Malcolm, and James McFarlane, eds. *Modernism.* New York: Penguin Books, 1976.

Braester, Yomi. "Shanghai's Economy of the Spectacle: The Shanghai Race Club in Liu Na'ou's and Mu Shiying's Stories." *Modern Chinese Literature* 9:1 (Spring 1995): 39–57.

Brewer, Anthony. *Marxist Theories of Imperialism.* London: Routledge, 1989.

Broers, Bernarda C. *Mysticism in the Neo-Romantics.* Amsterdam: H.J. Paris, 1923.

Buck-Morss, Susan. "The Flâneur, the Sandwichman and the Whore: The Politics of Loitering." *New German Critique* 39 (Fall 1986): 99–139.

Burgwinkle, William. "Veiling the Phallus: French Modernism and the Feminization of the Asian Male." In *Gender and Culture in Literature and Film East and West: Issues of Perception and Interpretation,* edited by Nitaya Masavisut et al., 29–39. Honolulu: University of Hawaii and the East-West Center, 1994.

Butler, Judith. *Gender Trouble: Feminism and the Subversion of Identity.* New York: Routledge, 1990.

Cai Shangsi, ed. *Collected Materials of the Modern Chinese History of Ideas* (*Zhongguo xiandai sixiangshi ziliao jianbian*), vols. 1–4. Hangzhou: Zhejiang renmin chubanshe, 1982.

Calinescu, Matei. *Five Faces of Modernity.* Durham: Duke University Press, 1987.

Carpenter, Edward. *Love's Coming of Age.* Manchester: Labour Press, 1896.

C.C.F. [full name not given]. "Shanghai's Standard of Living." *The Chinese Nation* 1:51 (June 3, 1931): 1439, 1442–1443.

Chakrabarty, Dipesh. "Postcoloniality and the Artifice of History: Who Speaks for 'Indian' Pasts?" *Representations* 37 (Winter 1992): 1–26.

Chan, Stephen. "The Language of Despair: Ideological Representation of the 'New Woman' by May Fourth Writers." In *Gender Politics in Modern China: Writing and Feminism,* edited by Tani E. Barlow, 13–32. Durham: Duke University Press, 1993.

Chang, Sung-sheng Yvonne. *Modernism and the Nativist Resistance: Contemporary Chinese Fiction from Taiwan.* Durham: Duke University Press, 1993.

Chatterjee, Partha. *Nationalist Thought and the Colonial World: A Derivative Discourse.* Minneapolis: University of Minnesota Press, 1993.

———. *The Nation and Its Fragments.* Princeton: Princeton University Press, 1993.

Chen Duxiu. "On Literary Revolution" (*Wenxue geming lun*). In *Materials on the History of New Chinese Literary Movement* (*Zhongguo xinwenxue yundongshi ziliao*), edited by Zhang Ruoying, 40–44. Shanghai: Guangming shuju, 1934.

Ch'en, Jerome. *China and the West: Society and Culture 1815–1937.* Bloomington: Indiana University Press, 1979.

Chen Jingzhi. *Obstacles to the New Literature Movement* (*Xinwenxue yundong de zuli*). Taipei: Chengwen chubanshe, 1980.

———. *Women Writers of Early Modern Literature* (*Xiandai wenxue zaoqi de nüzuojia*). Taipei: Chengwen chubanshe, 1980.

Ch'en, Kenneth. *Buddhism in China.* Princeton: Princeton University Press, 1964.

Chen Quan. "The May Fourth Movement and the *Sturm und Drang*" (*Wusi yundong yu kuangbiao yundong*). *National Literature* (*Minzu wenxue*) 1:3 (September 1943): 1–6.

Chen, Sihe. *A Holistic Look at China's New Literature* (*Zhongguo xin wenxue zhengti guan*). Taipei: Yeqiang chubanshe, 1990.

Chen Song, ed. *Collected Essays from the Debate on the Question of Eastern and Western Cul-*

ture During the May Fourth Period (*Wusi qianhou dongxi wenhua wenti lunzhan wenxuan*). Beijing: Zhongguo shehui kexue chubanshe, 1989.

Chen, Xiaomei. "Rediscovering Ezra Pound: A Post-Postcolonial 'Misreading' of a Western Legacy." *Paideuma* 23:2 and 3 (Fall/Winter 1994): 81–105.

———. *Occidentalism: A Theory of Counter-Discourse in Post-Mao China.* New York: Oxford University Press, 1995.

Chen, Zishan, and Wang Zili, eds. *Research Materials on Yu Dafu* (*Yu Dafu yanjiu ziliao*). Hong Kong: Sanlian shudian, 1986.

Cheng Ma. *A History of Lu Xun's Studies in Japan* (*Lu Xun liuxue Riben shi*). Xi'an: Shanxi renmin chubanshe, 1985.

———. *Communication and Renewal: Exploring the Relationship between Lu Xun and Japanese Literature* (*Goutong yu gengxin: Lu Xun yu Riben wenxue guanxi fawei*). Beijing: Zhongguo shehui kexue chubanshe, 1990.

Chow, Rey. "Virtuous Transactions: A Reading of Three Stories by Ling Shuhua." *Modern Chinese Literature* 4:1 and 2 (Spring and Fall 1988): 71–86.

———. *Woman and Chinese Modernity: The Politics of Reading Between West and East.* Minnesota: University of Minnesota Press, 1991.

———. "Between Colonizers: Hong Kong's Postcolonial Self-writing in the 1990s." *Diaspora* 2:2 (1992): 151–170.

———. *Writing Diaspora: Tactics of Intervention in Contemporary Cultural Studies.* Bloomington: Indiana University Press, 1993.

———. "The Politics of Admittance: Female Sexual Agency, Miscegenation and the Formation of Community in Frantz Fanon," *UTS Review* 1:1 (1995): 5–29.

———. *Primitive Passions: Visuality, Sexuality, Ethnography, and Contemporary Chinese Cinema.* New York: Columbia University Press, 1995.

Clark, Suzanne. *Sentimental Modernism.* Bloomington: Indiana University Press, 1991.

Clifford, Nicholas. *Spoilt Children of Empire: Westerners in Shanghai and the Chinese Revolution of the 1920s.* Middlebury, Vt.: Middlebury College Press, 1991.

Cohen, Paul A. *Discovering History in China.* New York: Columbia University Press, 1984.

Coleman, James William. *Blackness and Modernism.* Jackson: University Press of Mississippi, 1989.

"Communist Literature," Shanghai Municipal Police File, reel 1, D-39, February 18, 1929.

Dai Wangshu. "Wangshu on Poetry" (*Wangshu shi lun*). *Les Contemporaines* 2:1 (November 1932): 92–94.

Daruvala, Susan. *Zhou Zuoren and the Alternative Chinese Response to Modernity.* Ph.D. dissertation, University of Chicago, 1993.

de Certeau, Michel. *The Practice of Everyday Life.* Translated by Steven Rendall. Berkeley: University of California Press, 1984.

de Gourmont, Rémy. *Decadence and Other Essays on the Culture of Ideas.* Translated by William A. Bradley. New York: Harcourt, Brace and Company, 1921.

DeKovan, Mariann. *Rich and Strange: Gender, History, Modernism.* Princeton: Princeton University Press, 1991.

de Man, Paul. *Blindness and Insight: Essays in the Rhetoric of Contemporary Criticism.* Minneapolis: University of Minnesota Press, 1983.

Denton, Kirk A., ed. *Modern Chinese Literary Thought.* Stanford: Stanford University Press, 1996.

Dickinson, G. Lowes. *Letters from John Chinaman and Other Essays.* London: George Allen and Unwin Ltd., 1946.

Dikötter, Frank. *The Discourse of Race in Modern China.* Stanford: Stanford University Press, 1992.

Dirlik, Arif. "Marxism and Chinese History: The Globalization of Marxist Historical Discourse and the Problem of Hegemony in Marxism." *Journal of Third World Studies* 4:1 (1987): 151–164.

———. *Anarchism in the Chinese Revolution.* Berkeley: University of California Press, 1991.

Doi Kochi. *James Joyce (Zhanmushi Zhushi).* Translated by Feng Cixing. Shanghai: Xiandai shuju, 1934.

Du Heng. *Nostalgia (Huai xiang ji).* Shanghai: Xiandai shuju, 1933.

Du Heng [as Su Wen]. "About Mu Shiying's Creative Work" (*Guanyu Mu Shiying de chuangzuo*). *Modern Publishing (Xiandai chubanjie)* 9 (January 1933): 10–11.

———. "Writers in Shanghai" (*Wenren zai Shanghai*). *Les Contemporaines (Xiandai)* 4:2 (December 1933): 281–282.

———, ed. *Debates on Literary Freedom (Wenyi ziyou lunbian ji).* Shanghai: Xiandai shuju, 1933.

Duara, Prasenjit. "Knowledge and Power in the Discourse of Modernity: The Campaigns Against Popular Religion in Early Twentieth-Century China," *Journal of Asian Studies* 50:1 (February 1991): 67–83.

———. *Rescuing History from the Nation: Questioning Narratives of Modern China.* Chicago: University of Chicago Press, 1995.

Duus, Peter, Ramon Myers, and Mark R. Peattie, eds. *The Japanese Informal Empire in China, 1895–1937.* Princeton: Princeton University Press, 1989.

Editorial Committee [of *La Nouvelle Littérature*]. "Words from the Editors" (*Bianji de hua*). *La Nouvelle Littérature* 2:2 (April 1930): 399–400.

Eliot, T. S. *The Sacred Wood.* London: Metheun & Co. Ltd., 1960.

Ellis, Havelock. See Pan Guangdan, trans.

Ellmann, Mary. *Thinking About Women.* New York: Harcourt, Brace and World, 1968.

Elvin, Mark, and G. William Skinner, eds. *The Chinese City Between Two Worlds.* Stanford: Stanford University Press, 1974.

Fabian, Johannes. *Time and the Other: How Anthropology Makes Its Object.* New York: Columbia University Press, 1983.

Fairbank, Wilma. *Liang and Lin: Partners in Exploring China's Architectural Past.* Philadelphia: University of Pennsylvania Press, 1994.

Fang Lingru, et al. "My Favorite Books of 1936" (*Er shi wu nian wo de ai du shu*). *Cosmic Wind (Yuzhou feng)* 32 (January 1937): 439–442.

Fang Xun. "Bergson's *Philosophy of Life*" (*Bogesen Sheng zhi Zhexue*). *Young China (Qingnian Zhongguo)* 1:7 (1919): 3–7.

Fanon, Frantz. *Black Skin, White Masks.* Translated by Charles Lam Markmann. New York: Grove Weidenfeld, 1967.

———. *The Wretched of the Earth.* Translated by Constance Farrington. New York: Grove Press, Inc., 1968.

Fei Jianzhao. "Irish Writer Joyce" (*Aierlan zuojia Qiao'ousi*). *Literature Monthly* (*Wenyi yuekan*) 3:7 (January 1933): 351–353.

Fei Ming [Feng Wenbing]. *Stories of the Bamboo Grove* (*Zhulin de gushi*). Beijing: Xinchao she, 1925; Shanghai: Beixin shuju, 1927.

———. "On Water" (*Shui shang*) and "Key" (*Yaoshi*). *Crescent Moon* (*Xinyue*) 4:5 (November 1932): 1–17.

———. *Bridge* (*Qiao*). Shanghai: Kaiming shudian, 1932.

———. "Window" (*Chuang*). *Crescent Moon* 4:7 (June 1933): 1–7.

———. "Lotus Leaves" (*Heye*) and "Untitled" (*Wuti*). *Xuewen Monthly* (*Xuewen yuekan*) 1:2 (June 1934): 27–41.

———. "On Modern Poetry: A Dialogue by Feng Fei-ming." In *Modern Chinese Poetry*, edited by Harold Acton, translated by Harold Acton and Ch'en Shih-hsiang, 33–45. London: Duckworth, 1936.

———. "Jottings" (*Suibi*). *Literature Magazine* (*Wenxue zazhi*) 1:1 (May 1937): 200–201.

———. "Light of Fireflies" (*Yinghuo*). *Literature Magazine* 1:3 (July 1937): 45–57.

———. "Morning Glory" (*Qianniu hua*). *Literature Magazine* 1:4 (August 1937): 117–129.

———. *Talking to Youth About Lu Xun* (*Gen qingnian tan Lu Xun*). Beijing: Zhongguo qingnian chubanshe, 1956.

———. *Collected Writings of Feng Wenbing* (*Feng Wenbing xuanji*). Beijing: Beijing renmin wenxue chubanshe, 1985.

———. *Selected Writings of Fei Ming* (*Fei Ming xuanji*). Sichuan: Sichuan wenyi chubanshe, 1988.

Fei Zhengqing [John K. Fairbank]. *The Cambridge History of Republican China* (*Jianqiao Zhonghua minguo shi*). Translated by Yang Pinchuan et al. Beijing: Zhongguo shehui kexue chubanshe, 1993.

Feng Jiannan. "About Fei Ming's Life" (*Shuo Fei Ming de shengping*). *Historical Materials on New Literature* (*Xin wenxue shi liao*) (February 1984): 106–112.

———. "On Fei Ming's Fictional Writing" (*Tan Fei Ming de xiaoshuo chuangzuo*). *Studies of Modern Chinese Literature* (*Zhongguo xiandai wenxue yanjiu*) 4 (April 1985): 140–151.

———. "Fei Ming—Outstanding Essayist" (*Fei Ming—jiechu de sanwen jia*). *Studies of Modern and Contemporary Chinese Literature* (*Zhongguo xiandai dangdai wenxue yanjiu*) (August 1988): 233–238.

Feng Youlan. *Scholarly Essays from Three Bamboo Studio* (*Sansong tang xueshu wenji*). Beijing: Beijing daxue chubanshe, 1984.

Fenollosa, Ernest. *East and West*. New York: Crowell and Company, 1893.

Fletcher, John Gould. "The Orient and Contemporary Poetry." In *The Asian Legacy and American Life*, edited by Arthur E. Christy, 145–74. New York: Asia Press, 1945.

Fogel, Joshua. *The Cultural Dimension of Sino-Japanese Relations: Essays on the Nineteenth and Twentieth Centuries*. New York: M. E. Sharpe, 1995.

———. *The Literature of Travel in the Japanese Rediscovery of China, 1862–1945*. Stanford: Stanford University Press, 1996.

———. "Akutagawa Ryūnosuke in China." *Chinese Studies in History* 30:4 (Summer 1997): 6–9.

———, trans. "Travels in China," by Akutagawa Ryūnosuke, *Chinese Studies in History* 30:4 (Summer 1997): 10–55.

Foster, Hal, ed. *Vision and Visuality.* Seattle: Bay Press, 1988.

Frank, Joseph. "Spatial Form in Modern Literature." *Sewanee Review* 53 (1945): 221–240, 433–456, 643–653.

Frankel, Hans H. *The Flowering Plum and the Palace Lady: Interpretations of Chinese Poetry.* New Haven: Yale University Press, 1976.

Freedman, Ralph. *The Lyrical Novel.* Princeton: Princeton University Press, 1963.

Freud, Sigmund. *The Interpretation of Dreams.* Translated by James Strachey. New York: Avon Books, 1965.

———. *Introductory Lectures on Psychoanalysis.* Translated by James Strachey. New York: W. W. Norton, 1966.

———. *Inhibitions, Symptoms, and Anxiety.* Translated by Alix Strachey. New York: W. W. Norton, 1989.

Freuhauf, Heinrich. *Urban Exoticism in Modern Chinese Literature, 1910–1933.* Ph.D. dissertation, University of Chicago, 1990.

Fu Donghua and Zheng Zhenduo, eds. *One Hundred Questions About Literature (Wenxue baiti).* Shanghai: Shenghuo shudian, 1935.

Fu, Poshek. *Passivity, Resistance, and Collaboration: Intellectual Choices in Occupied Shanghai, 1937–1945.* Stanford: Stanford University Press, 1993.

Furth, Charlotte, ed. *Limits of Change.* Cambridge: Harvard University Press, 1976.

Gao Juefu. *Gao Juefu's Essays on Psychology (Gao Juefu xinlixue wen xuan).* Shanghai: Jiangsu jiaoyu chubanshe, 1986.

Ge Momei. "Cinema and Women's Beauty" (*Dianying yu nüxingmei*). *Trackless Train (Wugui lieche)* 4 (October 10, 1928): 207.

Gelfant, Blanche H. *The American City Novel.* Norman: University of Oklahoma Press, 1954.

Giddens, Anthony. *The Consequences of Modernity* . Stanford: Stanford University Press, 1990.

Gikandi, Simon. *Writing in Limbo: Modernism and Caribbean Literature.* Ithaca: Cornell University Press, 1992.

Gilbert, Sandra M., and Susan Gubar. *The Madwoman in the Attic: The Woman Writer and the Nineteenth Century Literary Imagination.* New Haven: Yale University Press, 1984.

Gilman, Sander L. *Freud, Race, and Gender.* Princeton: Princeton University Press, 1993.

———. *The Case of Sigmund Freud.* Baltimore: Johns Hopkins University Press, 1993.

Girard, René. *Deceit, Desire, and the Novel.* Translated by Yvonne Freccero. Baltimore: Johns Hopkins Press, 1965.

Goldman, Merle, ed. *Modern Chinese Literature in the May Fourth Era.* Cambridge: Harvard University Press, 1977.

Grieder, Jerome B. *Hu Shih and the Chinese Renaissance.* Cambridge: Harvard University Press, 1970.

———. *Intellectuals and the State in Modern China.* New York: Free Press, 1981.

Gu Zhongqi. "The Last Letter" (*Zuihou de yi feng xin*). *Short Story Monthly (Xiaoshuo yuebao)* 14:8 (August 1923): 13–16.

Guénon, René. *East and West.* Translated by William Massey. London: Luzac and Co., 1941.

Guha, Ranajit. *Dominance Without Hegemony: History and Power in Colonial India.* Cambridge: Harvard University Press, 1997.

Gunn, Edward. *Unwelcome Muse: Chinese Literature in Shanghai and Peking, 1937–1945*. New York: Columbia University Press, 1980.

————. *Rewriting Chinese: Style and Innovation in Twentieth-Century Chinese Prose*. Stanford: Stanford Univ. Press, 1991.

Guo Moruo. "Poetic Theories of Futurism and Its Criticism" (*Weilaipai de shi yue ji qi piping*). *Creation Weekly* (*Chuangzao zhoukan*) 17 (September 1923): 1–6.

————. "Walter Pater's Critical Theory" (*Wate Feite de piping lun*). *Creation Weekly* 26 (November 1923): 1–5.

————. *Goddess* (*Nüshen*). Beijing: Renmin wenxue chubanshe, 1957.

————. *Guo Moruo on Creative Writing* (*Guo Moruo lun yishu*). Edited by Zhang Chenghuan. Shanghai: Shanghai wenyi chubanshe, 1982.

————. *Complete Works of Guo Moruo* (*Guo Moruo quanji*). Beijing: Renmin wenxue chubanshe, 1985.

Habermas, Jürgen. "Modernity—An Incomplete Project." In *The Anti-Aesthetic: Essays on Postmodern Culture*, edited by Hal Foster, 3–15. Seattle: Bay Press, 1983.

————. *The Philosophical Discourse of Modernity*. Translated by Frederick G. Lawrence. Cambridge: MIT Press, 1987.

Hao Wen. See Shao Xunmei [Hao Wen].

Hay, Steven N. *Asian Ideas of East and West: Tagore and His Critics in Japan, China, and India*. Cambridge: Harvard University Press, 1970.

He Lin. *Chinese Philosophy of the Last Fifty Years* (*Wushi nian lian de Zhongguo zhexue*). Shenyang: Liaoning jiaoyu chubanshe, 1989.

Hegel, Georg W. F. *The Philosophy of History*. Translated by J. Sibree. New York: Dover Publications, 1956.

————. *The Phenomenology of Spirit*. Translated by A. V. Miller. New York: Oxford University Press, 1977.

————. *Introduction to the Philosophy of History*. Translated by Leo Rauch. Indianapolis: Hackett Publishing Company, 1988.

Hei Ying. *Daughter of the Empire* (*Diguo de nüer*). Shanghai: Kaihua shuju, 1934.

————. "The Mu Shiying I Knew" (*Wo jiandao de Mu Shiying*). *Historical Materials on Modern Chinese Literature* (February 1989): 142–145.

Hershatter, Gail. "The Hierarchy of Shanghai Prostitution, 1870–1949." *Modern China* 15:4 (1989): 463–98.

————. "The Subaltern Talks Back: Reflections on Subaltern Theory and Chinese History." *positions* 1:1 (Spring 1993): 103–130.

Hirabayashi Hatsunosuke. "Commodified Modern Fiction" (*Shangpin hua de jindai xiaoshuo*). Translated by Qian Gechuan. *Beixin* 4:16 (August 1930): 49–55.

Hiyashi Fusao. *The Double Curved Lines of the City* (*Duhui shuang qu xian*). Translated by Shi'er. Shanghai: Shenzhou guoguang she, 1932.

Hobsbawm, E. J. *Nations and Nationalism Since 1780*. 2nd ed. Cambridge: Cambridge University Press, 1992.

Hoeveler, J. David, Jr. *The New Humanism: A Critique of Modern America, 1900–1940*. Charlottesville: University Press of Virginia, 1977.

Holcombe, Chester. *The Real Chinese Question*. New York: Dodd, Mead and Company, 1900.

Hong Suye. "Sadism and Masochism in Literature" (*Wenxue shang shi yinnuekuang yu shounuekuang*). *Literature Monthly* (*Wenyi yuekan*) 7:1 (January 1935): 96–106.

Howe, Christopher, ed. *Shanghai: Revolution and Development in an Asian Metropolis.* New York: Cambridge University Press, 1981.

Hsia, C. T. *A History of Modern Chinese Fiction, 1917–1957.* New Haven: Yale University Press, 1961.

———. *Love, Society, and the Novel (Aiqing, shehui, xiaoshuo).* Taipei: Cunwenxue chubanshe, 1970.

Hu Shih [Hu Shi]. *The Chinese Renaissance: The Haskell Lectures, 1933.* Chicago: University of Chicago Press, 1934.

———. "Tentative Proposals for Literary Reform" (*Wenxue gailiang chuyi*). In *Materials on the History of New Chinese Literary Movement (Zhongguo xinwenxue yundongshi ziliao),* edited by Zhang Ruoying, 27–39. Shanghai: Guangming shuju, 1934.

———. *Which Path Should We Take? (Women zou natiaolu).* Taipei: Yuanliu chubanshe, 1986.

Hua Shi [Feng Xuefeng]. "Revolution and the Intellectual Class." *Trackless Train* 2 (September 25, 1928): 43–50.

Huang Jundong. "Mu Shiying and His Work" (*Mu Shiying yu ta de zuopin*). *Four Seasons (Siji)* 1 (November 1972): 38–42.

Huang Renying. See Qian Xingcun.

Huang Ziping, Chen Pingyuan, and Qian Liqun. *Three-Way Dialogues on Twentieth Century Chinese Literature (Ershi shiji Zhongguo wenxue sanren tan).* Beijing: Renmin wenxue chubanshe, 1988.

Hutcheon, Linda. *Narcissistic Narrative: The Metafictional Paradox.* New York: Metheun, 1980.

Huyssen, Andreas. *After the Great Divide.* Bloomington: Indiana University Press, 1986.

Iriye, Akira. *China and Japan in the Global Setting.* Cambridge: Harvard University Press, 1992.

Jameson, Fredric. "Literary Innovation and Modes of Production: A Commentary." *Modern Chinese Literature* 1:1 (September 1984): 67–77.

———. "Third-World Literature in the Era of Multinational Capital." *Social Text* 15 (Fall 1986): 65–88.

———. "Modernism and Imperialism." *Nationalism, Colonialism, and Literature,* by Fredric Jameson, Edward Said, and Terry Eagleton, 43–66. Minneapolis: University of Minnesota Press, 1990.

Jeans, Roger B., Jr. *Syncreticism in Defense of Confucianism: An Intellectual and Political Biography of the Early Years of Chang Chün-mai, 1887–1923.* Ph.D. dissertation, George Washington University, 1974.

———. *Democracy and Socialism in Republican China: The Politics of Zhang Junmai, 1906–1941.* New York and Boulder: Roman and Littlefield, 1997.

Jenner, W. J. F. "Is a Modern Chinese Literature Possible?" In *Essays in Modern Chinese Literature and Literary Criticism,* edited by Wolfgang Kubin and Rudolf G. Wagner, 192–230. Bochum: Studienberlag Brockmeyer, 1982.

Jiang Weitang et al., eds. *A Study of Beijing Women's Newspapers and Journals, 1905–1949 (Beijing funü baokankao, 1905–1949).* Beijing: Guangming ribao chubanshe, 1990.

Jones, Andrew. "The Violence of the Text: Reading Yu Hua and Shi Zhicun." *positions* 2:3 (Winter 1994): 570–602.

Kang Yi [Ji Kangyi]. "Hearing a Flute at Shanyang: Remembering the 1930s New

Sensationist Writer Mr. Mu Shiying" (*Lindi shanyang: daonian yiwei sanshi niandai xin'ganjuepai zuojia Mu Shiying xiansheng*). *Anecdotes* (*Zhanggu*) 10 (1972): 48–50.

Karatani Kōjin. *Origins of Modern Japanese Literature*. Translated and edited by Brett de Bary. Durham: Duke University Press, 1993.

Karl, Frederick. *Modern and Modernism: The Sovereignty of the Artist 1885–1925*. New York: Atheneum, 1988.

Katagami Noboru. "City Life and Modern Literature" (*Duhui shenghuo yu xiandai wenxue*). Translated by (Han) Shiheng. *New North* (*Beixin*) 2:20 (September 1928): 39–43.

Kataoka Teppei. "An Experience" (*Yige jingyan*). Translated by Ge Momei. *Trackless Train* (*Wugui lieche*) 7 (December 1928): 376–381.

———. "The Poverty of Art" (*Yishu de pinkun*). Translated by Guo Jianying. *La Nouvelle Littérature* (*Xin wenyi*) 1:1 (September 1929): 105–143.

Keene, Dennis. *Yokomitsu Riichi: Modernist*. New York: Columbia University Press, 1980.

Keene, Donald. *Dawn to the West: Japanese Literature in the Modern Era*. New York: Henry Holt and Company, 1984.

Kern, Stephen. *The Culture of Time and Space, 1880–1918*. Cambridge: Harvard University Press, 1983.

Kim, K. H. *Japanese Perspectives on China's Early Modernization*. Ann Arbor: University of Michigan Press, 1974.

Kinkley, Jeffrey. *The Odyssey of Shen Congwen*. Stanford: Stanford University Press, 1987.

Kirby, Kathleen M. *Indifferent Boundaries: Spatial Concepts of Human Subjectivity*. New York: Guilford Press, 1996.

Knox, George William. *The Spirit of the Orient*. New York: Thomas Y. Crowell & Co., 1906.

Kon Hidemi. "The Pain of Mr. Mu's Unexpected Death" (*Mu kun no furyo no shi o itamu*). *Literary World* (*Bungakukai*) 7 (September 1940): 184–186.

Kong Lingjing, ed. *Letters of Modern Chinese Writers* (*Xiandai Zhongguo zuojia shuxin*). Hong Kong: Yixin shudian, 1971.

Kristeva, Julia. *Desire in Language: A Semiotic Approach to Literature and Art*. Edited by Leon S. Roudiez. Translated by Thomas Gora, et al. New York: Columbia University Press, 1980.

———. *Revolution in Poetic Language*. Translated by Margaret Waller. New York: Columbia University Press, 1984.

Kuriyagawa Hakuson. "Abnormal Sexuality and Literature" (*Bing de xingyu yu wenxue*). Translated by Fan Zhongyun. *Short Story Monthly* 16:5 (May 1925): 1–9

———. "Art and Sexual Desire" (*Wenyi yu xingyu*). Translated by Fan Zhongyun. *Short Story Monthly* 16:7 (July 1925): 1–4.

———. *Symbols of Mental Anguish* (*Kumen de xiangzheng*). See Lu Xun, trans.

Kusano Shinpei. "Regarding Mr. Mu Shiying" (*Mu Shiying shi no koto*). *Literary World* (*Bungakukai*) 7 (September 1940): 176–178.

Lacan, Jacques. *The Four Fundamental Concepts of Psychoanalysis*. Edited by Jacques-Alain Miller. Translated by Alan Sheridan. New York: W. W. Norton & Company, 1981.

Laclau, Ernesto and Chantel Mouffe. *Hegemony and Socialist Strategy*. London: Verso, 1985.

Lahiri, Amar. *Japanese Modernism*. Tokyo: Hokuseido Press, 1939.

Lamaitre, George. *Four French Novelists: Marcel Proust, André Gide, Jean Giraudoux, Paul Morand.* London: Oxford University Press, 1938.

Lao Tzu [Laozi]. *Tao Te Ching (Daodejing).* Translated by D. C. Lau. Harmondsworth, Middlesex: Penguin Books, 1963.

Larson, Wendy. "Realism, Modernism, and the Anti-'Spiritual Pollution' Campaign in China." *Modern China* 15:1 (January 1989): 37–71,

———. *Literary Authority and the Modern Chinese Writer.* Durham: Duke University Press, 1991.

Larson, Wendy, and Anne Wedell-Wedellsborg, eds. *Inside Out: Modernism and Post-modernism in Chinese Literary Culture.* Aarhus, Denmark: Aarhus University Press, 1993.

Lasek, Elizabeth. "Imperialism in China: A Methodological Critique." *Bulletin of Concerned Asian Scholars* 15:1 (1983): 50.

Lee, Gregory. *Dai Wangshu: The Life and Poetry of a Chinese Modernist.* Hong Kong: Chinese University Press, 1989.

———. *Troubadours, Trumpeters, and Troubled Makers: Lyricism, Nationalism, and Hybridity in China and Its Others.* Durham: Duke University Press, 1996.

Lee, Leo Ou-fan. *The Romantic Generation of Modern Chinese Writers.* Cambridge: Harvard University Press, 1973.

———. "Literary Trends: The Road to Revolution 1927–1949." In *The Cambridge History of China,* edited by Denis Twitchett and John K. Fairbank, 13:421–491. Cambridge: Cambridge University Press, 1983.

———. *Voices from the Iron House: A Study of Lu Xun.* Bloomington: Indiana University Press, 1987.

———. "In Search of Modernity: Some Reflections on a New Mode of Consciousness in Twentieth-Century Chinese History and Literature." In *Ideas Across Culture,* edited by Paul A. Cohen and Merle Goldman, 109–135. Cambridge: Council on East Asian Studies, Harvard University, 1990.

———. "'Decadence' in Modern Chinese Literature and Its Writers" (*Zhongguo xiandai wenxue zhong de 'tuifei' ji qi zuojia*). *Con-Temporary (Dangdai)* 93 (January 1, 1994): 22–47.

———. "The Cultural Construction of Modernity in Early Republican China: Some Research Notes on Urban Shanghai." Typescript, 1996.

———. *Shanghai Modern: A Study of Urban Culture and Literary Imagination in China, 1930–1945.* Cambridge: Harvard University Press, 1999.

Lee, Tahirih V. "Introduction" to "Coping with Shanghai: Means to Survival and Success in the Early Twentieth Century—A Symposium." *Journal of Asian Studies* 54:1 (1995): 3–18.

Lerner, Michael G. *Pierre Loti.* New York: Twayne Publishers, 1974.

Leung, Ping-kwan. *Aesthetics of Opposition: A Study of the Modernist Generation of Chinese Poets, 1936–1949.* Ph.D. Dissertation, University of California, San Diego, 1984.

Levenson, Joseph R. "'History' and 'Value': The Tensions of Intellectual Choice in Modern China." *Studies in Chinese Thought* 55: 5 (December 1953): 146–194.

———. *Confucian China and Its Modern Fate.* Berkeley: University of California Press, 1958.

———. *Revolution and Cosmopolitanism: The Western Stages and the Chinese Stages.* Berkeley: University of California Press, 1971.

Li Jianwu. *A Selection of Li Jianwu's Creative and Critical Writing* (*Li Jianwu chuangzuo pinglun xuanji*). Beijing: Renmin wenxue chubanshe, 1984.

Liang Shuming. *Eastern and Western Culture and Their Philosophies* (*Dongxi wenhua ji qi zhexue*, 1921). Taipei: Liren shuju, 1983.

Liang Ssu-ch'eng [Liang Sicheng]. *A Pictorial History of Chinese Architecture*. Edited by Wilma Fairbank. Cambridge: MIT Press, 1984.

Liao, Ping-hui. "Hope, Recollection, Repetition: Turandot Revisited." *Musical Quarterly* 77:1 (Spring 1993): 67–80.

Lin Huiyin. "Embarrassment" (*Jiong*). *Crescent Moon* 3:9 (n.d.): 1–21.

———. "In Ninety-Nine Degree Heat" (*Jiushi jiu du zhong*). *Xuewen Monthly* (*Xuewen yuekan*) 1:1 (May 1934): 21–45.

———. "Meizhen and Them" (*Meizhen tong tamen*). *Literature Magazine* 1:1–3 (May–July 1937): 147–180; 111–140; 98–127.

Lin, Julia. *Modern Chinese Poetry: An Introduction*. Seattle: University of Washington Press, 1972.

Lin Shan. *Biography of Lin Huiyin* (*Lin Huiyin zhuan*). Taipei: Shijie shuju, 1993.

Lin Yü-sheng. *The Crisis of Chinese Consciousness*. Madison: University of Wisconsin Press, 1979.

Lin Yü-sheng et al. *May Fourth: Reflections from Multiple Perspectives* (*Wusi: duoyuan de fansi*). Hong Kong: Sanlian shudian, 1989.

Ling Shuhua. *Temple of Flowers* (*Hua zhi si*). Shanghai: Xinyue shudian, 1928.

———. *Collected Stories of Ling Shuhua* (*Ling Shuhua xiaoshuoji*). 2 vols. Taipei: Hongfan shudian, 1986.

——— [*Su Hua Ling Chen*]. *Ancient Melodies*. New York: Universe Books, 1988.

Lippit, Seiji. *Japanese Modernism and the Destruction of the Literary Form: The Writings of Akutagawa, Yokomitsu, and Kawabata*. Ph.D. dissertation, Columbia University, 1997.

Liu, Lydia. *Translingual Practice*. Stanford: Stanford University Press, 1995.

Liu Dajie. *Introduction to German Literature* (*Deguo wenxue gailun*). Shanghai: Beixin shuju, 1928.

Liu Na'ou. *Scène* (*Dushi fengjingxian*). Shanghai: Shuimo shudian, 1930.

———. "Below the Equator" (*Chidao xia*), *Les Contemporaines* 2:1 (November 1932): 166–174.

———. "A Lady to Keep You Company" (original English title). *Literary Landscape* (*Wenyi fengjing*) 1:1 (June 1934): 68–78.

———, ed. and trans. *Erotic Culture* (*Seqing wenhua*). Shanghai: Diyixian shudian, 1928.

———, trans. "On Paul Morand" (*Baoer Muhang lun*), by Benjamin Crémieux. *Trackless Train* 4 (October 1928): 147–60.

———, trans. *The Sociology of Art* (*Yishu shehuixue*), by Vladimir M. Friche. Shanghai: Shuimo shudian, 1930.

Liu Weichen. "Mu Shiying's 'Shanghai Foxtrot'" (*Mu Shiying de 'Shanghai hubuwu'*). *Modern Publishing* (*Xiandai chubanjie*) 7 (November 1932): 11–12.

Longenbach, James. *Modernist Poetics of History: Pound, Eliot, and the Sense of the Past*. Princeton: Princeton University Press, 1987.

Loti, Pierre. See Xu Xiacun, trans.

Lou Shiyi. "Shi Zhecun's New Sensationism" (*Shi Zhecun de xin'ganjue zhuyi*). *Literary News* (*Wenyi xinwen*) (October 26, 1931): 4.

Lu Tianshi. *Modern Literary Movements in Europe* (*Ouzhou jindai wenyi sichao*). Shanghai: Commercial Press, 1931.

Lu Xun. *Complete Works of Lu Xun* (*Lu Xun quanji*). Beijing: Renmin wenxue chuban-she, 1981.

―――, trans. *"Symbols of Mental Anguish" and "Outside the Ivory Tower"* (*Kumen de xiang-zheng; Chu le xiangya zhi ta*), by Kuriyagawa Hakuson. Beijing: Renmin wenxue chubanshe, 1988.

―――. "On the Power of Mara Poetry." Translated by Shu-ying Tsau and Donald Holock. In *Modern Chinese Literary Thought*, edited by Kirk A. Denton, 96–109. Stanford: Stanford University Press, 1996.

Luo Rongju, ed. *From "Westernization" to Modernization* (*Cong xihua dao xiandaihua*). Beijing: Beijing University Press, 1990.

Mani, Lata. "Contentious Traditions: The Debate on *Sati* in Colonial India." In *Recasting Women: Essays in Indian Colonial History*, edited by Kumkum Sangari and Sudesh Vaid, 88–126. New Brunswick: Rutgers University Press, 1990.

Mao Dun [Lang Sun]. "Manifesto on Reforming [the Magazine]" (*Gaige xuanyan*). *Short Story Monthly* 12:1 (January 1921): 2–4.

―――. "The Responsibility and Endeavor of Researchers of New Literature" (*Xin-wenxue yanjiu zhe de zeren yu nuli*). *Short Story Monthly* 12:2 (February 1921): 2–5.

Mao Zedong. *Selected Writings of Mao Zedong* (*Mao Zedong xuanji*). Beijing: Renmin chubanshe, 1968.

Marx, Karl, and Friedrich Engels. *The Marx-Engels Reader*. Edited by Robert C. Tucker. New York: W. W. Norton, 1978.

Masutani Tatsunosuke. "Mourning Mr. Mu Shiying" (*Mu Shiying shi tsuito*). *Literary World* (*Bungakukai*) 7 (September 1940): 172–173.

Matsumura Takeo. *Literature and Erotic Love* (*Wenyi yu xingai*). Translated by Xie Liu-yi. Shanghai: Kaiming shudian, n.d.

Meng Yue and Dai Jinhua. *Surfacing From History* (*Fuchu lishi dibiao*). Kaifeng: Henan renmin chubanshe, 1989.

Meng Zhou. "Devotion of the Silver Screen" (*Yinmu de gongxian*). *Trackless Train* 4 (October 10, 1928): 208.

Mianzun [Xia Mianzun], pref. and trans. "Mr. Akutagawa Ryūnosuke's Views on China" (*Jiechuan Longzhijie shi de Zhongguo guan*). *Short Story Monthly* (*Xiaoshuo yue-bao*) 17:4 (1926): 1–26.

Morand, Paul. "Laziness" (*Landuo bing*). Translated by Dai Wangshu. *Trackless Train* 4 (October 1928): 160–162.

―――. "New Friends" (*Xin pengyou*). Translated by Dai Wangshu. *Trackless Train* 4 (October 1928): 163–175.

―――. *Fancy Goods & Open All Night*. Translated by Ezra Pound. Edited by Breon Mitchell. New York: New Directions, 1984.

Mordell, Albert. *The Erotic Motive in Literature* (*Jindai wenxue yu xingai*, 1919). Translated by Zhong Ziyan and Wang Wenchuan. Shanghai: Kaiming shudian, 1931.

Mu Shiying. "Words About Myself" (*Guanyu ziji de hua*). *Modern Publishing* (*Xiandai chubanjie*) 4 (August 1932): 9–10.

―――. "My Daily Life" (*Wo de shenghuo*). *Modern Publishing* 9 (January 1933): 12–13.

―――. *Poles Apart* (*Nanbeiji*). Shanghai: Xiandai shuju, 1933.

―――. *Public Cemetery* (*Gongmu*). Shanghai: Xiandai shuju, 1933.

————. *Platinum Statue of a Female Nude* (*Baijin de nüti suxiang*). Shanghai: Xiandai shuju, 1934.

————. *The Love of St. Virgin* (*Sheng chunü de ganqing*). Shanghai: Liangyou tushu gongsi, 1935.

————. "'Licentious' and Dogmatic Pseudo-Realist" (*"Baiwu jinji" yu shuojiaoshi de ni xianshi zhuyi zhe*). *Morning Post* (*Chenbao*), May 5, 1935.

————. "The Mentality of Confusion Among Writers" (*Zuojia qun de mimang xinli*). *Morning Post*, September 13, 1935.

————. *The Complete Stories of Mu Shiying* (*Mu Shiying xiaoshuo quanji*). Shanghai: Xuelin chubanshe, 1997.

Mulvey, Laura. *Visual and Other Pleasures*. Bloomington: Indiana University Press, 1989.

Nandy, Ashis. *The Intimate Enemy: Loss and Recovery of Self Under Colonialism*. Delhi: Oxford University Press, 1983.

————. *The Savage Freud and Other Essays on Possible and Retrievable Selves*. Princeton: Princeton University Press, 1995.

————. "The Savage Freud." Talk given at the University of California, Los Angeles, April 25, 1995.

Ni Yide. *Autumn at Xuanwu Lake* (*Xuanwuhu zhi qiu*). Shanghai: Taidong tushuju, 1924.

————. *The Shore of the Eastern Sea* (*Donghai zhi bin*). Shanghai: Guanghua shuju, 1926.

Noboru Shōmu. "Main Literary Trends in Contemporary Russia" (*Jindai Eluosi wenyi de zhuchao*). Translated by Chen Wangdao. *Short Story Monthly* (*Xiaoshuo yuebao*) 12, special issue on Russian literature (September 1921): 1–20.

North, Michael. *The Dialect of Modernism: Race, Language and Twentieth-Century Literature*. New York: Oxford University Press, 1994.

Osterhammel, Jürgen, and Wolfgang J. Mommsen, eds. *Imperialism and After: Continuities and Discontinuities*. London: Allen and Unwin, 1986.

Ostrovky, Erika. *Under the Sign of Ambiguity: Saint-John Perse/Alexis Léger*. New York: New York University Press, 1984.

Palandri, Angela Jung, ed. *Women Writers of Twentieth-Century China*. Asian Studies Publication Series. Eugene: University of Oregon, 1982.

Palumbo-Liu, David. "Universalisms and Minority Culture." *differences* 7:1 (1995): 188–208.

Pan Guangdan, trans. *The Psychology of Sex* (*Xing xinlixue*), by Havelock Ellis. Beijing: Sanlian shudian, 1987.

Pan Hannian [Ya Ling]. "New Hooliganism (1)" (*Xin liumang zhuyi yi*). *Oazo* (*Huanzhou*) 1:1 (October 1926): 1–8.

————. "New Hooliganism (5)." *Oazo* 1: 6 (December 1926): 261–264.

Parker, Andrew et al., eds. *Nationalisms and Sexualities*. New York: Routledge, 1992.

Parmelee, Maurice. *Oriental and Occidental Culture*. New York: Century Co., 1928.

Peng, Hsiao-yen. *Antithesis Overcome: Shen Congwen's Avant-gardism and Primitivism*. Taipei: Institute of Chinese Literature and Philosophy, Academica Sinica, 1994.

Peng Xiaoyen. "Wandering in the World: The 1927 Diaries of Liu Na'ou" (*Langdang tianya: Liu Na'ou 1927 nien de riji*). *Chinese Literature and Philosophy Studies Quarterly* (*Zhongguo wenzhe yanjiu jikan*), forthcoming.

Perse, St. John. *Collected Poems*. Translated by T. S. Eliot, W. H. Auden, et al. Princeton: Princeton University Press, 1971.

Pincus, Leslie. *Authenticating Culture in Imperial Japan*. Berkeley: University of California Press, 1996.

Plaks, Andrew, ed. *Chinese Narrative*. Princeton: Princeton University Press, 1977.

Poggioli, Renalto. *The Theory of the Avant-Garde*. Translated by Gerald Fitzgerald. Cambridge: Harvard University Press, Belknap Press, 1968.

Pollard, David. *A Chinese Look At Literature: The Literary Values of Chou Tso-jen [Zhou Zuoren] in Relation to Tradition*. Berkeley: University of California Press, 1973

Prakash, Gyan. "Subaltern Studies as Postcolonial Criticism." *American Historical Review* 99 (1994): 1475–1490.

Pratt, Mary Louis. *Imperial Eyes: Travel Writing and Transculturation*. New York: Routledge, 1992.

Prusek, Jaroslav. *The Lyrical and the Epic*. Edited by Leo Ou-fan Lee. Bloomington: Indiana University Press, 1980.

Pyle, Kenneth. *The New Generation in Meiji Japan: Problems of Cultural Identity*. Stanford: Stanford University Press, 1969.

Qian Liqun. *A Biography of Zhou Zuoren (Zhou Zuoren zhuan)*. Beijing: Shiyue wenyi chubanshe, 1990.

Qian Liqun et al. *Thirty Years of Modern Chinese Literature (Zhongguo xiandai wenxue sanshinian)*. Shanghai: Shanghai wenyi chubanshe, 1987.

Qian Xingcun. "Yu Dafu" (1933). In *The Grand Collection of China's New Literature: 1927–1937 (Zhongguo xinwenxue daxi)*, edited by Zhao Jiabi, 1:629–649. Shanghai: Shanghai wenyi chubanshe, 1987.

Qian Xingcun [Huang Renying], ed. *Contemporary Chinese Women Writers (Dangdai Zhonggue nüzuojia lun)*. Shanghai: Guanghua shuju, 1933.

Qian, Zhaoming. *Orientalism and Modernism: The Legacy of China in Pound and Williams*. Durham: Duke University Press, 1995.

Qian Zhixiu. "Study of Dreams" (*Meng zhi yanjiu*). *Eastern Magazine (Dongfang zazhi)* 10:11 (May 1914): 7–8.

Ransome, Arthur. *The Chinese Puzzle*. Boston and New York: Houghton Mifflin, 1927.

Rao Hongjing et al., eds. *Materials on the Creation Society (Chuangzao she ziliao)*. Fuzhou: Fujian renmin chubanshe, 1985.

Rubin, Gayle. "The Traffic in Women: Notes on the 'Political Economy of Sex.'" In *Feminist Frameworks*, edited by Alison M. Jagger and Paula S. Rothenberg, 155–71. New York: McGraw-Hill Book Co., 1984.

Russell, Bertrand. *The Problem of China*. New York: Century Co., 1922.

Said, Edward. *Orientalism*. New York: Vintage Books, 1979.

———. *The World, the Text, and the Critic*. Cambridge: Harvard University Press, 1983.

———. *Culture and Imperialism*. New York: Alfred A. Knopf, 1993.

Sakai, Naoki. "Subject and/or *Shutai* and the Inscription of National Culture." Paper presented at the "Imaging Japan: Narrative of Nationhood" conference, Stanford University, May 13, 1993.

Sato, Barbara Hamill. "The *Moga* Sensation: Perceptions of the *Modan Gāru* in Japanese Intellectual Circles During the 1920s." *Gender and History* 5:3 (1993): 363–81.

Satō Haruo. *Melancholy of the City (Duhui de youyu)*. Translated by Zha Shiyuan. Shanghai: Huatong shuju, 1931.

————. *Stories by Satō Haruo* (*Zuoteng Chunfu ji*). Translated by Gao Ming. Shanghai: Xiandai shuju, 1933.

————. *Regeneration* (*Geng sheng ji*). Translated by Zha Shiyuan. Shanghai: Zhonghua shuju, 1935.

Schaefer, William. "Kumarajiva's Foreign Tongue: Shi Zhecun's Modernist Historical Fiction." *Modern Chinese Literature* 10:1–2 (Spring/Fall 1998): 25–70.

Schnitzler, Arthur. See Shi Zhecun, trans.

Schwartz, Sanford. *The Matrix of Modernism: Pound, Eliot, and Early Twentieth Century Thought.* Princeton: Princeton University Press, 1985.

Schwartz, Vera. *The Chinese Enlightenment: Intellectuals and the Legacy of the May Fourth Movement of 1919.* Berkeley: University of California Press, 1986.

Scott, Bonnie Kime, ed. *The Gender of Modernism.* Bloomington: Indiana University Press, 1990.

Scott, Paul D. "Introduction" to a translation of Tanizaki Jun'ichirō's "Shanghai Friends" (*Shanhai kōyū ki, 1926*). *Chinese Studies in History* 30:4 (Summer 1997): 56–70.

————, trans. "Shanghai Friends," by Tanizaki Jun'ichirō. *Chinese Studies in History* 30:4 (Summer 1997): 71–103.

Sergeant, Harriet. *Shanghai.* London: Jonathan Cape, 1991.

Shao Xunmei. *Flower-Like Evil* (*Hua yiban de zui'e*). Shanghai: Jinwu shudian, 1928.

————. *Poems and Drawings of Beardsley* (*Piyacilü shihuaji*). Shanghai: Jinwu shudian, 1929.

————. "Treasures in Contemporary Art Scene" (*Jindai yishu jie zhong de baobei*). *Gold Chamber Monthly* (*Jinwu yuekan*) 1:3 (March 1929): 82–86.

Shao Xunmei [Hao Wen]. "Gambling" (*Du*). *Gold Chamber Monthly* 1:3 (March 1929): 45–50.

————. "After the Gambler Left the Casino" (*Duqian ren li le duchang*). *Gold Chamber Monthly* 1: 5 (May 1929): 40–43.

Shao Xunmei and Zhang Kebiao. "Colors and Flags" (*Secai yu qizhi*). *Gold Chamber Monthly* 1:1 (January 1929): 1–6.

Shen Congwen. *Collected Works of Shen Congwen* (*Shen Congwen wenji*). Hong Kong and Guangzhou: Sanlian shudian and Huacheng chubanshe, 1985.

Shen Qiyu. "The So-called New Sensationism" (*Suowei xin'ganjuepai zhe*). *Big Dipper* (*Beidou*) 1:4 (December 1931): 65–70.

Shen Songqiao. *The Critical Review Group: A Conservative Alternative to the New Culture Movement in the May Fourth Era* (*Xuehengpai yu wusi shiqi de fan xinwenhua yundong*). Taipei: Guoli Taiwan daxue chuban weiyuanhui, 1984.

Shi Pu, trans. *Flush* (*Fulaxi*), by Virginia Woolf. Shanghai: Commercial Press, 1935.

Shi Zhecun. "Fengyang Girl" (*Fengyang nü*). *La Nouvelle Littérature* 1:3 (November 1929): 453–477.

————. *The General's Head* (*Jiangjun di tou*). Shanghai: Xinzhongguo shuju, 1932.

————. "Inaugural Manifesto" (*Chuangkan xuanyan*), *Les Contemporaines* 1:1 (May 1932): 2.

————. "Editor's Note" (*Bianji zuotan*). *Les Contemporaines* 1:2 (June 1932): 337–338.

————. "Editor's Diary" (*Shezhong riji*). *Les Contemporaines* 2:5 (March 1933): 768–769.

————. "Again About the Poetry in Our Magazine" (*You guanyu ben kan de shi*). *Les Contemporaines* 4:1 (November 1933): 6–7.

———. *Biographies of Good Women* (*Shan nüren xingpin*). Shanghai: Liangyou tushu yinshua gongsi, 1933.

———. "Book Banning and Leftist Tendency in Thought" (*Shuji jinzhi yu sixiang zuoqing*). *Literary Landscape* (*Wenyi fengjing*) 1: 1 (June 1934): 39–43.

———. "Short English and American Poems" (*Yingmei xiaoshi chao*). *Literary Landscape* (*Wenyi fengjing*) 1:1 (June 1934): 95–103.

———. "Dialogues in Fiction" (*Xiaoshuo zhong de duihua*). *Cosmic Wind* (*Yuzhou feng*) 39 (April 1937): n.p.

———. "Some Words about 'Master Huangxin'" (*Guanyu Huangxin dashi de ji ju hua*). *Chinese Literature* (*Zhongguo wenyi*) 1:2 (June 1937): n.p.

———. "Supernaturalist" (*Chao ziran zhuyi zhe*). *Literary Tide Monthly* (*Wen chao yuekan*) 3:3 (July 1947): 1053–1056.

———. "Miscellaneous Remembrances of *Les Contemporaines* (1)" (*Xiandai zayi*). *Historical Materials on New Literature* (*Xin wenxue shi liao*) (January 1981): 213–20.

———. "Miscellaneous Remembrances of *Les Contemporaines* (2)" (*Xiandai zayi*). *Historical Materials on New Literature* (*Xin wenxue shi liao*) (February 1981): 158–63.

———. "Miscellaneous Remembrances of *Les Contemporaines* (3)" (*Xiandai zayi*). *Historical Materials on New Literature* (*Xin wenxue shi liao*) (March 1981): 220–23.

———. "About Modernism" (*Guanyu xiandaipai yixitan*). *Wenhui Daily*, October 18, 1983.

———. "Two Years at Aurora University" (*Zhendan ernian*). *Historical Materials on New Literature* (*Xin wenxue shi liao*) (April 1984): 51–55.

———. "We Ran Three Bookstores" (*Women jingying guo sange shudian*). *Historical Materials on New Literature* (January 1985): 184–90.

———. *Shi Zhecun*. Edited by Ying Guojing. Xianggang: Sanlian shudian, 1988.

———. "Miscellaneous Poems of a Floating Life" (*Fusheng zayong*). *Guangming Daily* (*Guangming ribao*), serialized February 11 to November 25, 1990.

———. "The Dawn of Chinese Modernism: A Dialogue with the Master of New Sensationism, Shi Zhecun" (*Zhongguo xiandai zhuyi de shuguang: yu xin'ganjue pai dashi Shi Zhecun xiansheng duitan*). Interview by Zheng Mingli and Lin Yaode. *Unitas* (*Lianho wenxue*) 69 (July 1990): 130–141.

———. Interview by Shu-mei Shih. October 22–24, 1990.

———. *Shi Xiu's Love* (*Shi Xiu zhi lian*). Beijing: Renmin wenxue chubanshe, 1991.

———. *Fog, Sea Gulls, and Meteor* (*Wu, ou, liuxing*). Beijing: Renmin wenxue chubanshe, 1991.

———, trans. "Neo-romanticism" (*Xin de langman zhuyi*), by Aldous Huxley. *Les Contemporaines* 1:5 (September 1932): 629–634.

———, trans. *Theresa: The Chronicle of a Woman's Life* (*Boming de Dailisha*), by Arthur Schnitzler. Shanghai: Zhonghua shuju, 1937.

———, trans. *Trilogy of Women's Hearts* (*Fuxin sanbuqu*) (includes *Bertha Galan* [*Duoqing de guafu*], *Frau Beatrice und ihr Sohn* [*Biyateliesi ji qi zi*] and *Fräulein Else* [*Aiarsai zhi si*]), by Arthur Schnitzler. Shanghai: Yanxingshe, 1947.

———, trans. "Modern Writers and the Europe of the Future" (*Xiandai zuojia yu weilai de Ouzhou*), by Ernest Toller. *Literary Landscape* (*Wenyi fengjing*) 1:2 (July 1934): 2–9.

Shi Zhecun and Du Heng. "Introduction to the Special Issue on Modern American Literature" (*Xiandai Meiguo wenxue zhuanhao daoyan*). *Les Contemporaines* 5:6 (October 1934): 834–838.

Shih, Shu-mei. Interview with Shi Zhecun. See Shi Zhecun, interview.

———. "Female Confessional Narratives in Modern Chinese Literature" (*Zhongguo xiandai wenxue zhong de nüxing zibai xiaoshuo*). *Con-Temporary* (*Dangdai*) 95 (March 1994): 108–127.

———. "Gender, Race, and Semicolonialism: Liu Na'ou's Urban Shanghai Landscape." *Journal of Asian Studies* 55:4 (November 1996): 934–956.

Shils, Edward. *Tradition*. Chicago: University of Chicago Press, 1981.

Shomu, Noboru. "Main Literary Trends in Contemporary Russia" (*Jindai Eluosi wenxue di zhuchao*). Translated by Chen Wangdao. *Short Story Monthly* 12 (September 1921): 1–20.

Shorske, Carl E. *Fin-de-Siècle Vienna: Politics and Culture*. New York: Vintage Books, 1981.

Silverberg, Miriam. "The Modern Girl as Militant." In *Recreating Japanese Women, 1600–1945*, edited by Gail Lee Berstein, 239–266. Berkeley: University of California Press, 1991.

———. "Japanese Modern Montage: Was the *Ero Guro* Nonsense?" Paper presented at the "Colonialism, Nationalism and Modernity in East Asia" conference, University of California, Santa Cruz, November 11–12, 1996.

Simmel, Georg. "The Metropolis and Mental Life" (1903). Translated by Edward A. Shils. In *On Individuality and Social Forms*, edited by Donald N. Levine, 324–39. Chicago: University of Chicago Press, 1971.

"Sino-Japanese Cultural Enterprises." *The Chinese Nation* 1:44 (April 15, 1931): 1165–1166.

Slemon, Stephen. "Modernism's Last Post." *Ariel* 20:4 (1989): 3–17.

Smith, Arthur. *Chinese Characteristics*. Shanghai: North-China Herald, 1890.

Smitten, Jeffrey R., and Ann Daghistany, eds. *Spatial Form in Narrative*. Ithaca: Cornell University Press, 1981.

So Chun-sop. *A Study of Korean Modernism* (*Han'guk modonijum yon'gu*). Seoul: Iljisa, 1988.

Som, Tjan Tjo. "The Meeting of East and West: the Oriental View." In *Eastern and Western World*, conference proceedings organized by Netherlands Universities Foundation for International Co-operation, 13–23. Hague: W. Van Hoeve Ltd., 1953.

Spivak, Gayatri. *Outside in the Teaching Machine*. New York: Routledge, 1993.

Stopes, Marie. *Married Love*. New York: G. P. Putnam's Sons, 1931.

Strand, David. *Rickshaw Beijing: City People and Politics in the 1920s*. Berkeley: University of California Press, 1989.

Su Wen. See Du Heng.

Su Xiaokang. "The Excitement and Confusion of Identity" (*Rentong de hangfen yu miluan*). *China Daily News* (*Shijie ribao*), November 12, 1995, A4.

Sultan, Stanley. "Was Modernism Reactionary?" *Journal of Modern Literature* 17:4 (Spring 1991): 447–65.

Sun Lianggong. *Studies on New Literature and Art* (*Xin wenyi pinglun*). Shanghai: Minzhi shuju, 1923.

Sun, Lung-kee. "Historian's Warp: Problems in Textualizing the Intellectual History of Modern China." *positions* 2:2 (Fall 1994): 356–381.

Sun Yat-sen. *Three Principles of the People* (*Sanmin zhuyi*). Taipei: Zhongyang gaizao weiyuanhui, 1950.

Sun Zuoyun. "On 'Modernist School' Poetry" (*Lun xiandaipai shi*). *Qinghua Weekly* (*Qinghua zhoukan*) (March 1935): 56–65.

Tanaka, Stepan. *Japan's Orient: Rendering Pasts into History*. Berkeley: University of California Press, 1993.

Tang Heyi. "The Rise of Neoromanticism" (*Xin langman zhuyi de boxing*). *Sixth Anniversary Issue of Chenbao* (*Chenbao liu zhounian jinian zeng kan*) (December 1, 1924): 229–251.

Tang Tao, ed. *A History of Modern Chinese Literature* (*Zhongguo xiandai wenxue shi*). Vols. 1–2. Beijing: Renmin wenxue chubanshe, 1979–1990.

Tang Tao and Yan Jiayan, eds. *A History of Modern Chinese Literature* (*Zhongguo xiandai wenxue shi*). Vol. 3. Beijing: Renmin wenxue chubanshe, 1988.

Tang, Xiaobing. *Writing a History of Modernity: A Study of the Historical Consciousness of Liang Ch'i-ch'ao*. Ph.D. dissertation, Duke University, 1991.

————. *Global Space and the Nationalist Discourse of Modernity: The Historical Thinking of Liang Qichao*. Stanford: Stanford University Press, 1996.

Tanizaki Jun'ichirō. See Paul D. Scott, trans.

Tao, Jingsun. *Concert Ditties* (*Yinyuehui xiaoqu*). Shanghai: Chuangzao she, 1927.

Tay, William [Zheng Shusen]. *Literary Relations* (*Wenxue yinyuan*). Taipei: Dongda tushu, 1987.

Teng Gu. "A Mural" (*Bihua*). *Creation Quarterly* (*Chuangzao jikan*) 1:3 (October 1922): 42–54.

————. "The Resurrection of the Stone Sculpture" (*Shixiang de fuhuo*). *Creation Quarterly* 1:4 (February 1923): 142–149.

————. *Ginkgo Nuts* (*Yinxing zhi guo*). Shanghai: Qunzhong tushu gongsi, 1925.

————. "The Suicide of an Antique" (*Gudong de zisha*). *Short Story Monthly* 16:1 (January 1925): 1–10.

————. "Motorcycle Ghost" (*Motuoche de gui*). *Short Story Monthly* 16:7 (July 1925): 1–10.

————. "On Longhua Road" (*Longhua dao shang*). *Short Story Monthly* 17:8 (August 1926): 1–8.

————. *Labyrinth* (*Migong*). Shanghai: Guanghua shuju, 1927.

————. *Extramarital Affair* (*Waiyu*). Shanghai: Jinwu shudian, 1930.

————. *Complete Stories of Teng Gu* (*Teng Gu xiaoshuo quanbian*). Shanghai: Xuelin chubanshe, 1997.

Teppei, Kataoka. "Melancholy and Beautiful Face" (*Yūutsu na utsukushii kao*). *Literary World* (*Bungakukai*) 7 (September 1940): 178–179.

Thomson, James C., Jr., Peter Stanley, and John Cutis Perry. *Sentimental Imperialists*. New York: Harper & Row, 1981.

Tian Han. "Neoromanticism and others" (*Xin langman zhuyi ji qita*). *Young China* (*Qingnian Zhongguo*) 1:12 (June 1920): 24–52.

————. "Poor Lüliyan—*Pauvre Lelian*" (*Kelian de Lüliyan—Pauvre Lelian*). *Creation Quarterly* 1:2 (August 1922): 1–15.

Todorov, Tzvetan. *Mikhail Bakhtin: The Dialogic Principle*. Translated by Wlad Godzich. Minneapolis: University of Minnesota Press, 1984.

————. *The Fantastic: A Structural Approach to a Literary Genre*. Translated by Richard Howard. Ithaca: Cornell University Press, 1987.

Trotter, David. "Modernism and Empire: Reading *The Waste Land*." *Critical Quarterly* 28:1–2 (1986): 143–153.

Trumbull, Randolph. *The Shanghai Modernists*. Ph.D. dissertation, Stanford University, 1989.

———. "Modernist Inscriptions of Traditional China." Paper presented at the annual meeting of the Association for Asian Studies, Los Angeles, March 1993.

Volsik, Paul. "Neo-Romanticism and the Poetry of Dylan Thomas," *Études Anglaises*, 42:1 (1989): 39–54.

Wang, David Der-wei. *Fictional Realism in Twentieth Century China: Mao Dun, Lao She, Shen Congwen*. New York: Columbia University Press, 1992.

———. *Fin-de-siècle Splendor: Repressed Modernities of Late Qing Fiction, 1849–1911*. Stanford: Stanford University Press, 1997.

Wang Hui. "The Fate of 'Mr. Science' in China: The Concept of Science and Its Application in Modern Chinese Thought." Translated by Howard Y. F. Choy. *positions* 3:1 (Spring 1995): 1–68.

Wang, Jing. *High Culture Fever: Politics, Aesthetics, and Ideology in Deng's China*. Berkeley: University of California Press, 1997.

Wang Shuming. "Pidgin Knight" (*Yangjingbang qixia*). *Les Contemporaines* 5:1 (May 1934): 209–212.

Wang Xunzhao et al., eds. *Research Materials on Guo Moruo* (*Guo Moruo yanjiu ziliao*). Vols. 1–3. Beijing: Zhongguo shehui kexue chubanshe, 1986.

Wang Yao. *Manuscript on China's New Literary History* (*Zhongguo xin wenxue shigao*). Shanghai: Shanghai wenyi chubanshe, 1982.

———. *Collection of Essays on Lu Xun's Work* (*Lu Xun zuopin lunji*). Beijing: Renmin wenxue chubanshe, 1984.

———. "Historical Connections between Modern Chinese Literature and Classical Literature" (*Zhongguo xiandai wenxue yu gudian wenxue de lishi lianxi*). *Beijing University Journal* (*Beijing daxue xuebao*) 5 (1986): 1–14.

Wang Zengqi. *Evening Green Essays* (*Wancui wentan*). Hangzhou: Zhejiang wenyi chubanshe, 1988.

Wang Zhefu. *A History of the New Chinese Literary Movement* (*Zhongguo vin wenxue yundong shi*). Beiping [Beijing]: Jiecheng yinshuju, 1933.

Washburn, Dennis. *The Dilemma of the Modern in Japanese Fiction*. New Haven: Yale University Press, 1995.

Weber, Max. *The Religion of China: Confucianism and Taoism*. Translated and edited by Hans H. Gerth. New York: Free Press, 1951.

Wei, Betty Pei-t'i. *Old Shanghai*. Hong Kong: Oxford University Press, 1993.

Widmer, Ellen, and David Der-wei Wang, eds. *From May Fourth to June Fourth: Fiction and Film in Twentieth Century China*. Cambridge: Harvard University Press, 1993.

Williams, Patrick, and Laura Chrisman, eds. *Colonial Discourse and Post-colonial Theory*. New York: Columbia University Press, 1994.

Williams, Raymond. *The Politics of Modernism*. London: Verso, 1989.

Wolff, Janet. *Feminine Sentences*. Berkeley: University of California Press, 1990.

Wong, Wang-chi. *Politics and Literature in Shanghai*. Manchester: Manchester University Press, 1991

Woolf, Virginia. *Flush*. See Shi Pu, trans.

———. *The Letters of Virginia Woolf, vol. 6: 1936–1941*. Edited by Nigel Nicolson and Joanne Trautmann. New York: Harcourt Brace Jovanovich, 1980.

Wu Fuhui. "The Rise and Fall of Chinese New Sensationism and Japanese Literature" (*Zhongguo xin'ganjuepai de chenfu he Riben wenxue*). *Japanese Literature* (*Riben wenxue*) 2 (1986): 231–244.

———. "A Comparative Study of the Beijing and Shanghai Schools of Fiction" (*Jingpai haipai xiaoshuo bijiao yanjiu*). *Studies of Modern and Contemporary Chinese Literature* (*Zhongguo xiandai dangdai wenxue yanjiu*) (October 1987): 199–204.

———, ed. *Selected Stories of the Beijing School* (*Jingpai xiaoshuo xuan*). Beijing: Renmin wenxue chubanshe, 1990.

Wu Lichang. *Psychoanalysis and Sino-Western Literature* (*Jingshen fenxi yu Zhong xi wenxue*). Shanghai: Xuelin chubanshe, 1987.

Wu Luqin. "Virginia Woolf and Ling Shuhua" (*Weijiniya Wuerfu yu Ling Shuhua*). In *Writers Respect Each Other* (*Wenren xiangzhong*), 5–33. Taipei: Hongfan shudian, 1983.

Wu Xiaoming. "The Self-Consciousness of Chinese Culture in Facing the West in the Twentieth Century" (*Ershi shiji Zhongguo wenhua zai xifang mianqian de ziwo yishi*). *Twenty-First Century* (*Ershi yi shiji*) 14 (December 1992): 102–112.

Wu Yun. *Modern Literature ABC* (*Jindai wenxue ABC*). Shanghai: Shijie shuju, 1928.

Xia Yande. *Comprehensive Study of Literature* (*Wenyi tonglun*). Shanghai: Kaiming shudian, 1933.

Xia Yuanwen. "A Preliminary Discussion of City Fiction" (*Duhui zhuyi xiaoshuo chulun*). *Suzhou University Journal* (*Suzhou daxue xuebao*) (January 1990): 79–87.

Xiao Qian. *Selected Writings of Xiao Qian* (*Xiao Qian xuanji*). Chengdu: Sichuan renmin chubanshe, 1983.

———. "The Talented Lady of a Generation, Lin Huiyin" (*Yidai cainu Lin Huiyin*). *Dushu* 10 (October 1984): 113–121.

Xie Liuyi. *A History of Japanese Literature* (*Riben wenxue shi*). Shanghai: Beixin shuju, 1929.

———. "New Sensationism" (*Xin'ganjuepai*). *Modern Literary Criticism* (*Xiandai wenxue pinglun*) 1:1 (April 1931): 1–10.

Xie Liuyi and Wang Fuquan, eds. and trans. *Lectures on World Literature* (*Shijie wenxue jiangzuo*). 13 vols. Shanghai: Beixin shuju, n.d..

Xie Zhixi. *Existentialism and Modern Chinese Literature* (*Cunzai zhuyi yu Zhongguo xiandai wenxue*). Taipei: Zhiyan chubanshe, 1990.

———. *The Extremities of Beauty: A Study of Modern Chinese Literary Aestheticist Decadence* (*Mei de pianzhi: Zhongguo xiandai weimei tuifeizhuyi wenxue sichao yanjiu*). Shanghai: Shanghai wenyi chubanshe, 1997.

Xiong Yuezhi. "On Shanghai's Image in History" (*Lishi shang de Shanghai xingxiang sanlun*). *History Forest* (*Shilin*) 3 (1996): 139–153.

Xu Xiacun. "Italian Literature of the Past Twenty Years" (*Ershi nian lai de Yidali wenxue*). *Short Story Monthly* 20:7 (July 1929): 1101–1110.

———. "Spanish Literature of the Past Twenty Years" (*Ershi nian lai de Xibanya wenxue*). *Short Story Monthly* 20:7 (July 1929): 1111–1118.

———. "Modern Girl" (original English title). *La Nouvelle Littérature* 1:3 (November 1929): 406–413.

———, trans. *Mme. Chrysanthème* (*Juzi furen*), by Pierre Loti. Shanghai: Shangwu yinshuguan, 1929.

Xu Zhimo. *A Collection of Xu Zhimo's Works* (*Xu Zhimo wenji*). 5 vols. Hong Kong: Shangwu yinshuguan, 1983.

————, trans. *Stories of Mansfield* (*Manshufei'er xiaoshuoji*). Shanghai: Beixin shuju, 1927.

Xu Zhimo et al. "The Attitude of the Crescent Moon" (*Xinyue de taidu*). *Crescent Moon* (*Xinyue*) 1:1 (March 1928): 3–10.

Yan Cunde et al., eds. *Dictionary of Chinese Literary Figures* (*Zhongguo wenxuejia cidian*). Chengdu: Sichuan renmin chubanshe, 1979. 4 vols. for the modern period.

Yan Jiayan. *Schools of Modern Chinese Fiction* (*Zhongguo xiandai xiaoshuo liupai shi*). Beijing: Renmin wenxue chubanshe, 1989.

————. Interview by Shu-mei Shih. Los Angeles, California, June, 1997.

————. "*Jingpai* Fiction and Modernism" (*Jingpai xiaoshuo yu xiandai zhuyi*). Unpublished paper.

————. "Tracking Down Mu Shiying's Novels" (*Mu Shiying changpian xiaoshuo zhuizongji*). Preface to *Complete Works of Mu Shiying* (*Mu Shiying quanji*). Guangzhou: Huacheng chubanshe, forthcoming.

Yang Yi. *A History of Modern Chinese Fiction* (*Zhongguo xiandai xiaoshuo shi*). Vols. 1–3. Beijing: Renmin wenxue chubanshe, 1986, 1988, 1991.

————. "The Cultural Causes and Aesthetic Attitudes of the Beijing and Shanghai Schools of Fiction" (*Jingpai he haipai de wenhua yinyuan ji shenmei xingtai*). *Research on Modern and Contemporary Chinese Literature* (*Zhongguo xiandai dangdai wenxue yanjiu*) 6 (1996): 83–93.

Yang Zhihua, ed. *Historical Materials on the Literary Arena* (*Wentan shiliao*). Shanghai: Zhonghua ribaoshe, 1944.

Ye Gongchao. "On New Poetry" (*Lun xinshi*). *Literature Magazine* 1:1 (May 1937): 11–31.

Ye Lingfeng. "Inside the Ivory Tower" (*Xiangya ta zhong*). *Oazo* (*Huanzhou*) 1:1 (October 1926): 1–3.

————. "On Editing the Journal" (*Bianhou suibi*). *Oazo* 1:1 (October 1926): 55–58.

————. "Flu" (*Liuxing xing ganmao*). *Les Contemporaines* 3:5 (September 1933): 653–658.

————. *Stories by Lingfeng* (*Lingfeng xiaoshuo ji*). Shanghai: Xiandai shuju, 1934.

————. "A Comet in the 1930s Literary Arena: Ye Lingfeng Talks About Mu Shiying" (*Sanshi niandai wentan shang de yike huixing: Ye Lingfeng xiansheng tan Mu Shiying*). *Four Seasons* (*Siji*) 1 (November 1972): 26–30.

————. *Jottings from Reading* (*Dushu suibi*). 4 vols. Beijing: Sanlian shudian, 1988.

Yeh, Michelle. *Modern Chinese Poetry: Theory and Practice Since 1917*. New Haven: Yale University Press, 1991.

Yeh, Wen-hsin. *The Alienated Academy: Culture and Politics in Republican China, 1919–1937*. Cambridge: Council on East Asian Studies, Harvard University, 1990.

Yeh, Wen-hsin, and Frederic Wakeman, eds. *Shanghai Sojourners*. Berkeley: Institute of East Asian Studies, 1992.

Yi Tong. "Remembering Liu Na'ou" (*Ji Liu Na'ou*). In *Historical Materials on the Literary Arena* (*Wentan shiliao*), edited by Yang Zhihua, 233–34. Shanghai: Zhonghua ribaoshe, 1944.

Yip, Wai-lim. *Ezra Pound's "Cathay."* Princeton: Princeton University Press, 1969.

————. *Lyrics from Shelters: Modern Chinese Poetry, 1930–1950*. New York: Garland Publishing, Inc., 1992.

Yokomitsu Riichi. "The Death of Mr. Mu Shiying" (*Mu Shiying shi no shi*). *Literary World* (*Bungakukai*) 7 (September 1940): 174–175.

———. *Shanghai. Japanese Literature* (*Nihon no bungaku*), vol. 37. Tokyo: Chūō kōronsha, 1966.

Young, Robert. *White Mythologies*. New York: Routledge, 1990.

———. *Colonial Desire*. New York: Routledge, 1995.

Yu Dafu. "The Road Modern Fiction Took" (*Xiandai xiaoshuo suo jingguo de lucheng*). *Les Contemporaines* 1:2 (June 1932): 205–211.

———. "Painting in the Heat Wave" (*Zai rebo li chuanxi*). *Les Contemporaines* 1:5 (September 1932): 642–43.

———. "Proclamation Addressed to the Japanese Police on the Assassination of Kobayashi" (*Wei Xiaolin de beihai xi Riben jingshiting*). *Les Contemporaines* 3:1 (May 1933): 4.

———. *Collected Writings of Yu Dafu* (*Yu Dafu wenji*). Hong Kong: Sanlian shudian, 1983.

———. *The Complete Short Stories of Yu Dafu* (*Yu Dafu xiaoshuo quanbian*). Hangzhou: Zhejiang wenyi chubanshe, 1991.

Yu Dayin. "Women and Literature" (*Funü yu wenyi*). *Time and Tide Literature and Art* (*Shi yu chao wenyi*) 2:2 (December 1943): 19–36.

———. "Women's Self-Expression in Literature" (*Wenxue li de nüxing ziwo biaoxian*). *Time and Tide Literature and Art* (*Shi yu chao wenyi*) 4:4 (December 1944): 42–54.

Yu Fenggao. *Psychoanalysis and Modern Chinese Fiction* (*Xinli fenxi yu Zhongguo xiandai xiaoshuo*). Beijing: Zhongguo shehui kexue chubanshe, 1987.

Yu Guangzhong. "Introduction" (*Zong xu*). In *A Comprehensive Anthology of Modern Chinese Literature* (*Zhongguo xiandai wenxue daxi*), edited by the editorial committee of the anthology, 1:1–11. Taipei: Juren chubanshe, 1972.

Yü, Lu K'uan, trans. *The Vimalakirti Nirdesa Sutra*. Berkeley: Shambala Publications Inc., 1972.

Yu Qingxiang and Mao Jiaming. "Metropolis Contorting Under His Pen" (*Dadushi zai tade bixia jingruan*). *Huazhong Normal University Journal* (*Huazhong shifan daxue xuebao*) (April 1989): 43–49

Yuval-Davis, Nira. *Gender & Nation*. London: Sage Publications, 1997.

Zavala, Iris M. *Colonialism and Culture: Hispanic Modernisms and the Social Imaginary*. Bloomington: Indiana University Press, 1992.

Zeng Zhongming. *Essays on French Literature* (*Faguo wenxue lunji*). Shanghai: Liming shuju, 1932.

Zeng Zhuowen. "The Death of Yu Dafu and a Lost Poem" (*Yu Dafu zhi si yu yishou yishi*). *Ming Pao Monthly* (*Mingbao yuekan*) (September 1995): 57–59.

Zhang Chenghuan, ed. *Guo Moruo on Writing* (*Guo Moruo lun chuangzuo*). Shanghai: Shanghai wenyi chubanshe, 1982.

Zhang Jingyuan. *Sigmund Freud and Modern Chinese Literature (1919–1949)*. Ph. D. dissertation, Cornell University, 1989.

———. *Psychoanalysis in China: Literary Transformations, 1919–1949*. Ithaca: Cornell East Asia Series, 1992.

Zhang Junmai. *Collected Works of Zhang Junmai* (*Zhang Junmai ji*), edited by Huang Kejian. Beijing: Qunyan chubanshe, 1993.

Zhang Kebiao. "Come, Let Us Soundly Sleep by the Crater of the Volcano and Rejoice in Our Dreams" (*Lai ba rang women chenshui zai penhuo kou shang huanmeng*). *Gold Chamber Monthly* 1:2 (February 1929): 1–5.

Zhang Ruoying, ed. *Materials on the History of the New Literature Movement in China* (*Zhongguo xinwenxue yundongshi ziliao*). Shanghai: Guangming shuju, 1934. Reprint, Shanghai: Shanghai shuju, 1985.

Zhang, Xudong. *Chinese Modernism in the Era of Reforms*. Durham: Duke University Press, 1997.

Zhang, Yingjin. *The City in Modern Chinese Literature and Film*. Stanford: Stanford University Press, 1996.

Zhang Yinlin. "Fenollosa on the Strengths of Chinese Written Characters" (*Fennuoluosa lun Zhongguo wenzi zhi youdian*). *Critical Review* (*Xueheng*) 56 (August 1926): 1–28.

Zhang Yuhong. "The Infiltration and Transformation of Modernist Thought" (*Xiandai zhuyi sichao de shentou yu xingbian*). In *Western Literary Thought and Twentieth-Century Chinese Literature* (*Xifang wenyi sichao yu ershi shiji Zhongguo wenxue*), edited by Yue Daiyun and Wang Ning, 124–166. Beijing: Zhongguo shehui kexue chubanshe, 1990.

Zhang Zongli, ed. *A Study of Modern Shanghai* (*Jindai Shanghai chengshi yanjiu*). Shanghai: Shanghai renmin chubanshe, 1990.

Zhao Jiabi. "Passos" (*Pasuosi*). *Les Contemporaines* 4:1 (November 1933): 220–229.

———. "The Growth of American Fiction" (*Meiguo xiaoshuo zhi chengzhang*). *Les Contemporaines* 5:6 (October 1934): 839–859.

———. "From the Crosscutting Novel to John Dos Passos" (*Cong hengduan xiaoshuo dao Dusi Pasuosi*). *Writers* (*Zuojia*) 2:1 (October 1936): 179–192.

———, ed. and trans. *Tendencies of the Modern Euro-American Novel* (*Jinri Oumei xiaoshuo zhi dongxiang*). Shanghai: Liangyou tushu gongsi, 1935.

Zhao Jingshen. "Modern Chinese Literature and Abnormal Sexuality" (*Zhongguo xin wenyi yu biantai xingyu*). *Yiban* 4:1 (January 1928): 204–208.

———. *World Literature in 1929* (*Yijiuerjiu nian de shijie wenxue*). Shanghai: Shenzhou guoguangshe, 1930.

———. *World Literature in 1930* (*Yijiusanling nian de shijie wenxue*). Shanghai: Shenzhou guoguangshe, 1931.

Zheng Boqi. "Bells of Alarm for New Literature" (*Xin wenxue de jingzhong*). *Creation Weekly* (*Chuangzao zhoubao*) 31 (December 1923): 1–4.

Zheng Mingli and Lin Yaode. See Shi Zhecun, "The Dawn of Chinese Modernism."

———. Zheng Peikai [Cheng Pei-kai]. "The Cultural Impact of Mei Lanfang on World Theater" (*Mei Lanfang dui shijie jutan de wenhua chongji*). *Con-Temporary* (*Dangdai*) 103 (November 1994): 26–43.

Zhou Quanping. *Bitter Laughter* (*Kuxiao*). Shanghai: Guanghua shuju, 1927.

Zhou Zuoren. "Humane Literature" (1918). Translated by Ernst Wolff. In *Modern Chinese Literary Thought*, edited by Kirk A. Denton, 151–161. Stanford: Stanford University Press, 1996.

———. *About Dragons* (*Tan long ji*). Shanghai: Kaiming shudian, 1930.

———. *Collected Essays of Zhou Zhoren* (*Zhitang wenji*). Shanghai: Tianma shudian, 1933.

———. *The Origin of Modern Chinese Literature* (*Zhongguo xin wenxue de yuanliu*). Beiping: Renwen shudian, 1934.

————. "Preface to *Dates* and *Bridge*" (*Zao he Qiao de xu*). In Fei Ming, *Bridge* (*Qiao*), 1–6. Shanghai: Kaiming shuju, 1936.

————. *About Tigers* (*Tan hu ji*). Shanghai: Beixin shuju, 1936.

————. *Representative Works of Zhou Zuoren* (*Zhou Zuoren daibiao zuo*). Edited by Zhang Juxiang. Zhengzhou: Huanghe wenyi chubanshe, 1987.

————. *Zhou Zuoren's Essays* (*Zhou Zuoren sanwen*). Edited by Zhang Minggao et al. Beijing: Zhongguo guangbo dianshi chubanshe, 1992.

Zhu Guangqian. [Meng Shi]. "Freud's Theory of the Unconscious and Psychoanalysis" (*Fulude de yinyishi shuo yu xinli fenxi*). *Eastern Magazine* (*Dongfang zazhi*) 18:14 (1921): 41–51.

————. *The Writings of Mengshi* (*Mengshi wenchao*). Shanghai: Liangyou tushu gongsi, 1936.

————. "My Hopes for this Magazine" (*Wo dui ben kan de xiwang*). *Literature Magazine* (*Wenxue zazhi*) 1:1 (May 1937): 1–10.

————. "Editor's Note" (*Bianji houji*). *Literature Magazine* 1:1 (May 1937): 221–225.

————. "*Bridge*" (*Qiao*). *Literature Magazine* 1:3 (July 1937): 183–189.

————. *Me, Literature, and Others* (*Wo yu wenxue ji qita*). Shanghai: Kaiming shudian, 1943.

————. "Modern Chinese Literature" (*Xiandai Zhongguo wenxue*). *Literature Magazine* 2:8 (January 1948): 13–17.

————. *On Literature* (*Tan wenxue*). Hong Kong: Wenyi chubanshe, 1961.

————. *Complete Works of Zhu Guangqian* (*Zhu Guangqian quanji*). Hefei: Anhui jiaoyu chubanshe, 1987.

————. "'I Am the Colorful Pen Transmitted in the Dream': A Brief Account of Fei Ming" (*Wo shi meng zhong chuan caibi: Fei Ming lue shi*). *Dushu* 10 (October 1990): 28–34.

Zhu Xiang. "*Lantern Festival* and *My Memory*" (*Shangyuan deng yu Wo de jiyi*). *La Nouvelle Littérature* 1:3 (November 1929): 551–552.

Zhu Yunying. "Japan Correspondence" (*Riben tongxin*). *Les Contemporaines* 3:1 (May 1933): 167–71.

AUTHOR/TITLE INDEX

SUBJECT INDEX

ABC Series Bookstore, 240
aestheticism, 113
African American modernism, 3n6
Ah-Qism, 77, 131
alterity: of China, 8; management of, 6; non-Western, 4; and Western modernism, 10. *See also* Other
anti-Manchu sentiment, 77
Artistic and Literary Magazine, 379
assassination, 246
avant-garde, 91

Beijing opera, 11
Beijing School. See *jingpai*
bifurcation: strategies of, 141, 231–33, 260, 340; of the West, 231–32, 277, 301, 304, 335, 374
Big Dipper (magazine), 239

capital, 68
capitalism: and Chinese new sensationism, 257–68; and commodification, ix; and commodity, 268–75, 339; and interiority, 349–54
Central Plain (magazine), 380
China: appropriation of, 10; exoticized, barbarized, 8, 10; Japan's view of, 19; as "Middle Kingdom," 19; as repository

of difference and femininity, 9; as Shina, 19–20; Western use of, 7, 9
"Chinese": *Qingguoren*, 77; *Zhinaren (Shinajin)*, 23, 77, 116–17
Chinese masculinity: and colonialism, 137; and emasculation, 119–20, 138, 279, 351–54; "hypermasculinity," 109, 279; and Japanese women, 118; and national inferiority complex, 24, 117–19, 138; and Teng Gu, 125–26; and Western masculinity, 137; and Yu Dafu, 120. *See also* modern girl; urban men
Chinese modernism: Euro-American literature and, x; and Fei Ming, 190–203; and Guo Moruo, 96–109; and Japanese modernism, 5, 16–30; and language, 68–72; and Ling Shuhua, 215–28; and Lin Huiyin, 207–15; in literary history, 40–45; and Liu Na'ou, 285–99; and Lu Xun, 73–1; and Mu Shiying, 302–38; and new global culture, 151–89; and Occidentalism, 13–15, 128–44; and psychoanalysis, 105–8; and semicolonialism, 30–40; and Shi Zhecun, 247–61, 367–69; and Tao Jingsun, 91–95; and Teng Gu, 123–27; and time, 49, 51, 53–55; and translated modernist philosophies, 58–68; and urban Shanghai, 231–

Text: 10/12 Baskerville
Display: Baskerville
Composition: Integrated Composition Systems